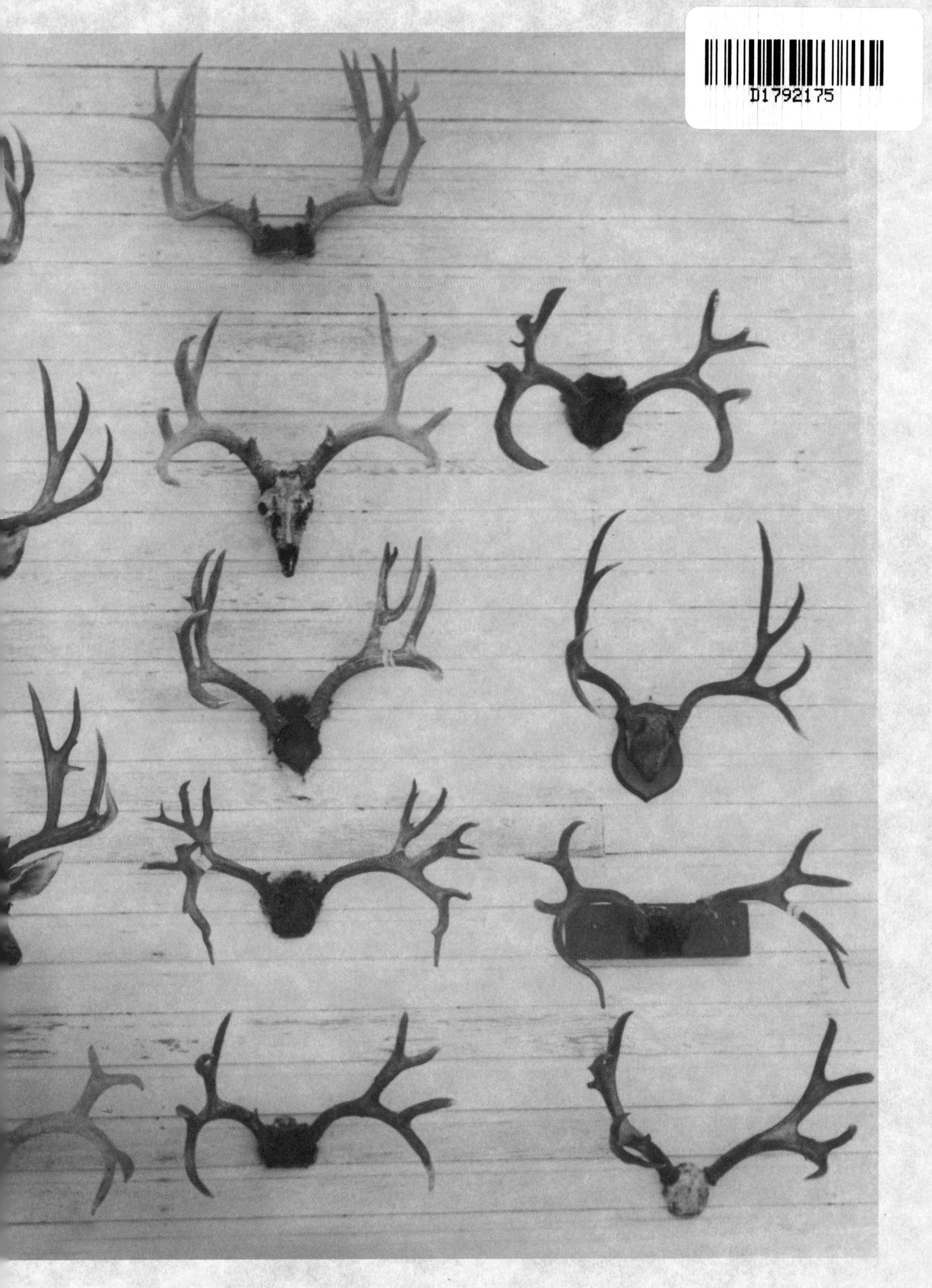

COLORADO'S BIGGEST BUCKS AND BULLS
and Other Great Colorado Big Game

Second Edition

"It is an incalculable added pleasure to any one's sense of happiness if he or she grows to know, even slightly and imperfectly, how to read and enjoy the wonder-book of nature. All hunters should be nature-lovers. It is to be hoped that the days of mere wasteful, boastful slaughter are past, and that from now on the hunter will stand foremost in working for the perpetuation of the wild life, whether big or little."

THEODORE ROOSEVELT
Author, Pastimes of an American Hunter

COLORADO'S BIGGEST BUCKS AND BULLS
And Other Great Colorado Big Game
Second Edition

Copyright © 2001 by Blue Mountain Publishing, Inc.
All rights reserved. No part of this work covered by the copyright hereon may be reproduced or copied in any form or by any means – graphic, electronic, or mechanical, including photocopying, recording, taping, compact disk, web site production, or any form of information storage and retrieval systems – without written permission of Blue Mountain Publishing, Inc.

Published in 2001

Library of Congress Catalog Card Number: 2001 135064
ISBN 0-9611376-4-9

Published in the United States of America by:

BLUE MOUNTAIN PUBLISHING, INC.
5425 Skyway Drive
Missoula, MT 59804

Phone: (406) 251-3372
FAX: (406) 251-5116
E-Mail: bluemountain@montana.com

    Every effort has been made by the author to insure accuracy and completeness while compiling this book. Hopefully, the accuracy has been attained as no expense in time, effort, or money has been spared in obtaining even the most minute detail. However, since the information obtained for this book has come from hundreds of supposedly reliable sources, its accuracy cannot be fully guaranteed.
    As far as completeness is concerned, the author knows there is room for expanding this work or for compiling similar publications. This is the second edition and is much expanded from the first edition by 200 pages and 500 new photographs. Should this second edition of **COLORADO'S BIGGEST BUCKS AND BULLS and Other Great Colorado Big Game** prove to be of particular interest to Colorado hunters, future editions will be considered. Anyone with photographs or materials of any of Colorado's big-game species, especially those that qualify for the Boone and Crockett Club, Pope and Young Club and the Longhunter Muzzleloading programs meeting minimum B&C score and fair chase requirements, should contact:

BLUE MOUNTAIN PUBLISHING, INC.
5425 Skyway Drive
Missoula, MT 59804

To the men, women and teenagers
who love to hunt in Colorado
and to the
Staff and Programs of the
Colorado Division of Wildlife

Acknowledgments

Jack Reneau, Director of Big Game, Boone and Crockett Club, for his assistance in providing B&C photographs and permission for reproduction of B&C score charts of big-game trophies from Colorado. He is also recognized for his assistance proofing the chapter on records-keeping programs.

Glenn E. Hisey, Records Committee Chair, Pope and Young Club, for his assistance in providing P&Y photographs and information about P&Y trophies. He is also recognized for his assistance proofing the chapter on records-keeping programs.

Terri Trowbridge, Director of Publications, National Muzzle Loading Rifle Association, for her assistance proofing the chapter on records keeping programs. **Joyce Vogel**, Executive Director of NMLRA, for proofing the big-game listings.

Frederick H. and **Amy S. Campbell** for their ongoing support and encouragement in this project.

Colorado Division of Wildlife (CDOW) current and retired staff for providing materials, data, and photographs that contribute substantially to the content of this book. Specifically, the author recognizes the following CDOW staff in alphabetical order: Tom Beck, Jackie Boss, Russ Bromby, Bob Davies, Pat Davies, Phillip L. Ehrlich, John Ellenberger, Marvin Gardner, Paul F. Gilbert, Bruce Gill, Pat Hayden, Bob Hernbrode, Bob and Scott Hoover, Rick Kahn, Mary Lloyd, Kathy McWright-Barton, Jeff Mekelburg, Jim Olterman, Chris Rushing, David Russell, Gene Schoonveld, Dave Seeber, Pat Trahey, Henrietta Turner, Mike Trujillo, Ron Velarde, and Steve West.

Russ Bromby of CDOW for his ongoing assistance throughout the entire research phase of the book production to its final printing.

Paul F. Gilbert of Hot Sulphur Springs, Colorado, for providing the author with dozens of photographs of Colorado trophies and their hunters.

Nancy Doerrfeld-Smith of Boring, Oregon, for her design of the book and its promotional materials.

Rick Kahn and **John Ellenberger** of CDOW for their review of the chapters on elk, deer, and moose in Colorado and feedback on content of each chapter.

Jackie Boss, research librarian for CDOW, for providing the author with dozens of scientific articles and CDOW game regulations throughout the 20th Century.

Pat Trahey, Editor, *Colorado Outdoors*, for her comments, recommendations, and effort to review the original book manuscript prior to publication.

Carol Kersavage, retired editor of Outdoor Writers Association of America (OWAA), for copy editing the entire book manuscript.

B&C Official Measurer **Bryon D. Long** of Dolores, Colorado, for his enthusiastic and comprehensive submissions of photographs and information regarding big-game animals taken in his area.

Sheridan Books of Chelsea, Michigan for the printing of this book.

B&C Official Measurer **Roger Selner**, owner of Trophy Show Productions, Inc., of Livingston, Montana, for his contributions of photographs and information on various big-game animals and their hunters.

Finally, special thanks are due to the hundreds of hunters and trophy owners who graciously contributed photographs, hunting stories, and unique photographs from family albums that add so richly to this book.

About the endsheet: The typical and non-typical mule deer displayed on this wall were taken by hunters in Colorado in the early 1960s. The photograph was used as a newspaper promotion in 1962 to entice hunters to Middle Park. A similar photograph with the hunters sitting below their trophies is reproduced elsewhere in this book.
Photograph by Paul F. Gilbert

Table of Contents

Dedication		iii
Acknowledgments		iv
Prologue by Rick Kahn		vi
Introduction by Susan Campbell Reneau		vii
Chapter I:	Deer Hunting in Colorado	1
Chapter II:	Colorado Typical Mule Deer Stories and Photographs	11
Chapter III:	Colorado Non-Typical Mule Deer Stories and Photographs	123
Chapter IV:	Colorado Typical and Non-Typical Whitetail Deer Stories and Photographs	177
Chapter V:	Elk Hunting in Colorado	195
Chapter VI:	Colorado Typical and Non-Typical American Elk Stories and Photographs	203
Chapter VII:	Shiras Moose in Colorado	231
Chapter VIII:	Shiras Moose Stories and Photographs	237
Chapter IX:	Other Great Colorado Big Game Stories and Photographs	247
	Bighorn and Desert Bighorn Sheep	248
	Rocky Mountain Goats	260
	Pronghorn	262
	Cougar	284
	Black Bear	306
Chapter X:	Photographs of Big-Game Trophies without Stories	319
	Typical Mule Deer	319
	Non-Typical Mule Deer	326
	Typical American Elk	331
	Shiras Moose	333
	Other Great Colorado Big Game	333-335
Chapter XI:	Trophy Judging and Care in the Field	336
Chapter XII:	Records-Keeping Programs of North America	339
	Boone and Crockett Club	339
	Pope and Young Club	340
	Longhunter Program for Muzzleloader Firearms	341
Chapter XIII:	Your Odds for a Colorado Trophy	343
Chapter XIV:	Boone and Crockett Club Official Score Charts	351
Chapter XV:	Photographs of Special Interest	365
Chapter XVI:	Places to Go and Things to See in Colorado	371
Chapter XVII:	Big-Game Listings from Colorado and Index	377-390
	Minimum Entry Scores for Awards and All-Time Listings in This Book	378

Prologue

For more than 35 years I have been a hunter. During that time I have been privileged to take a number of mule deer, whitetail deer and elk. None of these were trophies in the traditional sense; however, all were trophies to me. Each individual animal provided food for family and friends and equally as important, memories of times and places that I savor each day. I remember vividly the first elk I killed above Zimmerman Lake in Larimer County. It was a spike bull and to me as exciting and memorable as a 6x6 bull.

This second edition of *Colorado's Biggest Bucks and Bulls* will provide all hunters with the information and perhaps the inspiration to seek their own trophy in Colorado. As Susan Campbell Reneau has documented, they are out there from the brushy South Platte River bottoms of eastern Colorado where huge whitetail deer lurk to the oak brush tangles of southwest Colorado that is home to majestic elk. Colorado today has many opportunities for hunters to seek their own trophies. Most, like me, will not be successful in the sense of seeing the animals that grace the pages of a book like this. But, hopefully, each hunt will be a success, due to the memories, places and experiences that we all share as hunters.

Rick Kahn
Wildlife Biologist
Terrestrial Section
Colorado Division of Wildlife

Introduction

More than 20 years ago, my husband Jack and I wrote the first edition of COLORADO'S BIGGEST BUCKS AND BULLS, so I thought it was high time to do a second edition. This edition contains hundreds of new photographs and hunting stories as well as a plethora of historical photographs and photographs showing unique trophies and events. So many people have enjoyed the stories from the first book that many of them also are included in this edition since the first edition is long out of print. If you have a copy of the first edition you will recognize some of the story favorites but will delight in reading the new ones uncovered after six years of "hunting."

Hunting is precisely what I've been doing since 1995. By talking to taxidermists, guides and outfitters, officials with the Colorado Division of Wildlife, official measurers from Colorado and surrounding states, and friends and neighbors of big-game hunters, I've uncovered 273 stories and 400 photographs to delight those of us who love to hunt big game. The outdoor press, including my fellow members of Outdoor Writers Association of America, also have assisted by publishing short announcements in various publications that encouraged men and women to submit their stories and photographs to me. With the advent of the World Wide Web, an invention only dreamed of about twenty years ago by the likes of Bill Gates and the gurus of Microsoft, I have been able to track the phone numbers and addresses of hundreds of people who are listed as big-game hunters in various records books. When I located someone who possessed a terrific trophy I'd always ask for recommendations of other people they knew who also owned such trophies, and those recommendations led to even more outstanding animals. You can't imagine the fun I have had doing this.

My family and I enjoy the excitement and physical challenge of hunting big game. Between my husband, my three sons and myself, we have been blessed over the years in filling dozens of tags for elk, mule deer, whitetail deer, black bear, turkey, wild pig and pronghorn in Colorado, Wyoming, Virginia, Pennsylvania, Texas, Kentucky and Montana. Never have we come close to locating an animal that would rank as a Boone and Crockett trophy, but finding the largest rack, horn or skull has never been our incentive. Collecting a freezer full of meat, walking close to wildlife and savoring the great outdoors are our goals. Interviewing the lucky few who have collected lots of meat AND massive trophies provided me with an opportunity to see Boone and Crockett-quality trophies up close and personal, knowing with a twinge of regret that I'll probably never be so lucky. Meeting the men and women who hav-

The author with her first mule deer buck in 2000. Not a B&C trophy but a trophy to her, just the same.

taken these magnificent animals has been a distinct pleasure. Few of these hunters ever expected to come upon such a treasure and all have accepted their fate with grace and modesty.

Many of the hunters featured in the first book are no longer with us so it is with great gratification that new hunting stories are featured and recorded for future readers to savor. Over the years I have continued to receive letters and phone calls from people who have memorized the hunting stories from the first edition and wondered when the next edition would be produced. Fathers have told me they read the first edition to their children at bedtime. College students revealed that their professors of wildlife "borrowed" their copies to study and the books were never returned to them or the professors bought the books from them on the spot. Business owners have told of tales where the book "grew legs" and disappeared from their office bookshelves.

My excuse to not write the second edition of COLORADO'S BIGGEST BUCKS AND BULLS had always been that I was working on other books and raising a family. Since this book was first published in 1982, I have written 16 other books about big-game hunting and Western American history and raised three very handsome sons. The year 2000 was finally the year when I had no other book projects on my computer plate and my youngest son had just graduated from high school. This was the year to finish writing the second edition of COLORADO'S BIGGEST BUCKS AND BULLS. A comprehensive trip to Colorado in the summer of 2000 produced dozens of the new stories and photographs featured in the book as I logged more than 3,300 miles on my rented car in two weeks. From 1995 to 2000 I uncovered hundreds of photographs and stories, but the year 2000 was when I put the book together.

COLORADO'S BIGGEST BUCKS AND BULLS is a tribute to outstanding wildlife habitat management by the Colorado Division of Wildlife and private landowners and to the hunters who have supported this valuable work through their hunting licenses and hunting equipment purchases. Even with the increase of more than a million people from 1990 to 2000, Colorado remains the finest place to hunt mule deer and one of the finest places to hunt nearly every other type of big game that is indigenous to North America and legal to hunt. This book includes mule deer, whitetail deer and American (Yellowstone) elk stories and photos as well as stories and photos highlighting Shiras moose, bighorn sheep, desert bighorn sheep, Rocky Mountain goats, pronghorn, cougar or mountain

The author with her first pronghorn buck in 1999. Her guide for this hunt was her youngest son, Richard, age 16, shown to the left.

lions, and black bear. As a tribute to the other fine big game featured in this new edition, the subtitle has been added that reads, COLORADO'S BIGGEST BUCKS AND BULLS and Other Great Colorado Big Game.

The success of Shiras moose in Colorado and the explosion of trophy whitetail deer in the state are two big stories that have developed since the first edition, and chapters regarding those populations document their success. As more people have moved into Colorado in the last twenty years, more hunters have taken up primitive weapons use, which is also documented by the number of hunters who are featured in this edition. Happily for me, I was able to uncover more women hunters this time around, so the results of my efforts are documented. In the first edition we only featured one woman hunter, Lucille Gooch, but in this edition we have close to ten. It is incumbent upon all of us to encourage women to hunt since so many families now include a single mom with sons and daughters who might like to hunt but need a guiding adult for help and transportation to prime hunting areas. A mother who hunts will teach her children to hunt, and so the tradition will continue.

The number one reason the second edition was written was the simple fact that I enjoyed meeting lovely people across Colorado and the United States who had the unique distinction of taking Boone and Crockett, Pope and Young or Longhunter Muzzleloading big game in Colorado. My family first purchased land in Woodland Park in 1959 when that area and Colorado Springs were tiny towns that had the look of the Wild West about it. I was raised in Colorado Springs, Colorado, and graduated from Wasson High School in 1970 and the University of Northern Colorado in Greeley in 1974. I was married to Jack Reneau in the Colorado College chapel in Colorado Springs two weeks after college graduation and celebrated our marriage at a reception with friends and family at Rockledge Mansion in Manitou Springs. Jack and I now live in the Bitterroot Valley of Montana where the hunting tradition is equally well-documented and where we share a house with three black Labrador retrievers since our human sons are now in college or married.

COLORADO'S BIGGEST BUCKS AND BULLS is a permanent testament to the beauty of our state and the wildness of the West. We who know Colorado beyond the cities are truly blessed. A book is forever and will forever be read by generations of men, women and young people who love to hunt and who love the great outdoors. Hopefully you will enjoy the stories and photographs I've collected as much as I have enjoyed collecting them. Maybe next time I won't wait 20 years to produce the third edition.

Susan Campbell Reneau
Author
COLORADO'S BIGGEST BUCKS AND BULLS
And Other Great Colorado Big Game
Second Edition

Three happy Colorado hunters, left to right, include Eddie Stephenson, Jr. standing below his non-typical buck, Mark A. McCormick standing beneath his typical muley, and Wesley Bruce Brock beneath his typical muley. All three trophies were recognized at the Boone and Crockett Club's 18th Awards display in Dallas, Texas, in 1983. Eddie's buck received 2nd Award in the non-typical mule deer category with a final score of 272-4/8 points. Mark's buck scores 205-6/8 points and received 1st Award in the typical mule deer category. Wesley's Certificate of Merit buck scored 212 points.

— Chapter I —
Deer Hunting in Colorado

During the mid-1850s the pioneers arriving in the territory of what is now Colorado found vast numbers of deer, elk, bighorn sheep and pronghorn in the mountains west of Denver. Though most of these pioneers were initially in search of gold, many communities were established and, because trade and store goods were limited and difficult to obtain, wild game was the primary source of meat for many of these people.

As the communities became more permanent, their meat needs were supplied increasingly by professional exploiters of the abundant wildlife. Market hunters began to make such inroads on various big-game populations that the citizens became alarmed. Gilbert N. Hunter, former state game manager, estimated that 100,000 big-game animals per year must have been killed to supply Colorado's population at that time.

In 1897, the first game laws were enacted, which prohibited the taking of wildlife during the breeding season. Still no specific seasons or licenses were in effect, but game laws became increasingly restrictive. By 1903 the first deer hunting licenses were authorized at $1 for residents and $25 for non-residents. But elk, pronghorn and bighorn sheep seasons were still closed. Bison had disappeared from Colorado by the beginning of the 20th Century.

The early 1900s represented the low point in Colorado's big-game populations. For example, a total of 2,278 deer were harvested in 1903. Hunters were limited to bucks only and the success ratio was 15 percent. Annual deer harvest remained relatively low through 1912 when the season was closed. It remained closed through 1917. Even after the season reopened

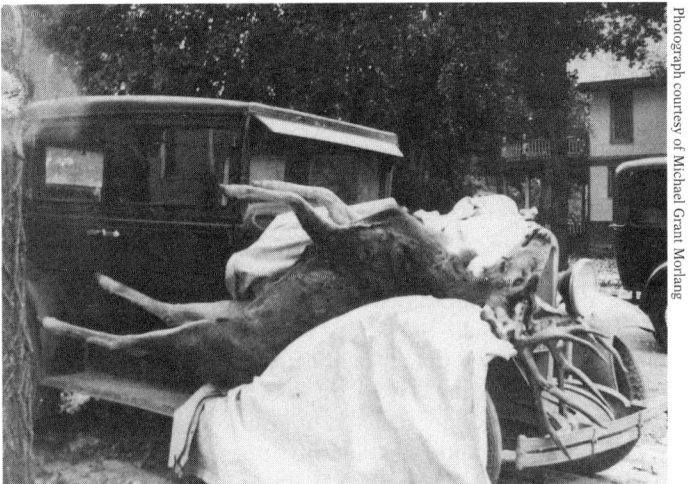
A trophy mule deer buck rests on the hood of a hunting vehicle, circa 1920.

in 1918, deer harvest statistics didn't really show any appreciable increase until beginning in 1939. Between 1918 and 1939 the deer harvest ranged from a low of 1,729 bucks taken in 1923 to a high of 14,500 taken in 1939. The average annual harvest for that time period was a mere 4,811 deer.

After 1940 Colorado's deer herds began to show an appreciable increase in numbers, and either sex seasons became commonplace. During the 1950s, however, the management of mule deer in the various Western states was affected throughout many different types of regulations and administrative philosophies. Regardless of the management approach, whether it was ultra-conservative or super-exploitive, the mule deer trend followed essentially the same pattern throughout the West; a gradual buildup of herds beginning in the 1920s, with a peaking somewhere in the late 1940s or early 1950s that extended into the early 1960s. This buildup was followed by a general decline during the remainder of the 1960s and into the mid-1970s. Beginning in the late 1970s and continuing through the early 1980s, big-game herds underwent a general buildup, reversing the trend of the early 1970s.

During the period 1940 through 1969, Colorado yielded a deer harvest of 2.3 million bucks, does and fawns for an overall success ratio of 42 percent in 1944 to the highest success ratio of 89 percent in 1957. During this 30-year period a total of 1.3 million bucks, representing an annual average of 43,300, were harvested. Broken down into three 10-year periods, the annual antlered harvest totaled 234,511 from 1940 to 1949; 455,804 from 1950 to 1959; and 532,239 from 1960 to 1969.

During the period 1970 to 1999, Colorado yielded a total deer harvest (bucks, does and fawns) of 1.8 million or an overall success ratio of a little more than 31 percent. The highest harvest success ratio during this 30-year period was 46 percent

Harsh winter conditions claim the lives of thousands of wildlife each year. Here, a typical mule deer skeleton lies as it died.

in 1972 and 1978. The lowest harvest success ratio was 28 percent in 1997. For the 10-year period from 1970 to 1979, the total number of antlered harvest was 477,542; the total antlered harvest from 1980 to 1989 was 535,881; and the total antlered harvest from 1990 to 1999 was 409,225. This downward trend of deer harvest reflects the growing concern for the mule deer populations of the state.

R. Bruce Gill and eight other contributors prepared a comprehensive report in November 1999 for the Colorado Legislature that was titled, "Declining Mule Deer Populations in Colorado: Reasons and Responses." The biologists who compiled the statistics concluded that wildly fluctuating numbers of deer apparently characterized mule deer populations. Numbers varied throughout the years, primarily in response to climatic fluctuations, habitat change and market hunting. Apparently mule deer were common but not abundant prior to European American settlement of the West. They were abundant in the late 1800s and scarce during the first three decades of the 20th century. Somewhere between 1935 and 1955 there were more mule deer in the West than at any time since. Mule deer numbers have fluctuated primarily in response to climatic conditions and effects of hunting. Deer numbers have been declining at least since the late 1950s and 1960s.

Henry "Huck" Roberts and his brothers, Russell and Ern, loved hunting on the Uncompahgre Plateau outside Grand Junction. Photographs of past hunts were saved by grandson Michael Grant Morlang of Grand Junction. Here we see the brothers hamming it up for the camera with their game in tow.

Today, mule deer populations in Colorado may number less than one-half of peak populations of the 1940s. The biologists further concluded that heavy browsing pressure and loss of prime mule deer habitat to human development has further influenced the decline of the mule deer population. As evidence of human impact, recently released Census 2000 figures show Colorado with a total population of 4,301,261, a rise in human population of 31 percent since 1990. When Colorado was a territory in 1870, the total human population was 39,864. In 1880, four years after Colorado became a state, the population jumped to 194,327 and rising population figures have never stopped.

Henry "Huck" Roberts on a deer hunt in the 1920s.

Five major factors seem to be responsible for the decline in mule deer populations. Decreases in amounts and quality of critical deer habitats, competition with elk and other grazing livestock, diseases, predators and hunting pressure were identified as the five factors. Elk populations have dramatically increased over the years as deer populations have declined. In 1997 estimates place the total deer population to be between 515,000 and 530,000. Elk populations were probably at their highest levels in 1999 with approximately 247,000 throughout Colorado.

The report to the Colorado Legislature in 1999 stated that by the late 1930s and early 1940s, wildlife managers thought there were too many mule deer. A 1940 survey of both mule deer populations and their habitats in the Gunnison Basin of southwestern Colorado showed approximately 22,000 deer while carrying capacity (ability to support a healthy deer population) was estimated to be 12,000 deer. In 1997 another wildlife survey was conducted by biologists in the same area of the state. They concluded that current deer numbers approximated the same carrying capacity estimates of 1940 and the current population seemed to have decreased since the 1940s. The biologists who conducted the 1997 survey also concluded that current mule deer population objectives might not be sustainable today because of increased human populations and destruction of mule deer habitat. Mule deer populations in 1997 for this area topped 10,000, but the carrying capacity for such a population has dropped since 1940 to below 10,000.

Mule deer populations in Colorado have widely fluctuated since the 1800s but seemed to decline after the peak numbers of the 1940s. Humans now occupy the same mid-elevation lands in mountain valleys that have been traditional deer habitat. Natural fire has been suppressed as human populations increased. Many shrubs and plants that need fire to enhance rapid growth haven't benefited from fire so forage for deer also has decreased. The expansive growth of noxious weeds has expanded its growth in areas where pinon pine and juniper plants used to dominate and since those plants are the ones mule deer love to eat, the noxious weeds help reduce their level of nourishment. Excessive grazing by cattle and other domesticated animals also damages wildlife habitat forage.

As elk populations have blossomed, mule deer populations have declined. Elk are much larger than mule deer and have the ability to walk through deep snow and eat plants that are higher on a shrub or tree than a mule deer can reach. Elk also have the ability to eat lower quality foods and still maintain their health in order to survive harsh winters and reproduce successfully. Elk young are able to join a herd much more quickly than mule deer young and the tendency is for a mule deer doe to remain apart from other deer, thus making mule deer more susceptible to predation. Mule deer can't subsist on dry grasses in the winter as elk can. They need easily digested plants and plant parts such as the leaves of evergreen shrubs to survive. Elk have the ability to eat lesser plants that still give them enough nutrition to survive and reproduce. Mule deer are also more susceptible to a variety of infectious, noninfectious and parasitic diseases, according to the 1999 report to the Colorado Legislature. The report emphasized that "most of these diseases affect individual deer and have not been detected at rates sufficient to affect deer population performance on regional, state or range-wide levels."

Dilworth Brothers Meats of Montrose was the site for seven hunters to pose in front of their eight bucks at the start of the 20th Century.

A wall of bucks from Colorado taken by hunters L.C. Denny, M.L. Schmidt and Earl Denny in the 1960s. The buck seen in the top row, third from left, is the B&C non-typical muley L.C. Denny took in 1961 that is listed in the B&C all-time records book.

Hunting pressure was also studied in 1999 and the report concluded that from 1940 to 1965, deer harvests increased steadily with much of the harvest in the 1960s directed towards antlerless deer to reduce deer populations. Harvests dropped dramatically following a severe winter of 1964-65 and antlerless seasons were reduced with harvest numbers stabilizing or slowly declining. Once mule deer populations dropped in the late 1950s and early 1960s, the ability for deer herds to renew their total population decreased. Significant in the statistics is that the record year for deer harvest in Colorado was 1963. Evidence suggests, though, that excessive hunter harvest over the years has NOT been responsible for the decline in mule deer populations. Biologists who wrote the 1999 report said that "if excessive hunter kill was the primary cause of declining mule deer numbers, ratios of fawns per 100 does should have increased rather than decreased." Data collected of over-winter mortality rates of mule deer fawns showed just the opposite.

Even though hunting pressure increased dramatically from after World War II to the present, evidence collected from biologists did not support the conclusion that low buck numbers were responsible for the drop in ratios of fawns per 100 does in the last 25 years. A 1999 study indicated that 93 percent of the does examined from the Uncompahgre Plateau were pregnant. The 1999 study stated that "if low buck numbers were responsible for the observed decline in fawn:doe ratios, both pregnancy rates and the average number of fetuses per doe observed should have been much lower, but they weren't." Change in habitat and wildlife predation were identified as the major causes of the mule deer population decline.

The CDOW responded to scientific and observational evidence by restricting buck licenses to a limited drawing season starting in 1999. This restriction will remain in effect until such time as the CDOW thinks mule deer populations are back to where they belong. Deer inventory procedures are being upgraded to allow frequent collection of deer population data and a variety of research projects are underway.

In contrast to concerns about mule deer populations in the mountains and mountain valleys of Colorado, whitetail deer populations seem to be on a healthy upswing if only by the number of Boone and Crockett Club trophies entered in their records keeping program since 1982. In the first edition of *Colorado's Biggest Bucks and Bulls*, only one hunter-killed and one picked-up typical whitetail buck were officially entered in the Boone and Crockett Club records program compared to a total of 13 typical and 11 non-typical bucks that have been added since the first edition of this book was published. An equally impressive number of typical and non-typical whitetail also were entered into the Pope and Young Club and one in the Longhunter Programs. The P&Y all-time records book lists 102 Colorado bucks that qualify for their all-time records book.

The lush grain fields of eastern Colorado have always attracted deer and this pattern continues in the new millennium. Prime hunting areas include habitat along the South Platte, Republican and Arkansas rivers. Recent records book whitetail have been harvested in the counties of Adams, Baca, Bent, Boulder, Cheyenne, Elbert, Kiowa, Larimer, Las Animas, Lincoln, Logan, Morgan, Otero, Prowers and Yuma counties. Reports of numerous whitetail deer bucks that make the Boone and Crockett Club's all-time records book continue to be heard but until the racks are measured the exact extent of whitetail trophies can't be calculated.

An unknown location for a hunting camp, circa 1900, that was possibly near Durango.

No permanent herds of whitetail deer existed in 1948 when Gilbert N. Hunter, a CDOW game manager, published a report titled, "History of White-Tailed Deer in Colorado." Hunter reported that in the past, small permanent herds did inhabit the lower Arkansas Valley, the San Isabel National Forest region and the Fisher Peak area near Trinidad but that such herds disappeared from the state during the late 1920s and early 1930s. In 1948 Hunter said that a small migrating herd of whitetails entered Colorado from New Mexico and spent summers in the Fisher Peak area but the main home range of these animals was the Sangre De Cristo region south of the Colorado border.

R. Bruce Gill, CDOW statewide mammals research program leader, was the first biologist to photograph a whitetail doe in the upper Colorado River Basin of Middle Park in 1970, which established the fact that whitetails have spread beyond the eastern plains into the mountain areas of Colorado. Gill was a wildlife researcher at the time and noted the populations of whitetail deer were in the valleys and forests around Kremmling, Hot Sulfur Springs and Meeker. Researchers have also identified whitetail populations in northern Colorado near the Wyoming border along the North Park of the Colorado River Basin and the Upper Yampa River Valley near Steamboat Springs and east of Meeker.

From a population of zero permanent whitetail herds in the late 1940s, best estimates by Gill place the population between 20,000 and 30,000 in 2001 with sightings not only in eastern Colorado but in the mountain regions of the state. Whitetail deer populations comprise about 5 percent of the total statewide deer population of deer that number between 400,000 and 500,000 bucks, does and fawns.

HUNTING SEASON DEVELOPMENTS

The 1970s were characterized by a number of innovative regulations designed to enhance big-game populations and reduce hunting pressure. A few of these regulations, as well as other highlights, are listed in Table II beginning with the second primitive weapons season held in 1970.

Faced with increasing numbers of hunters and dwindling acres of big-game habitat, the Division of Wildlife conducted separate deer and elk season beginning in 1971. The separate and later combined, seasons dominated the 1970s. From 1972 to 1973 deer season preceded elk season, and from 1974 to 1976 elk season preceded deer season. The year 1975 was the first year that the total harvest of antlerless deer was restricted to the holders of a limited number of either sex licenses during the regular deer season. That year was the first time in Colorado's history of wildlife management that such constraints on deer hunting were imposed to regulate the taking of antlerless deer so that mule deer populations could make a more rapid comeback than they could under the types of seasons previously held. Such changes in regulation allowed an adequate harvest in selected units where deer populations were up in relation to limited winter range or because of crop damage. This management philosophy was applied from 1975 to the 1980 deer seasons.

From 1977 to 1982 the CDOW conducted separate and combined (with elk) rifle deer seasons. This concept was adopted in an effort to maximize the harvest of excess animals and to spread hunting pressure between two different seasons thereby reducing hunter crowding. This approach served to give the deer hunter a choice, which was never before offered in Colorado. The management of the species was also

A hunting camp in 1902 includes, left to right, R.J. Sampson, W.W. Lippert, R. Smith (guide), W. Cook, Henry H. Zietz, Sr., and G. Smith (guide).

A lineup of 10 hunters with their 20 deer at the beginning of the 20th Century illustrates the bounty of Colorado. Licensed hunting in the modern era began in 1903 at a cost of $1 for residents and $25 for nonresidents. Hunting seasons closed from 1912 to 1917 and harvest figures really didn't grow dramatically until the 1940s.

enhanced by allowing the CDOW more flexibility in pinpointing needed pressure, or reducing in pressure over two seasons. An increase in deer numbers coupled with this seasonal structure accounted for an average rifle season harvest of 66,165 deer from 1978 to 1982. Overall, hunting pressure was better distributed due to the separate and combined deer seasons.

In 1981 the CDOW again departed from previous years with the elimination of either sex licenses in the regular rifle seasons. These licenses were replaced in all instances with limited antlerless licenses. This policy was extended for 1983. The CDOW documented poor fawn survival during the winter of 1979-80. They suspect that does surviving the winter of 1978-79 were unable to provide for fawns dropped during the spring of 1979. To the Colorado deer hunter this meant fewer bucks harvested and lower overall success ratios. In those herds hit by the winter of 1978-79, there were relatively few yearling bucks available to the hunter in the 1979 and 1980 seasons. Harvest statistics in 1981 indicated increased harvest and hunt success because of the large number of yearling bucks available from exceptional fawn crops in 1980.

The one and only hunt concept implemented in 1974 and the splitting up of the deer seasons significantly reduced hunter crowding. For example, in 1978 the 184,952 deer hunters were distributed so only a maximum of 88,106 hunters were in the field at any one time. The maximum occurred during the separate deer season.

In 1983 hunters were allowed to hunt a deer and/or elk in the separate seasons or they could hunt deer and/or elk in the combined season but they could not hunt one animal in a separate season and the other animal in a combined season. More than 190,500 hunters held deer licenses that included limited antlerless, unlimited antlered in combined and separate season, unlimited antlered only in separate and combined seasons, and limited antlered during an early high country season. If a deer hunter also wanted to hunt elk, he or she had to hunt in the same type of season for both deer and elk.

Heavy loss of deer and elk during the harsh winter of 1983-84 meant that hunting seasons were more restrictive in 1984 and the total number of deer hunters in the field that year dropped to a little more than 163,000. Limited antlered and antlerless seasons dominated what was available to hunters and only two unlimited either sex weeks each started on September 8. An unlimited antlered season for deer or elk only or combined was also offered. A special application was needed for most of the hunting seasons.

In 1985, all separate and combined hunting season antlerless deer licenses were considered additional licenses and if a hunter drew an additional license he or she could purchase one other license for the same season. Regulations that year also allowed a hunter to legally harvest an animal on either or both licenses. New in 1985 was a special season for big-game animals causing damage and 500 applicants were selected for each list that included regular firearm in the northwest, southwest, northeast or southeast regions of the state, muzzleloading rifle statewide, and bow and arrow statewide. Hunters could only apply for one region for regular rifle season and only for a maximum of three lists. This special season continued through 1989 for deer, elk and pronghorn.

Three regular rifle combined deer seasons were established in 1986 in October and November, and in most areas of the state, antler restrictions applied that required hunters to take bucks with at least three points on one antler. Starting in 1986, hunters were also required to keep some sort of evidence of sex naturally attached to the carcass for any big-game animal harvested so CDOW officials could check to make sure hunting license regulations were followed.

Unlimited archery deer licenses in November and December were issued in 1987 for the first time in selected eastern plains units but a hunter could not purchase an unlimited license for either the regular or late season. No unlimited licenses were issued that year for the muzzleloading rifle-only season and a hunter could only purchase one deer license for any one of the five deer seasons.

A deer was caught in a barbed wire fence and died near Yampa. Hundreds of deer annually suffer a fate similar to this deer shown in the above photograph.

Antler length for determining a legal buck was standardized to five inches in 1988 but in 1989 that antler length restriction was lifted for the third combined season from November 4 to 12 in certain units of northwest Colorado but not in the other combined seasons. Grand Mesa units saw continued antler length restrictions for the third combined season of 1989 and in other selected units of southwestern Colorado. An experimental late season on the Piceance Basin (Unit 22) allowed hunters to take two does using one license. For the first time in 1989, muzzleloading hunters had to specify if they were hunting for bucks or does.

Concern for the increased use of off-road vehicles prompted a new law to kick in on April 1, 1990, that all-terrain vehicles and unlicensed motorcycles (dirt bikes) had to be registered with the Colorado Division of Parks and Outdoor Recreation if they were used during hunting seasons. Starting January 1, 1991, owners of licensed motorcycles and four-wheel-drive vehicles had to pay an annual use permit fee if the vehicles were used on off-highway trails. Unlicensed and licensed out-of-state vehicles also had to pay for a use permit when vehicles were being used on off-highway trails.

Physically handicapped hunters received special licenses for the first time in 1991 if they were enrolled in a recreational therapy program of a licensed Colorado hospital or rehabilitation center. Limited either sex licenses were available that were concurrent with any one regular rifle season and were limited to ten licenses per unit or not more than 2 percent of licenses designated, whichever was greater. Californians who hunted in Colorado had to show an original state-issued hunter education card to purchase a Colorado hunting license if the hunter was born on or after January 1, 1949.

New in 1992 was a three-day buck season that required a hunter to take a buck deer only during the first three days of one of the three combined deer and elk seasons with an over-the-counter antlered deer license. Either sex deer licenses replaced doe deer licenses in many units during the three combined deer and elk seasons, and those licenses were limited in number and available through application and drawing only. "Private land only" licenses were instigated through a limited drawing that were the only "additional" licenses issued in 1992. Some units in Colorado issued the first-ever-combined license for cow elk and deer doe for the season from October 10 to 14. Except for eight game management units in western Colorado including west of Grand Junction, Delta and parts of Grand Mesa, Gunnison and White River National Forests had no antler point restrictions that year.

Two does could be taken for the first time in selected units or groups of units starting in 1993 using a drawing system for licenses. During the first three days of the season, hunters could take a doe or buck. After the first three days, hunters could take only does. Beginning in 1994, an early draw deer season was begun but if a hunter applied for that drawing he or she couldn't apply for a deer license during the other big-game seasons.

A new big-game season structure began in 1995 and continued through 1999 whendates were set for a five-year period. The CDOW returned to one drawing for limited big-game hunting licenses and a five-day buck deer season began. In the third season that year all buck licenses were limited in number and issued only through a drawing. Most either-sex licenses were available through a drawing and valid for a buck or a doe during the first five days and valid for only does after those first five days except in totally limited hunting units. As restrictions on hunting licenses continued, the number of hunters applying for licenses declined from 173,086 in 1995 to 80,649 in 1999. As the numbers of deer hunters declined, the rate of success rose to a 10-year high of 37 percent in 1999.

Special youth licenses were issued for the first time in 1997 for deer, elk and pronghorn. The licenses were available only through a drawing for young people ages 12 to 15. This year the heads (minus antlers and capes) of deer and elk had to be submitted from selected units to test for chronic wasting disease (CWD) in the northcentral area of Colorado near and along the

Wyoming border. The territory where heads of deer and elk needed to be collected to test for CWD expanded to game management units farther west and along the Wyoming border to the Nebraska border in the upper northeast section of Colorado.

One of the most significant developments in deer hunting history for Colorado began in 1999 when all or most deer hunting was limited to drawing, which continued through the start of the 21st Century.

New in 2001 were increases in nonresident hunting license fees for deer, elk, pronghorn and moose. Nonresident fees in 2001 for deer were set at $273.25 for adults and $103 for youth. Elk nonresident fees for adults were set at $453.25 and for youth at $103. Pronghorn nonresident license fees were established at $273.25 for adults and $103 for youth. Black bear nonresident fees for adults were $253.25 and Shiras moose nonresident license fees were set at $1,503.25. Bighorn sheep permit fees for nonresidents went to $1,503.25 while desert bighorn sheep licenses were not available for nonresidents. Rocky Mountain goat license fees went to $1,503.25 for nonresidents. The application deadline was April 3 with licenses mailed by June 22. New in 2001 unlimited either-sex elk licenses were available over the counter in the northeast plains for specific units. Additional licenses were made available for some units.

For detailed information about current hunting license regulations, printed CDOW information is available through any CDOW office or at stores where hunting licenses are sold. The CDOW Internet site is www.wildlife.state.co.us. The CDOW general information phone number is (303) 297-1192.

TROPHY HUNTS

Probably the seasons with the most historical significance to the Colorado trophy hunter are the trophy hunts initiated as early as 1963 and continued through 1976. These hunts, discontinued after 1976 but started again in the early 1980s, have been called high country, trophy or early rifle hunts. These seasons are held with the stated objective of providing a quality, wilderness hunt while the weather was relatively mild at high elevation levels.

Though a few exceptional bucks were taken during these seasons, they were somewhat controversial in that they proved to be difficult hunts and the bucks were still in velvet. In addition, there were other perceived and real conflicts with other recreationists and grazing livestock. After a five-year lapse in these special trophy hunts, the CDOW reestablished them for the 1982 season. No special trophy season was established in 1983 but in 1984 an early high-country rifle season was available from September 8 to 16 in selected units of the Holy Cross Wilderness, Maroon Bells-Snowmass Wilderness, Hunter-Frying Pan Wilderness and the Rawah Wilderness. Several early high-country seasons were established in 1985 in September for units in the Rawah Wilderness and parts of Routt National Forest area near Gould and in south central Colorado near Alamosa and parts of the Rio Grande National Forest. These hunts were above timberline.

Early seasons were established once again in 1986, 1987 and 1988 in the Rawah Wilderness Area above timberline at 10,000 feet. One early season was opened in 1989 in the Mt. Zirkel Wilderness Area. No early seasons were scheduled in 1990 but Mt. Zirkel area was open in 1991. Private land was open to early season hunts in 1992 along with selected units in Mt. Zirkel. Only private land in 1993 was available for early hunt permits and was also the case in 1994. Private land hunts during the early season was for antlerless animals only for the purpose of controlling game damage. The Rawah Wilderness was once again open in 1994 for early rifle hunts as well as units in Eagles Nest, Maroon Bells-Snowmass, Mt. Zirkel Wilderness and Holy Cross Wilderness Areas.

A combination of private and public land was available to early rifle hunters in 1995. In 1996 early rifle hunts were in units of Rawah, Mt. Zirkel, Eagles Nest, Maroon Bess-Snowmass, Holy Cross, and Hunter-Frying Pan Wilderness Areas. Nineteen early rifle hunts were available in 1997 on both private and public lands. The early season rifle hunts were available in 1998 from September 5 to 13 in 15 wilderness units and 14 were available in 1999, the same year that all deer licenses were by drawing only for the first time. The 2000 season also included 15 early rifle hunts in wilderness areas by drawing only.

As more people apply for hunting licenses and the population of Colorado continues to grow, early season hunts will continue their popularity as a way for hunters to get away from the crowds and come face to face with the wildness of nature.

L.R. "MAC" MCGRAW

Long-time Gunnison, Colorado, resident Mac McGraw began as a guide and outfitter in 1947 when he was 30 and continued his career in April 1950 when he was hired by W.A. "Monty" Moncrief who owned the Sportsman's Hotel. He worked for Monty until spring 1989 and took thousands of photographs of his hunters and their animals. His father, Clarence "Ray" McGraw, was a guide and outfitter with Mac starting in 1951 and took many photographs of his hunting adventures, which began in the 1920s. In 2000, Ray was 102 with many fond memories of hunts with Mac and Sportsman's Hotel clients.

Mac is the author of numerous books including *Mountain Tales, Faded Tracks, Hi-Jinks or (Wild and Wooly and Full of Fleas in the Early Days of Western Colorado), Hunters Attract Flies...Fishermen Do Too,* and *Cowboy Rhymes and Mountain Whimsies*. He provided a wealth of photographs of early Colorado hunting adventures. His books are available through Gunnison bookstores.

L.R. "Mac" McGraw Photographs

On October 15, 1929, five friends enjoyed a day of hunting near Gunnison. The men, from left to right, are Charlie Eilebrecht, Herman "Dad" Mauer, Vern Maurer, Max Werner and Bill Hartman.

A 1923 Nash dons hay for the horses and a buck on its hood for a hunt with style. The Nash was parked on Long Gulch, 15 miles south of Gunnison on October 16, 1927.

Mac McGraw with his young daughter Sharon in the early 1950s beside two massive bucks taken by Mac. Sharon now teachers school in Canon City. The bucks were taken in a patch overlooking Blue Mesa, south of the lake and west of Cebolla Creek. The photograph was taken on Moncrief Ranch, 19 miles west of Gunnison on land that used to be a part of the former town of Cebolla.

Six hunters and 10 mule deer bucks line the grass at the Moncrief Ranch in the 1950s. The far left hunter is Ray McGraw. Behind the line up of men is Dick Wobler and the far right man is Bill Wobler.

The club room of the Sportsman's Hotel in Cebolla, Colorado, in about 1900. Harry F. "J.J." Carpenter was the builder of the hotel and long-time owner. The original hotel burned in 1902 but was rebuilt by J.J. on the opposite side of the Gunnison River. The hotel was sold in 1937 and all the trophies were removed. In 1948, W.A. "Monty" Moncrief bought the ranch and Mac McGraw became his guide and outfitter in April 1950. J.J. Carpenter died of a heart attack in 1957 when he was 78 years old.

Truckloads of deer and elk were typical sights in the 1950s and 1960s when limits on hunting tags were much higher than they are today. In 1963 the Colorado Division of Wildlife allowed a three-deer limit.

Deer Hunting Harvest– Mule and Whitetail Deer

1903-1999

Year	Bucks	Does	Fawns	Total Harvest	Total Hunters	Percent Success
1999*	22,470	6,652	517	29,639	80,649	37%
1998	31,642	8,241	656	40,539	149,616	27%
1997	34,516	10,441	511	45,468	161,128	28%
1996	43,428	11,836	609	55,873	164,870	34%
1995	38,963	12,287	649	51,899	173,086	30%
1994	40,701	13,355	762	54,818	181,575	30%
1993	40,659	19,528	1,328	61,515	187,724	33%
1992	44,852	27,238	1,865	73,955	189,566	39%
1991	52,982	24,526	1,876	79,384	230,809	34%
1990	59,012	29,388	2,090	90,490	246,797	37%
1989	57,400	20,674	1,675	79,749	224,216	36%
1988	52,013	16,806	1,564	70,383	213,532	33%
1987	47,833	10,488	768	59,089	193,649	31%
1986	42,171	9,587	802	52,560	179,625	29%
1985	47,105	10,200	1,094	58,399	169,439	34%
1984	52,855	10,806	1,025	64,686	163,011	40%
1983	65,509	12,368	1,054	78,931	190,535	41%
1982	65,173	8,887	1,040	75,100	175,463	43%
1981	59,689	7,074	662	67,425	168,674	40%
1980	46,133	7,586	827	54,546	157,707	35%
1979	45,673	8,548	1,106	55,327	172,893	32%
1978	67,373	9,889	1,166	78,428	171,449	46%
1977	52,501	5,702	650	58,853	137,010	43%
1976	37,914	2,257	974	41,145	116,103	35%
1975	36,525	2,608	1,316	40,449	138,886	29%

— Before 1975, hunters and percent success based on license sales —

Year	Bucks	Does	Fawns	Total Harvest	Total Hunters	Percent Success
1974	43,968	9,688	1,648	55,304	165,417	33%
1973	51,858	21,430	3,754	77,042	190,818	40%
1972	51,177	14,667	1,394	67,238	144,663	46%
1971	40,413	276	60	40,749	102,262	40%
1970	50,140	18,237	1,877	70,254	173,886	40%
1969	46,777	31,784	8,801	87,362	179,585	49%
1968	44,087	30,506	7,951	82,544	181,598	45%
1967	41,200	29,541	6,996	77,737	172,701	45%
1966	37,062	32,330	9,462	78,854	178,818	44%
1965	44,716	46,056	12,260	103,032	225,629	46%
1964	59,422	47,535	11,883	118,840	236,297	50%
1963	65,594	62,163	20,091	147,848	233,247	63%
1962	66,758	59,391	16,649	142,798	214,830	66%
1961	68,263	59,261	19,817	147,341	198,021	74%
1960	58,360	38,511	12,848	109,719	163,242	67%
1959	54,632	39,640	12,848	107,120	154,910	69%
1958	43,509	30,149	10,579	84,237	137,891	61%
1957	60,458	42,272	11,799	114,529	129,234	89%
1956	47,805	30,403	6,930	85,138	112,596	76%
1955	41,700	23,706	4,634	70,040	111,987	63%
1954	45,576	23,386	4,488	73,450	115,405	64%
1953	39,828	26,330	6,217	72,375	109,418	66%
1952	40,404	25,853	6,852	73,109	109,817	67%
1951	44,045	25,741	5,003	74,789	105,705	71%
1950	37,847	23,434	3,901	65,182	96,565	68%
1949	33,787	30,328	7,104	71,219	87,445	81%
1948	40,328	21,470	4,878	66,676	89,087	75%
1947	32,883	12,048	1,735	46,666	81,126	57%
1946	36,695	14,446	2,124	53,265	81,446	65%
1945	22,804	5,397	63	28,264	55,673	51%
1944	19,850	5,089	246	25,185	59,924	42%
1943	25,271	5,375	—	30,646	58,910	52%
1942	20,551	4,742	—	25,293	42,187	60%
1941	16,917	2,773	—	19,690	34,948	56%
1940	21,874	2,310	244	24,428	36,995	66%
1903-1939	135,513	—	—	135,513	557,905	24%

* Totally limited drawing

— *Chapter II* —
Colorado Typical Mule Deer
Stories and Photographs

DOUG BURRIS, JR.
Location: Dolores County
Year Taken: 1972
Score: 226-4/8
Owner: Don Schaufler

Doug Burris began hunting the Dolores County area in 1969. On his first three Colorado hunts he took three nice bucks that any hunter would be proud to hang over his or her mantle. Little did Doug realize, however, that on his fourth trip he would shake the very foundations of the hunting community with a trophy that would surpass the World's Record by 9-4/8 points.

On opening day of the 1972 season, Doug and his three companions, Jack Smith, Robbie Roe and Bruce Winters, piled into their Jeep before dawn and headed out. Working their way up one of the many mountain roads on the San Juan National Forest, Doug dropped the hunters off at regular intervals. Robbie was the first, followed by Bruce, and then Jack. Doug continued on up the mountain. The day was rainy but all agreed to hunt until dark.

All the bucks the Texans saw that day were small and no one fired a shot. On the second day, Robbie and Bruce both took nice five-pointers, while Jack and Doug remained empty-handed.

On the third day, Doug decided to go after a buck a friend had seen the day before in Proven Canyon. About mid-morning, Doug spotted two nice bucks feeding in a clearing about 500 yards away. While he watched these two bucks, a third one came into view. Doug knew immediately that the latter buck had to be exceptional as he could see antlers even without the aid of binoculars. He decided to make the stalk.

For the better part of an hour Doug slowly and quietly worked his way through the oak brush. About the time he felt he had cut the distance in half, he nearly stepped on a doe bedded down in the underbrush. She exploded out of the brush and the three bucks Doug was stalking scattered in three different directions. Doug had time for one quick shot with his .264 Winchester Magnum and the largest buck folded in mid-stride.

Doug Burris with his World's Record typical mule deer that he took in Dolores County in 1972. His buck remains as the World's Record with a final score of 226-4/8 points.

World's Record
Sagamore Hill Award
First Place
15th B&C Awards Program

Upon closer examination Doug realized he had an unbelievable trophy. However, it wasn't until 1974 at the 15th North American Big Game Awards Program held in Atlanta, Georgia, that Doug's World's Record was confirmed. With a final score of 226-4/8 points, Doug's buck took the first-place award for the typical mule deer category. In addition he received the coveted Sagamore Hill Award for the finest trophy taken during the 15th B&C Awards Program. Doug's buck remains the World's Record typical mule deer and Number One in Colorado.

ROBERT L. INGLES
Location: Delta County
Year Taken: 1958
Score: 215-3/8
Owner: Fred Ferganchick

More than 40 years have past since Bob Ingles took this outstanding buck but the happiest memory about this deer hunt was that he finally hunted with his father. The story of the hunt was rather short. His memories in 2000 were as clear as they were more than four decades ago.

In 1958 when he and his father hunted in Delta County, each hunter could take two deer, so the two of them left home after taking their first buck in hopes they would collect a second deer to fill their tag. They drove their 1949 Chevy truck west of Eckert to the Hell's Kitchen area and stopped at the top of a hill where a church built by the Fuller family was located. They parked the truck on the hill next to a road and split up with Bob going right and his dad going left down the hill. As they walked along, Bob heard his dad shoot so he followed the sound to see what his dad had shot as he saw a monster buck walking out of a culvert below from a distance of about 125 yards. Bob raised his Winchester lever action 32 Special Marlin and dropped the buck in its tracks. "I guess it was a lucky shot," Bob recalled.

Bob split the body in sections and carried it back to the truck and didn't think anything about getting the buck's antlers measured because his goal was to collect meat for the family. Years later, in 1998, a family friend, Fred Ferganchick, offered to get the buck measured and it officially scored as one of the largest typical mule deer bucks ever taken in the world and ranks 3rd largest in Colorado. Bob celebrated his 81st birthday in the year 2000 and still remembers the hunt as if it were yesterday.

The official ranking for this magnificent buck won't be established until 2005 when the 12th edition of the Boone and Crockett Club's all-time records book, *Records of North American Big Game*, is published. If it was listed in the 11th edition it would have ranked 6th largest in the world.

Bob Ingles had his outstanding typical mule deer antlers measured by Roger Selner in 1998, 40 years after he hunted it near his home in Colorado. The buck is one of the world's largest ever taken and recorded with the Boone and Crockett Club.

PAUL A. MUEHLBAUER
Location: Gypsum Creek
Year Taken: 1967
Score: 214-3/8

Paul A. Muehlbauer hunted the last weekend of the 1967 combined deer and elk season with his sons, Rick and Steve. The sons had already filled some of their tags on opening weekend, but Paul still had unfilled deer and elk tags. The three arrived at their favorite campsite on Bear Gulch on the White River National Forest late Friday night and pitched camp.

The next morning they were up and off to Hardscrabble Mountain before daylight. They hunted all day without seeing anything. Late in the afternoon their Jeep developed fuel pump problems, and they returned to Eagle, found a mechanic, and had it repaired.

The next morning Paul and his sons were in the field long before daylight. Following their well-laid plans, they crossed Gypsum Creek and started up Red Table Mountain. There was an extremely heavy frost on the ground that morning and their footsteps crunched loudly. To avoid spooking deer, the three hunters took advantage of the many well-used game trails that crisscrossed the hillside. With the wind blowing in their faces, they had gone only a short distance when they caught the pungent odor of elk in the area. They knew there was an aspen-covered shelf above them and figured that was where the elk were located.

As they approached the shelf, Paul peered over the top and saw an exceptionally large buck not more than 25 yards away. Forgetting the possibility of taking an elk, Paul raised his .30-40 Winchester and let fly one round. The big buck staggered but took off. Rick and Steve each fired but missed as the buck dashed through a dense aspen stand. At about 100 yards, Paul got a second shot when the buck paused momentarily, but he missed again. The buck continued on over the hill that Paul and his sons had just ascended. It was out of sight when, seconds later, they heard it fall. They found it stone-dead wrapped around the base of a tree.

First Place
14th B&C Competition

To comprehend the size of Paul Muehlbauer's B&C typical mule deer a photograph with him holding the mount illustrates its massiveness. This photograph was taken in 1981 when the first edition of this book was written.

When they arrived at the Division of Wildlife's Idaho Springs check station, officials on duty recommended that Paul stop by their Denver office to have the antlers scored. Paul knew they were nice, but that was the first time he realized his trophy was something out of the ordinary.

Later an official measurer for the Boone and Crockett Club confirmed what the Colorado Division of Wildlife's personnel suspected. The rack scored a whopping 214-3/8 points to become the new state record at that time. They are presently the second largest set ever taken in Colorado. At the 14th Competition held at the Carnegie Museum in Pittsburgh, Pennsylvania, in 1971, Paul received the first-place award for the typical mule deer category.

Paul died in 1999 but his son Steve keeps his father's memory alive by having the buck on public display in Cabela's Sporting Good Store in Sidney, Nebraska.

ERROL R. RALEY
Location: Garfield County
Year Taken: 1971
Score: 212-7/8

**First Place
B&C 24th Awards Program**

Errol started hunting when he was 11 years old with his father, cousin and uncle. He got his first guide license when he was 18 years old and was a guide and outfitter for the next 18 years. At that time it was customary for the paying hunters to take the big bucks. In 1971 Errol got a chance to hunt this B&C buck but only had it roughly scored in 1977. At that time he figured the buck was about 8th largest in the world, based upon the Boone and Crockett Club's all-time records book listings.

The hunt took place on the third or fourth day of the deer hunting season when Errol and a friend, Rick Lyons, set off for a late afternoon hike into a draw running into Alkali Creek. The men hunted on Bureau of Land Management land well known to both of them. They had sighted the buck several times during the hunting season and felt confident they knew where the buck was located when they entered the draw for the stalk. Both men were hoping for a non-typical muley, but as soon as Errol saw his typical buck he knew he wanted it. Rick didn't, so without hesitation Errol raised his .270 Springfield Express from a distance of about 200 yards and fired a single shot using a 130-grain Bronze Point bullet. He remembers the buck had a field-dressed weight between 217 and 225 pounds.

For years after Errol took the buck he was satisfied with that unofficial score. In 1997, B&C official measurer Bob Black asked Errol if he could officially measure the buck. Until then all Errol had done with the buck was to mount it on a wooden plaque and hang it in his house. When Bob Black officially scored it at 212-7/8 points, Errol had no idea it would score so high. He was especially impressed at the care Bob took to measure and remeasure the rack 17 times before completing the official score sheet. The buck was invited to the B&C 24th Awards Program in 2001 held at Bass Pro Shop in Springfield, MO, where the Judges Panel confirmed its final score.

Errol took the buck to Darryl Powell of Darryl's Taxidermy in Grand Junction to have the antlers mounted in full shoulder position, and he's very glad he did because it was almost like bringing the buck back to the time when he had shot him.

HAROLD B. MOSER
Location: Jefferson County
Year Taken: 1967
Score: 207-1/8

Harold Moser had hunted deer with Ed Ladwig for years on Ed's spread in the foothills just west of Denver. Harold and Ed had often seen big bucks but nothing that compared to Harold's 1967 trophy.

Second Place
13th B&C Competition

On opening day of the 1967 season, Harold and Ed were accompanied by Harold's son, Neil, and grandson Russel. While Harold checked out a deep draw, the other three men worked a few dry gulches. When Harold peered over the edge into the draw, he noted nothing out of the ordinary except an isolated stand of aspen near the bottom. He was about to return to his companions when he recalled a tip his uncle taught him early in his hunting career. Supposedly, the big, smart bucks hide in the trees and waiting until the hunter is gone. When they feel it's safe, they quietly slip away undetected.

Harold really didn't think there was anything in the aspen grove but decided it was worth a closer look. Picking up a rock he tossed it into the near side of the trees. Instantly a large buck exploded out of the far side of the grove. Fortunately for Harold the buck had trouble negotiating the opposite slope because it was steep and slippery.

Harold raised his modified Springfield to his shoulder and fired. His first four rounds missed. Working his last round into the chamber he took a deep breath, squeezed the trigger and got his records-book trophy. It took Harold and his party the rest of the day to get it out of the field.

Unfortunately, while removing the cape, Harold cut the hide too close to the head. As a result he had to have the head mounted in a sneak position. Cutting the cape incorrectly, however, made no difference in the final score of this beautiful trophy. The antlers scored 207-1/8 points and placed second in the 13th Competition.

HENRY TRUJILLO, JR.
Location: Archuleta County
Year Taken: 1963
Score: 206-6/8

In 1963 Henry Trujillo and his hunting companions, John Chavez and Nobel Snow, hunted for several days early in the season without success. They passed up a few small bucks but saw no elk. The weather that year was unseasonably dry.

The second weekend, Henry and his companions decided to try hunting some of their more tried and proven stomping grounds in the high country. It was early Saturday morning as they unloaded their horses at the base of Middle Mountain in the San Juan Range in southwestern Colorado. The morning was crisp with the sun just turning the cloudless eastern sky red.

Henry and his two close friends had planned to make a sweep of Middle Mountain. As it was a combination deer and elk season that year, Henry instructed his companions to shoot bulls only. After all, they could get their bucks later where it would be easier to pack them out.

The three hunters parted company and didn't see each other the rest of the day. As he threaded his way up Middle Mountain, leading his packhorse, Henry felt he had made a good decision by going in the direction he had selected. By the time he hit the mountain's crest, it was 10 a.m. He hadn't seen a live animal, but felt it was due to all the nose he had made in the dry leaves going up through the timber.

Henry staked his horses, had a bite to eat and set out on foot in search of a respectable bull. After hiking for only 10 minutes, he came upon a large opening and his heart stood still. Standing no more than 80 yards away were two of the largest timberline bucks he had ever seen. Recalling the instructions he had given his partners four hours earlier, Henry raised his .30-06 Remington to his shoulder. Both bucks jumped at the same time and started quartering away from him. There was no time for any decision except to line up the cross hairs on the rear animal and squeeze the trigger. He fired as both bucks went out of sight.

Henry was positive he had hit his mark. He waited a few minutes and then slowly eased his way forward. At the edge of the clearing he found the biggest buck he had ever seen lying in the brush.

Henry knew he had taken an exceptional trophy and felt certain it would place high in the typical mule deer category of the Boone and Crockett Club's records book. Scoring 206-6/8 points, it was one of the biggest deer taken in the nation that year.

Henry Trujillo, Jr. just couldn't resist the impulse to take this Boone and Crockett Club buck (206-6/8 points) on his 1963 Archuleta County elk hunt.

PAT E. COURTIN, JR.
Location: Montrose County
Year Taken: 1972
Score: 206-2/8

Eddie Adams, Kenneth Woods and Pat Courtin had hunted in Colorado for several years prior to the 1972 season. Stanley Boykin joined the trio for this hunt. They hunted Dry Mesa on the Uncompahgre National Forest and jumped several nice bucks, but bulldozed dead trees and brush prevented them from getting clear shots. One afternoon they decided to spread out in a line and hunt the top of a promising looking plateau with windrowed brush piles between each hunter. They had frequently hunted together back home in Texas and believed they could safely use this technique in Colorado. Each man was 40 to 50 yards apart. Eddie was on Pat's left, with Kenneth next and Stanley on the far end of the line.

The men walked a quarter of the plateau's length when a huge buck jumped up under Eddie's feet. The proximity and noise startled Eddie enough to make him miss a snap shot as the buck promptly put dead brush between him and Eddie. When the buck broke out on the other side of the dead timber it was only 10 yards away from the plateau's edge and safety. The last thing the buck expected to see, however, was Pat standing in the middle of the escape route on the edge of the plateau. Both Pat and the buck were equally surprised and confused.

Pat couldn't back up because of the drop-off behind him so he instinctively sidestepped to his right to get out of the buck's way. The buck instantly made up his mind to keep on going whether Pat was standing there or not. Pat pulled the trigger while still side-stepping as the buck passed within two feet of the end of his rifle barrel, and it dropped with his forequarters hanging over the plateau's edge. Pat figured he could have taken the buck just as easily with a bayonet.

When it was all over Pat stood shaking and staring at the buck at his feet. The other hunters arrived and told Pat to keep his knife in its sheath because they figured he would cut himself the way he was shaking. Kenneth field dressed the buck while Pat relaxed. Eddie was not sure he had missed the buck until it was skinned. Only one bullet wound was found.

Pat received a lot of grief from his buddies on many subsequent hunts about his shot and making "The Book." They kept repeating the old adage, "It's better to be lucky than to be smart."

RICHARD COBB
Location: Garfield County
Year Taken: 1962
Score: 205-4/8

Richard Cobb's favorite deer hunting area was a choice piece of Garfield County real estate that served as important deer winter range. Ordinarily there were smaller bucks and does on hand for the opening day rush, but Dick knew the bigger bucks didn't usually arrive until snow pushed them out of the higher elevations.

As Dick had hunted the same area for six or seven years he figured it was as good a place as any to score opening day of the 1962 deer season. After a brief hike Dick sat down on one of the many ridges in the area. A few minutes later, around 8 a.m., a buck with an unusually large set of antlers passed below Dick's vantage point. With a single shot from his .308 Winchester, Dick filled his 1962 deer tag.

Dick knew he had taken a fine trophy, but it wasn't until he had it officially measured that he knew just how good it was – the 9th largest set of typical mule deer antlers ever taken in Colorado at that time.

At the final judging for the 11th Boone and Crockett Club's North American Big Game Competition held in 1964 at the Carnegie Museum in Pittsburgh, Pennsylvania, Dick's trophy took the third-place award with an outstanding score of 205-4/8 points. For many years it was on public display through the 1970s at the Hotel Colorado in Glenwood Springs when the Colorado Division of Wildlife had an office there but now it is in a private collection. CDOW Wildlife Biologist Gene Byrne, who remains stationed in the Glenwood Springs office, said that the CDOW office has moved three times since then, and the trophy was returned to the Cobb family. Originally, Richard Cobb gave the trophy to the CDOW office supervisor, Marvin Smith, who retired and is now deceased.

Third Place
11th B&C Competition

JOE M. GARDNER
Location: Montrose County
Year Taken: 1954
Score: 205-2/8
Owner: Zane Gardner Holland

A solitary figure walked into a clearing and saw, to his relief, a large log where he could sit, remove his shoes and rub his aching feet. He carefully propped his .30-06 rifle up on another log in front of him. Actually, he hadn't walked far from the spot where he and Ben Allison, his hunting partner, pitched camp the previous day after a long and grueling trip from Texas. He had been cramped in the truck for extended periods of time, and his feet and legs were simply killing him.

The lone figure was Joe Gardner. Joe was 64 years old, soon to be 65, and overweight. He tipped the scales at 245 pounds, and he was just shy of 6 feet. Joe was born on a remote ranch in Kimble County, Texas, in 1890, and had rarely ever left it. He had spent 13 months in France as a doughboy during World War I. When the war was over, he returned to the ranch to marry and raise a family. On another occasion, he left to hunt big mule deer in Colorado with Ben Allison, a World War II veteran and avid woodsman. That was 1954.

Hunting was a way of life, as well as a necessity, for Joe. Wild game was the family's primary source of fresh meat. Predators were hunted to protect the cattle, goats and horses. Joe spent his days working and hunting the hills and deep rocky canyons along Maynard Creek, site of the ranch headquarters.

Photograph by Zane Gardner Holland

When Ben Allison hunted, he wasn't concerned at all with creature comforts. He left camp before daylight and returned after dark. A meal to Ben was a can of tomatoes and an onion. He thought nothing of hiking great distances each day. His bedroll consisted of nothing more than a couple of blankets. Joe's Colorado hunt with Ben in 1954 was just such a hunt. He was not able to keep up with Ben's hunting pace, but he was happy to be in camp with Ben to hear his stories.

While Joe sat alone on the log near camp massaging his sore feet, he heard the leaves rustle. He quickly caught a glimpse of a large buck slowly moving through the clearing before him. Joe smoothly picked up his rifle and shot the deer. It was that simple for Joe to make the records book.

Joe died before anyone had the deer officially measured. But he had a great hunting story to tell Ben as they warmed themselves around the campfire that evening, about "the big one that didn't get away."

Joe died in 1963 so his daughter, Zane Gardner Holland, provided details of the hunt and made sure the buck was officially measured years later during the 21st North American Big Game Awards Program (1989-1991).

FRANK PETERSON
Location: Delta County
Year Taken: 1956
Score: 204-7/8

During the 1956 hunting season Frank Peterson was accompanied by his wife and younger son. That year the three of them hunted familiar territory in the upper reaches of Surface Creek in Delta County.

After considerable discussion, the trio planned a drive through an aspen stand about an eighth of a mile square. While Frank and his son took up their positions along the lower edge of the aspens, Frank's wife rode around to the upper end on their only horse. She hadn't been working the aspens long when she jumped a small herd of deer that headed in the direction of her husband.

Frank could hear the deer from his stand long before he saw them. When they came into view there was one exceptional buck preceded by five to six does. As the buck broke out of the aspen it swerved to Frank's right. He dumped it with one clean shot. As Frank was primarily a meat hunter, it wasn't until 1964 that this outstanding trophy was officially scored.

Photograph courtesy of Frank Peterson

Photograph courtesy of Colorado's Biggest Bucks and Bulls archives

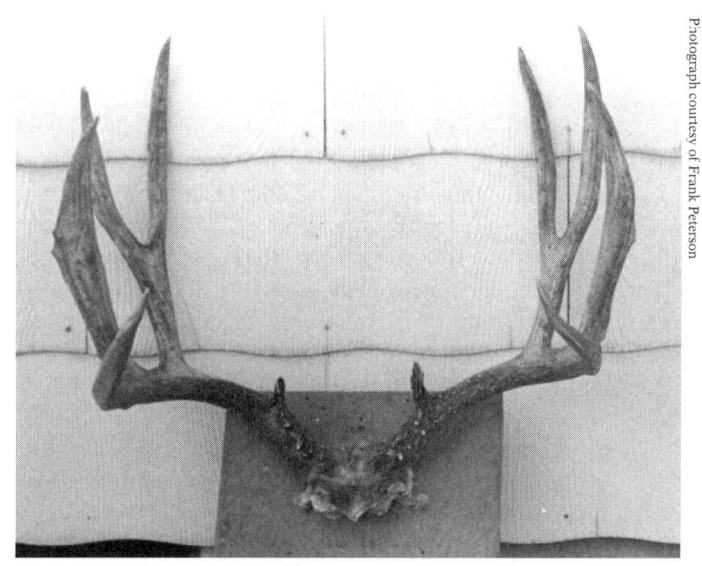

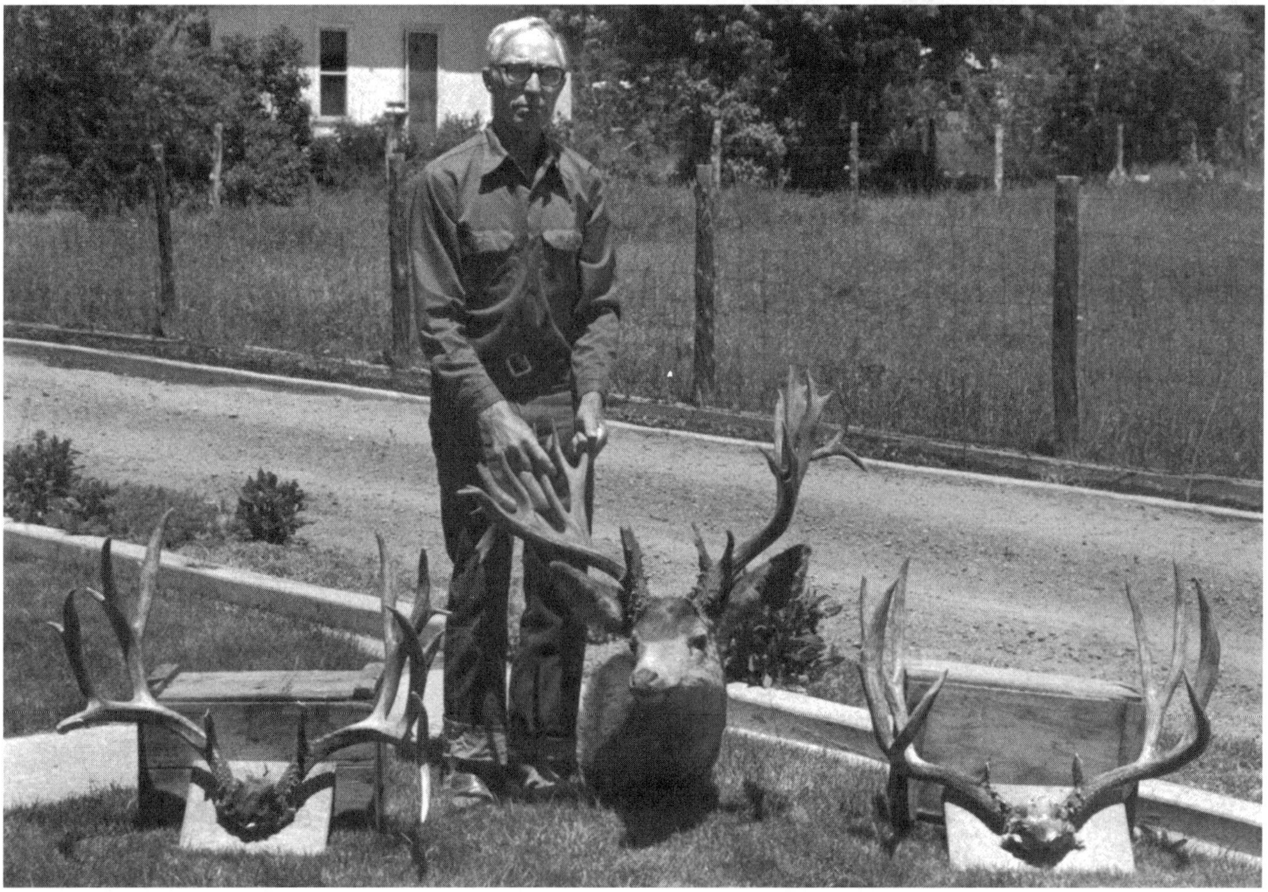

A lifetime hunting career has produced many fine Colorado trophies for Frank Peterson. Here, he poses with his B&C buck (lower right) from Surface Creek in Gunnison County and two other trophies.

NORMAN E. EBBLEY
Location: Hinsdale County
Year Taken: 1961
Score: 204-1/8
Owner: Jim Temple

A dusty set of antlers sat on a bookshelf for many years and became known as the bookshelf buck. Behind the antlers lies a story.

Norman Ebbley's hunt took place one sunny, fall day during the 1961 big game season. Duff, as Norman is known to his friends, and a now-forgotten rancher friend hunted a timbered draw on Big Blue Creek near Lake City. They were making their way down the draw when they spotted two exceptional four-pointers moving along a game trail in single file on the opposite hillside. They were only 150 yards away. Duff, using his Winchester Model 54, .30-06 with peep sights, dropped the lead buck with one shot while his friend cleanly nailed the second buck.

In 1992, more than 30 years after that momentous hunt, Duff's godson, Jim Temple, asked Duff if he could have the rack officially measured for the Boone and Crockett Club's records books. Duff agreed, and Jim contacted B&C official measurer Ray Boyd of Fort Collins, Colorado, to perform the measurement. Ray, conveniently in town for a convention, tallied the measurements on the official B&C score chart. The final score was an impressive 204-1/8 points. Duff's buck made "The Book" with plenty of room to spare.

Duff lives in a nursing home and time has erased most of the hunt's details from his memory. He does remember, however, that his hunting partner's buck was even larger than his. Duff's magnificent buck hangs with honor in Jim Temple's home as a tribute to the buck and to the hunter.

Jim Temple with his godfather's typical mule deer buck that scores 204-1/8 points.

JENS O. SOLBERG
Location: Pitkin County
Year Taken: 1950
Score: 204

On the morning of October 15, 1950, Jens Solberg and his hunting party of four others set out for McClure Pass in Pitkin County loaded with food, camping gear, horses and high hopes. Jens' brother John, his brother-in-law Russell Curtis, and two old hunting partners, Ab Harding and Whitney Scofield, were along on the hunt.

After hunting McClure Pass for three or four days without luck they decided to concentrate their efforts in the vicinity of Muddy Creek. Since they were unfamiliar with the area, they picked a spot at random and unloaded the horses.

They started riding east. Jens was on the north flank of the party when he suddenly spotted a huge deer on the opposite ridge approximately 300 yards away. When Jens put his field glasses on it, he noted that it was a buck bedded down and broadside to him. With his sights set for 200 yards, Jens aimed a little high and fired. The bullet from his trusty .270 Remington hit the buck behind the shoulder, downing it instantly.

Certificate of Merit
12th B&C Competition

Upon reaching his buck, Jens field dressed it alone. By the time he was finished, Russ, John and Whitney were there to help load the meat on Silver, his horse. Silver had other ideas and balked at the prospect of packing a deer. Jens' horse had no such problem with elk but always spooked around deer. Eventually, while Ab restrained the horse, Jens and his companions loaded the buck.

On the way home Jens had the deer checked at the Glenwood Springs check station. Colorado Division of Wildlife officials were greatly impressed with the trophy and suggested Jens get the rack officially measured. They even offered to pay for the mounting if Jens would leave it with them. Jens was flattered but decided to take it home and have it mounted by a friend of the family.

Jens waited nearly 16 years before he finally had the rack officially measured. The antlers easily made the Boone and Crockett Club's records book with a final score of 204 points. At the invitation of B&C, Jens sent his trophy to the Final Judging of the 12th Competition in Pittsburgh, Pennsylvania, where he received a Certificate of Merit.

Taken on Muddy Creek in Pitkin County in 1950 by Jens O. Solberg, this massive typical muley scores a hefty 204 points that received a B&C Certificate of Merit at their 12th Competition in 1956.

ED CRAIG
Location: Mesa County
Year Taken: 1951
Score: 203-7/8
Owner: Craig Family

When Ed Craig and his wife left the UC Cow Camp on the Uncompahgre Plateau to hunt deer in 1951, they were after venison. Neither had heard of the Boone and Crockett Club nor could they have cared less.

Hunting the ridge above South Fork Mesa Creek, the couple spied a large herd of deer with several big bucks at the bottom of a deep canyon. Realizing it would be quite a chore packing a deer out of the bottom of that canyon, the couple threw rocks at the deer in the vain hope of spooking a buck up the side of the canyon. When that didn't work, Ed selected one of the bigger bucks and dropped it with his .270.

After hiking down into the canyon, Ed prepared for the steep climb out. He first field dressed the big buck and then removed the antlers. Since he couldn't eat the antlers Ed left them hanging in a tree to cut down the weight of his load.

It wasn't until 1958, seven years later, that the antlers were found by one of Ed's ranch hands while herding sheep in the same canyon. When Ed saw the antlers for the second time, he thought he recognized them immediately. His suspicions were confirmed once the cowboy described where he had found them.

Ed's tremendous buck wasn't scored until 1958. Even though it probably shrank considerably in the intervening years, Ed's trophy still scored an impressive 203-7/8 points.

Ed Craig's massive buck is held by Colorado Division of Wildlife Senior Information Officer Bob Hoover (left) as Herschel Hendrickson (right), a friend of the Craig family, looks on in 1964. Herschel brought the mount to Bob to measure, and the photograph was snapped shortly after the measurements were taken. The Craig family currently owns the rack since Ed has passed away. The buck scored 203-7/8 points. Thanks to the Sherlock Holmes efforts of B&C Official Measurer Bob Black, identification of the photograph was complete.

EDISON A. PILLMORE
Location: Jackson County
Year Taken: 1949
Score: 203-7/8
Owner: Mrs. Edison A. Pillmore

**Sagamore Hill Award
First Place
6th B&C Competition**

Edison A. Pillmore collected this symmetrical set of antlers in 1949 on the Quarntance Ranch in North Park. His hunting companions on that memorable hunt were Clifford Alderson and Lee Moore.

As Edison stepped out of a stand of timber on the Quarntance Ranch and into a clearing, he spotted a small herd of deer with two of the largest bucks he had ever seen. Sensing his presence, the entire herd broke for cover. Before they could make it, though, Edison raised his .303 Savage to his shoulder and fired, dropping the larger of the pair.

Unfortunately, Edison never knew of the recognition his trophy received before he passed away in 1952. His widow entered his buck in the Boone and Crockett Club's 6th Competition in 1953. At the Final Judging, Edison's trophy scored 203-7/8 points. It not only took the first place honor for the typical mule deer category, but it also received the Sagamore Hill Award, the single highest award given at any big-game competition. In addition, his trophy was recognized as the new World's Record at that time.

Joe Neal, Bill Hensler, Ed Santye and Mr. Bergen (first name unknown), left to right, pose with deer they took near Meeker in September 1901. The latter three hunters were from Denver.

Robert Kinghorn, an official for the Colorado Division of Wildlife, measures a trophy mule deer buck at the check station on Hwy. 13 in the late 1950s.

OLEN J. HICKS
Location: Montezuma County
Year Taken: 1999
Score: 203-4/8

One day was all Olen Hicks had to hunt on the last day of the season for one of his favorite big game – the elusive mule deer, so he had to make his trip worthwhile.

Olen returned to his favorite hunting area near Mesa Verde National Park in Montezuma County in hopes of locating a big buck he saw at the beginning of the year that hung with another non-typical buck and a monster 4x4 typical. Olen sighted the buck twice within a canyon that day, so Olen started walking the canyon length for eight hours and close to 20 miles. Just before sunset, Olen saw two does feeding in willows, at first not realizing a buck was feeding about 30 yards away from them at a distance of 400 yards from where Olen scoped the scene. He estimated the buck to have a rack about 26 inches wide with three points and cheaters. He had no idea the buck was so big because the antler was hidden in the brush but he figured it was a respectable buck since he was at the end of the last day of the season and the sun was setting. With his first shot from his .270 Browning, semi-automatic rifle using a 150-grain bullet, Olen dropped the buck and the second shot finished it off.

For a one-day hunt, Olen did pretty well for himself.

Olen's massive typical mule deer buck was accepted into the Boone and Crockett Club's 24th North American Big Game Awards Program in 2000, and is one of the largest bucks ever taken in the hunting history of the state.

EARL L. MARKLEY
Location: Montrose County
Year Taken: 1968
Score: 203
Owner: Aly M. Bruner

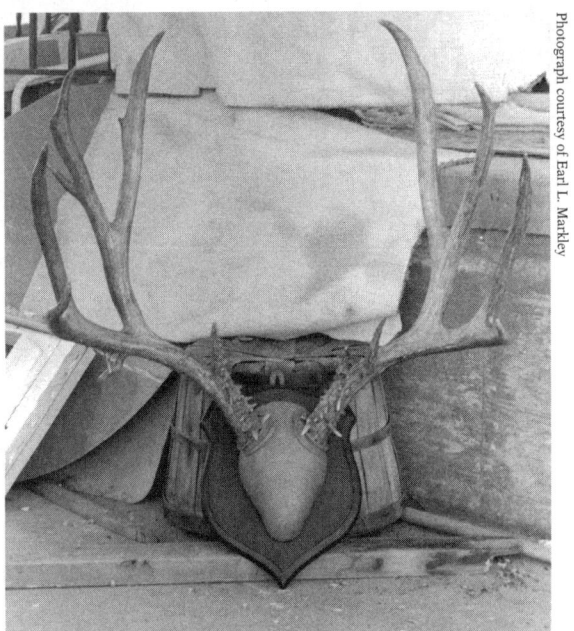

When Earl Markley returned to his partners, Don Ice and Clay Hanlon, after taking his first Boone and Crockett buck, both were beaming from ear to ear. They had just taken two really nice four-pointers and were convinced they had outdone Earl. Earl still smiles to himself to this day when he recalls their expressions upon seeing his 1968 buck.

Earl had hunted deer in Colorado for 25 years and had hunted with Clay for 20 of those hunting seasons. The men enjoyed each other's company and hunted on Kelso Mesa on the Uncompahgre National Forest. They had hunted there many times before and knew it was the place to find trophy deer.

It was a clear but ice-cold autumn day as the three men picked their way through one of the many draws of the mesa. Earl's attention was first caught by a small herd of does going out of the bottom of the draw. Glancing on the hillside above the does, two nice four-pointers materialized while a third exceptionally large deer was observed sneaking over the same hill. Afraid his buddies would shoot the largest buck if he pointed it out, Earl took off alone at a brisk pace in an effort to cut it off. After a good quarter-mile stalk, Earl took the first of two trophy bucks he has taken during his lifetime. In the meantime, Clay and Don had downed the other two four-pointers.

The three men packed their trophies back to camp on horseback. After the required drying period, Earl had his trophy scored by an official measurer of the Boone and Crockett Club. It had a final score of 203 points.

Earl Markley with his 1968 (right) and 1969 (left) Kelso Mesa bucks that made the records book with respective scores of 203 and 196-3/8 points. Earl is one of only a handful of hunters to have two Colorado trophies listed in the Boone and Crockett Club's all-time records book, Records of North American Big Game

JEWEL E. SCHOTTEL
Location: Ouray County
Year Taken: 1966
Score: 202-6/8

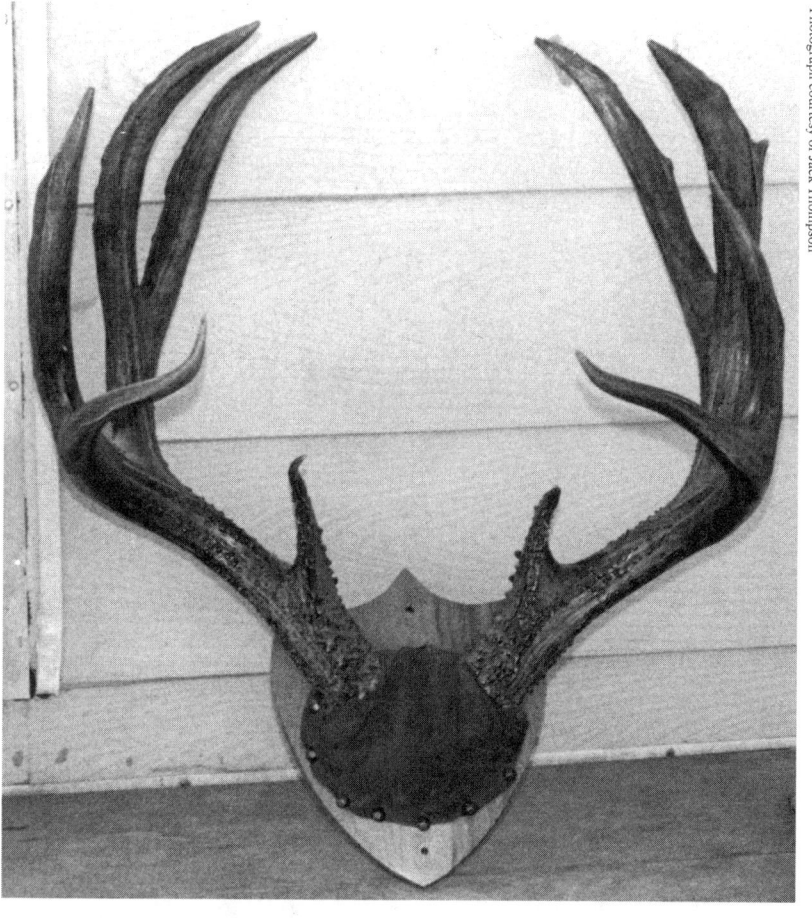

Photograph courtesy of Jack Thompson

As a dairy farmer, Jewel Schottel has to squeeze his big-game hunting in between milking and the countless other chores associated with farming. Usually he doesn't leave home for the field until 8 a.m. (after the morning milking) and returns before 4:30 p.m., in time for the evening milking. That is the exact schedule Jewel was following when he took his records-book muley in 1966.

On that particular day Jewel took his big buck while hunting on the Lee Ford Ranch near Montrose. Accompanying him on that hunt were Lee and Larry Ford, Preston Schottel, Pat White and Jerry Kitsmiller.

Hunting was extremely difficult that year. The weather was warm and dry. That made it extremely difficult to sneak up on any deer. In addition, the area they hunted was a series of draws densely covered with oak brush.

Jewel and his hunting companions arrived at their hunting site around 9 a.m. Each hunter went in his own direction with plans to return to the vehicle around noon for lunch. When they returned, they compared notes. Everyone had seen antlers, but no one was able to get a shot. The ground cover was so dry, and the brush was so dense, that all anyone caught was an occasional fleeting glimpse of a fleeing deer.

After lunch, Jewel paired off with Jerry with plans to cover some of the more densely covered draws on the Ford Ranch. Once Jerry was situated at the head of one such draw, Jewel worked his way around to the other end with the intention of coming up the middle. Utilizing this technique they hoped that at least Jerry would get more than a bouncing antler shot if any deer were jumped.

To get into position Jewel had to get down on his hands and knees and crawl through the oak brush. As he broke into the clearing over a rock cliff at the top of the draw he intended to work, he spooked two bucks bedded down at the base of the cliff. They looked like identical twins, but Jewel automatically focused his attention upon one of the bobbing heads and fired. His buck continued on down into the bottom of the draw while the other headed toward Jerry. When Jewel's buck hit the bottom it broke into an opening long enough for a second shot. The buck staggered but continued on. A third shot brought it down for good.

Jewel knew he had a nice buck but really didn't think it was records-book material. With a width of 19-2/8 inches, his trophy is one of the narrowest racks in the Boone and Crockett Club's all-time records book. Everyone told him it had to be at least 30 inches wide before a measurer would even consider looking at it. Thus, it wasn't until he got his hands on an article from Outdoor Life magazine that had scoring instructions that he gave any serious thought to having it officially measured. When he came up with a score of 196 points, he figured he better contact Smokey Till, the official B&C measurer in his area. After all, the minimum score at that time was only 185 points. Smokey scored Jewel's heavy and extremely symmetrical rack at 202-6/8 points.

JACK THOMPSON
Location: Mesa County
Year Taken: 1968
Score: 202-4/8

Photograph courtesy of Jack Thompson

In 1968 Jack Thompson of western Pennsylvania elected to hunt the Battlement area of Horsethief Mountain northwest of Collbran during the late season. That year Jack selected the late Jerry Byrum as his guide and outfitter. His hunting companion was Henry Leworthy of Dunkirk, New York.

The day Jack got his buck started off cold and snowy. When his hunting party awoke that morning they were greeted with about a foot of freshly fallen snow. After a warm breakfast, the trio left camp and traveled by Jeep to their hunting site. After parking, they began plowing their way through the snow up into the mountains.

Immediately they located deer sign everywhere. After climbing about halfway up the hillside, Jack's party jumped a herd of about 40 deer. There were little bucks, big bucks and does moving in all directions. Jerry assisted both hunters in selecting their deer. Henry took the first shot and brought his buck down with a single round at 150 yards. Jack took the next shot but missed on his first try. Another shot and Jack's name was in the all-time records for biggest deer ever taken with a final score of 202-4/8 points.

LEONARD J. ASHCRAFT
Location: Dolores County
Year Taken: 1958
Score: 201-7/8

Leonard Ashcraft and his family frequently hunted the Dolores River Drainage near Fish Creek in Dolores County. Accompanying him on his 1958 Dolores County deer hunt was his father, James, his mother, Evelyn, his brother, William, and a longtime hunting companion, William Strait.

Before dawn on opening day Leonard took a stand above a well-used game trail where his family had seen both deer and elk on previous big-game hunts. Shortly after daylight he heard something coming up the trail.

Waiting patiently, Leonard soon observed two nice four-pointers about 150 yards away making their way toward his stand. One had a nice rack but the antlers on the other seemed enormous. Leonard silently flicked the safety off on his .270 Winchester and sighted on the bigger buck.

Leonard's buck jumped at the sound of the shot and headed straight down the hill while the other buck headed uphill towards Leonard's mother and brother. The big buck's reaction indicated to Leonard that it had been hit.

Leonard quickly picked up the blood trail and followed it. After going no more than 100 yards he noted the antlers and head protruding above a fallen log. With a swift second shot the buck was downed for good.

Once his buck was field dressed Leonard caught up with his mother and brother who were field dressing the other buck that had accompanied his trophy. Leonard had heard their shots shortly after he got his buck.

Leonard's trophy scored 201-7/8 points. Since Leonard took his trophy, the new World's Record was taken in 1972 from the same area. Due to the similarity of his buck's rack to the World's Record, Leonard wonders if his buck might have been the great granddaddy of the World's Record typical mule deer. Of course, no one will ever know.

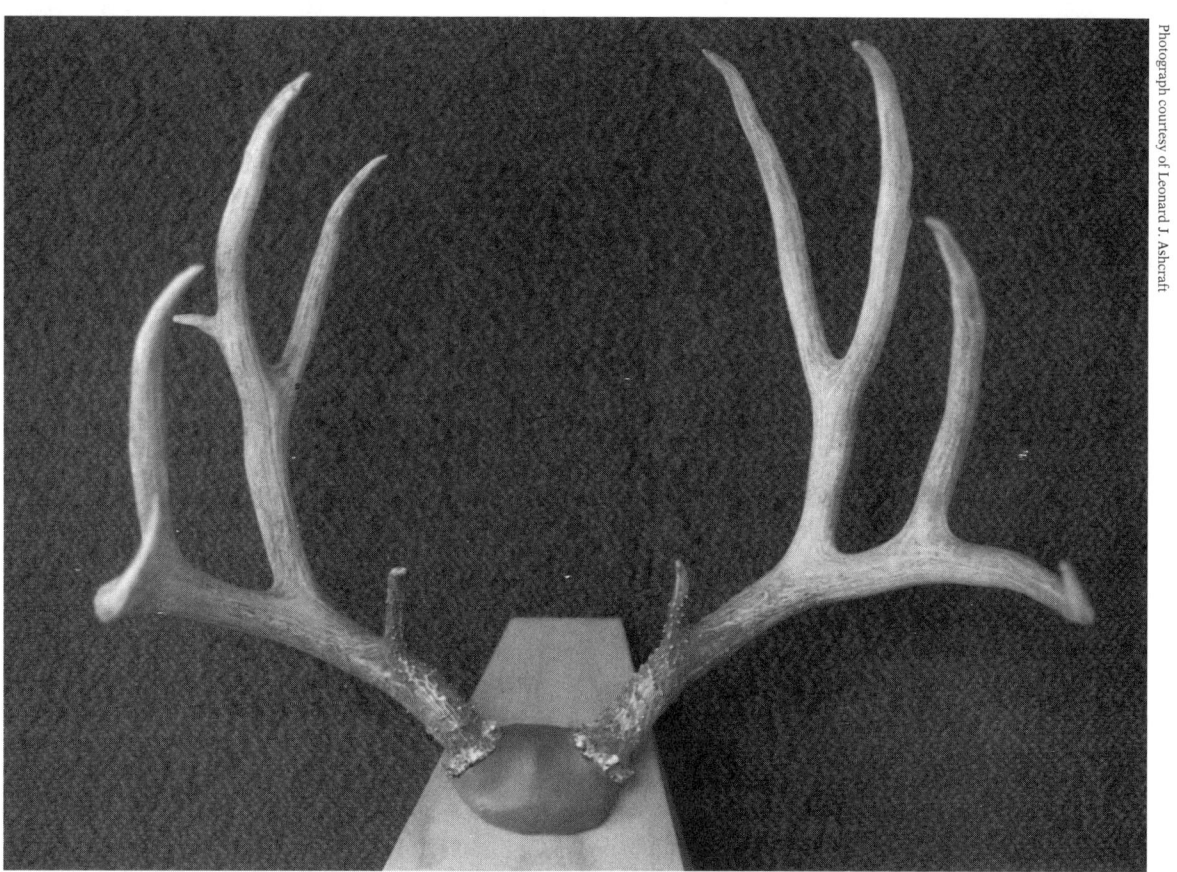

Photograph courtesy of Leonard J. Ashcraft

WILLIAM C. BYRD
Location: Mesa County
Year Taken: 1967
Score: 201-3/8

In October 1967, William Byrd and five friends from Kerrville, Texas, spent the first few days of deer season in Pinon Mesa, approximately 30 miles southwest of Grand Junction.

On the third day of the season William situated himself on the point of a bluff several miles from camp. The view was panoramic and the weather was cold. The longer William sat there the colder it got. Ultimately, he decided to move to a lower elevation on the same bluff to protect himself from the elements. After all, hunting wasn't that good from his vantage point as he had sighted only a few does and one small three-pointer. Carelessly working his way lower, William disturbed a buck bedded down only 30 yards away. As the buck bolted William realized it carried the largest and heaviest set of antlers he had seen in 15 years of deer hunting.

Immediately William had the buck lined up with the cross hairs of his scope. In the excitement he forgot to release the safety and the buck slipped out of sight before he could recover. Sick with anger and self-pity at losing such an opportunity, William continued working his way down the bluff. Suddenly the buck came back into view about 150 yards away. With a second chance at the trophy of a lifetime, William didn't make the same mistake twice. He dropped his records-book buck with a single round from his .270.

Six months later the rack was officially measured for the Boone and Crockett records program. The antlers scored 201-3/8 points.

GRANT MORLANG
Location: Montrose County
Year Taken: 1972
Score: 201-3/8

As a child Grant Morlang ran sheep on the Uncompahgre Plateau west of Montrose. He had hunted the same area for 33 years and knew the terrain well. Opening week of the 1972 hunting season found him in the Dry Creek drainage area.

Dale Ambrosini of Montrose and Ralph Gray of St. Louis, Missouri, were Grant's hunting buddies on that hunt. The weather conditions the first day of the season were miserable but the three men observed many big deer moving into the area from other parts of the Plateau. They did not hunt the first day but were eager and ready to go before daylight on the second day. The area was thick with oak brush and with a heavy snow falling, visibility was less than 50 yards.

The men still-hunted until 11 a.m. to the top of one of the many hills in the area. Once there Grant hunkered down in the rock foundation of an old building on the leeward side of the hill out of the weather. Glancing back down the hill the way he had come only seconds before, Grant watched as a large typical mule deer materialized out of the trees and snow, like an apparition. Right behind it came a large non-typical buck with 10 to 12 points on each antler. Both bucks sensed Grant's presence immediately and froze. Grant barely had time to get his rifle to his shoulder before both bucks whorled and headed for cover. Throwing his scope on the closest muley, the big typical buck, Grant had time for only one quick shot. Though he was convinced the 160-grain Sierra boattail had found its mark, Grant watched helplessly as the big muley continued on as though untouched. Grant immediately picked up the trail and found his buck gasping its last breath 50 yards later.

After field dressing the trophy, Grant drove the party's 4x4 Bronco to within a quarter mile of the buck. With the help of his companions Grant was able to get his buck back to the Jeep. Without the head and hide the hog-dressed buck weighed 269 pounds. Grant's typical mule deer scored 201-3/8 points in the 15th North American Big Game Awards Program.

Photograph courtesy of Colorado's Biggest Bucks and Bulls archives

ERNEST MANCUSO
Location: Mesa County
Year Taken: 1954
Score: 201

Third Place
7th B&C Competition

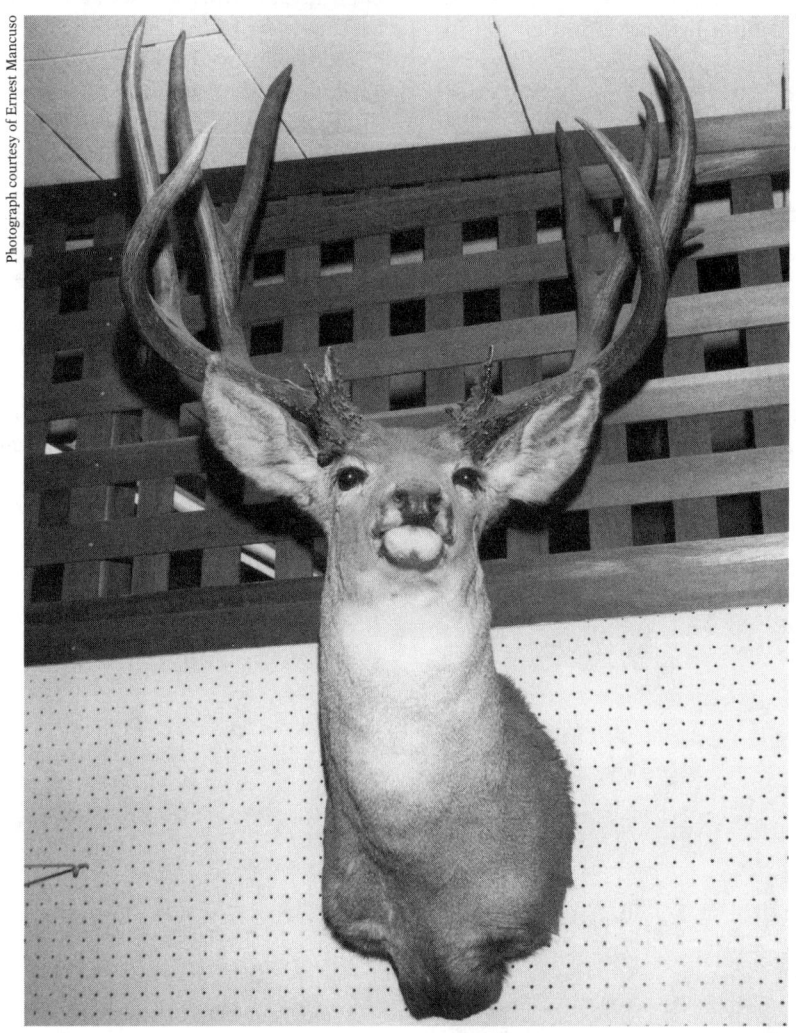

Ernest Mancuso was born and raised in Grand Junction but moved to California in 1939. For many years after he moved, he returned to Colorado for the big-game season.

In 1954 Ernest hunted with his brother-in-law, Jerry Crusos, on the Castro Ranch in Unaweep Canyon outside of Whitewater. On the third day of the season he sighted a very large muley in one of the fields as he drove by in his station wagon. Pulling to the side of the road, Ernest stepped out of the car, rested his .300 Savage on a fence post and fired. The buck ran a short distance, staggered and went down.

Ernest and Jerry dressed the animal and had some of the ranch hands assist in loading it into the station wagon. Back at the ranch Ernest skinned and hung the animal to cool. The field-dressed weight tipped the scales at 318 pounds.

Ernest's friend and taxidermist, Johnnie Dawson of Acampo, California, suggested he have the rack scored for the records book. The rack scored high enough to be invited to the Boone and Crockett Club's 7th North American Big Game Competition held at the American Museum of Natural History in New York City in 1956. It placed third in the typical mule deer category. The trophy scored 201 points.

JOHN ROBERTSON
Location: Eagle County
Year Taken: 1958
Score: 200-6/8

The first impression many Boone and Crockett trophy owners have of their trophy buck is that it looks like an elk. John Robertson was no exception when he first sighted his buck during the 1958 combined deer and elk season.

John was tracking a small band of elk early that morning at the head of Fisher Gulch, 14 miles southeast of Eagle. He was hunting alone, as was his custom, when he found where the herd had bedded down the night before. Continuing on their trail, he followed them up the ridge and east toward Mt. Adam. As he approached timberline, John caught a movement above him and to his right. He was ready to shoot but it turned out to be a string of 11 deer moving out in the same general direction as the elk he was tracking. They were alerted but not yet alarmed. One small four-pointer and two forked-horn bucks were in the herd. The rest were does and fawns.

Because the deer were headed in the same general direction as the elk John decided to hold tight for a few minutes. He figured if he spooked the deer he would probably also spook the elk he was tracking. After waiting four to five minutes he caught another flash of movement in the same general area where he had first detected the deer. As it began to materialize, John thought he could make out the large, dark form of an elk. When it moved in a little closer he could see

that it was an exceptionally large buck. It appeared nervous as it kept looking back the way it had come and was mighty uneasy about going on. When it was about 125 yards away the buck paused momentarily in an opening, broadside to John. After debating with himself a few moments, John decided to fill his deer tag that morning and hunt elk later that afternoon.

John knew he had a beautiful trophy but never thought to have it measured until a few years later when a friend, Jim Isabell, asked if he could take it to Denver to be measured. Laughingly, John consented, never believing for a second that it would make "The Book." Not only did John's buck make the records book with a final score of 200-6/8 points but it also came within 16-2/8 points of the world's record typical mule deer at that time.

John Robertson proudly displays his massive Eagle County Boone and Crockett buck that scores a hefty 200-6/8 points.

JACK STEVENS
Location: Eagle County
Year Taken: 1975
Score: 200-4/8

Jack Stevens' hunt actually began late in the afternoon of the last day of the 1975 elk season. That year elk season occurred one week prior to deer season. While working his way down a draw near Piney Peak on the White River National Forest, Jack's horse suddenly balked as a large antlered animal, with an elk-like gait, cut across the trail. Jack quickly dismounted but it wasn't until he had his rifle out of its scabbard that he realized it was a large deer. Disappointed, he stuffed his rifle back into the scabbard and vowed to return for that buck during the deer season.

One week later Jack and his wife Mary returned to the same area to search out Jack's big buck. It was the first and last time Mary ever accompanied Jack on a big-game hunt. She wanted to see what a hunting camp was like and get in a little hunting herself. However, since the last day of elk season, 18 to 24 inches of new snow had accumulated and the temperatures had fallen to 25 degrees below zero.

On opening day Jack and Mary left camp a half-hour before sunrise and set out for the same draw where Jack had seen the big buck. He placed Mary on a stand where he was certain she would get some shooting and proceeded 250 yards farther to another vantage point within sight of his wife. Both hunters remained at their stands for about two and a half hours until Mary got so cold that she decided to move up the ridge into the sunlight. When she did so Jack could no longer see her.

Within minutes of the time Mary moved to her new stand, a doe and Jack's trophy buck stepped out of the timber between Jack and his wife. While neither hunter could see each other both could see the deer. Jack held his fire since he didn't know Mary's exact location. When Mary reached for her rifle the doe bolted down the ridge towards Jack with the buck in hot pursuit.

When the buck was within 75 yards of his position, Jack fired. Without breaking stride both deer continued down the draw. Jack was sure he had scored but fired again when the buck reappeared on the opposite side of the draw. Again, both deer continued running until they were out of sight. Jack caught up with Mary at the top of the ridge who then pointed out a large spruce where she had last seen the buck. Just as Jack looked toward the big spruce, he saw the big buck collapse. His first shot had finally taken effect. The couple spent the next two and a half hours packing the animal out. Being a veteran hunter, Jack knew immediately that his buck was Boone and Crockett quality. Jack figured the live weight was round 325 pounds. The antlers were nearly symmetrical with a better than 31-inch spread. After the required drying time, Jack's antlers scored 200-4/8 points.

MITCHELL J. SACCO
Location: Mesa County
Year Taken: 1966
Score: 200-2/8

"Now, if I was an old buck, where would I go?"

That was how Mitchell Sacco selected the site for his 1966 trophy mule deer hunt. As he remembered, his method wasn't terrifically scientific but it worked for him.

Mitch and two fellow Texans, Calvin Riedel and Fred Reinarz, decided to hunt the Uncompahgre National Forest near 25 Mesa Road. The day of his "once-in-a-lifetime experience" dawned cold and clear. Scrub oak, sagebrush and bear brush covered the bench below the rimrock of the south rim of the mesa where they hunted. The bench was approximately 1,000 yards long and looked like the perfect spot to find a trophy buck.

The three men worked their way across the mesa towards Red Top. As they approached the sunny side of the bench, Mitch noticed the old buck lying just below the rimrock. If the men had not been talking they probably would have walked past the buck without spooking it. But the noise and closeness of their presence was too much for the old buck's nerves. It bolted from the bear brush it had bedded down in and ran straight towards the rimrock, not more than 75 yards from the men.

Mitch fired first with his sporterized .30-06 Springfield, slightly wounding the buck, which then veered to its left and ran parallel to the rimrock. Cal and Fred joined in and together the three hunters brought the buck down for good. The field-dressed weight was estimated at more than 325 pounds. From the condition of its body and teeth, Mitch determined the buck was between seven and nine years old.

Mitch's only regret about the hunt was that it was his first trip to Colorado. After making 12 more hunting trips to Colorado, he has taken nothing that compares to his first Colorado buck. Mitch's trophy scores 200-2/8 points in the all-time records.

Photograph courtesy of Mitchell J Sacco

One of several sets of locked antlers found in the Buckhorn Exchange restaurant at 1000 Osage Avenue in Denver.

Another set of locked antlered mule deer perpetually spar in the lady's bathroom of the Buckhorn Exchange restaurant in Denver.

JOSEPH T. HOLLINGSHEAD
Location: Ouray County
Year Taken: 1967
Score: 200-2/8

Joseph T. Hollingshead's sole purpose for going hunting on October 22, 1967, was to bag a trophy buck. Accompanying him on his records-book hunt was his hunting partner, Don Tyson. Together the two hunters scoured the east side of Horsefly Peak, 20 miles south of Montrose, for big bucks.

Don got the first shot at daylight and took a buck that later missed the records book by a fraction of an inch. With his tag filled, Don spent the rest of the morning beating the brush for Joe. Shortly after noon Don was working one of the many ridges that intersected the area when he jumped a herd of eight deer. Joe looked them over closely but just sat tight and waited. Sure enough, a big buck was hanging back. After a few seconds it stepped hesitantly out of the oak brush and gave Joe a 180-yard broadside shot. Joe fired but surprisingly the buck stood perfectly still for 20 seconds before it attempted to move again. A second shot brought the monster down. Upon closer examination Joe discovered that his first shot passed through the chest cavity. The second shot killed it instantly.

Joe knew his buck was big but thought it didn't look much bigger than some of the other four-pointers he had passed up earlier that morning. Two months later his buck scored 200-2/8 points.

JOHN M. DOMINGOS
Location: Mesa County
Year Taken: 1965
Score: 200-1/8

Photograph courtesy of John M. Domingos

John Domingos and hunting companions Norman McKenzie and Floyd Bowman selected the Uncompahgre Plateau as the site of their 1965 deer hunt. By the second day of the season the party had observed several nice bucks in the 30-inch class but did not have the manpower to hunt the area properly in order to score.

On the second day of the hunt, John and Norman chose to hunt the lower elevations of the Plateau while Floyd chased a big non-typical that Norman saw opening day. The first ridge the pair cleared, Norman spotted a buck breaking snow about 750 yards away and working its way toward the top of a distant ridge at a 45-degree angle. Norman realized immediately that it carried a rack better than any he had ever seen before. Both hunters further realized that there wasn't time for a long stalk as the big muley was breaking the skyline and would soon be out of sight.

While Norman prepared to "call the shots" if John missed, John advised Norman that he would hold high on his first shot. Both hunters felt that if the bullet passed over the buck it would also pass over the ridge and would not alarm the buck. However, if the shot were low, the buck would probably react.

Thus, when the buck did not react at the first shot, John lowered his sights and fired again. When the buck promptly collapsed Norman yelled, "My God! You flattened him! What a shot!"

With a spread of 32-1/4 inches, both hunters figured that the buck would easily make Boone and Crockett. With an official score of 200-1/8 points, both hunters were right.

DALE R. LEONARD
Location: Eagle County
Year Taken: 1976
Score: 200
Owner: David P. Moore

"Trophy hunting" is a great challenge and fills one with a sense of pride and accomplishment, but does little to fill one's freezer with badly needed meat. Seldom does success grace a dedicated trophy hunter's search, and the years between trophies become more numerous with each passing year. Dale Leonard has set his own strict guidelines for hunting trophy muleys. He won't shoot another buck unless he's sure it will out score his largest trophy at home.

In 1976 Dale left the decision of where to hunt up to his regular hunting partner, Bill Pipes. Bill selected an area 20 miles north of Eagle where he had taken one huge buck and had missed an even bigger one the year before. Dale knew nothing of the area but was eager to learn. Dale and Bill, along with Steve Lablanc and Jack Brittingham, left for Eagle on October 29, one day before the opening of the 1976 deer season. Sleep was impossible that first night, for tales of past hunts lasted nearly until dawn.

Opening day dawned clear but cold. An hour later Dale's party spotted one big buck feeding along a sagebrush flat, but it fled before they could get within range. They then decided to fan out along a high ridge. Bill took the top, Dale and Steve the middle, and Jack the bottom. Deer were everywhere, especially does, fawns and small bucks with antlers in the 20-inch to 25-inch class. Dale jumped a monstrous five-pointer that morning with a rack in the 35-inch class, but it ran over a ridge before he could fire. Bill got three shots off at the buck at about 300 yards but wasn't able to connect. Shortly thereafter, Bill downed a non-typical buck (8x8) after stalking it for a mile. Steve also connected with a non-typical buck (7x6) with a high, narrow rack and tremendous body.

That afternoon Jack and Dale got into a herd that contained three big bucks. Jack made a fine running shot on a big 5x6. The other two bucks took off and Dale gave chase. One of the bucks looked huge and Dale wanted a closer look. Dale ran about a half mile before he caught the bucks on a cedar-covered ridge as they paused for that one last look back. Dale flopped down on his stomach and lined up on the biggest bucks. When his .270 Winchester barked the buck collapsed and slid down the ridge.

Dale's buck was a trophy that would gladden any hunter's heart. It was a perfect five-pointer with a 32-inch spread. It later scored in at an official 200 points in the Boone and Crockett Club's all-time records book. With his trophy mule deer in "The Book," Dale accomplished what only two other Colorado hunters had managed to do at the time. He now has a Colorado buck and a Colorado bull listed in the all-time records book for North American hunters.

GEORGE S. BURTON
Location: Eagle County
Year Taken: 1967
Score: 199-7/8
Owner: George S. Burton Family

George S. Burton never knew his buck was a Boone and Crockett trophy, but thanks to the efforts of his wife, Betty, and his three sons, Larry, Lane and Lynn, his mount was officially measured and properly recognized in 1990, 23 years after it was taken in Eagle County. Following is George's hunting story as he told it to his sons.

In 1967 George met a rancher who invited him and a friend, Dale Cloud, to deer hunt on his ranch near Eagle. George and Dale met at the rancher's barn for breakfast at 3 a.m. on the opening day of deer season. After breakfast the rancher loaded them into his Jeep and then drove them to their deer stands. As he left the two hunters, the rancher told them not to move and that he would be back to pick them up later. George assured the rancher he wouldn't go anywhere.

George realized he was on a game trail above a meadow when it was light enough to see. He located a stump to sit on and settled in for the morning. After some time passed, he heard something while lighting a cigarette that made him look up. A monster buck stood close by, and the hunt was over in one shot. As George field dressed the buck, a 7x7 bull elk appeared 25 yards away, staring at George. He regretted he didn't have an elk tag. When the rancher returned to pick up the hunters he told George his buck was one of the largest he had ever seen.

George's antlers were mounted on a wooden plaque and hung on the den wall of his home for many years. Everyone who saw the rack called it the "monster buck." George never hunted again after taking this buck and always told his sons that he would start deer hunting again if one of them ever got a bigger buck.

In 1990, 23 years later, the family moved from California to Oregon. George had since passed away. The Burton's hadn't realized how large his trophy was until a friend, David Morris, told the sons the buck should be officially measured. When the buck was scored they found out it was the 17th largest buck entered in the Boone and Crockett Club's 17th Awards Program (1989-1991).

George's wife, Betty, and her three sons were delighted and so proud of George. They only wish he could have lived long enough to experience this tremendous achievement. Larry thinks maybe he knows. Betty died in 1994 so now the three sons are co-owners of this outstanding muley.

CHARLES W. PEARSON
Location: Archuleta County
Year Taken: 1995
Score: 199-5/8

Finding an uncrowded hunting area in Colorado was the primary goal of hunting partners Charles Pearson, Solon Smith and Lonnie Newsome in 1994. After considerable research, they selected an area to hunt on the San Juan National Forest near Durango. It wasn't until the second year they hunted that area, however, that Charles took his "trophy of a lifetime."

The first year they pitched camp next to a logging road at 9,500 feet above sea level. The weather was warm and sunny. Early the next morning, the men scouted the area and located several sites close to camp that looked very promising. These sites were heavily covered with fresh deer and elk sign. Unfortunately, the weather changed and it snowed the next three days. Twenty-four inches of the white stuff accumulated, and radio reports announced that several hunters were lost in the area.

Charles and his friends ventured out on the fourth day and promptly realized they couldn't hunt due to the deep snow. By the last day in camp everyone vowed to return in 1995 to try again.

The same three men, plus Eric Crawford, returned to the same area in October 1995. Solon, Lonnie and Eric scouted the mountain nearest to camp, and Charles returned to the same spot where he had seen extensive deer and elk sign the year before. The site was again covered with droppings, and every bush had been heavily browsed. Late that afternoon Charles settled on the exact area he intended to hunt the next day.

Charles hunted all day on opening day without seeing anything. He was, in fact, the only one in camp who didn't see anything. In spite of this, Charles vowed to hunt the same place all week since it looked so good. The next day everyone hunted the same general area where Charles had hunted. His partners planned to meet back at camp for lunch, but Charles intended to stay in the field all day.

About noon Charles heard a noise behind him. When he checked for the source, he observed a small buck standing 50 yards away in thick brush. Charles slowly raised his rifle to count the points on the buck's rack. As he scoped it out, he spotted one antler of the largest rack he had ever seen in his life. A large tree obscured his view so he took two slow steps to the right for a better view of the monster buck carrying it. One shot to the neck from his .270 laid it on the ground.

Everything happened so quickly Charles didn't have time to get excited. He hung his tag on the buck and returned to camp for help. This set his hunting partners on fire and they hunted more aggressively.

Several hunters stopped by camp during the next few days and admired Charles' buck. Someone suggested that it might make B&C. Charles couldn't wait to get home to have it officially scored after the 60-day drying period. When he did, he was excited to hear it made B&C's all-time records book at a score of 199-6/8 points.

All of Charles' friends tell him he is lucky, but Charles tells them he's just persistent.

Finding an uncrowded hunting area in Colorado in 1995 brought Mississippi hunter Charles Pearson to the San Juan National Forest where he located this B&C typical mule deer that scores 199-5/8 points.

KENNETH L. PETERS
Location: Dolores County
Year Taken: 1976
Score: 199-4/8

Kenneth L. Peters feels he was fortunate to have been born into a western Pennsylvanian family where deer hunting has long been a family tradition. During his early years he developed his deer hunting skills with his father and brothers who had a well-established record for taking big bucks.

Ken started hunting in Colorado in 1970, but it wasn't until 1976 that the story of his records-book buck began. That year Ken, his brother Frank and Wayne Pierce hunted three miles north of Dolores. On opening morning Ken was up and

ready to leave camp well before daylight. His party had decided to hunt a nearby ridge where Frank had previously taken two bucks in the 30-inch class. The morning dawned clear and the thermometer hovered around 20 degrees. There were patches of snow on the ground and the aspen had already shed their leaves.

As they moved up Frank's favorite ridge Ken became separated from the other hunters. At around 10:30 a.m. he reached the top of the ridge and continued still-hunting. He moved along quietly, being careful to make as little noise as possible. When he reached a 100-yard wide, aspen-covered depression, Ken cautiously stepped into it. Instantly, he detected the soft rustling of leaves and the cracking of twigs. Ken froze. He immediately detected movement about 75 yards away. The aspen trunks and underbrush were thick but Ken soon made out the form of a buck moving slowly along a well-used game trail. Though he couldn't see it clearly he knew it was large enough to uphold the family tradition.

Ken set his sights on a break in the trees, through which he figured the buck would pass. When it stepped into the opening, he fired. Strangely enough, however, the buck acted as though nothing had happened. Ken set his sights on another opening and touched off a second round as the buck entered it. That time the buck was gone in an instant. Ken approached the area where he figured the buck dropped but couldn't find it. He was convinced he had hit it and began to work a systematic pattern of circles looking for sign. Forty-five minutes later, Ken still hadn't turned up anything. Somewhat disappointed, he returned to the trail on which he had first spotted the buck. He got down on his hands and knees and began to carefully work the area over. A few minutes later his efforts were rewarded when he located his first speck of blood in a snow bank.

At that point, he was joined by Wayne. Together they worked out a blood trail good enough to follow. They tracked the buck a half mile before they found it lying on its side, stone dead. For Ken it was the culmination of many years of dreaming.

MUMMIFIED LOCKED ANTLERS
Location: Mesa County
Year Found: 1949
Score: 199-3/8
Owner: Greg Duff

Photograph by Susan Campbell Reneau

The story of this set of locked antlers starts in 1949, according to Gerald Blackwelder, a former owner of the antlers.

The father of Jerry Crim found the set in its present mummified state in 1949 while he was hunting near Gateway in southern Mesa County near Grand Junction. The fur and skin of the two deer had mummified to the skulls. Jerry, an employee of Gerald Blackwelder, sold the set to Gerald in 1986 or 1987. Gerald owns an outdoor advertising company in Grand Junction.

In 1991 Gerald sold the set to Kim's Taxidermy Studio, owned by Kim and Colin Fritzler. Greg Duff met Kim and Colin when he was doing construction work for the couple and became the owner of the antlers as payment for his construction work. Both locked antlers are outstanding but only one of them is Boone and Crockett quality. Gerald wishes he still owned that set of outstanding antlers, but he's happy they are enjoyed by Greg.

Greg had the antlers officially measured in 1997, and the one set was officially entered into the Boone and Crockett Club records-keeping program on May 10, 1997, 48 years after a hunter in Mesa County found them. The other set of antlers has a net score of approximately 144 B&C points. The mummified set remains intertwined as the massive bucks died.

ANTHONY W. DETOY
Location: Eagle County
Year Taken: 1978
Score: 199-2/8

For many years Pat Carlow owned The Game and Fish Deport in Eagle, Colorado. On the counter, Pat kept a photo album filled with photographs of wildlife, hunting and fishing trophies, and other outdoor momentos. After Pat sold the store and moved to another town, Pat packed the photo album away to gather dust in a closet. Recently, Pat found the album and while rifling through the pages, he came across photographs from a hunt in 1978 that triggered a flood of memories. It was a memorable hunt and is as clear in his mind as if it happened yesterday.

Larry Christensen and Troy DeToy made plans with Pat to go on a hunt at the spur of the moment. Pat received permission from a local rancher to pass through his ranch to public lands, and the men set out the next morning. Having hunted during the earlier archery season, Pat was free to help as a guide, an area he knew well.

The area they hunted was only about three miles north of Eagle. They left town too early and found themselves sitting in prime country well before daylight. Pat intended to make a series of drives through aspens, willows, and small canyons, but it was way too early for that. The men decided to wait in an area until daylight where Pat had spotted bucks on previous hunts rather than pass by prime country in the dark.

The hunters pulled over near the head of a long, shallow draw. Taking out a thermos of hot coffee and a pair of binoculars, they walked over to the edge of the draw and sat down to pass time until shooting light. Shortly after daybreak, a few does and fawns drifted along the draw about 300 yards out. A pair of forkhorns crossed; followed by a few more does and fawns. They were about to leave to execute their original plan when three decent bucks materialized out of the trees. They weren't trophy hunting, and both Pat's companions said they would be happy with a pair of those bucks.

As they prepared to shoot, a magnificent buck appeared behind the original tree. Even at that distance, there was no question he was a trophy. Since Pat was only glassing, he had plenty of time to study the buck. It

Larry Christensen, left, with his nice 4-point buck, and Tony DeToy, right, holding his B&C buck that scores 199-2/8 points on the day they took them. Larry, Tony and Pat Carlow enjoyed a hunt outside Eagle, Colorado, in 1978.

appeared to be a massive, near-perfect four point.

Tony shot first and missed. The buck didn't move so Tony's next shot dropped the buck in its tracks. It was hard for Pat to believe, but they had a trophy buck down, dressed, loaded, and tagged.

Shortly after taking this outstanding buck, Tony was transferred out of the area, and Pat Carlow always wondered if his friend ever entered the buck in the Boone and Crockett Club's records program. Sure enough, he did. Its final score is 199-2/8 points – a buck for the records book.

Pat Carlow provided details of the hunt.

RALPH CLOCK
Location: Garfield County
Year Taken: 1961
Score: 198-5/8

The year 1961 was a peak year for deer hunters in Colorado. According to the Colorado Division of Wildlife's statistics, a total of 68,263 bucks alone were harvested that year. That's more bucks than have been taken any other year since the Division started keeping records in 1903.

It was an especially good year for Ralph Clock, his brother Phil, and three other hunting companions, Tom Worth, Don Yunker and Ken Schonenbeck. The limit that year was two per hunter and in three days Ralph's party took their limit just south of Carbondale. One of Ralph's bucks made the Boone and Crockett records book. Ralph's hunt for his trophy buck actually began as his party was preparing to leave for home. After a late breakfast in Carbondale his group was headed back to camp to pick up their game. A short distance past the fish hatchery just south of town,

Ralph Clock in the field with his B&C buck.

Ralph started to ease his jeep up a steep incline. Glancing to one side he spotted a buck and two does running through the sagebrush about 100 yards out. Ralph dropped his Jeep into low gear, four-wheel drive and headed for the top of the hill as fast as his 60-horsepower engine could go.

By the time the young men had reached the crest of the hill and piled out of the Jeep, the buck was about 200 yards out and eating up more real estate with every passing second. Ralph laid his rifle across a rock, held a foot over the buck's shoulder and fired. Incredibly, the buck dropped in its tracks. It wasn't until after the buck was down that Ralph realized he had shot a real trophy. At 200 yards he could still see the antlers sticking above the sagebrush.

Several years later, Ralph had his trophy scored and entered in the 14th North American Big Game Competition. Ralph's magnificent buck is on public display at the Silver Tree Hotel in Snowmass Village, Colorado.

MARY ANN OTT
Location: Montezuma County
Year Taken: 1968
Score: 198-5/8

Growing up in Longmeadow, Massachusetts, a suburb of Springfield, Mary Ann Ott had no hunting experience prior to 1965 when she went on her first big-game hunt. Widowed in 1959, Mary Ann was determined to be a good companion to her second husband Jack by taking up hunting to share his passion for the outdoors.

Her method of hunting was equally straightforward; just follow Jack's directions to the "T." That first hunt in 1965 Jack had parked her on a log in a clearing. She waited patiently, enjoying the pristine silence of the morning and watching the sun's rays slide down the tall, leafless aspen. A majestic buck stepped quietly from the trees, pausing to survey the clearing. Mary Ann slowly raised her .30-06 and squeezed the trigger, downing the buck at 40 yards. Squirrels and jays erupted in a chatter of scolding. In a few minutes Jack appeared and found her bent over her kill and started dressing it out.

The Ott's primary goal was to harvest meat for their family of five sons and two daughters. Hunting and fishing skills, as well as preserving wild meat, were routine in their family life. Jack and Mary Ann recall returning from a convention of the Society of American Foresters to find their sons sitting around the kitchen table, cutting and packaging elk. Mary Ann can't recall how many big antlers were left in the woods due to their excessive weight and lack of meat. She revealed that antlers were even turned into buttons for the many outfits needed to clothe a growing family.

Mary Ann and her Boone and Crockett buck, taken in 1968, scores an impressive 198-5/8 points.

Mary Ann's trophy buck was shot in 1968. This was the first year their oldest son, Bill, hunted in the high country. After trudging down an old logging road in the pre-dawn light, Mary Ann took a stand in a clearing while Jack and Bill went deeper into the woods. Within a short time, she heard two shots and Bill's excited shouts that he had shot his first bull elk. Later, Mary Ann shot her trophy buck. Her first reaction was that the antlers would make good handles to drag the animal through the snow. Her sons insisted on mounting the rack.

The following year, Mary Ann and her son Woody went hunting together near their home, as Jack had to take the older children to a high school band competition. Woody went ahead down a draw to see if he could drive out a deer. Mary Ann had a doe license that year, and, sure enough, a doe sprang up from the draw and she shot it. They dragged it home with ample time for Mary Ann to freshen up and serve tea at the golden anniversary of her local chapter of P.E.O., an international women's organization. She was president that year. Few of her sisters knew how she had spent her morning.

Mary Ann joins a very small group of women who have taken any big-game animal entered in the Boone and Crockett Club's records-keeping program. Her buck was accepted into the B&Cs 24th North American Big Game Awards. The buck's final score is 198-5/8 points, making it one of the largest typical mule deer ever taken in Colorado.

LLOYD D. KINDSFATER
Location: Routt County
Year Taken: 1966
Score: 198-4/8

There's little doubt that Boone and Crockett bucks get big because they're smart. If Lloyd Kindsfater's buck was any indication of just how smart they can be, there's little wonder why there are so few trophies in the records book.

While sitting on a ridge in unfamiliar territory, approximately 10 miles north of Hayden, Lloyd observed his friend, Jack Groves, working up a draw in his direction. Slightly ahead of Jack, and 250 yards from his observation point, Lloyd caught a movement in the brush. Though he couldn't tell how big it was, Lloyd could make out the form of a buck bedded down behind a log. Jack continued on up the draw and passed within 30 feet of the buck. It remained as stationary as the log.

Lloyd Kindsfater with his heavy-beamed Routt County buck (198-4/8 points) taken in 1966. This buck lay hidden while Lloyd's friend, Jack Groves, walked within 30 feet of it.

When Jack caught up with Lloyd, Lloyd pointed out the buck. Together, they both checked it over for 20 minutes. Finally, Lloyd decided to take it and sighted his .300 H&H Magnum on the eight inches of the buck's back showing above the log. Three shots later, Lloyd's cunning Boone and Crockett buck was down for good. It wasn't until the two hunters reached the massive animal that they realized just how big it was. It took four men to drag the hog-dressed carcass 200 yards to their Scout. The field-dressed weight was later certified at 260 pounds. The antlers officially scored 198-4/8 points in the Boone and Crockett Club's all-time records book.

LUCILLE GOOCH
Location: Moffat County
Year Taken: 1951
Score: 198-3/8
Owner: George Gooch

**First Place
15th B&C Competition**

Only a handful of women have ever taken a mule deer that was large enough to make the Boone and Crockett Club's all-time records book. Lucille Gooch is one of only a few women from Colorado to have achieved such a distinguished recognition in the 20th Century.

According to Lucille, the hunt on which she took her buck was one of the most enjoyable hunts of her life. Her enjoyment was partially attributable to the fact that she took her trophy on her own ranch near Craig with the assistance of her late husband, George. The big buck had bedded down for the day in a dense stand of sagebrush and lay hidden among the brush except for its face. The sunlight reflecting off the buck's noble features caught Lucille's attention. Lucille never missed anything out of the ordinary on her ranch. The moment she saw the buck she knew it was a beauty. With her trusty .30-06 Savage, it took Lucille only one shot to collect her prize.

Since Lucille and George were only two miles from the ranch house they loaded the buck into their pickup and dressed it at home. The field-dressed weight was more than 300 pounds. Because of its exceptional quality, Lucille decided to have the head mounted in Laramie, Wyoming, by her taxidermist, Jim Gay. Being a Boone and Crockett Club official measurer, Jim informed Lucille that she had a real trophy and suggested she enter it in the Boone and Crockett Club's Competition. The rack scored 198-3/8 points in the all-time records book.

HUNTER UNKNOWN
Location: Colorado
Year Taken: Prior to 1989
Score: 198-1/8
Rick Heitman, Owner

Rick Heitman and his beloved grandfather, Phillip J. Donahue, visited a swap meet north of Seattle, Washington, in August 1989, three years before the latter's death at age 95. For 30 years Phillip had shared his love of hunting and outdoor adventure with his grandson, and it was at the swap meet that Rick found the largest mule deer rack he had ever seen.

Rick and Phillip stalked up and down the rows of vendors closely examining the trash and treasures for sale. Phillip wasn't in the best of shape, so the pace was slow and calculated. Years earlier, Phillip had taught Rick to be alert and to absorb his surroundings. He taught Rick that peripheral vision was the key to success. Suddenly, Rick spotted the telltale shine of antler tips 40 yards away among a forest of entangled items. Rick froze, and his grandfather sensed Rick's focus. Rick knew it was the largest set of antlers he had ever seen, but Phillip wasn't impressed.

"What do you want that old thing for?" Phillip asked.

Phillip must have trusted Rick's judgment at this point. Rick didn't have enough cash to buy to rack, so Phillip loaned his grandson $50 without another word. The old, tattered mount with one missing eye cost Rick $65, part of a beautiful day and a couple of hours with his grandfather, but the swap meet visit turned out to be the most successful hunt Rick has ever been on.

Rick Heitman holds his swap meet trophy buck he "hunted" with his beloved grandfather, Phillips Donahue, in 1989. The buck scores 198-1/8 points.

Buzzi Cook of Olympic Taxidermy, North Bend, Washington, remounted the buck in 1989. Buzzi, who is an official B&C measurer, scored it for Rick at 198-1/8 points. Rick entered this magnificent buck, which he fondly refers to as "Butch," in Boone and Crockett Club's 21st Big Game Awards Program. He feels that it may not be a trophy to many because the actual hunter is unknown, but he feels it deserves recognition in the hunting fraternity. To him it represents the efforts of hunter/conservationists who have worked since the turn of the century to preserve our heritage.

The vendor who sold the rack to Rick said he purchased the antlers at a church rummage sale east of Seattle. Rick traced the rack back to an elderly woman who said she and her second husband brought the rack with them from Colorado when they moved to Washington. She couldn't remember if her husband or his brother had taken the trophy, but she remembered it was taken in Colorado.

ALAN LEE VANDENBERG
Location: Hinsdale County
Year Taken: 1978
Score: 198

Lee and his party of five hunters pitched camp near Vallecito Reservoir on October 16, 1978. Lee's hunting party included his father Bud, two brothers Andy and Wayne, and two close friends, Bob Robinson and Russ Alderich. By Saturday of the opening week of hunting season all the men had filled their tags except Lee.

Since Lee had taken a week's vacation from his job, he intended to spend the entire time hunting. Several of the men headed home after filling their tags while Russ and Lee stayed behind to tend camp. Lee remembered sleeping late on the Monday morning that became one of the most eventful hunting days of his life.

Russ and Lee didn't leave camp until late afternoon when the deer began to move. Just before dusk, they reached a dark canyon and flipped Lee's good-luck charm, a Mexican peso, to decide whether Lee would hunt the ridge or walk the draw. Lee figures his peso wasn't much luck because he hadn't fired a single shot during the entire trip, so he threw it into the draw after the toss. Ironically, minutes later, he shot his trophy buck in that same draw.

Slowly working down into the draw Lee spotted a huge buck trotting parallel to the game trail on which he stood. The buck was approximately 100 yards from Lee when he fired his first shot. Lee missed and the buck dropped into a hollow and disappeared. Because Lee was familiar with the terrain, he knew there was a clearing 50 yards from where he first shot at the buck. He dropped back and waited. By now it was almost dark and Lee realized it would soon be too late to hunt. After a short wait, the buck appeared in the clearing about 50 yards from Lee. Lee aimed his .270 Winchester and fired. The second shot hit the animal, dropping it instantly. Without examining the antlers, he pulled out his hunting knife and started field dressing his buck.

Russ heard the commotion and ran over to where Lee was cleaning the buck. Russ' first reaction was, "You shot an elk!" But Lee assured him that it was just a big buck. It wasn't until the next day when both men returned after daylight with horses to pack the deer out that they realized just how big it was. Both men had difficulty lifting the deer onto Lee's packhorse, Nugget Bars. The mare refused to budge with such a heavy load. This angered Lee so much that he hit her on the rump with the back of his hand breaking his hand. Eventually the men packed the meat out on Nugget Bars after several attempts to get her started in the right direction.

Bud VanDenBerg, Lee's father, recognized his son's buck as a Boone and Crockett trophy when he first examined the rack. After the 60-day drying period, Lee had his buck scored. His rack, which scored 198 points, was accepted into the Boone and Crockett Club's records-keeping program in 1979.

EDDIE D. PALMER
Location: Gunnison County
Year Taken: 1962
Score: 198

In 1962 Eddie and Kelly Palmer got their hands on an old white horse and a skinny mule and decided to try their luck at packing into a remote hunting area. The area the two brothers selected for their hunt was the West Elk Wilderness Area in western Gunnison County.

Ten miles into the wilderness area, they ran into a cowboy herding cattle who told them they were crazy to pack that far. But, he added, they had selected one of the best big-game areas in the state. After directing them to a good campsite near a clump of blue spruce, he invited the brothers for coffee. Together they chewed the fat and discussed the hunting potential of the area they were in.

The next morning Eddie and his brother left camp in different directions. When he was about a mile from camp, Eddie realized that in the excitement of opening day he had forgotten his pistol belt with his knife and extra cartridges. Leaning against a tree he debated whether or not to return for them. After a few moments he decided he could improvise if necessary. When he stepped away from the tree, Eddie spooked a small forked horn that bounced to the top of the ridge in front of him. Since he was looking for something more respectable, he passed it up.

Eddie continued on and the little forked-horned buck began to parallel his course. Every now and then Eddie glanced back and spotted the little buck watching his every move. About the time Eddie began to think that a wise old buck would never pull such a stunt, he glanced back and saw a second buck with the little forked horn. All he could see was the head and the antlers of a real monster watching him from 35 to 40 yards away. Without a moments hesitation, Eddie whirled and fired one offhand shot at the big buck. It crumpled to the ground instantly and never moved another muscle.

In 1964 Eddie entered his buck in the 11th Boone and Crockett Big Game Competition. It scored 198 points in the all-time records book.

LEE FRUDDEN
Location: Eagle County
Year Taken: 1978
Score: 197-7/8

Months of preparation and days of intensive scouting landed a Boone and Crockett mule deer for both Lee Frudden and Jim Caraccioli. Not only did they take their deer on the same hunt but also on the same day.

Back in July of 1978 Lee received notification from the Colorado Division of Wildlife that he, Jim and two other friends, Greg and Gary, had been drawn for the late season near Glenwood Springs in Eagle County. Lee and Jim immediately started making plans. They knew the area had a reputation for trophy deer from talking to game biologists and local guides. In preparation for the late season, Jim scouted the area during the regular November hunting season and saw several large bucks.

Then in late November, Lee and Jim arrived in the hunting area on Gypsum Creek near Gypsum, Colorado, two days before opening day. A light snow was falling as the men drove their 4x4 pickup over the terrain. Late in the afternoon on November 30, Lee scoped the oak brush and sighted a huge buck grazing three-quarters of a mile away. He estimated the buck's rack would score between 200 and 205 points in Boone and Crockett. Lee again spotted the same buck the next day before heading back to town to wait for Saturday's opening, on December 2.

Due to additional snowfall during the night, the men didn't reach the hunting area until 8:30 a.m. Shortly after arriving in the area, Lee spotted a good-sized buck feeding in heavy snow on the side of a mountain. Gary, a friend of Lee's, downed the buck on his first shot. Two miles farther Lee spotted a second nice buck with non-typical antlers chasing a doe. The men began the stalk when Lee noticed a third huge monster walking about 75 yards to their left. Greg fired but missed, so Jim downed the deer. A mile more and Greg finally nailed his buck.

Lee had Jim drive him to the exact spot where he had sighted the trophy buck two days in a row. Lee walked to the top of a knoll and heard a twig snap as he peered into a small basin of oak brush. A doe ran below him and right behind her was the huge buck Lee was looking for. The buck dropped down into a small draw and had started up the other side when it suddenly stopped in its tracks to eye Lee. At 150 yards, Lee had a clear shot. With one shot, the buck collapsed in the 18-inch cover of fresh snow. After a second shot the deer lay still.

Gary helped Lee drag the buck with its 32-inch wide rack a quarter of a mile back to the truck. The entire hunt was over by 2 p.m. on opening day of the late season. Lee's and Jim's deer each made the Boone and Crockett Club's records book with Lee's buck scoring 197-7/8 points in the typical category, and Jim's buck scored 245-5/8 points in the non-typical category.

RUSS H. WINSLOW
Location: Moffat County
Year Taken: 1967
Score: 197-4/8

With the sun setting on the last day of the 1967 hunting season, Russ Winslow had only a couple of hours left in which to fill his tag. The weather was pleasant, but he had to work that day laying oil for the Moffat County Highway Department on roads northwest of Craig. When he got off work late that afternoon, he and Pat Coniff, a fellow worker who also hadn't filled his tag, decided to take the long way home on County Road Number 8 and look for deer along the way.

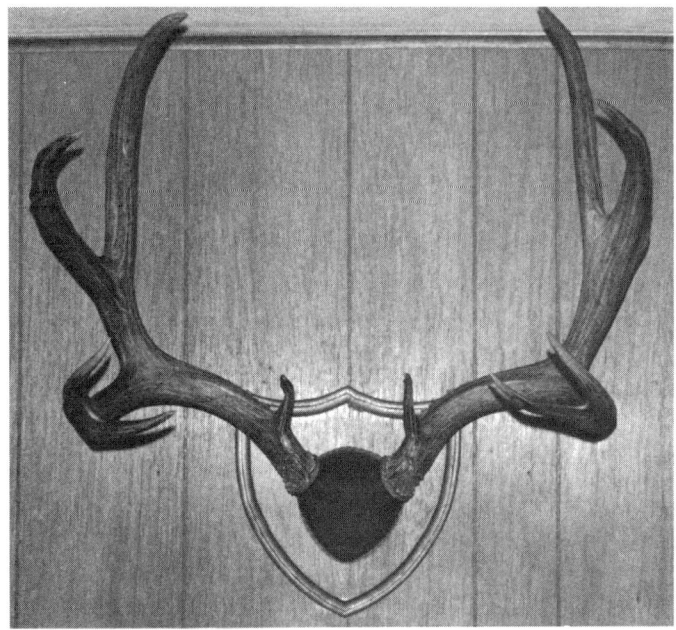

Going over a rise in the road, Russ glanced to one side and spotted a nice buck standing in tall sagebrush approximately 400 yards away. After pulling to the side of the road and parking, Russ offered his rifle to Pat and told him to take the first shot. Pat declined and returned the rifle to Russ, telling him to go ahead and shoot it himself as he probably knew his own rifle better than he did. They only had one rifle between them. Russ' first shot dropped the animal, but it was back up and running immediately. The second and third shots misfired, but the fourth one brought it down for good.

Russ knew he had a nice buck, but it wasn't until he took the antlers to Craig Sports to have them mounted on a plaque that he realized just how nice they were. At the suggestion of his taxidermist, Russ had his antlers officially scored by a B&C measurer. To Russ' surprise, they made the records book with plenty of room to spare with a total score of 197-4/8 points. They were well over the minimum score of the 185 points in effect at that time.

JEROME L. DEGREE
Location: Custer County
Year Taken: 1972
Score: 197-2/8

Jerome's hunt began early one morning in October 1972 in the Wet Mountains, southeast of Westcliffe. Jerome hunted that year with his brother, Robert, a friend, Jim Hall, and his cousin, Ron Vickerman. As the four hunters drove down a ridge in Ron's 4x4 pickup, three huge muley bucks crossed in front of them. In the blink of an eye, the trio disappeared down the ridge.

Everyone piled out of the pickup and hurriedly made plans for a series of drives to see if they could flush the bucks into the open for a shot. Jerome, Jim and Robert spread out to make a drive down the ridge where the bucks had vanished while Robert headed for the far end of the ridge to cut them off if they broke out of the timber.

Jerome went down the north side in the timber, Jim went along the top of the ridge and Robert crossed over to the next ridge to the north. Everyone gave Ron 30 minutes to get to the end of the ridge and get in position before they started the drive. Jerome finished his route a few minutes ahead of Jim and began discussing strategies with Ron. Suddenly, Jerome heard a rock roll behind him. He turned just in time to see the three bucks out in the middle of an opening scrambling for heavy timber on the other side. Both men fired but missed as the bucks went out of sight.

Jerome took off in hot pursuit and caught a glimpse of the bucks just as they disappeared for the second time. The smallest buck was in the lead, followed by Jerome's B&C buck, which was followed by an even larger typical buck with a 36-inch spread. Jerome trailed them for a half mile when he observed Robert motioning for him to head back. Robert informed Jerome that the bucks were two ridges away and that the largest buck had broken away from the other two. No one had the slightest clue where the bucks were so they ate lunch and plotted their next drive.

Jerome L. DeGree used his .30-40 Krag to down this massive typical mule deer buck in 1972 that scores 197-2/8 points.

Jerome DeGree stands below some of his outstanding Colorado trophies as he holds his .30-40 Krag rifle. His B&C buck is on the right.

After lunch, Jerome went to the far ridge to the north, Ron took the middle, and Robert went south. It was Jim's turn to take up a stand on the far end of the ridge. The three drivers were scattered across a half-mile of country when Jerome caught the two smaller bucks on the go about 500 yards away. When they were within 300 yards he took a shot at the bigger buck with his .30-40 Krag. He hit dirt. A second attempt was dead on and the buck dropped. Ron took the smaller buck and Robert dropped a third one he jumped on his way towards Jerome. Field dressed without the legs, head and hide, Jerome's buck weighed in at 203 pounds.

In 1991, at the urging of his son-in-law, Jerome finally had the rack officially scored by Boone and Crockett Club official measurer Stanley Ogilvie of Salida. His buck was accepted in the Boone and Crockett Club's 22nd Awards Program at a score of 197-2/8 points.

FRANCIS WILSON
Location: Elbert County
Year Taken: 1993
Score: 197-2/8

The landscape was still bathed in the warm glow of sunrise on opening day when Francis Wilson spotted a small herd of does feeding on a distant grassy ridge. While checking out that herd, he suddenly heard a rustling noise behind him. He turned and watched as five bucks casually browsed past him about 80 yards away and went over the hill out of sight. It was clear from the body language of the four smaller bucks that the other buck in the herd, with a massive rack, was regarded as the dominant male. Francis looked back for Jamie, his teenage daughter who had accompanied him on this muzzleloader hunt, and found her snoozing in the grass. He awoke Jamie and together they tracked the bucks until they crossed onto an adjoining ranch where neither had permission to hunt.

On the fifth day of the season Francis teamed up with his cousin Bill to hunt the same area. Francis dropped Bill off and drove another mile on down the road where he parked his Bronco. He then proceeded down a long, low ridge to a fence line, three-quarters of a mile away. As the sun rose, Francis spotted a herd of 11 deer feeding on a grassy hillside about 500 yards away. One of the bucks carried a rack that Francis estimated was 34-36 inches wide. The deer fed along a course that would eventually bring them within range of his .50 caliber Hawken. When several of the does were within 40 yards of him one snorted and the entire herd, including the big buck, bolted.

As a frustrated Francis watched the herd move to the south, a loud ruckus to the southwest caught his attention. Taking a closer look through his binoculars, Francis observed two bucks sparring on a low ridge. The click clack of the antlers attracted the attention of the other three bucks, including the buck with the wide rack. The big buck began to violently horn a bush.

Francis Wilson holds his B&C buck that he took with his .50 caliber Hawkin muzzleloader in 1993.

The herd continued to feed and walk off to the southeast heading towards an adjoining ranch where Francis couldn't hunt. He knew he had to reach the bucks before they crossed the fence line. He belly-crawled a couple of hundred yards to a slight draw in the prairie. The deer were close to the fence line and Francis was still out of range. He watched the does and the three bucks jump the fence.

Francis glanced back just in time to see three new bucks joining the herd near the fence line. One of the bucks was unusually large and he immediately recognized it as the same buck he sighted while hunting with his daughter on opening morning. Francis lined the iron sights up on the buck's chest and fired. Peering through the cloud of black-powder smoke Francis watched as the big buck ran off and stopped about 90 yards away under a small ponderosa pine. A second shot dropped the big buck for good.

A few days later Francis got a call from his taxidermist, Carl Devours, who told him that his buck would make the Longhunter Muzzleloading Big Game Record Book, as well as the Boone and Crockett Club's all-time records book. Francis then realized his buck was the blackpowder buck of a lifetime. Francis' buck is ranked 4th largest typical muley in the world to be taken by muzzleloader rifle.

Michael Duplan provided details of the hunt as told to him by Francis Wilson.

A belly-crawl for a couple of hundred yards brought Francis Wilson within sight of his trophy buck, which he downed with two shots.

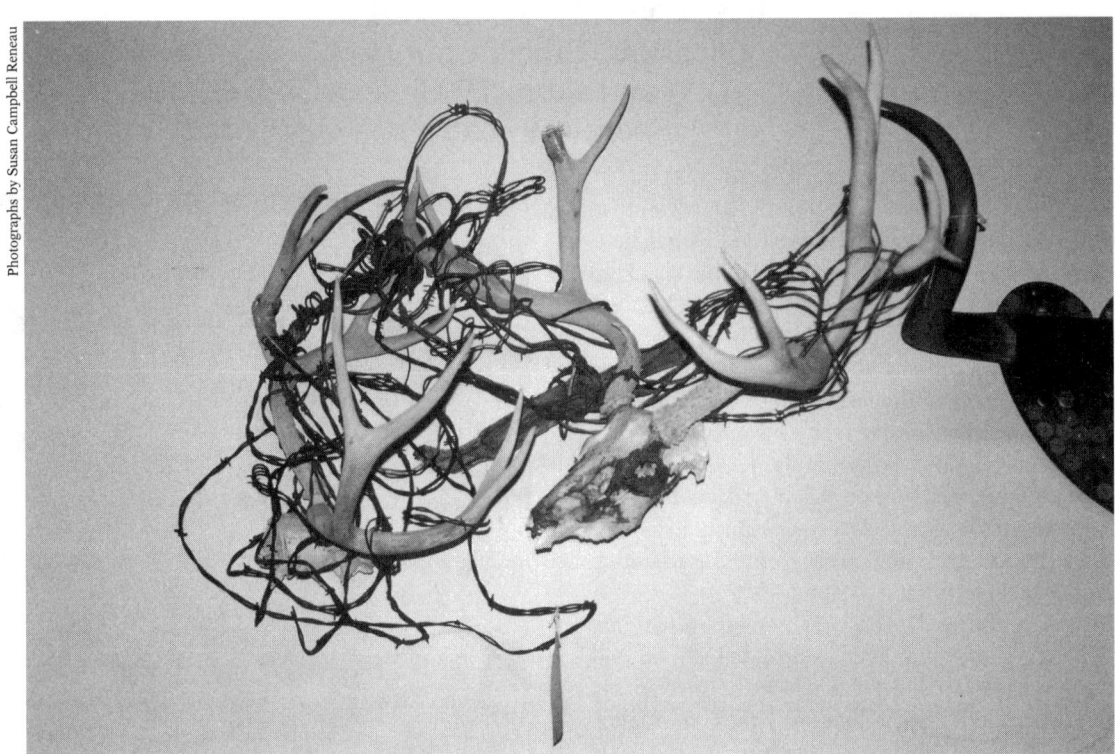

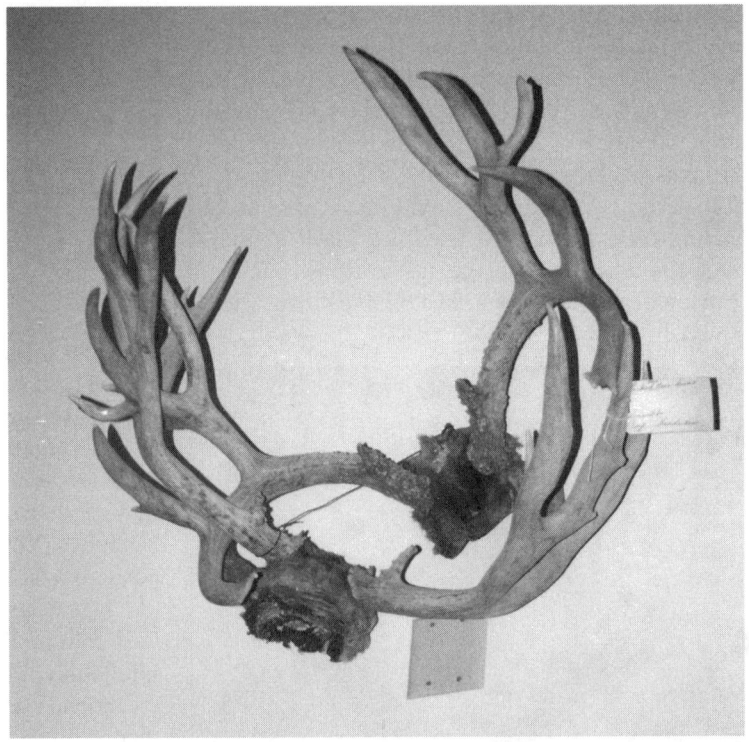

Two sets of locked mule deer antlers are on display at the White River Museum in Meeker, Colorado – a great local history museum to visit. The sets with barbed wire died as they twisted to release themselves from the wire. The name Curay Sanderson of Meeker was written on the museum tag. As for the locked antlers without barbed wire, the name Cup Sanderson is written on the museum tag.

HUGH W. GARDNER
Location: Archuleta County
Year Taken: 1971
Score: 197

Hugh Gardner will never forget the 1971 deer season. It was the first year he hunted in Colorado and the only year he bagged a Boone and Crockett mule deer. That year Hugh and his friend Ron Hunt, both of southwestern Oregon, hunted on the Continental Divide near Wolf Creek Pass. Both hunters were after trophy bucks and quickly became disenchanted with the area they were in as they only saw a few small bucks. Hoping to see something with bigger antlers, both men worked higher and higher and eventually took up stands about a half-mile apart overlooking opposite sides of a broad saddle.

Shortly after Hugh sat down and started glassing the area, he spotted a big buck, head held low, contouring the mountain mahogany-covered slope. Realizing he was in a difficult position and would probably get only one shot, Hugh glanced ahead of the buck and picked up a clearing, through

which he thought it would pass. Quietly, he set the sights of his 7mm Remington Magnum, Browning semi-automatic on the opening and prepared to fire.

When the buck entered the opening Hugh touched off a round and the buck dropped. After a brief pause to insure his buck wasn't going to move, Hugh caught up with it and finished it off. The weather that day was cool and partly cloudy, ideal for packing a big deer three and one-half miles back to their vehicle. Fortunately, the hike back was all downhill. Hugh's 1971 trophy scored 197 points in the Boone and Crockett Club's all-time records book.

Hugh Gardner was trophy hunting in Archuleta County in 1971 when he took this buck that scored 197. This low, wide rack has a spread of 35 inches.

MARVIN L. SHEPARD
Location: Delta County
Year Taken: 1960
Score: 196-5/8

Marvin Shepard and his father, Don, hunted the Grand Mesa together during the 1960 post season. Both men knew the terrain like the palms of their hands. They returned that year in search of one of the many large bucks they knew inhabited the area. The area was thick with pinon pine and oak brush that was covered with six inches of freshly fallen snow. It was a clear, crisp December day.

Before daylight the father and son team drove their Jeep to the end of an old Jeep road and downed a cup of steaming hot coffee while they awaited daybreak. As dawn began to break on the eastern horizon both hunters moved out. At the lower elevations they immediately spotted plenty of small bucks and does but nothing of any consequence. As they moved up into the steeper, rougher country, they saw larger bucks but still no keepers.

At about 8 a.m. Marvin spotted a very large-bodied buck standing behind a pinon but could not get a clear look at the rack. Marvin and his father then split up in the hopes that one of them would get a better look at the rack and possibly a clear shot if it turned out to be trophy-class. As Marvin moved

Marvin Shepard was only 17 when he took this Delta County buck on the Grand Mesa. Nearly symmetrical, it scored 196-5/8 points. This photograph was taken moments after he downed the buck on December 4, 1960.

to the right, the buck slipped out of sight and into the brush. There was a small clearing at the top of the opposite ridge, and Marvin watched as the big buck sneaked towards it with its head held low. Marvin was ready to shoot when the buck entered the clearing. However, when the buck didn't reappear after a few minutes he realized it had doubled back down the hill. Marvin's father, who had since rejoined him, pointed out the buck as it stepped behind another large pinon.

When the buck stepped from behind that tree only its head and rack were visible. At 175 yards, it stood looking straight at Don and Marvin. Both hunters got a good look at the buck and knew immediately that it was carrying the finest set of typical antlers either of them had ever seen. Carefully, trying not to spook the buck, Marvin placed the cross hairs of his .30-06 on the buck's neck and squeezed the trigger. The buck went down like the rug had been pulled out from under its feet and lay still. While Marvin worked his way through the brush toward the buck, his father stayed behind to spot for him. When he was about 75 yards from his buck, Marvin suddenly heard what he quickly determined to be his buck making a break for it. Don yelled for Marvin to watch the clearing at the top of the ridge.

Just as the buck entered that clearing, Marvin lined up the cross hairs for a second time, pulled ahead a few feet and fired. The buck promptly piled into the brush with one well-placed shot. At the meat locker the buck later weighed in at 285 pounds field dressed, less then hide, head and legs. Later Marvin had it officially scored and found that it made the all-time records book with a grand total of 196-5/8 points.

TRAN CANTON
Location: Moffat County
Year Taken: 1960
Score: 196-5/8

Tran Canton hunted in Colorado for 15 years, starting in the early 1950s, with great success. During the 1960 season he hunted with Roy Landucci, Bert Manual, Warren Chupp and Herm Foster north of Craig on the Pandella Ranch, which is located at the foot of the mountains. The weather was warm that year and, as a result, the hunting was slow. Some of the men thought of moving to a higher elevation, but Tran decided to go to town for groceries and gasoline and to take a bath.

When Tran was done with his chores, he headed back to camp. About two miles from where he had turned onto a dirt road he spotted some movement in the brush so he pulled off to the side of the road for a better look. Tran didn't expect to see any deer on the return trip. After all, if there were no deer around hunting camp, why should he expect to see any at a much lower elevation? However, upon checking a little closer, it didn't take him long to pick out a mule deer buck in the brush.

Tran's actions promptly flushed the buck, and it only took him a moment to realize that it was big enough for him. Tran fired and the buck dropped. He paused a moment or two before going to see what he had shot. When he reached the buck, Tran's first thought was, "He is big!"

Tran stepped back to collect his thoughts and decided this was the biggest deer he had ever seen. He field dressed it and returned to the truck. When he tried to load the buck into the back of his pickup, he realized it was too heavy to handle. Tran heard someone laughing and looked up to see two men in a passing truck. They too were surprised at the buck's size but offered to help load it into Tran's truck. He was sure glad they came along when they did and offered to help.

After the hunt, Tran returned home to California and never had the rack measured. When he retired in 1979 and moved to Nevada, a taxidermist, Don Barber, asked if he could get the trophy officially measured. Nineteen years after the trophy was taken, the rack scored 196-5/8 points, enough to make the Boone and Crockett Club's all-time records book in 1987.

The line up of men belonging to the Ouray Gun Club stop a moment for a photograph. The portrait was taken in 1910.

Quincy Hines (left) and Marvin Shepard (right) have hunted since the 1960s and on the lawn are some of the fruits of their labors.

ELMER NELSON
Location: Garfield County
Year Taken: 1962
Score: 196-4/8

In October 1962, Elmer Nelson and seven other hunters divided into two groups of four each, set out from central Michigan for Colorado with two campers, a _-ton Jeep, and a miscellaneous assortment of camping equipment. They traveled around the clock and stopped only to get gas, change drivers and eat meals prepared while the campers were rolling. The only meals eaten at restaurants were breakfast and a midnight supper.

Elmer's companions included Leo Blackhurst, Floyd Nagle, Dick Keller, Ken Fisher, Walt Schmock, Boyd Schoffner and Gerry Hart. Their final destination was Garfield Creek near New Castle.

Ordinarily each member of Elmer's hunting party hunted alone but on the third day of the season Elmer asked Boyd to accompany him. After leaving their Jeep they headed down a well-worn trail together and separated after going a short distance. While Boyd continued on down the trail, Elmer dropped off the aspen-covered hillside a few hundred feet. It was early and Elmer paused frequently to look and listen. Due to the dry leaves and loose rocks, it was nearly impossible to sneak along quietly.

Suddenly Elmer heard deer moving. He paused to listen and soon realized they were headed in his direction. A hundred feet below him a doe walked through the only sunlit opening on the hillside. Spotting a buck with a massive set of antlers heading for the same opening. Elmer dropped to one knee and trained the cross hairs of his 30-06 Remington, Model 740, on the opening. He followed the buck's movement for some time and fired when it stepped into the opening.

In the excitement Elmer did not see the buck go down nor did he see it go on. As a result, he scoped out the opening thoroughly and began a slow stalk. As he approached the opening he spotted a tangle of broken tree limbs that he soon made out to be the antlers of his buck. Since he wasn't sure the buck was dead, he purposely snapped a twig. The buck didn't react, and Elmer knew that additional shots wouldn't be necessary.

After admiring the exceptional qualities of his trophy for a few moments, Elmer took out his 8mm-movie camera and clicked off a few feet of film. While he did so he spotted Walt approaching in the distance. As Walt got closer Elmer paused and watched him intently. As Walt approached he kept straining his neck hoping to catch a glimpse of Elmer's buck. When he finally saw it, his eyes lit up and he said, "Now, that's what we've been looking for."

With a final score of 196-4/8 points, Elmer's buck is what plenty of Colorado's deer hunters are looking for.

RONALD CHITWOOD
Location: La Plata County
Year Taken: 1964
Score: 196-3/8

Early in the 1964 season, Ronald Chitwood borrowed his father-in-law's motorcycle and rode off to hunt the Bodo Ranch about seven miles southwest of Durango. Since he had an entire week to hunt, Ron leisurely worked his way up to the top of a ridge that overlooked a sagebrush flat. On his way up, Ron noticed a lot of deer sign in the area, but he saw no sign of other hunters.

Ron was looking over the pinons and oak spread out below him when he spotted a large buck watching him about 60 to 80 yards away. Ron had plenty of time to shoot, but he wasn't in any hurry since he still had the entire week left to hunt. As he watched, the buck turned and slowly threaded its way out of the oak brush into the open flats below. When the big buck reached the first clearing, Ron fired two shots and missed. By then the buck had it in high gear and was flat out moving out of the area. Ron watched as his buck disappeared into the distance.

Two days later Ron returned to the same spot with a college student who was boarding at his in-law's home. The pair of hunters climbed the same ridge Ron had hunted two days earlier. Immediately they spotted a small herd of deer. The college student was primarily after venison, so he downed a nice doe. Thinking the shot might have disturbed the big old buck, Ron maneuvered to a spot with a good vantage point. He immediately sighted the big buck again, but this time he didn't hesitate. The buck went down with one fatal shot to the chest.

The two men promptly field dressed the two deer and packed the doe out that night. They planned to return the next day for Ron's buck, so they hung it in a tree overnight. Ron returned the next day with his father-in-law. Since he wasn't required by law at that time to pack out the antlers, Ron decided to leave the head. Fortunately his father-in-law insisted that they take the antlers home. Upon returning to his home in Washington, Ron's friend and neighbor, Gary Sauer, recognized that the antlers had Boone and Crockett potential. With Gary's assistance, the antlers were measured after the 60-day drying period.

Ron's trophy scored 196-3/8 points in the 12th North American Big Game Competition. Although his trophy did not receive an award, he did send his trophy for display purposes to the awards banquet held in 1966 at the Carnegie Museum in Pittsburgh, Pennsylvania.

Ron Chitwood kneels beside the unmounted B&C typical mule deer he took in 1964.

MIKE MURPHY
Location: Rio Blanco County
Year Taken: 1971
Score: 196-2/8

In 1971 Mike Murphy's father, Pat, promised he would take Mike on his first hunting trip if he kept up his grades. Mike did so, and Pat took his 14-year-old son to Meeker, Colorado, that fall for the hunt of a lifetime.

Mike, Pat and Don, Mike's uncle, arrived in Meeker several days before the season, picked up needed supplies and set up camp at their cabin in the Price Creek area. Pat and Mike spent the next several days enjoying each other's companionship and fishing for trout. The weather was cold enough to freeze their lines, but they both caught their limit each day.

Opening day finally arrived and the trio spent the better part of the morning in a fruitless search for game near the cabin. They saw nothing but a handful of does. That afternoon, the hunters loaded their gear into their four-wheel drive Coot and set off down an old Jeep trail near the cabin for greener pastures. They had only gone about 500 yards when Mike's father spotted a buck and stopped the vehicle. Everyone piled out and agreed to let Mike have the first chance.

When Mike squeezed the trigger his first shot misfired. The second shell jammed his .30-30 so Mike's uncle backed him up and took the deer. Upon closer examination, Pat and Don both agreed that it was the biggest buck they had taken in 15 or 20 years of big-game hunting. It weighed about 250 pounds field dressed and had to be winched back to the Coot. After securing that monster on a sheet of canvas towed behind the Coot, Mike's party continued down the Jeep trail. They had gone another two and a half miles when Pat suddenly told Don to stop the vehicle. He had caught a fleeting glimpse of another deer. All three piled out again and hiked back up the Jeep trail searching for the deer.

The men had gone about 20 yards when they located it on the hillside about 100 yards away. It was partially hidden by the brush, but they could tell it was a nice buck. Don passed Mike his 6mm target rifle and told him that it wouldn't jam, and the buck would be a nice trophy for his first buck. As the rifle was too heavy for the 14-year-old lad, Pat knelt in the snow and let him use his shoulder as a rest. Two shots later Mike had collected his first deer. Both Pat and Don were impressed with the size of Mike's buck. It made the monster Don had taken earlier look like a baby. Mike's buck field dressed to 300 pounds and sported a 6x7-point rack.

On the way home Mike began composing an English term paper he was assigned for cutting a few classes. It was supposed to cover his Colorado trip. He had quite a story to tell. What a thrill it must have been for this young teenager when his first buck scored 196-2/8 points.

HARRY L. WHITLOCK
Location: Uncompahgre National Forest
Year Taken: 1968
Score: 196-1/8

Photograph courtesy of Harry L. Whitlock

While many people stumble onto their trophy bucks by chance or accident, careful planning and well-thought-out strategy pays off for others. Harry Whitlock falls in the latter group. He is a Californian who hunts solely for the bigger bucks. He had hunted nearly all the Western states and frequently returns home empty-handed by choice. He always sees deer but chooses to wait for the big one to come along.

In 1968 Harry hunted on the Uncompahgre National Forest with his father Stan Whitlock, his son Michael Whitlock, and friends William Sterbenk, Pete Page and Robert Hartner, Sr. The exact location of their hunt was Frank's Bench in the Blue Creek area. At daylight on the day he took his trophy buck, Harry and his companions left their pickup. Rather than spending an hour or so in the field, they planned on staying the entire day. In the hopes of bagging game, each hunter strapped on a packboard. They figured that if they got anything in that rugged country, they would have to pack it out in quarters.

At 8 a.m. Harry was one-and-a-half hours from the pickup. As the sun's fingers started reaching down into the shadowy side of Frank's Bench, Harry caught his first glimpse of his buck feeding about a half-mile away. With dawn's light reflecting off its antlers, Harry had no doubt in his mind that he had spotted a truly exceptional animal. When he checked it with his binoculars, he knew it was trophy quality.

Harry promptly pinpointed the buck's location below two small blue spruce and began working out his strategy for the stalk with his companions. He directed one companion to work across the top of Frank's Bench and another to work along its base. He contoured the slope between them and headed directly towards the two spruce. It took Harry an hour and a half to reach the point where he last saw his big buck. Slipping out of his packboard, he sat down and began glassing the area in a 200- to 300-foot radius of the two spruce trees. Immediately he spotted the gray muzzle of his buck. It was bedded down within 20 feet of the point where he had first spotted it and was watching his every move.

Sighting his .264 Winchester on the white spot of the buck's throat Harry squeezed off one round. Instead of fleeing the untouched buck stood up and began to slowly walk away. Harry's hasty follow up shots finished the buck. After field dressing it, Harry and his two companions quartered and hung it for the night. Another companion took a deer and Harry helped pack it out that evening. The next day they returned and packed out Harry's trophy. Ten days later the buck still weighed 263 pounds without the hide. One year later the antlers scored 196-1/8 points in the Boone and Crockett Club's all-time records book.

JERRY E. ALBIN
Location: San Miguel County
Year Taken: 1972
Score: 195-7/8

While many people only dream of taking a records-book buck, Jerry Albin is one of the few who actually fulfilled his dream.

On October 20, 1972, Jerry and his hunting companions, Don Larson and Don's two sons, left their home well before daylight and headed for lower Beaver Canyon. Jerry and his friends were after a B&C buck. Starting the hunt at daybreak, the hunting party began a six to seven mile trek up Beaver Canyon. Along the way each hunter passed up numerous smaller bucks in the hopes of bagging one of the larger muleys they knew inhabited the upper reaches of Beaver Canyon.

After a time Don and his sons moved ahead to take up stands while Jerry started driving for them. As Jerry broke over the rim of a deep canyon, four bucks broke out of the oak brush on the far side approximately 300 yards away. All four bucks were nice but it was immediately apparent to Jerry that the last one in line was exceptional. He promptly shouldered his .243 Winchester and fired as the lead deer began to drop out of sight. The last buck dropped instantly.

Don and his sons came running when they heard the lone shot. Don and one of his sons spotted the deer and held their position while Jerry and Don's other son worked their way

Beaver Canyon in San Miguel County yielded this 195-7/8-point typical mule deer to hunter Jerry Albin in 1972.

down the canyon and through the bush towards the deer. Being younger, Jerry's companion arrived at the buck first and yellowed back, "Mr. Albin, you've got a nice mule deer here."

When Don arrived he had no doubt that Jerry had bagged a records-book buck. His comment was, "Looks like you might have a Boone and Crockett trophy."

After appropriate congratulations were made the hunters hog dressed the buck and began their six-mile hike back to the vehicle. Jerry remembered the conversation all the way back centered around his trophy. The next day Jerry and his friends took two horses in to get the meat and trophy. Back home, the buck weighed in at 232 pounds field dressed. That year Jerry's deer was the number one hit in San Miguel County and the surrounding area. People came from miles around to see the trophy and to get the story of the hunt firsthand. After the required 60-day drying period, Jerry's deer officially scored 195-7/8 points.

Carl (left) and Addie (right) Doughty and Mrs. Cliff Allen (center) all of Cedaredge, pose with deer they took in the Meeker area, circa 1904. Note the long dresses and the all-terrain vehicle in the background used to travel from Cedaredge to Meeker.

Mrs. A.G. Wallihan of Lay, Colorado, and her trusted steed stand beside the buck she just downed with one shot from 130 yards, circa late 1800s. The photograph hangs in the lobby of the Meeker Hotel, Meeker, Colorado.

LARRY DELLA BITTA
Location: Montrose County
Year Taken: 1969
Score: 195-6/8

Larry Della Bitta has made many hunting trips to Colorado from his home in Northern California, but his 1969 hunt will probably remain his most memorable because that's the year he made the Boone and Crockett Club's all-time records book.

Early in November of that year Larry and five friends hunted the rolling, sagebrush-covered hills near the Black Canyon of the Gunnison in Montrose County. Larry's friends included Norm and Harold LeGore, Gary Portlock, Bert Mallich and Joe Daughbaugh.

On the day he got his trophy buck, Larry, Gary and Joe were working their way across a sage-covered ridge when Gary fired two shots at a monster buck. While he and Joe hollered back and forth at each other and looked for a possible blood trail, Larry took up a stand on a huge rock overlooking a shallow basin. Glassing the basin, Larry took up a stand on a huge rock overlooking a shallow basin where he promptly picked up a doe and a nice four-pointer standing in an isolated patch of brush looking back at Joe and Gary. Silently, Larry raised his 7x57 Winchester, Model 70 and fired. The shot missed the buck but alerted Gary and Joe who started yelling at Larry to find out what was happening. The buck was so intent on the two yelling hunters that it didn't even react to the gunshot.

Larry Della Bitta in his living room with his records-book buck. This set of antlers is extremely high and symmetrical.

Afraid he would spook the buck if he answered, Larry took his time and squeezed off two more rounds. The third shot found its mark, and the buck collapsed as if the ground had swallowed it up. It wasn't until after he located his buck in the brush that he realized his "nice four-pointer" was actually the same monster Gary had shot at first. Upon closer examination Larry determined that his was the only shot to hit the buck. Thus, in accordance with his hunting party's rules, the buck was Larry's.

Larry's "nice four-pointer" was actually a 5x7 and scored 195-6/8 points in the 14th Boone and Crockett North American Big Game Competition.

MIKE DISERT
Location: Huerfano County
Year Taken: 1954
Score: 195-6/8
Owners: Mike Disert and Janet D. Wasson

Recalling a mule deer hunt he was on more than 40 years earlier was a strain for Mike Disert's memory. However, he easily recalled that it was the best deer hunt of his life. Mike was just 14 years old when he took a buck of a lifetime.

Don Drury, Mike's future brother-in-law, was with Mike when the latter took his B&C trophy during the waning days of the 1954 hunting season. The two friends left before daylight one morning in an old Willys Jeep with high hopes of filling their elk and deer tags. Prior to that day, however, neither had seen anything larger than a tiny forked-horn buck.

They hunted on Mike's father's ranch in the Sheep Mountain area, which is about 30 miles west of Walsenburg. They jumped three does on the way into the area before they even got out of their Jeep. They didn't see another deer until 3 p.m., which was about the time the two tired, discouraged young men started to give up.

They were headed back to the Jeep in single file when Don stopped so suddenly that Mike plowed into him. "Did you hear that?" Don asked. Mike hadn't heard a thing; he was too busy talking. They moved into a little clearing to listen and watch the hillsides. Don needed his hearing checked, Mike thought, but he gave the hillside a thorough look. They were about to give up when halfway up the ridge behind them Mike spotted the largest set of antlers he had ever seen.

"Look at that. Is it a deer or an elk?" Mike said as he poked Don in the ribs. Don took a deep breath and said, "Who cares. We have tags for both. Let's go get it."

The distance was 250 yards and out of reach for Don's .30-30 and Mike's .348. The animal suddenly broke from the brush and bounded for the top. It was 20 yards from the top when the two boys fired simultaneously. The animal continued over the top and was gone.

"We missed. Let's see if he stops," Don said.

Mike admits today that he was young with very little between the ears; he ran straight up the side of the hill through the oak and brush. Don, who was smarter, went around. As Mike topped the hill, winded and blurry-eyed, he glanced about. He saw nothing, not even Don. Mike walked 30 feet when his feet became entangled in the brush. He went head over heels with his rifle flying one way and his body going the other. The "brush" was in fact

In 1990, Mike's daughter, Janet, and her new husband entered his buck in the Boone and Crockett Club's 22nd Awards Program at a score of 195-6/8 points. The buck now hangs in Janet's trophy room.

the massive antlers of his trophy buck. Both men's shots had hit the buck, but Don admitted Mike's .348 caused the fatal wound. The monster buck field dressed at 274 pounds and carried the biggest rack Mike had ever seen.

In 1990, Mike's daughter, Janet, and her new husband entered his buck in the Boone and Crockett Club's 22nd Awards Program at a score of 195-6/8 points. The buck now hangs in Janet's trophy room.

ROYCE JAY CARVILLE
Location: Delta County
Year Taken: 1974
Score: 195-5/8

Royce Carville had hunted hard in the warm weather for three days but only saw a couple of small bucks and a few does. His camp was located 10 miles southeast of Paonia on the Gunnison National Forest. His hunting partners included his father Ray, two brothers Randy and Robin, and an uncle fondly known as "Big John."

On the third night the weather changed and there were four inches of new snow on the ground by daylight. Not long after the snow had stopped falling, Robin and Royce picked up a fresh set of deer tracks that crossed a clearing in the oak brush. After they examined the tracks closely both hunters decided to follow them. By the time they had gone 800 to 900 yards, both hunters were convinced there was more than one buck in the area. The snow was crisscrossed with tracks. While Robin sorted them out, Royce moved ahead about 15 yards to a ridge overlooking a deep canyon. As he peered over the edge, Royce spotted his buck feeding with two does about 200 yards away. The antlers appeared to be three feet tall.

Royce J. Carville holds his trophy buck in 1974.

Royce eased back to get his brother without alarming the deer. Hoping they both might be able to score, the hunters scanned the area for another buck without success. By then Royce had a severe case of the shakes. About the time Royce was ready to shoot, the big buck lay down. After another brief pause, Royce fired. To his dismay his buck and another one, as large or larger than Royce's buck, jumped up and ran out of sight over the hill. Everything happened so quickly that neither brother was able to get off another shot.

Royce set off on the trail of the two big bucks while Robin skirted the ridge overlooking the canyon into which the bucks had disappeared. Within 50 yards or so, Royce found what appeared to be small flecks of blood in the snow. Then, much to his dismay, the bucks split up. One went up the canyon and the other went down. Royce wasn't sure which to follow, but he took the lower one, figuring the wounded buck was more likely to go downhill. Another 150 yards farther, Royce caught a movement under a large, low-lying cedar. It was his buck. He didn't have a clear shot, but he figured he couldn't miss at 40 yards. Royce fired, and for the second time his buck leaped to its feet and ran out of sight.

Royce took off running after the buck. As he crossed a small ridge he looked ahead, hoping to get another quick shot. About the time he looked up, he tripped and fell over his buck. It had only traveled 50 yards after the second shot.

Royce's buck weighed in at 278 pounds field dressed and scored 195-5/8 points in the records book.

C. JAY STOUT
Location: Grand County
Year Taken: 1981
Score: 195-5/8

Jay's hunting success in the fall of 1981 was so profound that he won all the bets and had to treat his friends to a round of drinks.

The story begins and ends near the Hot Sulfur Springs-Granby area in Grand County where Jay knew big muleys roamed. Jay set up a tent camp in a drainage with his father Leon, brother Jon and friend Tom O'Donovan and the men spent two days before the season scouting the area. After sighting many nice bucks, the men decided they needed to set up a little wager to make the effort more interesting, so the first person to take a buck would receive $5, $5 for the biggest buck, $5 for the first elk and $5 for the biggest elk. Everyone chipped in and the hunt began.

Opening morning the men were up dark and early to drive back into the drainage and drop everyone off in different places. Jay wandered up a mountain in hopes of reaching the top before the sun rose and tramped through about a foot of freshly fallen snow. As Jay caught his breath and readied himself to scope the area, a herd of elk walked nearby and he ended up taking a great 4x5 bull on opening morning. This was a time when hunters could hold both elk and deer permits and Jay had both. Jay thought, "Hay, I got the first elk. That's $5 each!"

Back in camp, Jay learned that Tom took the first buck, a small 5x5 mulie that Tom was certain to be the biggest buck of the hunt. Jay admitted the camp celebrated the elk and deer that night so the next morning they all overslept. By the time Jay dropped everyone off at their hunting spots and drove to his parking spot in preparation for a hike up the mountain, a couple of other vehicles were there. Jay's spirit sunk but he began hiking up the mountain and bumped into three hunters, so Jay was sure any hope of finding a buck was lost. After traveling another 200 yards above the third hunter, Jay saw a massive buck from 60 yards away picking its way through the forest on its way to high country. Without hesitation Jay threw up his Ruger m77MKII-7mm Remington Magnum and fired a single shot that immediately dropped the buck.

One of the strangers walked up to Jay after he started field dressing the buck and admired its size. When Jay returned to the parking lot, Tom and Jon were waiting and the first thing out of Tom's mouth was, "How big is he?"

"Oh, Tom. I don't know. He's probably pretty close to yours, but I do need some help getting it off the mountain," Jay said.

Tom knew he had lost the bet when he saw the size of Jay's buck. Jay's buck has a final Boone and Crockett score of 195-5/8 points in the all-time records book.

PICK UP
Location: Grand County
Year Found: 2000
Score: 195-1/8
Owner: Kevin Kaltenbaugh

From February to April each year, Kevin Kaltenbaugh walks hundreds of miles looking for antler sheds and 2000 was no exception except this year netted Kevin a full set of antlers that made the Boone and Crockett Club all-time records book.

Kevin celebrated his 39th birthday on March 24, 2000, by finding his trophy buck in Grand County, which he fondly called "Elvis." He estimated the buck had died six to eight weeks prior to his find. The skeleton was intact and the skin on the ribcage was mummified like jerky. Most of the hide was intact from the last rib forward and the hindquarters were stripped down to the pelvis and femur bones. Kevin found the buck by following its fur up a hillside that led to the body where it was crumpled under a tree.

What caused its demise has been the subject of hot discussion among Kevin and his friends since the only trauma Kevin noticed was a broken left femur several inches below the ball joint. Coyotes and birds had eaten the body. Kevin recognized the buck as the one whose sheds he had collected in previous years and he surmised that the buck might have died of natural causes curled against a tree he never left. Finding Elvis was one of Kevin's best birthday presents.

Kevin's birthday find was officially measured by Barry Smith with a final score of 195-1/8. Since this buck has not been entered into the Boone and Crockett Club it remains unranked.

Kevin Kaltenbaugh holds shed antlers from the typical mule deer shown hanging above him in the taxidermy shop of Barry Smith of Hot Sulphur Springs. Kevin found the skeletal and intact antler remains of the buck in 2000.

MICHAEL D. BLEHM
Location: Larimer County
Year Taken: 1972
Score: 195

Whereas many people travel thousands of miles in a lifetime to get a trophy, Mike Blehm dropped his B&C buck almost within sight of his home at age 19. When the first day of deer season rolled around on October 14, 1972, Mike was ready. In previous years he had his share of nice bucks, so that year he was after "something special." According to Mike's definition, "something special" is a buck with seven or eight points on each side or possibly one of the old "grandpas" running around. That year Mike decided to hunt a ranch in the Soapstone Hills northwest of Fort Collins where his family pastured cattle. Ray Griffy, the ranch manager, put Mike up the night before the season.

The next morning Mike accompanied Ray on his chores and assisted in checking for trespassers. By 10 a.m. the horses were saddled and Mike was ready to begin hunting. Ray only accompanied Mike in order to check fences and cattle and to guide him around the ranch. Mike's hunting rifle was a .30-30 Winchester, Model 94. He had used it on all his previous big-game hunts. "It is a super brush gun," according to Mike, "and can take a lot of the abuse characteristic of hunting from horseback." He had downed deer and antelope out to 250 yards with it.

Michael Blehm moments after arriving home with his trophy buck.

Mike and Ray decided to hunt the lower draws first and work their way up to the higher ones. In about the third draw both men spotted a buck in the brush approximately 125 yards away watching the hunters. Escape was 20 feet in either direction. At first glance Mike knew that particular buck was one of the "grandpas" he was after. He stepped off his horse, Jerry Pony, drew a bead and fired. The buck dropped instantly and rolled 40 to 50 feet down into the draw. The time was 11 a.m. on opening day. Mike had been hunting only one hour.

Mike and Ray estimated the buck's field-dressed weight at more than 300 pounds. Mike remembers, "It was the biggest bodied deer I had ever seen and was rolling fat." The buck was practically toothless and the few teeth that remained were broken or greatly worn down, a sure sign of old age.

At the urging of friends, Mike had it officially measured for the B&C records book. The rack scored 195 points, the minimum for entrance into the B&C records-keeping program at that time. The minimum now is 190.

JOREVA BEANE WELLBORN
Location: Mesa County
Year Taken: 1949
Score: 194-7/8

From the time she was 10 years old, JoReva hunted with her father, Joseph Hunt, near her home in Colorado and October 1949 was no exception. JoReva was a teenager at the time who enjoyed sharing time with a special dad in Mesa County.

The day was sunny and crisp when the hunting pair set out to find meat for the winter. JoReva remembered walking through thick oak and buck brush throughout the day and by the end of the day her shirt was shredded and tattered from the branches tugging at her. On the edge of the brush JoReva saw a huge buck standing and looking at her so she fired her .257 Roberts. The buck was mortally wounded but bounded away so she followed the blood trail until she reached the buck and delivered a second shot. Upon reaching the buck, JoReva and Joseph first noticed the size of the body but thought the rack was exceptionally large, too. After butchering the meat they hung the rack in the garage where it remained until friends and family encouraged JoReva to have it officially measured by Richard Keeney on October 29, 1999, close to 50 years after the buck was taken. Even after all those

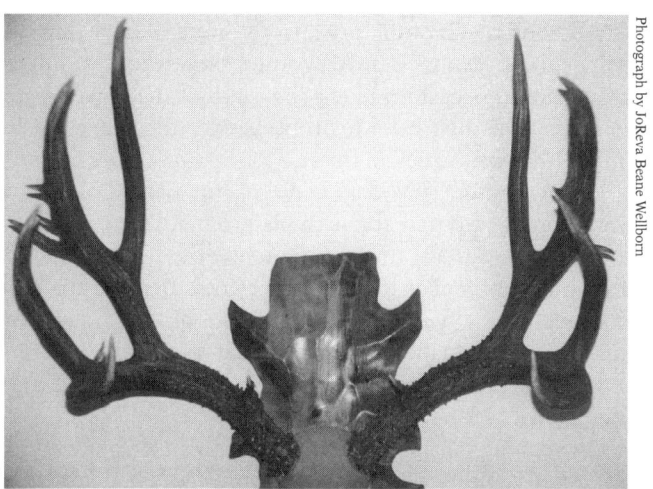

years of drying, the rack still measured well above the minimum score of 190 to be listed in the all-time records book.

JoReva no longer hunts but her memories of hunts with Dad remain strong in her mind as some special thoughts of childhood.

JoReva Wellborn stands along a downtown Grand Junction street beside her massive typical mule deer buck she took as a teenager in 1949.

DANIEL L. KRAFT
Location: Adams County
Year Taken: 1995
Score: 194-5/8
Owner: Douglas P. Kraft

Four or five months prior to the start of each hunting season, Danny Kraft scouted miles and miles of Colorado's eastern plains in search of the biggest mule deer buck. This had been his routine over the years but his hunt in 1995 was to be his finest.

Danny spotted "the buck" in August in Adams County and vowed to return to that site with his brother, Doug, when the season began. Several times he watched the buck in a small herd with four smaller bucks and six does. Deer on the eastern plains use the vastness of the land to protect them from danger by seeing and smelling predators before reaching them, so this challenge made a stalk to the herd a goal Danny anticipated.

On opening morning, Danny and Doug hiked to a vantage point about a mile from the area where Danny had last sighted the buck and watched for the sun to rise. Much to their dismay, no deer were found although they remained in the hunting area all morning. Instead of chancing a blind stalk, they decided to return later in the afternoon to try and spot the deer. The afternoon brought good luck when they saw the herd with the giant buck.

Danny and Doug crawled along the ground to avoid detection and got within 300 yards of the herd before they decided to stop the stalk for fear of spooking them. They knew

they would have only one chance to down a buck. Danny squeezed the trigger of his Remington Model 700, .30-06 and the buck dropped in its tracks. Doug also downed a nice buck as the herd took off across the plains. The many hours of searching the eastern plains paid off for both men.

On August 7, 1999, Danny Kraft died from an unknown illness after living only 33 years. His brother Doug honors his memory and their many hunts together with an impressive display of all their bucks at Colorado Clays Shooting Range in Brighton, Colorado, which is open to the public. Danny was an avid hunter of birds and big game and will be remembered as a champion clay shooter. To see the beautiful mule deer display, call the range first for times and days they are open at (303) 659-7117.

Danny with one of his favorite hunting companions during a duck hunt.

TOM BRODERICK
Location: Montezuma County
Year Taken: 1992
Score: 194-5/8

Loss of wildlife habitat is the single most profound negative impact on outstanding hunting locations, as evidenced by the hunting story of Tom Broderick.

The B&C buck Tom collected in 1992 was one of three massive bucks he collected in Montezuma County but that same area is now a subdivision. Tom's brother Earl saw no less than 10 bucks of the same caliber over the time he hunted this same area before the bulldozers arrived.

On the second weekend of the deer season, Tom returned to his favorite hunting spot after harvesting his elk in the high country. Tom's brother took the high country, and Tom decided to scout the draws and ravines in the lower country. As Tom maneuvered his way up a draw, he spotted a huge rump of a buck climbing in the same direction on the opposite side of the ravine. Tom's heart started pounding as he decided what to do next. Should he chase the buck? Should he go back down so he could see from the other side? Or, should he keep walking in the same direction of the buck? Tom selected the third option and continued watching the buck as it moved parallel to him. Tom followed an old fence line up a deep canyon and started working a side hill. The buck was angled a little toward the draw, picking its way through pinon pine and oak brush. He didn't like the shot so he didn't take it and hoped that the buck would eventually run into him at the top of the canyon. Tom took off knowing the buck never saw him. He stayed hidden as he sneaked over to a vantage point as he waited for the buck to reach the same general area.

The sun began to sink as Tom waited on his vantage point for the buck to arrive, so Tom thought he had really messed up. Just as Tom prepared to leave, a small buck bounded off the hill toward Tom. Tom immediately decided to hunker down to see if the big buck would materialize. Sure enough, a few minutes later a 4x4 buck with no kickers was seen walking at the bottom of the draw. Tom debated about taking this one even though he knew the first buck was biggest with kickers. He decided to wait and let this buck pass. Minutes later another nice buck was sighted trotting through the pinon as it moved with another buck. Tom fired but thought he missed when the fading sunlight flashed in his scope. He became equally concerned when he spotted a second big buck standing broadside to him minutes after he fired the single shot from his 7mm rifle use a 150-grain bullet. Should he shoot this buck or should he look for the first buck? What if the first buck was dead and he'd collect two bucks. The ethical questions were answered when Tom properly decided not to shoot the second buck and look for the first one even if it meant he didn't collect a deer that season. He watched the second buck trot out of sight his heart sank as he thought he had missed the first buck.

As luck would have it, Tom walked over the ridge to see the first buck lying dead where it had been shot. The single shot had hit its mark and Tom collected one of the finest bucks ever taken in Colorado. Upon closer examination, Tom figured the second buck may have received a larger score but the one he collected was fantastic even though the kicker points gave it a few deductions in the final B&C score.

By 1993 the subdivision bulldozing had begun and the outstanding hunting area had faded, but certainly not the memories of a buck and its partner that both made "The Book."

Tom's buck was accepted into the Boone and Crockett Club's 24th North American Big Game Awards Program.

Tom and his family with an assortment of outstanding game. Left to right we see a favorite dog, father Shorty, Tom, mother Sue and brother Earl.

QUINCY M. HINES
Location: Grand Mesa
Year Taken: 1962
Score: 194-4/8

Photograph courtesy of Quincy M. Hines

On Thanksgiving Day in 1962 three hunting buddies, Quincy Hines, Marvin Shepard and Gary Holsan, traveled to Chalk Mountain on the north side of the Grand Mesa where they had all taken big bucks on previous hunts. At the base of the south side of Chalk Mountain is a big "badlands-like" blowout with purple bentonite hills in a large desolate basin the trio wanted to hunt. The badlands are surrounded by thick stands of pinon and juniper, but there are very few trees within the badlands themselves. Hunting conditions were perfect that day with six inches of freshly fallen snow covering the ground.

The three hunters decided to split up and converge on the badlands from three sides. Marvin went up and over Chalk Mountain where he could view the entire basin from the north side. Quincy went up the bottom of the canyon that drained out of the badlands, and Gary closed in from the south side.

When Marvin saw Gary reach the top on the south side, he started into the blowout. He observed fresh, huge tracks everywhere when he reached the bottom. However, he hunted for nearly two hours without success. He knew, because of previous hunting trips to the area, that big bucks were hidden in the deep ravines and boulder fields.

Quincy reached the bottom end of his planned route and climbed onto a pinon ridge for a better view. It was near this ridge that Marvin encountered some tracks that headed into a rocky, brushy draw almost directly under Quincy. As Marvin approached the draw he heard deer clambering through the rocks and brush.

Four large bucks broke out of the brush right under Quincy and ran down the next ridge parallel to him. Quincy shouldered his 7mm Remington Magnum and dropped the largest of the four with one shot to the lungs. The buck had a really high and wide rack. As the sun was quickly setting, the three hunters promptly field dressed the buck, secured it in a pinon for the night and headed home.

Early the next morning, the three men started the long hike back up to get the buck. Marvin shot a 30-inch buck on the way up. After nearly eight hours of backbreaking work the men finally got the two bucks down to the Jeep. Marvin already had a buck in the Boone and Crockett Club's records book he had taken on the Grand Mesa two years earlier, so he was sure Quincy's was a "Booner," too. After the required 60-day drying period, Quincy's buck officially scored 194-4/8 points.

FRANK J. MOORE
Location: Garfield County
Year Taken: 1999
Score: 194-2/8

Frank Moore has hunted for more than 30 years but he's never taken anything as big as the buck he downed in 1999. Not many hunters have.

As a day of hunting ended for Frank during the third season, he settled himself at the edge of a clearing in one of his favorite hunting spots with a perfect view of the area that measured about the size of a football field. Less than 10 minutes after he sat down to prepare for a dusk hunt, a buck was sighted trotting across the clearing from a stand of live cedar. A forest fire created the clearing so the only cover was burned cedar. Frank watched the buck quickly flee to the opposite side of the clearing and back into more live cedars. The buck reached cedars and began to walk more slowly when Frank took aim through the trees. He raised his .25-06 Remington Model 700 and let fly a single shot using a 117-grain Federal premium bullet. The shot downed the buck immediately from a distance of about 200 yards.

Not until Frank reached the other side of the clearing and saw the rack did he realize the size of this buck. When Frank saw the buck the first time he knew it was the legal size, which that year was at least three points on one side. His buck certainly was legal. Not only did it make the Boone and Crockett Club with a final score of 194-2/8 points, but it made "The Book" with room to spare. Frank field dressed it and left to get a friend, Kevin, to help him haul it out of the field. After dragging the buck for a half-mile to the road, they were able to hoist it on Kevin's truck to get it home. Ironically, a few weeks later Frank spotted several more bucks of similar size near a golf course where he works.

"You just don't see big bucks like that anymore, so I was pretty pleased," said Frank.

REYNOLDS LEE VANSTROM
Location: Montrose County
Year Taken: 1960
Score: 193-6/8
Owners: Reynolds A. and Edra Vanstrom

The late Reynolds Lee Vanstrom was hunting on private land near Cimarron in 1960 when he took the prize buck of his hunting career. He was 22 years old at the time but passed away a few years later in a tragic automobile accident.

When it came to hunting styles, Reynolds preferred to hunt alone as he always hunted carefully and unhurriedly. During his hunting career he saw several trophy bucks but 1960 was the first year he was able to stalk his quarry and get close enough for a good, clear shot. His buck was the largest of several bucks he spotted in a herd that was obscured by heavy brush and trees.

Reynolds stalked the animal quietly and slowly through the brush and timber. He didn't want to take a chance of spooking it. As he got closer he noticed that the buck was suffering from an injured lower jaw. Because of that, he felt he had to get that buck, regardless of whether or not it was trophy-class. Fortunately, he was working into the wind, which made his stalk easier. Ultimately, Reynolds got to a place where the trees thinned out, and he could clearly observe the deer moving in his direction about 200 yards away. Though he had taken other deer at that distance, he patiently waited until it got closer. When he felt it was close enough for a clean kill, Reynolds dropped his buck with one shot. Although the antlers looked big when he first spotted the deer, they looked even bigger when he got to the spot where

it had fallen. He bled the deer and took off to enlist the aid of his friends. They returned and hoisted the animal into a position where they could field dress the skin it in preparation for the return trip home.

Because of the injury to the buck's lower jaw, Reynolds didn't have the head mounted. The antlers are presently the proud possession of his parents who find much consolation in having them on their livingroom wall. The antlers represent one of their son's finest hours of triumph and remind them of how happy he was while fishing and hunting. Reynolds' trophy scored 193-6/8 points.

MARVIN MEYERS
Location: Garfield County
Year Taken: 1982
Score: 193-4/8

Marvin Meyers and his hunting buddy, Jim Struble, decided to hunt only for trophies during the 1982 hunting season. Both had hunted hard all season and passed up many opportunities. However, they began to doubt the wisdom of their decision as the season waned and their tags remained unfilled.

On the morning Marvin took his Boone and Crockett buck, Jim was late. Jim was always punctual, but on this particular day the time had changed from daylight savings and he had not adjusted his alarm clock. Consequently, the men hunted one of their least favorite spots in the Bookcliff Mountains as they could get to the area quicker. Living in Grand Junction is an advantage because it is in the heart of one of the best mule deer hunting areas in the world and there are lots of options.

First light found the hunters working under the south rim of a large canyon. Marvin and Jim watched and glassed a herd of four bucks and eight does feeding and moving through the oak and pinions on the opposite side of the canyon. The situation was especially nerve-racking to Marvin because of all the other hunters in the area. Also, the herd was within sight of passing motor vehicles. They could spook at any moment.

Marvin and Jim determined that the three bucks feeding on the fringe of the does were large, mature animals. They tried desperately to get a good look at the single remaining buck feeding with the does. When it finally stepped into an opening, binoculars were dropped and rifles raised and shouldered. The buck was awesome. Marvin's .264 was sighted three inches high at 100 yards, so he held on top of the buck's back. Marvin and Jim fired simultaneously. The buck bolted but stopped after a few yards to determine the source of danger. Marvin elevated his cross hairs a few inches more and fired a second round. The buck's head dropped as it lunged forward and out of sight into the cedars.

Jim stood watch and marked the spot as Marvin hurried down the snow-covered canyon and up the opposite slope. Jim guided Marvin with hand motions to a blood trail in the snow. Marvin found his trophy buck in the cedars.

Marvin Meyers' B&C buck that scores 193-4/8 points.

Marvin Meyers of Grand Junction downed this outstanding typical mule deer with his compound Hoyt bow using a single arrow. Marvin was in a treestand in Garfield County when he collected this trophy with a final P&Y score of 181 points. Marvin took the buck on September 8, 1996.

BILL MORROW
Location: Gunnison County
Year Taken: 1960
Score: 193-2/8
Owner: Nancy Morrow and Tom Roatch

According to his son-in-law Tom Roatch, Bill Morrow road 12 to 15 miles on horseback into the Gunnison Wilderness Area in 1960 to locate the buck that easily makes the Boone and Crockett Club's all-time records book.

Bill worked as a superintendent for Denver builders, Wood Brothers' Homes, and delighted in his hunting adventures with some of the Wood family, including Pop Wood, J.D. Wood and Bob Wood. He began hunting in Colorado in 1953, one year after moving to the state from Ohio with his wife Nancy and their young children. He continued hunting each year until his untimely death in 1978 at age 48. Nancy recalled the hunting camp of 1954 as hot and dry. They camped in a small pup tent using kitchen supplies from home and a five-gallon can of water. Over the years their camp grew to include campers, motor homes, Jeeps and as many as 15 packhorses.

Tom Roatch inherited the rack from Nancy and asked Bob Tully of the Colorado Division of Wildlife to measure the rack in 1990. For many years the rack was hung in the basement of the Morrow's home, but the rack now holds a place of honor in the Roatch home as a tribute to Bill and his many hunting adventures. It was officially entered into the Boone and Crockett Club's records-keeping program by Tom during the 21st Awards Period.

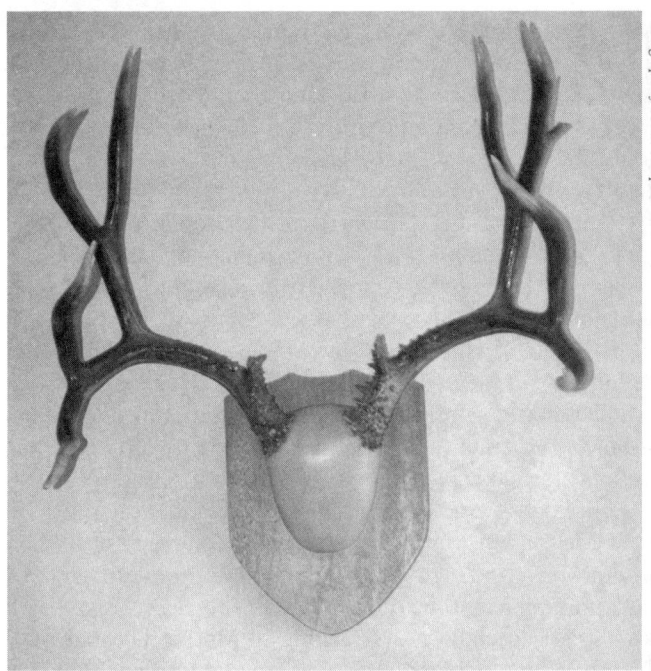

Bill died before his deer was officially measured so never lived to see his outstanding buck recognized by Boone and Crockett Club.

A hunt in 1955 was captured on film by Bill and Nancy Morrow as they successfully completed a deer hunt in DeBeque Canyon.

During the same 1955 hunt, Bill Morrow wipes pepper spray from his eyes after dowsing the buck to prevent flies from landing on the freshly skinned meat.

JAMES S. KENT
Location: Las Animas County
Year Taken: 1995
Score: 192-6/8

After six years of applying for preference points to the Fort Carson Pinon Canyon Maneuver Site of Colorado, James Kent finally drew a mule deer tag for the late November-early December 1995 hunt. If there was one piece of advice Jim remembered above all else it was the reminder not to shoot the first buck he saw because all the bucks were big. Jim arrived in the hunting area with full intentions of following this advice.

Jim was hunting with John Obringer, who also had been applying for the same area for six years and also received his permit in 1995. The men arrived late on a cool, windy, cloudy day because as faculty members of the U.S. Air Force Academy they couldn't do any advance scouting and had to arrive late on Friday afternoon after classes ended. By the time the staff in Pinon Canyon checked them in and gave them safety briefings with all the other requirements for hunting on a military installation, the time was Saturday at 9 a.m. The men had no real plans when they started out but they knew the area was filled with big bucks, open vistas, steep canyons and plenty of great muley habitat.

Jim and John drove about 10 miles into the site, took a little dirt road and stopped and started every mile or so as they glassed for game. They saw several bunches of does when they made another stop and saw a bunch of deer about a half mile

The vast expanse of the Fort Carson Pinon Canyon Maneuver Site provided the perfect habitat to grow a B&C buck. Jim Kent pauses with his trophy muley.

away. Jim turned to the left and saw at a distance of a quarter mile antler points spreading up from everywhere on one buck, a buck surrounded by a herd of eight to nine does. The men split up with Jim going downwind of the buck and John going upwind of it. Jim was fortunate to reach a gully that allowed him to sneak more closely to the buck as a doe bolted in front of him. He hunkered down to wait for the herd to come to him. The herd winded John, which motivated them to shift toward Jim. As they left the pinon junipers, Jim saw a few does and the huge buck.

The buck was looking for love in all the wrong places and was oblivious to Jim who was crouched in front of him. The does were alert and nervous but not the buck. He was in love and fully in rut. Jim located the buck in his scope at 80 yards when it crossed Jim's mind to heed the advice of everyone who had ever hunted in the area, but in the end, Jim disregarded everyone's advice and fired a single shot to the heart-lung area of the buck. In the first half hour of Jim's six-year wait to hunt this canyon, Jim's hunt came to an abrupt end with this single shot. The buck gave Jim plenty of time to debate whether to shoot but, in the end, Jim gave way to common sense and fired.

The buck field dressed to 225 pounds with an estimated full weight by area wildlife biologists of 300 pounds. The testosterone-laden meat tasted awful but Jim invited young and hungry Air Force Academy cadets over for dinner and they weren't as picky.

To this day, Jim doesn't regret his decision to take the first mule deer buck he saw that day on the Fort Carson Pinon Canyon Maneuver Site.

JAY N. CRUZAN
Location: Montezuma County
Year Taken: 1988
Score: 192-6/8

The common refrain from other hunters directed to Jay Cruzan after his first deer hunting season was that he'd probably never come close to taking a buck the size of the one he took in 1988.

He kept hearing comments like, "I've hunted for 50 years for a buck like this;" "You lucky little ##!!!??;" "That is just too bad. You're first year and you have been cursed by the Big Buck;" "You now may have many empty-handed seasons ahead. You have used a good 8 to 10 years of hunting luck during your first year."

Jay started the hunting season with his best friend, Billy Branson, his father, Terry and his dad's friend, Ray. On the fourth day of the season, they went to a portion of land belonging to Jay's grandfather, Ike Duncan, in Pleasantview. As soon as they started, three nice bucks jumped from their beds and were downed by Jay's hunting buddies and Jay was consumed with buck fever. Unfortunately, Jay lost his hunting partners that day when they all collected a buck so he was left to search for another hunting partner.

Jay's last and best option remained when he hunted his uncle's property and his uncle, Troy Oliver, volunteered to hunt with him. They hunted two mornings and two evenings without success On the morning of the last day, as they started their hunt at sun up Jay sat atop a knoll in a hayfield just as a massive buck crossed the road and walked toward Jay. One clean shot from his using a .270 Remington with a 150-grain bullet and the buck was his.

He didn't know what a huge buck he had downed until other hunters started talking to him. One of the hunters said he probably would be cursed after downing such a monster and, sure enough, it took four years of hunting before he bagged a second buck. Jay concluded, "No matter how magnificent or modest the animal, I will never lose my drive for the hunt."

Photograph by Byron D. Long

ERWIN R. PALMER
Location: Grand County
Year Taken: 1961
Score: 192-5/8

When Frank Rust and Erwin Palmer saw the snow fly, they knew it was time to take off to find a buck in Grand County.

Erwin worked the evening shift at the Dillon Dam in 1961 and when he saw the snow falling after his shift he decided to go hunting the next morning to find meat for the winter. The morning was cold, snowy and foggy when Frank Rust dropped Erwin off to begin his hunt. They agreed to meet at a big rock. As Erwin walked through pine trees the fog lifted and he saw an aspen knoll below him. There in the aspen he saw six or seven does and a single buck. He raised his .257 Roberts, Model 70 and fired a single shot to down the buck. Erwin skid the buck 200 yards down the hillside to his car with plenty of meat for the winter. Snow was certainly the motivation for a good hunt.

Erwin's buck wasn't entered into the Boone and Crockett Club's records-keeping program until 1999, but even after almost a half-century of drying, it still scored well above the 190 minimum.

TIM HAYS
Location: Gunnison County
Year Taken: 1981
Score: 191-2/8

It wasn't until January 1997 that Tim Hays found out what a trophy he really had. Tim took his mounted typical mule deer from Colorado to the Arkansas Big Buck Classic. It could only be entered into the category "The Best of Show." The Classic is mainly for whitetail deer. To Tim's surprise, his buck made the Boone and Crockett Club with a final score of 191-2/8 points. Tim wonders what the buck would have scored when he took it in 1981.

The story begins in 1981 when Tim traveled from his home in Arkansas to Gunnison County, Colorado, with his father Raymond and a friend Mack Cook. After scouting different places, he and his hunting group decided to set up camp just south of Crawford on Highway 92. The day before the season Tim found a flat between the buck brush and aspen just below the dark timber. It was a natural funnel spot where the deer would feed as they were moving through the area. Tim had talked to some cowboys who said they had seen some nice bucks in the area. Tim decided this was the place for him to take a stand.

Opening day Tim made his way to his stand in the cold, dark morning. As he sat there waiting for daybreak, Tim heard deer moving through the brush. As daylight broke, Tim made out the outlines of deer feeding. Most were does, but there were some smaller bucks. Tim continued to wait patiently and before long two larger bucks came walking in.

Tim, right, poses with his B&C buck (on the ground), his father, Raymond, and his father's buck (held by Raymond and Tim) in 1981 when Tim was 21. Not until 1997 did Tim discover his buck made "The Book" when he attended the Arkansas Big Buck Classic.

Tim picked out the larger buck, so far as body and antler size were concerned, and zoomed in on it. Tim had to reposition himself for a better shot but then the opportunity eventually presented itself. With the Buck at about 175 yards out Tim fired a single shot from his .30-06 Remington. The first shot was broadside and landed behind the shoulder. To Tim's surprise, the buck did not fall. Tim reloaded and took another shot as the buck broke over the rim of the flat, heading down the side of the mountain.

Tim marked the spot from where he knew he had shot and headed to where the buck was standing when he fired at it. Tim found a blood trail so he began to follow it. The buck had run approximately 70 to 80 yards across the flat. Tim found it just over the side going down the mountain. Both shots were good. Tim was speechless and could not believe his eyes at this beautiful creature that God created.

Tim returned to camp to get some help dragging the buck out. His father, Raymond, and a friend gave Tim a hand. This was Tim's first trip to this area and this hunt caused him to return again and again. Never was Tim so successful as he was in 1981 when he downed his Boone and Crockett buck. He started hunting in Colorado in 1978 and hunted there for a total of seven years.

LLOYD A. PALMER
Location: Grand County
Year Taken: 1959
Score: 191-1/8

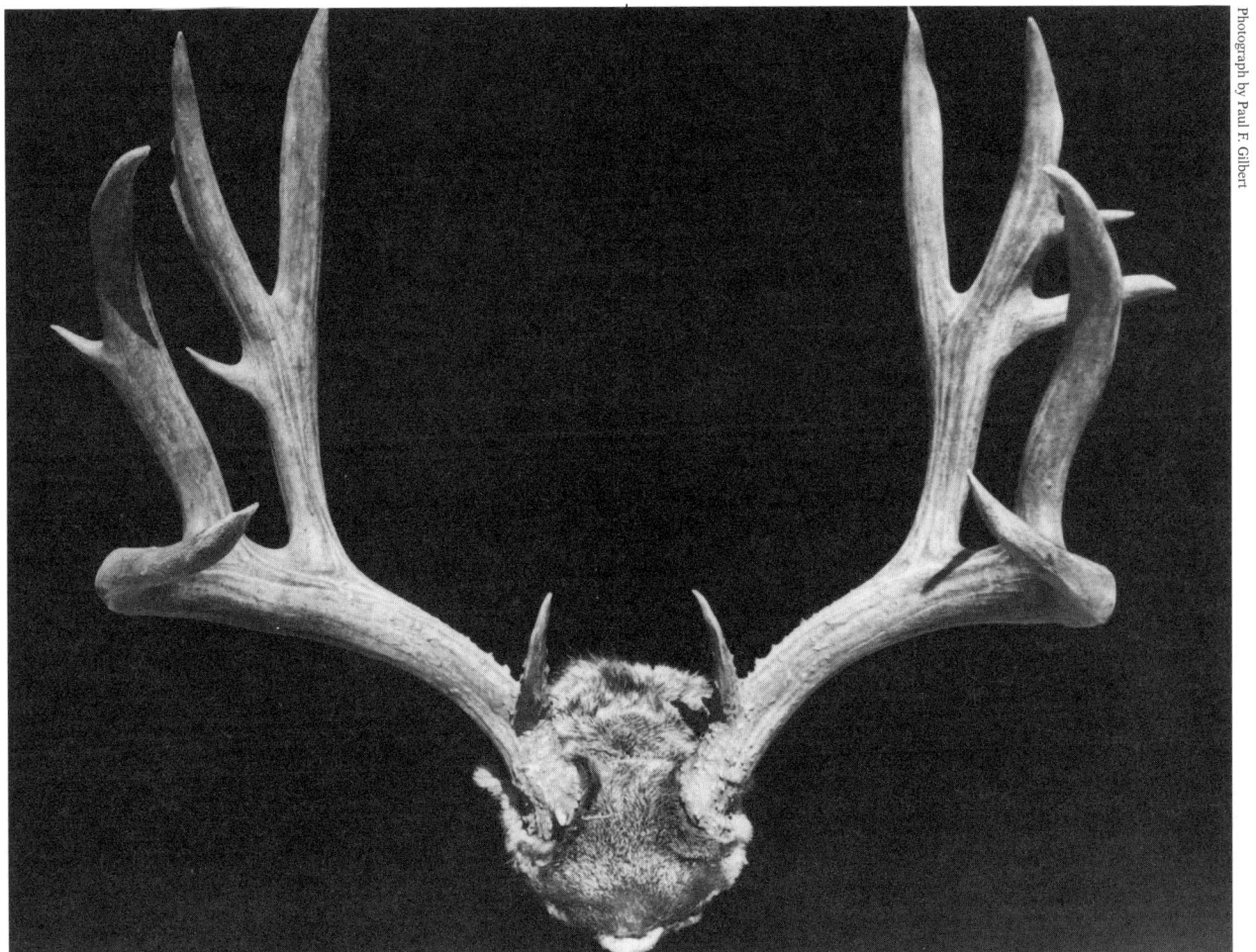

The Gore Range produced another B&C buck when Kremmling resident Lloyd Palmer hunted this outstanding 6x6 typical mule deer on October 25, 1959. Its greatest spread is 30-3/8 inches. Each main beam length measured more than 27 inches.

Lloyd Palmer and his brother, Erwin, hunted together during the 1959 regular hunting season near their homes in Kremmling. They hunted very remote areas away from the main stream of hunters and congestion.

It was late in the evening and both men were on their way back to their pickup when they stepped into the edge of a clearing in the Gore Range. At the upper end of the clearing they noticed a buck standing watching them. Lloyd identified it as a buck and whispered to Erwin that it would be a nice piece of meat to take home. Lloyd took aim with his Model 70 Winchester, .257 Roberts, and fired. The buck immediately dropped. It wasn't until the two men walked up to it that they realized what a massive buck Lloyd had just taken. They field dressed the buck, propped it open and returned the next day to pack it out with horses.

The buck was first listed in the 1964 edition of Boone and Crockett Club's all-time records book after official measurer Paul Gilbert scored and photographed it. Due to an increase in the minimum score for typical mule deer to 195 points in 1968, Lloyd's buck was dropped from the records book. It was reaccepted in 2000 when the minimum score for entry into the all-time records book was lowered to 190 points. Erwin also has a Boone and Crockett buck that was taken in 1961 and scored 192-5/8 points. Lloyd's son, Zane, also has a Boone and Crockett buck that measured 191-1/8 points.

Both Lloyd's and Erwin's bucks were accepted into the Boone and Crockett Club's 24th North American Big Game Awards Program that closed on December 31, 2000.

ROBERT D. DAVIDSON
Location: Las Animas County
Year Taken: 1995
Score: 190-7/8

Robert Davidson had hunted near Kim in South Central Colorado for four years prior to the 1995 season, but decided to stay home that year. He already had four outstanding trophies hanging on the wall, including one with a 32-inch spread, and figured he couldn't do any better.

Robert was home enjoying Thanksgiving with his wife, Christy, that year when he received an unexpected call from Rodney Ruebsahm who said he had to cancel his hunting trip to Kim at the last minute. Rodney wanted to know if Robert could substitute for him since it was Robert who had booked the hunt with T-7 Outfitters. Robert talked it over with Christy, cut his Thanksgiving short and headed for Kim. (He obviously has a very understanding wife.)

Robert drove to Kim with Steve Bonesio, another hunter who had booked the same hunt. They relived the excitement of their first hunt near Kim four years earlier and recalled the nice bucks they had taken on that trip.

The first three days of the hunt passed uneventfully for Robert. He spotted two very respectable bucks, which he tried to take, but both managed to get away. The first buck escaped when Robert missed it and shot a nearby fence post. Robert was preparing to take aim on a second very respectable buck when he knelt on a cactus. Needless to say the buck escaped during the subsequent commotion resulting from the pain in Robert's knee.

Texan Robert D. Davidson was near Kim in south central Colorado when he collected this 190-7/8-point typical muley.

On the fourth day, Robert was paired with guide Shane Goode. As they drove to a new hunting area, a tremendous buck accompanied by a doe jumped in front of their truck several minutes before legal shooting time. They hunted for the buck for four frustrating hours and returned to the camp house where Jamie Goode, Shane's mother, had prepared lunch for them.

Jamie informed them that the local bus driver had sighted the same massive buck at 7:30 a.m. standing at the edge of an open C.R.P. field. The buck casually meandered across a mile of open country, giving the local school children quite a show.

The men returned to the field where they glassed for five hours without sighting a single animal. During this time the weather turned on them. The temperature dropped and the wind picked up to about 30mph. Just as they were about to throw in the towel, Shane spotted the buck through his spotting scope about three-quarters of a mile away. With nightfall closing in on them, they quickly narrowed the distance to 200 yards. The buck looked like an elk on a small hill silhouetted against the red sky.

Robert centered the cross hairs on the walking deer. He squeezed the trigger on his 7mm Magnum and the buck collapsed. The men celebrated and were joined by Albert Goode, co-owner of T-7 Outfitters, and Steve Bonesio. After the required 60-day drying period, Robert had his buck officially scored. It made the Boone and Crockett Club's all-time records book, *Records of North American Big Game*, with a score of 190-7/8 points.

HAROLD WEIPPERT

Location: Douglas County
Years Taken: 1990
Score: 190-5/8

Location: Douglas County
Year Taken: 1994
Score: 186-2/8

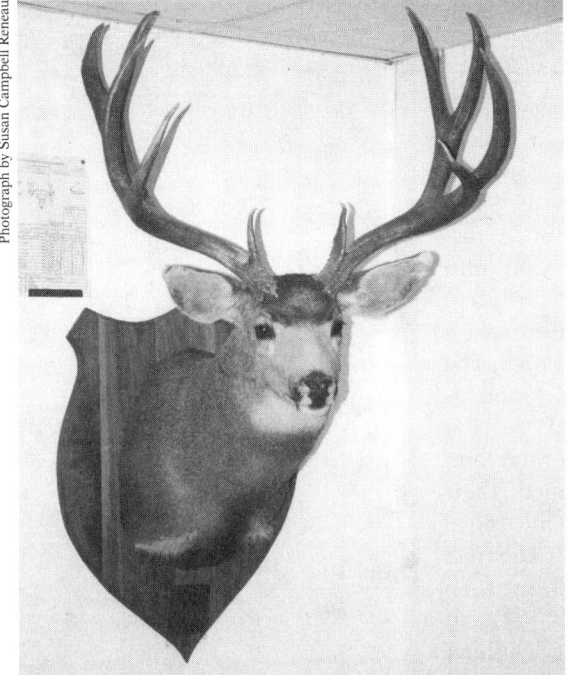

One of the most special aspects of Harold Weippert's mule deer hunts is his relationship with son Dan who has been his hunting companion and guide for years. Harold has taken many nice bucks over the years but the two that made Boone and Crockett Club stand out in his memory as special moments.

Ten minutes on opening day of 1990 was all it took for Harold to collect his first Boone and Crockett buck, thanks in large part to the sharp eyes of Dan who spotted five bucks at the start of the deer season. Harold wanted a big buck that year and told his son he wouldn't shoot unless it had a nice rack. They selected a favorite area in Douglas County and began walking down a draw into thicker and thicker brush. After passing up smaller bucks, Dan quietly called for Harold to stop and look at five bucks that had gone over the hill. Dan suggested they back up and crawl over the other hillside to sneak up on the herd. This accomplished, the men found themselves looking down on the five bucks that had not noticed the hunters at that moment.

"Dad, I know you're a pretty good shot but this has to be your best shot," Dan warned. One buck stood above the rest and was selected by Harold as the one to take. Harold raised his .243 Winchester at 250 yards and fired a single lung-heart shot that immediately dropped the buck. The sun has just come over the horizon when the hunt concluded.

"My son has such good eyes. He can see like a hawk," Harold said. Harold gave immediate credit to his son for his success.

A second Boone and Crockett Club buck taken by Harold in 1994 was again because of the sharp eyes of Dan. The men decided to hunt on a ranch near Franktown on the fifth day of hunting season. As the men walked through scrub oak over a hill into a valley, Dan saw a buck from 300 yards out that was walking away from them. Harold didn't want to shoot from that distance so he decided to follow the buck until it came to the next draw. When the men arrived at the next draw Harold noticed that the buck was oblivious to anything but a doe in the vicinity. This was late in the season and rut was in full force so the buck never noticed as the men positioned themselves for a clear shot. The buck was quartering away from Harold when he let loose with a single shot that stopped the buck in its tracks at about 250 yards. The buck stood there as though it was in a trance before it collapsed.

Harold collected his second B&C buck, thanks in large part to the guiding abilities of his son. Recently, Dan hasn't been able to guide for his father because of illness but both men have fond memories, especially of the two hunts that netted such outstanding trophies.

Harold included the write up for this book in his treasured hunting scrapbook and wrote in February 2001, "When I'm dead one day they will say Grandpa was a hunter." Yes, he is.

MARK W. STREISSGUTH
Location: Las Animas County
Year Taken: 1994
Score: 190-5/8

On October 1, 1994, Mark Streissguth and his guide, Pat Lancaster, were at the head of Cordova Canyon at sunrise hoping to locate a trophy buck before the deer bedded down for the morning. As luck would have it, the men eventually picked up two bucks in the optics a long ways down the canyon. One of the bucks appeared exceptionally large, but Mark needed a closer look to be sure.

The bucks were bedded down in the shade of the pinon and juniper trees along the rim of the canyon. The men took the road around the top end of Cordova Canyon and worked down out of sight behind the ridge separating Cordova from the next canyon. When they reached the area close to the bucks, they crawled to the top of the ridge for a better look. The smaller buck was visible while the larger buck was partially hidden behind a large juniper so they dropped back over the ridge and worked their way towards a mesa above the bucks.

This plan would have worked perfectly if it hadn't been for a third buck bedded down just above Mark's and Pat's route. This buck, with a wide rack and short forks, spooked and blew over the top of the butte and ran right between the two bedded bucks. The men continued their hopeless stalk to the edge of the mesa only to verify that all three deer were gone.

Pat and Mark returned to the same canyon the next day and sighted four bucks, including the two from the previous day, feeding in the same area as the day before. The big buck looked even better so Mark promised himself that if he got a clean shot, he would take it. The four bucks disappeared into a steep wash covered with oak brush. The men maneuvered to the ridge top and wormed their way into position. The oak brush was so thick Pat and Mark couldn't find the bucks from their new position.

It was time for "Plan B." Pat stalked around the ridge and out onto a mesa where he could glass the wash, hoping any deer he spooked would run by Mark. Mark waited for Pat to get into position. After glassing for 30 minutes, Pat motioned for Mark to join him.

Once Mark joined Pat, the pair belly crawled to the edge overlooking the wash where the deer had disappeared and glassed the area. The oak brush was thick and after 10 minutes Mark turned to Pat and whispered, "If he's in here I don't see why we can't spot him."

In the very next instant Pat said, "There he is," as calmly as if he were talking about the weather. The biggest buck Mark had ever seen on the hoof had just materialized at the bottom of the wash. Mark settled the cross hairs of his .300 Winchester Magnum behind the buck's right shoulder, eased off the safety and squeezed.

Time stood still as Mark checked the buck with his scope. Slaps on the back and congratulations erupted as the men realized they had a great trophy. That evening back at the ranch, they rough-scored the buck at 196 and change. The official B&C score is 190-5/8 points.

Mark Streissguth hunted at the head of Cordova Canyon in Las Animas County and collected with a single shot this outstanding typical mule deer that scored 190-5/8 points.

WILLIAM D. TATE
Location: Garfield County
Year Taken: 1978
Score: 190-4/8

Monty Long told William Tate that he had seen a buck in the Bookcliff Range in 1977 with antlers as wide as a refrigerator, but William dismissed the comment as an exaggeration. When he viewed his downed buck for the first time at the end of a hunt on the Long Ranch, William knew it was no exaggeration.

Bill Brewster, Doug Clark, Carlton Pittard and Lanny Tate were with William on his trophy, Bookcliff Range hunt in 1978, 23 miles north of Fruita. Monty Long's dad's ranch consisted of only a few hundred deeded acres, but it encompassed thousands of leased Bureau of Land Management acres. The terrain was covered with sagebrush flats and stands of quaking aspen and ponderosa pine.

William thought of Monty's comments about the large buck as he climbed the mountain overlooking their hunting camp long before daylight on the second day of the 1978 hunting season. Every coulee and pocket that day contained a small herd of deer with a few nice bucks.

Around 4:30 in the afternoon William was following Monty along a trail just below a ridge in thick ponderosa pine. The deer were bedded down and holding tight. The sky was blue. The day was unseasonably warm but cool in the shadows of the pines. Suddenly, an animal bolted down along the canyon wall, dislodging rocks and noisily snapping sticks as it ran. When the buck came into view in the thick brush it was running downhill from William's right to his left. Monty whispered those magical words, "take him." Without hesitation William swung his .300 Winchester Magnum through the deer's body and pulled the trigger just as he saw daylight between the cross hairs and the deer's chest. The buck disappeared and the forest fell silent. Monty simply said, "I think you will be pleased."

William Tate downed this massive buck in the Bookcliff Range using his .300 Winchester Magnum. His guide simply said, "I think you will be pleased."

The antlers were caught in a horizontal position about knee high in the brush. When William first saw the enormity and massiveness of the symmetrical rack he screamed to Monty, "He's huge!" Dragging the buck down the hill was the most physical part of the hunt. Darkness caught the men at the base of the mountain, so they field dressed the buck and returned to camp in the moonlight.

During the night a bear ate one of the hindquarters and covered the body with nearly a foot of dirt. The cape was not damaged. The men used all their strength to drape the remaining meat and cape over the saddle of the packhorse. They slowly walked the Dunn down the trail and calmed him with soft talk. The smell of bear on the carcass made the horse jittery.

That night in camp was one of the proudest evenings in William's life. There was talk of trophies, records books, and bucks with 30-inch spreads. There were both congratulations and a sense of envy in camp that night. There have been deer killed with larger racks, but hardly any more perfect. An artist molding a bronze sculpture could not make a more symmetrical set of antlers. It is the epitome of the B&C scoring system.

The outstanding rack was officially measured in 1995. William believes that the dream of taking such a trophy is what motivates hunters to go hunting again and again.

JAY GATES
Location: Private Ranch Outside Trinidad
Year Taken: 1996
Score: 190

Jay Gates with his outstanding typical mule deer buck scoring 190 points.

For the past two years Jay Gates had looked forward to hunting mule deer in Colorado prior to his hunt in 1996. These are early September hunts when bucks are in the velvet. These hunts also happen to take place on private ground in the southcentral part of the state. This is Spanish land-grant country with history predating Anglo settlement. It is also a land of vast contrasts, ranging from 6,000 to 10,000 feet above sea level and covered with thick scrub oak, pinon, juniper, ponderosa pine, spruce and fir.

As is the tradition, Jay's two good hunting buddies, George Cook and Steve Fennell, joined him in this hunt. They settled into camp the night before opening day, and Jay's guide, Chris, and Jay discussed plans for opening morning. Chris was interested in Jay's expectations and offered his suggestions. Jay wanted to get his feet wet by slowly driving ranch roads so he could regain his bearings and reestablish the lay of the land in his mind. They drove out of camp before first light, stopping intermittently to glass. West of camp, in a large grass field where they typically sight in their rifles, the men sighted a nice 25-inch, 5x5 buck. The two men stopped quite a few times during the early hours, glassing likely areas and enjoying the landscape. It was about 8 a.m. when they stopped and walked out to one of their favorite vantage points. Jay immediately picked up a pair of bucks a few hundred yards from where they sat and Chris spotted another buck to the left of the two Jay was watching. Jay guessed one of the two bucks he saw taped 28 inches wide and scored 185 to 190 points. Chris didn't think so, and was pretty sure the buck was much smaller. In any case it was a mute point, as Jay wasn't in the mood to finish his hunt on opening morning.

Chris and Jay hunted fairly hard the next few days during the mornings and late afternoons but didn't see any buck bigger than the first one they saw on opening morning. After returning to camp to discuss future hunting plans and compare notes with other hunters in the party, Chris and Jay resolved they had to go back for the first buck.

Chris and Jay parked in the time-honored spot and walked out to their favorite point. Jay was in the process of shedding his pack and taking a seat when Chris hollered that he was looking at a good buck. Jay unsheathed his spotting scope and took a hopeful glance at the buck. There was no doubt with that first glance that this was the same buck from the first morning.

A stalk was planned and executed perfectly. There was a tricky shot, but it worked. After the buck went down, Chris remained in the spot where Jay had taken the shot while Jay hustled over to the buck. It took perhaps 20 minutes to arrive beside the buck, fighting steep grades, tripping through oak tangle and fighting altitude. And then the buck was just ahead, about 30 feet away. Jay knew he had made a mistake scoring the buck. The buck was only 28 inches wide. He was indeed a 5x6, but it scored well over 200 points. It was a nice surprise, to say the least.

The official measurement after deductions totaled 190. The buck has not been entered in the Boone and Crockett Club so remains unranked.

A sampling of bucks Jay has harvested on a private ranch near Trinidad, Colorado, over the years. Left to right, Jay's 1995 buck with a gross score of approximately 191; the 1997 buck with a gross score of 193; and his 1998 buck with a gross score of approximately 187.

MARK S. PETRUCCI
Location: Delta County
Year Taken: 1989
Score: 189-3/8

"I can't hunt without these," Mark Petrucci said as he showed a fancy silver and turquoise wristband and matching ring to his cabin mates Ed Dentry, Charlie Russell and Aaron Pass near Paonia as they waited for the 1989 mule deer season to begin. Mark thought the Indian who had made the ring had cursed it. However, he took a 4x4 whitetail buck with it the previous year. As a result he figured it was good luck for him.

Aaron, a journalist, scowled at first and said that finding a good hunting location was more important for success. He later confided that he believes that if blood from another hunter's deer gets on him, his season will be wasted.

As the deer and elk rifle season wore on, Mark and his partners realized they needed some really strong "medicine" to improve their luck. "Hundreds" of does and fawns were everywhere, but no bucks. Elk lolled about at higher elevations just beyond their reach.

They searched for the cause of their misfortune and found road kill porcupine hair adorning two hunting hats in camp. After removing his offending amulet, Charlie bagged a handsome 3x2 muley. "You can't have road kill parts on your hat," Charlie postulated.

Mark offered another charm. If two bullet holes touch on the target when you sight in your rifle, you should never shoot the third, he said. That bullet is surely meant for a deer or elk. But, he missed a small buck Saturday, no thanks to a bullet that bounced through twigs like a steel ball in a pinball machine. Even religion had failed him, sort of.

Mark Petrucci prayed to see a big mule deer, and he did. His buck scores 189-3/8 points.

"I prayed to see a buck mule deer, and I saw one, all right," Mark told his hunting buddies. "But I forgot to say I wanted to kill it."

As snow fell on Sunday night, Mark sat in the cabin reviewing his "medicine" checklist. His wife, Mary, wished him good luck. Mark knew that if she got mad at him and didn't wish him good luck before he hunted, he might as well stay home.

On Monday morning Mark trudged through new snow to his blind in a slash pile. In the blind he saw fresh deer tracks so big he mistook them for elk. Mark tracked the deer in the snow and realized it was a deer when he was eyeball to eyeball with it. His 5x5 mule deer buck field dressed at 250 pounds and had an antler spread of 31 inches. It scored 189-3/8 points.

Mark thanks Diana, goddess of the hunt, or whoever arranges such things.

Details of this hunt were provided by Ed Dentry, outdoor editor of Denver's *Rocky Mountain News* and hunting partner of Mark Petrucci. Ed's column appeared in the Sunday sports section of the newspaper on October 22, 1989.

JAMES M. MALONIS
Location: Routt County
Year Taken: 1997
Score: 189-2/8

Rich Lombardi grabbed for Jim and pointed in the direction of the bull elk and told Jim to look below it. When Jim did, he spotted the largest buck he had ever encountered in the woods. Elk or massive mule deer—that was the decision he had to make. To understand this moment, a review of the hunt is in order.

On the morning of November 2, 1997, Jim hiked in about two miles to a piece of Bureau of Land Management (BLM) land he had hunted since 1970. He knew this area well. When he reached the top of the mountain, Jim heard a bull elk bugling. He then descended the mountain and picked an area where he could sit and scan the hill where the sounds were coming from. It wasn't long until he spotted elk. As they bedded down along the hillside, Jim returned to camp to see if anyone wanted to return with him for an afternoon hunt.

Rich Lombardi, who had made a successful stalk with Jim on two bull elk they collected on a previous hunt, eagerly volunteered to join him. As they crested the top of the hill they observed the elk feeding along the hillside. They worked their way down the mountain, hiding behind sage brush as they tried to get close enough to the bull for a clear shot.

Jim and Rich couldn't keep track of the big bull but spotted a satellite bull close to the bottom. As they got within shooting range, Rich grabbed Jim and said, "Look below the bull." There, below the bull in the draw, were two mule deer fighting over a young doe. The one deer was the biggest buck the two men had ever seen. They continued down the mountain hiding behind sage brush as they went. When they

To take an elk or a giant mule deer. That was the decision Jim Malonis had to make on a November day in 1997. The buck Jim decided to shoot scores 189-2/8 points – a true records-book buck.

reached a point where they could go no farther, Rich went back to look for a pair of glasses that he had dropped. Jim waited until Rich returned.

The huge buck looked up the hill and spotted the satellite bull walking down toward the other deer. He ran toward the bull with antlers down. As the buck did this the two other deer disappeared. Unable to find his glasses, Rich finally returned to their vantage point. Jim asked Rich if he was ready to shoot, but Rich said he couldn't because his breath had fogged up his scope. Hearing that, Jim picked an opening in the aspens through which the buck would pass. When it did moments later he fired one shot from his .300 Winchester Magnum. The deer collapsed and Jim collected his Boone and Crockett buck. A game biologist later estimated the buck's age at 9-1/2 years old.

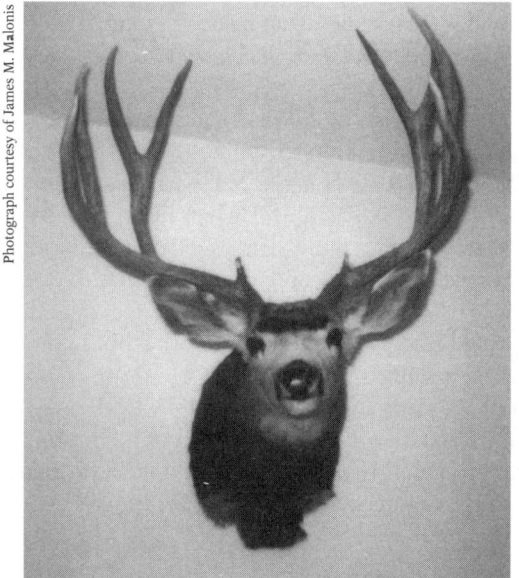

DANNY C. McNABB
Location: Archuleta County
Year Taken: 1996
Score: 189

On the last day of a five-day deer season, Danny McNabb realized almost every other hunter's dream by harvesting a mule deer that made "The Book." The date was October 16, 1996, and the area was near Pagosa Springs in Archuleta County.

At around 10 a.m. on the last morning of the hunt, Danny ousted his buck off its bed. All Danny saw was the left side of his antler frame and no shot was possible at the time so he cautiously made his way toward the buck's escape route. Danny thought he might catch the buck looking back, but it didn't. Danny was several miles from the location that his hunting buddy Ronnie Guess and he were to regroup, so Danny headed back, leaving the buck time to cool down from that first meeting.

Danny told Ronnie he saw a nice buck but couldn't get a shot but that he wanted to be back in the area by 2 p.m. After eating lunch, the two men headed back to the area where Danny saw the buck. The weather was changing by this time from rain, sleet, lightning and thunder, which isn't abnormal for this time of year in the Rockies. Several times Danny sprawled out on the ground away from any tall pines to escape the lightning. When the lightning moved on to the southeast, Danny resumed his trek in search of the mule deer.

Moving over the mountain with the wind to his face, Danny kept searching the sagebrush for a glimpse of the muley, ever ready for the buck to bust out as it had that morning. Danny inched along using his binoculars trying to uncover any movement, or views of an antler or body. The season was coming to an end quicker than Danny had wanted and his hopes for a shot of a lifetime were dimming fast. Slowly making his way back to his pickup point, Danny stood on a small draw that fed back to where he had jumped the buck. He noticed the sun slowly creeping over the western mountains, so he knew the last remaining minutes were upon them. At that moment, out popped the buck trotting up the hillside as though it was going back to its bedding area. Never more ready, Danny slipped off the safety of his .300 Weatherby magnum and lined up the cross hairs on its right shoulder. Danny squeezed off the round and sent the 180-grain Barnes-X on its way. The first shot hit but for insurance Danny fired a second time, which also connected. Danny walked 150 yards to the buck and knew this was the buck he saw that morning.

Danny's taxidermist suggested he get the buck officially scored and it made "The Book" with the greatest spread being 31-7/8 inches and a final net score of 189. The buck was recognized in the Boone and Crockett Club's 23rd North American Big Game Awards Program.

JAMES D. FOX
Location: Weld County
Year Taken: 1998
Score: 188-5/8

While scouting for a nice whitetail buck in 1998, Jim Fox located the mule deer of his dreams. When he did he abandoned his search for a nice whitetail and concentrated on the muley of a lifetime.

Being almost 48 years old, Jim has been after huge bucks and bulls for approximately 25 years. He credits all he knows about hunting to his father, Max, who took him hunting for years. Jim says his father has seen and done more deer hunting than most humans will ever experience.

In 1998 Jim drew a permit to hunt a unit east of Kersey near the Platte River in Weld County. Both whitetails and mule deer inhabit the area. Initially he hoped to locate a nice white-tailed buck. However, after he scouted 30 to 45 days before the season he realized the only bucks that excited him were the big muleys he saw. Once he located the buck he eventually took, he watched it twice a day, every day, before and after work. He familiarized himself with the buck's morning schedule and its evening schedule.

Jim was convinced that when opening day of the season arrived, he would quickly locate his buck and fill his tag. However, a week before opening day another buck whipped Jim's buck and chased it onto some adjacent private property that Jim didn't have permission to hunt. Jim continued scouting but didn't see his buck for four to five days. He was heartsick.

By early morning Jim Fox of Kersey downed this fantastic mule deer with a single shot in 1998.

Two days before opening day the big buck showed up again and Jim's hopes soared. On opening day, Jim found other bucks and does but not "his" buck. He located an area where deer fed at night and took up a stand nearby the next morning, but again he didn't see his buck. Because of work he wasn't able to hunt that evening.

On the third day of the season Jim watched from his stand as another buck moved into his area. It wasn't the buck he was looking for, but it was a respectable buck and he debated taking it. He hadn't seen his buck for awhile and was starting to think it had completely moved out of the area. Jim was ready to take this buck when a pair of does suddenly showed up. A short time later his buck came through "checking for things that big bucks check for." Everything was just as it was supposed to be. After all the watching and waiting things were quickly coming together.

Jim dropped it at 150 to 170 yards with his .270. It was so large that when it hit the ground it looked like its head was still up. When Jim got to his buck, it didn't suffer any ground shrinkage. It was everything that Jim knew it was when it was still alive. The buck's rack has a greatest spread measurement of 30-1/8 inches and scored 188-5/8 points.

PICK UP
Location: Purgatoire River
Year Taken: Early 1990s
Score: 188-5/8
Owner: Carl J. Wohlfert

While on a spring turkey hunt along the Purgatoire River in the Pinon Canyon area of Colorado, Carl found himself in thick brush along the river bottom with no visible way out.

As Carl picked his way through the brush to higher ground he saw something on the ground ahead of him. At first glance Carl thought it was the remains of a dead cow but upon further examination he saw complete skeletal remains of a very large mule deer buck. Carl checked for any broken bones or bullet wounds but found none so he guessed it died of old age or from a harsh winter. He brought the rack home where it remained in his trophy room for 10 years. As a Christmas present in 1999, Carl's wife gave him a copy of the Boone and Crockett Club's all-time records book, *Records of North American Big Game*, and as he reviewed the records of mule deer he compared his rack to the ones featured in the book. He called his friend Mike and together they rough-scored the rack only to discover it reached a gross score of about 200 points.

Carl called the Boone and Crockett Club for the name of an official measurer in his area and was given the name of Bob Davies of the CDOW who recorded the buck's final score at 188-5/8 points. The buck was accepted into the Boone and Crockett Club's 24th North American Big Game Awards Program.

Carl Wohlfert holds the antlers of his B&C buck he found in the Pinon Canyon area of Colorado in the early 1990s

JEFFREY B. BUNKE

Location: Eagle County
Year Taken: 1997
Score: 188-3/8

Location: Eagle County
Year Taken: 1995
Score: 180-2/8

Not many people in the world ever see, let alone take, a B&C trophy. In Jeff Bunke's case, however, he collected a B&C muley in 1995 and repeated his good fortune in 1997.

Jeff began researching for his first buck in 1984 while on a fly-fishing vacation with his family near Eagle along the Roaring Fork and Frying Pan Rivers. He kept seeing monster muleys so he spent time analyzing data in B&C records books. He first hunted in Eagle County in 1985 with his friend Gordon Ingram. In 1995 the pair were drawn to hunt an area they came to know well on an east-southeast exposure of sage and oak with deep drainages interspersed with aspen and black timber. The slope was four to five square miles with seven major ridges. His favorite hunting spot is near the center of this area, and he calls it, "The Big Plateau."

Very early the first morning Jeff pulled his truck off the trail in the Colorado darkness, and he and Gordon headed down the mountain by flashlight. Jeff arrived at his predetermined hunting spot before sunup as he had planned, and George made it to "The Big Plateau." George collected his buck first. After the customary congratulations, Jeff and George loaded up the meat and headed back to the truck. Jeff took a different route figuring he would hunt his way back, drop off the meat, and get in a late afternoon hunt.

Twenty minutes after he left George, Jeff caught a glimpse of a huge buck about 250 yards above him. Before he could shed his heavy backpack and take aim, the buck disappeared. Jeff traveled as fast as a Minnesota flatlander could go up the mountain with a pack load of his buddy's venison. When he spotted his buck again, it was about 300 yards away. When the buck turned broadside Jeff locked the cross hairs of his 12X Leupold scope on its shoulder and squeezed the trigger. When his rifle cracked, the great buck jumped ahead 10 yards, stopped broadside, and looked down in Jeff's direction. Jeff fired again and the buck disappeared. Jeff spent the next 10 minutes glassing with his scope to see if the buck would reappear. It didn't, and he found it after a brief search. Official Measurer Dave Boland scored the rack, and it made "The Book."

As for Jeff's 1997 B&C buck, George and he returned to Eagle County to hunt their favorite tract of BLM land. Opening day dawned with high winds and heavy snow. The snow had piled up, making spotting easy but walking difficult. Late in the afternoon Jeff spotted a heavy beamed 5x5 typical buck but it was too far down the mountain to try a stalk that day.

As he approached one of his favorite spotting sites the next morning, the same buck burst out of the brush 50 yards from him. The buck bolted and Jeff centered the cross hairs of his 12X scope in front of its left rear quarter and pulled the trigger. The buck dropped in its tracks. Jeff took his second buck less than a mile from where he shot his first B&C buck in 1995. Jeff had collected his second B&C buck on back-to-back hunts. It scores 188-3/8 B&C points.

Jeffrey Bunke took this B&C typical mule deer buck in 1997 with a score of 188-3/8 points.

Jeffrey Bunke took this B&C typical mule deer buck in 1995 with a score of 180-2/8 points.

Jeffrey Bunke grins ear to ear moments after collecting his first of two Boone and Crockett trophies.

ROY GUINN
Location: San Miguel County
Year Taken: 1965
Score: 188

Roy Guinn loved to hunt in Colorado so much that he and his son, Jack, made it an annual event. The day Roy harvested his records-book muley with his .30-06 Remington, he and a friend, Nate Rogers, were hunting along Dave Woods Road above the San Miguel River on the Uncompahgre Plateau. It was October 1965.

Jack was hunting in another area that day, and not with his father when Roy connected with his B&C buck. Thus, the precise details of the hunt and final stalk are not available as Roy passed away in 1993 at the age of 86 after a long battle with leukemia.

Elizabeth Guinn Wilson, granddaughter to Roy, remembers that her grandfather never had the rack scored, and that he always hung it on either the back porch or in the garage of his home in Fayetteville, Arkansas. She grew up with this deer staring at her whenever she was at Roy's house, and she even nicknamed it Henry. When her grandfather passed away, her father gave the trophy to Elizabeth and her husband, Doug Wilson. Her father knew the trophy meant a lot to both of them.

Doug always admired the trophy and had it officially scored by a B&C scorer in Springfield, Missouri, shortly after Roy's death. It scored a whopping 188 points. Doug entered it in the Boone and Crockett Club's 22nd North American Big Game Awards Program, and it was officially accepted on August 23, 1993.

Missouri hunter Roy Guinn used his .30-06 Remington to down this outstanding Colorado typical mule deer buck in 1965.

Unfortunately, Elizabeth's grandfather never knew he had taken a B&C qualifier. His trophy is now proudly displayed in Elizabeth's and Doug's house in Carthage, Missouri, where it reminds her of her childhood, her grandfather and the love that will never be forgotten.

Two nice bucks, one B&C and one not. The buck on the right was taken by Roy Guinn in 1965 with a B&C score of 188.

DAVID L. BIRDSALL
Location: Kit Carson County
Year Taken: 1995
Score: 188

Photograph by Susan Campbell Reneau

smaller 4x4 buck arose to investigate the approaching hunters as it bumped the larger 5x5 buck. When the 5x5 stood its grace and majesty left a lasting impression on David as he began to kneel and prepare for a single shot. As the buck turned to look from side to side with both ears pulled back, David's 430-grain maxi ball hit its neck, dropping the monster in its tracks.

David approached his downed buck with caution and reloaded his .54 caliber Thompson Center Hawkin just in case the buck jumped up. "Grasping the massive antlers, I realized my dream of harvesting a records book deer had come true. I was both thrilled and saddened beyond words to take such a spectacular animal," David explained.

Don estimated the antlers would score 190 points, only two points short of the final score after the 60-day drying period. As a taxidermist, David knew from the moment he downed the buck he wanted it mounted in a full-shoulder position. The mount reflects the memories of a fantastic hunt.

David's classic typical mule deer buck ranks as the 11th largest typical muley ever taken by a muzzleloader as ranked in the National Muzzle Loading Rifle Association's book, *Longhunter Muzzleloading Big Game Record Book, 3rd Edition*, published in 2000. The buck was accepted into the Boone and Crockett Club's 23rd North American Big Game Awards Program.

For David Birdsall, mule deer are one of God's most beautiful and majestic creatures. Hunting, filming, drawing, sculpting and doing taxidermy on mule deer are his greatest thrills in life, so it was no surprise that he jumped at the chance to hunt mule deer during muzzleloading season when he and his brother, Don, were drawn for the 1995 season.

On opening day David and Don glassed a small herd of deer in a large open basin in Kit Carson County. The men made a large circle to position the sun at their backs and the wind in their faces. They slowly began using the natural landscape cuts and vegetation to conceal them in attempts to approach the deer. Don spotted two respectable bucks at a distance of 165 yards bedded down in the shade and lying side by side, looking in opposite directions for any danger. The

WILLIAM E. CONDON
Location: Logan County
Year Taken: 1953
Score: 187-5/8

A friendly bet on the weight of the biggest buck made Bill Condon a winner in 1953, and he's never hunted a bigger one.

The story begins and ends on Oct. 24, 1953, when Bill set out on his ranch between Proctor and Crook to hunt for mule deer along the South Platte River. He'd been eyeing two big bucks in the brush on the opening day of the season when he saw a massive rack of antlers in the late afternoon. The buck bolted so Bill fired his .30-06 and the buck continued running, or so Bill thought. Turns out the first buck was standing side by side with the second buck and when Bill fired he dropped the first buck immediately. The second buck was the one that ran forward, and luckily Bill missed him when he fired the second shot.

When Bill reached the buck in the brush he immediately noticed its body size. The estimated hogged-dressed weight was 260 pounds, which beat Marv Gardner's buck weight by four pounds. Bill won the bet for biggest buck on the opening day of the deer season.

Bill's buck was recognized in the Boone and Crockett Club's 23rd North American Big Game Awards Program.

Bill Condon stands beside his barbed wire collection that was mounted against part of the tanned hide from his B&C buck.

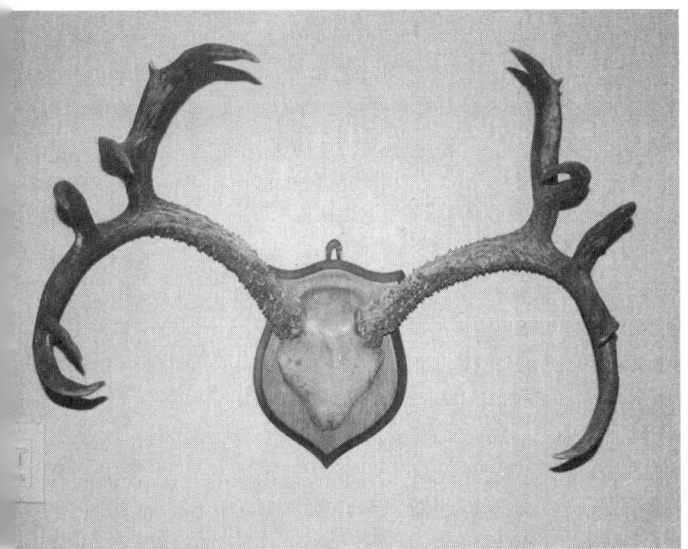

MARTEN A. PINNECOOSE
Year Taken: 1994
Score: 187-4/8

Marten Pinnecoose developed a keen interest in hunting while accompanying his dad and brothers on hunting trips long before he was old enough to shoot a rifle. He looked forward to the time he could hunt himself. However, before he was old enough to hunt, his family moved away from Colorado, and he was not able to move back for 20 years. Anytime he heard friends talk about their hunting experiences, looked at their hunting photographs or read hunting stories, he yearned to get back to Colorado to do some serious hunting.

As he got older, Marten first became proficient with the bow and arrow and took many "Pope and Young" qualifying prairie dogs and rabbits, but no big-game animals such as deer and elk. Marten later learned to handle a rifle while gaining considerable confidence in his hunting abilities. So far as Marten is concerned, it is not whether he hunts with a bow or a firearm, it's the hunt itself that he enjoys.

The day Marten took his B&C trophy started out like any other day. He got up and went to work. His body was at the work place, but his mind was elsewhere. All day long he anticipated the clock striking quitting time so he could go deer hunting.

As soon as Marten got off work the evening he took his B&C trophy, he changed into his hunting clothes, and he, his wife and children piled into their hunting rig. They only had an hour of daylight left, so they had to move fast. The first spot they checked out was a sagebrush flat in a river bottom where bucks were known to hang out. The area was close, and Marten figured it would be his best chance for a buck. It was an area where Marten's cousins had recently missed a 30-inch class buck. But they didn't see anything that evening.

Marten and his family then walked across the valley and headed into a stand of pinon and juniper trees. His wife was the first one who noticed the huge buck. She alerted everyone when she exclaimed, "Oh, my gosh!" Marten looked in her direction and exclaimed, "Oh, man!" A tall, wide 5x6 buck had just stepped out of the trees 60 yards away.

Marten ran to the edge of the trees and aimed the cross hairs low, behind the buck's elbow. He took a deep breath and squeezed the trigger. The buck bolted so Marten thought he had missed and prepared for another shot. However, after traveling only 20 yards, the buck reared up backwards and drove his antlers into the ground. He had made a heart shot.

Marten couldn't believe his good fortune. He wanted a "nice" buck, but the buck he had drawn was far superior to anything he anticipated. He was especially grateful that his wife and children were there with him to share in all the excitement.

Marten Pinnecoose (right) and his father, Guy, pause to enjoy Marten's B&C buck.

Marten Pinnecoose in the field moments after downing his typical mule deer.

TIMOTHY J. MOLITOR
Location: Eagle County
Year Taken: 1999
Score: 187-2/8 Points

Since the weather was warmer than a mid-October hunt should be but perfect for a fall hike in the mountains of the Holy Cross Wilderness, Tim Molitor and his hunting buddies knew the weather would be the challenge. The men set up tents and prepared their hunting camp with great anticipation for the eight- to nine-day hunt.

The first three days were slow hunting and on the fourth day a much-needed light snowfall began as the sun set. On Day Five hopes were rekindled by the men as they prepared for a long day of scouting and hiking. This was the last day to hunt deer, so Tim decided to return to a spot where he had taken nice bucks during previous seasons. Tim knew that deer were often found 600 to 1,000 feet below their camp with elk found lower in the canyons. The terrain includes steep slopes with ridges with strips of dark timber and aspen running through the area. As Tim entered the woods, he still-hunted by taking a few steps and glassing below as he worked into the breeze that ran out of the canyon. It seemed to take hours as he moved only a few hundred yards. The snow had disappeared and it was extremely dry. Tim heard deer steps as he crept through the woods but couldn't tell if the deer was a buck. Tim moved a quarter of a mile farther and spotted two does as they ran away upon hearing him. As Tim moved into a patch of dark timber, he came into an opening when he heard one of his friends shooting. Tim enjoyed a little competition with friends, so he became a little antsy as the day progressed and he couldn't find a decent shot.

Tim backtracked to the edge of the dark timber where to found a small covey of trees that provided a place to sit. He created a comfortable seat by clearing the sticks and leaves, enjoyed a snack and almost fell asleep. Thirty minutes later Tim almost left when something told him to stay and from the corner of his eyes he saw two tines appear from the timber. Tim quickly stood up and clicked off his safety on his .308 rifle. All Tim could see was the biggest set of antlers he had ever seen on a buck. Two does were to the right and two other bucks were above. The big buck had moved behind some trees and low bushes, so Tim moved toward another tree as he brought the rifle toward him in preparation for a shot. As he moved, Tim caught a branch and heard a "click." Tim immediately thought all was lost and fully expected the does to bolt, alerting the bucks to danger. Amazingly, none of the deer moved even though Tim was ready to shoot if the big buck stepped from behind the brush. The buck cautiously stuck its head out in front of a tree to look at Tim, giving Tim a 50- to 75-yard broadside shot through the trees. Tim didn't like the shot so he waited as he watched the does come closer. Through his scope, Tim lined up the cross hairs and fired at the buck just below its ears. The buck crumpled in its spot as the rest of the herd ran away and gave a fleeting glance to the big buck, thinking it might follow, but it never moved after Tim shot.

On the last day of the deer season, Tim thought he certainly collected a dandy. Tim's buck was accepted into the Boone and Crockett Club's 24th North American Big Game Awards Program.

A curvaceous mule deer rack graces the trophy Tim Molitor took in 1999 on a gorgeous fall day.

WILLIE JONES
Location: Routt County
Year Taken: 1976
Score: 186-6/8

Willie Jones moved to Colorado in 1969 to cut Christmas trees with his uncle, Bill Strickland, near Tonopas. During most of the year he lived with his uncle and his aunt, Patty. From September to November, however, he and his uncle lived in a tent on King Mountain while they cut Christmas trees. Even though he couldn't hunt during most of the season, Willie learned everything there was to know about the big game on King Mountain, especially their movement patterns.

Each year, around mid-October, hunters arrived at King Mountain from far away states such as Kansas, Texas and Missouri. They asked Willie about the game on the mountain, and he provided them valuable information that helped them fill their tags.

In 1976, after the hunters had gone home and the trees were cut, Willie took the opportunity to go hunting. Even then he didn't have much time to hunt because a severe winter storm was moving towards Yampa Valley and King Mountain. Strong winds indicated the weather front was on the way.

Willie Jones moved to Colorado in 1969 to cut Christmas trees and located a B&C buck a few years later on King Mountain.

The buck on the right has never been officially measured, but the one on the left is the B&C typical mule deer that scores 186-6/8 points.

Willie was hunting on the sunny side of King Mountain when he spotted two muley does through the aspens about 150 yards away. He dropped to his knees and waited. Suddenly, a 5x5 buck stepped into view. It didn't look very big, but Willie wanted to fill his tag before the storm hit. He touched off a round from his open-sighted .30-30 and hit the buck. A second shot was necessary.

After waiting 15 to 20 minutes, Willie worked his way towards the spot where he had last seen the buck and promptly found it, dead. He couldn't believe the buck's size. Not only was the buck so big that he couldn't drag it by himself, but the antlers were also exceptional. As he was the only one on the mountain, he had to go down the mountain to get help. Willie's buck weighed in at 300 pounds, twice Willie's weight, and sported a rack with a 31-inch outside spread.

While sitting alone in front of the campfire that night, Willie relived the events of the day over and over. He couldn't believe the size of the deer he had killed. The next day he broke camp and headed home.

Eleven years later, Willie saw an ad for the first edition of Colorado's Biggest Bucks and Bulls in a magazine. He ordered a copy and saw, for the first time, a Boone and Crockett Club score chart that was reproduced with the Club's permission. He contacted an official measurer and entered it in the Club's records books at a final score of 186-6/8 points.

L. JACK LYON
Location: Mesa County
Year Taken: 1952
Score: 186-6/8

Nearly 50 years ago, when Jack Lyon was a graduate student at Colorado State University, he drove halfway across Colorado with a couple of friends to hunt deer near DeBeque in Mesa County. Jack points out that there is no hunting story associated with taking this trophy other than being in the right place at the right time and spending an incredible amount of human energy dragging a rather monster deer down a very long ridge to the car.

The interesting part of the story began to develop after Jack returned to Fort Collins. An official measurer at the Denver Museum of Natural History scored Jack's trophy at 193-1/8 points. At that score it was ranked as the 9th largest typical mule deer ever taken in North America up to that time. Jack was then invited to send his antlers to the American Museum of Natural History in New York in 1953 for the 6th B&C Competition.

As it turned out, 1953 was a banner year for typical mule deer. The number of big muleys submitted to the 6th Competition Judges Panel that year was phenomenal. As best as Jack can remember, there were at least five trophies larger than the previous World's Record and an additional nine trophies larger than the one he submitted. The Judges Panel's final score for Jack's trophy was 186-6/8, and the Judges awarded it an Honorable Mention in the typical mule deer category.

Honorable Mention
6th B&C Competition

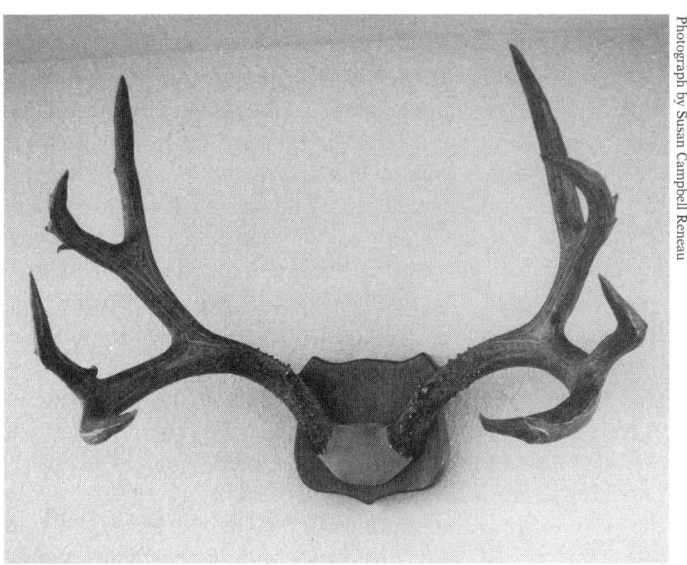

Jack Lyon stands beside his B&C typical muley he took in 1952 while attending graduate school at Colorado State University.

Since then, Jack's trophy has had quite an interesting history. When the 1958 all-time records book was published, Jack's mule deer had dropped to 63rd largest in the world at the time. Six years later, in 1964, the all-time ranking dropped to 348th with a four-way tie. Finally, it was not listed in the 1971 edition because the minimum score was raised in the interim to 195 points. The minimum score for the Awards records books was lowered in the 1990s to 180 points so Jack resubmitted his trophy. It was accepted once again into Boone and Crockett Club's 24th North American Big Game Awards Program in 1999, nearly 50 years after Jack took it.

As a sidebar story on this trophy, Jack has a limited edition print rendered by D. Noel Smith of Thol Arts, Inc. in Canon City, Colorado. It is a mule deer buck standing majestically on a rocky outcrop, and it is clearly his deer, right down to the particular small fork terminating the left main beam and a shortened first point on the left side. Thol Arts has gone out of business, and Jack has never been able to locate the artist. Jack's guess is that the painting, titled "First Snow," was done at least 20 years after his hunt, using a model several generations removed from Jack's granddaddy buck.

This beautiful typical mule deer buck proudly hangs in Jack Lyon's living room today next to the print by D. Noel Smith.

GERALD D. RICE
Location: Larimer County
Year Taken: 1962
Score: 186-6/8

Finding enough meat to feed a wife and four children was motivation enough for Gerald Rice who was a college student at Colorado State University in Fort Collins. The year was 1964 when he went alone to a new hunting area north of Horsetooth Mountain.

Gerald had never been in this area of Colorado so it was pure luck when he happened upon a buck that not only fed his family but also was a buck for the records books. Budgets were tight for this Korean War veteran who used the GI Bill to finish his college education, and the buck to carry them through the winter. Gerald remembered he drove to the hunting area and hiked down a creek bed for about a half mile when he startled the buck he shot with his .300 Savage. The buck had an estimated weight of 300 pounds, so dragging the buck down the creek bed was quite a chore.

No effort to measure the buck was made until a customer at the store where Gerald works challenged him in 1999 when debating about the size of a buck he took, saying he probably had a bigger buck then Gerald's. Gerald brought his rack into the store to show the customer and all debate ended. Within a short time period after the debate with the customer, Gerald had the antlers measured, and they made the Boone and Crockett Club, without a doubt.

Gerald Rice holds his 1964 mule deer antlers that easily made the Boone and Crockett Club records book 36 years after he took the buck.

For a man only looking for meat to feed his family, Gerald Rice received a bonus.

Gerald's buck was accepted into the Boone and Crockett Club's 24th North American Big Game Awards Program in February 2000, 36 years after he downed his 1964 muley.

NEIL C. NOSTRAND
Location: Gunnison County
Year Taken: 1986
Score: 186

Neil Nostrand and his friends, Dan Survillas and Bill Tubbs, have hunted together with near religious dedication for more than 30 years, and 1996 was no exception. Neil acquired a ranch on Colorado's Western Slope near Paonia in 1986 so this was the spot the three amigos gathered each big-game season to hunt on or near his ranch. The men selected the third combined deer/elk rifle season to improve their odds for snow and to facilitate tracking and animal visibility. They were chagrined, however, to see the Saturday opener dawn clear with little hope for cold weather. Sunday and Monday also lacked the desired weather elements, although they passed up numerous "last day bucks." On Tuesday they decided to hunt a familiar, higher elevation piece of BLM property consisting of open knolls and brushy ravines.

Tuesday morning the men began walking up the trail as an overcast sky dawned behind Mt. Gunnison. The shrill pitch of a bull elk shattered the silence somewhere to their left and a small herd was soon located, but no bull was seen. The men had elk tags so they debated whether or not to stalk the unseen bull. A second bugle made the men's hearts race and they agreed to continue up the mountain. This delay proved fortuitous.

Dan soon went to the right while Bill and Neil climbed steadily upwards. Neil glanced up towards a plateau 100 yards away and spotted antler tips moving slowly away from the men and vanishing just beyond the crest.

Photograph by Neil C. Nostrand

"There's a good buck just over the knoll," Neil whispered to Bill, and they continued to move silently up the ridge. At the top they peered over the edge with great anticipation.

The ridge gradually continued on up with steep ravines on both sides. A quick look into the right drainage netted nothing. Neil quickly ruled out the ridge in front of them as the low sagebrush provided insufficient cover. The left ravine remained with oak brush covering the near slope all the way up the draw. Neil and Bill listened for any sound. Still nothing. The buck had simply disappeared.

The heaviest cover was 150 to 200 yards in front of them near the creek bottom. Neil pointed at the only area he believed the buck could have gone. Neil asked Bill to go straight down into the draw to block a reverse sneak beneath them. As Neil again studied the possible hiding spot, a doe emerged from the brush, crossed the creek and walked slowly up the far slope about 175 yards away. Then, to Neil's delight, out stepped the buck, walking broadside 10 feet behind in full rut.

Neil didn't need binoculars to determine that this was a keeper buck. He hit the prone position, placed the cross hairs of his Leupold 4-power scope behind the shoulder of the animal, and squeezed off a round. The stunned buck was hit squarely but didn't immediately drop. A second shot dropped it in its tracks.

Bill and Neil crossed the draw and worked their way up to the downed buck. This 5x4 heavy-bodied buck, with high, wide, symmetrical antlers field dressed at 256 pounds. The antlers had a 27-inch spread that yielded a final score of 186 B&C points.

Neil proudly displays his trophy buck moments after taking it in 1986.

ANTHONY URWICK
Location: Pitkin County
Year Taken: 1982
Score: 186

Anthony Urwick hunted the Snowmass-Maroon Bells Wilderness on November 4, 1982, opening day of the late season, with Dion Luke, the owner of Ragged Mountain Outfitters of Glenwood Springs.

They still hunted and glassed down drainages throughout the day without success. As they headed back to camp about 4 p.m. they guided their horses along the edge of a plateau. This route provided a great view of the scrub oak-filled drainage 600 feet below. They suddenly spotted a huge typical mule deer buck as it was getting up out of its bed. The buck immediately began trotting away from them.

The buck, knowing he was spotted, made his way towards East Sopris Creek and black timber cover a third of a mile away. Anthony knew he was too far for a clear shot, so he rode his horse into the scrub oak-filled valley where he tied it up and started off after the buck.

Anthony suddenly caught a movement out of the corner of his right eye. The buck, with his head held low, was sneaking towards the dark timber on the far side of the creek. Anthony ran up the creek hoping to intercept the buck. He gasped for breath after sprinting 300 yards in his snow pack boots at 10,000 feet with his daypack on his back. The buck paused momentarily to glance back at Anthony as it reached the timber, and Anthony quickly realized that he had time for only one shot. He dropped to his knees, steadied himself and harvested the buck of a lifetime with one well-placed shot from his .270 Winchester.

The buck's nearly symmetrical rack is 27 inches wide and scored 186 Boone and Crockett Club points.

Anthony Urwick still-hunted with Dion Luke in the Snowmass-Maroon Bells Wilderness in 1982 where he downed this 186-point typical mule deer.

KELLY BROWN
Location: Rio Blanco County
Year Taken: 1999
Score: 186

Tracking a deer for a week and knowing its habitat was key for Kelly Brown in taking this outstanding typical mule deer.

Kelly saw the buck just as the season began but the property owner across the road from where the buck lived shot at the buck moments after the season began, and the buck bolted. The buck ran up a ravine so Kelly followed it to the next ridge in hopes of getting a clear shot. There was a big rock at the top of the ridge that Kelly used to lie down to set up a shot. The buck arrived on the opposite ridge and turned back to look down the hill, partially quartering away up the hill from Kelly. With his 7mm Magnum, Kelly fired a 165-grain bullet at its heart and the buck dropped in its tracks from 266 yards.

The buck was bigger and better than Kelly thought it would be with its 32-inch spread and huge body. Not only did Kelly take a great buck but also his hunting buddy, Don Robley, collected a great one.

Kelly's buck was accepted into the Boone and Crockett Club's 24th North American Big Game Awards Program in December 2000.

A big rock provided the perfect rest for Kelly Brown, who downed this massive typical mule deer with a single shot. The B&C buck scored 186 points.

GARY A. BAUDINO
Location: Las Animas County
Year Taken: 1996
Score: 185-6/8

The fact that Gary Baudino located a records book buck eight miles from home south of Aguilar, Colorado, certainly added to the enjoyment he felt from this 1996 hunt that started as a hunt for elk and ended with a Boone and Crockett mule deer.

On the opening morning of the hunting season, Gary spotted his trophy book buck from a distance of 60 yards in the Black Hills area of southern Colorado. The buck was looking directly at him but Gary could only see its head and neck. He placed the cross hairs of his Remington .270 on the neck and squeezed the trigger, but when he reached the area where the buck had been standing, he only found a small blood trail that disappeared within 50 yards. He continued to search for the disappearing buck for the remainder of the season and never found it. He combed the area within a three-mile radius of where the shot was fired, but to no avail.

On the last day of the hunting season, Gary and his son, Jason, 13, were combing the area on a four-wheeler when Gary spotted a buck that was about 400 yards ahead. Gary evaluated the buck through his binoculars to be a nice one so he got into a prone position over the four-wheeler and fired. The buck immediately dropped, and when Gary and Jason arrived at the area, he noticed the buck had a grazed neck, which was the same buck Gary shot at 10 days before.

Gary Baudino with his Boone and Crockett buck moments after he took it close to his home in Colorado.

The buck he first located at the start of the hunting season was finally his and his young son, Jordan, celebrated his 9th birthday on the same day of Dad's success on November 5. What a great way to celebrate a birthday.

Gary's buck was accepted into the Boone and Crockett Club's 23rd North American Big Game Awards Program.

MICHAEL E. ZIMMERMAN
Location: Eagle County
Year Taken: 1990
Score: 184-4/8

Michael Zimmerman and several friends selected the White River National Forest near Reudi Reservoir, Colorado, as the site for their 1990 deer hunt. Their hunt took place during the third rifle season. Bill Walker, who had moved to Basalt from Wisconsin some 20 years earlier, was their guide.

The day before the season opened, the men scouted the area. Michael and his friend, Rick Heinz, found a large clearing in a valley bordered on two sides by dark timber that they decided to hunt. There was a considerable amount of deer sign in the snow so Michael vowed to hunt this valley for the entire six-day stay if that's what it took to fill his tags.

Mike and Rick inadvertently arose late on opening morning and arrived at their area after sunrise. A light dusting of new snow had fallen and fresh tracks were everywhere. Michael headed for the top of a series of low-lying cliffs on the south side of the valley while Rick headed further south. The high altitude made the climbing a bit difficult for a flatlander like Michael, and he was profusely sweating when he reached the top of the cliffs.

Michael took his pack off at the top and settled in beside a large flat rock. He took out his binoculars and proceeded to glass a ridge to the far north and timberlines to the east and west. He estimated his field of view was 200 yards to the west and approximately 400 yards to both the north and the east.

Ten minutes after settling in several mule deer does wandered out of the black timber to the east to feed. Michael glassed them for about ten minutes when movement to his left caught his eye. A buck stepped into the opening. Even though he could only make out the left antler, Michael thought it was big. He brought his rifle up as the buck moved towards the does. The buck was only 175 yards away.

Michael thought he didn't want to shoot the first buck he saw but, at that moment, the buck looked straight up at him and forced him to make a decision. Michael put the cross hairs on the middle of the buck's neck and fired. The rifle kicked upwards, and the buck was gone by the time it came down. Michael thought his shot was good, but the deer was nowhere to be seen. He waited a few minutes, marked the spot, and climbed down to the area where he had last seen the buck.

Ten minutes of searching in fresh snow didn't produce any traces of blood or hair, so Michael began to doubt he had hit the buck. He stopped looking, took off his hat, and took a deep breath.

He needed a better view of the landscape so he started upslope to the east. Before he had taken more than a few steps to the east, Michael spotted his buck. Only the left antler was visible. He ran to the buck and pulled it out of the brush, thinking it might have only one antler. The buck was a massive typical 6x6 scoring 184-4/8 points. Rick and Michael both estimated the live weight to be more than 300 pounds.

People always ask Michael how far the buck traveled after the shot, and his reply is always the same, "About three feet, straight down."

Michael Zimmerman hunted on the White River National Forest in 1990 and collected one of the largest bucks ever taken in Colorado.

RANDY MOTZNER
Location: Eagle County
Year Taken: 1997
Score: 184

The buck stood broadside to Randy Motzner at the end of the 1997 hunting season but the distance between him and the buck was far, so a moment of decision had come for this hunter who had hunted hard all season.

The buck was across a draw and up a hillside from Randy in Eagle County at a distance of approximately 500 yards when Randy decided to grab his day pack and rifle and hightail it down the ridge to cut some distance between the two of them. Randy reached a small overlook about 100 yards closer to the buck and rested his rifle across his pack to check the distance. A single shot with his .270 Winchester, Model 70 and 130 handloaded grain bullet hit its mark and the buck ran downhill to its final resting-place.

When Randy reached the buck, he noticed the right eye was gouged out, the left ear was torn about halfway up and the nose sported several scars. Randy thought he'd sure like to see the other buck and wondered why this buck was so damaged. He imagined the damage was from a rut battle. Two of his friends, Steve and Bob Lake, had planned to help Randy with the hunt but they woke up too late. By the time Steve and Bob were up on horseback, Randy had dragged the buck down the hill, quartered it and hung the meat in the shade. When his friends caught up with Randy there wasn't much for them to do but admire the buck.

Randy Motzner poses with his B&C buck shortly after taking it in 1997.

On the seventh day of a nine-day hunting season, Nov. 7 1997, Randy had collected one of the largest bucks he had ever seen. For a man who started hunting small game at age 9 and big game at age 15, he had many years of experience from which to compare. The buck was collected at the end of the season but it was well worth the wait.

Randy's typical mule deer was accepted into the Boone and Crockett Club's 24th North American Big Game Awards Program in June 1998.

JERRY L. DeFRENCHI
Location: Montezuma County
Year Taken: 1999
Score: 183-5/8

Jerry DeFrenchi has taken many great mule deer bucks over the years but the buck taken on the last day of the third deer season in 1999 stands out in his mind.

Jerry tried to hunt another large buck that was living on his property but had no luck throughout the season and time was running out to fill his tag. He gave up on the buck when it went into hiding. Jerry remembered seeing big deer during archery elk season, so he decided to return to that area to see if he could locate more bucks. He parked his Jeep and started off toward a canyon where he normally hunted. He immediately saw a huge-bodied doe and continued hunting. Jerry was pressed for time because he needed to take his daughter to a doctor's appointment, so he knew he had only 45 minutes left in the hunting season to bag a buck.

After Jerry returned to the vehicle he saw a buck sneaking across through the oaks, so he slipped from the Jeep, loaded his rifle and prepared to shoot by creeping over to it. The buck bolted from the oak brush as Jerry fired a single shot to the front shoulder at a distance of less than 250 yards with his .300 Weatherby. For many hunters, 1999 had been difficult because of extreme dryness but not for Jerry. In addition to this Boone and Crockett Club buck he also took a nice 6x5 bull elk. Jerry, who is a professional taxidermist in Mancos, Colorado, was so delighted with his buck that he created a full mount that looks like a buck walking in the woods.

Jerry's full-mount typical mule deer that scores 183-5/8 points.

Jerry's buck was accepted into the B&C 24th North American Big Game Awards Program in February 2000 with a final score of 183-5/8 points. He also has two other outstanding bucks that are accepted into the Boone and Crockett Club's 24th Awards Program that scored 180-4/8 and 187-7/8 points.

Jerry's B&C buck that scores 187-7/8 points.

Jerry's B&C buck that scores 180-4/8 points.

BILLY E. GREEN
Location: Mesa County
Year Taken: 1986
Score: 183-1/8

South of Debeque in Mesa County is an ideal spot for Billy Green and his family to hunt year after year, but getting close enough to get a good shot at a big muley is another matter. Billy's luck turned in 1986 when he was in rim rock country leading up to Housetop Mountain and the Battlement Mesa. Billy loves this area of Colorado because he seldom sees another person once he gets away from a road or bike trail.

Billy was hunting the area in 1986 when he spotted two bucks in the morning. Both were nice 4x4s in the 20-inch to 25-inch range with thin horns, but nothing exceptional. Thanks to a skiff of snow just under the rim rock ledge, spotting for deer was made much easier.

Billy followed the rim rock for about a mile or so when two does and another small 4x4 jumped up and ran across a shale slide under the rim rock. They trotted out of sight, and Billy became concerned that he was moving too fast and spooking deer. While he was pondering the situation, a massive buck darted across the slide with two more does. The big buck paused giving Billy time to prepare for a shot. Billy fired four times at the buck while it moved across the shale. He thought he had missed it, but when Billy reached the area where he had last seen the buck it was lying there dead. The buck had traveled only 70 yards after it was hit.

The word got out and lots of people stopped by Billy's camp the see his buck. After the required drying period the buck was officially scored at 183-1/8 points.

Billy summed up the situation very well when he recently said, "My brother, myself and my dad have been hunting this area now for quite a few years. We have taken other nice bucks, but none like the big one from 1986. The area has giants and I have seen bucks as big or bigger but getting a good shot at them is another story."

South of Debeque was an ideal hunting spot for Billy Green when he downed this trophy buck that scores 183-1/8 points.

ROBERT B. CALDWELL
Location: Moffat County
Year Taken: 1975
Score: 182-1/8

Bob Caldwell made his first trip to Colorado in November 1975 to hunt the famed Colorado mule deer, and his expectations were more than satisfied when he collected a Boone and Crockett buck.

Bob and his older brother, Rudy, met some friends in Craig, bought food for the camp and headed to Bears Ear Peak in the Elkhead Mountains just north of Craig. The snow was absolutely beautiful, approximately 20 inches deep, but the temperature was a minus 10 degrees Fahrenheit. To put it bluntly, that's plenty cold for a Mississippi redneck.

Bob and his partners hunted Bears Ear Peak for two days and finally had to come down off the mountain as the temperature dropped to about minus 20 degrees Fahrenheit. They weren't physically or mentally prepared for that kind of weather. By chance they lucked out and ran into a gentleman who said they could hunt McIntosh Mesa, just down the mountain from Bears Ear Peak for a $25-per-day trespass fee.

On their first day on McIntosh Mesa, just prior to sunrise, Bob spotted a beautiful mule deer standing on the rim of a small hill, silhouetted against the morning sun. It was the most beautiful sight Bob had ever seen and he thought to himself, "God really knew what he was doing when he made this part of our country." This magnificent creature stood between Bob and the morning sun. Bob just couldn't believe his eyes. He started the long stalk never really believing he had a chance to get close to that trophy-class animal.

Bob Caldwell with "his baby," the buck that scored 182-1/8 points. Bob entered his buck in the Boone and Crockett 22 years after taking it near Craig.

At that time in his life, Bob had been fortunate to have taken some beautiful whitetail deer but nothing of this class. At about 8 a.m., Bob was walking along the rim of the hill where he had first spotted the muley. The buck suddenly jumped up and started running. Bob made the shot of a lifetime and just about fainted when the buck dropped in its tracks. Bob nearly broke his fool neck trying to get down the side of the hill to his buck. When he reached it, he was in shock. There stood a Mississippi redneck on his first hunting trip to Colorado with a buck of a lifetime lying before him.

Bob's buck wasn't officially scored until 1997 since he didn't know an Official Measurer who was qualified to score it. A friend in Tupelo, Mississippi, where Bob lives met one and scheduled an appointment to have the buck scored. Bob received his official B&C notification of acceptance on May 10, 1997. It scored 182-1/8 points and weighed in at 348 pounds on the hoof. Bob recognizes there are many mule deer out there that are bigger, but to him this is his trophy of a lifetime. It is one that he can tell his grandson about.

WILLIAM J. McEWEN
Location: Eagle County
Year Taken: 1996
Score: 182

Bill McEwen had hunted from dawn until dusk during the last deer season in 1996 and now it was the fifth day of a nine-day season.

An hour hike in Eagle County to a spot where Bill's friends had sighted a big buck brought Bill within 300 yards of this desired trophy. The buck was in love and totally out of its mind in rut so didn't pay attention to the human that was sneaking closer as it chased does. Bill developed buck fever and shot over the buck, shaving off some fur in the process. The buck bolted over the hill toward the does with Bill tracking right behind them. Luckily for Bill, four inches of fresh snow had fallen so tracking was easy. He tracked the buck a mile up hill and down. Bill reached the buck and does as the buck was madly chasing the does, so a single shot with his 7mm magnum at 250 yards dropped the buck without the buck ever noticing what hit him.

Bill shot the buck early in the day so he field dressed it and hung it in the shade to cool it off until the next day when hunting buddies Karl Steineck and Rick Yraceburu helped packed out the buck. The buck sported a rack measuring more than 31 inches wide and 24 inches tall so Bill knew the buck was big and when it was officially measured it met all his expectations. Hard hunting and knowledge of the hunting area paid off for this hunter.

Bill's buck was accepted into the Boone and Crockett Club's 23rd North American Big Game Awards Program in 1997.

Moments after Bill McEwen downed this records book buck, this picture was snapped.

RONALD E. MARKOW
Location: Washington County
Year Taken: 1991
Score: 181-6/8

A serious injury from an automobile wreck restricting climbs up mountains motivated Ron Markow to explore hunting opportunities in the flatlands of eastern Colorado, and he has never regretted that decision. Ron has mounted several hundred bucks in his lifetime as a professional taxidermist while living in the mountains at the time. He had never taken a buck as large as the one located outside Last Chance, Colorado.

Ron's story began in October 1991 when he traveled down Interstate 70 outside Denver to a farm loaded with wheat fields and flat land. Ron's friend, John, led him to weed patches standing eight feet tall where the men knew the bucks hid. The men examined several weed patches and came upon a large weed patch measuring 200 by 100 yards about a mile from the road in the middle of wheat. The men left their truck and circled around the patch, clapping their hands, wrapped on sticks and tried to make a little noise to rustle up a buck. Several does came out of the patch that left the patch, one by one, including a nice buck. When it left the patch the buck walked up a hill, 200 yards from the men. Ron's son-in-law thought another buck leaving the weeds was worth taking but John didn't agree so the men returned to the truck to explore another area of the ranch. Ron looked back toward the weed patch to see the bushes moving as though the wind was blowing, but there was no wind. That was when Ron realized the "wind" was antlers of a huge buck. The buck was stuck in the bushes trying to untangle himself from the brambles at a distance of 75 yards from Ron. As the buck moved from the cane weed, Ron fired a single shot that hit the buck in the neck and it went down. A second shot finished the job and Ron had collected his trophy buck.

Upon reaching the buck, the three hunters were in awe of its size. The estimated weight was 225 to 250 pounds and the men agreed that the only bucks they had ever seen of this size had hung on other people's walls. Ron couldn't believe his good luck. Not only was the rack huge but the meat was tender and succulent to eat. For a taxidermist to mount hundreds of bucks and never see anything this big, one can only imagine how rare a Boone and Crockett buck must be.

Ron, who is a taxidermist in Wheatridge, Colorado, and owner of Valley Taxidermist, entered his buck in the Boone and Crockett Club's 24th North American Big Game Awards Program in 2000.

BOB K. CARTER
Location: Delta County
Year Taken: 1998
Score: 181-6/8

The year Bob Carter graduated from high school, his good friend John Savage's father, J.L., took the young men mule deer hunting near Norwood, Colorado. Two days into the season they all had tagged out. J.L. didn't know it then, but he had ruined them. At that time Bob had hardly been out of his home state of Oklahoma. They've been going back to Colorado every year since that time and continue to return to Colorado each year. Now Bob takes his daughter with him on these annual treks as well as an assortment of nephews. They've tagged some nice bucks over the years, but the one on October 10, 1998, was the best.

Bob and his 12-year-old daughter Amy left early opening morning and made a big round about 10 to 12 miles on foot, saw lots of game and tagged out that morning. Amy got a 3x2 and Bob collected his 5x5 with his .308. It took him 18 years to find this big boy, but he did.

"God has really blessed us," Bob admits.

Bob's buck was accepted into the Boone and Crockett Club's 24th North American Big Game Awards Program.

On a glorious Colorado fall day Bob Carter kneels beside his outstanding B&C typical mule deer buck that scored 181-6/8 points.

VERNON D. HOLLEMAN
Location: Delta County
Year Taken: 1962
Score: 181-5/8

For many years Vernon has admired the crown The Good Lord used to adorn the heads of mule deer and considered it one of nature's greatest masterpieces. For him, this sentiment especially applies to non-typical antlers with their endless variety of forms.

In his younger days, Vernon passionately hunted mule deer with his brother, Dan. They packed into the high country during the early seasons and hunted the lower elevations during November and December. His first muley was a 5x5 that Vernon naively thought was a monster. His second was a 7x7 that he practically shot in self defense after it nearly ran over him. He and Dan shot another monster in 1965 that was tragically destroyed by fire before it could be officially measured. He estimated the score of that buck at around 191 points,

Occasionally, when Vernon and his brother tired of sleeping in an Army pup tent or in the back of a 1956 Chevy station wagon, they hired Sid Simpson, a Paonia guide, and paid him a hefty $20 a day for his services. Sid was a tough, old cowboy who lost a lung in WW II. What Sid lacked in breathing capacity, he made up for with his sharp vision. He never used binoculars, but he most often spotted deer before anyone who did.

Photograph courtesy of Vernon D. Holleman

After a comfortable night at Sid's house on November 19th, 1962, Vernon and his brother arose the next morning at 4:30 a.m., ate breakfast, saddled up and followed Sid into the mountains. Vernon doesn't remember all that happened that day, but he vividly remembers the sequence of events leading up to the successful taking of his Boone and Crockett trophy. They tied up the horses and sneaked over a ridge to glass the terrain before them. Sid, huffing and puffing from the short climb, excitedly whispered, "There he is!"

Binoculars weren't needed to size up this brute. Besides they had no time. The buck had sensed their presence and ran downhill towards the oak brush. Vernon readily admits his brother was the better hunter, but it was Vernon's single shot from his 6.5x55 Swedish military Mauser that hit its mark that day.

As Sid and Dan retrieved the horses, Vernon worked his way through the brush to the fallen trophy where he photographed his beautiful buck as it lay there in the snow. He then carefully removed the cape and antlers. Sid arrived shortly thereafter with the horses and eviscerated the carcass with as much tenderness as Vernon gave to the cape.

As Sid loaded the meat he said, "You can't eat them horns."

Vernon replied, "No, and you can't mount the meat." Still, Vernon knew Sid appreciated "them old big ones."

In 1962, Vernon Holleman stopped long enough for a photograph after field-dressing his B&C buck behind Sid Simpson's house in Paonia. In the background are the foothills of the mountains where Vernon hunted.

R. CHARLES PROSEK
Location: Rio Blanco County
Year Taken: 1993
Score: 181

Two days before the 1993 big-game season opened in Colorado, Chuck Prosek, Bob Germenis, Ed Allemand and B.O.B. Williams left their homes and drove straight through to Rangley, Colorado. The adventure they embarked on turned out to be the most memorable hunt in Chuck's life.

They arrived in Rangley at 5 a.m. on a Friday morning, ate breakfast, picked up supplies and headed for their usual campsite. By the time the men set up their mess tent and sleeping quarters it was late afternoon. Although they had slept little in the truck during the drive to Colorado, they decided to glass their hunting area during the remaining daylight hours.

Two hours before dawn, the men drove to the area they had previously scouted. Bob and B.O.B. headed off in one direction towards the cliffs, and Ed and Chuck headed for a large box canyon. Chuck walked up the right side of the canyon and Ed stayed near the bottom. Ed didn't want to hike up the canyon.

"Whatever you shoot, you better be able to drag it down yourself," Ed told Chuck. Chuck just laughed and took off up the canyon in the dark on his own.

A short time later he heard antlers rattling in the distance. When he was halfway up the ridge, Chuck spotted two deer fighting in a bowl. He scanned them with his 10x50 binoculars, but he still wasn't able to estimate their sizes. Chuck continued sneaking up the ridge hoping to get a better view. Once he reached the last place where he could maintain cover, he stopped and cranked his scope up to 9x to get a good look at both bucks. As he was debating which buck to shoot, a third buck stepped into view. There was no doubt in Chuck's mind that this was the largest buck he had ever seen.

The distance between him and the large buck was 250 to 300 yards, so Chuck assumed a prone position to get a steady rest. With heart pounding and an adrenaline rush, Chuck took a deep breath and squeezed off one shot. He then checked with his binoculars to see whether or not his shot hit its mark. Not seeing movement on the hill, Chuck picked several landmarks to guide him to the location where he hoped to find his buck.

It took Chuck 45 minutes to reach the location due to the steep terrain and snow on the ground. He reached the spot and found his buck after a brief search. It had jumped when Chuck shot and then slide down the hill about 15 feet. Chuck's hunt was over at 9:30 a.m.

After Chuck calmed down and returned to his senses, he realized he needed help getting the massive trophy back to camp. Ed arrived just as Chuck finished field dressing the buck and said, "Without a helicopter, we're not going to get this guy down the mountain." Chuck then left Ed to guard the deer while he went for help. Together the four hunters dragged and slid the buck down the hill and arrived back at their camp around 4 p.m.

Chuck's hunting buddies were glad he could only shoot one buck per season. It scored 181 B&C points.

By 9:30 a.m. Chuck Prosek downed his B&C typical 5x6 mule deer buck that made "The Book" with a score of 181 points.

PATRICK G. DIESING
Location: Douglas County
Year Taken: 1987
Score: 180-1/8

We all recall moments in our teen-age lives when skipping class was the best way to reach a favorite hunting spot away from the crowds of the weekend, and for Patrick G. Diesing, his high school skip day was no exception.

Patrick asked his mom to let him skip a few early morning classes to track mule deer near his home outside Denver in October 1987 during his senior year of high school. He promised Mom he would return to class by 9 a.m., so no harm would be done academically since his early morning classes were electives. Little did he know when he set out for his Wednesday hunt that this would be the day of his B&C trophy.

After borrowing his next door neighbors' Ford pickup with two-wheel drive, Patrick and his friend Andy Wood traveled 20 minutes from home into Douglas County to an area where he had hunted many times before. A skither of snow blanketed the ranch ground as the boys checked ridgetops. As they walked to the last ridgetop before heading back to school, they noticed fresh deer tracks heading west so as they walked over a small ridge where a massive buck was browsing in the scrub oak. The antlers rose above the brush like a tree trunk when Patrick saw him standing broadside from 30 yards away. Without hesitation, Patrick fired a round from his 270 Remington rifle but the bullet flew over the buck's back. Patrick blamed the miss on serious buck fever.

The buck wheeled around 180 degrees and started down the ridge, paralleling the boys at a distance of 50 yards when Patrick fired a second time and hit his mark. The buck ran another 20 yards and collapsed. They were a mile from the truck that couldn't drive through the snow, so needless to say, Patrick was late returning to school that day to tell all his buddies. He was way too excited to return to class, and as far as he can remember, his mom didn't even get mad at him for missing the rest of class that day.

Patrick's buck was accepted into the Boone and Crockett Club's 24th North American Big Game Awards Program in 1999.

Jonas Brothers, Inc. of Denver, a premiere taxidermy shop founded in 1908, is shown here in the 1920s.

The workroom of Jonas Brothers, Inc. in Denver, circa 1940.

— *Chapter III* —
Colorado Non-Typical Mule Deer
Stories and Photographs

LLOYD PYLE
Location: Montezuma County
Year Taken: 1972
Score: 306-7/8
Owner: Don Schaufler

Guide and Outfitter Rick Kirks, grandson to Lloyd Pyle, couldn't remember details of his grandfather's hunt in 1972, but he did have a family photograph of the rack. The buck was taken near Cortez in Montezuma County. Another family photograph shows three other racks with Lloyd's. Lloyd's rack is second from the left. The 16x18-point buck ranks 1st in Colorado and the 10th largest non-typical mule deer ever taken in the world. The buck received a Certificate of Merit for the 23rd North American Big Game Awards Program in June 1998 when ceremonies were held at the Reno Hilton in Reno, Nevada. Lloyd died on June 11, 1987, so he never lived to see the buck recognized.

The Lloyd Pyle non-typical mule deer rack, photographed before it was mounted. The antlers score 306-7/8 points, making it the largest non-typical muley ever taken in Colorado.

Certificate of Merit
23rd B&C Awards

The outstanding bucks shown in this picture were taken by hunters, left to right, Vic Hodges, Lloyd Pyle, Rick Kirks and Mark Smith.

STEVE HERNDON
Location: San Miguel County
Year Taken: 1954
Score: 306-2/8
Owners: V.D. and D.F. Holleman

Companionship was the most important facet of hunting for Norwood, Colorado, rancher, Steve Herndon. In fact, Steve's ranch was a gathering place for his friends and relatives each hunting season.

Each morning Steve was responsible for dropping his guests off at their appointed stands and for picking them up in the evening with their game. Shortly after he started to make his rounds one evening, Steve spotted a buck with the most massive set of antlers he had ever seen as it stepped out of the oak brush and into the clearing. With one carefully placed shot with his .30-30, the buck dropped.

With a Boone and Crockett Club score of 306-2/8 points, Steve's buck is the second largest non-typical mule deer buck ever taken in Colorado that is recognized by the all-time records book and the 11th largest non-typical mule deer buck taken in the world.

Steve's antlers weren't scored for B&C until 1965 when they were acquired by Texan Vernon D. Holleman. At the 12th Boone and Crockett Big Game Competition held at the Carnegie Museum in Pittsburgh, Pennsylvania, in 1966, Steve's trophy received a Certificate of Merit. Had it been entered at least five years earlier it might have won the first-place award and possibly even the Sagamore Hill Award.

Certificate of Merit
12th Competition

Photograph courtesy of Vernon D. Holleman

Steve Herndon's non-typical mule deer is the second largest antlered deer ever taken in Colorado. Steve collected this buck near Norwood in 1954. In this photograph it is the buck to the left of a respectable bull elk and an average-sized mule deer.

JAMES AUSTILL
Location: Eagle County
Year Taken: 1962
Score: 303-6/8
Owner: Don Schaufler

Long-term planning and knowledge of his hunting area paid off for James Austill who bagged the third largest non-typical mule deer ever taken in Colorado.

During the spring of 1962 Jim and five hunting buddies began preparing for a trophy mule deer hunt. They decided to take only four-pointers or better. Most of the men had hunted near the mining town of Minturn, so they decided to start the hunt from that point. They also decided to hunt late in the season to avoid the opening day crush.

In mid-November the six hunters set out from Minturn in a four-wheel drive Jeep and drove about eight miles over rough terrain to reach the area they felt would be the most productive. It was snowing lightly and the day was ice-cold. At 10,000 feet the air was frigid and thin.

On the first day the men split up along a ridge and downed five trophy deer. They took nothing less than four-pointers. Jim spotted his trophy buck that first day but did not get a clear shot. On the second day Jim walked along the top of a ridge and could hear hunters shouting across neighboring ridges to each other. He came upon a meadow and spotted a large animal through the trees. The sun's bright rays shone on the body of a huge buck bedded down in the grass. Fearing that the other hunters on the ridges around him would soon spook the buck, Jim quickly but quietly crept around the hill behind the unsuspecting deer. As the hunters approached, the buck stood up to flee. Jim took aim and downed the buck with one shot at 80 yards.

Jim ran to the deer and immediately realized he had a trophy. Later he noticed that the deer had only four well-worn teeth left in its jaw, indicating an older animal. He suspected that this deer would not have survived the severe winter that year.

Jim dressed it out and dragged it to the Jeep where it was taken back to his home. Although he had two tags Jim decided to stop hunting because his deer was so large. The venison was more than enough to feed his family. All of his hunting buddies decided to quit early and left camp on the morning of the third day with nine deer to their credit. The number of points on their racks ranged from four to 13.

When his trophy was later measured, it scored 303-6/8 points in the Boone and Crockett Club's records program. It was sent to the Carnegie Museum in Pittsburgh, Pennsylvania, in 1964 for the 11th North American Big Game Competition of the Boone and Crockett Club. The rack ranked second in the non-typical mule deer category.

**Second Place
11th B&C Competition**

ANDREW DAUM
Location: Elk Creek near Meeker
Year Taken: 1886
Score: 299-5/8
Owner: B&C National Collection of Heads and Horns

On November 9, 1999, Fred King, chair of the Museum Committee that oversees the Boone and Crockett Club's National Collection of Heads and Horns, delivered to the Club's national headquarters in Missoula, Montana, a truly spectacular non-typical mule deer head taken by Andrew Daum in 1886. This spectacular head is not an addition to the National Collection; it has been returned. It was stolen, along with 12 other specimens, from the National Collection in November 1974 when the Collection was still owned by the New York Zoological Society and housed at the Bronx Zoo.

Andrew Daum hunted this magnificent buck at Elk Creek, Colorado. Scoring 299-5/8 points, it is still one of the finest specimens of North American big game ever recorded. It was the first World's Record in its category when the Club adopted and copyrighted its scoring system in 1950. It was listed as the World's Record in the 1952 and 1958 editions of the all-time records books and dropped to fifth place in the 1964 edition. It currently ranks 20th in the 11th edition of *Records of North American Big Game* published in 1999.

The story of its return is quite simple. The mount was returned on the 25th anniversary of its disappearance from the Collection. It was recovered by Harry Batschelet, Jr., who called the Club's headquarters in May 1998 to say that he believed he possessed a mule deer stolen from the National Collection. He asked B&C to send photographs from their files of the stolen trophy to Tom Entinger, the owner of Trails West Taxidermy in Rawlins, Wyoming. After a brief exchange of photographs and telephone conversations with Harry and Tom, it was determined beyond a shadow of a doubt that the head Harry had acquired was indeed the stolen Daum head.

The Daum head, which was mounted by Tom Entinger, will temporarily hang in a conference room at the Club's headquarters in Missoula until it can be delivered to the Buffalo Bill Historical Center in Cody, Wyoming, where the National Collection is currently housed.

The two photographs show the Andrew Daum buck as it was recorded in 1886 (left) and its modern-day mount (right).

JACK AUTREY
Location: Larimer County
Year Taken: 1941
Score: 297-5/8
Owner: Linda Guy

Jack Autrey was discouraged and near despair as he drove up Rist Canyon in Larimer County on the fifth day of the 1941 deer season. The weather didn't help lighten his spirits any either as the day began with a heavy fog and mist. Even in mid-afternoon the valleys and gulches were filled with a thin fog, and dark clouds rested on all the higher peaks.

For the first four days of the season Jack camped at a cabin near Chambers Lake. He hunted far and near with one side trip down the Poudre River to as far as Eggan's Resort. For all his loss of sleep, and miles and miles of hiking and climbing, he didn't catch anything more than a few fleeting glances of deer in heavy timber.

On the fifth day of the season Jack was back home but couldn't resist the urge to check things out nearby. About mid-afternoon he grabbed his .25-35 Winchester, jumped into his 1935 Plymouth sedan and took a short spin up Rist Canyon to look around. About two miles from home a lone buck on a hillside caught his attention. Jack quickly parked his car and worked his way back down the road and up to a small point on the hillside. As he drew a perfect bead on a nice four-pointer, a clump of brush on the skyline about 350 yards away caught Jack's attention. It just didn't look like any clump of brush he had ever seen before. As he watched, the clump shook, and the biggest buck of his hunting career materialized before his very eyes. It turned broadside to look at Jack.

Jack didn't take long to get a bead on this exceptional buck and let one round go. He knew immediately he had hit the buck but had to fire again when it started to run. It took another dozen or so

Jack Autrey with his 1941 Larimer County buck draped over the fender and hood of his 1935 Plymouth sedan. Jack's buck, which hung in Vern's Restaurant north of Fort Collins until the restaurant burned down, scored 297-3/8 points. The trophy, along with everything else, was destroyed in the fire.

steps and went down in a flurry of cracking brush and rolling rocks. Jack hadn't been at all nervous or excited until he saw the buck go down. As he felt his rifle was bothersome, he leaned it against a tree and went on without it. When he was about halfway to the animal, he began to have doubts about the wisdom of such an action and ran back down the hill to get it. After all, he correctly figured he might need to finish the animal off if it got up and started to run.

When Jack saw the magnificent set of antlers his buck carried, his knees went weak. With a spread of 34-7/8 inches Jack's trophy was the 3rd largest non-typical mule deer buck in Colorado at that time, although it wasn't measured until 1981. There were 17 measurable points on the right antler and 15 on the left. There were 40 projections on which you could hang a ring. For many years this magnificent rack hung in Vern's Restaurant in Laporte, Colorado, until the restaurant burned down and the mount was destroyed along with everything else. This non-typical mule deer is preserved through photographs only.

HARRY JORDAN
Location: Rio Blanco County
Year Taken: 1932
Score: 295-5/8

Three bucks hang on the back wall of the Meeker Hotel lobby and are known as, "The Three Amigos." The center buck was taken by Harry Jordan of Meeker, Colorado, in October 1932 and was the winner of a big buck contest with a cash prize of $75 for greatest spread of 45 inches and $75 for greatest number of points with 34. The second-place winner was Leon D. Morris of Golden who downed a buck with a 38-inch spread and 24 points. According to Harry's son, Bill, the buck was taken outside Meeker in Rio Blanco County. When B&C official measurer Roger Selner scored the buck in 1997, he counted 15 points on the right and 17 on the left with the greatest spread officially measuring 44-2/8 inches.

Bill Jordan went home and brought back to Roger a copy of the newspaper article and the photograph shown on this page that recorded his father's accomplishment. The rifle in the photograph shows a .25-35 Winchester, which was likely the rifle that was used to take the buck. Bill remembered his father telling him that he shot the smaller of the two bucks that day. The trophy has never been entered in the Boone and Crockett Club records-keeping program so there is no ranking for this outstanding non-typical rack. The mount has hung in the Meeker Hotel lobby since the 1930s where it remains today.

The Three Amigos in the lobby of the Meeker Hotel. The center buck is the non-typical taken by Harry Jordan in 1932. This photograph was taken in 1982. All three bucks remain on display in the hotel's lobby.

A rare field photograph shows Harry Jordan (right) holding his 295-5/8-point buck as his friend and hunting partner, Tom Kilduff, left, looks on. The photograph hangs beneath the buck in the lobby of the Meeker Hotel.

Colorado's Biggest Bucks and Bulls

This photograph of bucks displayed on this barn wall was used in 1962 to promote mule deer hunting in Middle Park in statewide and local newspapers. Shown sitting beneath the bucks are the hunters who took them, and they are, left to right, county agent Bob Teagarden, rancher Charles Palmer, rancher Fred Palmer, merchant Lyman Brown, rancher Ernest Scherer, rancher Karl Knorr, rancher Lloyd Palmer, and rancher Irwin Palmer. The antlers on the diamond-shaped plaque and those with the complete skull are both listed in the Boone and Crockett Club's records books. A caption appearing below the photograph in The Denver Post on Sunday, March 18, 1962, noted that the Middle Park area produced more than 30 records-book bucks in two years.

The Ralston Brothers butcher shop at 00 Huerfano Street (presently Colorado Avenue) in Colorado Springs supplied the general public with elk and deer meat around 1901. Market hunting was big business in Colorado during the late 1800s as white settlers poured into the state. Market hunting led to the decline of several big-game species before the practice was outlawed with the instigation of game laws in 1897. In 1885 one Colorado hunting party supplied game to Laramine and Cheyenne, Wyoming, and Fort Collins, Colorado, citizens. They kept six wagon loads going at all times from Hog Park near Encampment River and were paid 3.5 cents per pound for elk and 3 cents per pound for deer.

DALE L. BECKER
Location: Eagle County
Year Taken: 1978
Score: 278-7/8

Colorado Division of Wildlife employees at the Idaho Springs check station told Dale Becker that his buck was the largest they had checked in 10 years. So recalled Dale about the Boone and Crockett non-typical muley he bagged during the 1978 combination hunting season near State Bridge.

In eight years of on and off big-game hunting, Dale's 1978 buck was the first deer he had ever taken. Accompanying him on his memorable hunt were his father Bob, two brothers, Jeff and Pat, and a close friend, Monty Moorman. Overall, Dale's party had quite a successful hunt that year. Around 9 a.m. on opening day Jeff and Monty simultaneously downed a five-point bull elk. On the second day of the season Dale's 14-year-old brother Pat dropped his first deer, a four-pointer. And on the third day, Dale took his Boone and Crockett non-typical muley.

At sunrise on the third day Dale awoke early and decided to work his way up a ridge near camp through a dense stand of black timber. Immediately, Dale jumped a few does but no bucks. He began to think that was all there was in his area when suddenly the buck of his dreams stepped forward out of the timber and gave Dale a broadside shot at 100 yards. For a moment Dale hesitated to fire because of a near disastrous case of buck fever. Fortunately, he pulled himself together before the buck sensed his presence. His first and only shot found its mark.

In addition to advising Dale that his buck was the biggest buck they had seen in 10 years, Idaho Springs check station officials estimated that his buck had weighed 400 pounds on the hoof. The final B&C score for Dale's trophy was a whopping 278-7/8 points. It has a spread of 42-1/8 inches and 12 points on each antler.

LARRY PREHM
Location: Garfield County
Year Taken: 1967
Score: 276-4/8
Owner: Spanky Greenville

As he headed for his redesignated stand on October 22, 1967, the last bit of advice Larry Prehm received from his father was a stern reminder not to shoot any deer as they were after elk. Even though the deer and elk seasons were combined that year, Ed did not want to ruin their chances of filling their bull tags by shooting at deer. When Larry got his first look at his records-book timber buck, he quickly forgot his father's stern warning.

The game plan for the day included an early morning, old-fashioned elk drive. As Larry took up his stand near an old cowlick, Ed and Larry's brother Mike began working a stringer of timber toward Larry's position. While facing the direction of the oncoming hunters, Larry suddenly heard a crashing noise behind him and whirled in time to see two massive bucks of equal size cutting through the aspen. The aspen was thick and the action fast, but Larry quickly set his sights on a narrow opening about 150 yards away through which he figured the two deer would run. As his lead was poor, he missed the first buck but hit the second. It went down, and he quickly dispatched it with two more rounds.

Larry didn't think his buck was big enough for the Boone and Crockett Club's records book, but his father insisted that the antlers be officially measured. The rack scored 275-5/8 points in the Club's 14th Competition.

EVERETT KING
Location: Gunnison County
Year Taken: 1957
Score: 275-6/8

Deer drives have long been one of the most popular, as well as effective, methods of hunting Colorado's muleys. In fact, the early settlers of Colorado probably used such drives to put meat on their tables.

It was in the fall of 1957 that Everett King not only scored on one such drive but also collected a records-book buck for himself. Accompanying Everett on that drive were fellow hunters Philip W. Jarvis, Jess Duchman and D.E. Hall, Jr. The location of their hunt was Ragged Mountain in northwestern Gunnison County.

While the rest of his party conducted the drive, Everett stood alone in an aspen stand hoping to intercept any deer that might be stirred up. It wasn't until around 11 a.m. that morning that Everett heard the heavy sounds of deer crashing through the timber. As the sounds drew nearer, Everett prepared to shoot. He realized that under those conditions a hunter usually only gets a quick shot.

When the big buck broke into view at 65 yards, Everett had no doubt in his mind that it was a legal buck. His fifth shot brought it down for good. It wasn't until he examined his buck up close that he appreciated its massiveness. After returning to camp to get help to bring in his trophy, Everett had trouble convincing his hunting buddies that he had shot an exceptional buck with 37 points. It wasn't until they saw it with their own eyes that they no longer doubted his word.

Everett's trophy wasn't measured until 1980 when his grandson, Jim Jarvis, contacted Jack Reneau, an official measurer for the Boone and Crockett Club. Upon Jim's request his grandfather's buck was measured. It scored an impressive 275-6/8 points. At the time it was taken it would have ranked approximately 8th in Colorado. It was entered in the Boone and Crockett Club's records-keeping program but was discovered to have a split skull so was removed. If the buck had been entered, its estimated rank now would be 14th largest ever taken in Colorado.

TODD MCKAY
Location: Mesa County
Year Taken: 1994
Score: 270-3/8

It was Saturday morning, November 5, 1994, opening day of Colorado's third hunting season, when Todd McKay, Mark Morrow and Trent Wright left Grand Junction and headed for an area they had previously hunted many times. The drive took 45 minutes, and they discussed the day's hunting strategy along the way.

The men arrived at their hunting area a half-hour before sunrise and discovered other hunters were already in their area. Todd knew the area well, so they moved to another canyon. Todd decided to work the bottom of the canyon and posted his friends on the ridges on top. Todd's goal was to jump deer towards his hunting buddies.

As Todd dropped into the canyon, he heard movement ahead of him. Instead of going all the way to the bottom, he skirted along the rim. He moved along slowly for a half hour but didn't hear or see anything.

Todd was contouring a steep slope when he first noticed a monster mule deer. He had heard stories about monsters like this one, but he had never seen one. He couldn't believe his eyes. The buck was 350 yards across the canyon, facing Todd with the sun behind it. Todd figured the buck saw him, but it held still except for a slight side-to-side movement of its head.

When Todd saw the buck, he hit the ground since he knew he was conspicuously visible in the open. He landed in an awkward position and wasn't able to take aim. Todd moved behind a cedar tree 5 yards away, but the tree's thick branches made a clear shot impossible, so he decided to move again. Todd noticed a dead cedar with a perfect gun rest about 5 yards below him. The buck remained motionless while Todd got in position.

Bright sunlight at the buck's back and the fact that the deer was facing him made a clear shot nearly impossible. Todd's heart pounded as he waited to fire his .300 Winchester when the buck turned sideways. He waited ten minutes for the buck to move, but when it didn't, Todd took matters into his own hands. He aimed high and squeezed off a round. As he jacked in another round, Todd saw the buck's head drop as it staggered backwards. The buck fell at Todd's second shot, but only the first shot connected.

When Todd approached his trophy, he knew it was a world-class deer. Todd was thankful to be so lucky to have taken such a buck. If you want to see his buck and visit with Todd, stop by the Mt. Garfield Bed and Breakfast in Clifton, Colorado, the next time you are in town. And, if you visit in the summer you might be lucky enough to enjoy a fresh peach from their orchard.

**2nd Award
23rd B&C Awards**

SHIRLEY C. SMITH
Location: Delta County
Year Taken: 1962
Score: 268-3/8

For one Colorado hunter, the 1962 Thanksgiving holiday will be remembered always as a time of great celebration. For Shirley Smith his November 17 hunt will probably remain his most memorable.

Shirley had received a late-season permit and was determined to fill his tag. He and a brother, Duane, and a cousin, Joe Smith, left for the Bureau of Land Management lands three miles north of Hotchkiss in Delta County. A foot of white power covered the ground. All had hunted the area regularly and were quite familiar with it.

Actually, Shirley and his hunting companions hadn't left home until early afternoon. The hunting area was only four to five miles from home. Shortly after their arrival, Joe spotted a deer he thought was a doe 350 yards away in the bottom of a long draw. He pointed it out to Shirley who promptly realized it was a big buck just by the way it carried its head as it sneaked through the underbrush.

Shirley asked Joe if he would mind if he took it. Joe indicated he didn't want it, and Shirley touched off his first and only shot. The buck dropped stone-dead in its tracks. After field dressing it, the three men hung it for the night. The next day they boned it out and packed it a half mile back to the Jeep. It wasn't a big deer, but it was one of the toughest Shirley ever remembered eating. That winter Shirley spent

First Place
12th B&C Competition

all his spare time mounting his trophy. He borrowed his brother's tools and books and mounted it himself. It was the first and last trophy he ever mounted.

Shirley's rack scored so high it was invited to Pittsburgh, Pennsylvania, for final scoring in 1966. It scored 269-3/8 points and ranked first in the 12th North American Big Game Competition in the non-typical mule deer category.

Shirley Smith received the first place award for this fine trophy that scored 268-3/8 points at the 12th B&C Competition.

JOSEF PEPI LANGEGGER
Location: Eagle County
Year Taken: 1967
Score: 267-1/8

Before Interstate 70 started to transverse the Western Slope of Colorado, this area used to be terrific big buck country according to Pepi Langegger, and it was in 1967 that he located this fabulous non-typical buck.

The buck was located about two miles from Pepi's house in Eagle County at the end of the hunting season. A heavy snow fell as Pepi spotted does being chased by two bucks during the rut. The largest of the two bucks chased the other within 60 yards of Josef, oblivious to the hunter and danger. A single shot from his .270 Weatherby using a 175-grain bullet downed this monster. Years later, an official measurer for the Boone and Crockett Club saw the buck and encouraged him to get the buck measured and entered into the records program.

The buck ranks as the 22nd largest non-typical muley ever taken in the state and is on public display for all to enjoy at The Tyrolean, a restaurant in Vail, Colorado, owned by Pepi's son, Sigmund.

GORDON E. BLAY
Location: Gunnison County
Year Taken: 1975
Score: 264-3/8

The night before opening day of the 1975 season, Gordon Blay set up camp in the West Elk Wilderness Area for himself and the five Californians he was guiding. Gordon's party hunted that year near Crystal Creek in Gunnison County.

Around 7:30 a.m. on opening day, Gordon spotted a buck with an exceptional set of non-typical antlers and sent two hunters after it. However, both quickly returned and reported that the big buck had apparently left the area. Feeling that it was probably still somewhere in the immediate vicinity, Gordon and his two clients returned for another check.

As Gordon had suspected they quickly sighted it sneaking off through the brush with four other nice bucks. One of the others was a nice typical mule deer that Gordon was certain would make the records book. Together with the two Californians, Gordon tracked the five bucks on horseback for about two and one half miles as the deer headed north into the West Elk Wilderness Area. When the deer dropped off a steep cliff, Gordon's clients decided they would call it quits for the day. Even though they could see the big non-typical bull at the bottom of a deep canyon, they felt it was too risky to go any farther.

Gordon still wanted to get that buck and asked his clients if they would mind if he went after it by himself. They advised him that it was okay with them and began cutting their way back to camp. Gordon followed that small herd of bucks for the next five hours, catching an occasional glimpse of them on distant ridges. Finally, he got a 350-yard shot and took the chance. The buck went down on the first shot but was quickly on its feet and running. When it suddenly paused Gordon got off two more rapid shots and the buck was his.

Gordon field dressed the buck and let his horse, Mr. Doolittle, drag it back to camp. As the load was heavy Gordon reached camp 15 minutes ahead of Mr. Doolittle. When the registered quarter horse finally plodded into camp, dragging the buck, everyone in camp was surprised, as Gordon had led them to believe he never caught up with the buck. Everyone had a good laugh.

Gordon's buck was so large and outstanding that it was invited to the final awards judging of the 16th North American Big Game Awards Program held at the Denver Museum of Natural History in Denver, Colorado, in 1977. His buck scored an official 264-3/8 points and took the first-place award in the non-typical mule deer category.

**First Place
16th B&C Awards
Program**

This outstanding monster from Gunnison County was taken in 1975 by Gordon E. Blay, guide and outfitter in Montrose, after his clients declined to pursue it over extremely rough terrain. It received the first-place award in the non-typical mule deer category at the 16th North American Big Game Awards Program held at the Denver Museum of Natural History in 1977.

ARTHUR A. GOSSAGE
Location: Meeker
Year Taken: 1934
Score: 261-6/8

Arthur Gossage, uncle to famous 22-year professional baseball relief pitcher Rick "Goose" Gossage, loved to hunt in the Meeker area with his brothers Arch, Jack and Bert. Arthur's sister-in-law, Sue Gossage, wife of Jack and mother to Goose, remembered Arthur always talking about the big buck he hunted. The hunting license was tacked to the back of the original mount with the date of October 12, 1934, as the date of kill. The buck was walking along a game trail near Meeker when Arthur shot it. Arthur hunted for meat so he gave the antlers to the Meeker Hotel for display in their lobby. The mount has remained on display since the 1930s.

Arthur died in the 1940s as a young man when he fell down a flight of stairs and hit his head on a marble floor in a Colorado Springs building. The rack was scored by Boone and Crockett Club official measurer Roger Selner when he visited the Meeker Hotel in 1996 to measure all of the trophies in the lobby during his World Record Elk Tour. Shoe's Taxidermy of Deer Lodge, Montana, remounted the head and antlers in 1999, so the mount is on display again in the Meeker Hotel lobby in its full glory along with the framed original hunting license. The score sheet has never been entered into the Boone and Crockett Club so the rack does not have a rank.

Arthur Gossage, far right with arms crossed, stands beside a large buck in the 1930s on a hunting trip with his brothers and a friend. Left to right are Gabe Brock, Arch Gossage, Jack "Jic" Gossage, Burt Gossage, and Arthur Gossage. This may be a photograph of the hunt on which Arthur took his trophy buck.

RACHEL PALMER
Location: Rio Blanco County
Year Taken: 1970
Score: 257-5/8

Rachel Palmer never thought of entering her outstanding non-typical mule deer in the all-time records-keeping program of the Boone and Crockett Club until 20 years after taking this magnificent buck, but she's glad she did. In fact, she suspects that her son and daughter-in-law, Doug and Susan, are more excited about the B&C acceptance than her.

She knew this was a monster from the moment she saw it but locating meat for the family was the motivation for hunting, not the rack. The hunt began and ended on the clear, cold day of October 20, 1970, in Rio Blanco County. As usual, three or four in her hunting group saddled up to hunt and drive the Breaks, a familiar hunting area, for deer while others took the Jeep to different areas of the Breaks. Because Rachel wasn't feeling well that day, she decided to ride in the Jeep with her young sons and a cousin rather than riding horseback as she had done for years. She passed the first crossing on the property and drove to a second where she hiked up a hill for a good view and a chance to sit.

A half hour after Rachel sat down to rest was when some of her hunting party on horseback fired their rifles and soon she saw a nice buck slip out of the brush 300 yards from her. She said to herself, "The drivers were doing their job so I'd best do mine." She raised her .270 and fired a single shot that immediately dropped the buck.

Rachel sat for a moment and dragged herself up to walk toward the buck. She was halfway to the buck when she saw the riders coming toward it, so she yelled for them to go to the buck. Rachel felt so poorly that she stopped and sat down again. Rachel's brother was the first to reach the buck and yelled to her that it was the biggest buck he had ever seen. Her first reaction was to think her brother was kidding her, so she didn't take his comment seriously until she saw the buck for herself and then she was appropriately impressed.

Years passed before the rack was measured but it was the persistence of Doug and Susan that the job was done and on March 5, 1990, almost 20 years from the date of the hunt. Doug and Susan enjoy seeing the buck each day since the mount hangs in their house, but their mother's memories will stay with her a lifetime.

Photograph courtesy of Rachel Palmer

RICHARD A. GORDEN
Location: Routt County
Year Taken: 1966
Score: 255

Richard Gorden had been hunting elk that cold, sunny day in October 1966, when he downed his Boone and Crockett buck. Fortunately for Richard, Colorado had a combination deer and elk season that year, and he still had an unfilled deer tag when he saw his buck.

Seven men hunted with Richard that year in the Beaver Flat Top area south of Hayden. The men had been camping and hunting on the Flat Tops for a week. The ground was covered with four to five inches of snow and the days were clear and cold. The land was relatively flat, and the canyons filled with aspen and Douglas fir were common.

The day Richard shot his record buck he had been hunting a deep hole with many side canyons. While on foot, he spotted a spike bull elk and began to stalk it. After several minutes the elk eluded Richard, and he sat down to rest. His resting spot conveniently overlooked several draws. When he heard shots to the east he looked in that direction.

There, standing 300 to 400 yards away was what Richard thought was a bull elk. Carefully, Richard edged closer for a shot. At 100 to 150 yards away he realized his elk was a huge buck. Richard remained motionless while the buck worked its way down the opposite ridge. When it was within 50 to 75 yards, Richard raised his .30-06 to his shoulder and downed the massive animal with one shot.

Richard Gorden stands beside his B&C buck in 1982, 16 years after he downed it from less than 100 yards. He thought the buck was an elk at first because it was so large.

Richard took over an hour to field dress and cape his buck. He immediately recognized his buck was a trophy and decided to have it mounted. Later his cousin Frank Major helped him pack out the venison. At a processing plant, where the meat was later cut and wrapped, the four skinned quarters officially weighed 287 pounds.

Richard had no thoughts of the Boone and Crockett Club until he took the cape and antlers to Jonas Brothers Taxidermy of Denver. Their official measurer scored his antlers after the required 60-day drying period and the rack made the records book with a score of 255 points.

GEORGE LAPPIN
Location: Clear Creek County
Year Taken: 1947
Score: 253-3/8
Owner: Doug Grubbe

None of the details of the hunt for this trophy are known as George Lappin suffered a fatal heart attack on November 5, 1953, while on another hunting trip near Craig. George was 69 at the time of his death.

Marjorie Perry, George's niece, stated in a letter dated May 12, 1981, that "George Lappin was born and raised in a time when hunting was an important way of life as it provided meat for the table. He was the seventh in a family of 12 children.

"He hunted up to the time of his death. He suffered a fatal heart attack while he and his party were breaking camp and starting home. He was taken to a hospital in Craig, Colorado, where he died two hours later."

George entered his buck in the *Rocky Mountain News-Max Cook Sporting Goods Company Big Game Contest* in 1947 and won the first-place award, which was a brand new Chevrolet automobile.

George's non-typical buck scores 253-3/8 points in Boone and Crockett Club's all-time records book.

George Lappin holds his 23-point Clear Creek County buck in 1947 shortly after he hunted it. The buck's score won for George a new Chevrolet automobile as the first-place winner in the Rocky Mountain News-Max Cook Sporting Goods *Contest. The buck scored 253-3/8 points.*

JOHN W. STOCKEMER
Location: Grand Mesa
Year Taken: 1969
Score: 252-1/8

John Stockemer didn't have lots of time to hunt so when he was on leave from the U.S. Navy in 1969, he decided to scout the Grand Mesa outside Delta, Colorado, with two friends.

John hunted down through a ranch that was just below Forest Service land when he heard deer coming along a fence line where John sat. The first buck jumped the fence and was probably a four pointer but the second buck was massive so John fired as it jumped the fence from a distance of 100 yards using his .30-06 Remington. He didn't realize the buck's size until he got up to it and stared at all the points. Two hunters from California came up after hearing the shot and thought the buck was an elk. They even commented that they didn't realize it was elk season.

John's friends were down another ridge when the shot was fired and met him at the bottom of Baker Ridge Loop. Together they returned to the buck and dragged it down the hill to field dress it. The estimated field-dressed weight was 420 pounds. John stayed with his Uncle Paul and hung the carcass without the head and antlers in the garage, so when Paul returned from hunting Pilot Mountain he thought the buck was an elk. He said to John, "Hey, what are you doing shooting an elk. You know this isn't elk season." John explained that it was a deer, and Paul was impressed.

The paperwork to submit his trophy for consideration in the Boone and Crockett Club's records-keeping program was not sent while John was in the Navy, including four tours of duty in Vietnam, so another 30 years passed before the trophy was officially recognized.

John has hunted since he was 14 years old but this is the largest buck he's ever taken and he expects this will be the largest buck he'll ever take in his life. This wasn't a bad buck to take on leave from the Navy.

John's muley was accepted into the Boone and Crockett Club's 24th North American Big Game Awards Program (1998-2000).

RICHARD G. LUNDOCK
Location: Eagle County
Year Taken: 1945
Score: 252

Seeing how close he can get to a herd of deer or elk without being noticed has always been a greater thrill for Richard Lundock than filling his tag. His primary objective when hunting is to enjoy the wildlife. He frequently sits there watching game and letting it walk off without firing a shot. He also hunts as much of the season as possible. Usually he passes up nice deer early in the season just so he can hunt the entire season.

Towards the end of the 1945 season, Richard hunted on Castle Peak north of Wolcott. He had hunted there on two or three previous occasions with his father and knew the area well. The weather towards the end of the season that year was wet and cold. Richard had hunted alone three to four days and passed up several bucks before he took his Boone and Crockett trophy. That morning he started early by working his way up one of the many draws around Castle Peak. The north and south sides of the draw were covered with aspens and pine, respectively, while the bottom was lined with isolated willow patches.

While working his way through the willows, Richard sensed movement above him. As he stepped out of the willows to get a better look, he spotted his trophy quartering away from him and about ready to step into timber. Immediately he realized that it was the buck he had waited for all season and threw his .30-30 Winchester, Model 1894, to his shoulder and sighted it right behind the buck's shoulder. The single shot stopped it in its tracks.

Richard had hiked a long way into the area where his buck was taken, so getting it out was no easy task. After removing the head and hide Richard cut the carcass in half. He spent the rest of that day and a half of the next sliding it back to the vehicle on the snow. Since Richard never hunted for trophies, he never considered having the antlers officially measured for the Boone and Crockett Club's records program until 1979 when a friend suggested the rack might make "The Book."

And, make the records book it did. With a total score of 252 points, Richard's non-typical mule deer made it with points to spare even after the 34 years of drying.

Photograph courtesy of Colorado's Biggest Bucks and Bulls archives

Horses pull a wagon load of deer and elk as they climb a hill going up Williams Fork. E.C. Peabody is the source of this photograph.

After hanging the meat in 1885, a gathering of big-game hunters stop for a photograph. Sitting, left to right, are Cooke Rhea, Hank Brown, Ed Gould, Oscar Sodagreen and Tobe Miller. Standing, left to right, are Bob Coe, Andy Boyd, Luke Wheeler, Charlie Miller, Billy Brown and Johnny Lord. Mrs. George J. Bailey was the source of this photograph.

JOHN M. RINGLER
Location: Gunnison County
Year Taken: 1956
Score: 251-5/8

On October 25, 1956, John Ringler was hiking around the north side of Flat Top Mountain looking for mule deer. It was around 9 o'clock in the morning on a slightly overcast day.

John knew there were large bucks in the area as he had downed a big one the year before in the same area. He was picking his way through a slide rock area and around aspen trees when he heard game coming through the slide rock higher up the mountain. From the sound of the running hooves, he was sure it was a herd of elk. Over the top of the hill came two huge bucks, instead of elk, running full speed in John's direction. The largest one was leading. Being young and relatively inexperienced, John developed a grand case of buck fever, especially after seeing the size of both specimens and the direction they were intending to go.

John aimed his .30-30 Winchester, Model 64, at the larger of the two and fired four times. Somehow all four shots missed, so John turned his attention to the second buck that made the fatal mistake of pausing for an instant to look over its shoulder. With one round remaining, John knew he had to make it count. His bullet was well-placed, and the buck tumbled to the ground.

Just to make sure he had not wounded the first buck, John tracked it 300 to 400 yards. He never located a blood trail, so he knew he had been shooting in the air. With the help of some friends, and a couple of packhorses, he was finally able to get the meat off the mountain and back to the Jeep. When the buck was dressed out it tipped the scales at 300 pounds. This fine non-typical mule deer was accepted into the Boone and Crockett Club's records archives in 1977 with a score of 251-5/8 points.

Photograph courtesy of John M. Ringler

ANTHONY MORABITO
Location: Garfield County
Year Taken: 1965
Score: 251-5/8

When Californian Tony Morabito took his Colorado dream buck in 1965 he had been hunting for 30 years. He had hunted in Colorado for only 11 of those years.

The first couple of years Tony hunted in Colorado he took nice deer, especially by California standards. He was satisfied with the deer all right but was disappointed to end his hunt on opening day both years. After all, he had come from California to hunt and still had the entire season ahead of him. It was all over too fast.

To get more satisfaction out of deer hunting Tony accepted the challenge of going after big bucks. In an effort to determine a good area for trophy bucks, he contacted the then State Game Manager Gilbert N. Hunter for assistance. To Tony's disappointment, Gilbert informed him that "trophy bucks are where you find them and no place in particular."

In 1965 Tony was accompanied by his brothers Joe and Dean and Colorado rancher Dale Burke. The latter was a good friend Tony had made while hunting in Colorado in 1956 and had hunted with ever since. According to Tony, 1965 was the toughest year they had ever encountered for hunting in Colorado. The weather was poor and the deer scarce.

On the day Tony took his records-book buck he was with Joe and Dale. They had hunted all morning and had seen only one doe. Around 1:30 p.m. they regrouped, had lunch, and discussed strategies for the afternoon hunt. Unanimously they agreed to try an area on Roan Creek that Dale knew well. Upon their arrival at the new hunting area, everyone elected to go in different directions. While Dale went one way Tony worked his way through a stand of aspen towards a ridge top along Roan Creek. Joe stayed below in case anything tried to sneak out below either of the other two hunters. The climb was steep and Tony had to stop periodically to check his progress and to take a breather. Each time he stopped he wondered why he was punishing himself so much. Not only was he sweating profusely from the steep climb, but also he was scratched and full of thorns from the wild berry bushes. At one point he stopped to check his progress on the edge of a 40-foot wide clearing. It was the only opening in the aspen, spruce, and brush-covered hillside that he had encountered during his entire climb. After passing through it, he paused again for that one last look back over his shoulder.

Instantly he spotted a set of monstrous antlers about to enter the clearing he had been in only moments before. For only an instant he thought it was an elk. He quickly threw his .270 Weatherby to his shoulder and fired as the old buck entered the opening. His single shot hit the massive buck in the neck bringing it down instantly. Tony couldn't believe he had killed anything so enormous even though he had been after one like it for years. Its heavy beans measured 42 inches wide and carried 24 points that projected in all directions. The antlers have a final score of 251-5/8 points.

Photograph courtesy of Anthony Morabito

ED BAAL
Location: Mesa County
Year Taken: 1988
Score: 248-3/8

The buck never knew what hit him when Ed Baal sat down to rest and enjoy a sandwich on October 28, 1988.

As Ed took a lunch break while hunting about one mile east of Powder Horn and Highway 65, he saw a massive buck out of the corner of his eye. He sat on a log smoking a cigarette in heavy down timber. A single shot downed the buck for good, without it ever knowing what hit him. Officials from the Colorado Division of Wildlife estimated its age to be 12 years. Most of its teeth were gone and the meat was not very appetizing, Ed remembered. This certainly was a sandwich Ed will always remember.

FRED JARDINE
Location: Hinsdale County
Year Taken: 1966
Score: 247-5/8

The thermometer hovered at minus 10 degrees Fahrenheit and one foot of snow blanketed the ground when Fred Jardine and his party of eight fellow Coloradans went after deer and elk in 1966. After several days of hard hunting, the party had taken several elk and one mule deer buck. The best trophy of them all was Fred's Boone and Crockett non-typical muley.

The nine hunters pitched camp in the Robber's Roost area near the Cannibal Plateau. Horses were used to pack in during the day. Fred had hunted the area for 15 years and knew it like the back of his hand. About 2:30 p.m. on October 20 Fred was hunting on horseback above timberline when he glanced back over his shoulder and saw a tremendous buck slipping along the edge of the timber. Fred eased off his horse and squeezed off one round at the buck's neck with his .250-3000 Savage. The buck whirled and traveled only 25 yards before collapsing.

The buck scored 247-5/8 points in the Boone and Crockett Club records book.

Fred Jardine holds his B&C buck soon after he took it in Hinsdale County.

THOMAS M. BOST
Location: Montrose County
Year Taken: 1967
Score: 247

Prior to 1967, Tom Bost had never hunted big game. As a resident of Addison, Illinois, he had plenty of opportunities to hunt small game, but he only dreamed of deer hunting in Colorado. He eagerly accepted the invitation to join his friend George Dempsey of Colorado Springs for the 1967 Colorado deer season.

Opening day of the big-game season found Tom, George and two other hunting companions, Chuck Hart and Louis Beebe, working the hills around the Black Canyon of the Gunnison for trophy deer. A two-hour early morning drive netted only failure for Tom and the rest of his party. Tom had a number of opportunities to take deer, but George cautioned him to be selective. After all, they had the entire week ahead of them.

After their first unsuccessful attempt at driving some of the draws, the men decided to work their way across one of the sagebrush flats in the vicinity of Poison Springs Hill. While working their way around a small cluster of oaks, the party kicked out a doe and fawn. Tom commented, "It sure is nice being close to deer like that."

On that note, George and the rest of the party decided to fan out. When George was in place 60 yards to Tom's left, he signaled and the group moved forward. Tom had moved only 20 yards when a deer exploded from the brush about 60 to 70 yards away, moving from Tom's left to his right. Tom realized immediately that it was a buck with "quite a bit of antler."

Tom Bost holds his 1967 Silver Bullet Award from the National Rifle Association as he stands beside his B&C non-typical muley that scores 247 points

With little time to react, Tom focused his scope on an opening in the brush. As the deer passed through the cross hairs, he fired. At the crack of the rifle the buck disappeared into the brush and Tom yelled, "I think I got him! I think I got him!" With that George and the rest of the party came running. After a brief search Tom located the buck 15 yards from the opening.

While Tom began field dressing his trophy, the rest of the boys congratulated him and started telling him about the Boone and Crockett Club. Tom had never heard of it before. The general consensus of the group was that Tom's buck would have probably made the book if it had just been "a little bit bigger." However, the longer the group looked at it, the bigger the buck seemed to get.

As it turned out the rack scored 247 points, well above the Boone and Crockett Club's minimum score of 225 in effect in 1967 for non-typical mule deer and well above the minimum score of 230 in effect in 2001. Tom's rack took first place in the non-typical mule deer category in the National Rifle Association's 1967 Silver Bullet Awards Program.

Tom was so impressed with the big-game hunting opportunities in Colorado that he packed up his family and moved to Colorado from Illinois two months after the close of the 1967 deer season. Besides, Tom felt that it would be cheaper in the long run to move to Colorado rather than making the 18-hour, 2,000-mile trip each hunting season.

WILLIAM M. NICKELS
Location: Eagle County
Year Taken: 1963
Score: 246-6/8

William Nickels hunted the 1963 post season with seven others, including his wife Barbara, near Castle Peak in Eagle County. That post-season hunt at Thanksgiving proved to be the ideal setting for William to down his Boone and Crockett buck.

Ten to 14 inches of snow had fallen just before the hunters set out at daylight. They hunted high that year figuring the numerous hunters below them would spook the game uphill. As the sun rose deer were sighted in great numbers in all directions. Immediately, Barbara and another companion filled their first tag with one deer each.

While helping to field dress his wife's deer, William spotted another deer with an extremely massive non-typical rack when it calmly stepped out of the timber approximately 300 yards away. Though William had not intended to shoot another deer after his wife got hers, he instantly flopped on his belly in the snow and quickly dispatched the buck with a single round.

At 9 a.m. that morning, William and his hunting partners regrouped back at the Jeeps for a cut of hot coffee. All told the seven hunters had already collected nine deer. As the limit was two each that year, they were still well within their legal limit. William's buck had an average-sized body, but the rack was outstanding. William remembers the meat was extremely tender and made good eating that winter. With four children, William was happy to supplement his grocery list with venison.

After the required drying time the rack was officially measured for the Boone and Crockett Club and made the book with a score of 246-6/8 points.

William Nickels stands beside his B&C buck that scores 246-6/8 points.

JAMES A. COOK
Location: Rio Blanco County
Year Taken: 1963
Score: 246-6/8

Jim Cook always carries a rifle in his truck so when he saw this outstanding non-typical buck on public land, Jim was prepared.

The year was 1963 and Jim was building fence for surrounding ranches in the Meeker area when he noticed a huge buck with a herd of does. Jim slid from his truck and steadied his rifle for a single shot from his .270 in Smith Gulch using 150-grain bullets. The lung shot immediately downed the buck. He stored the buck's antlers on his property for many years and even went to the trouble of having the buck measured but was told it wasn't big enough so he just saved the rack.

In 1999 Jim finally got the buck officially scored and this time the buck made "The Book."

CHARLES W. THORNBERG
Location: Eagle County
Year Taken: 1949
Score: 246-2/8

Each hunting season, Charles Thornberg and his cousins, Hugh and Jim Thomas, traveled from their homes in Denver to Eagle County for the annual deer-hunting season. Charles even remembered one season when he left high school for a month. Charles, who was 20 years old at the time, was with Jim and Hugh when he took the biggest buck of his life in 1949. This is what happened.

The young men were given permission to pass through a hereford ranch on State Ridge to the national forest where the young men camped and hunted. On an October morning just as the sun rose over the horizon the men hiked several miles from camp to a ridge overlooking an aspen-filled valley where they spotted a large herd of 150 does and bucks. One of the bucks outsized the rest of them by considerable proportions, so Charles took careful aim with his .300 Weatherby and fired. Unfortunately for Charles, the bullet whizzed over the back of the buck and the buck bolted away from him. Charles had recently inherited the rifle from a friend so he was unfamiliar with its capabilities. As the buck turned away from him, Charles fired a second time and hit the buck but the buck continued. Jim and Charles tracked the buck across the valley and up the other side in quick enough time to locate the buck. Charles finished the job with a third shot to the buck's neck.

Jim and Charles continued to fill their tags and ended up with two bucks each that year since that was the limit but Charles readily admits this was the largest buck taken that year. In the year 2000, Charles still enjoys hunting and still owns that same .300 Weatherby. His memories of hunts with his cousins remain as highlights of his life and this hunt remains as one of the grandest. "I was very blessed that year by being allowed to harvest two large deer," Charles recalled.

Charles Thornberg (right) crouches behind his newly harvested non-typical mule deer buck in 1949. Next to him is his hunting partner and Charles' cousin, Jim Thomas, who holds Charles rifle. The limit that year was two bucks per license and both young men filled their tags. The two bucks each man took are shown in this photograph.

Charles Thornberg holds his .300 Weatherby rifle he used in 1949 that downed his B&C buck, seen behind him in his living room in Colorado. The buck scores 246-2/8 points.

JOSEPH J. PITCHERELLA
Location: Mesa County
Year Taken: 1972
Score: 246-1/8

For years Joseph Pitcherella, a native Pennsylvanian, dreamed of a guided big-game hunt in Colorado. Finally in 1972 he and Paul Dombelski got their opportunity and signed on with the late Jerry Byrum. Accompanying Joe and Paul on their Colorado deer hunt were five other hunters from Michigan and New York.

On opening morning Joe's party started the day by driving isolated aspen stands. The hunters took turns driving or sitting on a stand. On the first drive, Joe and Paul were the drivers. As one might expect, none of the drivers got a deer on the first drive. However, several of the hunters on stands took deer and reported seeing some elk pushed out of the brush. Skeptical of their elk reports, Joe rather believed they had seen big deer. Jerry had informed him that there were no elk at that elevation at that time of year.

For the second drive of the day, Jerry posted Joe on a large boulder overlooking a deep draw. Shortly after he had positioned himself, a small buck came into view. While following its movements into the bottom of the draw, Joe caught a glimpse of another set of antlers coming right at him about 500 yards away. The massive buck continued deeper into the draw. It went out of sight momentarily and reappeared 375 yards away, cutting across a narrow talus slope. As Joe set his cross hairs on the buck's chest, another big buck stepped out of the brush a few paces behind the first. At that point Joe was confronted with a snap decision. If he didn't shoot quickly both bucks would soon be across the opening and out of sight.

Pennsylvanian Joseph Pitcherella holds the buck he collected on the day he collected it, which was October 14, 1972. The 22-point buck scores 246-1/8 points.

Joe decided the second one was the larger of the two and tried for it. When he fired, his buck froze momentarily while the other bolted for cover. Before he could chamber another round, his buck sauntered off into the brush, favoring its front shoulder. Adhering to Jerry's advice Joe held his stand and waited for help. Shortly thereafter, Jerry and Paul came out of the brush on the same side of the hill as Joe's buck. Through a series of hand signals and shouts, Joe informed them that he had a deer and directed them to it. While Jerry and Paul searched for his buck, Joe worked his way across the draw. When he got within earshot of his guide and Paul, he could hear them talking very excitedly.

As Joe drew closer, Jerry shouted, "I thought you came out here for a big buck."

Puzzled, Joe answered, "I did! Why?"

Jerry queried, "Well, why then did you shoot a doe?"

At that, Joe started to have second thoughts. He couldn't believe he had imagined the big rack, but he figured it was possible he could have hit a deer other than the one he had shot. When he finally caught up with his guide and Paul, Jerry pointed out his deer. There, lying on its side, was the biggest buck Joe had ever seen. Joe's non-typical mule deer scored 246-1/8 points.

CHARLES W. GROVE
Location: Rio Blanco County
Year Taken: 1934
Score: 245-5/8
Owner: Dorothy Shults

This trophy was collected in 1934 by Dorothy Shults' father, the late Charles W. Grove of Meeker. Dorothy, the current owner of this fine trophy, recounted the history of this buck.

On the first day of the 1934 season, Charles saddled his horse and packed it alone into the LO 7 Hill area, eight miles south of Meeker. Except for a few vittles and a coffeepot, he traveled lightly. After a long, cold day in the saddle and a warm meal of beans, boiled spuds and coffee, Charles crawled into the cold bed of a deserted cabin for the night.

The second day Charles was up and hunting early. He believed in sitting on a deer crossing and waiting for the deer to come to him. This he did, and late that day a beautiful buck came tripping through the brush in hot pursuit of two does. Charles heard them coming and waited until they got closer. He watched them for some time unnoticed and at an appropriate moment raised his trusty .30-06 Enfield with iron sights and shot the buck. It never knew what hit it.

Then the work began. After field dressing the buck, Charles tried to load it onto the horse, but it could not stand up under the weight. Thus, he quartered the buck and packed it back to the cabin in several trips. That evening he returned home and retired for the night after a hot supper.

The next morning Charles returned to the deserted cabin in his old Buick and packed the buck back to town. After the meat aged, he cut it up and Dorothy and her mother canned it. Charles caped out the scalp and put it in a brine to pickle for mounting. Using a book printed in 1905 titled, *Practical Taxidermy*, Charles mounted his own trophy. As an amateur he really didn't do a bad job considering he had to prepare his form from a couple of two by fours, excelsior and some plaster of Paris. Dorothy has thought of having the head remounted by an expert but has decided to leave it as her dear father mounted it. It was created by his own hands and means much to her.

Charles Grove's trophy was measured in 1978, and even after 44 years of drying, it still scored 245-5/8 points.

WALTER A. LARSEN
Location: Saguache County
Year Taken: 1962
Score: 245-3/8
Owner: Randy Clark

In 1962, Paul Hahn was one of the 30 fortunate Colorado hunters to draw a sheep permit for the Collegiate Range. Not wishing to risk hunting alone in the high country, Paul invited his longtime friend and world-renowned sheep hunter, Walter A. Larsen, to accompany him. Walt eagerly accepted with the intention of hunting deer at the same time during the early season, high-country trophy deer hunt.

The day before the season opened in mid-August, the pair backpacked into the high country on Antero Peak west of Bonanza to spend a few days with the sheep. They moved camp daily to follow the sheep but saw no legal rams in the _-curl or better class.

About the third or fourth day of the hunt, the two men got up early and set out to try a different area. Glancing down into a canyon about 1-1/2 miles away Walt spotted four nice bucks. One had an exceptionally board set of heavy-beamed antlers. Since the deer were so far away and, because they were really after sheep, Walt noted the location in his mind and forgot them for the time being. Later that evening the two hunters circled by the same spot. As luck would have it, Walt jumped the four bucks out of the warped, low-lying bushes characteristic of timberline. As they cut across a small opening in the brush in single file,

Walt felled the largest one bringing up the rear. With nightfall rapidly approaching, Walt caped out the head and packed it back to camp. The next day he and Paul returned to pack out the rest of the animal.

Although the buck seemed to be in its prime, the teeth were well-worn, indicating a relatively old buck. With a spread of 40 inches, Walt's trophy made the records book with a final score of 245-3/8 points.

On August 19, 1962, Walt Larsen (right) collected this impressive 10x7 non-typical mule deer buck during an early season, high country hunt on Antero Peak in the Collegiate Range. Shown here is the day that B&C official measurer Joe Jonas, Jr. (left) measures the buck. The buck has a right main beam length of 28-2/8 inches and a left beam of 24 inches. Its inside spread is 31-6/8 inches.

An extra wide buck is held by Ed Miles, right, who stands beside his hunting buddy Bill Law, a Meeker gunsmith, who also holds a respectable buck in their all-terrain vehicle. The biggest of the two bucks was killed about four miles from Meeker on Gore Pass in 1920. This rare photograph was taken shortly after the hunt occurred.

A window exhibit of deer mounts at Lathrop Hardware Store displays the taxidermy skills of Herbit Williams in 1925. The photograph was taken by Mr. Orr.

BOB RAMBO
Location: Eagle County
Year Taken: 1963
Score: 244-7/8

**Third Place
12th B&C Competition**

Good luck and a year of planning spelled success for Californian Bob Rambo in 1963. Two work buddies, Hall Christiansen and Walt Boyle, and Bob's brother John accompanied him on that trip.

Arriving in Walden after a better than 24-hour drive from California, Bob and his companions set up camp outside town in preparation for opening day of the late season. After scouting the area, everyone agreed that the area lacked suitable game but decided to try it anyway. So, after an unsuccessful opening day morning, the men decided to move camp to another late season area 20 miles north of Eagle. As they prepared to leave the first camp, news of President Kennedy's assassination reached them, and they considered returning home. Though they were disheartened, they knew there was nothing they could do and elected to continue their trip.

Late in the afternoon the next day, they arrived in Burns and spent $20 to sleep in a $10 cabin. It was well worth it as far as they were concerned, as a night's rest in a bed felt good to the four weary travelers. That Sunday the men arrived at their new hunting area in time to see everyone leaving at the close of the weekend. It seemed everyone was leaving for work the next day, and they had the entire area to themselves. On Monday morning, the group was up by 4:30 a.m. and ready for action. Quickly, Hal downed a nice four-pointer. He and Bob almost received frostbite while field dressing the buck, as the temperature was a nippy 5 degrees Fahrenheit. The men warmed up with coffee and immediately headed out for another attempt. The limit that year during the postseason was two deer each. John and Walt hunted north from camp, and Hal and Bob went south.

Early in the afternoon Hal and Bob spotted two gigantic bucks crossing a ridge. Even from 1,000 yards the men could clearly see large racks with their binoculars. Bob tracked them and eventually downed the smaller of the two, a nice four-pointer. The following day, Hal and Bob again hunted the same area. That day deer were abundant and seemed to be in all directions at the same time. Suddenly, Bob spotted what appeared to be a brush pile 75 yards away, bounding for timber. He fired two shots but much to his disappointment it thundered into the timber. Undaunted, he tracked the fleeing buck and quickly found a blood trail. Forty yards into the timber, he found the buck dead against the base of a tree.

Unfortunately, the other hunters in Bob's party had also shot at the same deer. So, the only fair thing to do was to draw straws. Bob drew the winning straw and had his trophy. Bob's non-typical rack scored 244-7/8 points at the Boone and Crockett Clubs' 12th North American Big Game Competition held in Pittsburgh, Pennsylvania, in 1966.

TOM HUNDLEY
Location: Mesa County
Year Taken: 1986
Score: 244-2/8

Alaska Master Guide Tom Hundley thinks Colorado is one of the best places to hunt. He has hunted in the state five times, beginning in 1976. Several of his trips were hosted by Craig Tigert and his uncle Kent Brayden. Tom became good friends with Craig while guiding him on four successful Dall's sheep hunts in Alaska over a period of 12 years.

Tom joined Craig for a hunt on the Grand Mesa National Forest in 1986. Tom's plan was to hunt the last season in hopes of catching the rut and taking a trophy animal. He had passed up lesser bucks over the years, only taking one four-pointer on the first hunt. Though empty-handed on the other hunts, Tom considered them well worthwhile as he was surrounded by the red rim rock and sagebrush country of Western Colorado each time.

Tom often said a little prayer in the field: "Dear Lord, let me see a mature, monster buck. You don't have to let me kill it. Just seeing one in this magnificent setting will be enough."

On November 6, 1986, Tom still-hunted across a small plateau that was densely wooded with pinon pine and cedar. Near the north end of the plateau, Tom jumped three deer at close range and caught a flash of antler through the brush as the deer scrambled for cover and bounded downhill into the rugged dry wash that flanked the hilltop.

Easing to the edge of the ravine, Tom observed a doe and two bucks moving downhill. One of the bucks carried a monster set of antlers. Tom watched a moment as the big buck trailed his companions out of sight into the jumbled landscape below his perch.

"Thank you, Lord. Thank you. At least I got to see one," Tom whispered to himself.

Seconds later, the smaller buck raced back uphill into view, pursued by the rutting larger buck. Tom knelt with his cross hairs posed on a patch of sunlight in a small clearing that was approximately 350 yards away. The young buck wove through the sunlit clearing, and adrenalin flooded through Tom's veins in anticipation of the larger buck's appearance. The big-antlered buck lunged into Tom's cross hairs, and the buck folded with one shot from his .308 Ruger Ultra Light. Overwhelmed by the sudden turn of events, Tom whooped like a banshee.

The symmetrical antlers, with an outside spread of just over 34 inches, sported 12 points on the right and 11 on the left. Tom hefted that massive rack and ran his hands over the spiked bases and the rough, dark-colored main beams, and he knew his dream was fulfilled.

"Dear Lord, let me see a mature, monster buck. You don't have to let me kill it. Just seeing one in this magnificent setting will be enough." This was the little prayer Alaska hunter Tom Hundley said each time he went into the field. In 1986, his prayers were answered when he downed this massive non-typical mule deer in Mesa County, Colorado.

LOUIS I. KINGSLEY
Location: Idaho Springs
Year Taken: 1981
Score: 243-4/8

Lou Kingsley was working on an I-70 highway construction project in 1981, about 25 miles west of Denver, when his supervisor, Rick Trujillo, told him about several large muleys he had spotted on a slope overlooking the construction site. Prior to hunting season the men watched the bucks on several occasions with the aid of a surveyor's transit. Of special interest were three large bucks on a slope about a half-mile away.

Elk hunting had been more important to Lou in previous years, and he even skipped deer hunting altogether some years. But, in 1981 he decided he would forget the long drive to the West Slope where he hunted elk and concentrate his hunting on the deer four miles from his home in Idaho Springs. Rugged, rough, rocky slopes with thick bunches of mountain mahogany typified Lou's hunting area.

Lou's primary ambition was to take a nice, average sized muley with his handgun, a .41 Magnum, Ruger Blackhawk with a short barrel. He had a keen interest in handgun hunting and had qualified to do so when he passed the written and shooting portions of the Colorado Division of Wildlife's handgun course in 1978.

On the morning Lou made the records book, he had hiked a quarter mile from I-70 hoping to get into position before any other hunters in the area. Ten minutes after legal shooting time Lou heard shots and shouting of other hunters above him so he hid next to a ponderosa pine. Shortly thereafter, two does trotted by heading away from the area where the shots were fired.

Louis Kingsley planned to collect an average-sized buck outside Idaho Springs, Colorado, but "settled" for a non-typical trophy that scores 243-4/8 points. Here, he holds the rack on the day B&C official measurer Paul F. Gilbert put a measuring tape to it.

As he moved onto a wide, flat, brushy area, Lou heard movement in the brush behind his left shoulder. He turned and glimpsed the top of a rack belonging to a huge buck slowly moving towards an open area ahead of him. He took up a kneeling position next to a large cedar tree and prepared himself for a shot.

The buck was 35 to 40 yards away from Lou, quartering in his direction. It momentarily paused for a second look when it noticed Lou. Lou thought the buck's massive rack looked like a tangle of driftwood, but he didn't take time to count the points. Rather, he quickly sighted his revolver on the deer's chest and squeezed the trigger before it could flee. The buck reared up and back over its left rear leg in response to the bullet's impact.

Lou sprinted after the buck as it disappeared down the hill. After traveling about 300 yards he hadn't found any sign he hit the buck and began to worry that he might lose it to other hunters. He had faith in his sight picture, but he was having second thoughts about his choice of firearm.

He started a circular search pattern in the area where he thought the buck should be. He was about to give up and search another area when he spotted the sun shining on the buck's hip and rack where it lay in the thick brush. Lou had walked within 20 to 30 yards of it earlier.

Paul F. Gilbert, an official B&C measurer from Hot Sulphur Springs, scored the rack at 243-4/8 points. It has 23 measurable points.

Louis Kingsley sits beside his outstanding mule deer buck moments after he downed it on October 24, 1981. From the smile on his face, Louis must have realized immediately that he had a trophy on his hands.

STEVE B. HUMANN
Location: Eagle County
Year Taken: 1982
Score: 240-6/8

It had been snowing heavily for several days when Steve Humann's party of five arrived at hunting camp on Friday evening north of the town of Dotsero near the Flat Tops. Joining Steve on this hunt were Larry Lang, Larry Lang, Jr. and Steve's two sons, Steve and Ray.

Steve, Jr., and Ray filled their tags on Saturday and Sunday and left Monday morning to return to their high school and college classes. On Sunday evening Larry and Steve made the decision to do some trophy hunting since their sons had filled their freezers with meat.

Snow continued falling as Steve and Larry followed the boys down the mountain to insure their safe departure. Even with four-wheel-drive and chains on all wheels, the men got stuck twice during the return trip to camp.

Monday afternoon and Tuesday morning Steve and Larry saw several average-sized bucks. The snow had stopped falling but the temperature hovered around zero. They had one more opportunity to hunt on Tuesday afternoon, November 2.

Steve was scanning a sage-filled meadow and a sage-covered hillside for any deer activity. About 200 yards up the 35-degree slope was a stand of aspen. Directly across from the aspen stand on the right was dark timber that went over the ridge. There were barely 10 minutes of shooting light left in the day when a massive mule deer buck stepped from the

aspen, hesitated a moment and broke for the dark timber. A single shot from Steve's .270 Winchester downed the buck before it made it to the other side of the clearing.

The snow was knee-deep, but Steve doesn't remember going up that hill. When Steve reached the buck he knew it was the largest deer he had ever seen in more than 25 years of hunting. The steep hill and deep snow made dragging relatively easy. The buck was so heavy that Steve and Larry could barely lift the buck up to the tailgate of Larry's Jeep Cherokee.

Taxidermist Joe Jonas, Jr., of Broomfield, Colorado mounted Steve's muley and scored it for the Boone and Crockett Club's records books. The 10x8 buck has a 39-inch outside spread and a total of 33 inches of abnormal points. It scores 240-6/8 points.

Steve B. Humann traveled to Eagle County from his home near Denver to collect this non-typical muley in 1982 using his .270 Winchester. Here, Steve holds his buck a few hours after it was taken north of the town Dotsero.

Photograph courtesy of Steve B. Humann

CULLEN D. WAGONER
Location: La Plata County
Year Taken: 1976
Score: 240-4/8

Cullen Wagoner, Gary Hardin and Harold Hansen were drawn for mule deer on the Southern Ute Indian Reservation during the 1976 hunting season. When they arrived at the reservation on December 11th, Cullen never imagined that his hunt-of-a-lifetime would culminate five hours later.

In 1976 Cullen Wagoner is shown holding his B&C non-typical buck in the field where he took it on the Southern Ute Indian Reservation. The buck scores 240-4/8 points.

Two of their friends had hunted the same area on the first week of the season and had collected two very respectable bucks in the 170- to 180-point class. They said they had seen a lot of nice bucks, which boosted the hunters' spirits and motivated them to go find their own trophies. Cullen, Gary and Harold began the hunt by driving up Sandoval Canyon as far as they could go. They then hiked to the top of a ridge and settled in near a large cedar tree that had fallen several years earlier. From their vantage point, the men could see forever. They started by glassing the closest draws first and working out from there. Cullen spotted several does about 1,300 yards out and figured bucks wouldn't be far away at that time of year. About 200 yards above them were two bucks with good antlers on both.

Harold and Cullen slipped back over the ridge and ran down to a ridge that put them to the right of the buck. They ran down the backside of the ridge and peeked over but were still about 700 yards away from them. The men decided to drop back over the ridge and run another 200 yards where they stopped. They had reached a saddle with not even a blade of grass on it for cover. The men peeked from behind a juniper bush and spotted the buck walking away. The buck Cullen wanted continued to walk slowly away from him, so Cullen used the juniper as a rest and fired a single shot from his custom made 7mm Remington Magnum. The buck dropped but jumped up and ran into a stand of scrub oak and it didn't come out.

Cullen ran down the saddle to the stand of scrub oak, stopped to catch his breath and started walking into the oak. When Cullen was 60 yards away from the buck, it jumped up again and ran down the hill. That's when Cullen saw how big the buck really was. The only thought that went through his mind at that time was, "Don't let him get away!"

The buck tried to make it up a small knoll but couldn't. It turned broadside at about 100 yards to go downhill. That's when Cullen said to himself, "That's far enough, my friend." His second shot ended his quest for a trophy buck.

As Cullen approached his buck he couldn't believe his eyes. He counted nine points on the right antler and eight on the left. The width was an impressive 34 inches. Cullen had planned for six months to savor this moment and now the moment was his. Five hours after the hunt began it ended.

The Southern Ute Indian Reservation was the location where Cullen Wagoner collected this outstanding B&C buck that scores 228 points. The buck has a greatest spread of 30-3/8 inches. The right antler main beam measures 25-3/8 inches and the left main beam measures 25-7/8 inches.

VERNON E. YOUNG
Location: Yuma County
Year Taken: 1995
Score: 240-2/8

A cornfield provided the perfect habitat for a fat and sassy buck in eastern Colorado.

Vernon Young drove his pickup a half mile down a dirt road on his ranch outside Brush in 1995 when he came upon a bedded down buck with several does. This was the first time Vernon had ever seen this buck, so when it stood up Vernon figured the snowstorm from the previous night had driven the buck into a more protected area between two circles of irrigated, unpicked corn. The buck eyed Vernon as he slowly eased from his truck, walked a few feet and fired his .243 Remington but the shells stuck in the chamber so all Vernon heard was a "click" and no "boom." The misfired rifle and Vernon's movement startled the buck so it bolted forwards about 50 yards and turned back to stare at Vernon a second time. That was its fatal error. Vernon quickly positioned himself against a fence post and waited as the buck reached a distance of about 200 yards from him in a northeasterly direction. On the second shot, the buck dropped and Vernon knew he had a big one.

Mike Trujillo, son-in-law to Vernon and his hunting companion, had scouted with Vernon throughout the season but on the day Vernon got his big one Mike told Vernon he couldn't go out with him that morning because he had to set up a check station for the Colorado Division of Wildlife along

Interstate 80. When Vernon downed his buck he called Mike and told him he had taken that little three-pointer they had seen earlier in the season. Mike became suspicious when Vernon asked him to come out to the house and measure it. Mike decided at that point to postpone going to the check station and he drove immediately to Vernon. They counted 11 points on one side and nine points on the other. Mike snapped the first pictures of the buck moments after Vernon took it and shared in his father-in-law's excitement. Mike is an official measurer for the B&C so he green-scored it close to its final score and made sure the buck was officially measured after the 60-day drying period.

The field-dressed weight was about 180 pounds, which wasn't the largest bodied buck he had ever taken, but it certainly was one of the best-eating bucks. Vernon said the meat was tender and tasty thanks in large part to alfalfa and corn from Vernon's ranch. And Vernon was darn happy that his non-typical buck liked eating his corn and alfalfa.

Vernon's outstanding non-typical mule deer was accepted into the Boone and Crockett Club's 23rd North American Big Game Awards Program (1995-1997).

Vernon Young collected this outstanding non-typical mule deer in the cornfields of his ranch in eastern Colorado in 1995 less than a mile from his home. The buck scores 240-2/8 points.

ED PETERS, JR.
Location: Garfield County
Year Taken: 1962
Score: 240

In December 1960 Ed Peters and his brother hunted deer in the hills above their home ranch near Grand Valley. The area they hunted that year was a three-deer area. If you bought two tags, you got a third one free. Ed was specifically after forked-horn bucks to provide venison for their family.

Ed and his brother saddled up and headed out early that eventful day. They had traveled about five miles above the ranch when they decided to hunt some isolated pockets of spruce. Ed set his brother on a stand and began working one of those pockets hoping to drive deer past his brother. Immediately, Ed stumbled onto a herd of approximately 300 does with a single buck. The entire hillside was covered with doe deer. There were none of the usual spikes, forked-horns or three-pointers usually associated with such a large herd of deer, just one buck with an extremely unusual set of non-typical antlers. It was standing in the middle of the herd about 100 yards away.

Ed laid the open sights of his .30-30 Winchester on the buck's chest and fired. He was so nervous the first two shots he fired missed the deer completely. In fact, he wasn't sure he had even hit the hillside on which the deer stood. His next two shots brought it down for good.

Not only had Ed taken a trophy with an exceptional set of antlers, but he also had taken one with plenty of venison steaks for his family. Though they never weighed the big buck, the two hunters nearly strained themselves getting it onto one of the horses. Even the horse thought it was too heavy. It lay down twice on the trail back home. It never did that for some of the spiked bull elk it had carried for Ed.

Ed's exceptional rack with 22 measurable points scored 240 points.

A photograph of Ed Peters in 1962 at age 17 shows him holding his outstanding non-typical mule deer buck that he collected near Grand Valley in Garfield County. Ed's buck scores 240 in the B&C all-time records book.

Photograph courtesy of Colorado's Biggest Bucks and Bulls archives

DAVID BLAKE
Location: La Plata County
Year Taken: 1977
Score: 239-6/8

David Blake arrived in Durango two to three days before Colorado's combined deer and elk season in November 1977 to hunt an area called Carbonate Basin at the foot of Miller Mountain. He had tags for both deer and elk. It snowed the night before the season opened setting the stage for something good to happen.

David rose at 4 a.m. on opening morning and hiked down into Carbonate basin after downing breakfast. He plunked himself down beside a pile of rocks at the bottom and scanned a stand of evergreens that extended from the bottom of the basin to within 100 yards of the top. While he sat there several cow elk came over the top of the basin and dropped into the trees about 75 yards above him.

While David watched the cows travel north to a saddle at the top of the basin he heard branches breaking above him where the cows had first appeared. His first thought was, "bull elk!" David watched, expecting a bull to step from the dark timber at any moment. When nothing happened for an hour, he decided to move to where the cows had gone over the saddle. He traveled nearly a mile north and went around the west side of Miller Mountain. He reached the top of Miller Mountain and dropped down its backside to the top of the basin where he had first seen the cows.

David Blake holds his B&C buck in 1996.

David with his caped-out buck a short time after he hunted it in November 1977. David waited almost 25 years to have the trophy officially measured, but when it was it easily made the B&C.

David located a 40- to 50-pound rock that was on the edge of the timber and worked it loose with his feet. He deliberately rolled it down the slope into the dark timber hoping to make lots of noise. He waited expectantly for something to spook from the brush. Sure enough, out jumped the biggest buck David had ever seen so he fired five times using his .270 Winchester, pre 64, Model 70. The first four bullets kicked up snow behind and over the deer but the fifth bullet didn't kick up snow as the buck sprinted across the basin into the dark timber on the other side. He thought he might have hit it with his last shot.

David was sick. He was 27 years old and had just blown a chance at the biggest buck he had ever seen. He followed the tracks in the snow and soon realized his fifth shot had also missed. The buck had crossed the basin and started up another small mountain. When David reached the peak and looked down the buck stepped out into a small park about 300 yards away. David dropped to the snow, steadied himself, and squeezed off another round at the buck's shoulder. This time David made good on his second chance and the buck immediately dropped. This was the greatest moment of David's life.

David admired his Colorado buck for almost 25 years before he entered it in the B&C's records-keeping program.

FRED H. PALMER
Location: Summit County
Year Taken: 1959
Score: 239-1/8

Fred Palmer's recollections of his 1959 hunt in 2001 is as clear now as it was the day he collected his Boone and Crockett buck.

In October 1959, Fred hunted on property that was two miles east of his family's ranch about 25 miles south of Kremmling in the heart of mule deer country. His grandfather had homesteaded to this area of Colorado in 1895, so Fred was born and raised in that area. Fred was hunting with a friend when they spotted two nice bucks traveling over a ridge. The snow was piled so high that the deer couldn't jump over the snow so they ran back toward the men. When the bucks were within 30 feet of Fred, he fired his .364 Winchester Model 7 that was rechambered to a .300 Weatherby Magnum. The buck dropped immediately and his friend took the other one. Fred remembered both bucks had big bodies but only his buck had the nice rack.

Years after Boone and Crockett Club Official Measurer Paul Gilbert measured the buck, Fred entered it in the records-keeping program and it was accepted into the 23rd B&C North American Big Game Awards Program in 1997, so almost 40 years passed before the buck was officially recognized. Even with 40 years of drying the buck still made the all-time records book with nine points to spare.

Fred admits that this buck was the largest set of antlers he ever saw except for a buck he spotted before World War II. No other buck since 1959 has come close to this buck's size.

Fred Palmer holds the antlers of the typical mule deer buck taken by his friend, Harold Taylor, in Eagle County in 1960. The buck scores 206-3/8 points and received the Certificate of Merit for Harold's trophy at the 10th B&C Competition. The greatest spread is better than 32 inches and remains as one of the largest muleys ever taken in Colorado. This photograph was taken in 1962 shortly after Fred accepted the award for Harold. The 10th B&C Competition was held at the American Museum of Natural History in New York City.

Fred Palmer in 2001 with his massive non-typical mule deer that makes the all-times records book.

JAMES D. GREER
Location: Uncompahgre National Forest
Year Taken: 1969
Score: 238

More than 30 years passed before James Greer had his magnificent non-typical mule deer officially measured, but he knew this was a Boone and Crockett muley from the moment he saw it.

James traveled to the Uncompahgre Plateau in October 1969 from his home in Missouri and secured a hunting license that was good for the Uncompahgre National Forest, Unit 62. The day before the start of the season, James scouted the area and located five good bucks, so he knew this was the right place.

The hunt began on opening morning and was over a few hours later when the buck was downed at 10 a.m. He was starting to leave his tree stand when he jumped his buck that was bedded down right below him. James fired twice using his Remington .308 automatic but missed but dropped it immediately with the third shot before it disappeared over the crest of the mountain.

James has hunted in Colorado since 1961 on the same mountain range where he has harvested many outstanding animals, but this is certainly one of the finest. The buck was not officially measured until January 2001 by Donald Roper who lives near James' home. The buck easily made the minimum to be entered into the Boone and Crockett Club with a final score of 238 points, a tidy eight points above the 230 minimum score needed to be listed in the all-time records book.

James Greer holds his 238-point non-typical buck that he took in 1969. The buck was only officially measured in 2001 and has not been entered into the B&C so remains unranked.

JACK E. MOERMOND
Location: Gunnison County
Year Taken: 1970
Score: 234-1/8

When Timothy S. Moermond of Michigan was three years old in 1970, his father, Jack, went to Colorado to hunt mule deer for the first time. Tim remembers telling his dad to "Have a great time and bring me home a reindeer."

Gordon Dean joined Jack on this hunt that included five days of adventure in the wilds of Gunnison County. On the third day, after not seeing a single deer, the men decided to relocate higher on the mountain. The roads were in good condition so they drove as far as possible. They eventually ran into other hunters who had filled their tags and who informed Gordon and Jack where they had sighted mule deer. They had 2-1/2 days remaining in the season to fill their tags.

That first afternoon in their new area Gordon and Jack saw deer but took no shots. On the next day, they split up as they worked their way to the top of the ridge. Jack hadn't gone far when he heard Gordon shoot. Gordon had filled his tags with a button buck and a forked horn. It took the two men all day to field dress the bucks and haul them back to camp. That left Jack the final day of the season to fill his tags.

Jack awoke long before sunup in hopes of reaching the top of the ridge before sunrise. Early in the morning he shot a doe. Shortly thereafter Gordon showed up with lunch and dragged the animal back to camp, allowing Jack more time to hunt. All the exercise in the thin air had tired Jack so he sat down to rest and to watch for deer. While he sat there, a buck

suddenly ran out from behind him. From a sitting position, Jack had to twist at the waist to shoot. The buck disappeared and Jack thought he blew it.

Before he could reload, the buck returned from the direction where it had just disappeared, and again Jack fired at the running deer. This time the buck stopped and shook its head. Jack knew he had one shot left so he pivoted into a prone position and fired. The buck flipped over backwards and kicked his way out of sight. After 15 minutes Jack couldn't take the suspense any longer and went in search of his buck. When he found it his first thought was, "Timmy has his reindeer."

Jack knew he was a long way from camp and darkness was descending, so he left his buck for the night. Luckily for Jack there was a full moon to provide much-needed light. Gordon had heard the shots but thought it might have been Jack's signal for help. When Jack arrived in camp, Gordon was setting out lanterns to guide Jack in. Gordon was relieved to see Jack enter camp, but he didn't believe Jack when he described his buck as having at least six or seven points on each side. When they reached Jack's buck the next morning, however, Gordon said, "You didn't lie one bit." They estimated the field-dressed weight to be 300 pounds. After much effort in an ever-worsening snowstorm, the men dragged the buck to camp and maneuvered their truck down the mountainside and headed for home.

Jack Moermond stands beside his B&C buck that scores 234-2/8 points.

ROBERT E. BUCKLES
Location: Rio Blanco County
Year Taken: 1960
Score: 233-6/8

Bob Buckles' massive non-typical mule deer rack hung in his barn for years but when his son encouraged him to get it officially measured in 1997, Bob dragged it to Meeker. It was scored by Boone and Crockett Official Measurer Roger Selner who came to town with his World Record Elk Tour.

The hunt was in 1960 when Bob's goal was to locate enough meat for his family. He and Ellis Sedgley always hunted together and that year was no exception. The men split up with the plan to meet at the top of a hill. Bob arrived at the top first and looked across a draw where his buck stood. When he put up his 2-1/2 power Carl Ziess scope, Bob's eyes nearly popped out. Normally he aimed for the neck or head but he didn't want the rack ruined, so he aimed his .30-06 for the heart. The buck flinched, staggered and ran down the draw so Ellis offered to scout for the buck. Less than 300 yards down the draw, Ellis came upon the buck, dead as a doornail.

Ellis and Bob guessed the hogged-dressed weight to be more than 300 pounds. Between the two of them they couldn't lift the buck off the ground so they retrieved a Jeep to finish pulling the body up the hill. Bob remembers the meat to be as good as anything he had ever eaten, so not only did he collect outstanding antlers, but also he collected outstanding meat for his family.

The rack hung in his barn until 1997 when it was finally measured and entered into the Boone and Crockett Club. The rack now hangs in the sunroom of Bob's house and not the barn. Bob started hunting and fishing in Colorado in 1953 and continues until today but this buck was the whopper he'll always remember.

Photograph by Susan Campbell Reneau

UNKNOWN COLORADO HUNTER
Location: Colorado
Year Taken: Prior to 1900
Score: 232-3/8
Owner: Melvin A. Mitchell, Jr.

This non-typical mule deer trophy hung in S.O. Fisher's Sporting Goods Store in downtown Lynchburg, Virginia, for as long as most people could remember. As a child growing up in the 1940s, Melvin Mitchell used to visit the store and admire the rack where it hung in as place of honor over the front door.

In 1966, Melvin, as a professional taxidermist, was asked to locate a new cape and remount it. When he took it apart, Melvin discovered that the old mount contained the entire original skull. He sawed the antlers off the skull and remounted them using a cape from the state of Washington. Melvin saved the original manikin with the skull and teeth intact to show people how trophies were mounted.

Several years after Melvin remounted it, the store's owners died. When it closed, Melvin acquired the mount. He did considerable research on his newly acquired trophy and discovered it was taken in Colorado before 1900. The store itself opened around 1870.

Melvin started part-time taxidermy work in 1948 at the age of 14. He worked as a quality control engineer for Babcock and Wilcox Fuel Division in Lynchburg, Virginia, and retired after 34-1/2 years. He is now a full-time taxidermist and has hunted big game in Wyoming, Montana, Colorado and Quebec. Over the years, Melvin has taken six bull elk and six mule deer bucks near Durango, Colorado.

TED R. RAMIREZ
Location: Eagle County
Year Taken: 1996
Score: 230-3/8

On the day Ted Ramirez took his trophy buck, he awoke at 4:30 a.m. to prepare for a full day of hiking and hunting. He was on the trail by 5:30 a.m., hiking deep into the mountains. Eight inches of snow had fallen a few days before making tracking easier. Ted hunted a small valley with a creek at the bottom. From one side of the valley he could view open meadows through small openings in the dense trees. Ted paused at each opening to search for any movement. Two hours later he came across fresh deer tracks that meandered on and off the game trail. He thought, "Buck!"

Ted prepared himself by removing the lens cap from his scope and chambering a round as he continued his Quasimodo-like movements to the next opening, ever alert to any movement. Ted caught a movement in a large meadow about 300 yards away and realized it was the largest buck of his life. He slowly stepped back behind a small pine tree, dropped to his knees and removed his coat and backpack. Ted kept his eyes glued on the buck as it headed for the black timber 50 yards above it.

Ted quickly closed the distance between him and the buck by 100 yards by half running and half walking while trying not to make any noise. The babbling creek covered any noise he made as his feet crunched in the snow. When he reached some large pine trees and willow, Ted scanned the area for the buck only to realize it stood broadside to him, looking in his direction. Ted froze for at least five minutes as he watched the buck and listened to his heart pound. The buck eventually turned and walked at a steady pace for the dense forest above. Ted realized he had a poor shot between the trees; all he could see was the rear and rack of the buck.

Just as it was about to disappear into the woods, Ted dropped to a sitting position and prepared for a shot.

As Ted fixed the buck in his sights, it walked behind a large tree. In a last-ditch effort to attract the buck's attention, Ted gave a short, monotone whistle. The curious muley made the fatal error of taking one last look in Ted's direction and stepped partially away from the tree for a half broadside shot. Ted let one fly. The buck jumped and bolted toward cover, giving no indication it had been hit. Disappearing 50 yards from where Ted last saw it, Ted questioned his shot. He waited an hour and returned to the trail where he had first spotted the deer with plans to work his way up the trail in hopes of finding the buck. Seventy-five yards from where the buck disappeared, he spotted it at the base of a small tree. He observed the buck with his binoculars knowing it was hit but not knowing how well. Two hours later Ted spent 10 minutes working his way towards his buck. When he got closer he realized the buck had died instantly from a heart shot, but it slid to the base of a tree with its head up and its legs tucked under it, looking alert and ready to bolt.

Ted's buck was accepted into the Boone and Crockett Club's 23rd North American Big Game Awards Program (1995-1997).

Ted Ramirez thought his trophy non-typical buck was alert and ready to bolt at the base of a tree when in reality his shot to the buck's heart had killed it instantly. The buck scores 230-3/8 points.

MATT GILSON
Location: Mesa County
Year Taken: 1998
Score: 228-2/8

Matt Gilson had never traveled out West so when he arrived in Colorado from his home in Michigan in the fall of 1998, he was excited. Matt's dad hunted in Colorado for several years and had urged his son to come with him many times, but this was the first time Matt could go. Maybe it was a lack of funds or a lack of vacation time, but nonetheless Matt's time to go to Colorado had finally come.

When the men arrived they discovered that the first ranch they planned to hunt was full so they were sent to hunt with guide and outfitter Jody Poland. This turned out to be the best thing that could have happened to Matt, although at the time he had his doubts.

This was to be an unguided hunt but Jody's, brother, Josh, and his friend, Jim, were in camp to serve as guides if they were needed. Since this was Matt's and his brother-in-laws first Western hunt, Matt's dad thought it was good for the pair to use Josh and Jim for at least the first two days.

On opening morning the men didn't see much until late in the day when Josh took Matt to a place where he had shot a 30-inch buck a few years earlier. As soon as they got to the ridge from which they were going to glass, they spotted a small, forked-horn buck, so Josh walked around the brush to

Matt Gilson had never hunted in Colorado when he downed this B&C buck in Mesa County. The buck scores 228-2/8 points. Here he holds his buck moments after the hunt ended on October 17, 1998.

glass the other side of the mountain. Josh was only gone a few minutes when he called to Matt to check out a buck he had spotted more than 500 yards away. When Matt put the binoculars up for a good look he immediately decided this was the buck for him, so they took off down the mountain to close some distance between themselves and the massive deer. They didn't have much time since the buck was feeding in and out of the oak brush and could disappear forever at any moment.

Matt steadied himself as he fired his first shot. The buck hunched up and Matt knew he had hit the buck. Matt stayed at his vantage point while Josh went to locate the buck in the brush. A few minutes later Matt heard Josh screaming for him to shoot the buck again when it emerged from the protection of the oak brush. Two additional well-placed shots from about 200 yards downed the buck for good. As Matt approached the buck he thought its head was stuck in the oak brush. In fact, the rack was so huge that it stuck up over the bushes. It was a non-typical mule deer with 11 points on each side and a final Boone and Crockett Club score of 228-2/8 points.

To top off a perfect Colorado experience, Matt also collected a respectable 6x3 bull elk on the last morning of the hunt. The bull was icing on an already perfect cake.

Matt's buck was accepted into the Boone and Crockett Club's 24th North American Big Game Awards Program (1998-2000).

Hunter Gilson with his dad's B&C buck.

BRADLEY D. HERMAN
Location: Moffat County
Year Taken: 1999
Score: 223-2/8

A serious illness prevented Brad Herman from hunting with bow and arrow during the fall of 1999, so he apologizes for not having a spectacular story.

Brad was drawn for Area 2, northwest of Craig, for the October hunt and scouted the area in July and August with his brother. Colorado experienced extreme dry and hot weather that year so the men only saw three bucks on opening weekend but the three bucks he saw were all trophy size. Brad's nephew kicked the buck to him from the sagebrush on the north side of Lookout Mountain and less than a mile from their truck. The buck was running 100 yards from Brad when he let loose a hand-loaded 165-grain partition bullet from his .30-06 700 Remington ADL rifle. The first shot was a fatal blow to the back and the second shot was to the heart at 4 p.m. on the opening day of the season.

From start to finish, Brad's hunt lasted only a few hours but the memories will last a lifetime, even if the story isn't as dramatic as a bow hunt.

Bradley's buck was accepted into the Boone and Crockett Club's 24th North American Big Game Awards Program in 2000.

Brad Herman in Moffat County with the non-typical buck he took with his .30-06 Remington 700 ADL rifle.

JOHN O. GARVIN
Location: Mesa County
Year Taken: 1962
Score: 220-6/8

John Garvin, Douglas MacMurphy, Don MacMurphy, Vic Bouday and Douglas Pleager began their third year in a row hunting mule deer together in 1962, and this time they went to Mesa County. This was an unguided hunt not far from DeBeque.

On the third day of the hunt John decided to hunt a canyon where he saw large buck tracks the day before. The evening before the hunt he suggested to the rest of his friends that it might well be worth trying since no one saw any bucks to that point larger than a 5x5 with a 24-inch spread. Don and Vic agreed to go with him the next day.

Early the next morning the three arrived at the starting point. Don and Vic started their climb up the left side of the draw, which appeared to provide a good climbing route with good visibility. John started his climb on the right side of the draw but was faced at first with wading through some heavy brush and steep climbing.

John realized after about 30 minutes of climbing that he had broken out of the heavy brush and was in position to overlook much of the other side of the canyon from about 75 yards directly below to the top of the ridge around 500 yards distance. Realizing this, he found a large rock and sat down to look over the hillside. Almost immediately, he saw his companions below him coming up the other side of the hill several hundred yards away.

Setting back on the rock John shouldered his rifle, a Remington specially chambered for the 30 Gibbs cartridge with a Weaver 2-1/2 x 8 scope, loaded with 150-grain Gameking Sierra bullets. The buck at this point was slowly moving up the hill, some 300 yards above Don and Vic but at a distance from John around 175 yards.

Taking steady aim, while resting the rifle on his knee, John placed the vertical cross hairs just ahead of the buck's front shoulder and pulled the trigger. Almost immediately the buck jerked and went down. To John's dismay, it came right back up and started going very fast up the hill. John shot two more rounds, missing each time. On his last round in the gun he connected again, and the buck went down, but again jumped up. This time, instead of continuing up the hill it turned and headed for a draw just below John. Having time only to put two more rounds in the rifle, John finally stopped the buck with one more shot at 75 to 80 yards.

John remembers directing Don and Vic to where the buck had dropped and yelling down to them if they could count the number of points on the rack. Don yelled back he thought the buck was a 10x10.

Photograph courtesy of John O. Garvin

Upon closer examination, John realized he had himself a trophy of a lifetime, but it wasn't until 1999, 37 years after the event, that John had this beautiful set of antlers measured for the Boone and Crockett Club. The measurements confirmed what he had thought all that time. The non-typical mule deer buck scores 220-6/8 points and was accepted into the B&C 24th North American Big Game Awards Program.

ANTHONY L. WEISS
Location: Rio Blanco County
Year Taken: 1974
Score: 220-5/8

Knowing your hunting area is one of the most important tips any experienced hunter can teach a new hunter, and Anthony Weiss' hunt was a classic example of this rule.

The Rangely area of Colorado was the terrain where Anthony hunted every year, so he knew the hills, draws and canyons inside out and had sighted his trophy buck before the season and had seen the shed antlers for several years. He knew the buck was living in the pinons and cedars, so Anthony worked the pockets and tracked him within 50 yards. A single shot from his .257 Weatherby downed the buck.

At one time, hunters could get up to three deer per license and Anthony and his friends thought the stream of trophy bucks from Rangely would never stop, so many of his bigger racks were given away. Anthony can't even estimate how many big racks he threw away or gave to friends. Luckily for him, one of his favorite racks was saved and was entered into the Boone and Crockett Club.

Although Anthony took this outstanding buck in 1974 it wasn't until the year 2000 that he entered the buck in the Boone and Crockett Club's 24th North American Big Game Awards Program. Anthony's buck is one of the largest deer ever taken in Colorado.

CALVIN TURNER
Location: Carbondale
Year Taken: 1966
Score: 220-2/8

Calvin Turner has hunted for many years in Colorado but his first hunt could be categorized as astounding.

Calvin and his first cousins L.D. and Jack Turner drove non-stop from their homes in Oklahoma to their hunting area in the Carbondale area of Colorado. They camped outside in the cold and got up early on opening day to begin their hunt. They each had a combined deer and elk tag but after a half day of hiking in deep snow L.D. downed a doe and Calvin decided to locate a game trail where he could sit. Calvin found an elk trail so he sat close to it and waited. By mid-afternoon he was still sitting near the trail when a monster buck was spotted walking down the trail toward Calvin. Without hesitation, Calvin fired his 7mm from a distance of about 200 feet and the buck was his. Since Calvin had never seen a mule deer before he thought at first it was an elk because it was so large. He found his cousins who confirmed when they saw the deer that it was a very large buck.

Calvin Turner of Oklahoma carried his non-typical mule deer mount to a game show in Oklahoma City to have the rack officially measured. Here he holds the rack after learning that it made the Boone and Crockett Club's records-keeping program.

The year was 1966 when three first cousins traveled non-stop from their homes in Oklahoma to an area outside Carbondale, Colorado, where Calvin Turner downed a B&C buck on his first deer hunt. From left to right, the photograph shows L.D. Turner, Calvin Turner and Jack Turner.

The three men were so cold after walking through 18 inches of snow they decided to drive home without filling the rest of their tags but they returned year after year and have many hunting tales to recall. Thanks to the persistent urging of his nephew, Danny Turner, Calvin finally got his buck's rack measured in 2000 and entered into the Boone and Crockett Club's records-keeping program with a final score of 220-2/8 points. The rack has eight main points on each side with six abnormal points totaling more than 19 inches.

STEVE L. KYLE
Location: Jefferson County
Year Taken: 1996
Score: 216-2/8

Steve Kyle paused for this photograph moments after taking this massive non-typical mule deer during the 1996 Colorado muzzleloader season. This buck is the 15th largest typical mule deer taken with a muzzleloader.

Steve hunted a 5,000-acre private ranch west of Denver on opening day of the 1996 Colorado muzzleloader season. During the previous eight years he hunted there Steve saw some monstrous bucks but never connected. With tag in hand, Steve was determined that 1996 was his year. As the shadows of opening day lengthened, Steve did some glassing with his Zeiss 10x40 binoculars from a favorite vantage point. He spotted herds of deer located in different areas up to two miles away and examined them closely with his spotting scope. One bachelor group of nine had two bucks that really looked promising. The largest buck had a great spread, mass and so many points Steve couldn't count them all. He spotted 17 bucks that first evening. As he descended the ridge, he couldn't wait to hunt the next day.

The next morning Steve returned to his vantage point as the day dawned and began seeing deer almost immediately. With the sun fully illuminating the countryside, the deer really stood out. There were now 11 bucks where he'd seen nine the evening before. Steve studied the largest buck, a 7x7, for more than two hours as the herd fed up over the ridge. He had seen larger bucks in past years, but the buck in view was the best he had seen that year. After watching this herd for four hours, he noticed one pine tree that stood out as a likely spot to make an ambush. The buck passed near this pine tree both times Steve had observed it so he decided to put up a tree stand in the afternoon while the bucks were bedded down for the day.

Steve set up his portable stand and used his rangefinder to determine the maximum shooting distance for his .54 caliber Knight muzzleloader. He figured he could accurately shoot it to 125 yards. The wind was wrong to hunt that first evening so Steve returned to his vantage point and did some more glassing. Later that evening he spotted his buck once again above the pine tree and immediately planned for the next morning's hunt.

As it turned out the next day passed uneventfully. Steve spotted two big bucks from his stand in the morning and did some still-hunting in the evening. He had a good shot at a respectable 5x5 during the day but passed it up in the hopes of getting the 7x7 from his stand the next morning.

Steve made a lot of noise slipping into his stand the next morning and worried he'd blown it. Three bull elk bugled a short distance away, and Steve decided to sit back and enjoy the morning. Thirty minutes later the 5x5 and 7x7 appeared and fed into the open broadside. Steve fired once and saw the bigger buck stumble before it was obscured by the smoke. The second shot also hit its mark but the third shot finished it. Upon reaching the buck he realized it was actually a 9x8 with a 28-inch spread.

Steve's muley ranks as the 15th largest non-typical mule deer ever taken with a muzzleloader according to the third edition of *Longhunter Muzzleloading Big Game Record Book* published in 2000.

— Chapter IV —
Colorado Typical and Non-Typical Whitetail Deer
Stories and Photographs

DAVID A. McCRACKEN
Location: Adams County
Year Taken: 1996
Score: 186-3/8

Dave McCracken, Joe Emily and Pat Murphy were plotting their afternoon hunting strategy at a local restaurant on opening day of the 1996 deer season when out of the clear blue a rancher they knew well stood up to pay his bill. This was the same rancher who owned property where Dave had spotted a massive whitetail buck, but he had only given Dave permission to hunt pheasants. Joe urged Dave to ask the rancher one more time for permission to hunt deer, reasoning they had nothing to lose.

"I saw a really good whitetail in your alfalfa pasture and sure would like a chance to get him," Dave said to the rancher.

Much to Dave's delight, the rancher responded, "Go ahead, Dave. Just don't take a bunch of people with you."

Dave figured he must have looked like a nut to the rancher as he thanked the man over and over again before returning to his table to share the good news with Joe and Pat. Dave felt like he had just won the lottery.

Pat and Dave returned to the ranch that afternoon without Joe and concentrated on a large patch of cattails. The men split up and went in opposite directions to circle the area. Pat was about 300 yards east of Dave when Pat started waving frantically. Dave looked left and saw a beautiful 5x5 buck running through the cattails about 200 yards away, but he didn't get a shot. When the pair got together again, Pat told Dave about a much larger buck he had seen. They vowed to return to the same area the next day.

Dave hit the snooze button at least three times before getting up at 6 a.m. the next morning. He debated whether or not to disturb the same area, but he eventually decided to return to the cattails for another look. He arrived in the area at first light. He walked only 50 yards when he spotted a deer with its head buried in the grass about 250 yards away. When it raised its head Dave knew it was the big buck Pat spotted the previous day. Dave carefully raised his rifle, rested it on a fence post and fired. The buck dropped from sight and Dave spent the next 45 minutes searching for it. Dave became discouraged and paused for four or five minutes gathering his thoughts when the buck suddenly stood up 60 yards from him.

Dave aimed at the buck's lower neck and fired. He watched as the buck disappeared into the brush where it kicked and thrashed before it fell silent. When Dave walked up to the buck he couldn't believe his eyes. It was a 7x7 with two abnormal points. He quickly realized he needed help getting the buck out of the cattails so he returned home to tell Chris, his wife, the good news and to locate Pat. Pat's reaction was the same as Dave's when he saw the buck. They spent more than an hour dragging it through the cattails. After field dressing and skinning it, Dave discovered the second shot was the only one that hit the mark.

Dave's once-in-a-lifetime trophy is the largest typical whitetail buck entered into B&C from Colorado.

Dave McCracken with his trophy whitetail buck that becomes the largest typical whitetail buck ever taken in Colorado. The buck scores 186-3/8 points.

IVAN W. RHODES
Location: Yuma County
Year Taken: 1978
Score: 182-5/8

There wasn't another hunter within sight or earshot of Ivan Rhodes all day on opening day of the 1978 deer season. Ivan had planned to hunt with his father and brother near Bonny Reservoir in Yuma County, but they had applied for the limited permits in separate envelopes and were not drawn with Ivan. They spent opening day on the Western Slope hunting mule deer.

The area Ivan hunted on the eastern plains is interlaced with ravines and branching lateral fingers. By late afternoon, all he had to show for his efforts was a pair of sore feet. He hadn't even spotted so much as a doe, let alone any of the sizable bucks that he had heard inhabited the area.

After one last break, Ivan began working his way back to his vehicle. He had gone only 50 yards when he spotted what appeared to be the ribs of a cow's skeleton in a small brush-covered depression. They were gray-white in color and only about 30 paces away. When the ribs suddenly shifted slightly, Ivan realized he was gazing at one of Colorado's most remarkable trophies. It was a massive whitetail buck bedded down for the day and facing downhill. Ivan instantly lined up the cross hairs of his .30-06 on the buck's neck just below the ear and fired. Charging forward, Ivan found his Boone and Crockett buck lying in the brush.

As there was only about an hour of daylight left, Ivan caped out the head and positioned the animal so that it would drain and cool during the night. Realizing that the car was still two miles away, he began his hike out. The next morning Ivan returned to the buck early and spent five hours packing it out, one half at a time. The two halves later weighed a total of 190 pounds.

Not only did Ivan's whitetail score high enough to make the Boone and Crockett Club's all-time records book, but it also became the first Colorado whitetail taken by a hunter to do so. The buck scored 182-5/8 points.

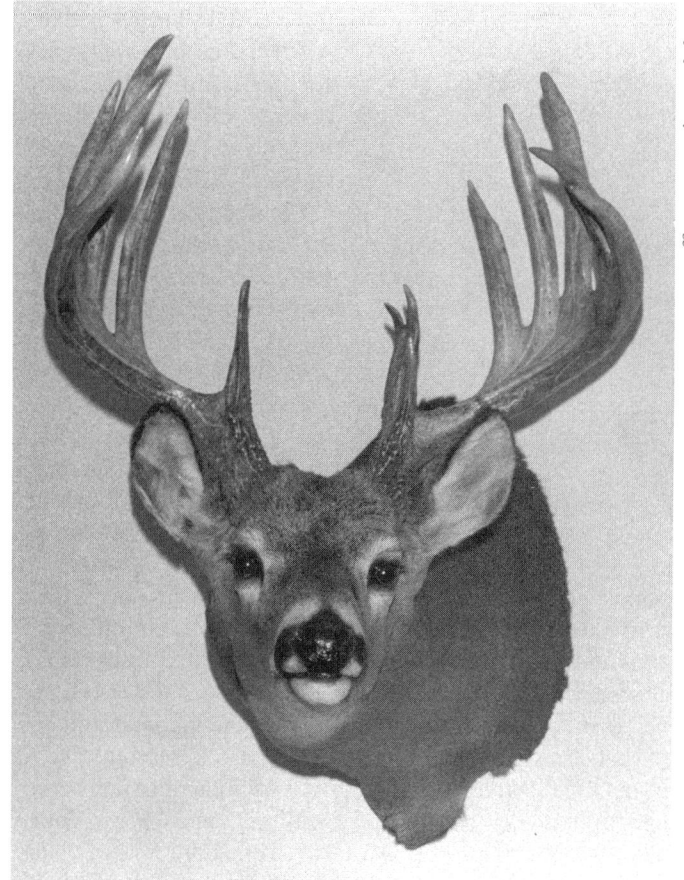

Photograph courtesy of Colorado's Biggest Bucks and Bulls archives

JEFF L. MEKELBURG

Location: Yuma County
Year Taken: 1989
Score: 180-2/8

Location: Yuma County
Year Taken: 1986
Score: 204-2/8

Jeff Mekelburg is one of a handful of people who has taken two Boone and Crockett Club whitetails and the only person in Colorado with such a distinction.

The first buck Jeff took was the non-typical whitetail in 1986 that he had watched for two years in Yuma County. On the day before the season opened, his hunt area in Yuma County received up to three inches of snow on the ground so when Jeff arrived on opening day tracking hoof prints was less difficult. He climbed on top of a hill and started searching for the buck, which he located with four other smaller bucks and a few does. That accomplished, Jeff decided to return to the ranch house to talk with friends and play some cards while he debated about returning and hunting the big buck he had located. No one believed Jeff when he told them the size of the antlers because no one else had seen the buck. After taking the break, Jeff returned to the field at 1 p.m. and stalked the buck for a half mile before taking it from 200 yards at 2 p.m. with his 7mm Moser. Unlike many bucks in this area that live in river bottoms, this buck remained in the sagebrush.

The buck had an estimated field-dressed weight of 220 pounds and an impressive rack but Jeff didn't imagine it was a Boone and Crockett trophy until later. His hunting buddy, Joe Kuntz, also took a nice buck that day but that one didn't make "The Book."

Jeff's second B&C buck was also taken in Yuma County and had first been sighted by Jeff's brother, Greg, who had hunted the same area the year before with a friend. The year was 1989 when Jeff put in for that area and received permission from a rancher to hunt it. When Jeff and his wife Dana arrived for the hunt, Jeff wasn't sure what the big buck looked like so when they saw a nice one, he wanted his wife to shoot first. She took the buck on opening day of the hunt with her .243 from 300 yards but Jeff didn't take it for another eight days. In the meantime, Jeff, his wife, his brother Greg and hunting friend Harry Snelling spent the time walking in the brush trying to kick up the buck.

On the second day, Jeff and Harry went to the right and Greg went to the left when he practically walked on top of the big one with no gun and no hunting license. Greg was amazed that the buck was only 100 yards from him and never bolted. Try as he might, Greg couldn't get Jeff's attention so the buck left the area only to reappear on the eighth day of the hunt. The rancher was certain Jeff would never see the buck again since this was a buck everyone was after, including the rancher. They all figured the buck would stay low and disappear until after the hunting season.

Jeff continued to hunt from sunup to sundown on this cool and sunny day and saw lots of bucks with racks measuring 150 or so but never seeing THE buck. On the eighth day, Jeff and his brother went up on a hill in the early morning and decided to ask permission of a neighboring rancher to look around his cornfield for the elusive buck. They walked around in some trees and were driving out of the area in their truck when they noticed large antlers sticking up in a little draw at the corner of the pasture on the first rancher's land. Greg grabbed a video camera as Jeff got out of the pickup. As he edged toward the buck it bolted and Jeff fired his .270 Ruger from 20 yards. Four shots all hit their mark and the buck dropped within 80 yards of where Jeff aimed.

Jeff Mekelburg continues to enjoy hunting in Yuma County but his two bucks from 1986 and 1989 were two highlights of his hunting career.

Jeff Mekelburg took this fine typical whitetail buck among the cornstalks.

A classic non-typical whitetail buck easily qualified for the Boone and Crockett Club. Jeff Mekelburg is one of a small handful of hunters with bucks listed in the non-typical and typical categories for whitetail deer.

PICK UP
Location: Logan County
Year Found: 1971
Score: 175-7/8
Found by Marvin Gardner

Marv Gardner worked as the wildlife technician III for the Colorado Division of Wildlife on the Tamarack State Wildlife Area from 1967 to 1998. While making his rounds one day in the fall of 1971, Marv came upon a road kill. The buck was a huge typical whitetail on Interstate 76 near the Tamarack State Wildlife Area, southeast of Proctor. Trophy antlers weren't on the minds of people as much as they are today, so the buck lay there for several hours before Marv had time to retrieve the rack. This is the first Boone and Crockett trophy whitetail recorded from Colorado. Marv's pick up buck ranks as the 6th largest Colorado typical whitetail buck ever entered into the B&C records program. The rack hangs in a place of honor in his living room as a tribute to an outstanding buck and was the first whitetail buck from Colorado to be recognized by the Boone and Crockett Club and listed in their all-time records book.

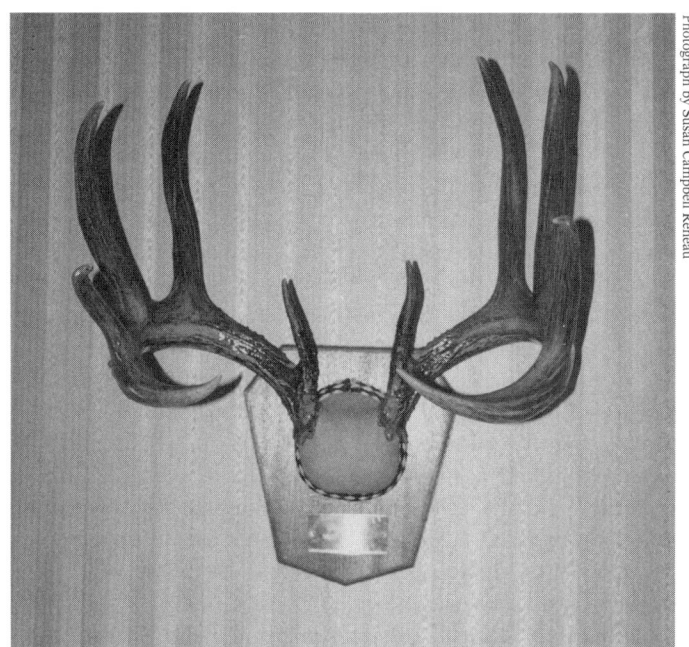

Photograph by Susan Campbell Reneau

RICK J. TOKARSKI
Location: Bent County
Year Taken: 1994
Score: 173-3/8

Rick Tokarski, a Wisconsin resident, and his younger brother, Eddie, bow-hunted whitetail deer in Bent County, Colorado, in the fall of 1994. He hunted over a scrape in a cottonwood tree grove.

When this massive buck passed within 35 yards of his stand, Rick let go an Easton XX75, 2216 arrow with a Zwickey broadhead. It was launched from his PSE Magna Flite bow set at 65 pounds. The shot was fatal, but it took a second shot to quickly finish the job. The buck has been accepted into both the Boone and Crockett Club's and Pope and Young Club's records books.

Contrary to a very popular misconception, Boone and Crockett Club does not keep records of trophies taken only with a firearm. The Boone and Crockett Club keeps records of all hunter-taken native North American big-game animals, regardless of the method of taking, as long as the trophy was taken in fair chase as defined by the Club. In addition, Boone and Crockett Club accepts trophies that die of natural causes or are of unknown origin.

Pope and Young Club has been granted permission to use the Club's copyrighted scoring system to record only those trophies taken with a bow and arrow. Because Pope and Young Club records only trophies taken with a bow, it has lower minimums for entering a trophies.

"The feeling I felt when I took this deer was overwhelming. I just could not believe the sheer size of the animal's body or antlers," Rick said. It is one of the finest whitetails ever recorded for the state of Colorado, a state that is more popularly known for producing trophy mule deer.

The whitetail buck Rick Tokarski took in 1994 is one of only a handful taken in Colorado that make the B&C and the P&Y. This fine typical whitetail scores 173-3/8 points.

LES OHLHAUSER
Location: Prowers County
Year Taken: 1997
Score: 173-3/8

Les located his buck in 1995 on private land near Lamar in Prowers County. He immediately secured permission to hunt on the land from the rancher, but he had to wait patiently until the permit arrived for the December 1997 season. The season began on Monday, but he couldn't leave until Friday after work. His boss noticed his lack of concentration on Friday so he gave Les permission to leave at noon. Les was grateful and left with his hunting buddy, Tony Clem.

Les and Tony arrived in time to glass the landscape and were blessed by the deer gods when they promptly located the buck feeding in a CRP field with a smaller buck. To get into the field and in position for the stalk, the men walked a half-mile around an irrigation ditch.

They spotted the buck feeding toward a neighboring pasture, and Les realized the buck would have to jump a fence to enter the pasture, so Tony and Les crouched down and began to eliminate the distance between themselves and the bucks. They stopped several times to glass the deer and noticed on one occasion that the smaller buck was looking right at them. The two bucks were separated by about 75 yards.

The larger buck continued to feed with its head down as it worked its way toward the fence, ahead of the smaller one. The smaller buck stopped in the field when the larger one reached the fence. Les decided it was "now or never," so he loaded his .284 caliber, Scott Carlson, custom-made rifle, and fired. The shot fell short, kicking up snow and scaring ducks off a nearby irrigation ditch.

The buck watched the ducks as Les made necessary adjustments for another shot. The second shot hit the buck with a very audible whop. It bolted toward the river bottom as more deer raised their heads to look at the men while the big buck ran toward the herd. Upon reaching the other deer, the herd started milling about. Les fired his third shot just as his deer lowered its head to antler another buck.

Les knew the third shot hit its mark. The other deer ran toward the river bottom but the big buck didn't follow. Tony said all the deer made it to the timber but Les was convinced the buck didn't. Using an old dead tree as a marker, Les worked his way toward the spot where he had last seen his buck. They separated with one going in a clockwise pattern to search for the deer while the other went counterclockwise. Les paused to clean the fog off his glasses. No sooner had he taken his glasses off, when Tony shouted, "Les, there he goes."

Les dropped his glasses, threw his rifle to his shoulder, squeezed off a shot, and the buck was down for good. Les had passed within 10 feet of his buck before Tony jumped it.

Les's hunt started at 3 p.m. and it was over at 4:22 p.m. Les quickly determined that his buck, which carried a 5x7 rack, was a Boone and Crockett trophy. His field estimates were correct, and after the required 60-day drying period, the buck officially scored 173-3/8 points. The deer gods were with Les that day in 1997, for sure.

JOHN O. CLETCHER, JR.
Location: Yuma County
Year Taken: 1985
Score: 171-2/8

Jackie Cletcher knew her husband, John, had dropped the biggest buck she had ever seen with one shot but John wasn't so sure.

Temperatures dropped to zero and below as John Cletcher began his late season deer hunt on opening day in December 1985. Winds gusted to 25 miles per hour as John and Jackie slowly drove their pickup on back roads to case out the hunting area near Bonny Reservoir, less than three miles from the Kansas border. The couple came to an abandoned homestead in the middle of a 180-acre wheatfield where they saw sod houses and buildings on the top of a ridge.

John surmised that deer might shelter themselves against the wild and cold by burrowing themselves near or inside the abandoned buildings, so they continued to drive closer to the structures. Jackie noticed movement near the buildings, so John slipped from the truck and started walking the 200 yards up the hill to the houses along a path through the field. John looked back at Jackie who was using their binoculars and saw her excitedly motioning him to continue. Moments later, within 100 yards of John, a small herd of five to six deer stood up, including two nice bucks, and stared at John and Jackie on the ridgeline.

While bracing himself against his knee, John fired a single shot and watched as the entire herd flew over the ridge. John's heart sank when he thought he had missed the big buck, but his wife had confidence in his shot. She urged him to go to where the herd had stood, so John guided the truck to that location only to discover the dead buck lying in the grass where it had been shot. Jackie was right; John had taken a trophy buck with a single shot.

Getting this buck back to the truck was quite a task for the two of them because of an estimated body weight of more than 250 pounds. He first field dressed it and lifted the hindquarters onto the tailgate of the truck and hoisted the rest of the body into the truck using a block and tackle.

Thanks to Jackie's sharp eyes and confidence in John's shooting abilities, the Cletchers have a Boone and Crockett Club whitetail. John's massive whitetail buck ranks as the 10th largest ever taken in Colorado with a final score of 171-2/8.

JOSEPH C. FOX
Location: Lincoln County
Year Taken: 1992
Score: 170-2/8

Joe Fox proudly holds his B&C whitetail buck moments after downing it with a single shot from his .30-06. Joe has collected one of a handful of B&C whitetail bucks taken in Colorado, although the number of trophy whitetail has increased dramatically since 1982 when only one hunter-killed whitetail was listed from Colorado.

Lots of people enjoy hunting for shed antlers but not many locate a Boone and Crockett-quality buck during the regular hunting season.

Joe spent a year searching for shed antlers in Lincoln County and during the regular hunting season of 1992 passed up several 30-inch bucks, knowing that a larger buck was out there based upon his year-long scouting. On the fourth day of the hunt, Joe moved along a creek at sunset when he spotted a massive buck bedded down in the sagebrush looking straight at him. Joe was about 100 yards from the buck, walking towards it and angling away from the sun. With a single shot from his .30-06 rifle, Joe collected his buck. He estimated the weight to be 350 pounds and the age to be 10-1/2 years based upon the wear on the teeth. Ranch roads were everywhere so to retrieve the buck from the field only meant driving up to it and hauling it away. Searching for shed antlers certainly helped this hunter collect his buck.

Joe's buck ranks as the 12th largest typical whitetail deer ever taken in Colorado as listed in the all-time records book of the Boone and Crockett Club.

MICHAEL A. FRANEK
Location: Elbert County
Year Taken: 1993
Score: 162-7/8

Upon receiving their 1993 Colorado buck tags through the lottery, Matt and Michael Franek decided they could not, and would not, fill their tags with just any buck. They had hunted the Simla area for years and knew there were many exceptional bucks in the area. In fact, Michael had spotted just such a buck during the previous archery season. That whitetail, which he called "Big Ed," had safely crossed 80 yards out in front of his stand.

The 1993 rifle season started slowly for the brothers. They hunted hard for eight days in their usual haunts only to find many smaller bucks that couldn't possibly fill their expectations and tags. Michael passed up 32 legal bucks during those eight days. A few days later, Michael's friend Jeff Brown called and told Mike he had a doe tag for the same area. They discussed their options and made plans for a Halloween Day hunt.

On Halloween morning Michael, Matt and Jeff hunted one of their favorite areas together but didn't see a single fresh track. They then moved closer to Simla and hunted on some property belonging to a mutual friend. They parked their vehicle and headed for a creek bottom. After they had traveled about 200 yards they spooked a small herd of does with one small buck. Five hundred yards beyond the herd, however, Michael spotted a buck with the aid of his binoculars. Once he was focused on the buck, Michael nearly dropped his binoculars. It was a buck Michael wanted to tie his tag to.

Jeff and Matt stayed put as Michael slowly edged his way back to cover to begin his stalk. Michael had to walk a half mile along a crunchy creek bottom to get within rifle range. He sprinted down the sandy sections of the creek bottom to quickly narrow the distance. When Michael paused to relocate the deer with his binoculars, the buck was standing there looking directly at him.

Michael needed to reach a fence line about 100 yards away to have a chance of hitting the majestic buck, but the only way to do it was to get down and crawl. Upon reaching the fence, Michael determined the buck was about 150 yards away. The antlers were huge and Michael kept reminding himself to aim for the lung area, not the rack. He took a deep breath to calm himself and to steady the dancing cross hairs. Michael squeezed the trigger and the deer dropped out of sight so fast he wondered if he had actually seen the buck or if it was just a vision.

Michael sprinted the 150 yards to where he had last seen the buck and was greeted by Matt and Jeff who were whooping and hollering. The men admired the buck and shook hands for what seemed like an hour. The single shot had hit the buck square in the chest.

Michael didn't realize the nature of his achievement until he showed the antlers to a taxidermist who told him they made B&C. After the required 60-day drying period, Michael's antlers officially scored 162-7/8 points. The buck was a deer to remember, and the hunt provides Michael with memories that flood back any time he glances at the mounted antlers.

TROY CUNNINGHAM
Location: Otero County
Year Taken: 1995
Score: 160

On November 18, 1995, while hunting on a private ranch in eastern Colorado along the Arkansas River bottom, Troy Cunningham was perched 13 feet up in a big old cottonwood tree, standing along a natural bottleneck of the Arkansas. Around 4:30 p.m. Troy looked up river in the same grouping of cottonwoods when he spotted a large buck trotting out of a dark bedding area going in the opposite direction from Troy's tree stand. Instantly, Troy tried grunting at the big buck, but it was traveling in the opposite direction approximately 150 yards away and gave no response.

Troy realized he needed to do something fast so he grabbed his 130-inch class rattling antlers and began smacking them together. The buck quickly turned in his direction. He knew exactly where these two other bucks were fighting. Looking down the cottonwoods Troy saw this amazing buck coming in his direction. He needed to react motionlessly and quickly to rehang his rattling antlers, grab his 64-pound handmade long bow and prepare to shoot.

At 40 yards, the buck stopped and looked in Troy's direction while Troy knocked his arrow and kept telling himself not to look at the buck's antlers. This big buck was closer now – about 20 yards – and it was hard not to admire its massive rack as it came closer. The buck dropped his nose, sniffed right where Troy had a darsle drag, and slowly walked down the mail trail, which led right to Troy. The buck was even closer – now 10 yards away. What a sight. Troy was pumped, to say the least, and released a single yellow- and white-feathered arrow, which hit the buck directly in its center. The buck ran 20 yards down river as Troy watched it drop in its tracks.

Troy Cunningham and his P&Y records book buck that scores 160 points.

Troy's first reaction was that this was Boone and Crockett material. After climbing down from his tree stand, Troy worked his way toward the buck and noticed its 3rd tine on its right antler was broken. That caused an 18-inch deduction, which took him out of B&C all-time records book contention but plenty of room to spare in the Pope and Young Club's all-time records book, Bowhunting Big Game Records of North America, 5th Edition, published in 1999. The buck qualifies for the Boone and Crockett Club's awards program if entered.

MICHAEL J. OKRAY
Location: Cheyenne County
Year Taken: 1992
Score: 258-2/8
Owner: Bass Pro Shops

The first shot flew over the back of the biggest buck Mike Okray had ever hunted in his life and he wondered if he had time to shoot again.

Such was the dilemma facing Mike on October 21, 1992, when he aimed at a non-typical whitetail deer as he hunted on private land in Cheyenne County with his friend and guide Greg Pink. On the first day they sat in a small wooded lot watching for deer and only saw scrape marks. On the second day, Greg told Mike that bucks lie down in the willows so he offered to walk around the willows in a zigzag pattern, in hopes that his movement would drive bucks to Mike who sat by a game trail next to the willow field. Greg explained that if he started a drive he would stand up and wave his hands to attract Mike's attention so Mike could prepare for the flushing of a buck in his path.

Shortly after these arrangements were made, Greg began waving his arms in the willows and motioning to Mike. Make thought Greg wanted him to prepare for bucks coming out of the willows so he stayed in his position and waved back at Greg to acknowledge the start of a drive. Greg continued to wave at Mike and Mike at first didn't know what to think until Greg motioned for Mike to crawl to him rather than staying at the trail. This accomplished, Mike got within 75 to 100 yards when Greg pointed to a location where he whispered a buck was standing broadside to him within 50 yards. When Mike tried to see the buck he couldn't and didn't shoot. Greg again motioned for Mike to shoot but Mike only saw its body and not the antlers. After several moments of hesitation, Mike trusted Greg's effort to get him to shoot and he fired a round using his 7mm magnum Lazar Blazer R-94. The bullet flew over the back of the buck, much to the astonishment of Mike and Greg, so he fired a second time and the shot hit its mark.

Greg ran to the buck and threw his jacket over the rack to prevent Mike from seeing its size and told Mike the rack was unusual. Mike's first thought was disappointment, thinking that he shot a small buck or one with freak antlers but upon reaching the buck and seeing the rack, all doubt melted away.

The buck was estimated to be 9 years old and a full body weight of 312 pounds. The buck ranks as the largest non-typical whitetail buck taken in Colorado that is ranked in the Boone and Crockett Club's all-time records book.

This magnificent buck is on public display at the Bass Pro Shop at their headquarters store in Springfield, Missouri. Bass Pro Shops Outfitter World at 1935 S. Campbell in Springfield is open 364 days a year and only closed on Christmas Day. Call first for hours the store is open. The shop includes more than 300,000 square feet of wildlife displays mixed with outdoor merchandise. Michael's non-typical

whitetail buck is one of more than 80 trophies featured in the "King of Bucks" collection, a registered name for the Bass Pro Shops exhibit of big game. Bass Pro Shop in Springfield was the gracious host of the B&C 24th North American Big Game Awards Program in June, 2001 including an exhibit of all award-winning big game entered from 1998-2000.

SCOTT TENOLD
Location: Pueblo County
Year Taken: 1994
Score: 239-2/8

Story by Riley A. Fletschock

When Scott Tenold was going to chiropractic school he met a man from Colorado named Doug Kuhns. They became friends and kept in touch, with deer hunting a common interest. Doug, who had gone into an outfitting business, would send Scott videos and stories of the big bucks they shot in Colorado. Over the years, Doug invited Scott to come out to hunt, but it took until the 1997 hunting season before Scott journeyed to Colorado.

Scott had drawn a rifle permit in an area where a huge non-typical whitetail was hanging out. Just a few days before Scott arrived, Doug had filmed the great buck again.

The first day of Scott's hunt was December 7, 1997. Having seen the buck at a distance in the morning, they headed back to the hayfield for the afternoon hunt. Set up in an irrigation ditch, with some piled up hay bales as a blind, Scott and Doug were ready. Does and fawns came out to feed, followed by some smaller bucks. Then they saw the huge non-typical step out of the river bottom cover. Doug got the camcorder running as they observed the monster chase a big doe out into the hayfield and stop some 250 yards from the hunter. Scott leveled his STW rifle on the buck and squeezed off a shot. The buck never knew what hit him. He went about 40 yards before dropping. Doug captured the whole episode on film. The buck was 8-1/2 years old, with a

Scott Tenold holds his B&C whitetail buck near his home in Wisconsin.

live weight of 270 pounds and 22 scorable points. This 13x9 whitetail buck has a score of 239-2/8 points. It ranks as the Number Two non-typical whitetail in Colorado.

What Scott remembers most about the hunt is the generosity of his friend, Doug Kuhns. Doug could have hunted this buck himself, but he unselfishly let Scott take this trophy. Scott said he doesn't know anybody in the world who would let someone else have a chance at such a great buck.

After hearing that Scott got the non-typical, Tony Perry, the man who had shot at and missed this buck during the 1996 season, flew in from Vale, Colorado, to give Scott the 1995 sheds from the buck. The right shed scored 108-7/8 and the left scored 93-0/8.

Scott would like to thank his friends for such a memorable hunt.

In the field moments after taking this outstanding whitetail buck in Pueblo County, Wisconsin hunter Scott Tenold takes time for a winning photograph. The buck is the second largest non-typical whitetail buck ever taken in Colorado.

RAYMOND A. VERTOVEC
Location: Pueblo County
Year Taken: 1994
Score: 233-3/8

Alfalfa and wheat fattened a trophy whitetail buck all year and many people knew its whereabouts, but it was farmer Raymond Vertovec who collected it in 1994. Who says the big ones don't exist in Colorado?

Ray leases land between Colorado Springs and Pueblo in Pueblo County so he is often in the field when spotting wildlife. The property totals more than 1,000 acres of ideal habitat for whitetails, so Ray spent every morning and some afternoons during the 10-day hunting season searching for a buck. On the second to last day of the season, Ray was feeding hogs when he spotted a herd of whitetails so he watched and noticed a buck chewing wheat stubble in a ditch. This was the first time Ray noticed the buck but after he harvested it others in the area said the buck was noticed. Without hesitation, Ray raised his .243 Browning lever action and fired a single shot while resting his rifle on a fence. The buck dropped from a distance of 70 yards. The buck was so heavy that he couldn't pick it up so he called his brother Matthew to help load it onto his pickup truck.

The buck is one of the largest non-typical whitetail bucks ever taken in Colorado as listed in the 11th edition of Boone and Crockett Club's all-time records book, *Records of North American Big Game*, and is currently on display at Valentine Taxidermy in Pueblo, Colorado, where many outstanding and unmeasured whitetail bucks are on display.

PAUL D. MIRLEY
Location: Prowers County
Year Taken: 1997
Score: 209-1/8

Paul Mirley of Massachusetts began hunting the Lemar area of southeast Colorado in 1996. His hunting companion, Scott Steinkruger of Amarillo, Texas, invited him to hunt on a piece of private property bordering the Arkansas River. Scott took home a nice 10-point whitetail buck and the men saw many smaller deer.

An early season blizzard covered the region with 2 to 3 feet of snow around opening day of the 1997 season from October 25 to November 5. The difficulty getting around the property the first couple of days was an understatement. Because of the early snow, the property owner was not able to cut his standing corn, which was a magnet to the whitetails. Paul and Scott saw several bucks in the 140-class the first couple of days and Scott collected a nice non-typical scoring in the high 140's. The next morning they were driving in the truck at mid morning when they saw a massive whitetail buck with another buck and doe, feeding by the corn. By the time they saw the deer, the deer were already running for the Tamarak State Wildlife Area for safety.

The following afternoon Paul decided to hunt a drainage slew in the area where they saw the deer from the morning before. By now the snow was melting rapidly from rising temperatures. The slew was almost bare of snow with the grasses and scrub brush flattened by the snow. Because of the wind direction and the lack of cover, Paul had difficulty finding a

place to take a stand for the afternoon. The only place Paul found was a cattle feeder made out of a tractor tire turned on its side with the sidewall cut off to create a bowl. The feeder was empty so Paul made the decision to squeeze into it.

Paul figured he looked pretty ridiculous sitting in the tire, but it worked. A doe came screaming out of the bush and ran within 10 feet of his stand. Several minutes later a buck came running out of the bush 300 yards away, but it was gone before Paul could get off a shot. As Paul sat dejectedly for missing the opportunity, a doe stepped out of the bush only 40 yards away from his position, followed by the massive buck Paul searched to find. While the buck looked for the doe, Paul raised and fired his .300 Winchester Magnum. At the report this incredible buck was Paul's. When Paul walked up to it for a closer examination, Paul could not believe his eyes. Paul shook uncontrollably. After anxiously waiting the required 60-day drying period, the buck was officially scored by a Boone and Crockett Club measurer with a total of 209-1/8 points. The buck has 20 scoreable points and a 28-inch outside spread.

Paul Mirley waited in a cattle feeder made from a cut tractor tire and downed this massive whitetail buck with a single shot at 40 yards from his .300 Winchester. The buck scored 209-1/8.

DAVE SANFORD
Location: Baca County
Year Taken: 1996
Score: 200

Who ever said that success in hunting often begins with a lot of good luck has never heard Dave Sanford's story.

Dave decided to hunt on a ranch in Baca County in eastern Colorado for the fall 1996 season. The rancher didn't allow driving while hunting because of dry conditions, so Dave walked along river bottoms and through the woods for a day and a half. Dave's friend, Arden Nicodemus, and his son Austin, were hunting with him, and as they walked along Austin jumped over a deadfall and stepped on Dave's buck that was bedded down. The buck bolted toward Dave and Arden. Arden couldn't shoot because the buck was in line with Austin and Dave couldn't shoot because Arden was in line with the buck, so they both had to wait for the deer to run past them before any shots were fired. As soon as there was a safe shot within 30 yards, Dave raised his 7 Magnum Ruger No. 1 Single Shot rifle and fired a 160-grain bullet.

The bullet hit its mark and Arden went to cut the throat when Dave hollered, "Stop!" Dave knew this was a set of antlers and a cape he wanted to keep. The buck had an estimated live weight of 330 to 340 pounds and a field-dressed weight, without head or a cape, of 262 pounds. Dave said the buck had received several bullet wounds, including a damaged shoulder that had healed and scars from other bullets

Dave Sanford (right) in the field moments after he downed his B&C non-typical whitetail buck. Dave's whitetail is one of only 13 bucks from Colorado listed in the B&C and P&Y.

hitting its body. Dave estimated the buck had been around for a long time.

Dave was at the right place at the right time to collect this outstanding whitetail buck. Who says good luck doesn't count for something?

Dave's outstanding non-typical whitetail buck was accepted into the Boone and Crockett Club's 24th North American Big Game Awards Program.

MICHAEL L. FURCOLOW
Location: Morgan County
Year Taken: 1997
Score: 199-1/8

Mike Furcolow knew the South Platte River bottom like the back of his hand since he managed some of the private property in Morgan County, and he knew where two huge whitetail bucks lived. The year was 1997 when he finally was drawn to hunt in the area.

Mike found shed antlers from the same buck in 1991 or 1992 but for several years afterwards Mike didn't see it. On the year he drew his permit, Mike located a monster eight-point buck during the summer before the season started so he was on a mission to hunt this deer when the season began in early December. Mike believes in slipping quietly into a hunting area without bothering the deer and he doesn't do deer drives. He likes to rattle up the bucks when they're in rut and sneak close to them so he can get a clear shot without the rest of the deer knowing what has happened. Mike deliberately waited a few days after the season opened to avoid bumping into other hunters that terrorize the deer with their shooting and movements. The other hunters would scare deer onto the property where Mike hunted, so waiting a few days was the best plan.

Thursday, December 4, 1997, Mike scouted his area, making sure to avoid the willows and grape cover in the river bottom that he calls the "honey hole," with steep draws that go up to a hill with cornfields on top. Mike's plan was to sit on one of the draws near the cornfields as the bucks filed back to the river bottom but he decided to walk with his wife, Terry, on the other side of the river to glass around. As he and Terry walked through a gate, standing in the open, were two monstrous bucks chasing a doe out of the river bottom. One of the bucks was the eight-pointer and the other was a non-typical. The bucks and doe saw the humans but didn't startle; all they did was return to the river bottom within a quarter mile from Mike and Terry. Mike knew they went toward a dyke and cover and was waiting to decide whether to follow them or not when the bucks came back through shoulder-height weeds toward Mike, oblivious to Mike thanks to being in full rut. The bucks spared with each other and chased the doe out in the open so Mike and Terry positioned themselves along the dike to have a better view.

The eight-point buck dug at the non-typical buck and took off with the doe down the river and the non-typical started coming up the river toward Mike and Terry along a fence within 300 yards of the hunters. As Mike thought of ways to stalk closer to the buck, the buck started walking toward Mike within 150 yards, standing broadside. Because the buck stood in the weeds, Mike couldn't see all the points so Mike debated about whether he should shoot after only five minutes into his hunting season. Mike quickly changed his mind and fired a single shot – which missed. The buck stood still, looked back at Mike and Mike downed the buck with another shot.

And the eight-pointer is still out there somewhere.
Mike's symmetrical non-typical whitetail buck was accepted into the Boone and Crockett Club's 24th North American Big Game Awards Program.

Michael Furcolow holds his non-typical whitetail buck in the field where it was downed in 1997.

Michael Furcolow holds the skull and antlers of his B&C buck.

Photograph courtesy of Denver Public Library, Western History Collection

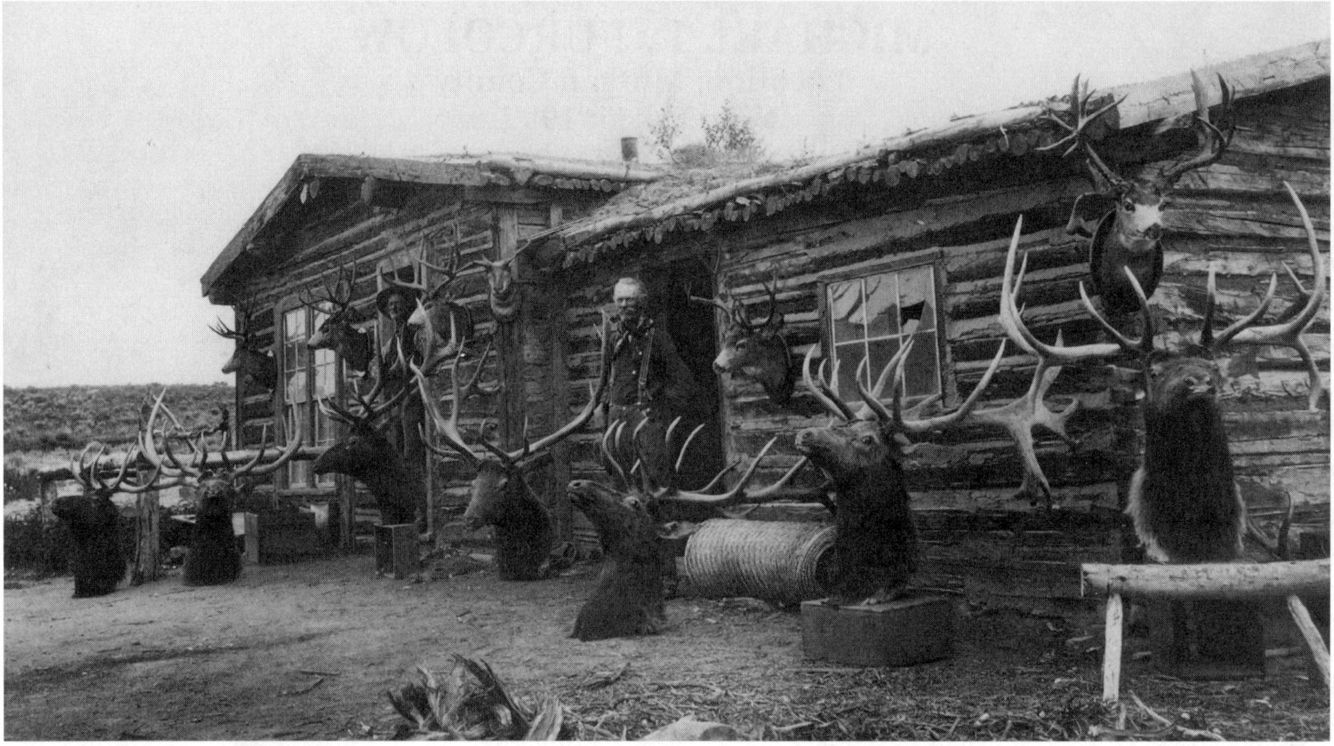

Renowned 19th Century wildlife photographer Allen Grant Wallihan photographed "Dummy" Smith (standing in rear door) and an unidentified friend in the doorways of his taxidermy shop near Lay, Colorado, circa 1894. While compiling material for this book, the author met a customer in the Norwood Hardware Store who recognized Dummy Smith, a popular character from the turn of the century, in this phenomenal photograph. As far as anyone knows, none of these bull elk racks have been officially scored. Care to wager a few guesses?

Photograph courtesy of Animas Museum, Durango, Colorado

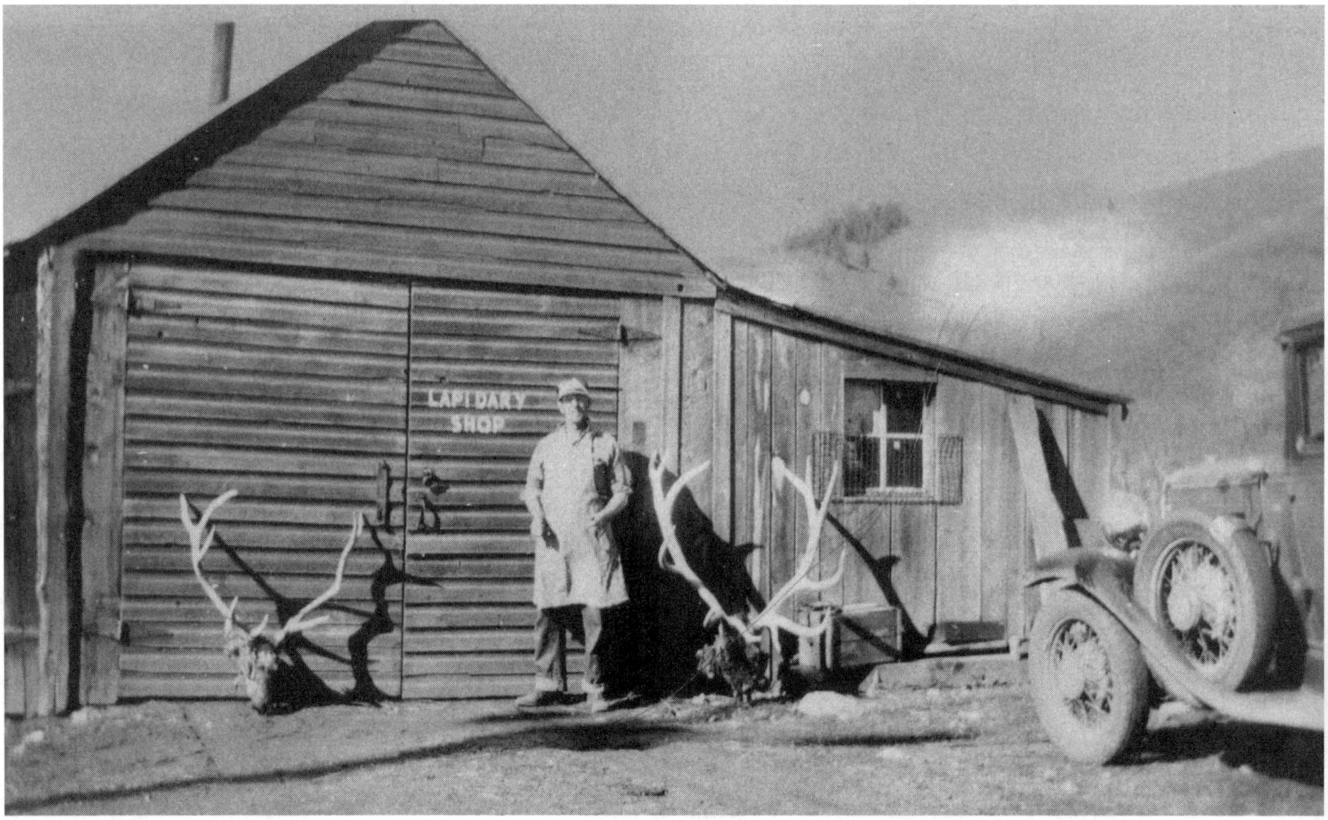

Bill Little stands between two massive elk in front of his lapidary shop near his home in Mayday, west of Durango, circa 1920.

— Chapter V —
Elk Hunting in Colorado

Elk populations in Colorado are at their all-time high but such was not always the case. Today, elk populations exceed 264,000 but in 1903 the total only numbered 1,000 and that may have been a high estimate.

No elk-hunting license was required during the period 1897 to 1902 and all elk hunting was closed from 1903 to 1929. Through protection and transplanting elk to several areas from Wyoming, the population increased to the point that a season was held in 1929. That first season yielded a harvest of 895 bulls. The elk population continued to increase to the extent that cows and calves could be taken beginning in 1940.

Table III lists the license and harvest data from 1903 to the present, and is an indication of the elk population during this period. From 1940 to 1982, the elk population initially increased more rapidly than did the number of hunters. A steady growth in license sales began in 1954, and has continued almost unabated to the 1999 all-time population high and a high of 254,913 elk hunting licenses sold in 1998. An expanding elk population in fact has been cause for concern on the part of Colorado Division of Wildlife (CDOW) officials and hunters alike who see mule deer populations dwindling as the elk population blossoms. Studies are underway now to examine the causes of this disturbing deer population trend.

During the 1940s, elk seasons were of the "boom or bust" type with a year of either sex hunting, followed by two years of antlered only season and a renewal of the same cycle throughout the decade. During the 1950s, the innovation of limited numbers of antlerless permits was begun. In the mid-1960s, a refinement was initiated in selected units whereby the total number of licenses were specified for both antlerless and antlered elk where uncontrolled elk hunting pressure was excessive.

The CDOW initiated a number of innovative elk management techniques in the 1970s to better control the harvest and distribute the take among ever-increasing numbers of hunters. By 1974 the hunter population had risen to more

Pennington Camera Company took this photograph in 1929 on the first day of the reopening of the elk-hunting season. Shown are seven bull elk and their hunters along Main Street in front of Gardenswartz Sporting Goods Store. The man standing in the doorway may be Lester "Buzzy" Gardenswartz. Gardenswartz opened in 1928 and has remained open on Main Street in Durango ever since. Pennington's has been open since 1906 and remains open today near Gardenswartz.

The legendary Otto "Ott" C. Peterson, state game warden in Delta from 1917 to 1932, waits at the Delta Railway Depot to ship five bulls to Denver for distribution to the poor during the Great Depression. These bulls lived on John Burtard's ranch on Hubbard Creek for five years while the Colorado Division of Wildlife (CDOW) paid damage claims.

than 133,000 licenses sold compared with 55,000 licenses in 1964. After many years of combined elk and deer, they were separated in 1971. In addition, the elk season was shortened, cow licenses were reduced by 25 percent from 1970 and spike bulls were protected. As a result, an all-time low of 13 percent success was reached that year.

In 1972, hunters were further restricted in seven elk areas where they were permitted to take only bulls having at least four points on one antler. Elsewhere, any antlered elk could be harvested and the 25-percent reduction of cow licenses was lifted. As a result, hunting pressure and success increased to 86,208 hunters and 22 percent, respectively.

In 1973, the regular elk season opened 15 days after the start of the general statewide deer season. In addition, there were three days of no big-game hunting between the closing of deer season and the opening of the regular elk season.

Three new specified areas were added. In these areas, as well as in a couple of early season areas, a hunter could participate only if successful in acquiring a license through application and public drawing. Almost all other elk habitat was open to bull hunting for regular elk license holders and antlered elk were legal with no four-point minimum restriction. A designated number of antlerless licenses were issued through public drawing for the hunting of cows and calves in 51 areas. Elk hunting was not allowed in all or part of six elk areas of low elk populations. In addition, only bull hunting was allowed in all or part of seven other elk areas.

The season started on October 12 and ran through October 22 in 1974 for a total of 11 days. This was the earliest the season had started since 1971. The early season drew many complaints from hunters who like to hunt in the snow that normally occurs late in October. The harvest of 23,940 elk that year was the highest on record up until that time. A record number of hunters up to that time totaled 133,352. The high harvest generally reflects Colorado's high elk population. An increase in nonresident hunting pressure was partially attributed to the cost of an elk license, which was relatively lower than those of the other major elk-producing states. Two pre-season elk hunts took place in 1974. Early seasons were established in Unit 201 in the northwest corner of the state and in Unit 40 west of Grand Junction to achieve a harvest that probably could not have been achieved during the regular season.

In 1975 there were again pre-seasons in game management Units 201 and 40. The regular season opened on day earlier than in 1974 from October 11 to 21, for 11 days. While the elk harvest of 22,632 was the second highest ever-attained in Colorado to that year, a total number of elk licenses sold topped 143,000 – a new record high.

The 1976 seasons were similar to those of 1975 with early season in Units 201 and 40. Regular elk season proceeded deer season, opening on October 16 for 11 days. The harvest of 23,839 elk by 130,720 hunters yielded a success ratio of 18 percent. The 1976 regular elk season harvest was the second highest ever-achieved in Colorado to that date.

Starting in 1977 the CDOW conducted separate and combined rifle elk seasons. That is, the Colorado hunter had a choice between the separate elk season or the combined deer and elk season. If the hunter chose to hunt during the separate elk season then he or she couldn't hunt during the combined deer and elk season. Vice versa was also true. The separate and combined elk season has continued through 1982.

This concept was adopted in an effort to maximize the harvest of excess elk and to spread hunting pressure between two different seasons, thereby reducing hunter crowding. This approach served to give the elk hunter an opportunity never before offered in Colorado. The management of the species was also enhanced by allowing the CDOW more flexibility in pinpointing needed pressure or reducing pressure with two seasons.

A continued increase in elk numbers coupled with this season structure accounted for a record harvest of 30,309 elk in 1981 to date. The second and third highest elk harvests prior to 1983 were in 1982 and 1978, respectively.

As a result of the separate and combined deer and elk seasons, hunting pressure was greatly reduced. For example, the maximum number of elk hunters in the field during any given season in 1978 was 77,246 even though there was a total of 158,029 elk licenses sold.

Adding to the popularity of elk hunting in Colorado were the low license fees of $16 for residents and $135 for non-residents in 1982 with unrestricted either-sex archery hunting beginning August 28 and rifle seasons starting on October 16. Beginning in the early 1980s an early drawing was held for most restricted rifle bull elk licenses and preference points were assigned if a hunter's first choice was not granted.

Starting in 1983, the CDOW began managing for quality elk hunting in Units 1, 2, 201, 10, 20, 29, 40, 46, 48, 481, 49, 50, 500, 501, 56, 57 and 61 in areas generally located around Dinosaur National Monument, Mesa and Montrose Counties, Pike National Forest near Leadville and Fairplay, San Isabel National Forest, Salida, and Chaffee, Park and Jefferson Counties. In addition, Unit 76 in the Upper Rio Grande River drainage was studied to become a quality elk hunting area. These units were managed as totally limited elk areas in which the number of bull and cow licenses were totally controlled. By reducing hunter pressure, each area produced

The interior of Gardenswartz Sporting Goods Store in 1929 with some of the elk taken on the first day of the reopening of elk-hunting season.

good elk populations with significant numbers of bulls in the older age classes.

License fees rose to $25 for residents and $210 for non-residents in 1984 using all legal methods of hunting. From the time that elk populations were tracked to this year, elk populations rose from 1,000 at the turn of the century to in excess of 165,000 head. Success rate rose to 21 percent of the 149,342 hunters in the field, which was the highest rate of success since 1977 when the success rate was 22 percent. Efforts to inform hunters about the difference between elk and moose began in 1985 as more hunters accidentally or deliberately shot moose they thought were elk when they didn't have the special permit for moose. A simple flier was produced that was inserted into the 1985 hunting regulations showing basic physical characteristics of both animals. Hunters were warned that shooting a moose without a special permit meant a fine of $1,000.

Carl Scheuerman, shown here with his trophy elk in Montezuma County, guided for most of the 1949 elk season with his brother-in-law, and didn't have much time to get out in the field for themselves. On the last day of the season they were hauling out camp in their Model A Ford pickup truck. As they drove out of Cottonwood Canyon on the West Dolores River, Carl saw this massive bull elk lumbering up the canyon. A second shot uphill downed the bull for good. It was late in the day so Carl field dressed the meat and carried the head and rack out that night. Before returning to pick up the meat the next morning, Carl tried to pick up the rack and could barely move it, yet the night before he had packed it out without a care. Amazing what a little hunting adrenaline can do for a guy. Carl's son, Tom, recalled the details of the hunt.

Photograph courtesy of Bryon D. Long

lished from September 7 to 20 as well as a special season for archery hunters that ran from August 13 to September 20. Three combined rifle seasons were set from mid October to mid November. For the first time the antler length for determining legal buck deer, antelope and elk was standardized to five inches. All doe licenses and any deer or elk license obtained in the "leftover" drawing were additional licenses and fees for eliminated the charge for application processing so the price dropped by $3 to $25.25 for residents and $210.25 for non-residents. Muzzleloading rifle season was by drawing only.

During the first and second combined rifle seasons in 1989 any bull elk had to have four or more points on one antler to be legal in all units open to hunting with a general season license. This was a new development in elk hunting regulations, as was the fact that there were no longer antler restrictions in totally specified units except in Unit 76, which included parts of Mineral County between Silverton and Creede. Check stations were set up around the state to collect biological data and enforce laws. A total of 172,644 elk hunters were in the field and 24 percent of them came home with an elk, cow or calf.

For the first time in 1987 there were no unlimited licenses available for the muzzleloading rifle only season. The only archery season was from August 15 to September 20 and rifle (regular and muzzleloading) was divided into three seasons in October and early November. The archery season also allowed hunters to take a bull only from August 15 to 31 and from September 1 to 20 hunters were allowed to take either sex.

The elk population blossomed to an estimated size of more than 181,000 in 1988 with more than 151,000 hunters in the field and a success rate of 21 percent. An elk license for residents rose slightly to $28.25 and $213.25 for non-residents to cover the cost of application processing and search and rescue. A special season for muzzleloading rifles was estab-

New in 1991 was the requirement of California hunters had to possess an original, state-issued hunter education card, not a California hunting license, in order to purchase a Colorado hunting license if the hunter was born on or after January 1, 1949. Special licenses were made available for physically handicapped hunters for the first time this year with certain requirements of eligibility. Resident license fees rose to $30.25 and non-residents paid $250.25. Even though fees jumped dramatically for non-residents, the total number of hunters continued to rise dramatically with 194,434 elk hunters in the field and of those, 24 percent filled their tags. Private-land-only licenses were the only limited licenses issued in a drawing that year, which meant that hunters who possessed a private land only license could also purchase an over-the-counter deer, elk or antelope license for any season. The following year the license fees rose to $33.25 for residents and $253.25 for non-residents.

In 1994, fees dropped slightly from the previous year to $30.25 for residents and $250.25 for non-residents. The CDOW began its new licensing system called the Colorado Outdoor Recreation Information System (CORIS) that required hunters to complete a conservation certificate containing the name, address, driver's license number, phone numbers, birth date, weight, height, hunter safety certificate number and license dates of each hunter. The hunter then purchased stamps to attach to the certificate indicating whether they were hunting, fishing or trapping. The certificate was valid for multiple years to be used for all over-the-counter licenses.

For 1995 one drawing for limited big-game hunting licenses was held two months earlier than previous years in April. New in 1995 was the regulation that "private land only either sex elk" licenses were not considered additional licenses. Elk taken on those licenses were counted toward the annual bag limit that meant a hunter could not purchase an over-the-counter elk license if the hunter drew a "private land only either sex" license. Other "private land only" licenses were considered additional. A youth license fee structure began in 1995 for young people ages 12 to 15. The cost for such a license when a child was with an adult mentor was $10 for residents and $75 for non-residents. By 1995, the elk population statewide

In 1932 the CDOW paid Otto Ott's son Frank, seated on the cab of the 1931 Chevy pickup truck, and one other hunter $3.33 for a day's work to assist in removing the animals from John Burtard's ranch.

exceeded 203,000 with 219,000 hunters in the field and a 16 percent success rate.

Four special restricted archery and muzzleloading units were opened for the first time in 1996 in the White River National Forest that allowed the CDOW to study the effects of early hunting on elk movements in the area. Elk populations jumped to 216,000 with 234,283 hunters in the field.

New in 1998 unlimited either-sex licenses were sold over-the-counter in many West Slope units for the second and third rifle elk seasons but antler-point restrictions continued to be in effect. Additional limited antlerless antler elk licenses were made available in ten units located in parts of Alamosa, Archuleta, Conejos, Costilla, Grand, Gunnison, Huerfano, Rio Grande, and Saguache, Summit counties. Elk populations swelled past 229,000 that year with 51,477 elk harvested. Total number of elk hunters rose in 1998 to 254,913 with a 20 percent success rate.

For the first time in 1999 up to 15 percent of the antlerless elk licenses, along with doe antelope and antlerless deer, established for each hunting unit were available to qualified youth ages 12 to 15 by application and drawing. Free hunting permits to qualified hunters with disabilities were also distributed in 1999 if these hunters had first applied unsuccessfully for the same license through a regular drawing before applying for a special license.

New in 2000 was a separate limited rifle elk season prior to the regular combined rifle deer/elk seasons that were by drawing only. This was also the first year that four regular rifle seasons were established. The first season was a separate limited elk season by application only for October 14 to 18. The second to fourth seasons were for combined deer and elk from late October to mid-November and with all deer licenses limited. Another first for 2000 was a late youth elk hunt if young people had not filled their earlier season tag and if they hunted with an adult mentor in specified late or private-land-only antlerless seasons. The elk population exceeded 265,000.

As far as the future of elk hunting in Colorado is concerned, the prospects never looked brighter for hunters. In the early 1960s there was considerable discussion as to what the optimum population of elk might be in the state. The conclusion was that 50,000 were the optimum. Statistics from 2000 have proven that estimate to be dramatically incorrect.

The Colorado Division of Wildlife increased the cost of a non-resident elk-hunting license from $250 to $450 in 2001. That license price is now in keeping with surrounding states. New in 2001 were over-the-counter, either-sex elk licenses available in the northeast plains for specific units. In the northern hunting units of the state (units 7, 8, 191, 9, 19, 20, 94, 951, 95, 29, 91, 93 and 92) chronic wasting disease was diagnosed in elk and deer so licenses in those units were limited. Nonresident license fees rose to $453.25 for adults and $103 for youth. In comparison, adult residents paid $33.25 and youth residents paid $13.

The history of hunting elk in Colorado is one of great success, not only for the hunter but also for the animal.

Elk Hunting in Colorado

Russ Behram of Maybell found this set of locked bull elk antlers on a private ranch in Moffat County in October 1996. Russ guides hunters on elk, deer, pronghorn and cougar hunts so he has many opportunities to scout the territory. He spotted a freak-antlered bull elk several times. A few weeks after the bull disappeared Russ found it dead and locked up with a six-point bull.

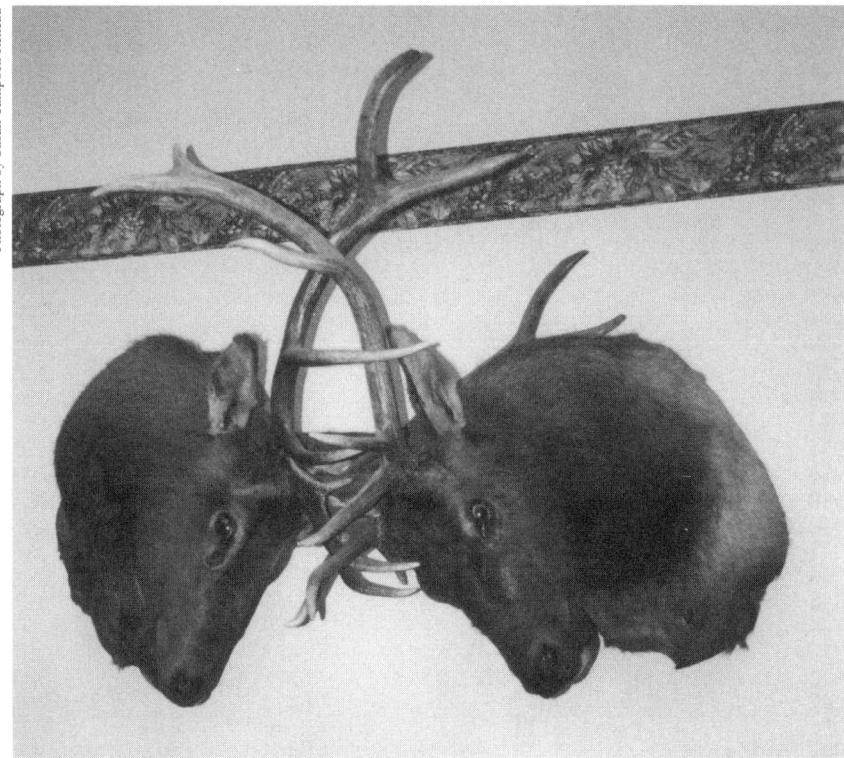

A rare locked antler mount of elk hangs from the wall of Discount Liquors, 305 South Camino del Rio in Durango, Colorado. Two bull elk sparred on October 19, 1996, when two hunters, Jeff and Donald Ray, happened upon them battling for their lives. The two elk fought from 7 a.m. to 2 p.m. Since the bulls' battle probably would have been fatal for both, the hunters decided to fill their elk tags just before the bulls drowned in 4 feet of water on a private ranch six miles west of Navajo Lake near Arboles, Colorado. The two hunters took the bulls on the last day of the hunting season. Video footage was taken by taxidermist Bob Peck and final production of a 17-minute videotape was created by Gary Brown, owner of Discount Liquors. The videotape of the battling bull elk is sold at Discount Liquors. Jeff and Donald Ray decided to have the two bull elk mounted as they died.

Elk Hunting Harvests 1903-1999

Year	Bulls	Cows	Total Calves	Total Harvest	Hunters	Percent Success
1999	21,453	16,392	1,837	39,682	239,109	17%
1998	22,380	25,949	3,148	51,477	254,913	20%
1997	21,697	18,597	2,210	42,504	234,283	18%
1996	29,004	22,454	2,620	54,078	222,309	24%
1995	20,014	14,561	1,596	36,171	219,852	16%
1994	22,390	20,389	2,624	45,403	217,900	21%
1993	21,122	23,348	2,895	47,365	225,080	21%
1992	27,125	20,385	2,624	50,134	207,178	24%
1991	25,574	18,354	2,392	46,320	194,434	24%
1990	27,391	21,507	2,697	51,595	192,907	27%
1989	23,073	16,077	2,126	41,276	172,644	24%
1988	19,018	11,871	1,584	32,473	151,347	21%
1987	13,304	8,495	1,287	23,086	138,136	17%
1986	11,847	8,758	1,277	21,882	122,939	18%
1985	13,902	8,314	1,133	23,349	139,033	17%
1984	18,499	10,632	1,521	30,652	149,342	21%
1983	19,264	8,645	1,148	29,057	181,814	16%
1982	20,369	8,614	1,225	30,208	181,170	17%
1981	20,671	8,634	1,004	30,309	174,214	17%
1980	17,883	8,643	1,097	27,623	160,912	17%
1979	19,213	7,645	1,013	27,871	144,567	19%
1978	20,685	7,176	1,054	28,912	141,664	20%
1977	18,718	6,665	911	26,294	121,083	22%
1976	16,055	6,225	1,559	23,839	120,047	20%
1975	15,745	5,500	1,387	22,632	132,608	17%
— Before 1975, hunters and percent success based on license sales —						
1974	16,208	6,501	1,237	23,946	133,352	18%
1973	14,548	4,611	771	19,930	116,338	17%
1972	13,017	5,082	935	19,034	86,208	22%
1971	7,275	2,945	473	10,693	82,015	13%
1970	12,660	3,944	632	17,236	94,788	18%
1969	13,851	5,989	1,100	20,940	78,970	27%
1968	8,676	5,324	1,088	15,088	69,008	22%
1967	7,913	4,484	791	13,188	59,939	22%
1966	7,812	4,752	1,158	13,722	56,751	24%
1965	8,972	3,943	680	13,595	56,902	24%
1964	9,734	4,492	749	14,975	55,002	27%
1963	8,114	3,377	629	12,120	51,672	23%
1962	6,343	3,307	703	10,353	46,919	22%
1961	7,413	3,820	510	11,743	44,406	26%
1960	6,806	3,358	675	10,839	39,495	27%
1959	6,823	3,306	691	10,820	37,223	29%
1958	5,290	2,776	532	8,598	31,589	27%
1957	4,869	2,748	538	8,155	29,639	28%
1956	5,137	2,725	510	8,372	27,261	31%
1955	4,640	2,052	345	7,037	24,006	29%
1954	4,512	1,361	283	6,156	22,302	28%
1953	4,158	934	207	5,299	19,400	27%
1952	2,977	26	3	3,006	20,317	15%
1951	4,581	4,240	1,509	10,330	29,302	35%
1950	4,061	2,519	866	7,446	25,266	29%
1949	3,641	3,481	1,126	8,248	25,379	32%
1948	3,831	5,154	1,643	10,628	24,278	44%
1947	3,849	700	244	4,793	18,708	26%
1946	4,114	3,185	1,129	8,428	28,945	29%
1945	1,481	1,452	428	3,361	7,517	45%
1944	2,827	1,104 **	3,931	53,729 ***		NA
1943	3,932	2,216 **	6,148	55,458 ***		NA
1942	3,558	1,335 **	4,893	9,376		52%
1941	1,680	707 **	2,387	8,436		28%
1940	2,375	612 **	2,987	33,540 ***	****	****
1929-1939	11,475	—	—	11,475	179,824	****
1903-1928	—	—	—	No Season	None	—

** Cow, calf breakdown not available for the years 1940-1944.
*** Deer or elk.
**** Information not available.

— *Chapter VI* —
Colorado Typical and Non-Typical American Elk
Stories and Photographs

JOHN PLUTE
Location: Gunnison County
Year Taken: 1899
Score: 442-3/8
Owner: Ed Rozman

John Plute of Crested Butte, a bachelor and mountain man of the first order, shot this huge bull in the Dark Canyon of Anthracite Creek in 1899 with a .30-40 Krag rifle. He gave the rack to saloon keeper John Rozich in payment for a bar bill. Ed Rozman, stepson to John Rozich, became the owner of the rack when he acquired the saloon many years later.

Ed and Tony Rozman made the first effort to officially measure the antlers in 1955, and the score was sent to the Boone and Crockett Club headquarters in New York City. However, it wasn't until September 1961 that Charles Whadford of the Hotchkiss Elks Lodge had it officially scored by Jesse Williams of the Colorado Division of Wildlife. At the close of the 10th Awards Competition, the trophy was invited by the Boone and Crockett Club to the American Museum of Natural History in New York for final judging. In February 1961, the Plute antlers were officially certified as the new World's Record typical American elk with an official score of 442-3/8 points.

Photographs do not do justice to this massive 8x7 rack with a basal circumference of one antler measuring greater than a foot. The length of the main right beam measures 55-5/8 inches and the left main beam measures a whopping 59-5/8 inches. Total number of inches for this rack is 459-7/8 inches with only 17-4/8 inches of deductions.

Through the efforts of the American Sportsman's Club, Plute's antlers were mounted by Joe Jonas, Jr., a Denver taxidermist, who mounted them using a cape from the largest bull he could find. The head then hung in the ASC's Denver regional office for a number of years before it returned to Crested Butte where it was on display at the Crested Butte Hardware and Conoco Station. When not on loan or on tour, the trophy is currently on display at the downtown Crested Butte Chamber of Commerce Visitor's Center.

The Plute elk is no longer the world's record typical American elk. In 1995 an antler collector located a rack that scored 442-5/8 points. The hunter who took the bull did so in the White Mountains of Arizona in 1968, but the rack wasn't officially measured for another 37 years. Whether or not the Plute elk is the World's Record it remains Number One in the hearts and souls of Colorado hunters and Number Two in the world by a mere 2/8 points.

Certificate of Merit
10th B&C Competition
Former World's Record

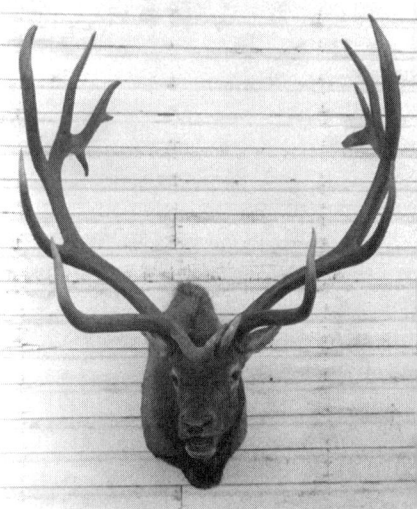

A rare photograph (circa 1900) of Crested Butte resident John Plute (far left) with a line up of hunting friends. John took the World's Record typical American elk in the Dark Canyon in 1899. The other hunters are unidentified but may include Kapse, George Snepenger, Grehk, George Volk and Jake Saja.

Wildlife Conservation Officer Larry Huck of the Colorado Division of Wildlife holds the John Plute typical American elk (442-3/8 points) with an unidentified typical mule deer mount in Paonia. The John Plute bull was the B&C World's Record from 1961 to 1998.

UNKNOWN HUNTER
Location: Colorado
Year Taken: Prior to 1906
Score: 427-3/8
Owner: Meeker Hotel and Café

This massive typical American elk has fallen from the wall of the Meeker Hotel several times, so the measurements are unofficial since several points have been repaired, but the mount is something special. A rare historical photograph shown on this page includes this same elk hanging in the Meeker Hotel lobby in 1906. We know that the mount has been on display for at least that long. Roger Selner, an official measurer for the Boone and Crockett Club, scored the rack in 1996 at 427-3/8 points, so if it could be entered in the B&C it would rank as one of the largest typical bull elk in the world.

Photographs courtesy of Roger Selner, Trophy Show Productions, Inc.

JOHN R. BURRITT
Location: Gunnison County
Year Taken: 1970
Score: 397-2/8

Physical endurance and marksmanship both play a significant role in many big-game hunts, especially for elk. As a biathlon competitor (cross-country skier and marksman) in the 1960 Winter Olympic Games held in Squaw Valley, John Burritt had the opportunity to have both skills honed to a fine edge. In fact, John feels that his experience as a biathlon competitor probably contributed greatly to the success of the hunt on which he took his Boone and Crockett bull.

On the first day of the 1970 elk season, John hunted with his brother on Electric Mountain approximately 13 miles north of Paonia. Unfortunately, the area was crowded and neither hunter saw any game. Thus, when John's brother asked him to return to the same area the next day John turned him down with the excuse he wasn't feeling well. John had already made plans in his mind to hunt alone the next day on Mount Gunnison about 12 miles southeast of Paonia.

After a leisurely breakfast the next morning and a short drive, John parked his Studebaker Lark at a wide spot in the road about two miles above the Davenport Ranch. From there John spent the rest of the morning working his way uphill in the knee-deep snow. Other than a few does, the only other signs of game John saw were tracks and a lone coyote. He was tempted to shoot the coyote but passed it up since he figured he'd rather eat elk than coyote. He felt that shots would likely ruin his chances for taking game.

That afternoon John began working his way down the face of Mount Gunnison in big loops hoping to drive something out. When he got within shooting distance of his car, John figured he had been beaten for the day and fired a random shot into a rocky outcrop. He remembers thinking, "I know they're here; I guess I'll wake them up before I leave."

About another 30 yards down the hill John glanced at the opposite hillside and there stood an old bull looking straight at him about 500 yards away. John dropped to a sitting position and fired. As the bull turned to move John cranked his scope up to 8x and prepared for another shot. When John looked through the scope again he couldn't believe the antlers he saw. Even at 500 yards they seemed exceptional. He fired again and the bull disappeared into the oak brush.

Though he thought he might have missed, John quickly picked up the bull's trail. The bull had been hit, and John found it lying in the underbrush after trailing it for only 30 yards.

JAMES A. BALLER
Location: Jackson County
Year Taken: 1969
Score: 392
Owner: North Park State Bank

Not many hunters can say they have ever had trophy elk feeding in their backyard. But for Jim Baller, the owner of the Baller Livestock Company, this actually occurred a number of years ago.

During the 1969 elk season, Jim hunted his ranch unsuccessfully the first two days of the season. Towards the end of the season Jim noted that four bulls were feeding on the haystacks in one of his meadows and decided to make one last attempt to fill his tag.

At daylight on the last day of the season, Jim and a hired hand approached the meadow in their pickup where the bulls fed during the night. The four bulls were spotted, but they were already headed for an adjacent stand of timber. The two men quickly drove to the edge of the meadow where they abandoned their truck. They then ran until they were close enough for a good shot. Jim downed the largest bull with a single shot from his .308 Winchester, Model 88, while the hired hand dropped another.

Shortly thereafter another local resident, Russ Crowder, and the two game wardens, Don Gore and Jack Hogue, approached Jim and his hired hand from another direction. The disappointed trio had been stalking the same bulls from another angle. None of the three had been able to get a shot at the remaining two bulls.

With the assistance of the three other hunters and Jim's father, Pete, who had arrived shortly after the shooting, Jim field dressed the bull. The big bull was then dragged into Jim's pickup with the aid of another truck. Jim later estimated that his bull weighed 750 pounds field dressed. Jim's bull scored 392 points in the all-time records book.

Jim's outstanding bull elk has been on public display at several locations over the years but is currently on display at Corkle's Little Market that is now known as North Park Super's in Walden, Colorado. Prior to 1980 it was displayed in the lobby of the North Park State Bank in Walden and the Rand Store in Rand, Colorado. For 15 years it was in the private cabin of Rosa Mae Nelson from 1980 to 1995 until it was moved to its current public display area at the Walden supermarket.

Two old-time Colorado Division of Wildlife game wardens are George Steele (left) and Rooster Wilson (right). These game wardens were on duty in the early 1900s.

An unidentified woman hunter overlooks the outskirts of Montrose at the beginning of the 20th Century, circa 1900 to 1910.

HUNTER UNKNOWN
Location: Mt. Evans
Year Taken: 1874
Score: 391-4/8
Owner: Frank Brady

Frank Brady, the current owner of this magnificent set of elk antlers, first remembers seeing this head hanging behind the meat counter of his grandfather's grocery store in Idaho Springs. It was the center of attraction, with large deer heads flanking it on either side.

No one knew exactly where the antlers had come from as they came with the store when his grandfather purchased it in 1911. However, everyone agreed that it probably came from the Mount Evans area.

In 1945 Frank's grandfather retired and leased the store. While cleaning it out, he asked Frank to take the old heads to the dump. Fortunately, Frank recognized the uniqueness of his grandfather's elk mount and decided to keep it himself.

In the early 1960s Frank took the head to Joe Jonas, Jr., to have the antlers scored. His trophy scored 391-4/8 points and ranked 12th in the world at that time.

Later the head mount began to deteriorate so Frank disassembled it. Stuffed inside the head was a copy of The Denver Times (Territory of Colorado) dated July 1874. Thus, this exceptional animal was probably taken even before Colorado became a state in 1876. The exact date of kill is unknown but estimates place it in 1874.

After almost 88 years this trophy was recognized for its outstanding qualities by receiving a Certificate of Merit at the Boone and Crockett Club's 10th North American Big Game Competition held in Pittsburgh's Carnegie Museum in 1962.

**Certificate of Merit
10th B&C Competition**

JOHN HOLZWARTH
Location: Grand County
Year Taken: 1949
Score: 391-3/8

**Certificate of Merit
9th B&C Competition**

According to John Holzwarth, Jr. his father and he would be millionaires today if elk could have been legally raised and sold. The bull his father has listed in the records book is one of numerous elk that annually fattened themselves on the haystacks of the Holzwarth's "New Summer Ranch" near Granby.

In 1949 John and his father were working in the fields when John noticed a huge bull feeding on one of their many haystacks. He pointed it out to his father who then told him to get the butchering tools ready. AT a distance of approximately 200 yards, John Holzwarth, Sr. downed the bull with his sporterized Remington .30-06. It was a crisp, clear fall day and the bull was "easy pickings."

As was custom at that time, the Holzwarths shared some of the meat with their neighbors and the rest was packed away in 55-gallon drums and buried in the snow. This was the only freezer they had and the meat kept beautifully. Since the Holzwarths had plenty of ranch hands to feed daily, the meat went quickly and was greatly appreciated.

For many years the antlers lay in the front yard of the Never Summer Ranch. It wasn't until 10 years later that a Boone and Crockett official measurer Paul Gilbert stopped by and offered to score them. Even after 10 years of weathering, the massive rack still scored 391-3/8 points. The antlers were awarded the Certificate of Merit at the 9th Boone and Crockett North American Big Game Competition held in 1960. The antlers disappeared off the front yard of John's ranch and have never been found again by his family.

John Holzwarth leans against his B&C bull elk antlers (391-3/8) that were on display in his front yard for many years at his Never Summer Ranch near Granby. The rack was stolen from his yard, and the rack's whereabouts are unknown.

PICK UP
Location: Douglas County
Year Picked Up: 1999
Score: 387-5/8
Owner: Colorado Division of Wildlife

This massive typical American elk was killed when a van hit it as it tried to cross Highway 85, south of C-470 Highway in Douglas County in November 1999. The beautiful mount continues to be a popular display at various outdoor shows and at the Colorado State Fair booth for the Colorado Division of Wildlife. John L. Gardner of Wildlife Expressions in Durango did the taxidermy work.

The elk is on permanent public display at the Denver headquarters of the Colorado Division of Wildlife at 6060 Broadway, but look for it at popular wildlife and hunting conventions and shows.

This massive bull elk permanently bugles to visitors who come to the Denver headquarters of the Colorado Division of Wildlife at 6060 Broadway.

Phillip L. Ehrlich, B&C official measurer and Colorado Division of Wildlife official, holds the typical American elk he measured in 2000 that scores 387-5/8 points.

BERT JOHNSON
Location: Delta County
Year Taken: 1974
Score: 386-2/8

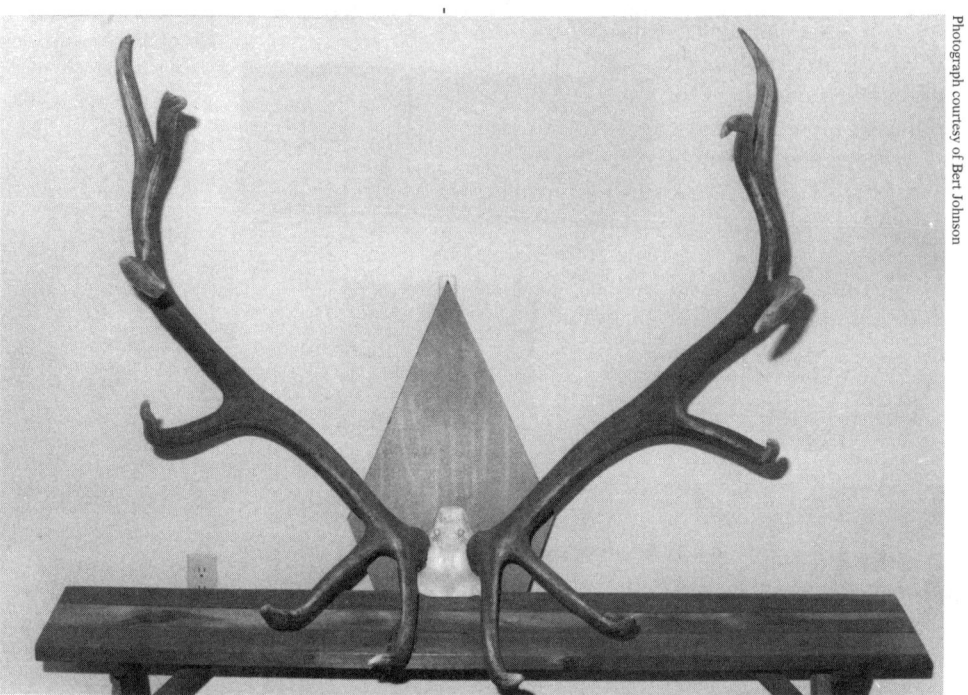

Retirement for Bert Johnson meant more time to enjoy his favorite pastime – hunting. Bert had just retired from the Washington State Highway Department in 1974 when he decided to try his luck on a Colorado elk hunt.

Bert and Ed "Casey" Casebeir wrote for hunting information and secured their licenses in preparation for the trip. In mid-October the pair left Washington for Cedaredge, 50 miles east of Grand Junction. There they were met by Casey's brother, Loren, who joined them for the hunt. They repacked their gear into Loren's camper and headed for Woods Lake near Norwood.

After four days of uneventful hunting the three men received word through the "Buckskin Network" on a local radio station of a death in Casey's family. As a result, the camp was dismantled and the trio returned to Cedaredge empty-handed. While in town, Casey's cousins Erwin and Dick Casebeir asked Bert and Casey to join them at their camp on the Uncompahgre Plateau near Escalante Canyon in Delta County. Their camp was complete with packhorses. Both were eager to accept the invitation.

Long before daylight on October 18, Bert and Casey awoke after only a few hours of sleep, ate a warm breakfast and headed for Bald Knob about four miles northeast of camp. As they planned to be gone all day they packed a lunch. It was a clear day. The foliage was in full color of bright autumn hues and the leaves were beginning to fall – a great day for hunting.

About an hour after daylight the pair reached an excellent vantage point about a half-mile south of Bald Knob. Glassing the area, Bert spotted a small herd of elk feeding in a clearing about a mile and a half away. They couldn't see antlers as the sun was in their eyes, so they decided to work in a little closer. After they had gone a half mile, they got another look at the herd and spotted a bull with a large set of antlers. The men split, with Bert working off to the left and Casey circling to the right through a draw. Cautiously, Bert worked his way through the oak brush and into the junipers near where he last saw the herd. Taking up a concealed position, Bert grew tense when he saw elk coming through the brush. Five cows passed within 50 yards of Bert before he saw the antlers coming above the brush.

Bert raised his .30-06 Savage, Model 110, aimed just below the ear as the bull came into view, and fired. The elk dropped instantly. Together, Bert and Casey field dressed the 900-pound animal and hurried back to camp to get a vehicle. Luckily, the men were able to get within 100 yards of the elk. Not until much later did Bert realize what he had taken. A Division of Wildlife employee roughly measured it and classed it as 38th in the all-time records book at that time. After the required drying period, Bert had the bull officially measured and it scored 386-2/8 points.

MARSHALL SHERMAN
Location: Summit County
Year Taken: 1966
Score: 382-4/8

About 4 inches of freshly fallen snow covered the ground when Marshall Sherman and his two sons, Mike and Marshall, Jr., pitched camp near their favorite elk hunting spot in the Gore Range in 1966. Marshall always enjoyed hunting, but that year was extra special because his sons accompanied him. It was Marshall, Jr.'s second season, but Mike was still too young to get a license. He just went along for the fun of it and the experience.

Marshall and his two sons left camp at daybreak that day and hiked directly to their favorite hunting spot four miles away. Upon reaching the exact area they had planned to hunt, the three of them fanned out about 100 yards apart to cover the area. The area was comprised of heavy brush and low-lying ridges. Marshall, Jr. took a ridge top and quickly jumped a lone bull. The only thing he saw were the tracks it left. Fortunately, it headed in the direction of his father and brother.

When Marshall and Mike first saw the big bull heading in their direction, it was looking back over its shoulder towards the ridge from where it had just come. All that was visible above the brush were the bull's neck and head. Marshall's first shot was a little high and burned a one-foot furrow of hair off the bull's back. As the bull turned, Marshall fired again. It went down in its tracks about 50 yards from his position. The three hunters did not realize the size of the bull until they found it in the brush. Even then Marshall did not think to consider B&C. With the aid of eight other hunters, Marshall was able to drag his bull a mile to his waiting vehicle. Marshall believed the old bull probably field dressed somewhere around 900 pounds.

Marshall's 6x7-point bull was light in color, almost white and extremely thin. His bugle teeth were worn down to the gums. The meat wasn't the best they'd eaten, but the Sherman family ate it all.

Marshall's elk scored 382-4/8 points and was such a sensation that it was featured in the *Middle Park Times* and the *Denver Post*.

EARL L. ERBES
Location: Jackson County
Year Taken: 1972
Score: 381-3/8

The second day of the 1972 elk season is a day that Earl Erbes will long remember. That was the day he became one of the few Coloradans lucky enough to take a bull elk big enough to make the Boone and Crockett Club's records book.

Earl and his friend Gary Weinmeister hunted elk that year in eastern Jackson County. The weather on the second day of the season was cold, and snow fell heavily all day. The two men decided to split up and work a mountain near their camp. While Earl went down the side of the mountain with plans to work his way along the bottom and back up the other side, Gary worked his way along the top. Earl had gone no more than 200 yards when he located three sets of fresh elk tracks, which he decided to follow.

Earl followed the tracks for more than two and one-half hours without ever knowing whether he was following bulls or cows. With every step the snow fell harder, and Earl considered turning back for safety several times. Each time he was pushed on with the urge to see what he had been tracking for such a long time. As Earl stepped off one of the many

Earl Erbes tracked his Jackson County bull (381-3/8 points) for nearly three hours in a blinding snowstorm.

logs he had to cross, he snapped a branch hidden under the snow. Instantly, three elk bedded down no more than 100 yards away went crashing off through the timber. Even though he couldn't tell what sex they were, he had to do something.

Taking off after the three elk, Earl followed them over a windswept ridge into another stand of timber. When he heard some rocks sliding down the steep slope above him, he dropped to his knees to look under the branches of the pine trees. The view he got would make any hunter's heart skip a beat. There, standing in a clearing a short distance above him was three bulls looking down at him.

With little time to spare, Earl raised his Model 70, .30-06 and aimed at the largest of the three. As one bull spooked and the others started to move, he figured it was now or never. He fired. Three shots later the largest bull rolled down the hill within 25 yards of where Earl stood. Earl's trophy scored 381 3/8 points in the Boone and Crockett Club's records book.

ANTON PURKAT
Location: Chaffee County
Year Taken: 1972
Score: 380-5/8

According to Anton Purkat, the 1972 hunt on which he took his Boone and Crockett bull was probably his easiest hunt. While that may have been the case, it actually took him the entire season to locate his trophy.

Anton and his brother, Joe, hunted every weekend during the 1972 season, as well as many evenings. It wasn't until the last day of the season on a Sunday, however, that things began looking up. Within minutes of their arrival to their favorite hunting site in Lost Canyon in Chaffee County, Anton and Joe picked up the trail of a small band of elk. After tracking them for only 20 minutes they jumped the herd bull. Anton quickly got off one shot with his .270 Remington. When the bull didn't even flinch, he got off two more shots in rapid succession. The bull went down for good. When he saw it up close, Anton knew immediately that it was trophy-class. Everything happened so quickly that morning that Anton was able to get his bull and make it back home in time to attend Sunday morning church services. Anton's bull has a final score of 380-5/8 points.

Photograph by Paul F. Gilbert

WALTER R. DUCEY
Location: Routt County
Year Taken: 1961
Score: 379-7/8

When the October 1961 elk season opened Walter Ducey found himself and three other men camped on the west side of the Quaker Mountains, south of Bears Ears on Black Mountain.

The day before they hunted hard and that evening drank more than they should have so were reluctant to get up the next morning to go hunting. Walter decided he'd go and one of his friends, Joe Clark, said he'd come along. Walter planned to hunt the top of Quaker Mountain where there were nice open parks. The men drove to the potholes, parked their truck and started walking up the north side of the mountain. The sun was coming up and Walter complained it was getting late, so they picked up their pace. About three quarters of the way up the hill the men paused to catch their breath and sit down a spell. They looked back down the hill and saw a big bull walking out below them, looking up the hill to see what went by. In one single movement, Walter turned his gun down the hill and shot the bull in the chest using his .308 lever action Winchester from a distance of 50 yards.

Walt Ducey stands beneath his B&C bull elk that hangs in his White River Resort.

The bull was huge with not one ounce of fat on it. Walter noticed the bull had a scar across the bridge of its nose and another one that ran the length of its ribs on the left side. The bull sported a black head and the hair on its neck was like wire. It had long black legs and its body was almost white. Walter guessed this old bull had survived many fights in its day. He took it to long-time B&C official measurer, Carroll Grounds, in Craig and learned it was around 377 points. He never entered the bull until 1997 when it was officially scored at 379-7/8 points. In 1978 he gave the antlers to his oldest son who had them mounted using a young bull cape. In 1992 Walter purchased a resort on the White River and asked his son if he could display the antlers in his resort. The shoulder mount remains on public display at Ducey's White River Resort, 14 miles up river from Meeker.

ROD B. MORRISON
Location: Moffat County
Year Taken: 1996
Score: 379

A bellow like a rut-crazed bull elk broke the silence as Rod Morrison opened an envelope from the Colorado Division of Wildlife revealing his elk tag in 1996.

First order of business for Rod was to call his hunting partner, Craig Goodrich, who also drew a tag because they had applied together. The men knew the hunting area in Moffat County because they had made several short trips over the years in anticipation of this day when a tag was procured. They met Dee Allred who had drawn the coveted elk tag the year before and graciously revealed prime locations where bulls hung out. Rod's scouting trips were cut short because he and his wife Lesa were in the process of building their log house.

Opening day finally arrived for the pair and they spotted several dandy bulls including a 6x6 and a 6x7 that impressed them. The first few days of the hunt didn't go so well because hunters had beaten them to their "secret" spot before daylight. They saw plenty of bulls but not the two bulls they were after.

Day three the men spotted the 6x6 bull. It had broken one side of its main beam off clear down to the trez. That must have been some fight, the men thought. Craig and Rod split up to check out different bulls that were bugling, and Craig downed a nice 6x6 that morning. They spent the rest of the day packing his bull back to camp.

Day four found Rod anxious for sunrise because he had seen the big 6x6 the day before as it bugled back and forth with another bull. He had passed up a stalk of the big one for fear of spooking it and vowed to return the next day. The men returned to the "honey hole" before dawn to the music of bugling bulls. After looking over many bulls they settled on the one Rod wanted. The stalk was long because so many elk were in the way, but the end finally came. Rod stalked the herd within 200 yards but a cow saw him and spooked the entire herd. Rod cow-called and the bull turned around for a final look, which also became its final breath. One well-placed shot and the bull was Rod's.

That bull certainly looks good as a shoulder mount hanging in Rod's and Lesa's new log home.

Rod Morrison in the field with his B&C bull elk that scores 379 points.

LEO W. WELCH
Location: Gunnison County
Year Taken: 1972
Score: 377-4/8

Though it was the last weekend of the 1972 elk season, Leo Welch and Sal Harns decided to give it one last try. The area they hunted was in the vicinity of Soap Creek on the Gunnison National Forest.

Leo and Sal had hunted all day Saturday without success. On Sunday, the last day of the season, they debated at breakfast whether or not they should return home to Denver. Sal was all for returning home, but Leo wanted to give it one more try.

As they sat in their camper discussing the matter, Leo glanced out the window. There was a light snow falling, which made the countryside picturesque. As he glanced out the south window, he suddenly made out the form of a massive bull cutting across the wall of a distant canyon. It was a long distance away, but Leo knew immediately that it was a respectable bull as he could see the antlers without the aid of his binoculars. Abruptly cutting off their discussion, Leo stepped outside with his .280 Remington and braced himself against the camper. As he touched off the first round, Sal rocked the camper trying to get out, and the shot went wild. The bull spooked, and both men hastily made plans to outwit it.

While Sal attempted to intercept the bull, Leo decided to pick up the trail. Having hunted elk for a number of years, Leo figured there was a good chance the old bull would backtrack anyway. After quickly closing the distance between the bull and himself, Leo slowed his pace. He took a few steps and paused to listen. He continued this pattern for some time when suddenly it seemed as if the entire mountain jumped up 25 to 30 yards in front of him.

Leo pulled his scope down on the big bull to make a quick, clean shot. Nothing happened. The bolt on his rifle had not locked due to the extreme cold temperatures. After that, Sal and Leo got together and tracked their bull until three or four that afternoon. They saw it several times during the day. Ultimately Leo got close enough to put a finishing shot into the animal.

In 1973 Leo's bull scored 377-4/8 points in the 15th North American Big Game Awards Program co-sponsored by the Boone and Crockett Club and the National Rifle Association of America.

MELVIN VAN LEWEN
Location: Grand County
Year Taken: 1961
Score: 376-5/8
Owner: Colorado Division of Wildlife

The late Melvin Van Lewen was a truly dedicated elk hunter. Prior to taking his records-book elk during the 1961 season, Mel had been on a fruitless week-long elk hunt. His companions on his second attempt were Charles Nelson, a fellow member of the Front Range Chapter of the Isaac Walton League, and Gerald Park, with whom Mel worked at the U.S. Geological Survey's Denver Office. They set out together for the North Park area near Rand on a Friday evening.

Tracking conditions were ideal on Saturday and early in the afternoon Mel picked up a set of elk tracks that he began following. There were about 14 inches of snow on the ground, and the day was overcast with snow flurries. After some time, Mel got within 85 yards of a massive royal bull elk and hit it with one round from his customized 6.5 Swedish Mauser. The big six pointer ran downhill a short distance where it became entangled in the brush and expired. After field dressing the big bull, it was taken out on a small toboggan in three trips. Mel got 502 pounds of meat from the carcass.

For the return trip home Mel placed the head on the front of Charlie's Jeep and created a major sensation along the highway. Cars that passed Mel would pull over farther down the road and wait until he passed. Once Mel had gone by, they would fall in behind him and pass again so that all the occupants could get a second look. When the hunting party reached the Colorado Division of Wildlife's Idaho Springs check station, the checkers became very excited at the size of the head and immediately began taking pictures.

Mel's bull scored 376-5/8 points in the Boone and Crockett Club's 11th North American Big Game Competition in 1963.

Knowing that few people would see it if he kept it at home, Mel donated the trophy, which was mounted by the curator of the Denver Museum of Natural History, to the CDOW for display in their Fort Collins office. It is still there for anyone to enjoy and view.

Ironically, and very tragically, Mel and two hunting companions were victims of carbon monoxide poisoning on an elk hunting trip in early November of 1969.

Melvin Van Lewen's typical American elk is held by a Colorado Division of Wildlife official. Melvin's trophy scores 376-5/8 points and was taken on October 20, 1961. Mel died in early November 1969 from carbon monoxide poisoning while on another elk hunting trip.

GERALD J. OBERTINO
Location: Gunnison County
Year Taken: 1986
Score: 376-3/8

A massive bull elk stood guard over a herd of 25 cows as Jerry Obertino bugled to him, and the bull's compulsion to protect the herd would be his demise.

Jerry hunted northeast of Lake City along Mineral Creek in September 1988. On the second day of his hunt, Jerry rode horseback for one and a half hours until he reached an area filled with willows. As the herd of 25 cow elk fed, the massive bull entered the herd and began feeding away from them just as Jerry began bugling to him. The bull answered as it rounded up the females and led them away from the willows. Jerry waited 45 minutes and bugled to the bull again. The bull stepped from the protection of the timber and bugled back just as Jerry prepared to fire his muzzleloader within 100 yards of the bull. A single shot using a 54-caliber bullet brought down the bull. Three trips back to the hunting site using horses was what it took to haul all the meat out of the woods and Jerry did the butchering himself.

DALE R. LEONARD
Location: Park County
Year Taken: 1961
Score: 375-6/8

At the start of the 1961 elk season Dale Leonard told his father, "This year I'm going to get that old orange bull." It was the same bull that Dale, his father and brother had tracked for six years. That year Dale was confident he had finally figured out the old fellow's habits.

The old monarch lived within 30 miles of Denver in an area not usually considered typical elk habitat. Rather, the old bull haunted an area comprised of ranch country and mountain subdivisions. The elevation was 8,500 feet, and the terrain was covered with pine, aspen and hay meadows. The old orange bull and his herd lived in the area year-round.

Dale enlisted in the military in 1958 and, except when stationed overseas, had always planned his annual leave during the Colorado hunting season. He was stationed in California in 1961, so when deer season rolled around, Dale found himself driving toward his home in Bailey, Colorado. By then all of the local populace knew about the old orange bull, but no one except the Leonard family knew his hiding places during hunting season.

Opening day found Dale working through the old boy's backyard. Fresh snow was falling on top of an already accumulated 1-1/2 feet of powder. About 7:30 a.m. Dale cut the bull's tracks. He took up the chase by walking 10 yards, kneeling to glass ahead, and then continuing.

Dale realized he had to get above and ahead of the old guy by paralleling its general direction. He climbed to the top of the ridge and continued glassing the elk trail below him every so often. As he glanced over the hillside for the umpteenth time, he choked, for there, no more than 50 yards away, was a tremendous bull elk under a low-hanging pine looking at its back trail. For a fleeting moment Dale hesitated to shoot because it was not the old orange bull. When the fleeting moment passed, Dale's .270 Winchester, Model 64 cracked and the bull hit the ground not knowing what had happened. While Dale's trophy wasn't the biggest bull on the mountain, it was a perfect 6x6 with 13 inches around at the burr.

Backtracking his bull's trail Dale found where the old orange bull split off the trail and left his friend to run the gauntlet for him. Dale never did get that old orange bull. In fact, no one ever did. Old age, winter and a barbed wire fence were its demise. It was found a couple of years later hung up on a barbed wire fence that it had tried to jump.

Dale's bull was too big to hang in the house, so he hung it on the barn wall. Besides, he couldn't afford the taxidermy fee at the time for mounting. The antlers hung there until 1965 when he became trophy conscious and had the rack and head mounted. Even after drying and weathering for five years in the elements, it still made the Boone and Crockett Club's records book with a final score of 375-6/8 points.

Dale Leonard's typical American elk's antlers hung on a barn wall until 1965 exposed to the elements when he finally had them measured. They easily made the all-time records book with a final score of 375-6/8 points.

TOM C. SMITH
Location: Sangre De Cristo Mountains
Year Taken: 1996
Score: 362-1/8

Hunting with his father each year was something Tom Smith anticipated with great excitement. He and his dad, Clifford, had hunted together for 28 years, so it wasn't unusual that the two men were together when Tom took his Boone and Crockett Club bull. Fall hunting season of 1996 was a tough season for hunters and the two had hunted hard to get where they were now. Tom had endured back surgery shortly before the season began, but he never regretted that medical decision because of the end results. It would take more than the back surgery to stop him from hunting with his best bud, his dad. After all, he IS the one that taught him to be a good and safe hunter.

Clifford had taken a five-point bull early in the morning and the men had returned to camp to be met with a strong wind. Tom got bored in camp so he decided to take a walk into a big canyon on his ranch in the Sangre De Cristo Mountains, just south of the Spanish Peaks on a private ranch. The lone bull Tom took was bedded down under a big old pine tree at the bottom of the canyon as Tom dropped down into it. They had been hunting hard for about a week when Tom found the bull. The hunt had been hard with lots of wind and blowing snow. The day of the hunt the wind was blowing hard with 3 to 4 inches of snow on the ground. Tom got within 150 yards of the bull before the bull saw Tom and lunged forward.

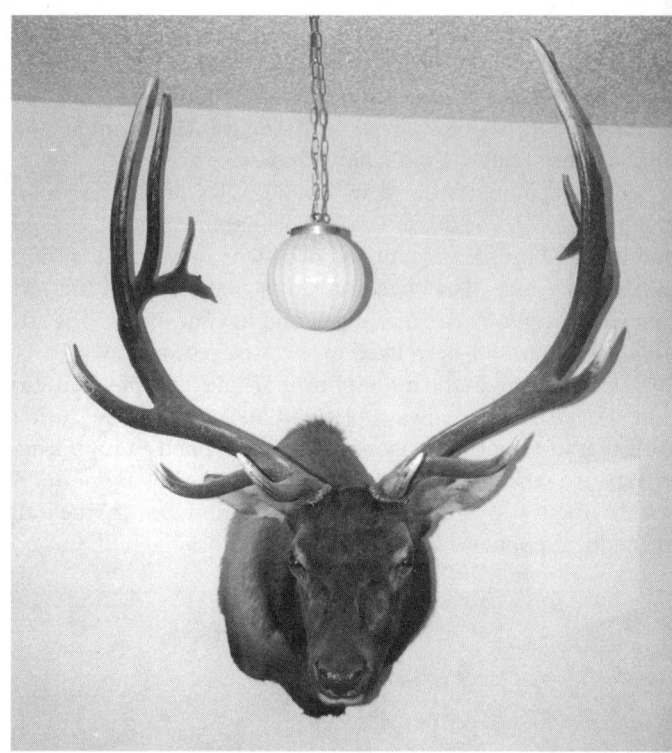

Tom Smith in the field with his massive typical bull elk that scores 362-1/8 points.

The bull scrambled to its feet as it moved forward at the same time Tom fired his Remington Model 700, .270 Winchester, hitting the bull in the lungs right behind the front shoulder. The bull disappeared and ran down a canyon a quarter of a mile, so Tom followed, knowing he had hit the bull but he wasn't sure how hard. Tom heard the bull snorting and bugling. The bull turned upwards because he had heard Tom coming down the canyon walls, so Tom followed the bull upwards to an old logging road that crossed through the area. The bull spotted Tom sitting under an aspen tree and moved toward the hunter.

"He was mad and headed right towards me looking for a fight," Tom remembered.

Tom shot a second time in the neck, and after a few steps the bull dropped dead in its tracks. Tom ran up to the bull and immediately knew it was the largest elk he had ever taken without a doubt. Clifford heard Tom shoot and yelled over to Tom asking if the bull was a good one. Tom toyed with him by yelling back that is was only a four pointer. Naturally, when Clifford reached the bull his opinion of the bull changed quickly. Of the 15 bulls Tom took in his lifetime, this is the one that was the most impressive and the most impressive for his dad.

A lifetime of hunting by father and son culminated with a trophy for the records books.

ROB LUCERO
Location: Spanish Peaks
Year Taken: 1992
Score: 360

A herd of 40 bull and cow elk milled about on top of a ridge in the Spanish Peaks when Rob Lucero and three other friends reached an opposite ridge. The men had spotted the herd from a distance of several hundred yards and knew several bulls would be perfect for the taking.

Rob maneuvered himself into shooting position on the second weekend of the elk hunting season on Sept. 6, 1992, as the herd slowly worked its way up the side of a hill, opposite to Rob. As the herd moved forward, Rob and his friends started to bugle. One of his friends got within 15 yards of a huge bull before releasing an arrow from his bow. Seconds later, another huge bull stepped out broadside to Rob and Rob released an arrow from his 80 lb. PSE bow. The arrow hit its mark and after one final shot, the bull dropped.

Upon reaching the bull, Rob knew this was the largest elk he had ever seen. Rob's friend regretted he had taken the first bull after seeing the size of Rob's. After the required 60-day drying period, Rob had the antlers measured for the Pope and Young Club records-keeping program and would also qualify as a Boone and Crockett trophy because of its size. Rob's bull is listed in the P&Y all-time records book, *Bowhunting Big Game Records of North America, 5th Edition*, that was published in 1999.

Rob Lucero rests against the rack of his Pope and Young bull elk that scores 360 points.

PAUL DUNN
Location: Colorado, probably near Meeker
Year Taken: 1936
Score: 447-2/8

Paul Dunn stands with his 447-2/8-point non-typical bull elk moments after taking it in 1936. To pack the meat and rack out of the woods, the rack was sawed in half, so the trophy cannot be entered in the Boone and Crockett Club's records-keeping program. The bull has been on tour with the World Record Elk Tour but will return to the Meeker Hotel in Meeker, Colorado, for permanent display after the tour ends. The mount has been on display in the hotel's lobby since the 1930s. No other information is known about Paul's hunt, but the rack deserves recognition in this book.

ROBERT HELVEY
Location: Unknown
Year Taken: Prior to 1918
Score: 441-3/8
Owner: Meeker Hotel and Café

Alice McGomery, granddaughter of Robert Helvey, stands beside his massive non-typical elk moments after Roger Selner measured it for the Boone and Crockett Club.

This non-typical American elk was taken by Robert Helvey prior to 1918. Here we see Robert's granddaughter, Alice McGomery, with the elk while it was on display during the World Record Elk Tour in 1996. The elk is on permanent public display at the Meeker Hotel and Café. The massive rack has not been entered in the Boone and Crockett Club even though it was measured by B&C official measurer Roger Selner who operates the World Record Elk Tour in 1996, so there is no rank for this trophy.

CHRIS WHITE
Location: Southwest of Denver
Year Taken: 1993
Score: 404-1/8

Chris White scouted Area 461, which starts a few miles southwest of Denver, all summer in 1993 and found many well-traveled game trails used by elk, deer, bears, and even wild turkeys. He followed these trails whenever he could, hoping to make sense out of them. He did figure out that the elk rested in the heavy timber on the north-facing slopes in the heat of the day and traveled down to feed and drink in the evening.

In late summer Chris observed that every little tree was a target for any buck or bull with the urge to rub the velvet off its antlers. Some rubs were eight feet above the ground.

A week before the black powder season opened on September 11, 1993, Chris located some active wallows and decided to hunt them. Paul Bianchi joined him for the opening day hunt.

Chris and Paul left camp after a quick breakfast of coffee and reached the wallows as the sun peeked over the horizon. Fresh tracks, thrashed earth, and mud splattered high on nearby trees told the men it was an active wallow. The pungent odor of elk hung in the air.

Chris and Paul set up under low hanging spruce limbs and blew the bugle, imitating an immature bull. They followed this with their best cow call. Nothing happened so they moved 100 yards uphill of the wallows and called again. Again nothing happened.

As they discussed their strategy a bugle sounded in a distant valley. A squeaky bugle without any follow-up grunts followed it. Chris figured it was a spike bull and answered with another immature bull call. This time he got an immediate

World's Record for Muzzleloader Longhunter Program

answer. He waited a few minutes, which seemed like hours and blew on his cow call. A bull responded, but much closer this time. Chris bugled again, imitating an immature bull, trying not to spook the little guy by imitating a herd bull.

Chris had actually left his elk call in his buddy's truck and was calling elk with a Quaker Boy coyote killer call that sounds similar to a spike bull. Between his bugles and cow calls, Chris must have sounded convincing. He "talked" to the bull from 7:30 to 9 a.m. without losing any ground.

Chris finally made his move. He kept the wind in his face and slowly moved forward. He took three to five steps, stopped, looked, listened, and sniffed the air. He traveled 150 yards through thick lodge pole pines and aspens in this manner before he finally caught a glimmer of antlers and a flash of tan. Any bull was legal so without hesitation Chris squeezed off a round from his .50 caliber CVA Frontier rifle. He quickly passed through the smoke and saw a bull, his bull, with more points than he had fingers moving up the mountainside 40 yards away and showing no signs of being hit. Chris started to reload and was overcome with a classic case of "bull fever." The bull went another 10 yards and lay down for good. It was 9:45 a.m.

Chris's bull, which scores 404-1/8 points, has seven points on the right and nine on the left. It is the second largest non-typical American elk ever recorded by the Longhunter Program. This bull elk is also entered into the B&C.

The muzzleloader World's Record non-typical American elk was taken by Chris White on September 11, 1993. It now ranks second largest in the world for an elk taken by blackpowder firearm. Here he is in Jefferson County just outside Denver with his bull moments after harvesting it.

WILLIAM C. PARRISH
Location: Mesa County
Year Taken: 1994
Score: 400-6/8

After 15 years of hunting the same ranch in Mesa County, Bill Parrish was familiar with the terrain and the lay of the land so he set out to locate his 1994 bull elk.

Bill hunted with John Boylen on September 10 near a wooded area that was loaded with cow and bull elk. A huge herd was observed by the men all morning but they couldn't get into the area so they decided to walk back to their vehicle to maneuver to another area of the ranch. As Bill walked up a hillside he turned back to see a massive bull with four or five cows standing broadside on the opposite hillside from a distance of about 450 yards. Bill raised his 7mm Magnum and fired a single shot and watched as the bull immediately dropped without moving a muscle. Unbeknown to Bill, John had been watching the bull and its herd using a scope.

Upon reaching the bull, Bill realized he had a giant that surprised him. He called the rancher from the hillside using his cell phone to say the bull hanging at his house could fit inside this bull's rack. Bill returned to camp and retrieved a 4-wheel drive vehicle to pull the elk down the mountain to a flatbed truck. A winch was needed to hoist the 1,200-pound animal into the truck to transport it to the butcher. After fully packaging the meat, the weight totaled 546 pounds.

Bill's outstanding non-typical elk is one of only three to be listed in the Boone and Crockett Club's all-times records book taken in Colorado and ranks as the 54th largest (two-way tie) in the world.

Bill Parrish with his massive non-typical American elk, one of only three recorded in the Boone and Crockett Club taken in Colorado.

WILLIAM E. GOOSMAN
Location: Routt County
Year Taken: 1939
Score: 400

Final plans for the 1939 elk season were made. Bill Goosman and his brother-in-law, Clyde Annand, decided to hunt in Cyclone Park near the eastern end of the Beaver Flattops. Both men were very familiar with the area and knew it was prime elk range. They planned to hunt on horseback beyond the area where foot hunters could travel from motor vehicles.

They saddled up a day before the season's opener and headed to their favorite campsite. Since they hunt from a "light" camp, they only used one packhorse. After setting up camp, they scouted the area around camp. The presence of fresh elk beds and tracks in the surrounding parks convinced both men that elk were "in residence" in the Cyclone Park area.

Bill and Clyde left camp at daybreak on opening morning after breakfast. Bill planned to hunt north of camp and Clyde went west. They agreed to meet back at camp by dark, if not sooner. Bill hunts elk by smell, so he headed for the thick timber. Soon after reaching the timber, Bill found fresh elk tracks. He worked his way into the blow downs and soon picked up the pungent odor of a bull. Bill followed his nose upwind towards the smell.

Easing up on a log, Bill froze when he saw a slight movement about 45 yards away in some small pines. Closer observation revealed the right shoulder and antler of an elk. The bull took another step and its right side was completely exposed. Bill fired a single shot from his .250-3000 Savage, Model 99, with peep sights into the lung area, and the elk was his.

Bill was surprised at the size of the 6x7 rack, but didn't think to have the trophy mounted until after World War II. By mid-morning

Bill Goosman of Meeker scored thousands of big-game trophies for hunters as a B&C official measurer from 1967 to 2001. Here he stands with his magnificent non-typical American elk in 1996 that he took when he was a young man in 1939.

Bill was back in camp, waiting for Clyde. Clyde didn't fire a shot until late the next day when he connected with a five-pointer.

Bill's trophy received the recognition it deserved when it was accepted into the Boone and Crockett Club's 21st Awards Program in 1989, 50 years after it was taken. There are two reasons for Bill's delay in entering it into the Club's Awards Programs. First, Bill's bull did not make the typical category because of the deduction for 13 inches of abnormal points. Secondly, the Club did not establish a non-typical category for American elk until the early 1980s.

Bill passed away in early 2001 after complications from cancer, and his dedicated service to the Boone and Crockett Club as an official measurer from 1967 to 2001 will always be remembered by the thousands of men, women and teenagers who came to him over the years to measure their trophy big game. He also has the distinction of taking one of only three B&C non-typical American elk ever recorded from Colorado.

MARK MARTIN
Location: Douglas County
Year Taken: 1998
Score: 389-5/8

Who says a hunter can't get close enough to land a whopper of a bull elk? Mark Martin began his hunting career with a rifle and scope but found muzzleloading rifles and bow and arrow much more challenging. This type of hunting also required that he sneak very close to the game, which added to the enjoyment.

For the hunting season of 1998 Mark spent the first half of September filming and photographing elk in the field and not hunting. One morning as Mark sat on a ridge looking down 400 yards he heard two big bulls bugling. When the bulls stepped into a clearing, one of them was the bull Mark eventually downed and the other was a bit bigger. Mark watched as the bulls bugled and started moving closer to each other as they sized each other up. He continued watching their movements and dowsed himself in elk urine to mask his human scent so he could sneak closer for a clear shot but he wasn't successful. Mark set up camp and tried to sleep in the thick of things as bulls bugled and racks clicked and rattled all night. The next morning Mark sneaked up to the large bull that by then had 30 to 40 cows surrounding him but never got a clear shot even though at one point the big bull was within 60 yards.

On September 13 Mark headed in a different direction and ran into the bull he eventually harvested. It was late in the morning and the big elk had stopped responding to his calls as it was more intent upon mating. Mark moved closer to the herd using the Scheery and Lonesome Cow calls. The bull started moving toward Mark and was about 60 yards away when it suddenly bolted with the cows due to a mother bear and her cubs in the draw. The elk moved over two draws so Mark stayed in the brushy timber as he moved close to the big bull. He reached the bull and its harem in a tiny washout basin. Mark made his stalk but the big bull kept herding its cows away from Mark. Mark hit the Hyper Hot call, which caused the bull to turn, look in Mark's direction and bugle. Mark hit his Power Bugle call and the bull charged toward him for about 30 yards as he tipped its back and bugled. The bull jumped into some brush and was thrashing as Mark hit the Lonesome Cow call one more time. The bull was interested but was still in the wrong position for Mark to get a good draw on it. The man and animal bugled back and forth until finally the majestic bull stepped out just far enough to give Mark a perfect broadside shot as it started bugling again from a distance of only 20 yards.

The bull's nose was flaring almost inside out as Mark let an arrow fly. The arrow hit perfectly as it crashed into the brush. An hour later Mark began tracking the bull, which seemed to take half the night, but the mission was finally accomplished and Mark collapsed next to the dead bull for a night of slumber. The next morning Mark packed out the meat to his truck and placed the meat safely on ice.

The bull was displayed with the World Record Elk Tour that traveled around the United States. Details of the hunt were provided by Roger Selner of the World Record Elk Tour. Mark's 7x7 non-typical elk ranks as the 8th largest bull in the world from this big-game category as listed in the latest edition of Pope and Young Club's all-time records book, *Bowhunting Big Game Records of North America, 5th Edition*, published in 1999. Because of its size, it would also qualify for the Boone and Crockett Club if it were entered.

Colorado's Biggest Bucks and Bulls

Net gunning during the Rio Grande transplant in February 1993.

Darting Shiras moose during a 1978 transplant

— Chapter VII —
Shiras Moose in Colorado

Shiras or Wyoming moose first made their appearance in Colorado in the 19th century but never seemed to take up permanent residence until a concerted effort was made by wildlife biologists, sportsmen and conservation groups in the 1970s to reestablish moose in North Park.

Gene Schoonveld, Colorado Division of Wildlife (CDOW) Northeast Regional Biologist, reported in 1995 that efforts to transplant moose to Colorado were discussed more than 20 years before the first transplant took place in 1978.

Wildlife Biologist Andre Duvall and District Wildlife Manager Steve Porter of the Colorado Division of Wildlife completed the moose management plan for the North Park area. It stated, "A recent theory is that moose have been slowly moving their range southward and would have eventually reached Colorado. This southward movement has been associated with recent establishments of moose populations in southern Wyoming and northern Utah. The documented sightings of moose in Colorado prior to 1978 and 1979 were probably transient animals, but were perhaps the first immigrants in the natural establishment of a population." Documented sightings of moose in Colorado were in the mid-1950s and in 1976 when a cow moose was illegally shot during the elk hunting season on Independence Mountain, according to Schoonveld.

Bud Smith, regional information officer in 1987 for the CDOW based in Fort Collins, reported that efforts to plan for a moose reintroduction began in earnest in the winter of 1974-75 when CDOW and Routt National Forest officials studied the feasibility of moose introduction in the North Park area. The John B. Farley Foundation of Pueblo stepped forward and offered the CDOW a $5,000 grant if moose were released in Colorado in 1976. Wildlife biologists from Idaho and Wyoming were brought to Colorado to inspect and evaluate several potential moose release sites, and the Powderhorn-Cebolla-Cochetopa area in the Gunnison River drainage was selected as a spot that could support up to 500 moose. The reintroduction didn't take place when the plans didn't mesh with the wilderness management plans of the U.S. Forest Service and the Bureau of Land Management (BLM) because moose were not native to the area.

Later an additional study was conducted by CDOW, BLM and Routt National Forest officials, and the Big Bottom area of the Illinois River drainage at the southern end of North Park was approved as the first Colorado moose release site. A combination of willows, aspen, spruce, fir and lodgepole pine habitat was determined to be ideal for moose, Schoonveld said. A carrying capacity of 150 moose was estimated based upon the riparian willow habitat. Scientists estimated that a conservative moose winter carrying capacity for the southern end of North Park was determined to be 300 moose.

Raising the necessary funds to accomplish this moose reintroduction became the challenge when state funds weren't authorized by the Colorado Legislature to finance the transplant. Approval for the transplant was given only with the stipulation that private funds would be raised. A special bank account was established called the moose fund and $5,000 was received by the John B. Farley Foundation. Sportsmen's clubs, private corporations and individuals pitched in with additional donations, including the National Wildlife Federation, the Wildlife Management Institute, Safari Club International, Energy Fuels, Colorado Fuel and Iron and the Public Service Company of Colorado. More than $15,000 was raised to permanently bring moose back to Colorado.

The Denver Chapter of Safari Club International purchased insurance to cover any moose damage, other than personal injury, not specifically covered by Colorado wildlife damage laws. The Loyal Order of the Moose fraternal organization sold bumper stickers to raise funds and Safari Club International donated radio transmitters for use in tracking the movements of Colorado moose. By March 1978 all the money was in place and 12 moose were captured on the North Slope of the Uinta Mountains by officials from the Utah Division of Wildlife Resources and transported to the Illinois River area in North Park, southeast of the town of Rand. This release included four bulls and eight cows, including one cow calf.

A second release took place in January 1979 when 12 additional moose were captured from Moran Junction, Wyoming, and taken to the same site on the Illinois River thanks to cooperation between Wyoming Game and Fish Department and CDOW officials. The moose in this release included one bull, six adult cows, three yearling cows and two cow calves.

Officials worried that the moose would stray back to Wyoming and not stay in North Park but when radio telemetry equipment was monitored and moose checked, they learned the Utah moose had stayed within 10 miles of the release site and all the Wyoming moose were within one mile of their release site, except a cow and calf found in the Laramie River Valley and another cow that had wandered 25 miles south on Willow Creek to Middle Park.

Poaching has been a problem ever since reintroduction began. During the first 10 years of the reintroduction effort, through early 1987, CDOW logged 32 illegal kills and six natural mortalities or accidental deaths. The cow and her calf that wandered into Laramie River Valley were illegally killed in 1981. Limited permit hunting seasons begun in 1985 provided stringent restrictions to moose hunting and harvest figures confirmed that 80 to 100 animals per year were harvested in Colorado in the late 20th century. Law enforcement efforts continue to work on keeping poaching numbers low, but the battle continues. Kufeld said that moose are sometimes mistaken as elk by hunters or are poached for their meat. Cases of moose being shot and left in the field to rot have also been reported. "Illegal harvest may approach 50 percent or more of the legal harvest once unreported illegal kills are considered," Kufeld reported.

Jim Olterman, senior wildlife biologist in the CDOW's Southwest Region, estimates the total moose population in late 2000 to be in excess of 1,000 animals. He expects limited permits to hunt moose will continue since the total population is relatively low but healthy. CDOW officials admit that counting moose are more difficult than counting elk or deer because they stay isolated and alone and conceal themselves in thick willow bottoms.

From the initial transplant efforts, wildlife biologists and the general public saw moose in Middle Park, Rocky Mountain National Park, the Laramie River Valley, South Park and near Gunnison, Leadville, Yampa and west of Denver. Once again public support for an additional transplant provided the encouragement to provide 10 cow moose and two bull moose in February 1987 from a private ranch in Wyoming within Grand Teton National Park. Schoonveld of CDOW and U.S. Forest Service Biologist Steve Mighton provided the planning and paperwork necessary to successfully accomplish the moose transplant that brought the animals to the Laramie River Valley. The effort was coordinated with CDOW and Roosevelt National Forest officials. The moose thrived in the Laramie River willow bottoms near the Tunnel Campground.

A final transplant area was identified by biologists as areas in the upper Rio Grande and adjoining San Juan and Gunnison basins. An environmental assessment and plan was devised by U.S. Forest Service and CDOW officials to release up to 100 moose over a 10-year period to allow time to locate moose available for tranplanting. DCOW officials began shopping for moose in the summer of 1991 by contacting Utah and Wyoming game and fish agencies. Utah officials agreed to provide 20 moose in return for bighorn sheep from Colorado so CDOW officials made plans to go to northeastern Utah in January 1992 to capture and transplant the animals to the Rio Grande-San Juan-Gunnison area.

Schoonveld offered five additional moose from his moose study when he and other CDOW officials in the northeast region of Colorado discovered that their capture operation was going so smoothly as they radio-collared the moose population in North Park. Snowmobiles for herding animals and a sled to haul fresh hay toward the transport trailer worked like a charm and on December 11, 1991, the first moose left the trailer on the Rio Grande 13 miles west of Creede. The additional 22 moose (10 bulls and 12 cows) from the Uinta Mountains of Utah arrived in the same area in January 1992. The Utah operations involved darting moose from a helicopter and transporting the darted moose using a sling connected to a second helicopter that carried the animals to the trailers. Part of the expense of helicopter use was offset by donations from members of Safari Club International chapters in Denver and Glenwood Springs and from the John B. Farley Foundation.

In 1992 and 1993 Schoonveld reported 26 cows and 20 bulls were captured in North Park and released in the Upper Rio Grande using a combination of drug tranquilization and aerial net-gunning operations. Another 12 bulls and 17 cows were captured in southwestern Wyoming at Smith Fork and released in the upper Rio Grande near the river's headwaters where the moose population is thriving. The transplants that took place in the early 1990s were the last that took place in Colorado since the moose population was so healthy. The moose were released near Creede but have been tracked to Blue Mesa Reservoir and as far away as the Grand Mesa area.

Wildlife Researcher Ron Kufeld reported in July 1995 that a moose research project begun in 1991 included 71 moose that were captured and radio-collared in the east and southeast portions of North Park. These animals were monitored for up to three and a half years by radio tracking at approximately two-week intervals, mostly by aircraft. This study showed an estimated moose population in North Park of 450 to 525.

Schoonveld and Kufeld said public interest and support of the Colorado moose population continues, especially by nonconsumptive users who enjoy seeing and photographing the largest deer in North America. In fact, the Colorado General Assembly designated Walden as the moose viewing capital of the state through recent legislation. Viewing of moose has become a major contribution to the economy of Jackson County.

Significant to the history of moose in Colorado is the 20 moose that have been harvested by hunters that qualify as Boone and Crockett Club trophies. As early as November 17, 1987, when Donald I. Poeschl took a Jackson County bull moose, trophy moose have been taken in Colorado. The fac

Trapped Shiras moose from Wyoming waiting for transport to North Park, Colorado in 1979.

that trophy moose exist in Colorado when reintroduction of the species only began in the late 1970s speaks volumes about the health of the moose population and its habitat. The first Boone and Crockett bull was taken less than 10 years after the first moose stepped foot on Colorado soil. The largest bull moose taken in Colorado with an official B&C score of 194-4/8 points is just a few points off of the world record that scores 205-4/8 points. The moose taken by Dr. Jack Anderson, with an official rank of 8th in the world as stated in the 11th edition of *Records of North American Big Game*, was collected in 1995 – just 17 years after the first moose transplant took place.

The first hunting season in 1985 took place November 16 to November 24 in selected units in the Jackson Creek Drainage, the Illinois River Drainage and the South Fork of the Michigan River Drainage. A total of 485 individuals applied for five bull permits with three bulls harvested for a 60 percent success rate. The cost of an in-state permit was $200. Non-residents weren't allowed to apply for a moose permit that first season.

The hunting seasons from 1986 to 1988 only allowed three bull permits and between 253 to 395 people applied each year. The hunters drawing a permit were all successful for a 100 percent success rate. License fees for resident hunters rose slightly in 1988 to $203.25 that included $3 for an application fee and 25 cents for the Search and Rescue Fund.

In 1989 and 1990 CDOW allowed five bull moose permits with less than 300 people applying each year. The rate of success each year was 100 percent. Seven coveted bull permits were issued in 1991 and 397 people applied. The success rate was once again 100%.

The year 1992 was the first year dozens of bull and cow permits were issued thanks to the dramatic and healthy increase of moose populations in the state and non-residents were allowed to apply for a moose permit. The cost for a resident permit remained the same but the non-resident fee was $1,003.25. That year 32 bull and 30 cow permits were issued and 2,084 people applied.

The following year saw a dramatic increase in moose permits issued – 54 bull and 60 cow permits with an 88% success rate. A total of 2,179 hunters applied. The year 1993 was also the first time CDOW had special moose seasons for archery, muzzleloading rifle and regular rifle hunters starting in

Radio collaring a moose in North Park in December 1991.

September for archery and muzzleloading and October and mid-November for regular rifle. This year a mandatory check was required for all moose taken. A hunter had to present the antlers attached to the skull plate of the animal to a CDOW official within five days after the close of the season hunted. For 1994, CDOW issued 49 bull and 63 cow moose permits with 2,282 people applying. The success rate was 83 percent.

The number of hunters applying for moose permits jumped dramatically starting in 1992 when the number of applicants rose from 397 in 1991 and went to 2,084 in 1993. Since then, the number of moose hunter applicants has steadily risen to an all-time high of close to 6,000 in 1999. Success rates for hunters have ranged from a high of 100 percent between 1986 and 1991 to a low of 68 percent success rate in 1997. A chart in this chapter illustrates the history of moose hunting permits, number of licenses issued, population totals, percent of success and post-hunt population estimates from the start of hunting in 1985 to 1999.

Up until 1995 only hunters 14 and older could hunt moose but starting in 1995 young people from 12 years and up could participate if they were accompanied by an adult "mentor" through age 15. New to 1996 was the institution of a single bull moose raffle license that was drawn on March 2 at the annual banquet and fundraiser for the Colorado Chapter of Safari Club International.

Starting in 1998 a single preference point was earned by each hunter who was unsuccessful in being drawn for a tag. A hunter could use this preference point each year for future applications but the hunter had to apply at least once within five consecutive years for moose or all preference points would be purged. If a hunter were drawn, all preference points earned would drop to zero since the hunter was successful at drawing a tag.

Units for hunting moose were expanded in 1999 with the addition of the Hinsdale, Lake City and Mineral areas of the state added to the areas on the Routt and Arapaho National Forests and in the Jackson and Walden areas of the state. Significant for the 2000 moose season was the reduction of hunting dates for the regular rifle season. Archery season was September 9 to 24 and muzzleloading season was September 9 to 17 but only one regular rifle season was allowed from October 1 to 9. This compares to three regular rifle seasons in previous years.

When all is said and done, the fact remains that transplanting Shiras moose in Colorado is a raging success. And even though the looks of a moose reminds someone of an animal designed by an ungainly committee, one Colorado biologist summed up the popularity of the creature when Bud Smith quoted him as saying, "I think moose are cute."

That says it all.

Moose Hunting Harvest 1985-1999

Year	No. of Applicants	Number of Licenses Issued		Harvest			Percent Success
		Bulls	Cows	Total	Bulls	Cows	Total	
1985	485	5	0	5	3	0	3	60
1986	395	3	0	3	3	0	3	100
1987	267	3	0	3	3	0	3	100
1988	253	3	0	3	3	0	3	100
1989	221	5	0	5	5	0	5	100
1990	273	5	0	5	5	0	5	100
1991	397	7	0	7	7	0	7	100
1992	2,084	32	30	62	29	28	57	92
1993	2,179	54	60	114	47	54	101	89
1994	2,282	49	63	112	40	52	92	82
1995	2,918	54	74	128	50	54	104	81
1996	3,325	44	70	114	34	56	90	79
1997	3,650	40	68	108	29	46	75	69
1998	5,165	43	36	79	33	21	54	68
1999	5,868	48	32	80	34	22	56	70

— Chapter VIII —

Colorado Shiras Moose

Stories and Photographs

JACK A. ANDERSON
Location: Jackson County
Year Taken: 1995
Score: 200-6/8

Jack Anderson and his friend, Craig Jobe, arrived at Red Feather Outfitters on October 13, 1995, where they were greeted by the owners of Red Feather Outfitters Todd Peterson and Arnie Schlottman. Todd told Jack and Craig that he had spotted a couple of nice bull moose the day before while packing in a drop camp for some elk hunters. Craig didn't have a permit but agreed to help any way he could and videotape the hunt. Both men were encouraged and excited with Todd's observations.

Arnie pounded on Jack's and Craig's cabin door at 4:30 a.m. the next morning. Trisha and Marty provided a great breakfast and sack lunch. Jack figured Trisha and Marty knew the men would be out all day and would need extra fuel to face the task ahead of them. The men drove south of Gould to the South Fork of the Michigan River. When the road deteriorated, they left the Suburban behind and took an ATV the last two miles to the Never Summer Wilderness Area trailhead. The sun was starting to rise over Baker Pass, a perfect time to start hiking into the Michigan River drainage.

As the men hiked, Craig filmed several cow moose and calves from no more than 50 yards away. They looked strong, healthy and in excellent shape.

Wyoming moose were reintroduced into the North Park area about 12 years earlier. The habitat was ideal for moose and the herd had grown to about 500 head. Jack thanked God

Jack Anderson in the field with his Shiras moose that measures 200-6/8 points becomes the largest moose ever taken in Colorado. He downed this great trophy in 1995, only 17 years after the Shiras moose was introduced to the state in North Park by officials from the Colorado Division of Wildlife – a true wildlife success story thanks to hunters who financed the effort.

for the beautiful scenery, clear skies, his bull moose tag and the opportunity for this hunting experience.

Jack and Craig ran into a party of elk hunters at 10 a.m. When Jack told the hunters he had a bull moose tag, the elk hunter said he had observed a large bull with a cow about 10 minutes earlier up the drainage. Jack and Craig put their effort into overdrive. When they reached the designated area they spotted a cow grazing approximately 500 yards away on the other side of a meadow. Jack's heart rate accelerated. While glassing the cow, he spotted the rear end of another moose drinking from the river. When it lifted its head, Jack and Craig immediately knew it was a keeper. They had never seen a Wyoming moose with such large palms. Jack's pulse went to redline.

Jack knew he needed to get closer so they ran through the snow to their right trying to keep some cover between the bull moose and themselves. The cow and bull started walking towards the timber away from them. Jack lay down on a big rock and Craig turned on his video camera. As Jack sighted on the massive bull with his Zeiss 3x9 scope, the cross hairs jumped all over it. Jack told himself to get a grip. After relaxing and collecting his thoughts, Jack fired several well-placed shots with his .340 Weatherby and the trophy bull was down. Virgil Hyatt, a Redfeather outfitters packer, was hired to pack the moose out in quarters.

Jack's trophy received the First Place Award at the Boone and Crockett Club's 23rd Awards Program in Reno, Nevada in 1998.

STEVEN P. KUGLER
Location: Jackson County
Year Taken: 1995
Score: 177-2/8

Photograph by Susan Campbell Reneau

Steve Kugler thought he would find his moose in the marshes but, as time would tell, his best luck was in heavy, dark timber.

The November 1995 season was the year Steve was drawn for a moose permit that allowed him to hunt in the Illinois River drainage near Rand. His brother Bruce and a friend Jim Carver joined him as they searched for elk and helped rustle up a moose. Steve wanted to take his moose with a muzzleloader but after four days of no success and no sightings of bull moose, Steve decided he better carry his .270 Ruger as insurance.

On the fifth day of the season, Steve was hunting in heavy timber when he spotted a bull moose coming through the timber to the edge of a clearing on a logging trail within 150 yards of Steve. The moose stopped and stood broadside to Steve as Steve fired. After several shots, the .270 finally did its job, and the moose dropped.

Steve knew the bull was big but didn't know how big until people started encouraging him to have the rack measured. The front quarter of the moose was the same height as Steve – 6 feet, 5 inches. After the required 60-day drying period, the rack official measured 177-2/8 points and ranks as the 2nd largest Shiras moose ever taken in Colorado and 56th largest Shiras bull moose in the world (two-way tie).

NANCY SOMMER
Location: Jackson County
Year Taken: 1994
Score: 171-7/8

After 12 years of applying for a moose permit, Nancy Sommer finally received word from the Colorado Division of Wildlife that 1994 was her year of the moose.

Nancy readily admits that she never would have hunted if it hadn't been for her husband Mick. They celebrated their 23rd anniversary in 2000 and started hunting together one year after their marriage. Nancy figured she could either sit at home alone during the hunting season or join Mick. She has never regretted those times together and has shared hunting experiences with family and friends, including her Uncle Vern.

Scouting for moose became Nancy and Mick's passion for three or four weeks before the season. They arrived in Jackson County and located one remaining cabin reservation in the middle of nowhere but exactly where they wanted to be for moose.

Mick's advice was to get there first and shoot straight, so that's what they did on opening day and their efforts were rewarded with a sighting of two nice moose far away from them – the one Nancy took and a smaller one. Nancy decided to go down in the lower creek to see if they could sneak closer just as clouds rolled in. They walked through the marsh and swamp but never got close enough for a clear shot. The remaining portion of the first day was spent squishing around in the mud and getting familiar with the lay of the land.

Day Two found the couple up early to trek to the same area. Nancy went up on a ridge while Mick walked farther up the ridge to help drive a moose to Nancy when she spotted a

small moose close to her. As she debated about the distance of a shot, another much larger moose came into view, so Nancy decided to watch it for awhile from her vantage point part way down the ridge. She finally took a few shots with her .30-06 from a distance of about 350 yards, and knew she hit it but the clouds rolled in as the snow blew. The wind and blowing snow and fog made visibility down to zero, so Nancy and Mick decided to return to the cabin to change into dry clothes and replot their efforts to track the wounded bull.

When they went back out Nancy returned to the same place where she had shot and Mick looped around in hopes of flushing the moose from the brush. Nancy traveled down in a valley and looked up the hillside and around the edge of the hill. There standing broadside, was her bull, except that Mick was standing in a direct line beyond the moose. Nancy maneuvered herself to have a clear shot and fired three quick rounds. When the bull dropped and they field dressed the meat, she found a cluster of three shots precisely where she had fired. It took three shots from 220-grain bullets to down this massive bull. Since the sun was setting when the moose dropped, they returned the next day to carry out the 500 pounds of meat.

The rancher, his ranch hands and officials at the check station near Walden all encouraged Nancy to have the rack measured, and her moose became one of only a handful of moose ever taken in Colorado to make "The Book." And, they hosted a fine moose party for all their friends.

Nancy Sommer with her B&C Shiras moose.

DENNIS W. MACY
Location: Jackson County
Year Taken: 1991
Score: 162

Dennis Macy has hunted elk in the Colorado State Forest on the western side of the Rawah Wilderness Area near Walden, Colorado since 1983. Each year while hunting elk he noticed increasing evidence of moose in this area, but it was not until 1991 that he applied for one of only seven moose permits given for the entire state of Colorado.

Luck was with Dennis, and he drew his bull moose permit for Area 6. He decided to hunt the state forest where he hunted elk for so many years. Dennis knew very little about moose behavior but acquired several books on moose and moose hunting while fishing in Alaska that summer. The moose season began November 10 following the last rifle elk season.

Jim Warson, a long-time hunting partner of Dennis, and Tom Macy, Dennis' brother, accompanied Dennis on the elk hunt. Dennis knew big-game hunting was a team sport and it was unlikely he could drag a 1,000-pound bull moose by the antlers and sling it into the back of a pickup without help.

The two men walked through 2 feet of snow and survived 30 degrees below zero that froze their wine and beer. The elk had vanished from the area so the three men spent much of their time scouting for moose. They located ten bull moose, including two near an old lumber mill site, the evening before the opening of moose season. They decided to try for one of the big moose near the lumber mill the next morning as there was a nice bull there. The Macy brothers rose long before sunrise and hiked to the meadow at the mill site to wait for daylight. As dawn approached the men spotted the two bulls standing in the meadow 200 yards away. The largest bull was at the farthest distance.

Dennis felt his .30-06 wouldn't be effective at that range so he decided to close the distance to 100 yards. Both bulls became spooked and started towards the black timber. Dennis fired five rounds, all of which hit their mark as the moose dashed out of sight into a stand of thick willows. After reloading, he slowly hiked through the deep snow toward the fallen moose. When Dennis was within 50 yards of the moose, the bull stood up and started to charge. Two more rounds were quickly discharged and the bull permanently fell. Dennis knew it was a trophy as soon as he saw it.

Dennis quickly removed the measuring tape from his backpack and couldn't believe his eyes. The rack was 55 inches wide. The work began as the two hunters began to skin the 1,300-pound animal. However, Tom became altitude sick at the 9,500-foot elevation and had to return to camp with Dennis halfway through the field-dressing process. Dennis returned to the moose a few hours later and wrapped the animal in sweaty clothes to protect it from predators since he couldn't finish the job by himself that day. The next day Tom and Dennis returned and finished the job. Not until Dennis showed the moose to officials with the Colorado Division of Wildlife did he realize just how big the bull was. The moose received a final Boone and Crockett Club score of 162.

Minutes after Dennis Macy collected this outstanding Shiras moose, a photograph was taken to capture the moment. The bull is one of 24 taken in Colorado that qualifies for the B&C, a significant wildlife management achievement considering that Shiras moose were only introduced into the state in 1978.

WAYNE R. KROFT
Location: Jackson County
Year Taken: 1999
Score: 161-2/8

Wayne Kroft scouted throughout the summer of 1999 in Jackson County without seeing moose, so he asked one of his best friends and experienced moose hunter, Don Fenner, to help. Two days before the season began, Don and his wife Diana joined Wayne to scout for moose in several promising drainages.

The men drove up one drainage the day before the season and saw plenty of good moose sign. Opening day led them back to this same area long before sunup to scope a huge ridge that measured at least a half mile in width and one mile in length with ponds and thick willows.

Wayne decided to drop off the ridge to skirt the timber and Don and Diana began hunting for elk along the ridge. An hour and a half after sunup, Wayne noticed something in a willow bog with a shape that looked like a large hawk. When he put his binoculars to the area he realized the "hawk" was part of a set of moose antlers belonging to a massive bull that was moving from the timber into the marsh area. Wayne noticed the wind was blowing up the drainage, so he decided to parallel the moose. Wayne dropped down to the right and got into 12- to 15-foot willows as Don and Diane stayed up top.

Wayne angled his way through the willows, using various tree landmarks to keep him going in the right direction. He came out straight on to the moose with the antlers peaking over the willows in front of him. Wayne looked up to see the massive rack but had no view of the head or body. A beaver pond was

on one side and a creek on the other, so his only choice was to go forward but he feared he would spook it. Wayne skirted the beaver dam, and as he stepped out below the dam he saw the bull standing with a cow that was positioned broadside to the bull with its head slumped over her rump. Both noticed Wayne so he decided to use a cow call in hopes that the cow would move away from the bull for a clear shot. The bull immediately started calling back to Wayne and both cow and bull became nervous. The cow moved four steps ahead of the bull to Wayne's left. The bull was positioned broadside to Wayne, partially hidden in the willows. Throughout Wayne's stalk, the cow and bull stood nose to tail like horses. As Wayne stood in mushy water he searched for a clear shot through the willows and finally found it approximately 60 yards from the moose. He fired his Remington 700 7mm Magnum, but the bull showed no reaction of being hit. It took one step and turned straightaway.

Wayne waited as the bull turned to the right, took two steps and walked into another opening. Wayne fired a second shot, and the moose took 10 to 12 steps, staggered and collapsed into the marsh. Both shots delivered a fatal blow since they were separated by two inches in the lungs. Wayne guessed the field-dressed weight to be 1,000 to 1,200 pounds with more than 500 pounds of meat. It took the three friends 10 loads to drag the meat out of the woods. Wayne, Don and Diana all shared in the moose's bounty. This was a hunt for the records books and for memories.

Miserably cold weather conditions with thick, fluffy frost covering everything greeted Wayne Kroft on opening day of the moose season when he downed this magnificent bull with two well-placed shots in 1999.

BOB GOETTL
Location: Jackson County
Year Taken: 1994
Score: 160-6/8

Winning the moose lottery was a dream come true for Bob Goettl. Routt National Forest was a new area for Bob, so he spent every weekend in the summer and early fall scouting the territory before the season opener in November.

Bob used four different maps to scout the area as he drove down roads in the unit while taking pictures of the area and filming it with his video camera. By the third weekend he had narrowed his hunting choices to Silver and Porcupine Creeks where he often saw a herd of five bulls with nice racks, several cows and a calf. On opening day, November 5, Bob only saw a cow and calf. That night he decided to head back to Silver and Porcupine Creeks. He figured hunting pressure from earlier elk, deer and moose seasons had pushed moose up the mountain.

The second day of hunting was even nicer than the first. Bob grabbed his backpack and planned to make a day of it in the woods. He left early and sneaked along Silver Creek. If he stepped on something or made a noise, he blew his cow call a couple of times and paused for five to 10 minutes before continuing the stalk. He reached dense cover consisting of dead and down timber at 10:30 a.m. Bob made lots of noise when he accidentally stepped on a limb. He heard a loud thump and looked straight ahead. He was looking into the face of a huge bull moose within 50 yards.

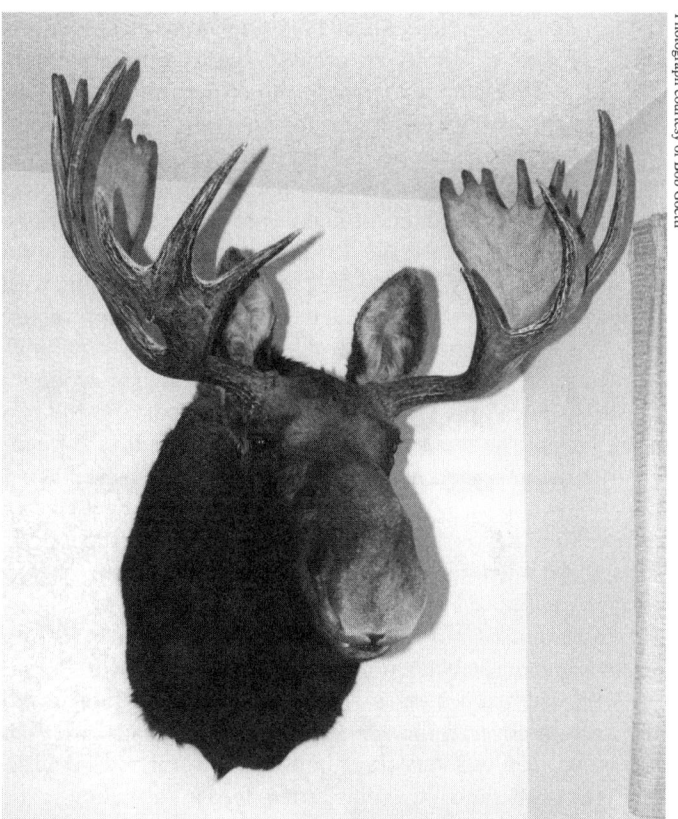

Man and moose stared at each other for a couple of seconds as Bob heard more moose moving to his right. The moose ran and Bob felt the ground rumble as they circled him and raced up the mountain. Bob couldn't take his eyes off the bull in front of him. Two shots from his Browning 7mm and the bull was down for good.

The rest of the day was spent field dressing his trophy. Bob took special care to save the cape and rack as he knew this was a trophy he wanted to mount. The first trip back to camp Bob carried the head and cape, which weighed 105 pounds. He knew he needed help, so he found two men, Bob and Murph, with horses who offered to pack out the meat. Word spread quickly throughout the area that Bob had taken a trophy moose. The bull's trophy status was confirmed after the 60-day drying period when it was officially measured for Boone and Crockett Club's Awards Program.

Bob Goettl is dwarfed by the massiveness of his Boone and Crockett Shiras moose towering over his shoulder. The bull easily makes the all-time records book with a final score of 160-6/8 points.

RONALD W. MADSEN
Location: Jackson County
Year Taken: 1996
Score: 160-4/8

Lady Luck smiled on Ron Madsen in 1996 as he was one of only a handful of people to draw a moose tag in Colorado that year. The common refrain repeated by anyone who heard of Ron's good fortune was, "You lucky dog!"

Ron prepared for his fall hunt by talking to Colorado Division of Wildlife (CDOW) officials and other hunters who had successfully filled moose tags in previous years. Everyone advised him not to take the first bull he saw but to wait for a big one. However, when Ron began hunting and talking with archery elk hunters in the field, he always heard about moose they saw last year but this year they weren't seeing anything.

On his third day Ron found two bulls hanging around a meadow area with willows a couple of miles past the end of a road. One of the moose sported a set of antlers Ron estimated at 48 inches wide. He tried three stalks during the next couple of days and once got within 30 yards. His arrow deflected on a willow branch and stuck in the ground under the moose. After three attempts the massive moose decided enough was enough and moved out of the area.

After more exploring, Ron found a drainage loaded with willows and dense black timber right up to the edge of the willows. Moose had beaten trails through the willow tangle, and moose sign covered the edges of the black timber. Late that afternoon Ron watched three bulls and several cows emerge from the timber during a rainstorm to feed in the willows. The largest bull was even bigger than the bull he had missed earlier. Ron was optimistic, but with fading daylight, and con-

cerns the rain would wash away any blood trail, he decided to wait until morning to try for the bull.

That next morning Ron found the three bulls at the timber's edge without the cows. He stalked to within 30 yards of the big one and waited for a clear shot. When the opportunity presented itself Ron's arrow hit the big bull in the shoulder blade and barely penetrated. The bulls scattered but for some reason the big bull ran back in front of Ron. Ron didn't lead him enough so the second arrow hit too far back. All three bulls disappeared into the timber.

An hour later Ron found the big bull bedded in thick brush. His third arrow ricocheted off a limb, hitting the bull at a glancing angle. The moose sprang up and for a few seconds looked like it would charge but then turned and ran off. Ron waited and then followed the trail until he lost it in a clearing. After hours of unsuccessful attempts to follow the trail, two archery elk hunters from Virginia, Bud Nichols and D.J. Delgado, joined in the search. Together they found Ron's bull bedded down in the willows where one well-placed arrow put the big guy down for good. Ron could not have asked for better assistance than that which he received from Bud and D.J.

Ron's bull is listed in both the Pope and Young Club's and Boone and Crockett Club's records-keeping programs with a score of 160-4/8 points. The greatest spread of Ron's rack is 50-4/8 inches.

Bowhunter Ron Madsen collected his 1996 bull moose with a well-placed arrow and the searching efforts of two Virginians.

RONALD L. ELKINS
Location: Jackson County
Year Taken: 1999
Score: 140

Thirteen years were spent applying for a moose permit when Ron Elkins finally received word from the Colorado Division of Wildlife that he would hunt moose in North Park of Jackson County in 1999.

For all of those 13 years Ron had applied with his friend, Roger Viefhaus, so the moment he received written notification about his selection, the first person Ron called was Roger. At first, Ron called Roger to ask for permission to use Roger's four mules to pack out the meat, but the moment he called, Roger said he wouldn't just loan his mules to Ron, he wanted to be a part of the hunt. From that day forward, Roger took off from work during the five-day moose season to help Ron locate a moose. Riding with them were Ron's wife Sharon and Ron's son-in-law, Matt Bowman.

Ron celebrated his birthday on October 8, the day before the season started, and spent the next five days scouting for moose. They saw moose almost everyday and by Tuesday morning had decided to return to a meadow where moose had been sighted earlier in the week. Sharon and Ron saw two cow moose but no bulls so they headed back to camp for lunch.

Ron Elkins waited 13 years for a moose hunt of a lifetime, and he was rewarded with a B&C bull scoring 140 points.

After lunch Roger suggested they take the mules and go to the area where elk hunters saw bull moose and a couple of cows walking down a draw. When the hunters reached the area, a lone bull moose walked into the draw down a little valley without noticing Ron and the other people on mules. Ron pulled up to shoot as the moose went behind a tree. Ron waited for the moose to come into the clear but it had turned and was running away from Ron. Ron knew he had a limited amount of time to place a fatal shot, so he fired his .308 Savage Model 99 using a 180-grain softpoint bullet, and the moose dropped.

The meat processor in Yuma County near where Ron and Sharon's daughter lives and the butcher had never worked with a moose, so he was quite excited and told everyone in the town about the hunt. The bones from Ron's moose were donated to Liberty School so the students could compare cattle bones with moose bones.

No thought of measuring the rack took place until Thanksgiving when Matt started making rough measurements using a Pope and Young Club score sheet as a guide. When the score came close to the minimum for Boone and Crockett Club, Ron decided to have an official measurer score the rack. Raymond Boyd of Fort Collins, a B&C measurer, officially scored the moose and announced that Ron had "made the Book."

Collecting a beautiful moose and sharing the experience with dear relatives and friends made the 13-year wait for Ron Elkins all worthwhile. Ron's Shiras moose was accepted into the Boone and Crockett Club's 24th North American Big Game Awards Program.

The 1961 Boone and Crockett Club's 10th Competition included an impressive exhibit of Dall's, Stone's, desert bighorn and bighorn sheep that received recognition. The 10th Competition was held at the American Museum of Natural History in New York City and was the last B&C Competition to be held there before relocating to the Carnegie Museum in Pittsburgh, Pennsylvania.

— Chapter IX —
Other Great Colorado Big Game
Stories and Photographs

The taxidermy and fur shop of C.L. McFadden & Sons at 412 17th Street in Denver, circa 1910, includes a large collection of full-body mounts of pronghorn, shown in the center of the photograph, along with bighorn sheep, Rocky Mountain goats, bear, American elk, mule deer and every other type of big-game animal and varmit.

Bighorn Sheep 1953-1999

Year	Rams	Ewes	Total Harvest	Total Hunters	Percent Success
1999	113	38	151	284	53%
1998	114	36	150	320	47%
1997	125	42	167	351	48%
1996	140	21	161	325	50%
1995	127	27	154	345	45%
1994	133	32	165	357	46%
1993	139	24	163	356	46%
1992	142	23	165	360	46%
1991	121	18	139	343	41%
1990	116	18	134	340	39%
1989	143	22	165	341	48%
1988	127	20	147	366	40%
1987	132	23	155	398	39%
1986	121	6	127	382	33%
1985	101	11	112	375	30%
1984	105	6	111	402	28%
1983	97	16	113	384	29%
1982	102	9	111	393	28%
1981	84	6	90	310	29%
1980	76	3	79	305	26%
1979	85	3	88	253	35%
1978	86	6	92	208	44%
1977	78	0	78	188	41%
1976	53	3	56	177	32%
1975	28	0	28	123	23%
1974	35	0	35	172	20%
1973	29	0	29	114	25%
1972	26	0	26	96	27%
1971	24	0	24	92	26%
1970	15	0	15	98	15%
1969	37	0	37	145	26%
1968	32	0	32	131	24%
1967	36	0	36	205	18%
1966	33	0	33	285	12%
1965	40	0	40	205	20%
1964	59	0	59	207	29%
1963	66	0	66	228	29%
1962	61	0	61	229	27%
1961	46	0	46	210	22%
1960	40	0	40	176	23%
1959	25	0	25	148	17%
1958	37	15	52	212	25%
1957	39	21	60	218	28%
1956	34	0	34	177	19%
1955	45	0	45	179	25%
1954	58	21	79	239	33%
1953	58	0	58	169	34%

Desert Bighorn Sheep 1988-1999

Year	Rams	Ewes	Total Harvest	Total Hunters	Percent Success
1999	6	0	6	6	100%
1998	6	0	6	6	100%
1997	5	0	5	5	100%
1996	5	0	5	5	100%
1995	5	0	5	6	83%
1994	6	0	6	6	100%
1993	6	0	6	6	100%
1992	3	0	3	3	100%
1991	2	0	2	2	100%
1990	4	0	4	4	100%
1989	2	0	2	2	100%
1988	2	0	2	2	100%

Before 1975, hunters and percent success based on license sales.

DONALD W. SNYDER
Location: Cuchara Peaks
Year Taken: 2000
Score: 195

Pennsylvanian Don Snyder was the successful bidder for the Colorado bighorn sheep tag at the national convention of the Foundation for North American Wild Sheep (FNAWS) in 2000, so it was with great anticipation when he set out to fill his tag in the fall with Al Vallejo of Ram's Horn Outfitters.

Al directed Don to Units 50 and 51 where he thought the big ones lived. Don's goal was to take a ram that scored at least 190 points. When they arrived in Unit 50 the first rams they saw were dead, which they suspected had been hit by lightening. Several bears were having a feast on the carcasses. The men spent five hot days looking over several rams but decided to move to Area 51. Day Seven they were glassing from a 13,000-foot ridge in Cuchara Peaks. Al spotted a large ram after watching him for several hours. The men thought this was the ram Don wanted but weren't able to maneuver into shooting position.

That evening Don and Al watched the ram until dark. Shortly after daybreak they located the ram with eight other rams. The men were pinned down for more than three hours by five rams so they belly-crawled to some higher rocks. The five rams spotted the men and started to move off as Don prepared to fire his .300 Winchester Magnum. Don's first shot misfired, and the big ram looked straight at the men. Don made a quick shot using a 150-grain bullet, and the ram collapsed. When they reached the ram it was bigger than first estimated.

The ram was entered in the Boone and Crockett Club's 24th North American Big Game Awards Program.

Pennsylvanian Donald Snyder was high bidder at the Foundation for North American Wild Sheep auction for a bighorn sheep permit. He landed this massive trophy in the fall of 2000.

GENE MOORE
P&Y World's Record
Location: El Paso County
Year Taken: 1983
Score: 191-3/8

Bowhunter Gene Moore began his bighorn sheep hunt at 5:30 a.m. on opening day of the 1983 sheep season. He felt a little unprepared as he hadn't spent any time scouting. However, he had hunted the area two years earlier and knew where a big ram lived.

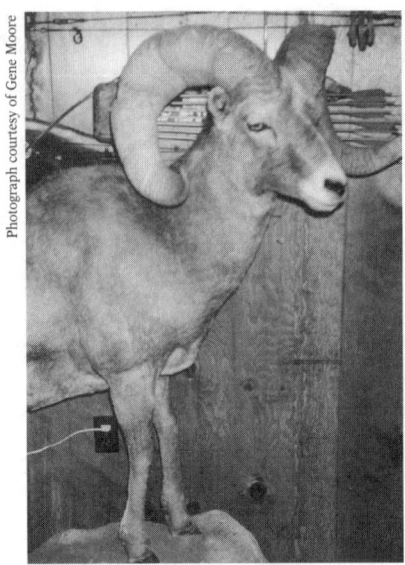

A second outstanding bighorn ram was taken by Gene Moore in 1998 that scores 177-7/8 points in the P&Y. The ram was from Chaffee County.

By 8:35 a.m. Gene was within 30 yards of the massive ram. It was bedded down with its back to him. When Gene stepped back to ready himself for a shot and inadvertently dislodged some rocks. The ram jumped up and disappeared in one bound. Gene would have followed it in previous years, but that year he simply returned to camp, believing the ram was headed for Queens Canyon. It is an area the ram frequented when it was pressured. Besides, Gene still had 29 more days to hunt.

Two days later Gene hiked across two ridges to where he believed he would find the ram. The time was 8:40 a.m. when he arrived at his predetermined destination and decided to take a nap. He knew the sheep in that area didn't usually start feeding until around mid-morning. At 10:15 a.m. he awoke and walked over to a rock outcropping to glass the area. Gene spotted the ram 600 yards below him. It was closely watching him from its bed. A smaller, half-curl ram joined the big ram and hooked it a couple of times. The big ram got up, and the two started feeding together. Gene realized that this would make his stalk more difficult as there were now two rams to outwit.

To silence the sound his boots would make, Gene placed heavy woolen socks over them. With his stalk substantially muted, Gene took one and a half hours to creep up on the majestic critter. He was within 25 yards of the bedded ram and 11 others that had joined it. Gene realized that it might now be next to impossible to get a clear shot.

Three and a half-hour later, the ram arose and the rest of the herd followed. They fed to Gene's right at the same elevation. Gene saw a small opening through the timber 15 yards ahead of them. He knew he would get a clear shot if the ram passed through it.

Gene Moore took the World's Record bighorn sheep listed in the Pope and Young Club on September 12, 1983, near Colorado Springs in El Paso County. Gene is an avid bowhunter, and his ram is the largest ever taken by bow and arrow.

The ram did pass through the opening, so Gene drew his 70 lb. Martin Cougar II and let an arrow fly. Gene inadvertently aimed high, and the arrow went over the ram's back, scattering the herd. Gene's ram ran 30 yards and stopped broadside, which was the shot Gene was looking for. Gene nocked another arrow and was beginning to draw when the ram turned and headed for the same opening where Gene shot at him the first time. Gene couldn't believe it; he was going to get another shot.

Ten minutes later the ram fed its way to a point where Gene let go his second shaft. The ram turned, walked 20 feet, and lay down. As Gene was taking pictures, the ram unexpectedly made a final effort to get up and charge him, but it collapsed at his feet. After years of scouting and hunting this magnificent ram, Gene gently touched his ram and felt a twinge of sadness now that the hunt over.

Gene's bighorn sheep is the World's Record bowhunter-taken ram with a Pope and Young Club score of 191-3/8 points. Because of its size this ram also qualifies for the Boone and Crockett Club but is not registered with them as of March 2001.

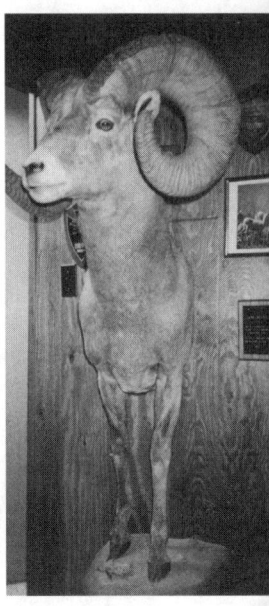

TIMOTHY K. RUSHING
Location: Huerfano County
Year Taken: 1997
Score: 191-2/8

Tim Rushing applied 15 years for a Colorado bighorn sheep permit without any luck and 1997 was no exception. But, this time Tim had purchased a single raffle ticket for a bighorn permit from the Rocky Mountain Bighorn Society (RMBS) and this time his wife called to say he had won. This drawing entitled him to hunt for Colorado bighorn in any open sheep unit across the state. Tim scouted alone and with his father, Ken, throughout the rest of the summer in preparation for the official opening of the season. On August 9 Tim and his father, Ken, started searching near Gunnison but later focused their attention in the Walsenburg area where Tim spotted a huge ram with heavy horns.

A day before the season opened, Tim backpacked into the rugged area outside Walsenburg with his father and a Fort Collins friend, James. Late afternoon lightning storms kept the men in camp until next morning. They were one sunrise away from opening day and anticipation was building. The men climbed for several hours but instead of spotting the ram, they only saw lambs and ewes. For the next few days the men maintained the traditional hunter's ritual: wake up before sunlight, climb as many mountains as possible, glass until there is a need for some Advil, return to camp late, cook dinner in the rain and drop into bed. Tim's confidence in even finding a ram was dwindling.

Photograph by Susan Campbell Reneau

Tim's pattern of hunting continued for 29 days. He and his father had endured countless lightning storms, physical and mental exhaustion, damp boots, frozen toes and fingers and freeze-dried food, but finally, Tim spotted "his ram" that he had first located in late August bedded amidst a clutter of talus rocks and a few spindly spruce. Tim maneuvered into a shooting position, using a small rock outcrop as a dead rest for a 325-yard shot all the while his father walked very slowly back and forth to distract and keep several ewes from spooking the ram. The clever strategy worked and Tim touched off his 7mm when the ram turned at a slight forward angle. Tim's friend, Joe Boucher, screamed, "You got him...You got him...He humped up." Tim, his dad and Joe hopped around a bit, hugging and hollering, but in the end they stood back to admire the massive horns and deep brown coat. The ram sported 39-3/4-inch horns and 15-3/8-inch bases. The final Boone and Crockett score totaled 191-2/8 points.

A cell phone call was placed atop the 12,000-foot mountain by Ken to Tim's mom, Carol, telling her of Tim's success. When Tim and Ken pulled up to Tim's house, Ken first went inside and asked Tim's wife, Jimel, and children to come outside to help unload the camper since Tim was so sick. When the family stood at the back of the truck and the camper door opened, they looked in, and discovered Tim's ram. Dad wasn't so sick afterall.

Tim Rushing with a grin as the whole outdoors as he holds his B&C ram.

TRACY ATKINSON
Location: Rawah Wilderness Area
Year Taken: 1999
Score: 190

Tracy Atkinson was at the base of the Matterhorn Mountain in Switzerland when his daughter called to say he was the 1999 winner of the bighorn sheep permit raffle sponsored by the Rocky Mountain Bighorn Society (RMBS) and the Colorado Division of Wildlife (CDOW). Better yet, Tracy would hunt in the reopened Rawah Wilderness Area that had been closed to bighorn hunting for more than a decade. The raffle tag holder could hunt any open sheep area across the entire state.

Tracy called Scott Limmer, owner of Comanche Wilderness Outfitters, who had spotted a big ram he named Chiphorn that eventually was known as the Poudre ram. Scott was delighted when he was asked to hunt the area with Tracy and another hunter, Roger Berends, who drew one of the two draw-issued tags. Scott invited his friend, Tim Rushing, who took a B&C ram in 1997. Tim and Scott set up two camps about a week before the season in two different drainages so the hunters would have two locations in case the ram moved out of one area.

On opening day, Tracy awoke long before the alarm went off at 3:30 a.m., pacing the tent floor like an expectant father-to-be. The hunters and guides finally arrived at a concealed glassing spot not far from where the rams had been spotted. Moments after the sun rose above the horizon, they spotted the rams in a rocky chute about halfway up the mountain above timberline on a near vertical slope from which they had a commanding view. There were eight rams, including the Poudre ram. The rams alternately fed and sparred but never moved more than a couple of hundred yards from where the men had watched them for the past three days. The men planned their route and tried to remain hidden while they stalked the keen-eyed band.

The men inched closer to the herd but cover was scarce as they neared a small knob that would completely conceal them. A small half-curl spotted the men so Tim whispered for everyone to freeze until it returned to grazing. When the ram returned to feeding, the men moved slowly and deliberately to a better vantage point. That accomplished, the men knew they were out of sight so they hustled up the steep bench and crept over the top to a small bunch of krummholz brush and rocks that offered a clear shot. They crawled on hands and knees as they tried to relocate the herd as Scott led the way. Upon reaching an outcrop, Scott saw the Poudre ram standing broadside, so Tracy set up in a prone position using two day packs as a rest.

After 15 minutes of patient waiting, Tracy's and Roger's rams moved into perfect shooting position so both hunters fired a single shot. Tracy's ram reared up on its back legs, took a few steps uphill and crumpled. Roger's was located a few minutes later piled up at the far edge of the talus rock where the men stood. The Poudre ram has joined the ranks of other great rams for its place in Colorado hunting history.

Tim Rushing and Scott Limmer provided the details of this hunt.

Tracy Atkinson and his Poudre Canyon ram.

PICK UP
Location: El Paso County
Year Found: 1989
Score: 187-5/8
Owner: Michael D. Swanson

The full-curl ram on the distant slope in Michael Swanson's optics was an awesome sight, exciting him more about the upcoming archery sheep season. He was one of only nine residents to draw a permit for an outstanding sheep area in Colorado's south-central mountains that year. Michael's wife Cathy suggested they hike in for a closer look, but Michael was reluctant, believing the ram would still be in the vicinity when the season opened two weeks later.

It was a hot summer day when Michael, Kathy, his wife, and their two sons, Ryan and Corey left their home north of Denver. They welcomed the cooler air as they reached the higher elevations. They again spotted the spectacular ram and passed it as they drove up the winding road on the southern edge of his hunting area. They reached the mountaintop but didn't see any additional sheep, so down the mountain they went.

As they approached the spot where they had previously seen the huge ram, Michael spotted it lying in the shade of a pinon tree. The rush of seeing a huge ram quickly returned, but as he glassed it Michael realized something was wrong. The ram's head rolled in a clockwise direction, and its legs stuck out instead of being tucked beneath it. Cathy grabbed the binoculars and saw the same mannerisms. They realized the ram was sick and dying, and wondered if it was the victim of an unsuccessful poaching attempt.

They drove back to Colorado Springs to report their suspicions to the Colorado Division of Wildlife. A sheriff returned to the site with the Swansons by 10 p.m. They had difficulty locating the ram in the dreary and drizzly darkness, but Michael eventually found it where they had last seen it earlier that afternoon. It was dead. The sheriff called the Colorado Division of Wildlife, and Nick Pinell responded.

Nick determined that the ram was the victim of a power struggle with another big ram. A large piece of horn was lost from the crest of the curve of the horn. The opening extended all the way to the horn core and created a prime location for infection and disease. Nick told Michael he could cape out the ram since it had died from natural causes. The Swansons returned to the division office with Nick at 2 a.m., took pictures, and "plugged" the horns.

Later in the morning, after two hours of sleep, Michael took the ram to his taxidermist, Barry Smith, of Hot Sulphur Springs, for mounting. Barry suggested the ram was Boone and Crockett quality. After the required 60-day drying period, the final B&C score was 187-5/8 points.

BOB RENNER
Location: El Paso County
Year Taken: 1979
Score: 183-2/8

The year 1979 was Bob Renner's fifth year to hunt bighorn sheep in Colorado. Back then Colorado had a "once-in-a-lifetime" rule for sheep hunters. That is, you could hunt for more than one season, but as soon as you harvested a sheep, you couldn't take another one during your lifetime.

The first two years Bob hunted sheep, he hunted Mt. Princeton in the Collegiate Range. The third year he hunted in the Sangre de Christo Mountains, and on his fourth and fifth years he hunted in the Rampart Range.

It was during his second season in the Rampart Range in 1979 that Bob spotted a ram that would satisfy him for his once-in-a-lifetime trophy. After arriving at his destination, Bob backpacked into a remote area with many tree-covered ridges about one mile from the closest road and high on a ridge above where Bob had spotted a 190-class ram the previous year known as "Old Grand Dad." Many hunters tried to harvest this ram, but it eluded them all and died of natural causes a few years later.

As Bob approached a rock outcropping that looked like a good vantage point, he slipped out of his backpack and climbed up on some boulders. After glassing east for five minutes into the drainage where Bob planned to hunt, Bob got an uneasy feeling. He turned and looked behind him down the ridge he had just crossed. Bob immediately spotted a tremendous ram to the west and below him about 600 yards away,

standing on another rock outcropping. Bob watched the ram and the ram watched him. As Bob formulated plans for his final stalk, he spotted two more rams. He was watching a massive full-curl ram and two ¾-curl rams.

The approach through the pine trees mixed with aspens was easy. When he was within 100 yards, Bob paused long enough to put on heavy woolen socks over his hiking boots. Bob eventually got too close and spooked the three rams as they fed through the timber in his direction. He was within 10 yards of them when they spooked. Fortunately, they only ran 20 yards and stopped. It was then that Bob got a fatal shot at the largest ram.

After a rather long and difficult search with three friends and some hikers, Bob was able to recover the magnificent ram. This ram became the P&Y World's Record for two years. It now ranks as the third largest bighorn ever listed in P&Y from Colorado and the 13th largest bighorn ram ever taken with a bow and arrow as listed in the P&Y all-time records book published in 1999. The ram is large enough to qualify for the B&C all-time records book if entered.

Bob Renner took this outstanding P&Y bighorn ram in 1979 from a distance of 20 yards.

RALPH HEJNY
Location: Saguache County
Year Taken: 1992
Score: 182

A young son urging a father to shoot the big one was what it took for Ralph Hejny to collect his Boone and Crockett ram during the 1992 hunting season.

Ralph asked his wife, Marcia, to join him for the first week of scouting and hunting in Saguache County outside Grand Junction but saw nothing. For the second week, Marcia brought their young son, Seth, age 12, to help scout for his father in the Middle Creek area. Ralph and Seth walked up a mountain early in the morning and as Ralph paused to catch his breath two nice rams ran past. Seth urged his father to shoot because he was convinced a better one wouldn't be found, but Ralph decided to wait. Ralph promised his son that if he didn't take a ram as big as those two he'd let Seth kick him. "That's a deal, Dad," Seth said.

The next week was the start of school, so Seth stayed behind and Ralph returned to his ram quest outside Grand Junction. Ralph spotted 14 rams late in the day of the third week so he decided to return to that area before sunup the next day. Ralph hiked up the mountain, starting at 4 a.m., and missed the ridge where the herd of rams was bedded down. He spooked another animal and thought he had blown the entire hunt. Late in the day Ralph located the herd and decided to wait until the next early morning for the stalk. To avoid

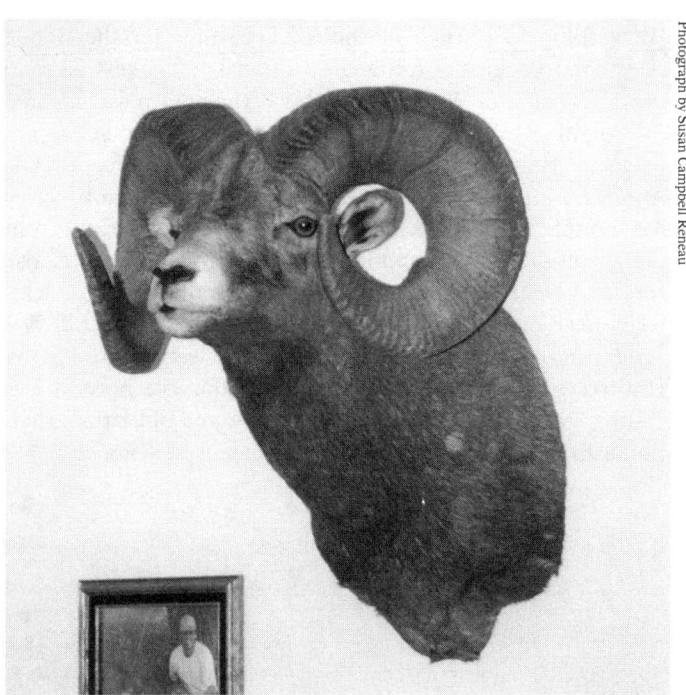

missing the ridge he waited for the sunup, and when he reached the right area he looked over a rock outcropping just as a rabbit bolted away. Ralph thought he had blown a stalk again but soon realized a small herd of rams had spooked the rabbit as they slipped through an opening. Ralph tried to loop around the herd but they were long gone, and again Ralph thought he had blown his hunt. The rams were feeding up hill, and he was above some of them. Ralph decided to hunt downhill in hopes more rams were in the area that hadn't run over the ridge.

As Ralph walked downhill he thought he heard something so he sat down for about 10 minutes and began to rise again when he stepped on a twig. The crack of the twig echoed across the silent landscape as the remaining rams burst out of there and scattered as Ralph's heart sank. He resolved he would shoot the first decent ram he saw. Ralph maneuvered himself within the herd. Small rams were to his right and several nice rams, including the one he took, ran to the left as they jumped off a ledge. Ralph pinpointed the biggest ram and waited for it to run straight away from him. The ram stopped and turned part way toward Ralph to glance at him as Ralph fired. The ram dropped in its tracks, and Ralph had collected his trophy ram with his .270 Remington Model 700 BDL.

"He walked on thin air for two weeks, " Marcia said.

Ralph Hejny walked on air for two weeks after taking this B&C ram during the 1992 season.

PICK UP
Location: Las Animas County
Year Found: Prior to 1994
Score: 182
Owner: U.S. Army

Phillip L. Ehrlich, an official measurer for the Boone and Crockett Club and an official with the Colorado Division of Wildlife, said this bighorn ram was located by a female U.S. Army pilot who was flying her helicopter over the Bravo Canyon and Purgatoire River area of Las Animas County. She was helping to conduct a raptor survey for the U.S. Fish and Wildlife Service and saw the skull from the air on the Fort Carson Pinon Canyon Maneuver Site. The ram had been dead for some time and the bones were scattered near the skull with the horn sheaths off the skull. The skull was cleaned, bleached and horns were mounted by Huffman's Taxidermy of Aguilar, Colorado. The horn shows eight growth rings but they are broomed and older than that. Phil estimates the ram to be approximately 10 years old.

The sharp eyes of a female Army pilot spotted this outstanding bighorn ram from the air above the U.S. Army Pinon Canyon Maneuver Site in 1994 as she assisted officials from the Colorado Division of Wildlife with wildlife surveys.

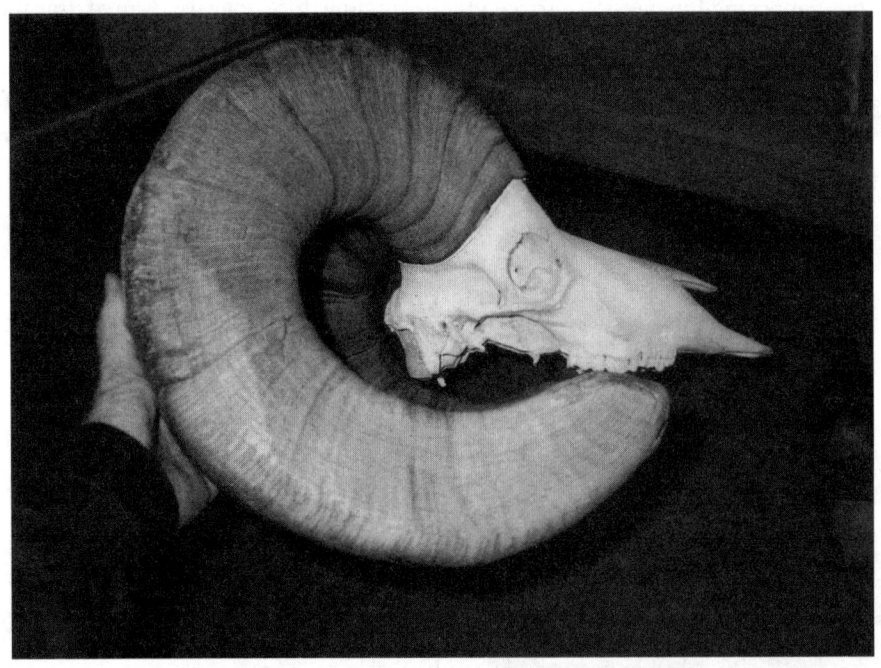

DARREL L. MOBERLY
Location: Saguache County
Year Taken: 1994
Score: 181-4/8

Putting in for bighorn sheep permits over a 30-year period was getting to be a routine for Darrel L. Moberly. He tried for a permit in the Pikes Peak area for 18 years but finally switched to the Sangre De Cristo area where he finally drew a permit in 1994.

Darrel knew this was a special hunt, so he decided to hire a guide for the first time in his life. He heard of Ed Wiseman and hired him, a decision he never regretted. "He's a great guide," Darrel said.

Ed knew where to hunt, so Darrel relied on him to help locate big rams. The season was September 26 to October 4, so they met a couple of times before the season to work out details of the hunt. Darrel arrived in the hunting area on September 25 and was met by Ed's assistants, Don and Mack, who helped load the horses. They rode from the Creststone trailhead and basked in the glory of the blazing yellow colors of aspen leaves as they turned for the winter. The men reached spike camp several miles back into the wilderness, and walked out from there. Ed knew where the big rams hung out, so one day they spotted a herd Darrel wanted to pursue. They left camp early the next morning to begin the hike to the herd's location.

"Ed said we must have bloodied their nose because they saw us, and away they went," Darrel explained. It was a good thing they ran because the ram in the herd wasn't as big as the one Darrel eventually took.

After several days of hunting they planned to move to another area when they got into the worst weather Darrel had ever experienced in his life. Blizzard. Rain. Snowstorm. Cold. Wind. They socked in from that storm, so after it let up a bit they went up on a ridge to spot for rams. Darrel walked down from the ridge and saw a huge ram standing there, but when he stepped back to load his gun, the ram took off running to the left into the trees. Darrel hit the ram at 150 yards as it ran down through the trees and found it a few yards away. Not only did he take a Boone and Crockett Club ram, but he took it with one shot.

The date was October 1, 1994, and Darrel had collected one fine ram. Ed was pretty sure the ram was Boone and Crockett quality, and it was. It was late in the day when the men field dressed the ram and took pictures as the sun set. They returned the next day to pack the meat out and Darrel returned home to a chorus of grandchildren who wanted to eat bighorn and macaroni and cheese, especially the youngest grandchild, Kenny. The meat was great to eat and Darrel remembered it as succulent, and one he will never forget.

Darrel Moberly in the Sangre De Cristo Mountains in 1994 with his B&C ram.

CHARLES W. HANAWALT
Location: Clear Creek County
Year Taken: 1990
Score: 180-1/8

Learning the area where he planned to hunt on opening day was the goal of Charles Hanawalt when he finally drew a permit to hunt Rocky Mountain bighorn sheep in Clear Creek County in 1990. What he didn't know at the time was that his hunt would put him so close to the sheep that they stood right next to him on a mountaintop.

Two weeks prior to the hunting season Charles glassed an area along the eastern side of the Continental Divide. On opening morning at daybreak, he located a herd of sheep with a massive ram. As the herd fed along a high grassy basin, Charles sat on an adjoining mountainside. Getting to the herd took another half day but when he came to the area where he had seen them, the herd had disappeared, so the next day he was fortunate to locate them again. Charles located the herd toward the end of the season on September 13, but the wind had turned to the southwest on September 14 so he came in from another direction to make sure the wind was in his favor.

When Charles reached the area where he thought the herd was located, he spent the next couple of hours waiting for the sheep to come out in the open. He saw some sheep come out above and thought he had misjudged his distance to the herd. As he sat trying to figure out how to reach the herd, he heard click, click, click to his left about 50 yards away and saw a herd of five mature rams coming out of the timber. They came across a rock outcropping as the wind blew from the sheep directly to Charles as Charles sat near the edge of some timber with a small pine tree in front of him. A log had blown down next to him, so Charles lay down beside the log as the sheep milled about toward Charles. The five rams were in two groups; Charles' ram and another one were in front of the other three. When the three rams tried to move in closer to the other two rams as they grazed, Charles' ram charged them and knocked one down with the blow. As this took place, Charles watched the scene unfold trying to decide which of these two huge rams he should take because both were equal in size.

The rams got so close to Charles that he couldn't move for fear of spooking all of them. Within five feet of Charles the rams munched grass, allowing him to hear them chew and breathe. To draw his bow accurately, Charles waited for the five rams to feed away from him so finally the time came for him to come to a full draw – the first time in his life he had to do this while lying flat on the ground. The ram he wanted was behind the other and by the time he could draw his bow the rams had fed 40 yards away. Added to the challenge was the fact that he had to shoot the arrow over the back of the front ram to hit the ram he wanted using his 70-pound Hoyt compound bow. The arrow hit its mark perfectly as the ram walked 60 yards to the rock outcropping, stood quietly as blood gushed from him and eventually lay down as if to go to sleep. The other rams followed Charles' ram to the outcropping while tapping paws nervously on the rock, not knowing what had happened. Charles walked up to the herd as the rams stayed close to their fallen leader. Eventually they melted back into the timber as Charles arrived at the ram's side.

Charles credits a southwesterly wind blowing his human scent away from the rams and the fact that he had dried his clothes and body after climbing the mountain, which eliminated additional human odor before completing the final stalk. Upon examining the horns, he knew he had a big one but darkness was descending and he needed help carrying the meat and horns off the mountain. Charles covered the body with his shirt and T-shirt and hiked down the mountain to his truck. He drove to Georgetown and called his friend, Ray Ault, for help. Next morning the two men climbed back to the rock outcropping and transported the animal to the truck.

Never had Charles come so close to a herd of massive bighorn sheep, and the hunt will be one he will recount for a lifetime.

Charles Hanawalt used his 70-pound Hoyt compound bow and a lot of patience to down this outstanding B&C bighorn ram in 1990.

P. CRAIG PIERCE
Location: Gunnison County
Year Taken: 1999
Score: 177-1/8

Craig Pierce credits the advice of experienced sheep hunter, Dick Simillion, as the reason for his success on August 14, 1999, when he downed his Boone and Crockett ram.

Several weekends of scouting with hunting buddy Mike Brickley had netted nothing for Craig and Mike when it came to locating rams so after consulting with Division of Wildlife District Manager Tom Henry, they decided to ask local hunters. Dick not only helped Craig locate hunting areas near Gunnison but also offered four different places to locate rams and estimated how many rams he'd find in each location. Dick works for Western State College and passionately observes the bighorn sheep near Gunnison on a year-round basis. In fact, Craig said he knows the bighorn so well he has practically named them.

Dick offered advice on how to hunt, too, and made Craig and Mike vow they would never reveal his secret hunting places. He said to go up a certain trail, camp there, get up on a certain ridge early on opening morning, look over the edge on one side and then the other, move slowly down the ridge and continue to scout the edges. When Craig and Mike followed all of Dick's suggestions, they finally found a herd of not just one nice ram but 13 of them lying down in a bunch.

Craig Pierce in the field with his B&C ram moments after he collected a trophy that ranks as one of the largest bighorn rams ever taken in Colorado since records were kept.

One ram was a 7/8th curl and the rest were 5/8 to 3/5 curls so Craig made his way into shooting position as Mike observed the herd through binoculars. Craig selected the largest of the rams from a distance of 150 yards and fired his Winchester .30-06 where the ram lay using a 125-grain bullet. The ram stood up and Craig fired a second time, hitting it in the chest as it turned and faced him. The third shot in the neck was insurance that the ram was down for good although Craig was certain the chest shot did the trick.

Craig thanks Mike and Dick for bringing his hunt to a positive conclusion. He also thanks God for a hunt of a lifetime. Craig's ram was entered in the Boone and Crockett Club's 24th North American Big Game Records Program on January 24, 2000.

Rocky Mountain Goat Harvests

1964-1999

Year	Male	Female	Total Harvest	Total Hunters	Percent Success
1999	103	59	162	173	94%
1998	100	58	158	178	89%
1997	84	41	125	134	93%
1996	60	26	86	107	80%
1995	71	23	94	114	82%
1994	51	34	85	96	89%
1993	49	19	68	80	85%
1992	58	34	92	104	88%
1991	63	42	105	121	87%
1990	59	43	102	110	93%
1989	53	34	87	100	87%
1988	43	27	70	81	86%
1987	40	34	74	91	81%
1986	41	16	57	84	68%
1985	21	24	45	80	56%
1984	34	26	60	88	68%
1983	41	19	60	81	74%
1982	22	28	50	77	65%
1981	35	16	51	65	78%
1980	33	21	54	77	70%
1979	30	19	49	66	74%
1978	37	21	58	71	82%
1977	27	14	41	53	77%
1976	20	14	34	46	74%
1975	20	15	35	40	88%
1974	13	5	18	20	90%
1973	10	2	12	14	86%
1972	0	0	0	0	---
1971	0	0	0	0	---
1970	0	0	0	0	---
1969	13	7	20	21	95%
1968	6	9	15	19	79%
1967	8	6	14	18	78%
1966	3	0	3	7	43%
1965	3	0	3	6	50%
1964	4	0	4	6	67%

JANICE L. HEMINGSON
Location: Clear Creek County
Year Taken: 1988
Score: 51

Janice Hemingson never intended to take a Boone and Crockett Club billy goat when she left for her hunt with husband Jim and friends, Steve Pickett and Larry Lindholm, in September 1988, but she did anyway.

For three years, Janice applied for a Rocky Mountain goat permit so receiving a permit was a thrill. Twice she and Jim scouted in Colorado's Mount Evans area before the season. She began her first day of hunting when she left home at 3 a.m. and arrived at the base of the mountain to begin an assent to 12,500 feet. The going was dark and challenging as Janice and the men picked their way for three and a half miles through a bog with tall grass reaching their knees. They maneuvered to a bowl in the mountain with rocks on all sides that hunters called the Bachelor's Pad.

Daybreak was just cracking over the horizon when Janice reached the edge of the bowl to search for the elusive goats that frequented the area. Disappointment flooded over Janice and her companions when they couldn't locate any goats. After much glassing they finally located a single billy goat farther up from them, so Janice and Jim started the stalk. Larry remained up high where glassing began as Janice and Jim picked their way down the sides and around the bowl to avoid being sighted by the goat. An hour later, Janice and Jim arrived within 50 yards of the goat without being noticed.

Steve was ahead of Janice and Jim was behind Janice when Steve suggested she stand on a rock and shoot, but when Janice readied herself, the goat had its rear end to Janice. A second billy goat was grazing with the first, but they didn't see it until Janice was ready to shoot after climbing upon the rock. Janice didn't want to take that shot but at that moment, the second billy came into view, broadside to Janice, so with a standing shot using her .30-06 Winchester, Model 70, Janice fired a round that hit its mark perfectly. The billy dropped without a sound or movement, never knowing what hit it. Steve thought Janice had shot the smaller goat, but when they started to examine the horns, they all realized this was a trophy animal.

Janice was simply looking for a clear shot when she collected her outstanding billy goat, but for Janice, this was a hunt of a lifetime. She de-boned it for the trip down the mountain and carried the rifle and packs while Jim carried the head and the hide. The other men transported the meat. Janice, a teacher, asked a former student and taxidermist, Greg Brown, to mount the head and Greg had the horns officially scored.

The goat is one of only nine Rocky Mountain goats from Colorado that qualify for the B&C records book and is ranked Number Two in the state.

Janice Hemingson, surrounded by her hunting companions, sits beside her B&C Rocky Mountain billy goat in 1988 when she became one of only three hunters in Colorado to collect a trophy mountain goat. The goat scores 51 points.

Pronghorn Harvests

1949-1999

Year	Bucks	Does	Fawns	Total Harvest	Total Hunters	Percent Success
1999	4,314	3,659	286	8,259	12,798	65%
1998	4,612	3,508	358	8,478	13,486	63%
1997	5,534	4,153	323	10,010	15,051	67%
1996	5,562	4,522	389	10,473	14,971	70%
1995	5,214	3,933	391	9,538	13,690	70%
1994	5,197	4,021	282	9,500	12,791	74%
1993	5,262	3,887	313	9,462	12,317	77%
1992	4,816	3,522	272	8,610	11,729	73%
1991	4,310	2,803	202	7,315	10,016	73%
1990	4,956	3,450	215	8,621	11,851	73%
1989	4,931	3,369	232	8,532	11,456	74%
1988	4,557	3,083	295	7,935	11,064	72%
1987	4,520	2,712	290	7,522	11,113	68%
1986	4,684	2,979	228	7,891	10,989	72%
1985	4,303	2,910	262	7,475	12,380	60%
1984	5,336	4,101	438	9,875	16,173	61%
1983	5,298	4,250	361	9,909	14,924	66%
1982	5,693	3,568	381	9,642	13,341	72%
1981	4,885	3,164	408	8,457	11,612	73%
1980	4,503	2,146	224	6,873	9,091	76%
1979	3,448	1,131	124	4,703	5,767	82%
1978	3,206	1,401	158	4,765	5,864	81%
1977	3,101	1,026	122	4,249	5,273	81%
1976	2,731	616	391	3,738	4,728	79%
1975	2,384	670	492	3,546	4,398	81%
— Before 1975, hunters and percent success based on license sales —						
1974	2,132	860	161	3,153	4,514	70%
1973	2,279	867	206	3,352	4,897	68%
1972	2,580	1,273	310	4,163	5,686	73%
1971	3,007	1,595	411	5,013	6,793	74%
1970	3,722	1,709	202	5,633	7,243	78%
1969	3,286	1,706	230	5,222	6,827	76%
1968	3,484	1,829	177	5,490	6,742	81%
1967	3,527	1,982	326	5,835	7,280	80%
1966	3,800	2,088	304	6,192	7,120	87%
1965	3,127	1,635	283	5,045	6,435	78%
1964	2,948	1,635	302	4,885	5,785	84%
1963	2,750	1,118	155	4,023	4,512	89%
1962	1,869	621	98	2,588	2,905	89%
1961	1,205	597	103	1,905	2,153	88%
1960	1,156	472	85	1,713	1,825	94%
1959	1,317	520	63	1,900	2,237	85%
1958	1,467	694	101	2,262	2,715	83%
1957	2,056	1,048	198	3,302	4,021	82%
1956	1,974	891	104	2,969	3,440	86%
1955	1,830	1,227	110	3,167	3,900	81%
1954	1,905	1,327	106	3,338	4,033	83%
1953	2,882	1,426	148	4,456	4,951	90%
1952	1,231	598	93	1,922	2,125	90%
1951	1,019	528	99	1,646	1,893	87%
1950	1,314	699	135	2,148	2,396	90%
1949	682	374	73	1,129	1,279	88%

BOB SCHNEIDMILLER
Location: Weld County
Year Taken: 1965
Score: 91-4/8

Robert "Bob" Schneidmiller heard his name called over the office PA system as he returned from lunch, and fate stepped in to change the direction of his hunting decision.

For decades Bob Schneidmiller and Reg Thornburg hunted together, so when Reg didn't draw his pronghorn permit for the 1965 season and Bob did, Bob decided to chuck the permit because he didn't want to hunt alone. Richard "Butch" Farmer, an old high school classmate of Bob's, worked with Reg and heard about Bob's dilemma, so that is what prompted him to page Bob at work and ask Bob to join him with another friend. Bob's answer was a resounding, "yes," so planning began. The one thing they were missing was a tent and the one person who had the tent was Reg, so reluctantly Bob called Reg. Reg gave Bob a bit of a hard time but happily loaned the tent to Bob.

The men left the day before the season opened and arrived at a ranch in the Pawnee Grasslands about 20 miles north of New Raymer around 4 p.m. They made camp near a cattle watering trough and a sizable orchard. By dawn the next morning and after Bob made breakfast, the three hunters piled into Butch's Jeep to slowly cruise an area south of a nearby big butte. They had driven only two miles when Butch stopped the Jeep and slipped into a shallow arroyo. Moments later and 15 minutes after the season began, Butch collected his buck with a single shot from 75 yards. The men continued to hunt and even took time for a short nap in the afternoon but they decided to be selective since they already had a nice buck.

The men were greeted by bone-chilling drizzle on the second day and Butch's friend collected his first buck pronghorn after sneaking close to a small herd and crawling through mud.

On the third and last day of the hunt, the men were met with more cold drizzle so they debated whether or not to stay or break camp. Bob convinced them to stay another hour to drive toward the ranch house and north. They remained rain-drenched for an hour, and Bob was wiping down his rifle to put it back in the gun case when they saw three pronghorn standing in the rain-soaked road ruts.

Bob eased from the Jeep as the animals ambled slowly over a low bluff into a small bowl. Bob kept a hillside distance from the threesome as he carefully stalked them. A quick glance through his spotting scope confirmed that one of the three was a massive buck. When Bob finally knew he was only a short ridge away from the small herd, he crawled on the ground to the rise to peek over the edge only to discover the three couldn't be bothered with anything but each other. The smaller buck was vying for the attention of the doe and the bigger buck was defending his territory. Bob raised his 7mm Remington Magnum and released a 160-grain Sierra boat-tail bullet that hit its mark with a whop. The buck turned out to be the largest pronghorn ever taken in Colorado and ranks in the Boone and Crockett Club's all-time records book as the 5th largest pronghorn buck ever taken in the world.

Bob hasn't hunted pronghorn since that day, long ago, when he took one for the record books.

PRESTON J. ESSEX
Location: Moffat County
Year Taken: 1997
Score: 87-4/8

As Preston Essex crawled through the underbrush in search of a pronghorn buck on September 15, 1997, in Moffat County all he could think about was the possibility of crawling over a rattlesnake. Luckily, he never touched a rattlesnake, but he certainly found something even more special on this hunt.

Photograph courtesy of Preston J. Essex

Brad Baker and Don Laisure joined Preston on his first pronghorn hunt, which took place in Moffat County. Preston had finally drawn a permit for that area after receiving refunds the previous six years. The men set up camp near their unit on the eve of opening day and did some last minute scouting as they had also done the previous weekend.

On opening morning, they arose at daylight. Brad immediately took a nice little buck and began field dressing it as Don and Preston began a stalk on another herd. Preston singled out a nice buck and missed a shot. He also missed four other bucks that morning but didn't become discouraged because he was enjoying the hunt. As he puts it, he was becoming anxious.

That afternoon Brad caught up with Don and Preston again and together they pursued another herd of pronghorn. They singled out a nice buck, fired, and missed. Another herd of pronghorn was spotted, and they began the stalk. When they were within range, Brad spotted an exceptionally large buck in the herd and frantically whispered for either Don or Preston to shoot. Brad didn't care who shot. All he could say was, "It's huge! Somebody take him!"

Don fired four times at the buck, which was 150 yards away, and missed each time. Preston then stood up and tried his luck on the fleeing buck. As luck would have it, Preston hit it on the first shot with his .30-06, which was throwing a 180 grain soft point bullet. The buck piled up in a cloud of dust. Preston stood there in disbelief not believing what he had just accomplished. The buck was his. All the previous misses meant nothing to him as he had just collected a Boone and Crockett buck that ranks as one of the finest pronghorns ever taken in Colorado.

SCOTT E. RAUBACH
Location: Jackson County
Year Taken: 1995
Score: 86-6/8

To shoot or not to shoot, that was the question Scott Raubach and his hunting buddy, Dennis Johnson, debated at the crack on dawn on the opening morning of pronghorn season in Jackson County on September 30, 1995.

The weather was fantastic and the stalk was less than 50 yards. Dennis had spotted the buck from the road as they drove by the area but the two men debated as to whom should shoot first. Five or 10 minutes later, after walking into a ditch, Scott fired a single shot with his Winchester Model 70 Pre 64 .270 and the buck was his. That's why the men had debated about shooting because they had waited four years for a buck permit and the hunt would end if one of them fired and was successful. Moments after Scott fired, the area game warden pulled up to check the buck and licenses, and other hunters in the area showed up with a tape measure.

Less than 10 minutes after the season opened for Scott, it closed. He had his buck and now it was time to go fishing.

Photograph by Susan Campbell Reneau

RODNEY D. GLASER
Location: Bent County
Year Taken: 1992
Score: 86-6/8

Ten years of hunting in southern Colorado has netted several 14-inch pronghorn bucks for friends Veryl Hays and Rod Glaser.

The men only saw small does and bucks on the first day of hunting season in 1992, but on the morning of October 4, they saw pronghorn at as estimated 1,000 yards. They circled behind a bluff and got to within 250 yards. When they reached the top of the bluff, two does and a big buck broke into a run. Rod hit the buck in the lungs on the second shot using a .243 Remington 700 BDL with a 6x Leopold scope. The distance was paced out at 340 yards. Rod and Veryl knew this was a B&C buck.

The pronghorn was mounted by D&S Taxidermy of Loveland, Colorado. The buck was officially entered into the Boone and Crockett Club's records program on December 6, 1992.

The fourth largest pronghorn ever taken in Colorado was taken by Rodney D. Glaser in 1992. The buck scores 86-6/8 points.

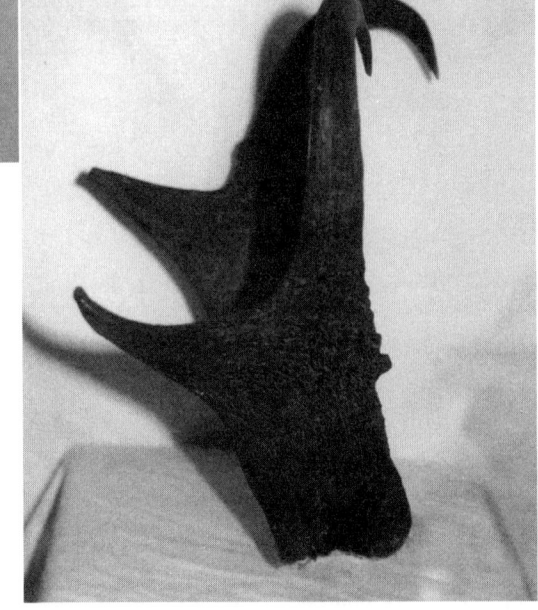

NICHOLAS R. RUSSO
Location: Las Animas County
Year Taken: 1996
Score: 86-4/8

Records are made to be tied and broken. Competition is always a challenge in sports, but in the world of hunting Mother Nature has more to do with it.

New Yorker Nick Russo accomplished what few hunters do when he harvested a B&C buck in 1996. Added to the enjoyment of the hunt was the companionship of his friend and guide, Les Ohlhauser, and his wife, Theresa, who was on her first hunt. This was Nick's first time to hunt Colorado pronghorn, although he had hunted big game with Les several times. In fact, Nick dubbed Les "The Beast Master" because of his ability to locate game and to get Nick to it.

Nick and Les outfitted Theresa with a .243 Winchester, while Nick carried a Scott Carlson custom-made rifle in .284 caliber created by Atwood, Kansas, gunsmith Scot Carlson. The couple flew to Denver where Les met them, and together they traveled to a ranch near Trinidad for their hunt. Les leased the ranch for his clients and only allowed eight hunters on it each year. This helped to maintain the quality of the herd.

Les' party arrived early enough to do some scouting, and together they sighted several outstanding bucks. Les spotted an exceptional buck just at dusk, so they discussed how it should be hunted the next day. Theresa was to get the first shot.

When they arrived on the ranch, well before sunrise, the yucca plants looked like pronghorn. In the predawn light they changed into their actual configuration. Together they searched for the big buck but couldn't find it. Theresa successfully stalked and took another nice buck, much to the delight of her hunting companions. Her eyes filled with tears as she recalled her two years of hard work preparing for that moment.

A photo session ensued with Theresa and her buck. When they finished field dressing it, they gathered their belongings and headed back to the ranch to hang it. On the way there, Les stopped to glass the horizon. He spotted three bucks and several does in the distance but what really caught his attention was a lone buck that was running directly towards them. It chased some smaller bucks trying to run them off. Les quickly determined this was the massive animal he had sighted the night before. Les warned Nick to prepare for a shot when the buck stopped near the herd. Sure enough, just as Les had predicted, the buck stopped within 300 yards of the hunters near the herd. Without hesitation, Nick fired a single shot that immediately dropped the massive buck.

As the men approached the buck Les informed Nick that he had just taken a B&C trophy. High fives and many of photos later, both first-time pronghorn hunters had collected their bucks in less than two hours.

Nick Russo on the plains of Colorado where he took this outstanding B&C pronghorn buck.

But the story doesn't end there. Les celebrated his birthday on this hunt, and as a token of his friendship and appreciation for many years of great hunting, Nick handed Les a card and gun case. The note read, "Thank you for a wonderful hunt and the friendship. The Beast Master is yours." Unknown to Les, Nick had Scott Carlson engrave "The Beast Master" on the rifle barrel in anticipation of presenting the rifle to Les. It was now Les' turn to shed the tears.

Les Ohlhauser provided the details of this hunt.

MAURICE CUTTING
Location: El Paso County
Year Taken: 1981
Score: 86-2/8

Details of this hunt were fondly remembered by son Aaron who was with his father when they sighted one of the largest pronghorn ever taken in Colorado, and to add to their enjoyment, the buck walked right to them.

One week before the season began, 16-year-old Aaron and his dad scouted the ridges and draws on an 80,000-acre ranch in El Paso County in hopes of locating a buck for each of them. Aaron remembered seeing pronghorn everywhere he looked, and he knew they would have a successful hunting season. Maurice Cutting felt lucky to have permission to hunt in prime pronghorn country rich in grass halfway to his knees, sharing a 20,000-acre pasture with only one other hunting party.

A hunt of a lifetime included the father-son team of Maurice (right) and Aaron Cutting in 1981. Maurice's buck scores 86-2/8 points, making it the one of the largest pronghorn taken in Colorado.

Father and son arrived at long before sunrise on a September morning in 1981 to check in with the ranch foreman where they were assigned a large pasture. Aaron's leg was in a cast, so Maurice drove his son down a road when they spotted a nice buck on a ridge several hundred yards away. Aaron left the truck and fired a single shot at the buck from a distance of about 150 yards. The buck dropped behind the ridge and they located the buck a few minutes later. Aaron thought his buck was outstanding (horns measuring 12 to 13 inches) – until he saw his father's buck.

That opening day was so hot that Maurice remembered wanting to find a buck and get Aaron's buck home as soon as possible. He was in a big hurry after they field-dressed Aaron's buck and prepared to locate one for himself. Shortly after preparing Aaron's meat, Maurice spotted two small bucks – barely legal – so he piled out of the truck and started chasing after them on foot over a rise in a ridge toward a stock water tank at the bottom of a draw. Maurice spotted an animal drinking from the tank and at first thought it was a coyote. Upon more careful examination using binoculars, both hunters concluded it was a very large buck antelope. For no particular reason, the buck started walking toward the hunters, oblivious to its impending demise but curious about two humans who were watching it. Maurice figured the pronghorn was familiar with cowboys working the ranch but didn't recognize a human on foot since the cowboys were only seen by pronghorn when they rode a truck or horse. The buck kept trotting toward the hunters until it got within 75 yards when Maurice started firing. Maurice remembered firing four times before hitting the buck dead center because the buck kept jumping each time Maurice fired the rifle. The fifth shot was a good one and the buck was his. Aaron remembered hopping up and down and yelling to his dad not to miss the buck. Maurice took his buck with a .30-06 Ruger 77.

Rising above the grass was nothing but buck horns. Aaron said the buck looked grotesque because the horns were so big and the body was average sized. Maurice figured he deserved good luck once in his life. Aaron knows this is a hunt he'll never forget.

Maurice's pronghorn was indeed huge. His pronghorn buck ranks as one of the largest pronghorn buck ever taken in Colorado.

JAMES R. DAWSON
Location: Gunnison County
Year Taken: 1995
Score: 86

James Dawson is quick to tell you he is basically a meat hunter. However, he is also just as quick to point out that he is a meat hunter who was fortunate to take a very large pronghorn.

Opening day of the 1995 pronghorn season was a long time in coming for James. He had applied for a pronghorn tag near his hometown of Gunnison for seven years before being notified of his success. After applying for so long, this hunt was going to be an exception to his meat hunting tendencies.

The hunting unit James drew was close enough to his home in Gunnison to scout for game after work and on weekends. He scouted the unit for a month and a half before the season opened. By the Friday night before his hunt, James had located the buck he wanted, but it was not far from the home of another hunter he knew who had also drawn a pronghorn tag. James hoped the other hunter wouldn't be after the same animal.

Early opening morning, James picked up his son-in-law, Gabe Wright, who volunteered to accompany him on the hunt. This was Gabe's first experience with pronghorn hunting. They stopped the pickup just under the ridge that formed one rim of the large basin where James spotted the buck. James knew animals in the area were especially vehicle shy, so he took special care not to prematurely spook them.

James and Gabe walked about a mile into the middle of the basin by sunrise and positioned themselves near where James figured the buck would be in the early morning. Gabe watched a small herd of pronghorn with his binoculars, but the men couldn't find the big buck. The hunt was in the middle of the rut so James knew the buck wouldn't be too far from the does.

The men moved a quarter of a mile to the top of a hill and quickly found a herd from their new vantage point. By the time the men reached the hilltop, the big buck had joined the herd. The men dropped off the backside of the hill and used a draw to get within 500 yards of it.

The stalk began and quickly became a prolonged crawl. James was able to close the distance to 350 yards before the sagebrush cover ended. He flipped down the legs on the Harris bipod he borrowed from a friend and jockeyed around for a solid prone position. Gabe hung back 50 yards to call the shot through the spotting scope. James' rifle was solid and his sight picture was good when he fired.

James heard the bullet strike and watched the buck trip over itself as it went down. The buck ran-walked about 20 yards towards the men before dropping. They paced the distance at 340 yards.

When James and Gabe approached the buck, they couldn't believe the size of the massive horns. The buck's head was huge in comparison to other pronghorn James had taken in years past. A short time later, wildlife officer Tom Henry drove into the basin and joined their celebration. He had watched the entire stalk from a distant ridge top.

And, James is happy to report the meat from the pronghorn was great!

Meat for the family was James Dawson's motivation for hunting, but in 1995 he also brought home a B&C pronghorn buck.

PATRICK G. DIESING
Location: Moffat County
Year Taken: 1998
Score: 84-4/8

Gary Morrow won the straw draw to shoot first, but generously allowed Patrick to do so on opening day of the 1998 pronghorn season. This was a decision Gary learned to regret.

The men began their hunt at sunup in Moffat County on opening day when they located dozens of nice bucks. As they drove down a back road in a pasture Gary spotted a buck crossing the road at a distance of 125 yards ahead but when they reached that location, the buck was nowhere to be found. Upon turning back, Patrick saw the buck 30 yards off the trail but it was Gary's turn to shoot. At this point the buck had run another 125 yards away from the men and was standing broadside to them. Gary generously offered to let Patrick shoot first but Patrick knew this was a big buck so he asked Gary again if it was okay to shoot. When the answer was in the affirmative, Patrick raised his .243 Remington mountain rifle and lobbed a single shot, which immediately downed the buck. From start to finish on his first pronghorn hunt, Patrick had collected one of the largest pronghorn in the world in less than five hours on opening day of the season. Not bad for the first time out.

The buck was a beauty so when Gary and Patrick reached it they pulled out a tape and green-scored it within the limits of B&C. After the required 60-day drying period, Patrick had it officially scored and entered for inclusion in the next all-time records book. Gary has shot many great pronghorn in his hunting career but nothing that comes close to the size of Patrick's buck, so Patrick will always be grateful to his friend who let him shoot first when it was his friend's turn.

Patrick's outstanding pronghorn buck was accepted in the Boone and Crockett Club's 24th North American Big Game Awards Program in August 1998.

M. WAYNE HOEBEN
Location: Weld County
Year Taken: 1989
Score: 84-2/8

If the politeness and thoughtfulness of relatives hadn't come into play, Wayne Hoeben wouldn't have been given the first shot on opening morning of the 1989 pronghorn season.

Wayne hunted with his son Steve and brother-in-law Bud on the Pawnee National Grasslands area in Weld County in September. Crawling out of a warm sleeping bag at 4 a.m. and discussing hunting strategies for the day as they downed a quick breakfast was the routine for opening day. As light cracked over the horizon, the men's plan was to split up along a ridge, separating them by approximately a half mile in a northward direction away from camp. When the men approached the first gully on the east side of the ridge all three noticed movements ahead of them. Steve dropped to his knee to look through his scope and exclaimed, "Oh, my God!"

Bud also intently eyed the same location as Wayne spotted a huge buck picking its way toward the men at a distance of 75 yards. Both Steve and Bud motioned to Wayne to fire his .58 caliber plains rifle, much to the puzzlement of Wayne at the time. Later, Wayne learned that both men wanted Wayne to take the first shot since he needed the short distance because he used a muzzleloader. They also admitted that if Wayne had missed, they would have quickly fired their modern rifles.

The buck was within 60 yards of Wayne when he let loose a single shot that hit its mark perfectly and dropped the buck in its tracks. When the rifle was fired, smoke completely obscured Wayne's vision so he didn't know if he had taken the buck but shouts from Steve confirmed that he had. The patched roundball had entered the chest and exited behind the offside shoulder. Bud and Steve also took their bucks by mid-morning so the three hunters decided to return home in the afternoon to care for all the meat.

Years after Wayne took his massive buck, Steve encouraged him to have the animal officially measured and the buck easily made the Boone and Crockett Club and National Muzzle Loading Rifle Association's Longhorn records books. It is the former World's Record pronghorn buck taken with muzzleloader and is currently listed in the third edition of *Longhunter Muzzleloading Big Game Record Book* in late 2000 as the eighth largest in the world.

"Had it not been for a series of unplanned but fortunate happenings, plus a couple of pretty classy fellows who yielded to a hunter with a muzzleloader, this story would not have been told," Wayne said.

WILLIAM R. KINCADE
Location: Baca County
Year Taken: 1997
Score: 84-2/8

Photograph by Susan Campbell Reneau

Teaching young people how to hunt pronghorn was the reason why Bill Kincade was in the field at sunup on opening day of the 1997 season, but Bill walked away with more than just a good feeling.

The three youngsters were on their first or second hunt and Bill had no plans to take a pronghorn that day. He needed to find a legal buck for the kids to take before they went to school, so time was limited. As the hunting party drove around the equivalent of eight huge ranches, Bill passed up several modest-sized bucks on his quest to help the children. They drove down one of the back roads when they spotted a small herd on one side and a trophy buck with two does on the other side, up on a ridge. They debated about what to do and decided to drive two miles south to the corner of the property where two guys were sent up a hill towards a gully in case the buck spooked toward them.

Bill went up a canyon for about a half-mile stalk. The buck remained out of sight feeding on a side hill, so the stalk through a canyon was pretty easy for Bill. Bill got within 250 yards of the buck when he decided to move a little closer for a better shot. When Bill got within 200 yards he fired once, and the buck looked up. Bill thought he had missed so he fired a second time and the buck dropped. Upon reaching the buck he discovered the first shot had hit its mark but the effects of the bullet took its time.

This was Bill's 11th pronghorn buck but certainly his finest

STEPHEN H. PORTER
Location: Jackson County
Year Taken: 1994
Score: 83-6/8

Stephen's adventure began in mid-August of 1994 as he drove home from work. Stephen first observed his buck west of Walden near Peterson Ridge. As it came into focus in his spotting scope, Stephen knew he was looking at an exceptional animal. The buck's massive, dark horns and heavy body dwarfed a respectable 14-inch buck that accompanied it.

Keeping track of the buck until September became Stephen's primary goal. In spite of a considerable amount of pre-season scouting, however, he never saw the buck again. Six weeks later, on the evening before the hunt, Stephen was joined by Timothy Rolan, Ed Neilson, and Tom Landini. Tom and Stephen had licenses, and Ed and Tim went along for the "experience."

Opening morning broke crisp, clear, and cold with the promise of warming up as the day progressed. Tim and Stephen located several herds of pronghorn. Stephen made several successful stalks but turned down all the shots in hopes of locating the big buck he saw in August. Tom connected with a nice 14" buck in the afternoon on Peterson Ridge after missing a buck earlier at Hebron Sloughs.

On the second morning, Tim and Stephen hunted around MacFarlane Reservoir to look at several nice bucks he saw the previous day. As they headed in that direction just before sunrise, Tim spotted a group of pronghorn running across a meadow on the Arapaho National Wildlife Refuge. A quick glimpse with his binoculars at those large, stumpy horns told Stephen he had just relocated his buck.

The big buck trailed four does that quickly disappeared on private property in the Soap Creek drainage. Stephen quickly obtained permission to hunt the private property, and the hunt was on. Tim and Stephen began their stalk while Ed and Tom stayed at the vehicles to watch the action. Tim and Stephen relocated the herd 700 yards across an open draw containing no ground cover. Tim wanted to continue the stalk, but Stephen stopped to observe the pronghorn behavior. He feared a stalk would spook the entire herd.

Stephen admired the big buck for nearly an hour and watched as one of the does began running back and forth. She returned to the bottom of the draw and walked up Soap Creek. The herd followed as they moved out of sight around the point of the ridge. Tim and Stephen sprinted in the herd's direction, using the ridge as cover. Stephen crawled on all fours over the ridge crest for another look. The big buck stood broadside at 175 yards, looking straight at Stephen.

Dropping to a prone position, Stephen saw nothing but sagebrush through his scope, so he crawled forward several yards for an unobstructed view. Stephen sucked in several deep breaths, took careful aim, squeezed the trigger and fired his .270. The pronghorn buck Stephen saw in August was his.

Photograph courtesy of Stephen H. Porter

Tim leaped up and did an impressive victory dance, which further increased Stephen's flow of adrenalin. They ran to the buck and realized he was every bit as large as they had imagined from a distance. Ed and Tom joined the two hunters and everyone gathered around the buck to admire the massive horns. Stephen felt lucky to share this remarkable hunt with exceptional friends. This was a very special North Park pronghorn hunt, indeed.

DELMAR BREWER
Location: Weld County
Year Taken: 1993
Score: 83-3/8

As Delmar Brewer crawled closer to the buck, the buck seemed to get bigger. Could this be the Boone and Crockett trophy he sought?

It was the second day of a sunny and hot pronghorn season in Weld County on September 26, 1993, and Delmar's six friends had filled their tags. Delmar was willing to hold out for a buck that was bigger than the ones already taken, and he was willing to crawl through cactus to accomplish his goal. At 2:30 p.m. Delmar saw a huge buck through his spotting scope standing a mile away so he dropped around the southwest side of the animal and started to crawl. Crawling on his hands and knees for an hour and 48 minutes until he reached the edge of a wheat field where the buck stood in a hole. The buck didn't notice Delmar due to the rut but 20 does in the herd bolted, which alerted the buck who then broke up over a hill in front of Delmar and out of the hole. The buck was within 80 yards of Delmar so without hesitation Delmar swung around and fired a single shot from his Winchester Model 70, Pre 64 .270.

When Delmar reached the buck he couldn't believe its body and horn size. He estimated the weight to be 180 to 190 pounds, which produced lots of summer sausage and jerky. Delmar is a professional taxidermist and his mount of the buck received "Best Pronghorn" award from the Wyoming Taxidermy Association and "Best Game Head" in the professional division in Nebraska's taxidermy association.

The Boone and Crockett Club buck he sought was his.

Delmar's outstanding buck was accepted into the Boone and Crockett Club's 24th North American Big Game Awards Program.

STANLEY W. BOUSE
Location: Jackson County
Year Taken: 1999
Score: 83-2/8

Two hours after the pronghorn season began, it was over for Stan and Barbara Bouse.

Stan and Barbara always hunt together and the 1999 season was no exception. They had driven to their favorite hunting spot out on the flats about 20 miles from Walden to wait for the sun to rise when Stan saw a single pronghorn buck walk from a draw. Stan scoped him and knew it was a nice buck but at the time didn't know how nice. When the buck reached the top of the hill, Stan squeezed off a single shot with his .270 using a 130-grain Nosler bullet. After dressing out the buck and returning to the ranch, Stan was encouraged by ranch staff to save the cape as well as the horns because they recognized its massive size. In fact, its body was so large that it looked like a deer although no one weighed it. The meat from this buck was delicious even though it had been in full rut.

From start to finish, Stan's hunt was over in less than two hours with a Boone and Crockett Club trophy to show for his brief efforts. This impressive buck was accepted into the Boone and Crockett Club's 24th North American Big Game Awards Program.

Photograph by Susan Campbell Reneau

MARVIN L. SHEPARD
Location: Moffat County
Year Taken: 1987
Score: 83

Two days before the 1987 pronghorn season, Tom Schultz, his son Mark, and Marvin Shepard arrived in northwestern Colorado to scout for trophy pronghorn. Tom and Mark didn't draw permits but wanted to go along to learn how to judge trophy bucks.

Early the next morning the men scouted Vermillion Creek, the badlands and the rolling sage-covered country next to the Wyoming border. They saw lots of 13-inch and 15-inch bucks all day. Just before dark, Marvin spotted a large buck about a half mile away in Wyoming. The buck appeared to have 17- or 18-inch horns, but was unique. Its right horn tipped forward towards its nose about 20 degrees. The closest water hole was just below the men in Colorado, so Marvin planned to stake it out on opening morning.

A cold, 30-mph wind blew at dawn on opening morning as the men approached the waterhole. Marvin saw some nice 15- to 16-inch bucks, but not the big crooked horned buck. He started glassing farther into Wyoming where he had seen the crooked horned buck the night before and noticed a small dust cloud. When he focused on it, he saw the crooked horned buck fighting another large buck with an audience of 20 does.

Marvin Shepard hunted with Tom Schultz and his son Mark during the pronghorn season of 1987. He took this outstanding buck in Moffat County with his .300 Winchester. The buck scored 83 points.

The crooked horned buck chased the other buck farther into Wyoming while the herd of does ran into Colorado below the water hole and dropped behind a big purple bluff. Marvin asked his partners, Mark and Tom, to keep an eye on the buck as he headed for the bluff, thinking the crooked horned buck would follow its does when it tired of chasing the smaller buck.

"Here he comes," yelled Mark as the big buck returned to the does.

Marvin reached the bluff nearly out of breath and peeked over the edge. The big crooked horned buck was passing about 175 yards below Marvin following the does. The buck was now in Colorado. Pulling up his .300 Winchester Magnum, Marvin touched off a shot just as the buck came into his cross hairs. The buck piled up in a cloud of dust. When Marvin approached his buck he quickly realized that it was not only a trophy, but also that it would probably make "The Book."

Mark and Tom showed up shortly after Marvin's shot and helped field dress the buck. They spent the afternoon hunting sage grouse and then headed to the Division of Wildlife's checkpoint in Maybell. The wildlife officer told Marvin that it was the largest buck he had checked in 22 years.

CHARLES J. CESAR
Location: Jackson County
Year Taken: 1985
Score: 83

Chuck Cesar had helped his other friends collect nice pronghorn bucks and now it was the last day of the season and a buck was heading toward the fence onto private property where he couldn't hunt.

The men were hunting on the Arapaho National Wildlife Refuge when Chuck sighted a nice buck – nothing special – moving toward a fence with a herd of does that separated the refuge from private property. Chuck was on the road when he saw them so he slowly left his truck in hopes he could cut them off before they left the refuge. He didn't think the buck was of Boone and Crockett quality because it was short and squatty but this was the end of the season and he wanted to fill his tag. He worked his way closer to the herd and the herd quartered itself away from the men without running.

When the herd acted like it was getting nervous, Chuck sat down to prepare a shot. He fired the first time from 150 yards and the buck immediately dropped. The does took off just as Chuck had predicted and scooted under the fence with the wounded buck trying to follow them. A second quick shot from a distance of 40 yards permanently downed the buck but the cape was ruined when the bullet pierced the neck. Years later, after Chuck had taken another nice buck, he had the horns mounted and the buck's Boone and Crockett Club score entered.

HAMMOND R. COLLINS
Location: Rio Grande County
Year Taken: 1995
Score: 82-6/8

The alarm clock blared at 5:30 a.m. on opening day of the 1995 pronghorn season for Hamm and Sue Collins. They were already running late when their feet hit the floor.

Hamm's wife, Sue, listened as Hamm went through his angry, irritated, frustrated, aggravated, record-breaking, panic-inspiring, coffee-making, truck-loading, rifle-checking, coffee-spilling, dog-blaming tirade until they were headed down the straight track to their hunting area north of Del Norte at 65 mph. As they raced north from Del Norte, Sue wondered out loud, "Well, we are on our way, can't we slow down?" Inspired by her patience and self-control, Hamm did just what she suggested. He also began to reflect on what had happened in the past, and what it was that brought them to this point.

Hamm Collins was late getting to his hunting area near Del Norte but it didn't matter. He still came home with a trophy pronghorn buck that scores 82-6/8 points.

Hamm was introduced to his favorite trophy pronghorn-producing area north of Del Norte in 1985 when he accompanied some friends from Creede on his first archery hunt. He recalled that on the opening day of the 1985 archery season that he saw more trophy pronghorn than he had ever seen anywhere in his life.

He was thinking if he knew in 1985 what he knew in 1995, he would have certainly bagged a trophy antelope back then. He had bowshots at four different pronghorns within the first six hours of opening-day daylight that year. Near noon he observed a herd of 20 to 25 animals with at least five Pope and Young qualifiers in it. He also saw an antelope with a normal horn on one side, while the other horn ran down the length of the buck's face. The horn tip protruded at least three inches past its nose, and the brow tine appeared to encircle the buck's eye.

Because of the memories from his 1985 archery hunt, he started applying for an antelope rifle license in 1990. It wasn't until 1995 that he was finally drawn.

A few moments before legal shooting light Sue said, "Look at all those antelope." Hamm slowed down and took a look at what he would have passed up because he was reflecting on the past while Sue was paying attention to the present. A buck with his harem of eight does was standing out there at about 250 yards. Even in gathering daylight, Hamm could make out a buck chasing a doe as the others watched. Hamm took off with his .30-06 Winchester, 1958, Model 70, to scope the herd. When he got set up, he could plainly see that this buck was "love sick" and that it had found the cure.

Minutes later, Hamm slipped off the safety, set the cross hairs 8.5 inches high to allow for bullet drop at 250 yards and squeezed off a round. The bullet impact was the loudest Hamm had ever heard. When the scope settled on his buck again, Hamm watched it run a short distance, stumble and drop.

Hamm waited five years for a pronghorn permit and spent five minutes collecting his B&C buck. Sue videotaped the celebrations and the hunting experience was complete.

MICHAEL J. ATWOOD, SR.
Location: Saguache County
Year Taken: 1986
Score: 82-4/8

Michael Atwood holds his B&C pronghorn buck he downed in 1986.

Michael Atwood applied for a pronghorn tag for seven years before being drawn in 1986. His permit was for Area A-73 east of the Continental Divide and north of the La Garita Mountains.

Michael and his son scouted the area two weeks before the season opened and set up his camper. Michael remembered seeing plenty of pronghorns while passing through the area on previous elk hunting trips. After two days of scouting, however, they only located three does. The weather was hot and dry, and Michael prayed for snow at the higher elevations to push the bucks out of the high country.

The day before the season opened, Michael drove back to the camper and scouted the area again. He only saw 11 pronghorns, including one small buck. Temperatures ranged from 12 degrees in the morning to 65 degrees by 1 p.m., and the hunting went poorly. On the sixth day, Michael awoke at 3 a.m. to wind and rain shaking and pounding the camper. He figured the pronghorn would be on the move, but he didn't think he would be able to move due to poor road conditions. Snow began to fall at 5 a.m., and Michael knew after 50 years of hunting that these weather conditions would cause game to feed and move late.

Michael dressed warmly, put his truck into four-wheel drive, and moved slowly up the valley, stopping periodically to glass the meadows and ridges. He noted a large herd leaving an adjacent meadow and going over the next ridge, so he decided to drive ahead of the herd and sneak back. After he parked, he grabbed his rifle and took off. He sneaked along the bottom of the ridge close to the rocky bottom. The snow had stopped falling and the wind was in his favor. He was a half mile from his truck and 400 yards from the head of the meadow where he had last seen the herd so he decided to wait them out.

Within 10 minutes he heard rocks tumbling on the other side of the ridge next to him. He crept over the rocky ridge to within 10 yards of the top and heard what sounded like a large rockslide. Michael reached the top as a herd of 60 pronghorns sped away from the ridge. Michael followed, with his scope, three bucks that broke from the herd to the right and looked like they would come around the end of the ridge Michael was on.

Michael selected the lead buck to fill his tag. He flipped the safety off and fired two shots. After the second shot, his buck lay down while the other two trotted off after pausing only long enough to look back at the downed buck. Michael figured his buck was dead, so he headed back to the truck to drive it closer to the pronghorn. He didn't want to drag it more than necessary. Before it was all over, however, Michael had to relocate his buck and put it down for good with one more shot. When he went to retrieve the truck, his buck had gotten up. It was trotting along the mountainside with its head down when he relocated it. This was Michael's first pronghorn, and it made the B&C records book.

CHARLES W. KLAASSENS
Location: Moffat County
Year Taken: 1981
Score: 82-4/8

It was late July 1981 when Charles Klaassens and his brother-in-law, Mark Bergmann finally decided to do some scouting in the area for which they had drawn permits. After all, the season was quickly closing in on them. Combining their trip with a fishing expedition, they spent a good half-day scouting out their area. They saw lots of pronghorns but nothing to brag about. They still planned to hunt the same area, figuring that where there were does, there would be some nice bucks.

Charles and Mark took an extra day off from work to set up camp and prepare for opening morning. The next day they awoke at 4 a.m., downed a big breakfast, and left camp in different directions. Charles followed a dry creek bed and remained hidden. He was about a mile from camp when he detected movement 300 yards away. It was 7:12 a.m. when Charles grabbed his binoculars to check it out. He could hardly believe his eyes. There were two big pronghorn bucks in his field of view that were facing east toward the sun. Charles inched closer to the bucks on his knees through the cactuses while the bucks continued to graze.

When he was within 200 yards of the pair, Charles calmed himself and took a deep breath. The buck on the left was larger, so he placed the cross hairs on the buck's shoulder and squeezed the trigger of his .270 Winchester. At the crack of the rifle, Charles' name entered the records books.

Two trophy pronghorn bucks hung on Charles Klaassens' living room wall until he sold the mount on the right before having it measured. The buck on the left is his 1981 B&C trophy. Charles said the buck on the right was taken five years after the other buck and within 100 yards of where the B&C buck was taken.

That was the end of Charles' 1981 season, but he knew he had a good one. Not knowing much about the B&C Club's scoring system, Charles really didn't realize what a spectacular trophy he had just collected. In fact, it wasn't until he talked to two game wardens who later checked his buck that Charles realized he might have a real trophy. An official measurement after the required 60-day drying period revealed the fact that Charles' "nice" buck was indeed a B&C trophy.

Charles was very happy with the news. He has hunted the same area for the last 14 years and has had the good fortune to take two other big bucks. Both were two inches shy of the minimum score necessary to enter a pronghorn in "The Book."

The exact area Charles hunts is Area 3 north of Craig in northwestern Colorado. It is a very popular pronghorn area and anyone who applies for this area can count on at least a five-year wait. In spite of the long wait, Charles feels it is well worth it.

Charles Klaaassens is an avid hunter who especially enjoys pronghorn hunting. This trophy buck was collected by Charles in 1981 while hunting with his brother-in-law, Mark Bergmann.

TERRY OMAN
Location: Moffat County
Year Taken: 1991
Score: 81

Terry Oman has hunted the rugged beauty of Colorado for more than 25 years, but in 1988 he decided to get serious about bringing home a trophy pronghorn buck. Terry waited the four years to accumulate preference points to pull a buck tag. The area he wanted was about an hour's drive northwest of Craig. Terry hunted this area many times with his brothers and friends, and they'd shot does but noticed some sizable bucks they thought were trophy material.

Opening morning was cold and clear and all the more full of anticipation since it was the first year Terry's 10-year-old daughter Ashlie had come along with him to accompany him on the hunt. At sunrise, the two of them took off on foot across the rolling hills, silently winding a path through the scrub oak and cactus. As they approached the area where Terry expected to see a pronghorn cross, Ashlie was the first to spot seven pronghorn on a knoll 300 yards off. Terry slowly raised his binoculars and determined that one buck in the herd was very large and tempting. Terry suffered from opening day optimism and thought he could do better. The same situation was true of the next herd Ashlie spotted a little while later.

Although the sun had been up for more than an hour, it was just now breaking over the ridge and the two hunters were still feeling the cold. For a diversion, they stopped and dug into the backpack for the goodies Terry's wife always packs. As they enjoyed the treats, they had an animated conversation about Terry's promise that Ashlie could hunt rabbits later in the day and would be eligible to pull a doe tag of her own in just two years.

Terry and Ashlie Oman proudly pose with Terry's Boone and Crockett pronghorn buck on the exact spot where the trophy was downed. The buck scores 81 points.

With renewed enthusiasm and energy, Terry and Ashlie set out for a new vantage point with Ashlie walking just head of Terry. As they trudged along, Terry wondered to himself if he should have tried for that first buck. He was still wondering when they came up over the top of the ridge and both of them instinctively froze at the sight of a monster buck, running all alone about 150 yards away. The buck saw the humans at about the same instant and stopped dead in its tracks. As they stood staring at each other, suspended in time for what seemed like an eternity, Terry whispered to Ashlie, "If he looks away, drop down on one knee."

The moment came within a minute or so when the buck glanced to the side and Terry and Ashlie dropped silently to their knees in a single motion. The buck looked right back at them and they froze again. The buck finally looked at the ground in front of him, so Terry pulled up his rifle in a smooth motion and sited down the scope. He sucked in his breath when he saw the buck's size, and the adrenaline started to flow.

In a low whisper that was barely audible, Terry said, "Ash, this is the one. Cover your ears." The buck looked straight at Terry again so Terry squeezed down on his 7mm for a single shot. The buck flinched and ran but Terry knew it was a clean shot. The buck ran 50 yards before it fell. Terry collected his B&C trophy and completed his first hunt with his daughter. Ashlie continues to hunt with her father, and Terry always remembers his buck of a lifetime.

JOHN R. OLSON
Location: Rio Grande County
Year Taken: 1997
Score: 80-6/8

Several weeks of scouting in Rio Grande County had convinced John Olson this was where he wanted to hunt for big pronghorn bucks but he had no idea his total hunt would be only two hours on opening morning.

John and a hunting partner set out on opening morning to stalk a small herd but nothing in the herd was large enough so they went to a new hunting area. A large buck stood on top of a hillside when the men reached the new area, so John decided to go after it. When he reached the top of the ridge, the buck had disappeared. His friend motioned to John to look below, and there stood the buck. John raised his .25-06 and fired a single shot, dropping the buck where it stood.

Upon reaching the buck John noticed the huge heart-shaped horns measuring more than 16 inches and its massiveness. From start to finish, the total hunt lasted two hours and John had collected his Boone and Crockett Club trophy. John's pronghorn buck was accepted into the Boone and Crockett Club's 24th North American Big Game Awards Program in August 1998.

PAMELA S. COBURN
Location: Moffat County
Year Taken: 1993
Score: 80-2/8

Pamela Coburn and her husband, Jerrell, applied unsuccessfully for Colorado pronghorn permits for five years before they were drawn for Area 2 in July 1993. They had planned to leave for a trail ride in the Collegiate Range with Glen Roberts when they received their tags. As a result, they extended their vacation by two weeks allowing time to scout for pronghorn. Glen, an outfitter from Buena Vista, showed them a great time. And they felt fortunate to see several flocks of bighorn sheep and Rocky Mountain goats.

With detailed county maps in hand, Pam and Jerrell headed northwest to Moffat County. Brad Pelch, a game biologist from Maybell, informed them the severe winter of 1992-93 might have stunted horn growth in Colorado's pronghorn herds for the upcoming season. On the plus side, Brad told them that some of Wyoming's antelope were pushed into their unit because of the same weather patterns.

Pam and Jerrell scouted for three days on Bureau of Land Management land covering most of their unit. Each day they saw more than 50 different bucks plus an assortment of elk, mule deer, golden eagles and bands of wild horses. Pam and Jerrell highlighted the areas on their maps they planned to hunt in September. They saw one pronghorn buck with exceptionally good prongs, and she told Jerrell it was the buck she wanted to hunt when the season opened.

Less than two months later they were on their way back to Colorado. Their first stop was at the Taylor Ranch east of San Luis. Jerrell hunted for five days during the rut and took a nice 6x6 bull elk.

They then headed towards Moffat County. They arrived on a Friday evening and set up camp. Scouting was out of the question that evening as it was too late. Pam and Jerrell set out long before sunup on opening morning and drove to the area where they had spotted the trophy buck in July. It took them 45 minutes to get to the location where they had previ-

Pamela Coburn waited five years to receive a pronghorn hunting permit and for her efforts she collected this outstanding pronghorn buck in Moffat County in 1993 that scores 80-2/8 points.

ously seen the big buck. They sat and waited for sunrise.

Thirty minutes later as the sun's rays cracked on the horizon, Pam's buck materialized in the distance. It took her only a few minutes to get into position. Her first shot hit solidly, but the buck stood there. Pam fired a second round and her buck never even twitched when it hit the ground. Pam had tagged along with Jerrell on many hunts, but this was her first hunt and it certainly wasn't her last.

Jerrell and Pam hunted hard for the remainder of the season and saw dozens of bucks each day, but nothing compared to the first pronghorn buck Pam was lucky enough to take.

Cougar or Mountain Lion Harvests

1967-1999

Year	Male Harvest	Female Harvest	Total Harvest	Total Hunters	Percent Success
1999	263	211	473	1,178	40
1998	209	193	402	1,242	32
1997	223	191	414	1,157	36
1996	213	178	391	971	40
1995	180	137	317	905	35
1994	187	129	316	826	38
1993	167	130	297	781	38
1992	175	120	295	681	43
1991	143	94	237	692	34
1990	143	97	240	576	42
1989	115	68	183	520	35
1988	104	74	178	416	43
1987	---	---	180	365	49
1986	---	---	166	310	54
1985	---	---	155	363	43
1984	---	---	101	257	39
1983	78	47	125	362	35
1982	77	60	137	327	42
1981	67	40	107	248	43
1980	41	41	82	200	41
1979	49	25	74	209	35
1978	48	43	91	243	37
1977	44	39	83	195	43
1976	44	21	65	152	43
1975	47	43	90	143	63
1974	27	25	52	185	28
1973	33	27	60	115	52
1972	29	6	35	72	49
1971	19	10	29	33	88
1970	23	24	47	---	---
1969	31	23	54	---	---
1968	---	---	50	---	---
1967	---	---	58	---	---

* No hunting regulations and season before 1967.
** After 1983, total harvest based on mandatory check forms.

Possible members of the Harry Jackson family celebrate a successful cougar hunt around 1910 near Durango. From left to right, Ella (daughter), Louisa (Mother), and Marquerite (daughter). The lady in white and the two little boys are not identified.

THEODORE ROOSEVELT
Location: Meeker
Year Taken: 1901
Score: 15-12/16
Owner: Smithsonian Institution's Museum of Natural History, Washington, D.C.

President Theodore Roosevelt and members of his hunting party in 1905 outside Glenwood Springs in Garfield County. The photograph was taken by Harry H. Buckwalter. President Roosevelt loved to hunt in Colorado.

Killed by Theo. Roosevelt Feb. 14, 1901, at Meeker, Colorado.
Skull length – 9-5/16 inches
Skull width – 6-3/8 inches
Length of animal (tip to tip) – 96 inches
Wgt. (weight) – 227 lbs.
Specimen #108681
Skull of largest male puma *(Felix concolor hippolestes)* taken to date in the Americas

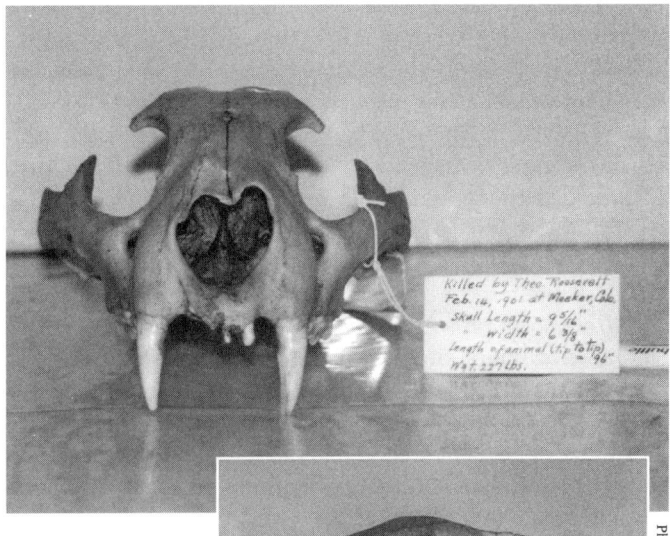

Two photographs show the cougar skull of Theodore Roosevelt's trophy taken in 1901 in Meeker. President Roosevelt died in 1919, long before the Boone and Crockett Club established a big-game measuring system, but the skull was eventually measured and given to the National Museum of Natural History in Washington, D.C.

While on a trip to Washington, D.C., in August 2000, the author of this book met the curators of the Museum of Natural History that maintain the skulls, skins and skeletons of all North American animals, including this cougar skull. The author knew that the Smithsonian Institution owned this skull based upon listings in Boone and Crockett Club records books, but did not know where the skull was stored. After several days of calling to various museum offices, she was invited to visit the Suitland, Maryland, storage facility where the Smithsonian's natural history collections are found. The curator who escorted her to the facility was impressed by the size of the skull compared to other cougar specimens and did not know that this cougar ranked as the largest ever taken in Colorado.

There, attached to a modest-looking cougar skull, was the original specimen tag created when President Theodore Roosevelt gave his treasured cougar skull to the collections. The tag is shown in the photographs, but in case the reader of this book can't read the label, this is the exact wording:

DARRYL POWELL
Location: Mesa County
Year Taken: 1997
Score: 15-9/16

A trade of expert guiding services for job referrals was just the right informal agreement among friends for Scott Barnes and Tracy Clark of Lazy House Outfitters to take Darryl Powell out on the Grand Mesa to locate a trophy cougar.

"I reasoned with them that since I had a lion tag and there were only a few days left in the season, if they would take me out and get me a lion, I could certainly send some business their way," explained Darryl.

The Christmas holidays were the days set aside to find a mountain lion. Early on December 26, 1997, Tracy called Darryl to say he had located some fresh tracks, so within minutes the two met at a convenience store on a highway close to Darryl's house in Grand Junction. Darryl followed Tracy in his truck through the sagebrush flats at the base of the Grand Mesa to cedar and juniper hillsides. They hiked up a hill to the fresh tracks and released three of Scott's hounds, surmising that the cougar had been down in the lower country just hours before feeding on deer when it decided to travel up the hill to the location where the dogs were released.

Several hours later, as the men followed the howls and barking, the hunters determined the dogs had treed a cat in a ponderosa. Darryl worked his way up a steep hillside to within 18 yards of the cat and fired his Jennings Buckmaster compound bow and let fly his Eastman aluminum arrow with a Thunderhead broadhead.

Getting the cat down the mountain became the rest of the story. Tracy and Darryl saw their truck two miles down the mountain, so they decided to go straight down the slope since there were only a couple of hours of light remaining in the day. Tracy put a 10-foot rope around the lion's neck and slid the lion down the slope in the snow as Darryl broke trail ahead. They came to several rugged and

Darryl Powell's Mesa County cougar.

steep cliff areas and one in particular was difficult to maneuver around easily, so Darryl turned to Tracy to suggest they find another route just as Tracy lost his footing on a slippery snow-covered rock. Tracy was dragged down the slope by the weight of the lion, so he let go of the rope and shouted to Darryl to look out.

As the lion slid toward Darryl, Darryl only had time to spread his legs in hopes the cat would slip through them but a claw from the cat's paw hooked on his pant leg and dragged Darryl off a 20-foot cliff. Darryl spun through the air, crashing through a ponderosa tree and landed on his back and shoulder with the lion resting beside him. Darryl knew he had broken bones, so when Tracy asked if everything was all right, Darryl responded that he needed to get to an emergency room. At the base of the mountain, Darryl was loaded into the truck, and Tracy and Scott raced to the nearest hospital.

X-rays showed that Darryl had a dislocated shoulder, cracked scapula, fractured head of the humerus and a broken acromion bone. But, Darryl had his trophy cat, and thanks to the efforts of Scott and Tracy, the cat was finally retrieved off the mountain. This massive cougar is registered with the Boone and Crockett Club and the Pope and Young Club as one of the top cats in the world.

Darryl Powell moments after he downed his records-book cougar that scores 15-9/16 points in the Boone and Crockett Club and Pope and Young Club records programs.

PICK UP
Location: Las Animas County
Year Found: Prior to 1994
Score: 15-5/16
Found by Phillip L. Ehrlich

Phil was coyote hunting during the winter of 1993-1994 in a remote section of the Mesa DeMaya just north of the New Mexico border in southeastern Colorado when he stumbled upon an old, moss-covered cougar skull with a missing jawbone, never imagining that this was a Boone and Crockett skull. He even debated about carrying the skull back with him from the mesa because it was so old and grungy looking.

As Phil walked along the edge of a shallow draw lined with junipers and oak brush, he kicked something that turned out to be an aged cougar skull. His job with the Colorado Division of Wildlife often involves making presentations to school children so he often took the skull with him to pass among little fingers. The skull was even dropped once during a presentation and he had to glue back the teeth several times. When Phil was selected to become a B&C official measurer, he measured the skull as practice for the class and discovered its size. Needless to say, he no longer passes the skull around in classrooms or during hunter safety training and treats the skull like fine china. The skull has been mounted on a plaque and hangs proudly on his wall.

And, to think this skull might have never been measured.

Phil Ehrlich holds the Boone and Crockett cougar skull he found while coyote hunting near the New Mexico border during the winter of 1993-1994.

WILLIAM KALLISTER
Location: Delta County
Year Taken: 1995
Score: 15-5/16

January 4, 1995, found Illinois resident Bill Kallister winging his way to the Grand Junction airport to meet guide and outfitter Lawrence Zeldenthius who planned to take him to the Uncompahgre National Forest for a cougar hunt. Conditions were dry so no snow had fallen and Lawrence told Bill this would be their challenge on the hunt.

The morning after Bill landed, he and Lawrence arose at 4 a.m. to find that the bowhunting gods had smiled on them. Six inches of fresh snow had fallen overnight to aid in their ability to locate fresh tracks. After loading up the dogs and picking up Doug McCauley at his taxidermy shop with some friends in Delta, Bill and Lawrence drove up a back road on the forest as the other hunters drove another route. They had driven a few miles when Lawrence suddenly stopped the pick-up upon spotting fresh tracks that crossed the road. Lawrence told Bill these were the tracks of a big tom, so he let out the dogs to see if they could pick up the trail.

Bill was given a walkie-talkie so Lawrence could communicate with him in the field as Bill waited in the truck. Bill was 65 years old at the time, and Lawrence was in his 30s and in great shape to climb up and down mountains, so Bill wanted to make sure the trail led to a cougar before he started to follow Lawrence. Before leaving the truck, Lawrence radioed to Doug that he had located a tom and to meet them at the truck. Shortly after Doug reached Bill, Lawrence radioed back that he had jumped the lion so Doug and Bill took off to meet him.

Sometime later, which seemed like an eternity to Bill, Doug said he could tell by the dogs' baying that the lion was treed. When they got within 200 yards of the lion, Lawrence and the dogs, Bill seriously doubted if he could make it. Just then the lion bolted from the tree and took off with the dogs in hot pursuit. Bill told Doug he couldn't continue but as he spoke the dogs treed the cat again, which energized Bill to continue the hunt. They reached Lawrence, the dogs and the cat high up in a tree and Bill worked to catch his breath. As Bill prepared to shoot, Lawrence directed him to aim for the cat's shoulder. Bill released a single arrow but the guides thought he had missed. In fact he had not, and the arrow traveled through the tom. Five seconds after the shot the cat was Bill's, and Bill had collected a cougar that not only qualified for Pope and Young's records book but also for the Boone and Crockett Club's records program.

"This was a fantastic conclusion to a very, very lucky one-day lion hunt in the fabulous mountains of Colorado," said Bill.

The snow couldn't have fallen at a more perfect time.

MARK TURNER
Location: Clear Creek County
Year Taken: 1995
Score: 15-3/16

On the last day of the cougar season, March 28, 1995, in Clear Creek County Mark Turner was searching for his elusive goal when he located fresh tracks. The chase was on.

Smokey, his blue-tick hound, and several pups were released to track the big cat and after crossing a couple of ridges the cougar was located. Connie and Gary Renfro joined Mark in the four to five mile hike up and down hill and dale. When the three reached the place where Smokey and the pups had treed the cat, Mark saw the cat in a tall ponderosa pine tree overlooking a cliff. He fired his 65-pound recurve Pitsley Predator bow and the tom jumped from the tree.

Mark knew the cougar was big by the measurement of its eyes and nose. After the 60-day drying period, the cat was officially scored for the Pope and Young Club and is ranked 8th largest (five-way tie) in their 5th edition of the P&Y all-time records book, *Bowhunting Big Game Records of North America*, published in 1999. Because of its size, this cougar would also qualify for entrance in the Boone and Crockett Club if entered.

Smokey died in 2000 but her legacy lives through the pups who Mark said are as outstanding at tracking cougar as their teacher.

Connie and Gary Renfro pose with Mark Turner (center) and his Pope and Young Club cougar.

BRAD F. PFEFFER
Location: La Plata County
Year Taken: 1998
Score: 15-2/16

A first-time cougar hunt, deep snow, fresh tracks, great guides and outstanding hunting dogs all combined to create one of the best hunts in his life for Brad Pfeffer during the winter of 1998.

A friend of Brad's, George Lyons, offered to take him on his first cougar hunt near Durango with his son, Brian, and Brian's friend, John Floyd, but warned Brad that when he called, Brad would need to come quickly. Several months after George's offer, he called Brad to say fresh tracks had been sighted in fresh snow, and could Brad come immediately. Brad had business commitments the next day but reached George in Durango that evening in time to hunt on Saturday, January 10. He tossed and turned that night, worried that the snow would melt. George, Brian and John and their trained tracking dogs accompanied Brad to the hunting area as the snow melted, and after a day's worth of tracking a set of paw prints, up mountains and down, the men decided to wait until the next day in hopes more snow would fall.

On Saturday night 6 inches of fresh snow fell, much to the delight of everyone, so tracking another set of paw prints was made much easier on Sunday. Shortly after arrival in the hunting area, the dogs cut a fresh track and were off as the cat led them up mountainsides and down, through snowdrifts up to their thighs and through almost impenetrable ground cover. The dogs finally treed a tom after several miles of tortuous tracking, and the dogs were leashed as Brad fired a single shot with his .357 revolver.

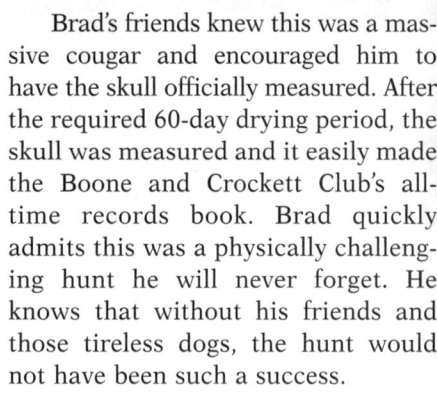

Brad's friends knew this was a massive cougar and encouraged him to have the skull officially measured. After the required 60-day drying period, the skull was measured and it easily made the Boone and Crockett Club's all-time records book. Brad quickly admits this was a physically challenging hunt he will never forget. He knows that without his friends and those tireless dogs, the hunt would not have been such a success.

Cougar

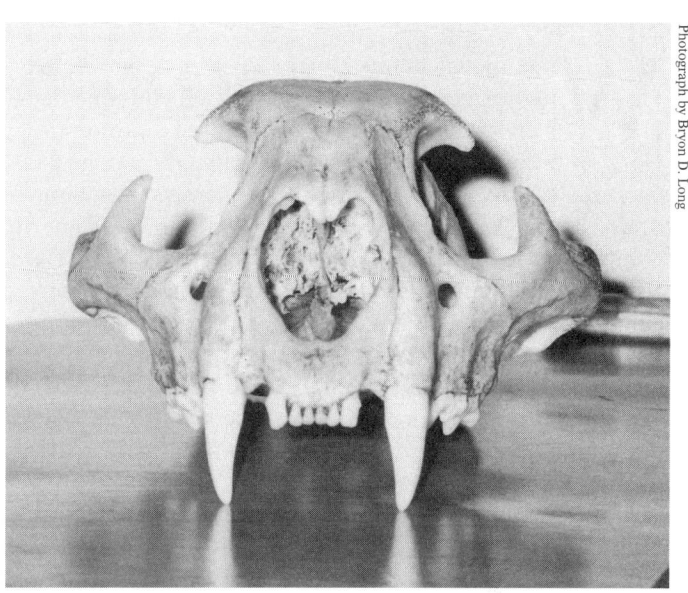

Montezuma County produced another fine trophy-book cougar. This time the honors went to a cougar that scores 15-2/16 B&C points that was collected by Terry Amrine of Dolores on February 5, 1999.

Michael R. Treinen tracked this outstanding cougar in the Cortez area in January 1997. The tom scores 14-9/16.

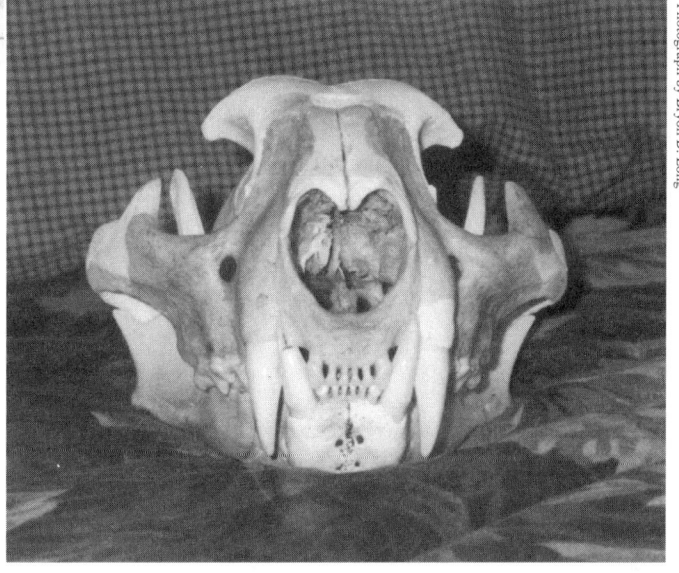

ANTHONY S. WAGNER
Location: Dolores County
Year Taken: 1990
Score: 15-1/16

When the telephone rang at 11:30 p.m. on a Sunday night, Anthony and Tammy Wagner immediately knew it was Colorado guide and outfitter Tony Hoza, of Dolores, Colorado. Tony was calling to say he unexpectedly had five days open to take Anthony cougar hunting again. Three weeks earlier Anthony and Tammy came up empty handed while hunting with Tony and Gary Hoza. Before they left, Anthony had made arrangements for Tony to call if he came up with any free time.

Anthony was on the plane the next day by 2 p.m. and arrived in Montrose that evening. When he disembarked, he was amazed at the amount of fresh new snow. He figured maybe this time those big toms wouldn't be as lucky as tracking conditions were perfect.

The men located a large set of tom tracks heading into a deep canyon on the first day. The tracks were two or three days old, so they didn't let the dogs loose. Rather, they circled the area on foot to see if the cat had come out. They found some smaller lion tracks, but not the big one. On the second day, things remained slow and nothing happened.

The hunting pace picked up on the third day, however, when Tony and Anthony dropped into a valley filled with elk and deer tracks. Anthony pointed out a set of cat tracks to Tony, and Tony told him, "This is what we have been looking for." The dogs were released, and in moments their baying was heard on a distant ridge. Adrenaline pumped in the

hunters' veins as they neared the dogs' barking only to discover they had treed a 30-pound kitten. Not far from the kitten, the men noticed where the big tom had killed a 4x4 elk. The kitten and the female were feeding on the elk when the dogs jumped them. The men then redirected the dogs back onto the tom's tracks.

Just before dark the dogs caught the tom on the face of a cliff, but the men were unable to find it in the crevices before darkness fell. As the men returned to the truck, one of the dogs, Daisy, broke loose after the tom, and they had to leave her on the mountain that night.

The men returned to the same area early the next morning and found Daisy sitting in the middle of the road. She had chased the big tom all night but had given up when it crossed the road. After a quick meal, Daisy and the others were back on the cat's trail again. The dogs chased it to another rock ledge, but when the hunters arrived, the cat gave the dogs the slip. They watched the tom cross the canyon floor closely followed by the dogs in hot pursuit.

Eventually, the dogs cornered the tom in a small cave near the top of the canyon where they were pulled from the cave one by one and tied to a tree. Anthony had hoped to take his cougar with a bow, but due to the small cave opening, he switched to Gary's .357 Colt Python. A single, well-placed shot behind the shoulders, and Anthony had his B&C trophy. They estimated its weight to be between 170 and 180 pounds.

Anthony Wagner used a .357 Colt Python pistol to collect this B&C cougar that scores 15-1/16 points. Here he holds his cougar as his dog Pilot stands nearby.

NORMAN R. NOE
Location: Las Animas County
Year Taken: 1996
Score: 15-1/16

The hunting trip probably won't go down in the records books as the longest but it certainly netted a records book cat.

The hunt began and ended February 3, 1996, when Norman met his friend and hunting guide, Albert Goode, plus assorted blue tick and walker dogs. After locating a fresh set of tracks, the dogs were released and within three-quarters of a mile from the starting point, the dogs had treed a massive tom cougar. One of the dogs had the courage and motivation to climb the tree with the cat and begin growling at it. The cat turned and faced the dog so the two commenced a growling contest. Since the two were inches apart, Norman decided to use a more precise rifle rather than his .357 Magnum revolver. Carefully making sure not to shoot the hound, Norman aimed his .223 Remington rifle using a 55-grain Sierra soft point bullet. That single, well-placed shot downed the cat.

Norman knew this was a large animal so he had Phil Ehrlich measure it for Boone and Crockett Club after the 60-day drying period. The cat easily made the all-time records book with a final score of 15-1/16 points.

H. MICHAEL HOCKER
Location: Archuleta County
Year Taken: 1999
Score: 15

Three days of hard hunting by a father-daughter team netted for this family one of the largest cougars ever taken in Colorado and the world. The story begins in Archuletta County outside Pagosa Springs on Devil's Mountain in January 1999.

Michael and his daughter, Ann, have hunted together for more than 23 years or since Ann was 16 years old, so tracking a tom cat up hill and down was commonplace for them. Two days before the large tom was located, they awoke each morning at 3 a.m. and spent all of daylight searching for elusive cougar tracks. Fresh snow fell on the third day of Michael's hunt providing 12 to 36 inches of white cover with 10 degree below zero temperatures. When the fresh cougar tracks were located by the hunters, an eight-hour hike began. Five dogs belonging to Michael's friend were released at 7 a.m., but they didn't locate the treed cougar until 3 p.m. at the top of a 60-foot conifer tree. A single shot from his .44 Remington Magnum rifle using a 210-grain bullet brought down the cat.

Michael and Ann dragged the cougar out without field dressing it so when they reached Pagosa Springs they weighed the cat at 187 pounds. To get the cat out of the mountains, its body was wrapped in a tarp and loaded onto a snowmobile that carried them back to their truck. The Hockers enjoyed 60 pounds of dense, sweet meat that tasted much like pork. Not only did Michael down a great cougar, but also Ann collected a female cat on the same hunt.

This was a team effort by a father and daughter on a hunt they will never forget.

The father-daughter hunting team of Michael and Ann with his B&C cougar in the winter of 1999.

LAWRENCE C. GLASS
Location: Mesa County
Year Taken: 1985
Score: 15

Big cat tracks, deer tracks, and blood in the snow told Larry Glass and his hunting guide Blaine Atwood about an age-old struggle that had occurred. The hunter had descended the ridge and stalked its prey. It pounced, drew blood, and lost its grip releasing its prey. Now it was Larry's turn to hunt the hunter.

The hounds were released and took off up a ridge, down a valley and up the other side. Eventually the day ended with confusion because there were just too many tracks in the snow. The next day, Larry and his guide discovered some new tracks, which resulted in a long chase that ended at dark.

The next weekend Larry had fresh tracking snow. Blaine told Larry, "This is a perfect day," adding, "We're on to a big tom." Larry just smiled back wondering if Blaine was serious.

Leaving Blaine's house on the Colorado River, they rode horses up Alkali Creek through sagebrush, junipers and into the national forest. The south sides were dry and the north sides were deep in snow.

Eventually they found some big cat tracks and were off in hot pursuit. The slope was too steep and icy for the horses, so Blaine sent his stepson, Larry, with Larry Glass to follow the dogs on foot. Blaine's last words were, "Stay with Sadie. She's my best hound." Over the icy rock ledges they went, pulling themselves from tree to tree. The dog pack split; Sadie went uphill and the rest of the pack went downhill. Both Larrys followed Sadie until she disappeared over a ridge.

At that point they gave up on Sadie and went back to investigate the main pack. When they caught up with it, Larry could see where the hounds had danced around the base of a fir tree. Searching from branch to branch, Larry and his guide eventually spotted the giant hairball crouched on a branch. The guide corralled the dogs downstream and told Larry to, "Make sure the lion is killed. I don't want the dogs torn up."

Larry Glass drew his .357 Magnum from its holster, thinking how anti-climatic this moment was turning out. He had hunted for 5 days for this chance at a nice cat. When he fired, the tom cascaded down the tree in an avalanche of snow and branches. A second shot missed, and a third shot hit the cougar as it jumped away from the base of the tree. The cougar saw the dogs and ran upstream, made a 90-degree turn, and headed straight towards Larry.

Larry's next shot parted the skin between its ears. Larry's mouth dropped open because the cougar had not dropped dead. It ran past Larry and he fired again. The dogs went crazy and broke from Larry the guide. The cat ran 70 yards and halfway up a pinon tree. The guide yelled and dogs howled. Larry was four thumbs and 12 fingers trying to reload. Two more shots and the cat fell dead. They dragged the 160-pound cougar to the packhorses, and everyone, including the taxidermist, said it was very large.

Larry smiled and said, "Sure."

BARRY GENE HASTEN
Location: Las Animas County
Year Taken: 2000
Score: 15

While hunting mule deer in Colorado in fall 1999 Barry Hasten explored the possibility of hunting mountain lions. His long-time mule deer guide Chris Furia suggested lion guide Rob Padretti of Canon City. He talked to Rob and told him he wanted to bring his 10-year-old son Austin and 8-year-old son Quentin. Rob agreed, and they set the hunt for the third week in December 1999.

As the date approached, Austin and Quentin became more excited. Being from Texas, Barry's kids had never seen much more than skiff of snow. When they reached Raton, New Mexico, the boys asked Barry pull off the road so they could play in a ditch full of snow. The night before the hunt there was a good snow, making for good lion hunting. They arrived at a ranch outside Trinidad at daylight. Barry's friend, Chris Furia, took his boys in one truck, and Rob and Barry went in another. They drove all day but didn't see a track. The boys and Barry saw a number of elk, turkey and lots of snow. That night they were tired, but the boys were still excited and spirits were high.

There was another snow on the second night and they reached the ranch at daylight. About 11 a.m. they ran across a track. Rob looked at the track carefully and determined it was probably a small male or average female. They discussed what to do and decided to go after it since it was more important for the boys to be on a hunt than the size of the lion. They followed the track and cut the dogs loose.

The dogs hit the trail hard and within about 20 minutes Barry looked across the valley and saw the lion being chased by the dogs. Barry told Rob that the lion looked pretty big. Chris, the boys and Barry went back to the truck and drove around while Rob followed the dogs. They got out on a mountain overlooking where the dogs had gone. It sounded like the dogs split up, treeing in two different places. Rob said on the radio that he didn't know why his dogs were barking up an empty tree, but he then added, "Get down here. We've got a monster!" Rob responded.

Chris, the boys and Barry walked about a mile until they got to the tree where they found an awesome lion that was unquestionably the most beautiful, captivating animal Barry had ever seen. The boys were speechless. It looked more like a female African lion than a cougar.

As Rob rounded up the rest of his dogs that had treed another lion, the rest of the hunting party stood speechless under the tree for about 45 minutes waiting for his return. The look on the boys' faces was unforgettable. They were a little scared but clearly impressed. When Rob returned, Barry fired a single shot with his .273, but the cougar came out of the tree and ran as if it wasn't hit. They followed the blood trail 75 yards down the valley where Barry found it. There were lots of hugs and handshaking and a profound respect for what Barry had just harvested. After the required 60-day drying period, the cougar easily made the Boone and Crockett Club's all-time records book with a final score of 15 points.

Barry Hasten with his sons, Quentin (left) and Austin (center), moments after Barry downed one of the largest cougars ever taken in Colorado.

PAUL F. GABEL
Location: Chaffee County
Year Taken: 1966
Score: 14-14/16

Bob "Cat" Peters met Paul Gabel and his wife, Rose, in Salida on December 4th and led them back to his hunting camp. The Gabels found camp well equipped with dogs, horses and a nice little sleeping trailer. Bob's wife, Vona, did the cooking and accompanied Rose on arrowhead hunts while the men hunted lions.

The first few days were spent searching for cat tracks without success, and the evenings were spent in camp taking it easy. The mountains were covered with snow, and the sun shone brightly.

Bob had six hounds in camp, but he only used two each day. While sitting around camp one day, another fellow offered Bob $1,600 for Chief, one of his best hounds. Bob told him that Chief wasn't for sale even at twice that price.

Paul intended to take his lion with a .357 Magnum revolver so Bob checked out Paul's shooting abilities in camp. Paul had to shoot at a one gallon can 15' to 20' away, and passed with flying colors.

A hot cat track was located at 10 a.m. on the fourth day, and they caught up with it at 5:30 that evening. Bob quickly realized that the cat in the tree was a trophy-class animal and told Paul, "Don't shoot it in the head." The cat moved up and down the tree making things difficult for Paul, but he eventually got in a lethal shot. It was late in the day so Paul and Bob positioned the cat on a rock for the night with plans to haul it out with packhorses the next morning.

Paul still had three days left of his seven-day cougar hunt, so Bob asked him to stay a while longer to hunt bobcats. Since December in the Rockies can get quite nasty, Paul decided that he and Rose should leave early. As it turned out, there were nine inches of new snow on the ground when they left in the morning.

Paul has taken three moose, three pronghorns, one bear, and eight deer, but he feels this hunt was by far and away his best hunt. It was also his toughest. Rose said she enjoyed the hunt, too, but Paul is convinced that Rose went along just to see what Paul looked like after the lion finished with him.

Paul knew he was lucky to get a trophy lion on his first try. He recalls that this hunt cost him $400 in 1966, and figures that it would probably cost many more times that today. In addition, Paul feels people should have to pay just to live in such a beautiful state as Colorado.

Paul Gobel holds the massive paw of his B&C cougar to illustrate the size of this majestic animal. From nose to the end of its tail, Paul measured the cougar at 8 feet, 6 inches.

STEVE W. CHIN
Location: Rio Blanco County
Year Taken: 1999
Score: 14-13/16

For someone who had never hunted cougar, Steve Chin didn't do too badly for himself. The hunt began in January 1999 with Monte Elder of Rimrock Outfitters near Dinosaur National Park and ended three days later with one of the largest toms ever taken in Colorado.

The first day was spent searching for fresh cat tracks, but the men and the dogs found nothing. Up before sunrise and back in camp at sunset was the daily routine. Ravens slowly circling overhead led Steve to a fresh elk kill by a cougar, so the men decided this was a place to locate fresh cougar tracks, although the dogs found nothing. The men returned to the elk kill the next day and noticed fresh cougar tracks inside the men's tracks from the day before. Four dogs were released, and the chase was on. Steve chased the dogs over two mountains and came to the treed cat. Using his 70 pound PSE Carol Intruder II bow, Steve delivered a single fatal shot from a distance of 10 yards.

Steve Chin with his Boone and Crockett cougar taken in 1999.

Hunting for a cat, Steve discovered, required days of endurance as the hunter hiked through sagebrush, pinon pine, rim rock and juniper brush. Hunting for cougar was not simply releasing dogs and finding a cat but a series of 12- to 15-hour days up and down mountains. Not many hunters bag a Boone and Crockett Club trophy the first time in the field, but for Steve this became a reality and an experience he'll never forget.

Steve's cougar was entered in the 24th North American Big Game Awards (1998-2000) of the Boone and Crockett Club in November 1999. Because this cougar was taken with bow and arrow, it would also qualify for entry into the Pope and Young Club's records program.

SAM B. RAY
Location: Archuleta County
Year Taken: 1992
Score: 14-13/16

Sam Ray has hunted cougar for many years. As a guide and outfitter, he has made it possible for many hunters to achieve their dreams of harvesting a trophy cougar.

In 1991 Sam spent nearly two months counting cougars on the Southern Ute Indian Reservation in southwestern Colorado with Director of the Wildlife Department Mike Olguin and Head Biologist Sam Diswood of the Southern Ute Indian Reservation. They covered countless miles on foot and with snowmobiles and determined that the mountain lion density was high enough to support a cougar season in 1992.

For Sam, it was a long wait until the season opened on January 1, 1992. He waited the first six weeks of the season doing what he does best – guiding clients to trophy cats. It wasn't until February 21 that he had an opportunity to do a little lion hunting himself. Sam left home early, pulling a sled loaded with dogs behind a snowmobile and headed for a cat track he had located the day before. Toby, the lead dog, hit the track running, his deep, double-bark echoing off the canyon walls. The rest of the pack streamed behind like a roiling river of bawling dog flesh. Sam shouldered his pack, strapped on his snowshoes and began slogging through the deep snow after the dogs.

Two miles is a long distance to cover on snowshoes when the powder is four feet deep, but the music of the hounds kept Sam moving. With each difficult step he appreciated the dogs more. He kept wondering how big the cat was and how much farther he and the dogs would have to chase it to find out. As he topped the next ridge he realized the trailing barks had changed. The dogs were barking treed in the canyon below. Sam was as excited as if it was the first lion he had ever treed when he charged off the north slope of the hill. It seemed to take forever to reach the bottom of the canyon where he spotted blood in the snow. Sam started to run, hoping the dogs were not hurt, but he soon spotted the carcass of a five-point bull elk the cat had killed and fed upon. The cascading pack had continued on after the lion. Sam continued on up the other side. By then, he was nearing the cat that had treed high in a towering ponderosa pine. As soon as Sam saw the tom, he knew it wasn't the giant cat that had made tracks near his home but it was a splendid trophy. He decided to take it home.

Sam tied up the dogs, drew his bow and released an arrow. The lion spat back and ran out on a limb and then back. It was a clean shot but Sam sent another arrow in the cat's direction for a clean kill. The tom dropped from the tree, stone dead, and Sam was soon busy skinning it and packing the meat for the return trip.

Sam Ray with his B&C and P&Y records book cougar moments after he collected it with his bow and arrow.

After the 60-day drying period, Sam's cat scored 14-13/16 points. It was large enough for entry into both the Boone and Crockett Club's and Pope and Young Club's records books. It is the first cougar Sam put in the records books by himself, and he is still excited about it.

Susan Ray provided the details of this hunt as told to her by Sam.

TOMMY L. TUCKER
Location: Montezuma County
Year Taken: 1997
Score: 14-12/16

Guides and outfitters Rick Kirks of Cortez and Donny Moffat of Bayfield had hunted with Tommy Tucker for three years as he looked for the largest mountain lion possible. The time had come to make a decision about taking the tomcat that peered down at him.

On March 1, 1997, the men started out at 4 a.m. in the Cortez area of Montezuma County in search of cat tracks in the 8 to 10 inches of fresh snow. Conditions were perfect for hunting as Rick traversed a mesa following an old road and Donny and Tommy set off in the opposite direction. Rick was the first to locate fresh tracks so he called Donny on his cell phone to transmit the exact location and to order the release of the dogs. The men and dogs took off on foot in 2 feet of snow along the north side of a hill. They found the cat staring down at them in an 80 to 90-foot tree.

A debate ensued as to the cat's size but the guides were confident this was the big one Tommy wanted. The cat jumped off a fresh calf kill, so the men trailed it. A single shot with his .222 Remington using a 50-grain Speer hand-loaded bullet downed the cat, and Tommy collected a cougar that eventually was measured as a Boone and Crockett trophy. Its live weight was 180 pounds with an estimated age of 6 years. Three years of tracking paid off big for Tommy Tucker.

Tommy's cougar was recognized in the 23rd North American Big Game Awards (1995-1997) of the Boone and Crockett Club as one of the largest cougars ever taken in Colorado.

Tommy Tucker with his cougar after the hunt ended.

JOHN PETE PIOTROWSKI
Location: Custer County
Year Taken: 1998
Score: 14-12/16

Jenny the dog knew she found a cougar and wouldn't let it out of her sight. It was Jenny who led the men to the biggest cougar Pete Piotrowski saw in his life in the San Isabel area of Colorado.

Ron Sniff, Jenny's owner and Pete's guide, let the dogs out at 8 a.m., two hours after the men started hunting, and the pack immediately located a clear cougar track. The men had experienced a lot of dry runs on the previous eight to 10 attempts, but this track was clear and fresh. The dogs followed the tracks down a draw, up a hillside and across three or four other draws as they barked and howled. The men decided to park their snowmobiles that had carried them into the backcountry and hike to the treed cat.

Ron commented they were lucky to find fresh snow because under that layer was 2 feet of hard crusted snow, which allowed the hunters to walk on top of the snow without snowshoes. The men continued tracking the barking dogs in a northwestern direction as they climbed from the bottom of a draw. Ron originally thought the dogs were at the base of a steep cliff about a quarter or half mile away but in actuality, the dogs were at the top of the steep ridge. The men spent the next half hour climbing the ridge to the top and following the direction of the barks and howls. The side of the ridge was covered with slippery boulders that made foot travel difficult.

Pete raised his binoculars to locate the cat in the tree. He noticed blood that may have come from prey the cougar had captured to eat. The area seemed to be the cougar's den. Moments later, Pete raised his .357 Ruger pistol for a single shot to the cat's shoulder. The tom leaped from the tree and ran about 50 yards, where it dropped.

Jenny chased all the other dogs away and guarded "her" cat, a cat with an estimated weighed of 195 pounds. The distance hiked by the men to track the cat from the point of release by the dogs was five miles uphill. The men field dressed the cat where it dropped because of its extreme weight. The meat and hide were lashed onto a plastic sled that easily moved the animal down the mountain to the snowmobile, and four and a half hours later, the hunting party was back to the truck. From the moment of Pete's shot at 11:45 a.m. the men were in their truck by 6 p.m. with the cat in hand.

Officials from the Colorado Division of Wildlife thought the cougar was the largest taken that year and encouraged him to have the skull measured. The cougar was one of the largest in Colorado with a final score of 14-12/16 points. The cougar was recognized in the 24th North American Big Game Awards (1998-2000).

Pete Piotrowski and Jenny the hound.

John Pete Piotrowski and his grandson Scott hold Pete's B&C cougar skull as the mount crouches above them ready to pounce.

EDWARD A. PETERSEN
Location: La Plata County
Year Taken: 1993
Score: 14-10/16

It was Sunday, February 7, 1993, and Edward Petersen was cougar hunting with Sam Ray, a guide and outfitter, near Pagosa Springs. He ate a breakfast big enough for two men before getting into a truck with Sam and Sam's dogs. They were joined by Sam's guides, Rob Pederitti and Brian Williams, more dogs, and more equipment. Snow covered the ground, and temperatures hovered around 20 degrees above zero with predictions it would rise to the low 30s.

Dozens of deer scattered along the roadside as the men drove through the darkness toward the Southern Ute Indian Reservation. They reached the reservation near dawn and drove along plowed roads looking for lion tracks in the snow. At about 8 a.m. Sam spotted two sets of tracks, one from a female and the other a big tom, off to the side of the road. After a brief examination, Sam released the dogs, one at a time and they took off like rockets after the cats. The loud, incessant barking quickly faded into the distance.

Sam pulled out a measuring tape and measured the length of the track and the cat's stride. He then told Ed, "This looks like a good one. Maybe even a record-book lion. He's probably about 170 pounds and 7 feet long." During the chase the men paused several times to listen to the dogs. Sam told Ed that it was possible to tell when the dogs were in pursuit and when they had treed the cat just by listening to their barking. After several stops to listen, Sam announced the dogs had treed a cougar. Not understanding a single bark of dog language, Ed took Sam's word for it.

Bowhunter Ed Peterson moments have he downed this outstanding mountain lion in 1993 on the Southern Ute Indian Reservation.

The chase was not easy for someone like Ed who sits behind a desk all day at sea level. For someone who is short Ed had serious difficulties moving through snow that was hip-deep in places. He was convinced that Sam was part snowshoe hare. The pair went up and down several canyons. As they got closer to the baying dogs, Ed was sweating like it was August and gasping for air like someone had been holding him under water.

Sam suddenly stopped as the two men approached the top of another hill. He turned to Ed and announced, "Two cats in the same tree." Sam had never seen Ed so excited. Resting on a limb high up in the tree was a big old tom Sam called "Old Crooked Ear." The female stood on another limb a short distance away. Both were big. Sam told Ed that if Ed didn't take the big tom, he'd take it. Ed wanted the tom.

After a brief search, Ed found an opening through the branches about a foot square that lined up with the big tom's chest. Rob and Brian arrived with more dogs just as Ed began to draw his bow. Ed was painfully aware that he was being watched by three experienced hunters so he told himself to, "Pick your spot." Ed released the string and the Easton XX75 arrow with its Thunderhead 125 broad head successfully connected. Ed's companions thought he was a regular William Tell. He didn't tell them he had missed six whitetails back home in New Jersey during the past season.

DENNIS A. SWANSON
Location: Rio Blanco County
Year Taken: 1992
Score: 14-9/16

It was about an hour before daylight on January 7, 1992, when Dennis Swanson and his 20-year hunting buddy, Doc Heykoop, were easing along a two track in Bianco Canyon, southwest of Meeker, Colorado. The men were looking for cougar sign in a 4-inch layer of fresh snow. Their guide, Chris Corbin, came up on the hunters riding his snowmobile and said he found a set of tracks that looked good.

When the three men saw the tracks, Dennis decided he'd go for it. By the time Dennis grabbed his Marlin .356 rifle and his back pack, the dogs were running hot and almost out of hearing range. Chris told Dennis to follow the dog tracks as he traveled cross country after the pack. Chris was ten years younger and in much better shape, so he was quickly out of sight.

The snow was about 18-inches deep on the flat but the going wasn't too tough for about the first half mile when Dennis saw the dogs had jumped the cougar out of its bed. From that point on, things changed. The cougar ran this way and that in the sloping and fairly open area, but once it came to a mountain it went straight up one side and straight down the back side and then straight up the next one. Following that tom cat was the most physically exhausting thing Dennis had ever done. Yet, when the hunt ended Dennis realized it was also one of the most satisfying things he had ever done.

Seven hours and six grueling miles later, Dennis reached the tree where Chris, the dogs and the cougar were located. Setting on a limb about 20 feet up was the tom. Two hours later at the bottom of the canyon, Dennis built a fire to dry off while Chris walked the four and one half miles to their truck where Doc sat. The cougar measured 7 feet, 6 inches from tip to tip and weighted approximately 140 pounds.

"I started hunting when I was eight years old, beginning with rabbits and on to other small game to whitetails, mule deer, bear, elk and moose, plus a lot of other animals, but it is this one hunt that comes to mind first whenever someone asks me about hunting," Dennis said.

Thick snowflakes fell as Dennis Swanson reached his massive B&C tom cougar that scores 14-9/16 points. This hunt was the highlight of his life.

TERRY L. ELLISON
Location: Fremont County
Year Taken: 1986
Score: 14-8/16

After successfully hunting most of Colorado's big game, including bighorn sheep, Rocky Mountain goats, and black bear, Terry Ellison was excited when he was invited to hunt cougar near his home in Montrose. Guide and Outfitter Ray Parmley offered to take Terry lion hunting on the Uncompahgre Plateau. Just as they were getting ready to go after a big tom, the Colorado Division of Wildlife closed the area to hunting for a 10-year study. Terry's heart sank, but Ray assured him that they could shift gears and find another area.

Another season passed and hours were spent chasing hounds in several counties with no success. Ray called Leonard, a friend and fellow hounds man, in Fremont County near Cotopaxi. Ray asked Leonard to keep an eye open for mountain lion activity.

Ray called Terry a few weeks later to tell him to meet him in the morning at Blue Mesa Reservoir as Leonard had located a large set of cougar tracks. Terry and Ray met Leonard on December 16, 1986, at 3 a.m.

Terry found himself trudging through thigh-deep snow in Spruce Basin and wondering if he would ever see the hounds that were making such a racket in the distance. After climbing out of the bottom of a hole that seemed like the Grand Canyon, Terry finally reached the dogs. They had a tom treed near the top of a 50-foot ponderosa pine, and it wasn't about to come down. Ray admonished Terry to make his shot count, as he didn't want a lion in the middle of his pack. Terry took careful aim with his .357 S&W pistol, and the lion was down permanently. Terry was impressed with its size and relieved the hounds didn't tear the hide to pieces.

After the required 60-day drying period, the late Smokey Till officially scored Michael's cougar at 14-1/16 points. Michael's cougar is mounted life-size and is on public display at the GMC dealership showroom in Montrose.

ROBERT DEE OWENS
Location: Rio Blanco County
Year Taken: 1998
Score: 14-8/16

The one and only time Dee Owens hunted cougar was on February 13 and 14, 1998, when he not only tracked and took a huge cat but a female cat to boot.

Dee went with his son, Rod, and four of his hounds into an area of Rio Blanco County where Dee picked up tracks the day before he took the massive female cougar. On Valentine's Day, the men set out to relocate the tracks and they did. For more than three miles, up and down hills, the men and hounds followed the tracks. Several times it ran up trees and jumped down again. When it went into a tree for the final time, Dee fired a single shot with his 9mm camp rifle at a distance of 15 to 20 feet and the cat crumbled to the ground.

The taxidermist grossed weighed it at 160 pounds and the meat tasted much like beef but drier. Dee donated most of the meat to a lady who requested it. Although he enjoyed the hunt, Dee doesn't plan to cougar hunt in the future. The cougar was officially entered into the 24th North American Big Game Awards of the Boone and Crockett Club in February 1999.

A rare Boone and Crockett female cougar became Dee Owens' trophy in February 1998.

Bear Hunting Harvest 1957-1999

Year	Boars	Sows	Total Harvest	Total Hunters	Percent Success
1999	621	364	983	11,299	9
1998	349	204	553	9,006	6
1997	265	193	458	8,936	5
1996	326	195	521	8,408	6
1995	313	220	533	8,305	6
1994	217	143	360	6,106	6
1993	175	103	278	4,060	7
1992	348	135	483	1,450	33
1991	317	158	475	3,852	12
1990	259	153	412	3,514	12
1989	398	194	592	3,872	15
1988	424	249	673	4,477	15
1987	401	215	616	4,029	15
1986	330	205	539	3,861	14
1985	400	217	617	—	—
1984	245	171	—	—	—
1983	487	246	733	9,871	7
1982	588	260	848	10,045	8
1981	391	268	659	8,736	8
1980	394	257	651	8,454	8
1979	440	341	781	8,577	9
1978	429	217	646	7,766	8
1977	429	226	655	6,771	10
1976	331	179	525	6,058	9
1975	—	—	895	13,899	6
1974	265	216	561	6,570	9
1973	208	165	373	7,469	5
1972	154	97	251	5,738	4
1971	134	48	199	7,466	3
1970	240	131	452	24,561	2
1969	—	—	406	2,672	15
1968	—	—	438	—	—
1967	—	—	519	—	—
1966	—	—	614	—	—
1965	—	—	728	—	—
1964	—	—	672	—	—
1963	—	—	570	—	—
1962	—	—	478	—	—
1961	—	—	586	—	—
1960	—	—	392	—	—
1959	—	—	555	—	—
1958	—	—	584	—	—
1957	—	—	552	—	—

A Pagosa Springs hunter from the late 1800s sits besides numerous bear pelts.

James J. Donnelly stands between two massive black bears that were taken by John Lough in 1909 (bear to the right) and by Clarence McKimpson in 1911 (bear to left). Beside Mr. Donnelly is the dog that treed the bear.

QUINCY M. HINES
Location: Delta County
Year Taken: 1967
Score: 21-12/16

Quincy Hines had just returned home from active duty in Alaska where he had taken an Alaska-Yukon moose and a Dall's sheep when he called his old friend Marvin Shepard to plan a hunt. After mulling over their options, they decided to hunt for bears on the Uncompahgre Plateau south of Grand Junction in the latter part of May 1967. Marvin had previously taken two bears there while working for the U.S. Forest Service during Quincy's tour of duty with Uncle Sam. Since military service had interrupted their hunting trips together, this was not only a chance for them to renew their friendship, but it also was a chance for Quincy to do some bear hunting.

On their way to Kelso Mesa, where they planned to hunt, they had to break their way through a few snowdrifts. They knew that the steep, south-facing slopes of Escalante Canyon were prime places to find bears coming out of hibernation. After parking their Jeep the pair decided to split up. Quincy paused long enough for Marvin to get to the bottom of the canyon before he took off along a flat bench well above Marvin. The steep canyon dropped off to the south below him and a steep, brush-covered slope extended to the north. The hill was capped with majestic ponderosa pines.

Almost immediately Quincy noticed a set of bear tracks on the trail he was following. He followed the trail for about a half-mile, pausing often to step off the trail and to look down into the canyon for bears. He was headed back to the trail after looking down into the canyon when he noticed a black spot 50 yards away on the steep slope above him. After focusing his binoculars on the object, he realized he was looking directly into the eyes of a very large back bear standing on its hind legs. It was peering down at him over the 6' tall scrub oak.

Quincy pulled up his 7 mm Remington Magnum, aimed at the throat, and fired. The bear dropped on the spot, and it wasn't long before Marvin, summoned by the gunshot, joined Quincy to admire his trophy. The bear measured eight feet six inches long from the tip of its nose to the tip of its tail. The big old boar later scored an impressive 21-12/16 points.

Marvin Shepard provided the details of this hunt.

ROBERT W. JACKSON
Location: Garfield County
Year Taken: 1980
Score: 21-8/16

The lure of hunting the West was a dream for Pennsylvanian Bob Jackson. His dream came true in 1977 when he traveled to Wyoming to hunt mule deer and pronghorn. The trip was such a success that it was only a matter of time before he planned another Western hunting trip.

In July 1980 Bob returned to the West, this time Colorado, with friends Doug Tjaden and Reggie Bishop. The trio booked a black bear hunt with guide Cap Atwood and Cap's son Holis. Temperatures, which rose to 115 degrees during the day, were not particularly conducive to hunting for three hunters from the Keystone State who were accustomed to hunting black bears back home in cool weather three days prior to Thanksgiving.

The focal point of their hunting activities was in Garfield County on the White River National Forest northeast of Rifle. Doug and Reggie teamed up with Cap, and Bob went with Holis. Doug took a 250-pound bear on the first day. The ensuing four days were spent in the saddle eating dust during the heat of the day while following dogs that chased bears but couldn't bring them to bay. Despite misgivings and shortcomings, Bob gained a great appreciation of Cap's dogs on the last day of the hunt.

On the morning of the last day, the men came upon six sheep that had been killed by a bear. Stokes, Cap's strike dog, was released to pick up the bear's hot trail. Holis released the remaining dogs that took off at a dead run behind Stokes, baying all the way. Stokes, a dog with a good heart, was about to chase his last bear. The men pursued the howling dog pack across two ridges and knew from the sounds they were getting closer. When they got closer, they paused and through a big, knowing grin, Holis said, "He's treed!"

After traversing the last ridge, Holis tied up the horses and told Bob what to do when they reached the bear. As they approached the treed bear, Bob knew it was the largest bruin he had ever seen. The bear stood on two branches 20 feet up a tree, looking down on the men and dogs. Bob placed the cross hairs of his Springfield .30-06 on the white, diamond-shaped, fur patch on the boar's chest and slammed a 180-grain Remington core-lokt bullet into it. The shot echoed across the valley, and the bear was on the ground dead with nine dogs swarming all over it. The bear looked big up the tree, but on the ground it looked even larger. Holis and Bob estimated its weight to be 400 to 450 pounds. What really impressed the hunters, besides its overall size, were the size of its massive head and its reddish-blond color.

After handshaking, backslapping, and picture taking, the celebration was tempered when Holis suddenly realized that Stokes, his strike dog, was not present. After a brief search, Stokes was found dead about 50 yards away. From the looks of the area, he must have put up a heck of a fight with that bear.

Eventually, Bob's bear was officially accepted in the Boone and Crockett Club's records book at a score of 21-8/16 points. It is one of the largest bears ever taken in Colorado.

Bob Jackson was especially impressed with the reddish blond fur and huge head of his B&C black bear.

ROGER L. BELL
Location: Trinidad
Year Taken: 1999
Score: 21-2/16

Roger Bell had hunted black bear in southern Colorado for almost 10 years but on opening day of the September 1999 season, he decided to scout an area near Trinidad in Majestic Canyon. From the very start of the hunt, Roger located huge bear tracks in the mud, so he knew this was the bear he wanted. He knew to look in the scrub oak where bear love to eat acorns as they prepared for winter hibernation. Roger made his way down a ravine to the bottom where a washed-out dam was located and noticed scrub oaks were busted out where the bear fed. Roger plunked himself down for the remaining part of the morning to see if the big bear materialized, but it didn't.

Roger decided to break for lunch so he traveled six miles using a four-wheeler back to his hunting trailer for lunch and vowed to return to the same ravine location after eating. Upon returning to the washed out dam, Roger proceeded to fall asleep as he stood waiting for the bear. He jolted himself awake and decided to sit down to avoid unnecessary injury if he fell over the ravine, so down he went to sit and wait for the bear. As he predicted, Roger fell asleep and awoke to the swish-swash of a large animal walking through the mud within 30 yards of him coming up from the bottom without acknowledging Roger's presence. Roger thought the bear might have smelled him but it didn't react as it continued to walk past him.

Moments after Roger Bell dropped this outstanding black bear in the mud using his .30-06, he holds his trophy.

The bear walked another 40 yards before it conveniently and thoughtfully turned sideways and walked directly under Roger as it headed toward the scrub oaks. Roger fired a single shot with his .30-06 and the bear dropped into the mud. Roger estimated its body size to be 400 pounds, so getting the bear out of the woods and back to the trailer was quite a task. He settled on cutting the body in half and carrying it back on the four wheeler so he could flag his hunting buddy, Dan Rodrigez, to get the rest of it out.

Months after taking the bear, Roger attended a sports show where a Boone and Crockett Club official measurer scored the skull and determined it was records-book quality. The black bear was entered in the Boone and Crockett Club's 24th North American Big Game Awards Program (1998-2000).

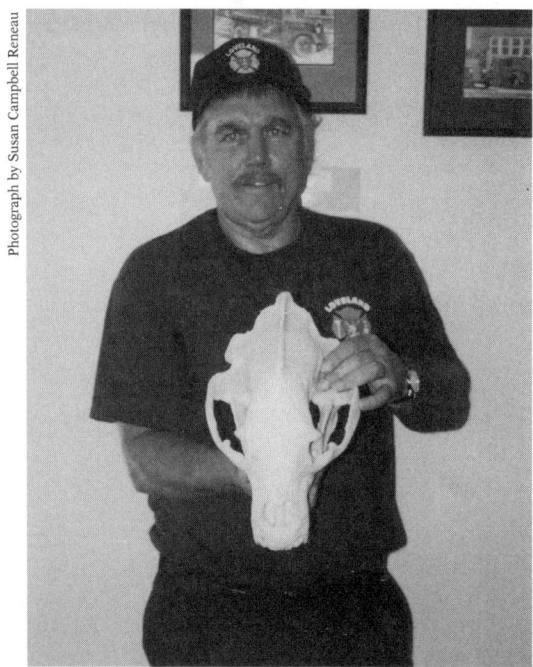
Roger Bell holds the skull of his B&C black bear he collected in 1999 near Trinidad.

JOE W. BRUNNER
Location: Montezuma County
Year Taken: 1998
Score: 21

The trophy bear hunt Joe Brunner was on in 1998 started out with a videotape filled with chipmunks and deer.

A few weeks before the season, Joe spent time scouting his hunting area in Montezuma County. He set up a stand on a little pass through oak brush on some high ground. He also noticed for the last couple of years that the area contained an ample amount of food for bear. Bear traveled back and forth between different food sources, so he decided he was in the right place.

On the first day of the season, Joe sat in his stand for two hours as his friend, Joe Brunner, videotaped deer and chipmunks. They had so much fun videotaping the deer and chipmunks that the batteries in the video camera died before they could film the actual bear hunt. Joe sat in a tree lower down the hill looking at a small clearing about 20 yards wide by 30 yards long with a trail coming through the oak brush. Joe couldn't see much from that location but as he watched, a nice bear wandered into the picture. It didn't seem as large as the bear he took the previous year, which had a fatter body and was jet black. Joe decided it was a good bear so he aimed

his 7mm Magnum using a 175-grain bullet and fired from a distance of 40 yards. The bear jumped a little and dropped where it walked. At 7:30 a.m. on opening day, Joe collected his bear, which after the 60-day drying period, measured as a Boone and Crockett trophy. He estimated the weight to be 500 pounds. Bryon Long officially measured the black bear with a final score of 21.

Joe's advice to anyone is to know your area and carry extra batteries for a video camera to capture all the activity, even the black bear. Preparation really pays off.

The black bear was officially scored by Bryon Long of Dolores, Colorado, and entered in the 24th North American Big Game Awards Period (1998-2000) of the Boone and Crockett Club.

Joe Brunner with his Boone and Crockett black bear that scores 21 points.

TERRY L. PIERCE
Location: Gore Mountain Range
Year Taken: 1982
Score: 20-13/16

A life-threatening fall in the Gore Mountain Range in 1981 was the start of Terry Pierce's 1982 black bear hunt.

Terry was hunting for trophy mule deer with a muzzleloader in the fall of 1981 at timberline in the Gore Mountain Range in north central Colorado. He fell off a downfall and broke five ribs. His oldest brother Larry, Terry's wife, Nita, and some grouse hunters saved his life by getting him to the Kremmling hospital intensive care unit. Terry grudgingly missed the rest of hunting season but vowed to make up for lost time next year.

By the time spring of 1982 rolled around, Terry was chomping at the bit to get back into the mountains to hunt. He applied for bighorn sheep, Rocky Mountain goat and pronghorn permits for the fall, fall muzzleloading tags for elk and deer and a spring bear hunting permit. When May arrived, Terry picked up his bear license and made plans to hunt in late May. Deep snow on trails in late May convinced Terry to return in mid June.

The second Friday of June 1982 found Terry, Nita, Larry and Larry's wife, LeEllen, four-wheeling up five miles to bear camp. Terry went west to an old game trail where Terry's best friend, Larry Smith, took a huge bear and where Terry usually found the first spring bear tracks in the Piney area. Larry headed east from camp to check a small creek drainage at the foot of the nearest ridge.

Two days of scouting turned up nothing. They went to bed thinking they may have come to hunt bear too early in the season. About 2 a.m. Terry awoke to the sounds of a bear walking around his tent. The tent shook violently and LeEllen sat up in her sleeping bag to ask, "What was that!"

Things were looking up. Terry headed to the old game trail and found bear tracks heading east toward a low ridge. Nita and Terry left camp at 6:30 p.m. to explore the base of that ridge and a small creek next to it. Larry headed north. Nita and Terry skirted a beaver pond and five minutes later found an overgrown fire break filled with new growth and old downfalls. They followed this trail as Nita searched for tracks and Terry searched for movement in the woods. As they walked the trail, timber along the trail was thinning as the couple entered a small clearing. Movement to Terry's left caught his attention as he scanned the meadow. A big bear stood halfway through the clearing, heading towards a heavy stand of aspen and spruce trees.

Without thinking, Terry lifted his rifle to his shoulder, put the crosshairs on the bear and fired. The first shot hit its mark and the second shot finished the job. The whole experience happened so quickly Nita hadn't seen the action. She stood next to the bear as Terry ran back to camp to get help. When Terry delivered the hide to the taxidermist, the taxidermist said it was the largest bear he had seen in a long time. Although the hunt took place a long time ago, Terry said it seems like yesterday.

Terry Pierce's brother, Larry, joins Terry to celebrate the taking of his B&C black bear that was collected in 1982 after Terry survived a life-threatening fall in the Gore Mountain Range the year before.

MICHAEL R. ELLIOTT
Location: Mesa County
Year Taken: 1995
Score: 20-8/16

Michael Elliott, Pete Larson, and Charlie Brown received an invitation to hunt on Bill Hardin's ranch. Bill's ranch, which butts up against Grand Mesa National Forest, is situated just outside of Collbran. The men selected the first hunting season thinking the weather could get a little too rough for them during the later seasons.

While they were buying their licenses, Bill Hardin suggested that Michael purchase a bear license because he had been seeing quite a few bears. Michael had only seen one bear in the wild in 20 twenty years of hunting but thought, "What the heck."

During the first few days of the hunt, the men took two nice 5x5 bucks and played hide-and-seek with a few bulls. The weather during the day was clear and warm so the elk were holing up on the north facing slopes in black timber during the day. On the fourth evening, Michael positioned himself beside a well-used elk trail at the bottom of a bowl looking uphill with the wind blowing in his face. He was surrounded by a herd of cow elk for about an hour when they suddenly left. Michael heard a noise behind and below him, which made him think one of his hunting buddies was walking uphill towards him.

A few seconds later, Michael turned around to see who it was and to his surprise a young black bear was walking straight towards him. He figured the bear was two years old and weighed in at about 150 to 175 pounds. Michael had doused himself with a "no scent" spray earlier in the day, and it appeared that the scent was working. The bear passed downwind of Michael within five feet and stuck its nose in the air. It sensed something was not right. It lumbered up the hill and out of sight. Michael felt that with all the game he was seeing around him, he was in the right spot.

The next day, which was also the last day of the hunt, Michael returned to the same location around 3 p.m. and saw nothing. As time passed, he was getting a little discouraged. With about 45 minutes of daylight left, Michael saw something black moving down the hill. He thought it was the cub again at first, but as the bear walked closer, it got bigger and bigger and bigger. At 70 yards, Michael pulled the trigger of his Remington 7mm Magnum and the bear raced downhill. When the bear showed no evidence of being hit, Michael became worried that his scope had been damaged earlier during the hunt. Michael fired a second shot, hitting an aspen. The bear ran another 50 yards and piled up. The first shot was a clean one.

Michael knew the bear was big, but he didn't realize just how big until the next morning when they returned with the 4-wheelers and horses to fetch his bear. It weighed in at 450 pounds and was almost 7 feet long.

Three friends located a great black bear near Collbran in 1995. Shown are, left to right, Mike Elliott, Charlie Brown and Peter Larson.

WOODY OTT
Location: Dolores County
Year Taken: 1999
Score: 20-8/16

Halloween turned out to be a perfect treat in 1999 for Woody Ott when he located the largest black bear he had ever seen in his life.

Woody was with his dad Jack, brothers Bill and Johnny, and two friends, Mike Guillette and Bill Ryter, in the Slick Rock area of southwestern Colorado when they set out to hunt for deer and elk. Woody has hunted in the La Plata Mountains since he was old enough to carry a rifle.

The men spread out from the cabin where they were staying and moved onto a mesa. On the last day of hunting, the hunters teased Woody about not going into Summit Canyon because he had many times hiked in the roughest terrain and many times his hunting companions had to help him carry out the meat. After scouting the countryside, Woody decided his best chance to see game was in the canyon, so he descended toward a bench.

As he worked down the canyon, and after traversing the steep slope to about 1,200 feet down its side, he saw a large bear lying down on a rocky ledge facing him from a distance of about 100 yards. The bear grazed on acorns, and it raised its head to watch Woody. Woody evaluated the bear's head size. Woody knew it was large but when he looked up the canyon to calculate what it would take to get the bear out of the canyon, he paused to reconsider. He also remembered the advice from his father not to shoot anything down in the canyon.

The bear didn't give Woody a chance to reconsider for long when it stood up and Woody knew he had to shoot even if the trip up the canyon would be difficult. Without hesitation, Woody fired his 8mm custom Mauser 8x57 at its chest and the bear spun around as it ran up the canyon. The bear paused when Woody let loose a second shot to finish the job, and the bear was Woody's. Thankfully, a small tree anchored the bear's body before it fell over a cliff.

Johnny heard Woody's shots and arrived at the top of the canyon with the rest of the hunting party. Jack suggested that the younger guys go down the hill to the bear, including Mike, who looked up and said, "You mean me too?"

Woody, Bill, John and Mike spent the next four hours getting the meat up the canyon, all 180 pounds of it. The fat on the bear averaged 7 to 9 inches in thickness and the meat was delicious. Woody knew this was an amazing bear, so he

Woody (right) and Jack Ott (left) hold up Woody's B&C bear during the summer of 2000 with the help of Woody's children, Wesley, age 9, and Angela, age 6.

took care to skin out the hide and skull, which weighed 150 pounds all by themselves. Bill Ott, district ranger for the Uintah National Forest in Utah, estimated its age to be 16 to 20 years. Its total body weight was 640 pounds with 9 inch paws and 3-1/2-inch claws. The hide measured 8 feet square. Woody was told that it was one of the largest bears any official had seen in years.

Not bad for a Halloween treat.

STEVE WEST
Location: Pueblo County
Year Taken: 1998
Score: 20-4/16
Owner: Jarred West

Hot temperatures soaring to 95 degrees and world record crops of mosquitoes made elk hunting miserable. As a result, Steve West decided to hunt black bear during the September 1998 season. Little did he know that this decision would take him to a runaway, star bruin, well known by Colorado Division of Wildlife officials.

Steve moved camp to just outside Rye, Colorado, where cooler temperatures prevailed. He quickly located abundant bear sign around the scattered oak brush patches. The next morning he spotted a couple of small bears and another very large bruin ambling through a meadow adjacent to a small pond. Steve didn't have much time to observe the bear since it spotted him first and quickly disappeared into the oak brush. He knew it was huge and couldn't get it out of his mind as he returned home.

Wednesday morning Steve was back at the same location after the big bear when he heard a "Woof!" A huge bear bounded out of the same pond into the woods. Steve kicked himself for missing an opportunity to shoot.

On Friday Steve and his son, Jarred, hiked into the same pond where Steve had already jumped the bear twice. As the men approached the pond, they notice massive bear tracks and discussed the size of the animal. At 3:30 p.m. they took a stand next to a ponderosa pine. Steve faced the pond, and Jarred watched an area about 90 degrees to his father's left. As Steve picked the last pinecone from under his rear, he spotted what looked like a brown bulldozer ambling out of the oak brush 90 yards away. The bear filled Steve's scope. As he prepared to shoot, he whispered to Jarred, "There he is!"

"Yeh, right!" responded Jarred sarcastically. His sarcasm changed to surprise when he turned and glanced down Steve's rifle barrel at the biggest bear he had ever seen. "Man! Dad! You better shoot!" he excitedly whispered in Steve's ear.

A runaway star bear became the B&C trophy for Steve West who located this massive bruin in 1998 outside Rye, Colorado.

Steve fired and the 250-grain soft point instantly entered the big boar just behind the shoulder. At the shot, the bear vanished into the underbrush. Steve and Jarred waited a few minutes and tracked it into the thicket. It was lying there stone dead 25 yards from where Steve shot it.

At the Colorado Division of Wildlife's check station, the men located a tattoo on the bear's lip that documented the fact that it was initially trapped in 1990 as a three-year-old dumpster raider. It was ear-tagged and released, only to be recaptured two years later after destroying beehives. District Wildlife Manager Bob Holder said he couldn't be certain that it was the same bear since the ear tags from the first encounter were torn off, and it wasn't lip tattooed before it was released the first time. When it was released the second time, however, the ear tags were in place and the lip was tatooed. "Mr. Big" was relocated the second time to Saguache Park some 200 air miles away. It had traveled across the San Luis Valley, the Sangre de Cristo Mountains and the Wet Mountain Valley to reach the pond where Steve had interrupted its travels. During this trek, the bruin had grown to Boone and Crockett proportions.

Three black bear skulls lined up and the largest is Steve West's Boone and Crockett trophy seen on the left.

TERRY L. SMALEC
Location: Garfield County
Year Taken: 1987
Score: 20-2/16

Feeding his young family was the motivation for Terry Smalec in 1987 when he searched for the biggest bear in the woods of Garfield County up on Douglas Pass.

Terry baited bear below a tree stand but nothing ever came in except little ones. Nothing was worth shooting until June 11 when the big black bear cautiously sauntered to the bait and sniffed the contents as it looked up in the tree stand at Terry. Terry was up 15 feet in the air when he heard the bear coming around behind the tree. Of all the bears Terry has ever shot, this was the most careful and leery of them all. As the bear continued toward the bait, Terry knew he had the right shot so he fired a slug from his 1918 16-gauge LaFever shotgun.

The bear took off running and climbed up the tree next to Terry's stand at a distance of 10 feet but totally out of sight. Terry didn't move and waited 30 seconds – which seemed like eternity – until the boar started crashing down through the branches to the ground. In one shot, placed from a distance of 20 feet, Terry collected his big black bear. He field dressed and skinned the bear in the dark and dropped into bed satisfied around 2 a.m. The 300-pound bear was delicious eating and much appreciated by this young couple.

Terry Smalec used his 1918 16-gauge LaFever shotgun to collect this outstanding B&C black bear that scores 20-2/16 points in 1987 in Garfield County.

CHARLES M. BETTERS
Location: Huerfano County
Year Taken: 1997
Score: 20-1/16

A life-size mount of Chuck Betters' B&C black bear impressively towers over Chuck in the foyer of his home. The bear scores 20-1/16 points.

Chuck Betters' bear was taken near a camp southwest of Walsenberg, Colorado, in October 1997. He and four buddies embarked on a guided elk hunt with Story Creek Outfitters not knowing they'd be returning with a trophy black bear.

Snow began falling as they reached their camp. By the following morning, more than 3 feet of snow had blanketed the ground, adding an impasse to an already challenging elk hunt. Most of the first day was spent trying to dig out of nature's little alteration.

Late the second day, Chuck and his guide startled a large black bear that was feeding on a kill. It quickly ran into some heavy brush. But the following day, while glassing for elk in the same area, they spotted the bear again. Chuck was convinced that it was time to go bear hunting. He and his guide left camp to purchase a bear tag. They arrived back at the camp and set up a post only to wait unsuccessfully for the bear's return that evening.

The next day, Chuck returned to the same area, finding his target eating from the same kill. Too much open space separated Chuck and the bear, so a clear shot was not feasible. His only option was about a mile and a half stalk to a better vantage point.

The harsh wind and crunchy snow only alerted the bear to the hunter's every move. Chuck and his guide got within 200 yards of the bear, but a small ridge separated them and the animal. Part of the bear's shoulder and its head were in view. Hoping to get in a better position, Chuck raised the scope of the .280 to his eye knowing this was the best shot he was going to get. The shot rang out and the bear retreated to some nearby brush. The hunting guide thought it was hit, so the pursuit was on. They found a blood trail but needed back-up to locate his bear.

While returning to camp, they crossed paths with another guide who told them he'd seen the bear running across a nearby hillside. Chuck and his guide rushed to that area in time to see the bear and get off another shot. The second shot was a clean hit, rolling the bear over. Chuck then delivered the third and final shot. It wasn't until Chuck reached the bear that he began to realize its magnitude.

The bear stretched out 78 inches and weighed 400 pounds. Scratch marks alongside the head indicated it was involved in a prior battle. The carcass that Chuck's bear was feeding on earlier turned out to be another bear it apparently killed in a fight. His bear was taken back to camp.

What started with 3 feet of snow and harsh conditions, ended with Chuck and his party bringing home a Boone and Crockett black bear, and three nice bull elk.

PATRICK T. STANOSHECK
Location: Livermore
Year Taken: 1993
Score: 20

Patrick Stanosheck's 1993 trophy hunt traced its origin back to 1991 when he hunted and filmed black bears on Carl Hansen's ranch. He had seen several nice bears that year but decided to hold out for a large, chocolate-colored one. Two years earlier he had taken a large black bear with a beautiful black pelt in British Columbia, so he could afford to be picky.

Patrick and his brother Tim set up camp on September 7, 1993, in the rocky foothills above the town of Livermore. They had both drawn muzzleloader elk tags and both planned to spend time hunting elk while Patrick also concentrated on filling his black bear tag.

It was a beautiful fall day on September 8 when Patrick and Tim started out early in the afternoon for a deep canyon where they intended to hunt for three bull elk they had seen earlier. Tim headed up into the canyon where he could look over three fingers of the canyon, while Patrick walked a half-mile down to the mouth of the canyon to scout for both elk and bear. There were berry patches along the creek where Patrick had seen black bears on previous hunting trips to the area.

Tim caught up with Patrick at 4:30 p.m. to tell him about a huge bear he had seen making its way down the canyon in Patrick's direction. The two men moved down the steep side of the canyon wall to a spot in the rocks about 80 yards above

the creek. Thirty minutes later the bear came into sight. They figured that if the bear stayed on course it would pass directly below them. As it turned out, luck was with Patrick and moments later he fired two shots. The bear dropped at the first shot, and the second was just for insurance.

After field dressing the big bruiser, the men called it a day and hiked back to camp for supper and a good night's sleep. The next morning they packed the meat out. Patrick checked the bear with the Colorado Division of Wildlife and then dropped the hide off at the taxidermist. Patrick returned later to hunt elk with Tim, but the elk were always one step ahead of them.

Patrick credits good luck and Tim's keen eyesight for the opportunity to take this great B&C trophy black bear. The two estimated its weight to be about 400 pounds.

"Colorado has been very good to Tim and me, and we return every year to hunt something," Patrick said. Between them, they have had the good fortune to have harvested several elk, deer, and antelope, as well as two bighorn sheep, two Rocky Mountain goats and one mountain lion.

Patrick thanks Colorado Rancher Carl Hansen and the Colorado Division of Wildlife for providing the hunting opportunity.

Patrick Stanosheck with the B&C black bear he took near Livermore, Colorado, in 1993.

— Chapter X —
Photographs of Big-Game Trophies
Typical Mule Deer

UNKNOWN COLORADO HUNTER

•

Location: Moffat County
Year Taken: 1982
Score: 213-1/8
Owner: David W. Blaker

Certificate of Merit 23rd B&C Awards

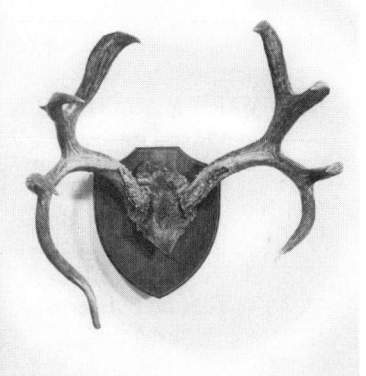

WESLEY BRUCE BROCK

•

Location: Grand County
Year Taken: 1963
Score: 212

Certificate of Merit 18th B&C Awards Program

UNKNOWN COLORADO HUNTER

•

Location: Boulder County
Year Taken: Prior to 1965
Score: 210-1/8
Owner: Don Schaufler

GEORGE SHEARER

•

Location: Garfield County
Year Taken: 1952
Score: 208-6/8
Owner: Richard L. Baker

ROBERT L. ZAINA

•

Location: Mesa County
Year Taken: 1960
Score: 208-5/8

Third Place 10th B&C Competition

W.L. BOYNTON

•

Location: Montrose County
Year Taken: 1973
Score: 206-7/8

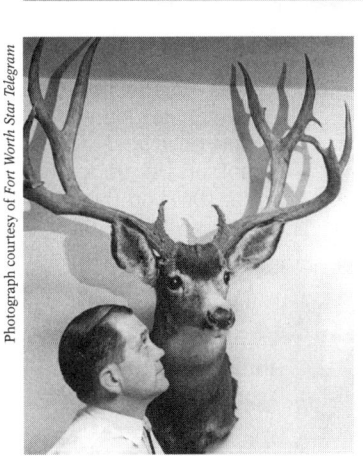

RICHARD V. PRICE

•

Location: Archuleta County
Year Taken: 1962
Score: 206-6/8

4th Place 11th B&C Competition

Colorado's Biggest Bucks and Bulls

HAROLD TAYLOR
•
Location: Eagle County
Year Taken: 1960
Score: 206-3/8
Owner: Fred Palmer

PICK UP
•
Location: Mesa County
Year Found: 1974
Score: 206-2/8
Owner: Darryl Powell

Harold L. Loesch's sons, Pat and Wayne, admire their father's Eagle County buck that scored an impressive 206 points. Harold took this typical muley in 1967 near Eagle, Colorado.

MARK A. MCCORMICK
•
Location: Eagle County
Year Taken: 1981
Score: 205-6/8

*1st Award
18th B&C Awards Program*

John Madden shot this typical mule deer in Delta County in 1953 but had the rack measured by Boone and Crockett Club official measurer Roger Selner in 1997. The B&C score is 205-2/8 points but the rack hasn't been entered in the official records-keeping program so it remains unranked.

NOLAN MARTINS
•
Location: Southern Ute Indian Reservation
Year Taken: 1967
Score: 204-7/8

Nolan Martins holds the monster typical mule deer buck he took on December 6, 1967, on the Southern Ute Indian Reservation. The reservation has a tradition of producing B&C muleys. Nolan's buck scores 204-7/8 points.

ROBERT V. DOERR
•
Location: Eagle County
Year Taken: 1982
Score: 204-5/8

*3rd Award
19th B&C Awards Program*

Photos—Big-Game Trophies

B.E. GRESSETT
•
Location: La Plata County
Year Taken: 1950
Score: 203-5/8

Photograph courtesy of Boone and Crockett Club

JOHN T. SEWELL
•
Location: Garfield County
Year Taken: 1985
Score: 203-4/8

*4th Award
20th B&C Awards Program*

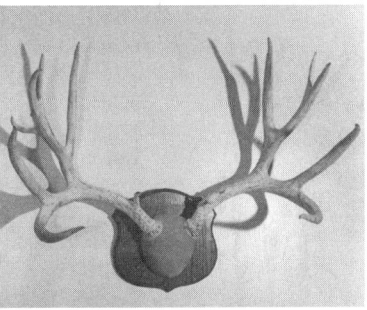

The World's Record typical mule deer taken by bow and arrow is this buck that scores 203-1/8 points. Bill Barcus hunted this massive buck on the White River National Forest in 1979. The buck has a greatest spread of 37-6/8 inches with a main right beam length of 28-5/8 inches. The left main bean is 27-6/8 inches in length.

Photograph courtesy of Boone and Crockett Club

JAMES S. HARDEN
•
Location: Garfield County
Year Taken: 1983
Score: 202-4/8

*Honorable Mention
19th B&C Awards Program*

DUANE YEARWOOD
•
Location: Archuleta County
Year Taken: 1973
Score: 202-2/8

Photograph courtesy of Robert D. Rader

ROBERT D. RADER
•
Location: Gunnison County
Year Taken: 1966
Score: 201-5/8

LES PATRICK
•
Location: La Plata County
Year Taken: 1966
Score: 201-1/8

Photograph shows Gary Patrick with rack.

Photograph by Paul F. Gilbert

Heavy snow and harsh weather conditions during the winter of 1959-1960 probably caused the death of this B&C buck that was found by rancher Bill Knorr of Kremmling along the Blue River in Summit County. The buck scores 200-1/8 points and sports main antler beams that measure 27 inches. Its greatest spread is more than 30 inches.

EMIL WARBER, JR.
•
Location: Delta County
Year Taken: 1966
Score: 200-6/8

GENE D. LINTZ
•
Location: Eagle County
Year Taken: 1974
Score: 200-3/8

A November day in 1985 netted Colorado hunter Nelson Harding this impressive typical mule deer from Montrose County that scored 200-2/8 points.

GEORGE B. BERGER, JR.
•
Location: Jackson County
Year Taken: 1934
Score: 199-7/8
Owner: Denver Museum of Natural History

Certificate of Merit 7th B&C Competition

PICK UP
•
Location: Mesa County
Year Found: 1975
Score: 199-6/8
Owner: Darryl Powell

KENNETH HUNTER
•
Location: Seven Miles North of Pagosa Springs
Year Taken: 1962
Score: 199-2/8
Owner: LeRoy Haug

Louis Ceriani of Kremmling found this outstanding typical mule deer prior to 1965 that has a greatest spread of 32-4/8 inches. The buck was found along Blue Ridge in Summit County and scores 198-2/8 points.

BOBBY JOE WATSON
•
Location: Gunnison County
Year Taken: 1975
Score: 198-2/8

Photos—Big-Game Trophies

EDDIE D. PALMER
•
Location: Gunnison County
Year Taken: 1962
Score: 198

LEROY FAILOR
•
Location: Garfield County
Year Taken: 1944
Score: 198

GARY L. BICKNELL
•
Location: Rio Blanco County
Year Taken: 1967
Score: 197-7/8
Owners: Dana Hollinger and Bob Howard

PICK UP
•
Location: Rio Blanco County
Year Found: Prior to 1957
Score: 197-3/8
Owner: Jack Thompson

JOE M. MOORE
•
Location: Archuleta County
Year Taken: 1962
Score: 197-3/8

Eight Mile Creek in Grand County was the location where Parshall hunter Woodrow W. Dixon downed this 197-point muley. This 5x5 had a greatest spread of 30-6/8 inches and was taken in 1962.

WILLIAM STYERS
•
Location: Mesa County
Year Taken: 1964
Score: 196-5/8

ALVIN T. STIVERS
•
Location: Mesa County
Year Taken: 1965
Score: 196

Colorado's Biggest Bucks and Bulls

RICHARD SCHMIDT
•
Location:
La Plata County
Year Taken: 1960
Score: 195-7/8
Owner: Southern Ute
Indian Reservation

RANDALL R. KIEFT
•
Location: Gunnison County
Year Taken: 1967
Score: 195-6/8

ELDON L. WEBB
•
Location:
Montrose County
Year Taken: 1965
Score: 195-1/8

GENE LAWRENCE
•
Location:
Rio Blanco County
Year Taken: 1977
Score: 195

When Jerry Capp had his 5x6 typical mule deer buck scored in 1962 by Paul Gilbert, it didn't quite make "The Book" since the minimum entry score was 195. Now the entry in the all-time records book is 190. This buck scores 194-7/8 points but has never been entered. The buck was harvested on Black Creek in Summit County.

The Gore Range in Grand County netted for this lucky hunter a typical mule deer that scored 193-3/8 points. The hunter, Kremmling resident Neil Hassler, harvested this buck on October 27, 1967.

UNKNOWN HUNTER
•
Location: Colorado
Year Taken: 1953
Score: 192-7/8
Owners: Dana
Hollinger and Bob
Howard

Fred Palmer of Kremmling took this impressive typical mule deer buck on October 28, 1961 along the Blue River in Summit County. Paul F. Gilbert measured the buck at 191-3/8 points.

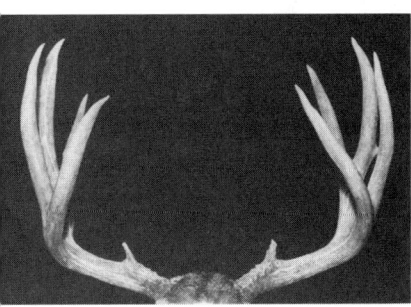
Ute Bill Creek in Grand County was the site where Delores Kendall located her trophy typical mule deer in October of 1961. Its final score was 191-1/8.

A mule deer buck with a 28-6/8-inch spread was collected by Oscar A. Spenard of Granby who took this buck on October 21, 1960 along the Fraser River in Grand County. Its final score was 190-6/8 points. At the time, this buck did not qualify for the B&C but now it does.

William B. Ainsley located this 6x6 trophy muley on October 18, 1966 along Willow Creek in Grand County. It scores 187-3/8.

Lyman Brown of Kremmling took this outstanding buck in October 1944 that scored 189-3/8 points.

DUANE CALHOON
•
Location: Montezuma County
Year Taken: 1976
Score: 186-3/8

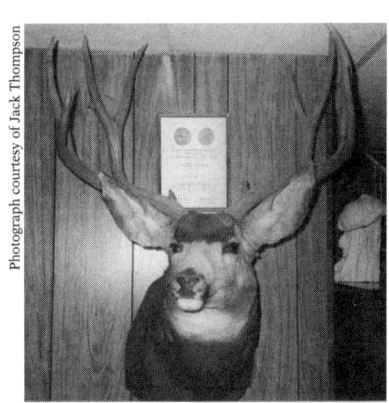
PICK UP
•
Location: Garfield County
Year Found: 1984
Score: 186-1/8
Owner: Jack Thompson

Arthur Cook took this outstanding typical mule deer in Glade Park in 1962 with bow and arrow. At the time, it was the world's largest typical mule deer taken by a bowhunter with a Pope and Young Club score of 184-1/8 points. In the latest edition of the Pope and Young Club all-time records book, *Bowhunting Big Game Records in North America*, Art's buck is now scored at 185-5/8 points and ranks 60th largest bow-killed typical mule deer buck in the world.

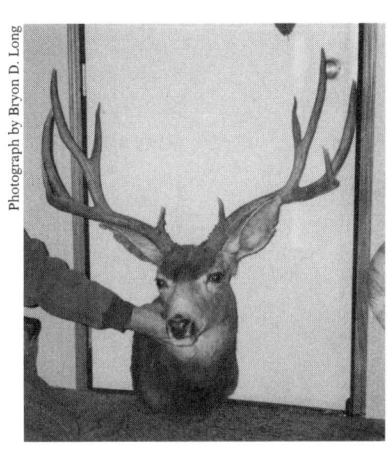
Jim Benauidez took this wide typical mule deer in 1987 and officially scores 184-6/8 points.

Non-Typical Mule Deer

LOUIS H. HUNTINGTON, JR.
•
Location: Delta County
Year Taken: 1965
Score: 302-4/8

*1st Place
13th B&C Competition*

GEORGE BLACKMON, JR.
•
Location: Mesa County
Year Taken: 1961
Score: 300
Owner: Don Schaufler

*Third Place
11th B&C Competition*

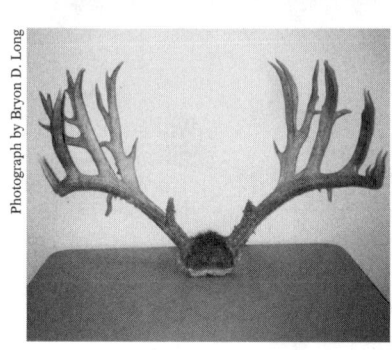

TRAVIS SHIPPEY
•
Location: Montezuma County
Year Taken: 1988
Score: 287-5/8
Owner: Don Shaufler

Keith Thaute holds his unusual non-typical rack from Blue Mesa in Montrose County that scored 278-7/8 points. In 1964 it was the third largest mule deer listed in the Boone and Crockett Club's all-time records book. Today it ranks 10th largest (two-way tie) in Colorado and 54th largest in the world (two-way tie) in the 11th edition of the B&C all-time records book.

The World's Record non-typical mule deer taken with bow and arrow was downed by Kenneth W. Plank in 1987 in Morgan County. Its final score is 274-7/8 points. Its greatest spread is 34-3/8 inches and its tip to tip spread is 27-3/8 inches. The rack sports 23 measurable points on the right and 12 points on the left. Because of its size, this buck easily qualifies for the B&C.

ROY RONEY
•
Location: Routt County
Year Taken: 1930
Score: 273-6/8
Owner: Colorado Division of Wildlife

EDDIE STEPHENSON, JR.
•
Location: Eagle County
Year Taken: 1978
Score: 272-4/8

*2nd Award
18th B&C Awards Program*

Photos—Big-Game Trophies

Mack Gorrod holds his Delta County non-typical mule deer buck he took in 1968 that has Boone and Crockett Club score of 271-2/8 points. The buck has not been officially entered in the B&C records-keeping program so remains unranked.

FRANK PETERSON
•
Location: Delta County
Year Taken: 1956
Score: 271

TRAVIS SHIPPEY
•
Location: Montezuma County
Year Taken: 1988
Score: 267-3/8
Owner: Don Schaufler

ROBERT L. PRICE
•
Location: Mesa County
Year Taken: 1963
Score: 263-4/8

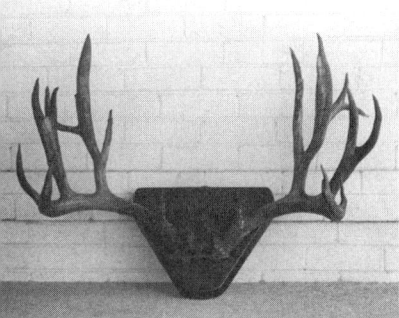

PETE TAULLIE
•
Location: Gunnison County
Year Taken: 1967
Score: 262-3/8

L.C. "KELLY" DENNY, JR.
•
Location: Rio Blanco County
Year Taken: 1961
Score: 261-1/8

L.C. "Kelley" Denny, Jr. (center) and his 1961 Colorado buck (261-1/8 points). Other nice Colorado trophies above include bucks taken by Kelley's brother, Earl (left), and the late M.L. Schmidt (right) of Texas.

R.V. RHODES
•
Location: Routt County
Year Taken: 1949
Score: 259-6/8
Owner: Cecil Weston

JOHN N. LUCERO
•
Location: Otero County
Year Taken: 1995
Score: 259-1/8

Colorado's Biggest Bucks and Bulls

GEIS NETTLEBECK
•
Location:
Rio Grande County
Year Taken: 1956
Score: 258-3/8
Owners:
Dana Hollinger and
Bob Howard

George McCoy smiles for the camera as he holds his Garfield County non-typical monster that scored 253-4/8 points in 1961.

FORREST F. PARHAM
•
Location: Delta County
Year Taken: 1961
Score: 253

Henry H. Zietz, Jr. hunted the Meeker area in 1955 when he downed this B&C non-typical muley that scores 251-1/8 points.

JOHN F. BALDAUF
•
Location: Eagle County
Year Taken: 1941
Score: 249
Owner: Lin F. Nowotny

WILLIAM A. WIEDENFELD
•
Location:
Garfield County
Year Taken: 1969
Score: 249

CLAUDE E. SHULTS
•
Location: Rio Blanco
County
Year Taken: 1956
Score: 248-1/8
Owner:
Claude E. Shults Family

VINCE PLASKETT
•
Location: Archuleta
County
Year Taken: 1970
Score: 247-4/8

Photos—Big-Game Trophies

FRED E. TROUTH, SR.
•
Location: Moffat County
Year Taken: 1960
Score: 246-7/8

This extremely non-typical mule deer buck was taken many years ago near Meeker and has hung in the Meeker Hotel lobby for as long as anyone can remember. The buck was scored by B&C official measurer Roger Selner in 1996 and measures 246-4/8 points. It has never been entered so remains unranked.

JIM CARACCIOLI
•
Location: Eagle County
Year Taken: 1978
Score: 245-5/8

NEIL A. BRISCOE, JR.
•
Location: Delta County
Year Taken: 1969
Score: 244-5/8

BEN CRANDELL
•
Location: San Miguel County
Year Taken: 1939
Score: 243-6/8
Owner: John Van Gaalen

*Certificate of Merit
8th B&C Competition*

PICK UP
•
Location: Grand County
Year Found: 1951
Score: 242-6/8
Owner: Karl Knorr

John T. Crook took this outstanding non-typical mule deer in 1938 near Meeker and gave the mount to the Meeker Hotel for public viewing in their lobby. The buck scores 242-3/8 points.

RICKY A. DIXON
•
Location: Grand County
Year Taken: 1978
Score: 241-7/8
Owners: Dana Hollinger and Bob Howard

Eddie Miller collected this excessively wide-racked mule deer buck on October 13, 1935, according to the hunting tag tacked to the back of the mount. The buck scores 240-6/8 points but has not been entered into the B&C records program so remains unranked.

UNKNOWN COLORADO HUNTER
•
Location: Colorado
Year Taken: Prior to 1970
Score: 240-6/8
Owner: Darryl Powell

A heavy-beamed non-typical buck was taken by Clayton Hill, shown here in 1949, along the Blue River in Grand Canyon. The muley scores 237-1/8 points. The right antler is 95-5/8 inches, and the left side is 92-7/8 inches. The buck was never entered in the B&C so remains unranked. At the time of its measurement the minimum score for entrance in the B&C was much higher.

PICK UP
•
Location: Montezuma County
Year Found: 1992
Score: 235-6/8
Owner: Tom Broderick

The year was 1925 when Bill Henry took this 10x17 non-typical buck that scores 234-5/8 points. The buck was never entered in the B&C. Its greatest spread was more than 34 inches.

UNKNOWN COLORADO HUNTER
•
Location: Colorado
Year Taken: Prior to 1992
Score: 233-7/8
Owner: Darryl Powell

An 11x7 non-typical muley was taken along Black Creek Ridge in Summit County by Howard Doig in 1929. The buck has 83 inches of abnormal points on the right antler and more than 92 inches on the left. Its final score was 230-2/8.

Photos—Big-Game Trophies

Typical American Elk

ROBERT G. YOUNG
•
Location: Summit County
Year Taken: 1967
Score: 407

*First Place
14th B&C
Competitions*

Ron D. Velarde waited seven years for a permit to hunt elk when he took this typical American elk in 1996 in Las Animas County. The rack sports a 47-4/8 inch width from widest tip to tip and the longest beam measures 58 inches. The antlers were measured at 393 points but have not been entered in the Boone and Crockett Club's records keeping program so remain unranked.

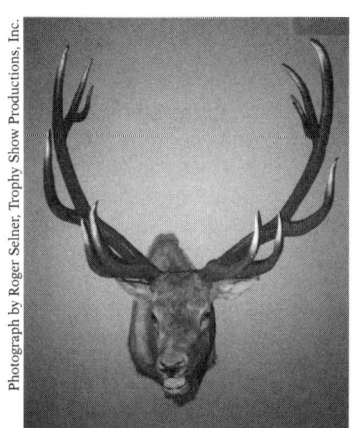

An unknown Colorado hunter gave this massive typical American elk to the Meeker Hotel and Café prior to 1906 and it's been on public display ever since in the hotel's lobby. The bull was officially measured by Roger Selner when he visited the Meeker Hotel and Café in 1996 and determined its score to be 391. It has not been entered in the Boone and Crockett Club's records-keeping program so remains unranked.

BYRON W. KNEFF
•
Location: Garfield County
Year Taken: 1954
Score: 385-1/8
Owner: Eugene Kneff

*Certificate of Merit
11th B&C Competition*

JOHN WALLACE
•
Location: Clear Creek County
Year Taken: 1973
Score: 384-3/8

NEWELL BEAUCHAMP
•
Location: Gunnison County
Year Taken: 1957
Score: 382
Owner: Bud Lovato

Art Wright (left) looks on as his hunting companion, "Sunny" Jim Orr (right), admires the long tines of Art's 1953 Boone and Crockett bull with a final score of 378-2/8 points. The bull was taken in the White River area.

Colorado's Biggest Bucks and Bulls

This outstanding Boone and Crockett typical American elk was taken in Dolores County by Audrea Holley in October 2000 and makes the all-time records book with a final score of 378 points. Audrea is one of only a handful of women to collect a B&C Colorado trophy of any kind.

Tom Nidey of Granby and his 377-6/8 points bull, which he took on the Routt National Forest on October 18, 1959.

John Schwartz took this fine trophy (376 points) in the vicinity of Doctor's Park near Almont, Colorado, with guide and outfitter Forrest Cranor. This photograph was taken shortly after John found success on October 21, 1961.

JOHN SCHWARTZ
•
Location: Gunnison County
Year Taken: 1961
Score: 376

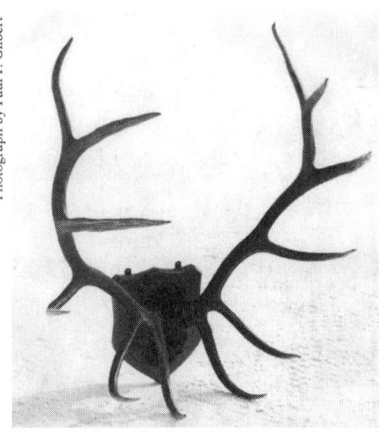

Radium, Colorado resident, Hank Hinton, downed this 6x6 typical American elk in October 1961 along Piney Creek in Eagle County. The bull's greatest spread is 44-7/8 inches. Its final score was 366-6/8, which at the time did not qualify for the Boone and Crockett Club's records book. Now it would easily qualify but is recognized in this book.

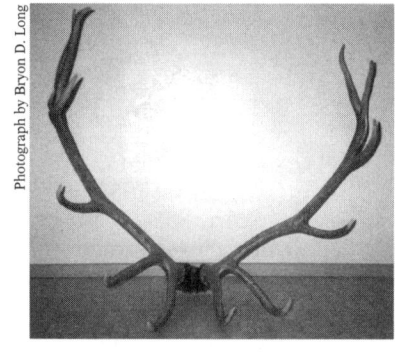

Renay Neely is one of the few women to have a Boone and Crockett elk in the records books. Her outstanding typical American elk scores 365-3/8 points. The bull was taken in October 1973 in Dolores County but was only measured in 2000.

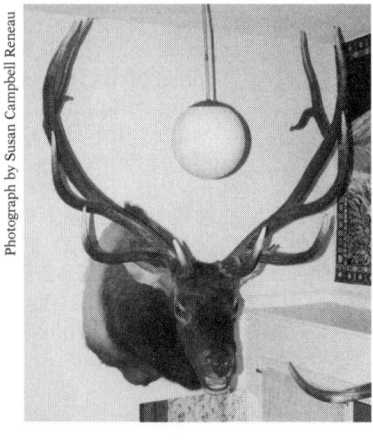

Darrel Lemon said the best thing about his 1993 elk hunt was the fact that he was completely alone on public land for two days with 12 inches of snow on the ground. Darrel downed his massive typical bull elk about an hour before sundown on October 30. His trophy, which he and his wife call Phreddie, scores 364-4/8 points and was accepted into the B&C 22nd North American Big Game Awards Program.

A joyful young man, J.R. Barnes, Jr., holds the trophy typical elk he took in October 1960 in Grand County. The 6x6 bull had a greatest spread of almost 48 inches. Its final score was 362-3/8 but it was never entered because at the time it did not have a high enough score. Now it would be recognized in the B&C Awards Program if entered.

Photos—Big-Game Trophies

Shiras Moose

This massive Shiras moose from Jackson County was harvested in 1998 by Colorado hunter Michael Tucker. It easily makes the B&C with a final score of 162.

Rick Karbowski located this P&Y Shiras moose in Grand County on September 18, 1998. It scores 159-1/8 and is large enough to also be accepted into the B&C.

Bighorn Sheep

Todd Clyncke holds the trophy bighorn ram he took in 1991 in Area 57 of Colorado. The ram scores 184-6/8, which qualifies it for Boone and Crockett Club and Pope and Young Club.

Moments after 15-year-old Steven Behunin took this massive ram, he poses for a picture. Steve is one of the youngest hunters to take a Pope and Young trophy. His ram, because of its size, also qualifies for the Boone and Crockett Club but has not yet been entered in the program as of spring 2001. Here is Steven, left, and his brother Cal.

This outstanding B&C bighorn ram was found by Henry H. Zietz, Jr. in 1947 on Sugarloaf Mountain. The ram scores 180-1/8 points.

Desert Bighorn Sheep

Steven Allan entered the hunting records books and made Colorado history by taking the first Colorado desert bighorn ram that is large enough to be listed in the Boone and Crockett Club. Steven's ram, shown here moments after Steven collected it with his .25-06, was within 70 yards of Steven when he fired two shots that hit their mark. Steven is shown with his 11-year-old son, Dustin, who joined him on the hunt in 1996 in Mesa County. The ram scores 169-5/8 points. As of June 2001, Steven's desert bighorn ram is the only one listed in the B&C from Colorado.

Rocky Mountain Goat

Lyle Willmarth is one of only nine men and women to collect a B&C-quality Rocky Mountain goat and holds the World's Record in the Pope and Young Club for taking the largest billy with bow and arrow. It scores 52-6/8 points and is listed in the B&C and P&Y all-time records books.

Lyle Willmarth's full mount Rocky Mountain goat was taken in Park County in 1988. Its greatest spread is 8-1/8 inches. Its right horn scored 26-5/8 inches and the left horn scored 26-2/8 points.

Colorado bowhunter Marv Clyncke looks at his P&Y trophy Rocky Mountain goat from Chaffee County that he downed with bow and arrow in 1978. His wild goat scores 48-2/8 points and would qualify for the Boone and Crockett Club because of its size.

Pronghorn

This pronghorn that Henry H. Zietz, Jr. collected in 1965 in Boyero, Colorado, scores 83 points.

Using a 53-pound St. Joe River longbow from 28 yards, Marv Clyncke downed this beautiful pronghorn buck northwest of Craig, Colorado in 1998. Marv shot a wood arrow with a Bear razor head. Because of its size (82), this buck also qualifies for B&C's records-keeping program.

RODNEY S. COOK
•
Location:
Rio Blanco County
Year Taken: 1999
Score: 81-4/8

GLEN A. FILENER
•
Location: Moffat County
Year Taken: 1989
Score: 80-4/8

Cougar

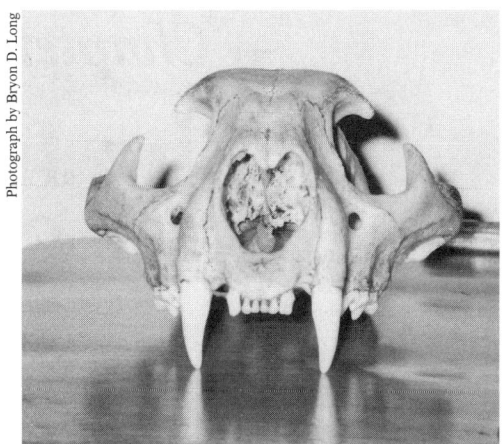

Montezuma County produced another fine trophy-book cougar. This time the honors went to a cougar that scores 15-2/16 B&C points that was collected by Terry Amrine of Dolores on February 5, 1999.

Black Bear

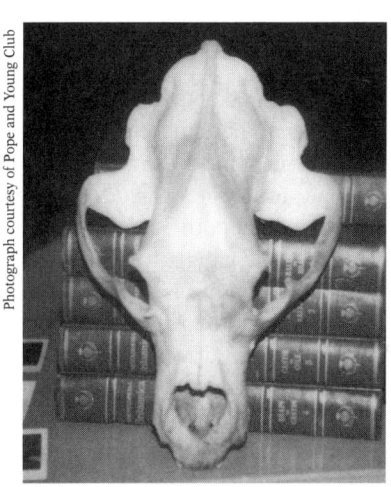

The highest Pope and Young Club honor, the Ishi Award, was presented to this 22-4/16-point black bear during the 12th Recording Period (1979-1980) that was taken in Colorado in 1978 by Ray Cox. This black bear is the largest ever taken in Colorado. It was harvested along Sinbad Ridge.

— Chapter XI —
Trophy Judging and Care

If there is any doubt as to whether or not a particular big-game animal is outstanding, then it probably isn't. Generally, when a hunter sees a Boone and Crockett animal in the field for the first time, there is little doubt in a hunter's mind that this is a massive animal. Except in a few cases where antlers and horns are partially obscured, a hunter who sees a B&C animal in the field is truly impressed. In fact, the spotting of a B&C trophy is frequently followed by a malady that can affect even the best and most experienced hunter – buck fever.

The two key characteristics that make an animal trophy-class are massiveness and symmetry. There just has to be lots of antler material. In the case of typical mule deer, there must be at least four normal points per antler, not including brow tines. Elk must have six or more normal points per antler. For a bighorn ram a ¾ or full curl is a good gauge. A bull elk with antlers that tip all the way back to the rump is a safe bet that this is a massive trophy. The horns of pronghorn and Rocky Mountain goat that seem to go on forever upwards toward the sky is another indication. Cougar and black bear with wide, bulky heads are also an indication of trophy size since their skulls are the source of measurement. A Shiras moose that reminds a hunter of an Alaska-Yukon moose probably is looking at a B&C specimen. The 20 moose featured in this book sported wide palmation and numerous points rippling from each palm.

The one point to keep in mind when judging a trophy is the simple fact that the entire B&C, P&Y and Longhunter measuring systems are based upon massiveness and symmetry.

JUDGING A TROPHY

If there is any question as to whether or not a certain trophy makes "The Book," there are a couple of techniques recommended for determining trophy quality. Both are quite simple.

The first method will work only for mule deer. In this case, the hunter uses the buck's ears like a ruler, keeping in mind the distance between ear tips is approximately 21 inches on adult mule deer. Usually, if a hunter has a clear enough view of a buck's antlers, the hunter can also see the ears. Thus, if the antlers extend several inches past each ear tip, and they are equally tall and heavy, they are probably trophy-class.

A second technique for judging trophy quality of mule deer and elk in the field has been recommended by Clyde Ormond in his book, *Complete Book of Hunting*. In the case of mule deer, he indicated that a buck (Figure 3) is probably trophy-class "if the antlers are at least one-half the animal's height from withers to ground, or if either antler overhangs the body by at least the body width."

Ormond also stated that a bull elk (Figure 4) is trophy-class "if the antlers approach body length." In either instance the hunter must make a mental effort to compare the antlers to the animal's body.

Several words of caution, however, are necessary when using any method that compares antlers with ears or body size. First, the body size and proportions of adult deer vary considerably between individuals. A set of antlers that looks average on a large-bodied deer may look exceptional on a small-bodied deer. Secondly, there is considerable variation between racks listed in the records books. There are numerous low, wide racks, as well as many tall, narrow racks. To get a feel for what trophy racks look like on a deer, carefully examine the photographs of the mounted trophies beside the hunter or owner. If a mount takes your breath away, chances are good that this is a B&C trophy.

FIELD CARE

The single biggest mistake that any hunter makes when preparing a big-game animal in the field is to wrap it in a plastic bag. Buzzi Cook, a Washington taxidermist who has written extensively about trophy care for hunting books and national publications, says that wrapping a big-game animal in plastic constrains body heat and does not allow the natural body heat to escape. The body heat held inside causes fur to slip. A second bit of advice is to not cut the throat and to field dress the game immediately without waiting to return to hunting camp. Anything a hunter can do to cool down the body will not only preserve the cape but also the meat.

Clean potato sacks or other types of simple burlap sacks are best for wrapping the field-dressed game because such material allows for ventilation. Any cloth sack with holes in it can be used to properly preserve meat in the field. The prepared meat and cape should be hung in the shade of a tree or

Figure 3.

Figure 4.

Illustrations by Doug Pifer

placed in some cool place until the cape, horn, antler, skull and meat can be transported to a meat packer's cooler or a home freezer. Skinning an animal on the spot where it was taken is critical to preserving the meat and hide. Dragging big game out of the woods is another moment when a cape can be seriously damaged, so Buzzi recommends that a plastic tarp or child's plastic sled be used to pull the field-dressed animal from the field. If these simple procedures are followed, a hunter will properly care for their big-game trophy in the field. Common sense should be the guide in any situation.

TROPHY CARE

Once you have your trophy and have made the decision to have it mounted, it is essential that it get the proper field care if it is to be preserved properly. Unless you have prior experience at removing capes and antlers, it is an operation best left for a trained taxidermist. However, if you are in a situation where you must remove the cape and antlers or horns yourself in order to transport or preserve your trophy, you can do so by taking the following steps. The procedures listed here apply to any big-game animal you take in the field, although the illustration shows a modest-sized mule deer.

1. Skin heads as shown in diagram. Make initial cut circling the body behind the front legs. A second cut up the back of neck to base of skull to form a "V" (see illustration) should be completed. Cut carefully around the antlers and cut the skin away from the base.

2. Cut ear cartilage from skull on the inside and clean meat away from base of ear. Skin down the skull, being careful not to cut through the skin, especially around the eyes and nose. Preserve the eyelids. Use the fingers of the free hand to guide on the outside to be certain you are not cutting into the lids and nose.

3. Before skinning past the lips, with the head facing you, reach inside the mouth cutting against the jaw bone on the lower lip, circling around to the upper lip leaving about one-half inch of the lip attached to the skin. Then turn the head around and continue taking the cape off and in doing so you will meet lip cuts you made on the inside. Place the one-half inch of lip that is left attached to the skin between your fingers and slip open for salting.

4. Saw off the top of the skull through the center of the eyes and above the ear hole after skinning is completed. Remove the brains, cut off the excess meat around the skull cap and then salt heavily.

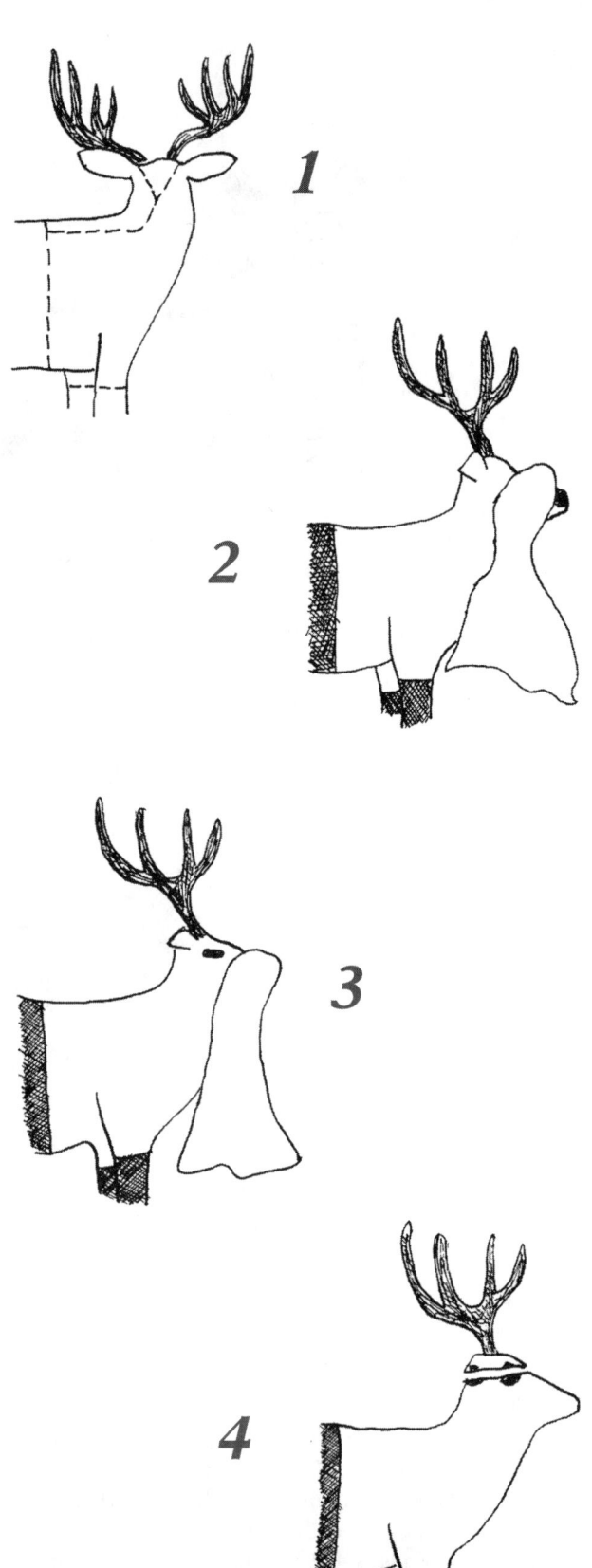

Illustrations courtesy of Gary Meyers

— Chapter XII —
Records-Keeping Programs for Big Game

Three well-respected organizations, the Boone and Crockett Club (B&C), the Pope and Young Club (P&Y) and the National Muzzle Loading Rifle Association's (NMLRA) Longhunter Program, collect and maintain the records of big-game animals in North America using the copyrighted measuring system created by the Boone and Crockett Club in 1950. With the recent addition of the tule elk during the 24th Awards Program, Boone and Crockett Club now accepts big game in 36 categories that are taken in fair chase by any legal means including modern rifle and pistol, bow and arrow, and muzzleloader firearms. Pope and Young only accepts the same big game taken with bow and arrow, and the Longhunter Program only accepts big game taken with muzzleloader firearms.

Their records books list and highlight the big game that are the biggest and the best when it comes to antler, horn, tusk or skull size, but more importantly, their books scientifically record the health of the big-game herds of North America and were not created to glorify the hunter. At the beginning of the 20th Century, that was not the case. By the time 1901 was celebrated as the start of the 20th Century, Roosevelt and many others feared that big-game animals such as elk, deer and moose would be extinct by the early 1920s. We in the 21st Century know that extinction did not come, thanks in large part to early members of the Boone and Crockett Club, professional wildlife biologists and hunters who have consistently been there to help wildlife of all types.

The records-keeping programs of B&C, P&Y and NMLRA document the success of wildlife management in the modern world.

BOONE AND CROCKETT CLUB

The Boone and Crockett Club was founded in 1887 by Theodore Roosevelt, George Bird Grinnell and a small group of men in New York City as they observed the destruction of natural resources, including wildlife, in the late 1800s. The Club's earliest achievements included the protection of the world's first national park, Yellowstone, and the establishment of Glacier National Park. The expansion of national parks was a result of Boone and Crockett Club members. Early members established a federal forest reserve system that eventually became the U.S. Forest Service. They established national and state wildlife refuge systems and wrote and passed wildlife protection laws. America's first hunting regulations were established by B&C members at the end of the 19th Century that stopped massive slaughter of wild game and ended market hunting. Today, B&C financially supports wildlife research projects across North America, funds a wildlife professorship at the University of Montana, operates the Theodore Roosevelt Memorial Ranch as a research, teaching and demonstration proj-

The Sagamore Hill Medal is the highest recognition given to a trophy, not the hunter, by the Boone and Crockett Club. The medal is given by the Roosevelt family in memory of Theodore Roosevelt (founder and first president of the B&C), Theodore Roosevelt, Jr. and Kermit Roosevelt. The medal was established in 1948 and has only been awarded 15 times, twice for Colorado trophies taken by Doug Burris, Jr. (typical mule deer scoring 226-4/8 points) and Edison A. Pillmore (typical mule deer scoring 203-7/8 points).

Photograph courtesy of Boone and Crockett Club

ect along the Rocky Mountain Front, and continues to promote conservation of all natural resources.

Most famous of the Boone and Crockett Club's activities is the records keeping of native North American big game. Their first formal recognition of outstanding North American big-game trophies was in 1932 with the publication of its first records book that featured a small number of big-game specimens and a modest measuring procedure that included length and spread of horns, antlers or skulls. The 1932 book was followed by the 1939 records book that included informative chapters on a variety of subjects related to big game and hunting. In 1947 B&C held its first "Big Game Competition" for outstanding trophies, ranking them by a series of measurements that were refined in 1950 into the Club's current copyrighted trophy scoring system. Since 1947 there have been awards programs, with the 24th North American Big Game Awards Program ending on December 31, 2000. The 25th Awards Program began on January 1, 2001 ends December 31, 2003. The famous B&C records book, *Records of North American Big Game*, is now in its 11th edition. The 12th edition will be published in 2005.

Trophy entry now occurs during a three-year period, followed by public display of the finest trophies entered in each big-game category and an Awards Banquet. Presentation of Boone and Crockett Club big-game medals and/or certificates recognizes trophy excellence. Only top trophies in each category are invited to the Final Awards Judging and only invited trophies remeasured by the Judges' Panel are eligible to receive awards. Other invited trophies, such as pick ups and invited trophies of unknown origin, are eligible only for a Certificate of Merit.

The Boone and Crockett Club publishes its all-time records book, *Records of North American Big Game*, after the completion of two Awards Programs or when significant changes have occurred in trophy rankings, categories or requirements. B&C also publishes other records books on big game of special interest to hunters, game managers and wildlife biologists.

The name Boone and Crockett is synonymous with trophy native North American big game. The long-time records keeping for native big game is but one of the many conservation activities of the Boone and Crockett Club. The Club's forefront role in conservation activities and leadership during the 20th Century is well documented in the book, *An American Crusade for Wildlife*.

Over the years the B&C records books have become valuable handbooks for the hunter, wildlife manager and serious student of big game. The current edition of the all-time records book contains more than 17,150 individual big-game trophy listings in 35 categories. Only big game meeting the minimum score requirements are listed.

For details about entering big game and for copies of score charts, call the Boone and Crockett Club at (406) 542-1888, or write 250 Station Drive, Missoula, MT 59801. Their web address is www.boone-crockett.org.

POPE AND YOUNG CLUB

The Pope and Young Club was founded in 1961 by Glenn St. Charles as a non-profit, scientific organization, and was patterned after the Boone and Crockett Club. The P&Y adopted the B&C method of measuring but lowered the entry scores for big game accepted into their program to account for the difficulty of taking wild game with bow and arrow. The P&Y advocates and encourages responsible bowhunting by promoting quality, fair chase hunting and sound conservation practices. Glenn established P&Y to upgrade the image of bowhunting as it relates to the rest of the hunting community.

Modern bowhunting began at the beginning of the 20th Century when Will "Chief" Compton and Saxon Pope introduced bowhunting to Art Young. The adventures of this trio of friends paved the way for other bow and arrow enthusiasts. In 1956 the National Field Archery Association (NFAA) established the Hunting Activities Committee headed by Glenn to work with state and Canadian provincial fish and wildlife departments to establish

Two Colorado trophies, a black bear and a typical mule deer, have received the highest recognition by the Pope and Young Club with the presentation of the Ishi Award. This award was first presented during the 4th Recording Period (1963-1964) and has only been presented 14 times. Ray Cox's black bear (22-4/16 points) was recognized during the 12th Recording Period (1979-1980), and Bill Barcus' typical mule deer (203-1/8 points) received the Ishi Award during the 14th Recording Period (1983-1984.)

Photograph courtesy of Pope and Young Club

bowhunting seasons. Glenn spent a year interviewing officials at state associations, state game departments and other interested individuals. He recognized that bowhunters needed to upgrade their image by demonstrating they believed in fair chase principles and sound conservation practices. Responses from questionnaires and interviews kept pointing to the establishment of a records-keeping program patterned after the prestigious Boone and Crockett Club. In the February 1958 issue of the NFAA national magazine, *Archery Magazine*, the entire program was presented to the NFAA members. NFAA John Yount requested and received permission from the B&C to use the B&C scoring system for bow-taken big game.

June 1958 was the first NFAA-hosted display and awards program in Grayling, Michigan. Later that same year the NFAA Hunting Activities Committee completely revised the Art Young Awards Program to eliminate from big-game status many small animals and domesticated wild animals, thus upgrading the bowhunter image. On June 29, 1960, the second awards program took place and 35 avid bowhunters gathered to discuss the formation of a separate club free to decide its own destiny in the field of records keeping. After much discussion with NFAA officials, the Pope and Young Club, named in honor of Saxon Pope and Art Young, came into being on January 27, 1961. Since then, P&Y has published five stunning editions of their popular all-time records book, *Bowhunting Big Game Records of North America*, with the latest edition released in 1999 at the close of the 22nd Awards Program. Unlike the Boone and Crockett Club with its three-year awards programs, the Pope and Young Club has two-year awards programs so the 23rd Awards Program began on January 1, 2001, and ends December 31, 2002. In addition to the 1999 edition, all-time records books have been published in 1975, 1981, 1987, 1993, or every six years after three awards programs.

Through the P&Y records program, the Club encourages quality bowhunting by awakening interest in outstanding examples of this continent's big-game animals. The Club records for posterity scientific data on North American big game taken with bow and arrow. It conducts ongoing recording periods and every two years presents appropriate recognition to the finest specimens submitted. These biennial presentations honor the quality of individual examples of various North American big-game species and promote the ideals of fair chase. Through the P&Y Conservation Program, members lead others to participate in protecting and promoting wildlife, wildlife conservation and the bowhunting-outdoor heritage.

To receive more information about the Pope and Young Club and their records-keeping program, call at (507) 867-4144. The Pope and Young Club address is 15 E. 2nd Street, P.O. Box 548, Chatfield, MN 55923. Their web address is www.pope-young.org.

NATIONAL MUZZLE LOADING RIFLE ASSOCIATION'S (NMLRA) LONGHUNTER PROGRAM

The National Muzzle Loading Rifle Association founded the Longhunter Muzzleloading Big Game Records Program for North American big game in 1988, although the association itself was established in 1933. This was the fourth attempt in 30-odd years within the United States to establish a muzzleloading big-game records-keeping program for the North American continent. NMLRA intends this to be the last effort.

Input from muzzleloading hunters in Canada and the United States set the tone for the new program as it was adopted by the NMLRA Board of Directors. With financial support from the Thompson/Center Arms of Rochester, New Hampshire, NMLRA and volunteer help from a core of avid muzzleloader hunting individuals, the die was cast for the establishment of the records keeping program. Since October 1988, the Longhunter Committee and the appointed staff from NMLRA headquarters in Friendship, Indiana, have worked diligently to establish a trophy measuring, scoring and records-keeping system for hunters who choose to pursue North American big game with a muzzleloading firearm. The basis for the Longhunter records-keeping program is the system established by the B&C and the P&Y, whose valuable input, hands-on help to the staff and generosity in allowing the Longhunter to utilize their official measurers and scoring system is deeply appreciated. The B&C also gave permission to reproduce examples of their score sheets in the Longhunter records book.

The Longhunter Records-Keeping Program does not host awards banquets but publishes their records book as directed by their Board of Directors. *The Longhunter Muzzleloading Big Game Record Book* was published in 1992, 1996 and 2000. The popularity of primitive firearms hunting is documented in the ever-expanding size of the NMLRA all-time records book. Its third edition contains more than 1,600 entries. In the first edition there were only 366 entries. The number of entries continues to grow as hunters discover the excitement and challenge of hunting with primitive firearms.

For more information about entry of big game into the *Longhunter Muzzleloading Big Game Record Book*, call the NMLRA headquarters at (812) 667-5131. Their address is P.O. Box 67, Friendship, IN 47021. The web address is www.nmlra@nmlra.org.

Table XVI
MINIMUM ENTRY SCORES FOR POPE AND YOUNG CLUB AND LONGHUNTER PROGRAM

Big Game of Colorado Taken with Bow and Arrow (P&Y) or Muzzleloading Firearms (Longhunter)

Big-Game Species	P&Y Entry Minimum	Longhunter Entry Minimum
Typical Mule Deer	145	146
Non-Typical Mule Deer	170	175
Typical Whitetail Deer	125	130
Non-Typical Whitetail Deer	155	160
Typical American Elk	260	255
Non-Typical American Elk	335	265
Shiras or Wyoming Moose	125	125
Bighorn Sheep	140	136
Desert Bighorn Sheep	140	125
Rocky Mountain Goat	40	41
Pronghorn	67	63
Cougar or Mountain Lion	13-8/16	16-13/16
Black Bear	18	18

Note: Minimum scores for P&Y and Longhunter Programs allow the hunter to enter big game in their all-time records keeping archives that do not meet B&C score requirements, but deserve recognition for the skill it takes to use primitive firearms and bow and arrow. P&Y and Longhunter Programs adhere to the B&C guidelines for fair chase.

— Chapter XIII —
Your Odds for a Trophy in Colorado

What are your odds for taking a trophy big-game animal in Colorado? Are they the often quoted one in a million? One in a hundred? Or, somewhere in between?

Before we really get into the meat of the subject at hand, we should analyze one key word – TROPHY. According to *The American Heritage Dictionary*, a trophy is, "a specimen or part, often mounted, preserved as a token of successful hunting."

Thus, through a liberal interpretation of this definition we could consider any big game or small game animal taken by a hunter as a trophy. A hunter's first deer or elk, irregardless of size or sex, is really a trophy. That teenager, woman or man will remember the final stalk for the rest of their lives.

As a Colorado hunter, your chances of taking such a trophy are better than hunters from most other states. In fact, in 1999 a deer hunter had a 37 percent success rate. For elk, a hunter had a 17 percent chance, and for Shiras moose, a hunter drawing a permit had a 70 percent chance of taking one. If a lucky hunter received a Rocky Mountain bighorn sheep permit, he or she had a 53 percent of filling their tag. A Rocky Mountain goat hunter had a 94 percent success rate in 1999, and 65 percent of the pronghorn hunters came home with their tag filled. Cougar hunters found a 40 percent success rate, and black bear hunters were least successful with a 9 percent success rate. Those are high percentages of success when you realize that nearly one out of every two deer hunters and one out of every six elk hunters went home with filled tags.

Another definition frequently used to describe any big-game trophy is "Boone and Crockett (B&C)" or "Pope and Young (P&Y)" or "Longhunter." While this isn't actually a dictionary definition, it is unlikely there are too many Colorado big-game hunters who are really not aware of what these terms mean. B&C, P&Y and Longhunter are synonymous with exceptional trophy quality and fair chase principles first established by the Boone and Crockett Club in the early 20th Century.

With this brief analysis of the word "trophy" out of the way, let's take a look at some facts and figures and answer a few questions. What are a Colorado hunter's chances of taking a records-book trophy? Where might a hunter go to have the best chances of getting one? And, are records-book trophies a commodity of the past only?

YOUR ODDS FOR A TROPHY MULE DEER AND ELK

While there are a few stories of Colorado hunters taking individual records book trophies they have deliberating pursued for days, weeks, months and even years, there are far more documented cases of hunters stumbling upon their B&C, P&Y or Longhunter trophy by chance. In fact, no less than 10 Colorado hunters stumbled on their B&C deer or elk on their first hunt. Within this book are other hunting stories of men, women and teenagers who took a trophy big-game animal on their first try.

Years of planning and preparation may help some hunters, but some degree of luck is a key ingredient in the taking of an exceptionally large animal. In fact, locating or even seeing a Boone and Crockett animal in the field is one of the most unique experiences any hunter will report. This fact is attested to by the simple fact that "neither love nor any amount of money" can guarantee a big-game hunter the taking of a Boone and Crockett animal. If it was easy, there would be a lot more big game and big-game hunters listed in "The Book."

In Colorado, a hunter has a better chance of seeing as well as successfully harvesting a B&C mule deer than in any other state or province in North America. For example, of all the typical and non-typical mule deer bucks listed in the 11th edition of the B&C all-time records book, *Records of North American Big Game*, 378 were taken in Colorado compared with the next best state for mule deer trophy production, Idaho, with a grand total of 207. The World's Record typical mule deer with a final score of 226-4/8 points was taken in Dolores County in 1972 by Doug Burris, Jr. Other states often referred to as outstanding producers of B&C mule deer bucks include Utah with a grand total of 169, Wyoming with 99, New Mexico with 92, and Arizona with 81. Colorado outshines the rest of North America for production of Boone and Crockett bucks.

The B&C non-typical mule deer category is also dominated by Colorado bucks, beginning with Lloyd Pyle's muley taken in 1972 that ranks Number 10 in the world with a final score of 306-7/8 points. Of the 473 non-typical mule deer bucks listed in the most recent edition of the B&C all-time records book, 117 are from Colorado. The closest competitor is Idaho with 93 bucks listed, followed by Utah with 72, Arizona with 44, Wyoming with 33, and Montana with 32.

Colorado mule deer trophies listed in Pope and Young and Longhunter all-time records books are equally impressive. Of the 1,820 typical mule deer listed in the latest edition of the Pope and Young Club's records book, *Bowhunting Big Game Records of North America*, published in 1999, 436 were harvested in Colorado, including the World's Record typical mule deer taken by Bill Barcus in 1979. As for non-typical muleys, 61 were from Colorado out of a total of 244 listed in P&Y, including the World's Record muley taken by Kenneth W. Plank in 1987. Other high P&Y mule deer trophy production states include Idaho, Arizona, Utah, New Mexico, Wyoming, Alberta, and Nevada, but no state comes close to trophy mule deer production as Colorado.

Muzzleloading hunters also find great success in Colorado with a total 36 from Colorado in the typical mule deer category out of a total of 218 listed trophies in their latest edition of the all-time muzzleloading records book, *Longhunter Muzzleloading Big Game Record Book, 3rd Edition*, published in late 2000. In the non-typical mule deer category, six are from Colorado out of a total of 53 accepted entries.

The number of big-game trophy entries in the typical and non-typical elk categories are not quite as spectacular in Colorado as listings are for mule deer, but the numbers are equally impressive. In the B&C all-time records book a count of all typical elk listings (359) nets 40 from Colorado. Arizona tops the list with 74 entries. Other top typical elk trophy producers include Wyoming with 55, Alberta with 36, Idaho with 33 and New Mexico with 29. Certainly Colorado is one of the top B&C elk producers in North America.

As for the non-typical elk listings in the B&C all-time records book, a total of 87 trophies are entered with three from Colorado. Other top trophy producing states include Arizona with 28, Montana with 21, Wyoming with 10, and Idaho with 6. Many outstanding non-typical elk officially measured by Roger Selner in 1996 at the Meeker Hotel and Café have not yet been entered in the B&C all-time records book, which would bump up the total number of non-typical elk entries from the state.

Elk listings from Colorado in the P&Y and Longhunter all-time records books are substantial and noteworthy. Of the 3,526 typical elk entered into the most recent edition of the P&Y records book, 443 are from Colorado, and 3 non-typical elk are entered into that big-game category out of a total of 61 animals. From the Longhunter muzzleloading records book, a whopping 82 of the 179 entered typical elk trophies listed are from Colorado, and in the non-typical category a total of 1 in 15 are from the state.

Top Colorado counties that consistently produce B&C, P&Y and Longhunter typical mule deer trophies include Eagle County with 21 listings, Montrose County with 19, Gunnison and Mesa Counties with 14 each, and Garfield County with 12. As for non-typical mule deer bucks, the best county to find them is Eagle County with 18 harvested, followed by Mesa County with 10, and Rio Blanco County with 7. Routt and Gunnison Counties each produced 4 typical elk trophies, and Las Animas and Larimer Counties each produced 3 trophies. Only 4 non-typical elk were taken in Colorado that make the all-time records book and one each were harvested in Jefferson, Mesa, Routt and Douglas Counties. Charts in this chapter show where all the mule deer and elk trophies were taken, organized by county.

YOUR ODDS FOR OTHER BIG-GAME TROPHIES

Other big-game species from Colorado fair well in records-keeping programs but are not as dramatic as the success ratio of mule deer and elk.

Twenty years ago, only one typical whitetail deer was listed in the B&C all-time records book as being taken by a hunter. In 2000, trophy whitetail listed in B&Y, P&Y and Longhunter that make the B&C all-time minimum entrance score total 18. Non-typical whitetail that qualify for the B&C records book total 13, so even though Midwestern states still dominate trophy whitetail deer production, Colorado bucks are making in-roads.

Shiras or Wyoming moose are the true success story of the state. As explained in the chapter about moose in Colorado, the number of bulls, cows and calves has expanded greatly since their re-introduction in 1978, and the number of bulls that qualify for the all-time records books is truly impressive. A total of 15 Shiras moose were accepted into the 1999 B&C all-time records book, with another 5 added from January to July 2000 during the 24th North American Big Game Awards Period, and P&Y lists 9 Shiras moose from Colorado out of a total number of Shiras moose listings of 256. Of the 13 Shiras moose listed in the Longhunter records book, none are from Colorado. The fact that 29 trophy-class Shiras moose grew in Colorado is a tribute to the health of the overall moose herds in the state. If you want a trophy moose in Colorado, Jackson County is the place to go with 11 harvested, followed by Grand County with 2. Single trophy moose have come from Park and Larimer Counties.

P&Y lists 105 bighorn sheep in their all-time records book as coming from Colorado out of a total of 245 entered in that big-game category, including their World's Record for bow and arrow taken by Gene Moore in 1983 with a score of 191-3/8 points. B&C lists 19 bighorn in their all-time records book from Colorado. Top trophy producing bighorn sheep include El Paso (3), Clear Creek (3), Huerfano (2), Fremont (2), Gunnison (2), and Saguache (2). A chart shows all the counties where rams were harvested in Colorado that qualify for the B&C all-time records book. Only one desert sheep has been listed in the all-time records books from Colorado but the seasons only opened by limited permit in 1988.

Your Odds for a Trophy

Certainly Wyoming is most noted for pronghorn hunting, but Moffat County is the number one producer of trophy-class pronghorn in Colorado with a grand total of 17. Jackson County follows with a total of 10, and Weld County produced 8. A chart shows all the counties where trophy-class pronghorn have been taken in the state.

The best three counties for harvesting trophy cougar in Colorado include Rio Blanco with 10, Mesa with 8, and Archuleta with 6, and the best counties for locating trophy black bear include Garfield (6) and Mesa (5). The community of Collbran has netted 3 trophy boars. Of the 484 cougar listed in the B&C all-time records book, 58 were taken in Colorado. In the P&Y all-time records book, 1,330 are listed, and of those, 309 are from Colorado. The Longhunter records book accepted 40 cougars and 9 are from Colorado. The counties of Rio Blanco, Mesa, and Archeleta were the highest producers of records-book cougars in Colorado, followed closely by Eagle, Huerfano, Garfield, and Montrose.

Only three Rocky Mountain goats are at or above the B&C minimum score of 50 that come from Colorado, including the World Record's P&Y billy taken in 1988 by Lyle K. Willmarth with a score of 52-4/8 points. This billy goat is also the Colorado state record. The P&Y all-time records book lists 80 goats from Colorado out of a total of 470 listings, but only one is largest enough to make the B&C. Park, Clear Creek, and Mount Antero were the areas where the trophy goats were taken. Two of the 18 goats listed in the Longhunter book are from Colorado but none make the B&C minimum score.

TOP COUNTIES

As the charts illustrate in this chapter, where you go makes a difference if you want to locate a trophy buck, bull, billy, ram, boar or tom taken by modern rifle and pistol, bow and arrow, or muzzleloader firearms. The numbers of animals taken represent calculations based upon the most recent editions of each all-time records book published by B&C, P&Y and Longhunter, and those animals that meet the minimum entrance score for the B&C all-time records book.

A quick analysis of Tables I and II reveals some very interesting facts to ponder regarding the most productive B&C mule deer and elk counties. Overall, the top county for trophy typical and non-typical bucks is Eagle County with 39 making the all-time records book. Second place honors are held by Mesa County with a grand total of 24 making the listings. Third place with 23 entries is Montrose County. Gunnison County is the top trophy typical elk producer but Douglas County is top for non-typical elk production.

One interesting sidelight in regards to mule deer is the simple fact that the top five typical mule deer counties are not the same as the top five non-typical mule deer counties, although the top county for both is Eagle. The top five counties for typical muley are Eagle, Montrose, Gunnison, Mesa and Garfield, while non-typical mule deer counties are Eagle, Mesa, Rio Blanco, Garfield, and Gunnison. Similar comparisons can be made throughout the entire mule deer listings.

Table I — Typical Mule Deer

Location	Number Taken
Eagle County	21
Montrose County	19
Gunnison County	15
Mesa County	14
Garfield County	12
Delta County	10
Archuleta County	9
Moffat County	7
Dolores County	6
Rio Blanca County	6
Southern Ute Indian Reservation	5
Pagosa Springs	5
Grand County	4
Mesa County	4
Bayfield County	3
Grand Junction	3
Huerfano County	3
Jackson County	3
La Plata County	3
Ouray County	3
Routt County	3
San Miguel County	3
Summit County	3
Boulder County	2
Carbondale	2
Collbran	2
DeBeque	2
Hinsdale County	2
Larimer County	2
Las Animas County	2
Moffat County	2
Pitkin County	2
Silt	2
Uncompahgre NF	2
Uncompahgre Plateau	2
Adams County	1
Amherst Mountain	1
Arapahoe County	1
Burns	1
Cameo	1
Chaffee County	1
Cimarron	1
Custer County	1
Dark Canyon	1
Del Norte	1
Disappointment Creek	1
Douglas County	1
Durango	1
Elbert County	1
Golden	1
Grand Mesa	1
Gypsum County	1
Hayden	1
Jefferson County	1
Kremmling	1
Marble	1
Maybell	1
Montezuma County	1
North Park	1
Park County	1
Piedra River	1

Continued on next page

Colorado's Biggest Bucks and Bulls

Location	Number Taken
Pueblo County	1
Saguache County	1
San Isabel NF	1
San Juan NF	1
Slater	1
Teller County	1
Weld County	1
White River	1
White River NF	1

Table II — Non-Typical Mule Deer

Location	Number Taken
Eagle County	18
Mesa County	10
Rio Blanco County	7
Garfield County	5
Gunnison County	4
Montrose County	4
Delta County	3
Glenwood Springs	3
Grand County	3
Hinsdale County	3
New Castle	3
Routt County	3
Columbine	2
Douglas County	2
Jefferson County	2
La Plata County	2
Meeker	2
Montezuma County	2
Norwood	2
Oak Creek	2
San Miguel County	2
Summit County	2
Arapahoe County	1
Archuleta County	1
Brush	1
Cedaredge	1
Clear Creek County	1
Costilla Valley	1
Craig	1
Elk	1
Garfield County	1
Grand County	1
Hayden	1
Harrison Gulch	1
Huerfano County	1
Larimer County	1
Middle Park	1
Minturn	1
Moffat County	1

Location	Number Taken
Monta Vista	1
Morgan County	1
Otero County	1
Pagosa Springs	1
Paonia	1
Pueblo County	1
Rabbit Ears Pass	1
San Juan NF	1
San Juan Wilderness	1
Saquache County	1
Silt	1
Yuma County	1
Unknown location	9

Table III — Typical Elk

Location	Number Taken
Gunnison County	4
Routt County	4
Larimer County	3
Las Animas County	3
Jackson County	2
Summit County	2
White River	2
Almont	1
Baca County	1
Buford County	1
Chaffee County	1
Clear Creek County	1
Costilla County	1
Craig	1
Crow Valley	1
Dark Canyon	1
Grand Lake	1
Granby	1
Hayden	1
Little Cimmaron	1
Moffat County	1
Mount Evans	1
Montrose County	1
Radium	1
San Miguel County	1
Slater	1
Trapper Lake	1

Table IV — Non-Typical Elk

Location	Number Taken
Douglas County	1
Jefferson County	1
Mesa County	1
Routt County	1

Table V — Typical Whitetail Deer

Location	Number Taken
Yuma County	4
Lincoln County	2
Logan County	2
Adams County	1
Bent County	1
Boulder County	1
Crowley County	1
Ebert County	1
Larimer County	1
Otero County	1
Powers	1

Table VI — Non-Typical Whitetail Deer

Location	Number Taken
Yuma County	2
Cheyenne County	1
Kiowa County	1
Logan County	1
Prowers County	1
Pueblo County	1

Table VII — Shiras Moose

County	Number Taken
Jackson County	11
Grand County	2
Larimer County	1
Park County	1

Table VIII — Bighorn Sheep

County	Number Taken
El Paso County	4
Clear Creek County	3
Fremont County	2
Gunnison County	2
Huerfano County	2
Saguache County	2
Cameron Pass	1
Glenwood Springs	1
Lake County	1
Larimer County	1
Las Animas County	1
Park County	1
South Platte Canyon	1
Sugarloaf Mountain	1
Texas Creek	1
Waterton	1
Unknown	1

Your Odds for a Trophy

Table VIX — Desert Bighorn Sheep

Location	Number Taken
Mesa County	1

Table X — Pronghorn

Location	Number Taken
Moffat County	17
Jackson County	10
Weld County	8
Las Animas County	3
Baca County	2
Washington County	2
Bent County	1
Boone	1
Boyero	1
Craig	1
El Paso County	1
Gunnison County	1
Larimer County	1
Limon	1
Logan County	1
Morgan County	1
Otero County	1
Park County	1
Rio Grande County	1
Rocky Ford	1
Saguache County	1
Thatcher	1

Table XI — Rocky Mountain Goat

Location	Number Taken
Park County	1
Clear Creek County	1
Mount Antero	1

Table XII — Cougar

Location	Number Taken
Rio Blanco County	10
Mesa County	8
Archuleta County	6
Eagle County	6
Dolores County	5
Huerfano County	5
San Miguel County	5
Garfield County	4
Montrose County	4
Las Animas County	4
Grand County	3
Larimer County	3
Rio Grande County	3
Canon City	2
Clear Creek County	2
Delta County	2
Douglas County	2
Montezuma County	2
Park County	2
Routt County	2
Meeker	2
Allison	1
Antelope Pass	1
Coal Canyon	1
Conejos County	1
Dotsero	1
Fremont County	1
Grand Junction	1
Moffat County	1
Ouray County	1
Sedalia	1
West Salt Creek	1

Table XIII — Black Bear

Location	Number Taken
Garfield County	7
Mesa County	5
Collbran	3
Ouray County	2
Buffalo Park	1
Delta County	1
Eagle County	1
Gunnison County	1
Hahns Peak	1
Huerfano County	1
Montrose County	1
Paonia	1
Pitken County	1
Rio Blanco County	1
Routt County	1
Sinbad Ridge	1
Snowmass	1
Steamboat Springs	1
Teller County	1
William Fork River	1
Uncompahgre NF	1
Unknown	1

TOP FORESTS

Colorado hunters are an extremely fortunate lot in that they have no shortage of prime big-game habitat at their disposal. There are nearly 18 million acres of public land on the Western Slope on which to hunt and an additional undetermined amount under private ownership.

The data of the 111 typical mule deer, 82 non-typical, 25 typical elk, and 7 non-typical elk collected to feature in this book were carefully scrutinized to determine exactly where the big ones were taken. Hunters who revealed public lands where they took trophy bucks and bulls said that 7 of the 11 Colorado national forests yielded the greatest number of trophies, followed by the Bureau of Land Management, the Southern Ute Indian Reservation, and the U.S. Army Pinon Canyon Maneuver Site. Of the seven national forests mentioned by trophy mule deer owners, the most productive mule deer forest was the Uncompahgre National Forest, followed by the San Juan and Gunnison National Forests. The White River National Forest was the third most productive. Top honors for elk hunters went to Gunnison National Forest, followed by White River and Arapaho National Forests.

BEST YEARS

How many times have you heard the statement, "All the big ones were taken years ago?" Did you ever wonder if there was any truth to that statement?

As a matter of fact, nothing could be further from the truth. First of all, Colorado's deer and elk populations during the first half of this century were so low that, in addition to extremely low harvest figures, there were closed seasons. There was no open deer season from 1913 to 1917, and elk season, which closed in 1903, did not reopen until 1929. In addition, when the seasons did reopen, hunters could only harvest bucks and bulls until 1940. That was the first year of either-sex licenses since the 19th Century. Sure, there are a few deer and elk in the records book from the first 50 years of the 20th Century, but there are *very few*.

Three charts show the years when B&C, P&Y and Longhunter mule deer and elk were taken. Only bucks and bulls that qualify for B&C minimum scores were analyzed as they are the largest, but the big game were listed in all three records books. The decades of the 1960s appears to have been the most productive for deer and elk. This is not happenchance as this data conicides very well with the peak deer harvest figures and the increasing elk harvest figures of the 1960s. The top years for taking a records-book typical mule deer buck during that decade were 1962 with 13, 1963 with 12, and 1965 to 1967 when 12, 14 and 15, respectively, were harvested. Another peak occurred in 1978 when 10 typical mule deer were taken that make "The Book."

Since 1980 when research on the first edition of this book was conducted, a whopping 47 new B&C-quality typical mule deer were entered into all-time records books, including two in 1999. To say only the big ones were taken in the "good old days" is statistically wrong. Prior to 1960 only 39 B&C-quality trophies were recorded in all-time records books from 1933 to 1959.

Less non-typical mule deer are taken that make the records books, but the peak for the highest number of trophy bucks was 1961 and 1962 when each year netted 7 "Booners." As for non-typical mule deer trophies, 33 bucks were harvested from 1980 to 1998 during an 18-year period. Compare that with the 1900 to 1959 time period when only 30 trophy bucks were registered in all-time records books. In the period 1960 to 1979, the total number of non-typical muley trophies recorded was 70. Modern wildlife management practices and hunting regulations have combined to create the best climate for hunting now, not during earlier years.

Elk trophies follow the same pattern as mule deer when it comes to trophy collection. The biggest and the best have been taken by hunters since 1960 and a substantial number of trophies, including those in the non-typical category, have been harvested from 1980 to 1998. As the chart shows, 13 B&C-quality bull elk have been taken and recorded in various records books since 1980, and 22 trophies were recorded from 1960 to 1979. The two best years for trophy elk production were 1993 and 1961 when each year produced 4 B&C bulls. Only 16 elk trophies were documented as being taken from 1850 (prior to Colorado becoming a state) and 1959 – a 109-year time span. If that doesn't convince a modern hunter that the best time is now, nothing will.

A sidenote must be made, though, that prior to 1947 when Boone and Crockett Club established their modern scoring system, few hunters kept heavy-beamed antlers that couldn't be eaten. Hunters in the early 1900s and 1800s needed meat to feed growing families, so we will never know how many outstanding racks were left in the woods and on top of mountains. We'll never know how many B&C-quality racks were thrown into a barn to be eaten by mice, shrunk by the elements, or cut in half to haul out of the woods on horseback. Antlers were also cut up to be used as buttons and other clothing decorations, too. It is intriguing to think of all the ways trophy antlers disappeared during the first half of the 20th Century, never to be measured and added to our chapter calculations. It is also fascinating to imagine how many trophy bucks and bulls remain uncounted that still hang in a deserted barn or hover above a fireplace on a family's livingroom wall. After the publication of the first edition of this book, many outstanding trophies were finally officially measured and entered into various all-time records books to recognize the health of the herds.

Chart I — Typical Mule Deer
Years of Harvest 1980-2000

Year	Number Taken
2000	0
1999	2
1998	0
1997	0
1996	5
1995	5
1994	2
1993	1
1992	1
1991	0
1990	4
1989	4
1988	2
1987	0
1986	2
1985	4
1984	1
1983	0
1982	5
1981	7
1980	2
Total	**47**

Chart II — Typical Mule Deer
Years of Harvest 1960-1979

Year	Number Taken
1979	2
1978	10
1977	5
1976	3
1975	3
1974	7
1973	4
1972	12
1971	4

Your Odds for a Trophy

Year	Number Taken
1970	2
1969	7
1968	9
1967	15
1966	14
1965	12
1964	5
1963	12
1962	13
1961	8
1960	11
Total	**70**

Chart III — Typical Mule Deer
Years of Harvest 1850-1959

Year	Number Taken
1959	5
1958	3
1957	4
1956	3
1955	0
1954	6
1953	1
1952	1
1951	4
1950	2
1949	3
1948	0
1947	2
1946	0
1945	0
1944	1
1943	1
1942-1938	0
1937	1
1936	0
1935	0
1934	1
1933	1
1850-1932	0
Total	**39**

Chart IV — Non-Typical Mule Deer
Years of Harvest 1980-2000

Year	Number Taken
2000	0
1999	0
1998	1
1997	2

Year	Number Taken
1996	3
1995	2
1994	4
1993	0
1992	1
1991	1
1990	0
1989	1
1988	3
1987	2
1986	3
1985	0
1984	2
1983	1
1982	1
1981	4
1980	2
Total	**33**

Chart V — Non-Typical Mule Deer
Years of Harvest 1960-1979

Year	Number Taken
1979	2
1978	5
1977	1
1976	3
1975	1
1974	3
1973	3
1972	2
1971	0
1970	6
1969	4
1968	0
1967	7
1966	4
1965	2
1964	1
1963	5
1962	7
1963	5
1962	7
1961	7
1960	6
Total	**70**

Chart VI — Non-Typical Mule Deer
Years of Harvest 1850-1959

Year	Number Taken
1959	2
1958	3
1957	0
1956	3
1955	2
1954	2
1953	0
1952	1
1951	1
1950	0
1949	2
1948	0
1947	1
1946	0
1945	1
1942-1944	0
1941	2
1940	0
1939	1
1938	0
1937	0
1936	1
1935	0
1934	1
1933	0
1932	1
1931	0
1930	2
1929	0
1928	1
1927	1
1926	1
1925-1918	0
1917	1
1916-1850	0
Total	**30**

Chart VII — Typical and Non-Typical Elk
Years of Harvest 1980-2000

Year	Number Taken
2000	0
1999	0
1998	2
1997	0
1996	1
1995	0

Year	Number Taken
1994	2
1993	4
1992	1
1991	1
1990-1988	0
1987	1
1986	1
1985-1980	0
Total	**13**

Chart VIII — Typical and Non-Typical Elk
Years of Harvest 1960-1979

Year	Number Taken
1979-1975	0
1974	2
1973	1
1972	3
1971	0
1970	1
1969	1
1968	0
1967	3
1966	3
1965	0
1964	1
1963	2
1962	0
1961	4
1960	1
Total	**22**

Chart IX — Typical and Non-Typical Elk
Years of Harvest 1850-1959

Year	Number Taken
1959	1
1958	0
1957	2
1956	0
1955	0
1954	2
1953	3
1952	0
1951	0
1950	0
1949	1
1948-1940	0
1939	1
1938	0
1937	0
1936	1
1935-1932	0
1931-1919	0
1918	1
1917-1907	0
1906	1
1905-1900	0
1899	1
1898-1891	0
1890	1
1889-1851	0
1850	1
Total	**16**

WHERE TO GO TO FIND THE BIG ONES

Only a handful of trophy animals were identified by contributors to this book as coming from a national forest or other public land, which is not to say more did come from public lands but are not documented in hunting stories and records keeping programs. Of the trophies identified by hunters and trophy owners as taken on public lands, Uncompahgre National Forest is the king producer of B&C, P&Y and Longhunter-quality racks.

Table XIV — Distribution of Boone and Crockett Trophies by Land Ownership
Typical and Non-Typical Mule Deer

Landowner	Typical	Non-Typical	Total
Uncompahgre National Forest	16	5	21
San Juan National Forest	14	1	15
Gunnison National Forest	8	7	15
White River National Forest	8	4	12
Grand Mesa National Forest	3	0	3
Routt National Forest	1	2	3
Rio Grande National Forest	0	2	2
Total	**50**	**21**	**71**
Other Landowners			
Private	22	10	32
Bureau of Land Management	0	3	3
Southern Ute Indian Reservation	0	6	6
U.S. Army Pinon Maneuver Site	1	0	1
Total	**23**	**19**	**42**
Typical and Non-Typical Elk			
Gunnison National Forest	4	0	4
White River National Forest	3	0	3
Arapaho National Forest	3	0	3
Routt National Forest	2	0	2
San Isabel National Forest	1	0	1
Uncompahgre National Forest	1	0	1
Other Landowners			
Private	15	7	
Unknown	2	0	
Total			**37**

Note: In the last edition of *Colorado's Biggest Bucks and Bulls*, the non-typical elk category did not exist in records books. The non-typical elk category was established in 1986 in time for the 10th Edition of *Records of North American Big Game*, that was published in 1993.

In all actuality, it is a fact that big-game trophies taken in the 1990s or uncovered from decades of storage and hiding will be entered into future editions of B&C, P&Y and Longhunter records books. After all, there is generally a time lag of several years from the time a trophy is taken until it is finally accepted in the records archives programs.

The future of Colorado big-game populations are strong and growing, even though hunters find growing restrictions on the application of hunting permits as demand for those permits continues to rise. Colorado will continue to lead North American states and provinces in its production of not only outstanding mule deer trophies but other trophies in the whitetail deer, elk, moose, bighorn sheep, pronghorn, black bear, cougar, and Rocky Mountain goat categories. Whether it is you the reader, one of your best hunting companions, or just some other lucky hunter you don't know, we all have the satisfaction of knowing there are still some big animals out there, and we are lucky enough to still have the opportunity to hunt them.

— Chapter XIV —
Boone and Crockett Club Official Score Charts

ENTRY AFFIDAVIT
For All Hunter-Taken Trophies

HUNTER'S NAME (please print)

CATEGORY

SCORE

For the purpose of entry into the Boone and Crockett Club's® records, North American big game harvested by the use of the following methods or under the following conditions are ineligible:

I. Spotting or herding game from the air, followed by landing in its vicinity for the purpose of pursuit and shooting;

II. Herding or chasing with the aid of any motorized equipment;

III. Use of electronic communication devices, artificial lighting, or electronic light intensifying devices;

IV. Confined by artificial barriers, including escape-proof fenced enclosures;

V. Transplanted for the purpose of commercial shooting;

VI. By the use of traps or pharmaceuticals;

VII. While swimming, helpless in deep snow, or helpless in any other natural or artificial medium;

VIII. On another hunter's license;

IX. Not in full compliance with the game laws or regulations of the federal government or of any state, province, territory, or tribal council on reservations or tribal lands;

Please answer the following questions only if the trophy in question is a bear, cougar or jaguar.

Were dogs used in conjunction with the pursuit and harvest of this animal? ☐ Yes   ☐ No

If the answer to the above question is yes, answer the following statements:

1. I was present on the hunt at the times the dogs were released to pursue this animal. ☐ True ☐ False

2. If electronic collars were attached to any of the dogs, receivers were not used to harvest this animal. ☐ True ☐ False

To the best of my knowledge the answers to the above statements are true. If the answer to either #1 or #2 above is false, please explain on a separate sheet.

I certify that the trophy scored on this chart was not taken in violation of the conditions listed above. In signing this statement, I understand that if the information provided on this entry is found to be misrepresented or fraudulent in any respect, it will not be accepted into the Awards Program and 1) all of my prior entries are subject to deletion from future editions of *Records of North American Big Game* 2) future entries may not be accepted.

FAIR CHASE, as defined by the Boone and Crockett Club®, is the ethical, sportsmanlike and lawful pursuit and taking of any free-ranging wild, native North American big game animal in a manner that does not give the hunter an improper advantage over such game animals.

The Boone and Crockett Club® may exclude the entry of any animal that it deems to have been taken in an unethical manner or under conditions deemed inappropriate by the Club.

Date: _____   Signature of Hunter: _____
(Signature must be witnessed by an Official Measurer or a Notary Public.)

Date: _____   Signature of Notary or Official Measurer: _____

Records of
North American
Big Game

250 Station Drive
Missoula, MT 59801
(406) 542-1888

BOONE AND CROCKETT CLUB®
OFFICIAL SCORING SYSTEM FOR NORTH AMERICAN BIG GAME TROPHIES

TYPICAL MULE DEER AND BLACKTAIL DEER

MINIMUM SCORES	AWARDS	ALL-TIME
mule deer	180	190
Columbia blacktail	125	135
Sitka blacktail	100	108

KIND OF DEER (check one)
☐ mule deer
☐ Columbia blacktail
☐ Sitka blacktail

Detail of Point Measurement

Abnormal Points	
Right Antler	Left Antler
SUBTOTALS	
TOTAL TO E	

SEE OTHER SIDE FOR INSTRUCTIONS				COLUMN 1	COLUMN 2	COLUMN 3	COLUMN 4
A. No. Points on Right Antler		No. Points on Left Antler		Spread Credit	Right Antler	Left Antler	Difference
B. Tip to Tip Spread		C. Greatest Spread					
D. Inside Spread of Main Beams		SPREAD CREDIT MAY EQUAL BUT NOT EXCEED LONGER MAIN BEAM					
E. Total of Lengths of Abnormal Points							
F. Length of Main Beam							
G-1. Length of First Point, If Present							
G-2. Length of Second Point							
G-3. Length of Third Point, If Present							
G-4. Length of Fourth Point, If Present							
H-1. Circumference at Smallest Place Between Burr and First Point							
H-2. Circumference at Smallest Place Between First and Second Points							
H-3. Circumference at Smallest Place Between Main Beam and Third Point							
H-4. Circumference at Smallest Place Between Second and Fourth Points							
			TOTALS				

ADD	Column 1		Exact Locality Where Killed:
	Column 2		Date Killed: Hunter:
	Column 3		Owner: Telephone #:
	Subtotal		Owner's Address:
SUBTRACT Column 4			Guide's Name and Address:
FINAL SCORE			Remarks: (Mention Any Abnormalities or Unique Qualities)

COPYRIGHT © 2000 BY BOONE AND CROCKETT CLUB®

Score Charts

Records of
North American
Big Game

250 Station Drive
Missoula, MT 59801
(406) 542-1888

BOONE AND CROCKETT CLUB®
OFFICIAL SCORING SYSTEM FOR NORTH AMERICAN BIG GAME TROPHIES
NON-TYPICAL MULE DEER

MINIMUM SCORES
AWARDS ALL-TIME
  215   230

Abnormal Points	
Right Antler	Left Antler
SUBTOTALS	
E. TOTAL	

SEE OTHER SIDE FOR INSTRUCTIONS				COLUMN 1	COLUMN 2	COLUMN 3	COLUMN 4
A. No. Points on Right Antler		No. Points on Left Antler		Spread Credit	Right Antler	Left Antler	Difference
B. Tip to Tip Spread		C. Greatest Spread					
D. Inside Spread of Main Beams		SPREAD CREDIT MAY EQUAL BUT NOT EXCEED LONGER MAIN BEAM					
F. Length of Main Beam							
G-1. Length of First Point, If Present							
G-2. Length of Second Point							
G-3. Length of Third Point, If Present							
G-4. Length of Fourth Point, If Present							
H-1. Circumference at Smallest Place Between Burr and First Point							
H-2. Circumference at Smallest Place Between First and Second Points							
H-3. Circumference at Smallest Place Between Main Beam and Third Point							
H-4. Circumference at Smallest Place Between Second and Fourth Points							
			TOTALS				

ADD	Column 1		Exact Locality Where Killed:
	Column 2		Date Killed: Hunter:
	Column 3		Owner: Telephone #:
	Subtotal		Owner's Address:
	SUBTRACT Column 4		Guide's Name and Address:
	Subtotal		Remarks: (Mention Any Abnormalities or Unique Qualities)
	ADD Line E Total		
	FINAL SCORE		

COPYRIGHT © 2000 BY BOONE AND CROCKETT CLUB®

Colorado's Biggest Bucks and Bulls

Records of North American Big Game

250 Station Drive
Missoula, MT 59801
(406) 542-1888

BOONE AND CROCKETT CLUB®
OFFICIAL SCORING SYSTEM FOR NORTH AMERICAN BIG GAME TROPHIES

MINIMUM SCORES

	AWARDS	ALL-TIME
whitetail	160	170
Coues'	100	110

TYPICAL WHITETAIL AND COUES' DEER

KIND OF DEER (check one)
☐ whitetail
☐ Coues'

Abnormal Points	
Right Antler	Left Antler

SUBTOTALS	
TOTAL TO E	

SEE OTHER SIDE FOR INSTRUCTIONS

				COLUMN 1	COLUMN 2	COLUMN 3	COLUMN 4
A. No. Points on Right Antler		No. Points on Left Antler		Spread Credit	Right Antler	Left Antler	Difference
B. Tip to Tip Spread		C. Greatest Spread					
D. Inside Spread of Main Beams		SPREAD CREDIT MAY EQUAL BUT NOT EXCEED LONGER MAIN BEAM					
E. Total of Lengths of Abnormal Points							
F. Length of Main Beam							
G-1. Length of First Point							
G-2. Length of Second Point							
G-3. Length of Third Point							
G-4. Length of Fourth Point, If Present							
G-5. Length of Fifth Point, If Present							
G-6. Length of Sixth Point, If Present							
G-7. Length of Seventh Point, If Present							
H-1. Circumference at Smallest Place Between Burr and First Point							
H-2. Circumference at Smallest Place Between First and Second Points							
H-3. Circumference at Smallest Place Between Second and Third Points							
H-4. Circumference at Smallest Place Between Third and Fourth Points							
			TOTALS				

ADD	Column 1	
	Column 2	
	Column 3	
Subtotal		
SUBTRACT Column 4		
FINAL SCORE		

Exact Locality Where Killed:

Date Killed: Hunter:

Owner: Telephone #:

Owner's Address:

Guide's Name and Address:

Remarks: (Mention Any Abnormalities or Unique Qualities)

COPYRIGHT © 2000 BY BOONE AND CROCKETT CLUB®

Score Charts

Records of North American Big Game

250 Station Drive
Missoula, MT 59801
(406) 542-1888

BOONE AND CROCKETT CLUB®
OFFICIAL SCORING SYSTEM FOR NORTH AMERICAN BIG GAME TROPHIES

MINIMUM SCORES

	AWARDS	ALL-TIME
whitetail	185	195
Coues'	105	120

NON-TYPICAL WHITETAIL AND COUES' DEER

KIND OF DEER (check one)
☐ whitetail
☐ Coues'

Abnormal Points	
Right Antler	Left Antler
SUBTOTALS	
E. TOTAL	

Detail of Point Measurement

SEE OTHER SIDE FOR INSTRUCTIONS				COLUMN 1	COLUMN 2	COLUMN 3	COLUMN 4
A. No. Points on Right Antler		No. Points on Left Antler		Spread Credit	Right Antler	Left Antler	Difference
B. Tip to Tip Spread		C. Greatest Spread					
D. Inside Spread of Main Beams		SPREAD CREDIT MAY EQUAL BUT NOT EXCEED LONGER MAIN BEAM					
F. Length of Main Beam							
G-1. Length of First Point							
G-2. Length of Second Point							
G-3. Length of Third Point							
G-4. Length of Fourth Point, If Present							
G-5. Length of Fifth Point, If Present							
G-6. Length of Sixth Point, If Present							
G-7. Length of Seventh Point, If Present							
H-1. Circumference at Smallest Place Between Burr and First Point							
H-2. Circumference at Smallest Place Between First and Second Points							
H-3. Circumference at Smallest Place Between Second and Third Points							
H-4. Circumference at Smallest Place Between Third and Fourth Points							
			TOTALS				

ADD	Column 1	
	Column 2	
	Column 3	
	Subtotal	
SUBTRACT Column 4		
	Subtotal	
	ADD Line E Total	
	FINAL SCORE	

Exact Locality Where Killed:
Date Killed: Hunter:
Owner: Telephone #:
Owner's Address:
Guide's Name and Address:
Remarks: (Mention Any Abnormalities or Unique Qualities)

COPYRIGHT © 2000 BY BOONE AND CROCKETT CLUB®

Colorado's Biggest Bucks and Bulls

Records of North American Big Game

250 Station Drive
Missoula, MT 59801
(406) 542-1888

BOONE AND CROCKETT CLUB®
OFFICIAL SCORING SYSTEM FOR NORTH AMERICAN BIG GAME TROPHIES

MINIMUM SCORES
AWARDS 360
ALL-TIME 375

TYPICAL AMERICAN ELK (WAPITI)

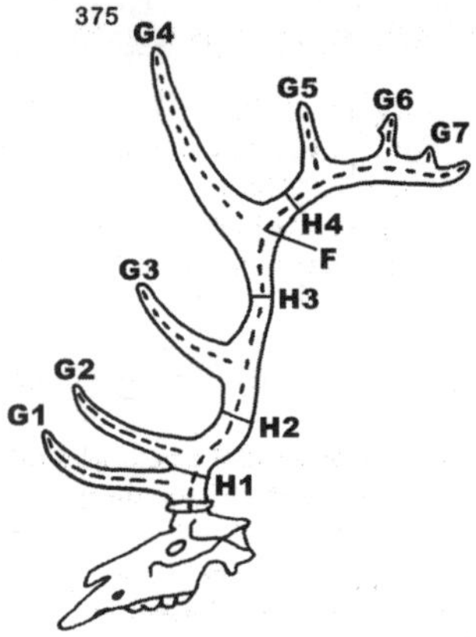

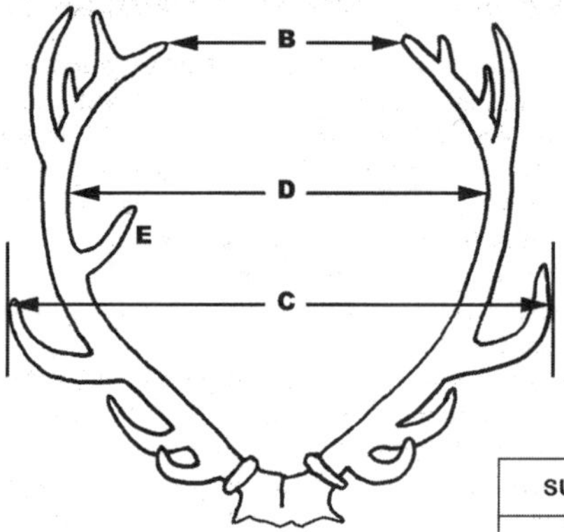

Detail of Point Measurement

Abnormal Points	
Right Antler	Left Antler
SUBTOTALS	
TOTAL TO E	

SEE OTHER SIDE FOR INSTRUCTIONS				COLUMN 1	COLUMN 2	COLUMN 3	COLUMN 4
A. No. Points on Right Antler		No. Points on Left Antler		Spread Credit	Right Antler	Left Antler	Difference
B. Tip to Tip Spread		C. Greatest Spread					
D. Inside Spread of Main Beams		SPREAD CREDIT MAY EQUAL BUT NOT EXCEED LONGER MAIN BEAM					
E. Total of Lengths of Abnormal Points							
F. Length of Main Beam							
G-1. Length of First Point							
G-2. Length of Second Point							
G-3. Length of Third Point							
G-4. Length of Fourth Point							
G-5. Length of Fifth Point							
G-6. Length of Sixth Point, If Present							
G-7. Length of Seventh Point, If Present							
H-1. Circumference at Smallest Place Between First and Second Points							
H-2. Circumference at Smallest Place Between Second and Third Points							
H-3. Circumference at Smallest Place Between Third and Fourth Points							
H-4. Circumference at Smallest Place Between Fourth and Fifth Points							
			TOTALS				

ADD	Column 1		Exact Locality Where Killed:
	Column 2		Date Killed: Hunter:
	Column 3		Owner: Telephone #:
Subtotal			Owner's Address:
SUBTRACT Column 4			Guide's Name and Address:
FINAL SCORE			Remarks: (Mention Any Abnormalities or Unique Qualities)

COPYRIGHT © 2000 BY BOONE AND CROCKETT CLUB®

Records of North American Big Game

250 Station Drive
Missoula, MT 59801
(406) 542-1888

BOONE AND CROCKETT CLUB®
OFFICIAL SCORING SYSTEM FOR NORTH AMERICAN BIG GAME TROPHIES

MINIMUM SCORES
AWARDS 385
ALL-TIME 385

NON-TYPICAL AMERICAN ELK (WAPITI)

Abnormal Points	
Right Antler	Left Antler
SUBTOTALS	
E. TOTAL	

SEE OTHER SIDE FOR INSTRUCTIONS

		COLUMN 1 Spread Credit	COLUMN 2 Right Antler	COLUMN 3 Left Antler	COLUMN 4 Difference
A. No. Points on Right Antler	No. Points on Left Antler				
B. Tip to Tip Spread	C. Greatest Spread				
D. Inside Spread of Main Beams	SPREAD CREDIT MAY EQUAL BUT NOT EXCEED LONGER MAIN BEAM				
F. Length of Main Beam					
G-1. Length of First Point					
G-2. Length of Second Point					
G-3. Length of Third Point					
G-4. Length of Fourth Point					
G-5. Length of Fifth Point					
G-6. Length of Sixth Point, If Present					
G-7. Length of Seventh Point, If Present					
H-1. Circumference at Smallest Place Between First and Second Points					
H-2. Circumference at Smallest Place Between Second and Third Points					
H-3. Circumference at Smallest Place Between Third and Fourth Points					
H-4. Circumference at Smallest Place Between Fourth and Fifth Points					
	TOTALS				

ADD	Column 1	
	Column 2	
	Column 3	
	Subtotal	
SUBTRACT Column 4		
	Subtotal	
	Add Line E Total	
	FINAL SCORE	

Exact Locality Where Killed:

Date Killed: Hunter:

Owner: Telephone #:

Owner's Address:

Guide's Name and Address:

Remarks: (Mention Any Abnormalities or Unique Qualities)

COPYRIGHT © 2000 BY BOONE AND CROCKETT CLUB®

Records of North American Big Game

250 Station Drive
Missoula, MT 59801
(406) 542-1888

BOONE AND CROCKETT CLUB®
OFFICIAL SCORING SYSTEM FOR NORTH AMERICAN BIG GAME TROPHIES

MOOSE

	MINIMUM SCORES	
	AWARDS	ALL-TIME
Canada	185	195
Alaska-Yukon	210	224
Wyoming	140	155

KIND OF MOOSE (check one)
☐ Canada
☐ Alaska-Yukon
☐ Wyoming

Detail of Point Measurement

	Abnormal Points	
	Right Antler	Left Antler
NUMBER OF POINTS		
TOTAL TO B.		

SEE OTHER SIDE FOR INSTRUCTIONS	COLUMN 1	COLUMN 2	COLUMN 3	COLUMN 4
A. Greatest Spread		Right Antler	Left Antler	Difference
B. Number of Abnormal Points on Both Antlers				
C. Number of Normal Points				
D. Width of Palm				
E. Length of Palm Including Brow Palm				
F. Circumference of Beam at Smallest Place				
TOTALS				

ADD	Column 1		Exact Locality Where Killed:
	Column 2		Date Killed: Hunter:
	Column 3		Owner: Telephone #:
Subtotal			Owner's Address:
SUBTRACT Column 4			Guide's Name and Address:
FINAL SCORE			Remarks: (Mention Any Abnormalities or Unique Qualities)

I, _____ , certify that I have measured this trophy on _____
         PRINT NAME   MM/DD/YYYY

at _____
      STREET ADDRESS   CITY   STATE/PROVINCE

and that these measurements and data are, to the best of my knowledge and belief, made in accordance with the instructions given.

Witness: _____ Signature: _____ I.D. Number ☐☐☐☐
                                              B&C OFFICIAL MEASURER

COPYRIGHT © 2000 BY BOONE AND CROCKETT CLUB®

Score Charts

Records of North American Big Game

250 Station Drive
Missoula, MT 59801
(406) 542-1888

BOONE AND CROCKETT CLUB®
OFFICIAL SCORING SYSTEM FOR NORTH AMERICAN BIG GAME TROPHIES

SHEEP

MINIMUM SCORES	
	AWARDS ALL-TIME
bighorn	175 180
desert	165 168
Dall's	160 170
Stone's	165 170

KIND OF SHEEP (check one)
☐ bighorn
☐ desert
☐ Dall's
☐ Stone's

PLUG NUMBER _____

Measure to a Point in Line With Horn Tip

SEE OTHER SIDE FOR INSTRUCTIONS		COLUMN 1	COLUMN 2	COLUMN 3
		Right Horn	Left Horn	Difference
A. Greatest Spread (Is Often Tip to Tip Spread)				
B. Tip to Tip Spread				
C. Length of Horn				
D-1. Circumference of Base				
D-2. Circumference at First Quarter				
D-3. Circumference at Second Quarter				
D-4. Circumference at Third Quarter				
	TOTALS			

ADD	Column 1		Exact Locality Where Killed:
	Column 2		Date Killed: Hunter:
	Subtotal		Owner: Telephone #:
SUBTRACT Column 3			Owner's Address:
FINAL SCORE			Guide's Name and Address:
			Remarks: (Mention Any Abnormalities or Unique Qualities)

I, _____, certify that I have measured this trophy on _____
    PRINT NAME   MM/DD/YYYY

at _____
   STREET ADDRESS   CITY   STATE/PROVINCE

and that these measurements and data are, to the best of my knowledge and belief, made in accordance with the instructions given.

Witness: _____ Signature: _____ I.D. Number ☐☐☐
                                      B&C OFFICIAL MEASURER

COPYRIGHT © 2000 BY BOONE AND CROCKETT CLUB®

Records of North American Big Game

250 Station Drive
Missoula, MT 59801
(406) 542-1888

BOONE AND CROCKETT CLUB®
OFFICIAL SCORING SYSTEM FOR NORTH AMERICAN BIG GAME TROPHIES

ROCKY MOUNTAIN GOAT

MINIMUM SCORES	
AWARDS	ALL-TIME
47	50

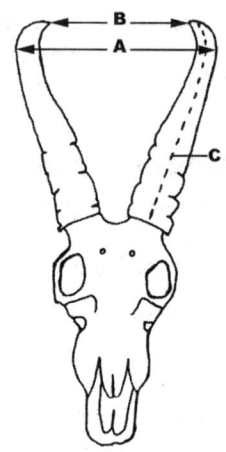
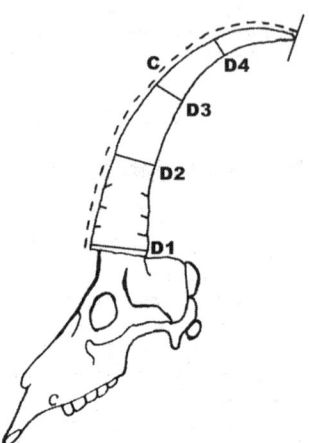

SEE OTHER SIDE FOR INSTRUCTIONS		COLUMN 1 Right Horn	COLUMN 2 Left Horn	COLUMN 3 Difference
A. Greatest Spread				
B. Tip to Tip Spread				
C. Length of Horn				
D-1. Circumference of Base				
D-2. Circumference at First Quarter				
D-3. Circumference at Second Quarter				
D-4. Circumference at Third Quarter				
TOTALS				

ADD	Column 1		Exact Locality Where Killed:
	Column 2		Date Killed: Hunter:
Subtotal			Owner: Telephone #:
SUBTRACT Column 3			Owner's Address:
FINAL SCORE			Guide's Name and Address:
			Remarks: (Mention Any Abnormalities or Unique Qualities)

I, _____ , certify that I have measured this trophy on _____
     PRINT NAME   MM/DD/YYYY

at _____
        STREET ADDRESS   CITY   STATE/PROVINCE

and that these measurements and data are, to the best of my knowledge and belief, made in accordance with the instructions given.

Witness: _____ Signature: _____ I.D. Number ____
                                        B&C OFFICIAL MEASURER

COPYRIGHT © 2000 BY BOONE AND CROCKETT CLUB®

Score Charts

Records of North American Big Game

250 Station Drive
Missoula, MT 59801
(406) 542-1888

BOONE AND CROCKETT CLUB®
OFFICIAL SCORING SYSTEM FOR NORTH AMERICAN BIG GAME TROPHIES
PRONGHORN

MINIMUM SCORES
AWARDS ALL-TIME
80   82

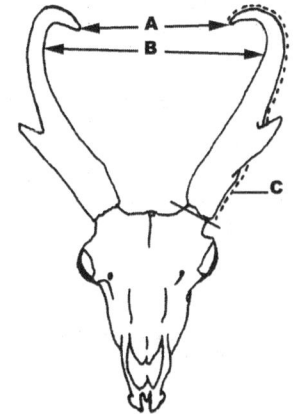
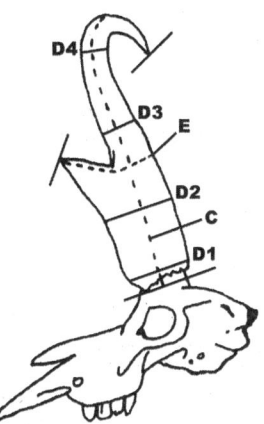

SEE OTHER SIDE FOR INSTRUCTIONS		COLUMN 1	COLUMN 2	COLUMN 3
A. Tip to Tip Spread		Right Horn	Left Horn	Difference
B. Inside Spread of Main Beams				
C. Length of Horn				
D-1. Circumference of Base				
D-2. Circumference at First Quarter				
D-3. Circumference at Second Quarter				
D-4. Circumference at Third Quarter				
E. Length of Prong				
	TOTALS			

ADD	Column 1		Exact Locality Where Killed:		
	Column 2		Date Killed:	Hunter:	
Subtotal			Owner:	Telephone #:	
SUBTRACT Column 3			Owner's Address:		
FINAL SCORE			Guide's Name and Address:		
			Remarks: (Mention Any Abnormalities or Unique Qualities)		

I, _____ , certify that I have measured this trophy on _____
PRINT NAME   MM/DD/YYYY

at _____
STREET ADDRESS   CITY   STATE/PROVINCE

and that these measurements and data are, to the best of my knowledge and belief, made in accordance with the instructions given.

Witness: _____ Signature: _____ I.D. Number ☐☐☐
                                                      B&C OFFICIAL MEASURER

COPYRIGHT © 2000 BY BOONE AND CROCKETT CLUB®

Records of North American Big Game

250 Station Drive
Missoula, MT 59801
(406) 542-1888

BOONE AND CROCKETT CLUB®
OFFICIAL SCORING SYSTEM FOR NORTH AMERICAN BIG GAME TROPHIES

COUGAR AND JAGUAR

MINIMUM SCORES

	AWARDS	ALL-TIME
cougar	14 - 8/16	15
jaguar	14 - 8/16	14 - 8/16

KIND OF CAT (check one)
☐ cougar
☐ jaguar

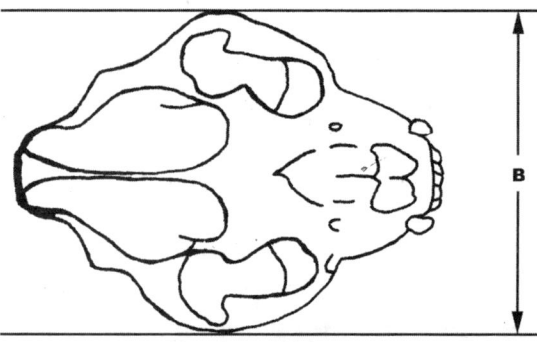

SEE OTHER SIDE FOR INSTRUCTIONS	MEASUREMENTS
A. Greatest Length Without Lower Jaw	
B. Greatest Width	
FINAL SCORE	

Exact Locality Where Killed:

Date Killed: Hunter:

Owner: Telephone #:

Owner's Address:

Guide's Name and Address:

Remarks: (Mention Any Abnormalities or Unique Qualities)

I, _____ , certify that I have measured this trophy on _____
         PRINT NAME   MM/DD/YYYYY

at _____
      STREET ADDRESS   CITY   STATE/PROVINCE

and that these measurements and data are, to the best of my knowledge and belief, made in accordance with the instructions given.

Witness: _____ Signature: _____ I.D. Number
                                         B&C OFFICIAL MEASURER

COPYRIGHT © 2000 BY BOONE AND CROCKETT CLUB®

Score Charts

Records of North American Big Game

250 Station Drive
Missoula, MT 59801
(406) 542-1888

BOONE AND CROCKETT CLUB®
OFFICIAL SCORING SYSTEM FOR NORTH AMERICAN BIG GAME TROPHIES

BEAR

	MINIMUM SCORES	
	AWARDS	ALL-TIME
black bear	20	21
grizzly bear	23	24
Alaska brown bear	26	28
polar bear	27	27

KIND OF BEAR (check one)
☐ black bear
☐ grizzly
☐ Alaska brown bear
☐ polar

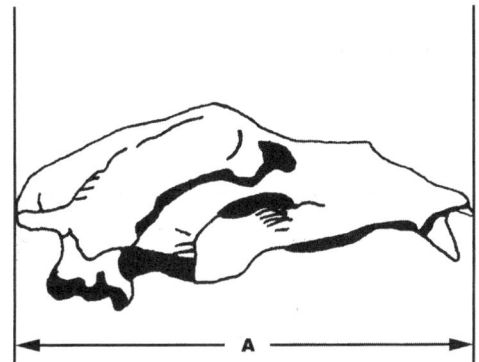
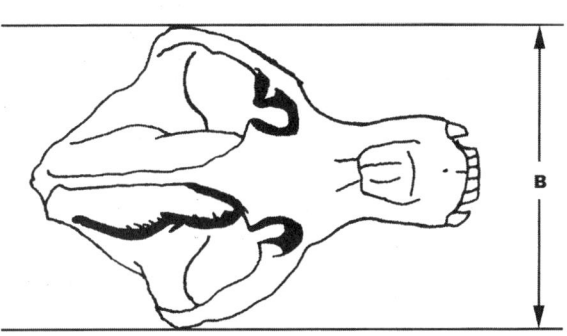

SEE OTHER SIDE FOR INSTRUCTIONS	MEASUREMENTS
A. Greatest Length Without Lower Jaw	
B. Greatest Width	
FINAL SCORE	

Exact Locality Where Killed:

Date Killed: Hunter:

Owner: Telephone #:

Owner's Address:

Guide's Name and Address:

Remarks: (Mention Any Abnormalities or Unique Qualities)

I, _____ , certify that I have measured this trophy on _____
   PRINT NAME   MM/DD/YYYY

at _____
   STREET ADDRESS   CITY   STATE/PROVINCE

and that these measurements and data are, to the best of my knowledge and belief, made in accordance with the instructions given.

Witness:_____ Signature:_____ I.D. Number ☐☐☐
                                           B&C OFFICIAL MEASURER

COPYRIGHT © 2000 BY BOONE AND CROCKETT CLUB®

A black bear in Colorado climbs with ease. Black bear hunters in 1999 totaled 11,299 with a harvest success rate of 9 percent.

— Chapter XV —
Photographs of Special Interest

John Robertson found this set of locked mule deer antlers in 1945 on Castle Peak, north of Eagle. He loaned the antlers to someone who took them to an outdoor show where they were rough measured with scores of more than 220 points each.

A castrated buck was photographed by Paul F. Gilbert who worked for the Colorado Division of Wildlife for many years before his retirement. He noted on the back of the photographs that if a buck is castrated before antler growth, it will never have antlers. If the buck is castrated after antler growth, the antlers will never be shed and will continue to grow in odd formations.

Marvin Shepard took this unusual and unmeasurable non-typical bull elk in Mesa County on Douglas Pass.

Cactus buck in the lobby of the Meeker Hotel and Café.

A badly deformed cactus buck is held by Allan Curtis Haskill prior to 1905. Haskill and his wife Auguste moved to Montrose in 1881 but ill health required him to move to a lower altitude in 1905. The Haskills lived on a farm at the foot of Haskill Hill. Their home was a stopping place for freighting teams and stagecoaches on route from Telluride to Montrose. Injuries to the head, atrophy of testicles or natural castration have been known to cause odd antler growth.

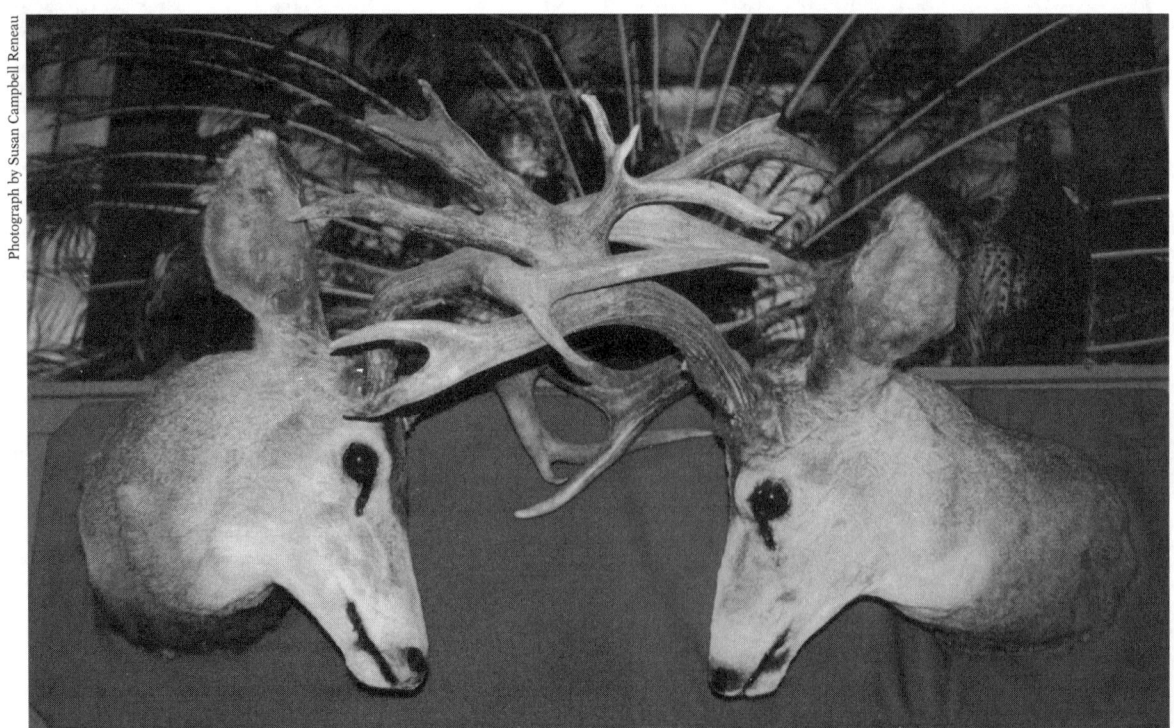

Two mule deer remain locked in combat for all eternity above the front door of Howard's Sporting Goods Store on Main Street in Cortez, Colorado.

Photographs of Special Interest

This impressive antler arch was seen by travelers and residents six miles north of Almont, Colorado, for many years until it was torn down in the 1980s.

On display at Traders Rendezvous store in Gunnison are several sets of locked mule deer antlers, including these two sets. Ralph Brown of Montrose found a set of locked antlers in 1952 and Randy Clark, owner of Traders Rendezvous, bought them in 1990. The biggest set of locked antlers on display at the store were found in Grand Junction in 1949 and purchased by Randy in the 1990s.

Marvin J. Gardner, wildlife technician III for the Tamarack State Wildlife Area for 31 years from 1967 to 1998, is shown with a pair of whitetail bucks around 1968 with locked antlers in the South Platte river bottom. The buck on the left is still alive and totally exhausted while the buck on the right has been partially consumed by coyotes and dead. A hunter on the wildlife area saw the locked pair and went to get Marvin. Marvin, known as Marv to friends, said the live buck was weak but eventually strong enough to bound off into the underbrush after the antlers from the dead deer were sawed. The Tamarack State Wildlife Area has 10,500 acres of prime deer habitat in eastern Colorado, especially for whitetail deer.

The shoulder mount of Henry Zietz's 2,000-pound bison is delivered to The Buckhorn Exchange in Denver in 1978 as the restaurant was redecorated. Henry took this massive bull bison in the 1930s. The bull still hangs in the restaurant today.

Three avid Colorado hunters pose for the cameras at the turn of the 20th Century. From left to right we see Henry Zietz, his father H. Shorty Zietz, Sr., and Henry's cousin Chester Zietz in 1912. Shorty Zietz founded Denver's famous restaurant and saloon, The Buckhorn Exchange, in 1893, and his son Henry took over management of the establishment after his father died in 1949.

Gerald Balciar stands on scaffolding as he assembles his impressive 18-foot bronze bugling elk sculpture in the early 1980s in Monument, Colorado. The finished sculpture greeted travelers along Interstate 25 in Monument until its move to Westminster, Colorado.

Balciar's 18-foot bronze of a bugling bull elk, called Challenge, greets all who visit the Westminster Sculpture Garden at City Hall in Westminster, Colorado.

A successful pronghorn hunt is documented in this early 1900s photograph on the JOD Ranch outside of Aroyo, Colorado.

An unknown woman and Mrs. Allan Grant Wallihan, right, stand beside a mule deer buck she downed with a single shot. Mr. Wallihan was a renowned wildlife photographer of the late 1800s who extensively photographed wildlife and hunting activities in Colorado. He used his wife as a model in some of his photographs because she loved to hunt.

— Chapter XVI —
Places to Go and Things to See in Colorado

Two views of the Meeker Hotel lobby in the early 1900s. The photograph showing the barbershop was taken in 1904.

MEEKER HOTEL AND CAFÉ

One of the more charming establishments to visit in Colorado is the Meeker Hotel and Café, which first opened in 1896 and continues in business today. The lobby is filled with 29 unique and massive deer and elk mounts as well as other big-game trophies and historical photographs.

In the spring and summer of 1996, Roger Selner and Don Stemler of Trophy Show Productions, Inc. visited the Meeker Hotel and Café and the town of Meeker to uncover some of the biggest Colorado bucks and bulls ever taken. Roger and Don remembered the hotel from visits during hunting trips in the 1960s and 1970s, so they wanted to return to the area. Roger is an official measurer for the Boone and Crockett Club, so he wanted to know what these massive antlers scored. He also hoped to locate trophies for the World Record Elk Tour that was sponsored in 2000 by the *Eastman's Hunting Journal*, Rocky

Mountain Elk Foundation, Realtree Outdoor Products, RedHead/Bass Pro Shops and Yellowstone Country Motors.

The brick Meeker Hotel was built in 1896 with the foundation being laid about June 9 and the final structure near completion on July 15. There was an earlier Meeker Hotel that was made of wood that was built prior to 1887. Billy the Kid signed the register on July 6, 1889, and a photograph exists dating to 1887. Charlie Dunbar and Susan Wright were the original owners of the hotel but when Charlie was shot and killed in a card game a few months after the hotel's opening, Susan joined forces with Simp Harp. She willed the hotel to her brother, Reuban Sanford Ball, before passing away in 1893. Under Ball's ownership, the new brick hotel was built with walls six-bricks thick. About 20,000 bricks were used to construct the new hotel. The east and west wings were added in 1904 and the ground floor of the east wing housed the Strehlke Bros. Drug Store, Dr. Bruner's office and the Colorado Telephone Company. That ground floor wing is now the café. The ground floor of the west wing was at one time a Safeway grocery store and an M&M store. It is now the Fawn Creek Gallery. The ownership of the hotel was transferred from the Ball family to Clarence P. and Lucille Mathis in 1923 and has had a variety of owners ever since. The present owner of the hotel and café is James Ritchie. Theodore Roosevelt stayed at the Meeker Hotel in 1901 while on a cougar hunt when he was governor of New York and the newly elected vice-president of the United States.

The trophies on display at the Meeker Hotel represent the history of hunting in Colorado. There are 16 trophy mule deer bucks, eight bull elk, two pronghorn, one caribou, one moose and one bear on display in the hotel lobby as well as a shed antler chair and numerous historical photographs. For further information about the Meeker Hotel and Café, call them a 970-878-5255 or www.meekerhotel.com.

Photographs by Susan Campbell Reneau

DARRYL'S TAXIDERMY SHOP

A fine mule deer display and collection is open to the public at Darryl's Taxidermy Shop in Grand Junction. Here is a fraction of the bucks on display. Out front visitors see the beginnings of a shed antler arch. Call first to learn of times and days when the shop is open for viewing the collection at (970) 243-2933.

DENVER MUSEUM OF NATURAL HISTORY

The Denver Museum of Natural History has some of the finest big-game and other wildlife dioramas in the world. Here we see (top to bottom) the spring mule deer, winter mule deer, American elk and whitetail deer dioramas. In the winter mule deer diorama, visitors look at the typical mule deer buck that sports the B&C antlers of a deer taken by museum trustee George E. Berger, Jr. in 1934. The antlers have a B&C score of 199-7/8 points. The buck received a Certificate of Merit during the 7th B&C Competition. The exhibits at the Denver Museum of Natural History are worth a trip to Denver.

BUCKHORN EXCHANGE RESTAURANT

Established in 1893 by Henry "Shorty Scout" Zietz, one of Buffalo Bill Cody's scouts, the Buckhorn Exchange at 1000 Osage Street at the corner of 10th Street and Osage in Denver is one of Colorado's most unique restaurants. Now in its 3rd Century of operation, the Buckhorn Exchange is packed with hundreds of big-game trophies, western history memorabilia and one-of-a-kind photographs dating to the 1800s when Shorty rode with Col. William F. "Buffalo Bill" Cody starting at age 12. It was during the years Henry rode with Buffalo Bill that the great Indian leader, Sitting Bull, dubbed him Shorty Scout due to his short stature. Shorty guided Theodore Roosevelt and his hunting party on their pronghorn and buffalo hunt between Glenwood Springs and Meeker and hosted many other celebrities at his popular establishment.

Not long after Shorty Zietz died in 1949, his son, Henry Zietz, Jr. took over its operation along with the help of his family. Henry was an outstanding hunter who collected most of the trophies on display at the restaurant. Three of his trophies from Colorado were entered into the Boone and Crockett Club's records program including a non-typical mule deer scoring 251-1/8 points taken in 1955 in Meeker, a bighorn sheep he picked up in 1947 that scores 180-1/8, and a pronghorn buck taken in 1965 in Boyero with a final score of 83 points. Their photographs are featured elsewhere in this book.

From the time of its founding in the 19th Century, the Buckhorn Exchange catered to cattlemen, miners, railroad builders, silver barons, roustabouts, gamblers, businessmen and women and great and near-great diners. The Buckhorn Exchange holds Colorado liquor license Number One. In 1978 the Zietz family sold the restaurant to a partnership of owners that has taken care to preserve the memorabilia and building that makes this Colorado landmark so special. Information about the Buckhorn Exchange can be found on the Internet at www.buckhorn.com. Their phone number is 303-534-9505.

The Buckhorn Exchange at 1000 Osage Street in Denver, Colorado.

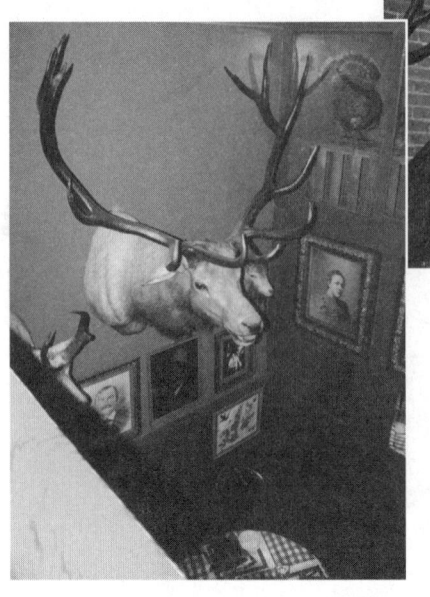

Upstairs at the Buckhorn Exchange the visitor finds a massive bull elk and a bison across from the bar. The 2000-pound bull Henry Zietz, Jr. collected in the 1930s was so heavy that when he tried to haul the meat out by truck, the truck broke down and the meat was spoiled.

TRADERS RENDEZVOUS

Traders Rendezvous is a fascinating store in Gunnison that contains 250 big-game mounts and up to 600 sets of unmounted elk and mule deer antlers. Owner Randy Clark started his collection in 1987 with two mounted heads and 15 sets of deer antlers. His love of antlers began years ago when his father, Harold, was a guide and outfitter. Harold now helps Randy with his business. Randy remembers collecting shed antlers around hunting camp when he was little and the hobby just grew and grew. He now ships antlers to Disney World's Frontier Land and all over the country where antlers and his gift items are in demand. He travels throughout the West to collect antlers of deer and elk. Traders Rendezvous is a place to visit when touring the Gunnison area. For more information, call them at (970) 641-5077 or view their web site at www.tradersrendezvous.com.

The entrance to Traders Rendezvous overwhelms the visitor with mounts, gift items and antlers.

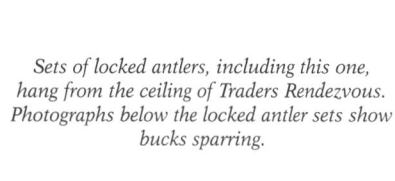

Sets of locked antlers, including this one, hang from the ceiling of Traders Rendezvous. Photographs below the locked antler sets show bucks sparring.

TRADERS OF THE BIGHORN

Canon City is the city where visitors find Traders of the Bighorn, a real western trade company containing collectibles, furs, leather, artwork, antiques, hide tanning, fur buying and much more. Check them out at 402 Royal Gorge Blvd. in Canon City along Highway 50. A wagon of shed antlers graces the front of the store.

THE BUCK STOP

The Buck Stop at 113 Main Street in Montrose, Colorado, is packed with trophy mounts to the delight of hunters.

ERNEST'S TAXIDERMY AND GIFTS

Antler arches, constructed of shed elk and deer antlers, are fairly common in other states, but this arch near Monte Vista is the only known antler arch still in existence in the state. A visitor to Monte Vista will find this arch three miles west of town on Highway 160.

— Chapter XVII —
Big Game Listings from Colorado and Index

To be listed in *COLORADO'S BIGGEST BUCKS AND BULLS and Other Great Colorado Big Game*, trophies need to be officially scored by a Boone and Crockett Club (B&C), Pope and Young Club (P&Y), or Longhunter Program measurer. Each hunter must meet the minimum fair chase and score requirements of the Awards Programs of the B&C. The trophy does not need to be entered into any of the records-keeping programs, but in a majority of cases the trophies in this book are included as the top big game in their categories in one or more of these famous records-keeping programs. Most of the trophies listed in this book are included in the *B&C Records of North American Big Game, 11th Edition* (1999), *P&Y Bowhunting Big Game Records of North America, 5th Edition* (1999), and/or *Longhunter Muzzleloading Big Game Records Book, 3rd Edition* (2000). For detailed measurements of the trophies, purchase copies of the records books from B&C, P&Y and Longhunter Programs. Check the chapter in this book on records-keeping programs in North America for details about ordering their books.

The chart on the following page lists the minimum scores necessary for a big-game animal to be listed in the B&C Awards books that are published once every three years at the end of each Awards Program. The chart also lists the minimum entry score for the B&C all-time records book that is published approximately once every six years at the end of two Awards Programs. The number of stories and photographs of each big game category from Colorado are also listed.

As for the big-game listings, all animals that qualify for this book are listed with the largest scores listed first. Only the final score, county where the animal was taken, year of kill, the hunter and the trophy owner are listed with the page number in the book where the photograph or story can be found. In the listings, PU represents "Picked Up" to a year listed; PR represents "Prior to" the year listed; NF represents "National Forest"; and IR represents Indian Reservation, especially as it relates to the Southern Ute Indian Reservation.

Table XV
MINIMUM ENTRY SCORES FOR AWARDS AND ALL-TIME LISTINGS IN THIS BOOK
Big Game of Colorado Taken by Modern Rifle and Pistol, Bow and Arrow, and Muzzleloader Firearms

Big-Game Species	Awards	All-Time
Typical Mule Deer	180	190
Non-Typical Mule Deer	215	230
Typical Whitetail Deer	160	170
Non-Typical Whitetail Deer	185	195
Typical American or Yellowstone Elk	360	375
Non-Typical American or Yellowstone Elk	385	385
Shiras or Wyoming Moose	140	155
Bighorn Sheep	175	180
Desert Bighorn Sheep	165	168
Rocky Mountain Goat	47	50
Pronghorn	80	82
Cougar or Mountain Lion	14-8/16	15
Black Bear	20	21

TYPICAL MULE DEER

Score	Location	Year	Hunter	Owner	Story	Photo	Page in Book
226-4/8	Dolores Co.	1972	Doug Burris, Jr.	Don Schaufler	Yes	Yes	12
215-3/8	Delta Co.	1958	Robert L. Ingles	Fred Ferganchick	Yes	Yes	13
214-3/8	Gypsum Creek	1967	Paul A. Muehlbauer	Muehlbauer Family	Yes	Yes	14
213-1/8	Moffat Co.	1982	Unknown	David W. Blaker	No	Yes	319
212-7/8	Garfield Co.	1971	Errol R. Raley	Errol R. Raley	Yes	Yes	15
212	Grand Co.	1963	Wesley B. Brock	Wesley B. Brock	No	Yes	319
210-2/8	Southern Ute IR	1963	Jack D. Johnston	Jack D. Johnston	No	No	
210-2/8	Delta Co.	1972	Tom Donaldson	Tom Donaldson	No	No	
210-1/8	Boulder Co.	PR 1965	Unknown	Don Schaufler	No	Yes	319
209-5/8	Montrose Co.	1974	Mike Thomas	Mike Thomas	No	No	
209-2/8	Amherst Mtn.	1963	Herbert Graham	Mrs. W.J. Graham	No	No	
209	Saquache Co.	1967	William B. Pennington	William B. Pennington	No	No	
208-6/8	Garfield Co.	1952	George Shearer	Richard L. Baker	No	Yes	319
208-5/8	Mesa Co.	1960	Robert L. Zaina	Robert L. Zaina	No	Yes	319
207-3/8	Mesa Co.	1972	Wally Bruegman	Wally Bruegman	No	No	
207-2/8	Montrose Co.	1974	Bill Crouch	Don Schaufler	No	No	
207-1/8	Golden	1967	Harold B. Moser	Harold B. Moser	Yes	Yes	16
207	Montrose	1966	Warren S. Bachhofer	Warren S. Bachhofer	No	No	
206-7/8	Montrose Co.	1973	W.L. Boynton	W.L. Boynton	No	Yes	319
206-6/8	Pagosa Spgs.	1963	Henry Trujillo, Jr.	Henry Trujillo, Jr.	Yes	Yes	17
206-6/8	Pagosa Spgs.	1962	Richard V. Price	Richard V. Price	No	Yes	319
206-3/8	Eagle Co.	1960	Harold Taylor	Fred Palmer	No	Yes	165,320
206-2/8	Mesa Co.	PU 1974	Picked Up	Darryl Powell	No	Yes	320
206-2/8	Montrose Co.	1972	Patrick E. Courtin, Jr.	Patrick E. Courtin, Jr.	Yes	Yes	18
206	Eagle Co.	1967	Harold L. Loesch	Harold L. Loesch	No	Yes	320
205-6/8	Eagle Co.	1981	Mark A. McCormick	Mark A. McCormick	No	Yes	320
205-4/8	Kremmling	1962	Larry Bell	Larry Bell	No	No	
205-4/8	Garfield Co.	1962	Richard Cobb	Richard Cobb	Yes	Yes	19
205-4/8	Gunnison Co.	1962	William T. Peacock	Ralph L. McKinley	No	No	
205-2/8	Delta Co.	1953	John Madden	John Madden +	No	Yes	320
205-2/8	Montrose Co.	1954	Joe M. Gardner	Zane G. Holland	Yes	Yes	20
204-7/8	Southern Ute IR	1967	Nolan Martins	Nolan Martins	No	Yes	320
204-7/8	Delta Co.	1956	Frank Peterson	Frank Peterson	Yes	Yes	21
204-6/8	Colorado	PR 1992	Unknown	Don Schaufler	No	No	
204-6/8	Colorado	PR 1990	Unknown	Dana Hollinger and Bob Howard	No	No	
204-5/8	Eagle Co.	1982	Robert V. Doerr	Robert V. Doerr	No	Yes	320
204-3/8	Grand Junction	1962	Charles M. Bentley	Michael N. Bentley	No	No	
204-1/8	Hinsdale Co.	1961	Norman E. Ebbley	Jim Temple	Yes	Yes	22
204	Pitkin Co.	1950	Jens O. Solberg	Jens O. Solberg	Yes	Yes	23
203-7/8	Mesa Co.	1951	Ed Craig	Craig Family	Yes	Yes	24
203-7/8	North Park	1949	Edison A. Pillmore	Edison A. Pillmore Family	Yes	Yes	25
203-6/8	Montezuma Co.	1970	Bob Meese	Don Schaufler	No	No	
203-5/8	Mesa Co.	1957	William P. Burger	William P. Burger	No	No	
203-5/8	La Plata Co.	1950	B.E. Gressett	B.E. Gressett	No	Yes	321
203-4/8	Garfield Co.	1985	John T. Sewell	John T. Sewell	No	Yes	321
203-4/8	Montezuma Co.	1999	Olen J. Hicks	Olen J. Hicks	Yes	Yes	27
203-2/8	White River	1943	Ron Vance	Ronald Crawford	No	No	
203-2/8	DeBeque	1962	Francis A. Moore	Francis A. Moore	No	No	
203-2/8	Collbran	1973	Joe R. Colingo	Joe R. Colingo	No	No	
203-1/8	Hayden	1959	M.W. Giboney	M.W. Giboney	No	No	
203-1/8	White River NF	1979	Bill Barcus *	—	No	Yes	321
203	Mesa Co.	1966	James K. Scott	James K. Scott	No	No	
203	Montrose Co.	1968	Earl L. Markley	Aly M. Bruner	Yes	Yes	28
202-6/8	Ouray Co.	1966	Jewel E. Schottel	Jewel E. Schottel	Yes	Yes	29

* Only listed P&Y all-time records book but qualifies for B&C.   ** Only listed in Longhunter's all-time records book but qualifies for B&C.   *** Listed in the B&C and Longhunter records books.
**** Listed in B&C and P&Y records books.   + Eligible for B&C but not registered.   # Ineligible for B&C because of damage but deserves recognition.

Big-Game Listings and Index

Score	Location	Date	Hunter	Owner	Col1	Col2	Page
202-5/8	Ouray Co.	1965	Louis V. Schlosser	Louis V. Schlosser	No	Yes	30
202-4/8	Mesa Co.	1968	Jack Thompson	Jack Thompson	Yes	Yes	
202-4/8	Garfield Co.	1982	James S. Harden	James S. Harden	No	Yes	321
202-3/8	Boulder Co.	1963	Bob Wallace	Bob Wallace	No	No	
202-2/8	Pagosa Springs	1960	Allen R. Arnwine	Allen R. Arnwine	No	No	
202-2/8	Archuleta Co.	1973	Duane Yearwood	Duane Yearwood	No	Yes	321
202	Montrose Co.	1966	Kenneth Klees	Kenneth Klees	No	No	
202	Gunnison NF	1963	James M. Newsom	James M. Newsom	No	No	
201-7/8	Dolores Co.	1958	Leonard J. Ashcraft	Leonard J. Ashcraft	Yes	Yes	31
201-6/8	Montrose Co.	1994	Allan K. Slafter	Allan K. Slafter	No	No	
201-5/8	Gunnison Co.	1966	Robert D. Rader	Robert D. Rader	No	Yes	321
201-5/8	Eagle Co.	1981	Richard C. Bergquist	Richard C. Bergquist	No	No	
201-4/8	Moffat Co.	1967	Carl E. Jacobson	Carl E. Jacobson	No	No	
201-4/8	Garfield Co.	1954	Unknown	Ronald E. McKinney	No	No	
201-4/8	Mesa Co.	1996	Michael W. Laws	Michael W. Laws	No	No	
201-3/8	Archuleta Co.	1962	Joe Moore	Joe Moore	No	No	
201-3/8	Grand Junction	1967	William C. Byrd	William C. Byrd	Yes	Yes	32
201-3/8	Montrose Co.	1972	Grant Morlang	Grant Morlang	Yes	Yes	33
201-2/8	Bayfield	1956	D. Rockwell	D. Rockwell	No	No	
201-1/8	Cameo	1962	Thomas C. Krauss	Thomas C. Krauss	No	No	
201-1/8	La Plata Co.	1966	Les Patrick	Les Patrick	No	Yes	321
201	Mesa Co.	1954	Ernest Mancuso	Ernest Mancuso	Yes	Yes	34
201	La Plata Co.	1978	Larry Pennington	Larry Pennington	No	No	
201	Dolores Co.	1978	Mark Loverin	Mark Loverin	No	No	
200-7/8	Collbran	1962	Homer O. Hartley	Homer O. Hartley	No	No	
200-6/8	Eagle Co.	1958	John Robertson	John Robertson	Yes	Yes	35
200-6/8	Southern Ute IR	1965	Jerry E. Morgan	Jerry E. Morgan	No	No	
200-6/8	Delta	1966	Emil Warber, Jr.	Emil Warber, Jr.	No	Yes	322
200-6/8	Gunnison Co.	1977	James B. Holbrooks	James B. Holbrooks	No	No	
200-5/8	La Plata Co.	1979	Unknown	Ronald F. Lax	No	No	
200-4/8	Dolores Co.	1988	James L. Horneck	James L. Horneck	No	No	
200-4/8	Eagle Co.	1975	Jack Stevens	Jack Stevens	Yes	Yes	36
200-3/8	Uncompahgre NF	1972	Richard M. Holbrook	Richard M. Holbrook	No	No	
200-3/8	Eagle Co.	1974	Gene D. Lintz	Gene D. Lintz	No	Yes	322
200-2/8	Mesa Co.	1966	Mitchell J. Sacco	Mitchell J. Sacco	Yes	Yes	37
200-2/8	Southern Ute IR	1966	Arthur Burch	Arthur Burch	No	No	
200-2/8	Ouray Co.	1967	Joseph T. Hollingshead	Joseph T. Hollingshead	Yes	Yes	39
200-2/8	Montrose Co.	1985	Nelson Harding	Nelson Harding	No	Yes	322
200-1/8	Mesa Co.	1965	John M. Domingos	John M. Domingos	Yes	Yes	40
200-1/8	Summit Co.	1959-60	Pick Up	Bill Knorr +	No	Yes	321
200	Silt	1961	George McCoy	George McCoy	No	No	
200	Piedra River	1960	Glenn A. Smith	Glenn A. Smith	No	No	
200	Garfield Co.	PU 1963	Picked Up	John F. Frost	No	No	
200	Eagle Co.	1976	Dale R. Leonard	David P. Moore	Yes	Yes	41
200	Park Co.	1971	Jim Fitzgerald	Rob Firth	No	No	
199-7/8	Eagle Co.	1967	George S. Burton	Betty Burton	Yes	Yes	42
199-7/8	Uncompahgre NF	1963	H.E. Gerhart	H.E. Gerhart	No	No	
199-7/8	Jackson Co.	1934	G.B. Berger, Jr.	Denver Museum of Natural History	No	Yes	322, 373
199-7/8	Disappointment Creek	1954	Clifford Le Neve	Clifford Le Neve	No	No	
199-6/8	Montrose Co.	1951	James O. McCleary	John E. McCleary	No	No	
199-6/8	Mesa Co.	1975	Pick Up	Darryl Powell	No	Yes	322
199-5/8	Archuleta Co.	1995	Charles W. Pearson	Charles W. Pearson	Yes	Yes	43
199-4/8	Pagosa Springs	1957	Perry Dixon	Perry Dixon	No	No	
199-4/8	Dolores Co.	1976	Kenneth L. Peters	Kenneth L. Peters	Yes	Yes	44
199-3/8	Silt	1961	V.M. Spiller	V.M. Spiller	No	No	
199-3/8	Mesa Co.	1949	Picked Up	Picked Up Greg Duff	Yes	Yes	45
199-3/8	Uncompahgre NF	PR 1933	Floyd Whitner	Jerome Burlingame	No	No	
199-2/8	Garfield Co.	1978	Gary W. Hartley	Gary W. Hartley	No	No	
199-2/8	Eagle Co.	1978	Anthony W. DeToy	Anthony W. DeToy	Yes	Yes	46
199-2/8	Eagle Co.	1965	Howard Stoker	Howard Stoker	No	No	
199-2/8	Archuleta Co.	1962	Kenneth Hunter	LeRoy C. Haug	No	Yes	322
198-7/8	Burns	1967	Charles D. Rush	Charles D. Rush	No	No	
198-5/8	Carbondale	1961	Ralph Clock	Ralph Clock	Yes	Yes	47
198-5/8	Colorado	PR 1960	Unknown	Don Schaufler	No	No	
198-5/8	Pueblo Co.	1986	James L. Bradley	ames L. Bradley	No	No	
198-5/8	Montezuma Co.	1968	Mary Ann Ott	Mary Ann Ott	Yes	Yes	48
198-4/8	Routt Co.	1966	Lloyd D. Kindsfater	Lloyd D. Kindsfater	Yes	Yes	49
198-4/8	Dark Canyon	1966	O.P. McGuire	O.P. McGuire	No	No	
198-4/8	La Plata Co.	1971	Pauline J. Bostic	Pauline J. Bostic	No	No	
198-4/8	Del Norte	1947	Esequiel Trujillo	Esequiel Trujillo	No	No	
198-3/8	Moffat Co.	1951	Lucille Gooch	George Gooch	Yes	Yes	50
198-3/8	Montrose Co.	1989	Allan K. Slafter	Allan K. Slafter	No	No	
198-2/8	Summit Co.	PR 1965	Picked Up	Louis Ceriani	No	Yes	322
198-2/8	Gunnison Co.	1975	Bobby Joe Watson	Bobby Joe Watson	No	Yes	322
198-1/8	Bayfield	1967	C. Ben Boyd	C. Ben Boyd	No	No	
198-1/8	Montrose Co.	1975	Robert A. Klatt	Robert A. Klatt	No	No	
198-1/8	Routt Co.	1968	William E. Goswick	William E. Goswick	No	No	
198-1/8	Colorado	PR 1989	Unknown	Richard A. Heitman	Yes	Yes	51
198	Gunnison Co.	1962	Eddie D. Palmer	Eddie D. Palmer	Yes	Yes	53, 323
198	Garfield Co.	1944	LeRoy Failor	LeRoy Failor	No	Yes	323
198	Eagle Co.	1978	Larry Schlasinger	Larry Schlasinger	No	No	
198	Hinsdale Co.	1978	Alan L. VanDenBerg	Alan L. VanDenBerg	Yes	Yes	52
197-7/8	Rio Blanco Co.	1967	Gary L. Bicknell	Dana Hollinger and Bob Howard	No	Yes	323
197-7/8	San Miguel Co.	1965	Everett Stutler	Everett Stutler	No	No	
197-7/8	Eagle Co.	1978	Lee Frudden	Lee Frudden	Yes	Yes	54
197-7/8	Chaffee Co.	1956	Marguerite Hill	Marguerite Hill	No	No	
197-6/8	Dolores Co.	1988	Jim Horneck *		No	No	
197-5/8	San Miguel Co.	1964	Virgil L. Burbridge	Jerry D. Burbridge	No	No	
197-5/8	Eagle Co.	1965	Joseph Sokel, Jr.	Steve J. Sokel	No	No	
197-4/8	Moffat Co.	1967	Russ H. Winslow	Russ H. Winslow	Yes	Yes	55
197-4/8	Gunnison Co.	1980	Thomas Gray, Jr.	Thomas Gray, Jr.	No	No	
197-4/8	Routt Co.	1969	William E. Goswick	William E. Goswick	No	No	
197-3/8	Montrose	1961	H.R. Clark	H.R. Clark	No	No	
197-3/8	Archuleta Co.	1957	Lansing Kothmann	Lansing Kothmann	No	No	

Colorado's Biggest Bucks and Bulls

Score	Location	Year	Hunter	Owner	Bow	Muzzleloader	Page
197-3/8	Pagosa Springs	1966	John D. Guess	John D. Guess	No	No	
197-3/8	Rio Blanco Co.	PR 1957	Picked Up	Jack Thompson	No	Yes	323
197-3/8	Gunnison Co.	1980	Mark L. Hanna	Mark L. Hanna	No	No	
197-3/8	Archuleta Co.	1962	Joe M. Moore	Joe M. Moore +	No	Yes	323
197-2/8	Custer Co.	1972	Jerome L. DeGree	Jerome L. DeGree	Yes	Yes	56
197-2/8	Elbert Co.	1993	Francis Wilson	Francis Wilson ***	Yes	Yes	57
197-1/8	Delta Co.	1977	B. Allan Jones	B. Allan Jones	No	No	
197-1/8	Mesa Co.	1978	Willis A. Kinsey	Willis A. Kinsey	No	No	
197-1/8	Gunnison Co.	1961	Ted Wolcott, Jr.	Ted Wolcott, Jr.	No	No	
197	Jackson Co.	1961	Alvin Bush	Jerry Haldeman	No	No	
197	Grand Co.	1962	Woodrow W. Dixon	Woodrow W. Dixon	No	Yes	323
197	Archuleta Co.	1971	Hugh W. Gardner	Hugh W. Gardner	Yes	Yes	59
196-7/8	Mesa Co.	PR 1966	Carl England	James B. Sisco III	No	No	
196-6/8	Eagle Co.	PR 1964	Picked Up	Don Schaufler	No	No	
196-6/8	Garfield Co.	1970	Walter C. Friauf	Walter C. Friauf	No	No	
196-6/8	Delta Co.	1968	Howard G. Reed	Howard G. Reed	No	No	
196-6/8	San Juan NF	1974	Wilford E. Seymour, Jr.	Wilford E. Seymour, Jr.	No	No	
196-5/8	Moffat Co.	1960	Tran Canton	Tran Canton	Yes	Yes	61
196-5/8	Maybell	1968	James W. Johnson	James W. Johnson	No	No	
196-5/8	Delta Co.	1960	Marvin L. Shepard	Marvin L. Shepard	Yes	Yes	60
196-5/8	Slater	1959	W.J. Bracken	W.J. Bracken	No	No	
196-5/8	Mesa Co.	1964	William Styers	William Styers	No	Yes	323
196-4/8	Garfield Co.	1962	Elmer Nelson	Elmer Nelson	Yes	Yes	63
196-4/8	Southern Ute IR	1974	William C. Forsyth	William C. Forsyth	No	No	
196-4/8	Summit Co.	1967	Steve Orecchio	Steve Orecchio	No	No	
196-3/8	Durango	1964	Ronald Chitwood	Ronald Chitwood	Yes	Yes	64
196-2/8	Rio Blanco Co.	1972	Max R. Zoeller	Max R. Zoeller	No	No	
196-2/8	Rio Blanco Co.	1971	Mike Murphy	Mike Murphy	Yes	Yes	65
196-1/8	Uncompahgre NF	1968	Harry L. Whitlock	Harry L. Whitlock	Yes	Yes	66
196-1/8	Eagle Co.	1981	Jeffery D. Harrison	Jeffery D. Harrison	No	No	
196	Delta Co.	1965	Alvin T. Stivers	Alvin T. Stivers	No	Yes	323
196	Huerfano Co.	1963	Frank C. Hibben	Frank C. Hibben	No	No	
195-7/8	Rio Blanco Co.	1951	Randy Kruse	Randy Kruse	No	No	
195-7/8	San Miguel Co.	1972	Jerry E. Albin	Jerry E. Albin	Yes	Yes	67
195-7/8	Southern Ute IR	1960	Richard Schmidt	Southern Ute Indian Reservation	No	Yes	324
195-6/8	Gunnison Co.	1972	George L. Hoffman, Jr.	George L. Hoffman, Jr.	No	No	
195-6/8	Eagle Co.	1954	Orlo E. Park	Orlo E. Park	No	No	
195-6/8	Gunnison	1967	Randall R. Kieft	Randall R. Kieft	No	Yes	324
195-6/8	Jefferson Co.	1947	Lloyd O. Rauchfuss	Lloyd O. Rauchfuss	No	No	
195-6/8	Montrose Co.	1969	Larry Della Bitta	Larry Della Bitta	Yes	Yes	69
195-6/8	Eagle Co.	1985	James B. Mesecke	James B. Mesecke	No	No	
195-6/8	Huerfano Co.	1954	Mike Disert	Janet D. Wasson	Yes	Yes	70
195-5/8	Delta Co.	1974	Royce J. Carville	Royce J. Carville	Yes	Yes	71
195-5/8	Mesa Co.	1989	John F. Stewart	John F. Stewart	No	No	
195-5/8	Grand Co.	1981	C. Jay Stout	C. Jay Stout	Yes	Yes	72
195-5/8	Pitkin Co.	1966	William F. Kirby	William F. Kirby	No	No	
195-5/8	Huerfano Co.	1989	Hub R. Grounds	Hub R. Grounds	No	No	
195-5/8	Archuleta Co.	1986	Matthew J. Arkins	Matthew J. Arkins	No	No	
195-4/8	Montrose	1969	Tony L. Hill	Tony L. Hill	No	No	
195-4/8	Garfield Co.	1969	Billy R. Babb	Billy R. Babb	No	No	
195-4/8	Gunnison Co.	1981	Celso Rico, Jr.	Celso Rico, Jr.	No	No	
195-3/8	Moffat Co.	1978	Frank J. Kubin	Frank J. Kubin	No	No	
195-2/8	Moffat Co.	1964	Orville R. Meineke	Craig Sports	No	No	
195-2/8	Marble	1968	David R. Allen	David R. Allen	No	No	
195-2/8	Montrose Co.	1965	Edward A. Ipser	Edward A. Ipser	No	No	
195-2/8	Gunnison Co.	1937	Herman F. Tomky	Russell J. Tomky	No	No	
195-1/8	Montrose Co.	1965	Eldon L. Webb	Eldon L. Webb	No	Yes	324
195-1/8	Grand Co.	2000	Picked Up	Kevin Kaltenbaugh +	Yes	Yes	73
195	Mesa Co.	1969	Paul Roddam, Jr.	Paul Roddam, Jr.	No	No	
195	Larimer Co.	1972	Michael D. Blehm	Michael D. Blehm	Yes	Yes	74
195	Rio Blanco Co.	1977	Gene Lawrence	Gene Lawrence	No	Yes	324
194-7/8	Mesa Co.	1949	JoReva Beane Wellborn	JoReva Beane Wellborn	Yes	Yes	75
194-7/8	Summit Co.	1962	Jerry Capp	Jerry Capp +	No	Yes	324
194-5/8	Adams Co.	1995	Daniel L. Kraft	Douglas P. Kraft	Yes	Yes	76
194-5/8	Montezuma Co.	1992	Tom Broderick	Tom Broderick	Yes	Yes	77
194-4/8	Eagle Co.	1984	William E. Pipes III	William E. Pipes III	No	No	
194-4/8	Grand Mesa	1962	Quincy M. Hines	Quincy M. Hines +	Yes	Yes	78
194-2/8	Garfield Co.	1999	Frank J. Moore	Frank J. Moore	Yes	Yes	79
194-1/8	Delta Co.	1977	Bill Rainer	Bill Rainer	No	No	
193-6/8	Montrose Co.	1960	Reynolds L. Vanstrom	Reynolds A./Edra Vanstrom	Yes	Yes	80
193-5/8	Eagle Co.	1995	William E. Pipes III	William E. Pipes III	No	No	
193-4/8	Garfield Co.	1982	Marvin A. Meyers	Marvin A. Meyers	Yes	Yes	81
193-3/8	Grand Co.	1967	Neil Hassler	Neil Hassler +	No	Yes	324
193-2/8	Eagle Co.	1959	Robert D. Pape	Rory Pape	No	No	
193-2/8	Gunnison Co.	1960	Bill Morrow	Nancy Morrow/Tom Roatch	Yes	Yes	82
193	Weld Co.	1996	Lance Hockett *	—	No	No	
192-7/8	San Isabel NF	1972	Donald D. Garrison *	—	No	No	
192-7/8	Colorado	1953	Unknown	Dana Hollinger and Bob Howard	No	Yes	324
192-6/8	Las Animas Co.	1995	James S. Kent	James S. Kent	Yes	Yes	83
192-6/8	Gunnison Co.	1968	Stephen A. Mahurin	Stephen A. Mahurin	No	No	
192-6/8	Montezuma Co.	1988	Jay N. Cruzan	Jay N. Cruzan	No	Yes	84
192-5/8	Grand Co.	1961	Erwin R. Palmer	Erwin R. Palmer	Yes	Yes	85
192-2/8	Uncompahgre Pl.	1973	Donald Click *	—	No	No	
192-2	Eagle Co.	1996	Ronald L. McCall	Ronald L. McCall	No	No	
192-2/8	Archuleta Co.	1965	John Richardson	John Richardson	No	No	
192	Arapahoe Co.	1996	Daniel K. Madajski	Daniel K. Madajski	No	No	
192	Delta Co.	1977	James W. Arellano	James W. Arellano	No	No	
192	Larimer Co.	PR 1990	Picked Up	John R. Steffes, Sr.	No	No	
191-7/8	Moffat Co.	1963	Howard Hageman	Aly M. Bruner	No	No	
191-3/8	Summit Co.	1961	Fred Palmer	Fred Palmer +	No	Yes	324
191-2/8	Gunnison Co.	1981	Tim Hays	Tim Hays	Yes	Yes	86
191-1/8	Moffat Co.	1959	Len E. Mayfield	Len E. Mayfield	No	No	
191-1/8	Grand Co.	1981	Zane Palmer	Zane Palmer	No	No	
191-1/8	Grand Co.	1959	Lloyd A. Palmer	Lloyd A. Palmer	Yes	Yes	87

Big-Game Listings and Index

Score	Location	Date	Hunter	Owner			Page
191-1/8	Grand Co.	1961	Delores Kendall	Delores Kendall +	No	Yes	325
190-7/8	Las Animas Co.	1995	Robert D. Davidson	Robert D. Davidson	Yes	Yes	88
190-6/8	Jackson Co.	1969	Guy Amburgey	Guy Amburgey	No	No	
190-6/8	Mesa Co.	1976	Allen Personious *	—	No	No	
190-6/8	Grand Co.	1960	Oscar D. Spenard	Oscar D. Spenard +	No	Yes	325
190-5/8	Douglas Co.	1990	Harold A. Weippert	Harold A. Weippert	Yes	Yes	89
190-5/8	Archulata Co.	1958	Lansing Kothmann	Lansing Kothmann	No	No	
190-5/8	Teller Co.	1982	Dan Mersman *	—	No	No	
190-5/8	Las Animas Co.	1994	Mark W. Streissguth	Mark W. Streissguth	Yes	Yes	90
190-4/8	Archuleta Co.	1985	James M. Russell III	James M. Russell III	No	No	
190-4/8	Garfield Co.	1963	Donald M. Alburtus	Dennis J. DaSilva	No	No	
190-4/8	Garfield Co.	1978	William D. Tate	William D. Tate	Yes	Yes	91
190-4/8	Arapahoe Co.	PR 1960	Ted Swanson	Michael D. Swanson	No	No	
190-3/8	Delta Co.	1996	Joe Alexander	Joe Alexander	No	No	
190-3/8	Mesa	1963	Robert W. Hill	Robert W. Hill	No	No	
190-1/8	Moffat Co.	1990	Glenn Pritchard *	—	No	No	
190	Trinidad	1996	Jay Gates	Jay Gates +	Yes	Yes	92
189-6/8	Cheyenne Co.	1991	Scott Anderson **	—	No	No	
189-5/8	Costilla Co.	1985	James M. Gray	James M. Gray	No	No	
189-3/8	Delta Co.	1968	Calvin R. Blake	Calvin R. Blake	No	No	
189-3/8	Gore Range	1944	Lyman Brown	Lyman Brown Family +	No	Yes	325
189-3/8	Delta Co.	1989	Mark S. Petrucci	Mark S. Petrucci +	Yes	Yes	93
189-2/8	Routt Co.	1997	James M. Malonis	James M. Malonis	Yes	Yes	94
189-1/8	La Plata Co.	1986	James L. Leyshon	James L. Leyshon	No	No	
189	Archuleta Co.	1996	Danny C. McNabb	Danny C. McNabb	Yes	Yes	95
189	Montezuma Co.	1983	Al Newkirk *	—	No	No	
188-6/8	Mesa Co.	1974	Bob Jensen *	—	No	No	
188-5/8	Weld Co.	1998	James D. Fox	James D. Fox	Yes	Yes	96
188-5/8	Purgatoire River	Early 1990s	Carl J. Wohlfert	Carl J. Wohlfert	Yes	Yes	97
188-5/8	Gunnison Co.	1992	Robert Hemmes **	—	No	No	
188-3/8	Eagle Co.	1997	Jeffrey B. Bunke	Jeffrey B. Bunke	Yes	Yes	98
188-3/8	Larimer Co.	1965	Fred W. Loy	Fred W. Loy	No	No	
188-3/8	Lincoln Co.	1997	Windell Penton *	—	No	No	
188-2/8	Eagle Co.	1976	H. Cruger Van Schaack IV	H. Cruger Van Schaack IV	No	No	
188-2/8	Gunnison Co.	1998	James J. Wilmes, Jr.	James J. Wilmes, Jr.	No	No	
188-2/8	Mesa Co.	1967	John Lamicq, Jr. *	—	No	No	
188	San Miguel Co.	1965	Roy Guinn	Elizabeth G. Wilson	Yes	Yes	99
188	Kit Carson Co.	1990	Thomas Aasbo	Thomas Aasbo	No	No	
188	Kit Carson Co.	1995	David L. Birdsall	David L. Birdsall ***	Yes	Yes	100
187-7/8	Pitkin Co.	1990	Kenneth N. Tucker	Kenneth N. Tucker	No	No	
187-7/8	Park Co.	1998	Drew L. Wright	Drew L. Wright	No	No	
187-7/8	Routt Co.	1986	Thomas Garvin **	—	No	No	
187-7/8	Montezuma Co.	1988	Jerry L. DeFrenchi	Jerry L. DeFrenchi	No	Yes	113
187-6/8	Weld Co.	1993	Randy Henderson *	—	No	No	
187-5/8	Logan Co.	1953	William E. Condon	William E. Condon	Yes	Yes	101
187-5/8	Moffat Co.	1971	Leonard Jefferson *	—	No	No	
187-5/8	Boulder Co.	1991	Jeff Biemiller *	—	No	No	
187-4/8	La Plata Co.	1994	Marten A. Pinnecoose	Marten A. Pinnecoose	Yes	Yes	102
187-3/8	Eagle Co.	1995	Osborne H. Linguist	Osborne H. Linguist	No	No	
187-3/8	Grand Co.	1966	William B. Ainsley	William B. Ainsley +	No	Yes	325
187-2/8	Rio Blanco Co.	PR 1987	Picked Up	Jack Thompson	No	No	
187-2/8	Rio Blanco Co.	PU 1982	Picked Up	Jack Thompson	No	Yes	
187-2/8	Eagle Co.	1999	Timothy J. Molitor	Timothy J. Molitor	Yes	Yes	103
187	Moffat Co.	1987	Warren C. Nuzum	Warren C. Nuzum	No	No	
186-7/8	Eagle Co.	1963	J.D. Jones *	—	No	No	
186-7/8	Garfield Co.	1986	Gary L. Hecht	Gary L. Hecht	No	No	
186-7/8	Uncompahgre Pl.	1973	Jerry Click *	—	No	No	
186-6/8	Garfield Co.	1995	Charlie M. Stewart, Jr.	Charles M. Stewart, Jr.	No	No	
186-6/8	Routt Co.	1976	Willie Jones	Willie Jones	Yes	Yes	104
186-6/8	Mesa Co.	1952	L. Jack Lyon	L. Jack Lyon	Yes	Yes	105
186-6/8	Larimer Co.	1962	Gerald D. Rice	Gerald D. Rice	Yes	Yes	106
186-5/8	Fremont Co.	1986	Donald B. Anderson, Jr.	Donald B. Anderson, Jr.	No	No	
186-5/8	Elbert Co.	1984	Loren Dellinger *	—	No	No	
186-4/8	White River NF	1977	Walt Seville *	—	No	No	
186-3/8	Montezuma Co.	1976	Duane Calhoon	Duane Calhoon	No	Yes	325
186-3/8	Douglas Co.	1994	Harold A. Weippert	Harold A. Weippert	Yes	Yes	89
186-2/8	Eagle Co.	1960	Robert D. Pape	Robert D. Pape	No	No	
186-2/8	Gunnison Co.	1973	Don E. Lampert *	—	No	No	
186-1/8	Garfield Co.	PU 1984	Picked Up	Jack Thompson	No	Yes	325
186	Gunnison Co.	1996	Neil C. Nostrand	Neil C. Nostrand	Yes	Yes	107
186	Pitkin Co.	1982	Anthony E. Urwick	Anthony E. Urwick	Yes	Yes	108
186	Rio Blanco Co.	1999	Kelly Brown	Kelly Brown	Yes	Yes	109
185-7/8	Routt Co.	1967	LeRoy S. Nelson	LeRoy S. Nelson	No	No	
185-6/8	Rio Blanco Co.	PR 1987	Picked Up	Jack Thompson	No	No	
185-6/8	Las Animas Co.	1996	Gary A. Baudino	Gary A. Baudino	Yes	Yes	110
185-5/8	Mesa Co.	1962	Art Cook *	—	No	Yes	325
185-5/8	Garfield Co.	PR 1982	Picked Up	Jack Thompson	No	No	
185-3/8	Delta Co.	1989	Mark S. Petrucci	Mark S. Petrucci	No	No	
185	Larimer Co.	1969	Don Lampert *	—	No	No	
185	Montrose Co.	1988	Darryl L. Coe *	—	No	No	
185	Clear Creek Co.	1996	Bradley John Kuhn *	—	No	No	
184-7/8	Mesa Co.	1983	James L. Peterson *	—	No	No	
184-6/8	Rio Grande Co.	1996	Joe R. Davis	Joe R. Davis	No	No	
184-6/8	Mesa Co.	1976	David L. Myers *	—	No	No	
184-6/8	La Plata Co.	1987	Jim Benauidez	Jim Benauidez	No	Yes	325
184-5/8	Douglas Co.	1995	Thomas L. Rea	Thomas L. Rea	No	No	
184-4/8	Eagle Co.	1990	Michael E. Zimmerman	Michael E. Zimmerman	Yes	Yes	111
184-1/8	Delta Co.	1963	Scott Kolb *	—	No	No	
184	Eagle Co.	1997	Randy Motzner	Randy Motzner	Yes	Yes	112
183-7/8	Moffat Co.	1966	Joel Hogan *	—	No	No	
183-5/8	Eagle Co.	1998	Jack T. Baumstark, Sr.	Jack T. Baumstark, Sr.	No	No	
183-5/8	Montezuma Co.	1999	Jerry L. DeFrenchi	Jerry L. DeFrenchi	Yes	Yes	113
183-4/8	Kiowa Co.	1968	Dave Moyer *	—	No	No	
183-1/8	Gunnison Co.	1997	William J. McCarthy, Jr.	William J. McCarthy, Jr.	No	No	

Score	Location	Year	Hunter	Owner	Story	Photo	Page in Book
183-1/8	Mesa Co.	1986	Billy E. Green	Billy E. Green	Yes	Yes	114
182-6/8	Las Animas Co.	1992	Donald P. Travis	Donald P. Travis	No	No	
182-6/8	Moffat Co.	1987	Glenn Pritchard *	—	No	No	
182-4/8	Mesa Co.	1985	Charles C. Perry *	—	No	No	
182-4/8	Mesa Co.	1986	David M. Gant *	—	No	No	
182-3/8	Colorado	1966	Eugene Schladoer	Eugene Schladoer	No	No	
182-3/8	Gunnison Co.	1976	Donald Turcke **	—	No	No	
182-2/8	Mesa County	1974	Robert C. Dawson *	—	No	No	
182-1/8	Moffat Co.	1975	Robert B. Caldwell	Robert B. Caldwell	Yes	Yes	115
182	Eagle Co.	1996	William J. McEwen	William J. McEwen	Yes	Yes	116
181-6/8	Washington Co.	1991	Ronald E. Markow	Ronald E. Markow	Yes	Yes	117
181-6/8	Delta Co.	1998	Bob K. Carter	Bob K. Carter	Yes	Yes	118
181-5/8	Delta Co.	1962	Vernon D. Holleman	Vernon D. Holleman	Yes	Yes	119
181-5/8	Wakely	1964	Lynn Grace *	—	No	No	
181-4/8	Garfield Co.	1967	Henry Wichers *	—	No	No	
181-4/8	El Paso County	1998	Craig E. Kimball *	—	No	No	
181-4/8	Archuleta Co.	1982	Dewitt Howell, Jr. **	—	No	No	
181-3/8	Montrose Co.	1981	John Lamb *	No		No	
181-2/8	Larimer Co.	1972	Wayne Eberhard	Wayne Eberhard	No	No	
181	Rio Blanco Co.	1993	R. Charles Prosek	R. Charles Prosek	Yes	Yes	120
181	Pitkin Co.	1992	James H. Calyer	James H. Calyer	No	No	
181	Garfield Co.	1996	Marvin Meyers	Marvin Meyers +	Yes	Yes	81
180-6/8	La Plata Co.	1988	Ralph RePola *	—	No	No	
180-4/8	Mesa Co.	1958	Jack Kruckenburg *	—	No	No	
180-4/8	Montezuma Co.	1987	Marvin Reichenau *	---	No	No	
180-4/8	Montezuma Co.	1986	Jerry L. DeFrenchi	Jerry L. DeFrenchi	No	Yes	113
180-3/8	Kiowa Co.	1994	Jeff Barber *	—	No	No	
180-2/8	Eagle Co.	1995	Jeffrey B. Bunke	Jeffrey B. Bunke	Yes	Yes	98
180-1/8	Delta Co.	1989	John R. Arellano	John R. Arellano	No	No	
180-1/8	Jackson Co.	1998	Darren F. Mumma	Darren F. Mumma	No	No	
180-1/8	Douglas Co.	1987	Patrick G. Diesing	Patrick G. Diesing	Yes	Yes	121
180	Mesa Co.	1970	Charles T. Joranco	Charles T. Joranco	No	No	

NON-TYPICAL MULE DEER

Score	Location	Year	Hunter	Owner	Story	Photo	Page in Book
306-7/8	Montezuma Co.	1972	Lloyd Pyle	Don Schaufler	Yes	Yes	124
306-2/8	Norwood	1954	Steve H. Herndon	V.D. & D.F. Holleman	Yes	Yes	125
303-6/8	Eagle Co.	1962	James Austill	Don Schaufler	Yes	Yes	126
302-4/8	Paonia	1965	Louis H. Huntington, Jr.	Louis H. Huntington, Jr.	No	Yes	326
300	Mesa Coo.	1961	George Blackmon, Jr.	Don Schaufler	No	Yes	326
299-5/8	Elk Creek	1886	Andrew Daum	B&C National Collection	Yes	Yes	127
297-5/8	Larimer Co.	1941	Jack Autrey	Linda Guy	Yes	Yes	128
296-2/8	Mesa Co.	PR 1981	Unknown	Don Schaufler	No	No	
295-5/8	Rio Blanco Co.	1932	Harry Jordan	Meeker Hotel and Café +	Yes	Yes	129
287-5/8	Montezuma Co.	1988	Travis Shippey	Don Schaufler +	No	Yes	326
286-3/8	Eagle Co.	1928	Albert L. Mulnix	Don Schaufler	No	No	
278-7/8	Eagle Co.	1978	Dale L. Becker	Dale L. Becker	Yes	Yes	131
278-7/8	Montrose Co.	1961	Keith Thaute	Keith Thaute	No	Yes	326
277-1/8	Colorado	1930	Native American	Charles McAden	No	No	
276-4/8	Glenwood Spgs.	1967	Larry Prehm	Spanky Greenville	Yes	Yes	132
275-6/8	Gunnison Co.	1957	Everett King	Everett King +	Yes	Yes	133
274-7/8	Delta Co.	1989	Robert G. Wilson	Robert G. Wilson	No	No	
274-7/8	Morgan Co.	1987	Kenneth W. Plank *	—	No	Yes	326
274-5/8	Pueblo County	PU 1988	Picked Up	Butler Ranch	No	No	
273-6/8	Hayden	PR 1930	Roy I. Roney	Colorado Div. of Wildlife	No	Yes	326
272-5/8	Glenwood Spgs.	1967	William L. Kurtz	William L. Kurtz	No	No	
272-4/8	Eagle Co.	1978	Eddie Stephenson, Jr.	Eddie Stephenson, Jr.	No	Yes	326
271-2/8	Delta Co.	1968	Mack Gorrod	Mack Gorrod +	No	Yes	327
271	Colorado	1944	Frank Peterson	Anita Peterson +	No	Yes	327
270-6/8	Colorado	1958	Floyd Hill	Don Schaufler	No	No	
270-3/8	Mesa Co.	1994	Todd McKay	Todd McKay	Yes	Yes	134
269-6/8	Morgan Co.	PU 1987	Picked Up	Aly M. Bruner	No	No	
268-3/8	Delta Co.	1962	Shirley Smith	Shirley Smith	Yes	Yes	135
267-3/8	Montezuma Co.	1988	Travis Shippey	Don Shaufler +	No	Yes	327
267-1/8	Eagle Co.	1969	Josef P. Langegger	Josef P. Langegger	Yes	Yes	136
264-3/8	Gunnison Co.	1975	Gordon E. Blay	Gordon E. Blay	Yes	Yes	137
263-4/8	Montrose	1963	Robert L. Price	Robert L. Price	No	Yes	327
262-3/8	Brush Creek	1967	Pete Taullie	Pete Taullie	No	Yes	327
261-6/8	Meeker	1934	Arthur A. Gossage	Meeker Hotel and Café +	Yes	Yes	138
261-1/8	Rio Blanco Co.	1961	L.C. Denny, Jr.	L.C. Denny, Jr.	No	Yes	327
259-6/8	Routt Co.	1949	R.V. Rhoads	Cecil R. Weston	No	Yes	327
259-1/8	Otero Co.	1995	John N. Lucero	John N. Lucero	No	Yes	327
258-3/8	Monte Vista	1956	Geis Nettlebeck	Dana Hollinger & Bob Howard	No	Yes	328
258-2/8	Mesa Co.	1976	David Glick *	—	No	No	
257-5/8	Rio Blanco Co.	1970	Rachael Palmer	Rachael Palmer	Yes	Yes	139
257-3/8	New Castle	1952	Unknown	A.E. Hudson	No	No	
256-5/8	Douglas Co.	1926	Adolph A. Larsen	Don Schaufler	No	No	
255-2/8	Eagle Co.	1936	Lloyd Murphy	Don Schaufler	No	No	
255-2/8	Garfield Co.	1932	Louis Lindauer	Louis Lindauer	No	No	
255-1/8	Eagle Co.	1980	Dennis Martinson	Dennis Martinson	No	No	
255	Dunkley Flat	1966	Richard A. Gorden	Richard A. Gorden	Yes	Yes	140
254-2/8	Columbine	1955	M.A. Story	M.A. Story	No	No	
254-1/8	Jefferson Co.	1994	Larry J. Jones	Larry J. Jones	No	No	
253-4/8	Silt	1961	George McCoy	George McCoy	No	Yes	328
253-3/8	Meeker	1917	George R. Howey	Robert L. Howey	No	No	
253-3/8	Clear Creek Co.	1947	George Lappin	Doug Grubbe	Yes	Yes	141
253	Delta Co.	1961	F.F. Parham	F.F. Parham	No	Yes	328
252-2/8	Garfield Co.	1973	B.J. Slack	Aly M. Bruner	No	No	
252-1/8	Grand Mesa	1969	John W. Stockenmer	John W. Stockenmer	Yes	Yes	142
252	Eagle Co.	1945	Richard G. Lundock	Richard G. Lundock	Yes	Yes	143
251-5/8	Gunnison Co.	1956	John M. Ringler	John M. Ringler	Yes	Yes	145

Score	Location	Date	Hunter	Owner	Col1	Col2	Page
251-5/8	Roan Creek	1965	Anthony Morabito	Anthony Morabito	Yes	Yes	146
251-1/8	Meeker	1955	Henry H. Zietz	Zietz Family	No	Yes	328
250-6/8	Pagosa Spgs.	1962	Thomas Jarrett	Thomas Jarrett	No	No	
250-3/8	Cedaredge	1963	E.K. Plante	E.K. Plante	No	No	
250-3/8	Moffat Co.	1960	Unknown	Aly M. Bruner	No	No	
250-2/8	Jefferson Co.	1994	Larry J. Jones *	—	No	No	
250-1/8	Montezuma Co.	1981	Jack E. Reed	Jack E. Reed	No	No	
249-5/8	Colorado	PR 1960	Unknown	Don Schaufler	No	No	
249-3/8	Routt Co.	1958	Howard Stoker	Howard Stoker	No	No	
249-2/8	Mesa Co.	1967	Gene Cavanagh	Gene Cavanagh	No	No	
249	Eagle Co.	1941	John F. Baldauf	Lin F. Nowotny	No	Yes	328
249	Garfield Co.	1969	William A. Wiedenfeld	William A. Wiedenfeld	No	Yes	328
248-3/8	Grand Co.	1987	Ricky Dixon	Ricky Dixon +	No	No	
248-3/8	Mesa Co.	1988	Edwin Baal	Edwin Baal	Yes	Yes	147
248-3/8	Costilla Co.	1988	Ronald E. Lewis	Ronald E. Lewis	No	No	
248-2/8	Colorado	PR 1980	Unknown	Dana Hollinger & Bob Howard	No	No	
248-1/8	Rio Blanco Co.	1956	Claude E. Shults	Claude E. Shults Family	No	Yes	328
248-1/8	Montezuma Co.	1973	Leland R. Tate	Leland R. Tate	No	Yes	
248	Columbine	1962	Bobby McLaughlin	Bobby McLaughlin	No	No	
247-7/8	Norwood	1951	Walter L. Reisbeck	Walter L. Reisbeck	No	No	
247-5/8	Hinsdale Co.	1966	Fred Jardine	Fred Jardine	Yes	Yes	148
247-4/8	Archuleta Co.	1970	Vince Plaskett	Vince Plaskett	No	Yes	328
247-3/8	Eagle Co.	1966	Earl M. Johnson	Earl M. Johnson	No	No	
247-2/8	Huerfano Co.	1997	Mike Komaroski **	—	No	No	
247-1/8	San Miguel Co.	1978	W.F. Grice	W.F. Grice	No	No	
247	Montrose Co.	1967	Thomas M. Bost	Thomas M. Bost	Yes	Yes	149
246-7/8	Craig	1960	Fred E. Trouth	Fred E. Trouth	No	Yes	329
246-6/8	Eagle Co.	1963	William M. Nickels	William M. Nickels	Yes	Yes	150
246-6/8	Rio Blanco Co.	1963	James A. Cook	James A. Cook	Yes	Yes	151
246-6/8	Mesa Co.	1976	Dean Derby II *	—	No	No	
246-4/8	Colorado	1996	Unknown	Meeker Hotel and Café +	No	Yes	329
246-3/8	Glenwood Spgs.	1959	Grady P. Lester	Grady P. Lester	No	No	
246-2/8	Eagle Co.	1949	Charles H. Thornberg	Charles H. Thornberg	Yes	Yes	152
246-1/8	Mesa Co.	1972	Joseph J. Pitcherella	Joseph J. Pitcherella	Yes	Yes	153
246	Mesa Co.		Harry A. Gay	Harry A. Gay	No	No	
245-7/8	Delores Co.	PU 1984	Picked Up	Mike Gassman	No	No	
245-5/8	Eagle Co.	1978	James Caraccioli	James Caraccioli	No	Yes	329
245-5/8	Rio Blanco Co.	1934	Charlie Grove	Dorothy Shults	Yes	Yes	154
245-3/8	Saquache Co.	1962	Walter A. Larsen	Randy Clark	Yes	Yes	155
244-7/8	Eagle Co.	1963	Bob Rambo	Bob Rambo +	Yes	Yes	157
244-5/8	Delta Co.	1969	Neil A. Briscoe, Jr.	Neil A. Briscoe, Jr.	No	Yes	329
244-2/8	Mesa Co.	1986	Thomas S. Hundley	Thomas S. Hundley	Yes	Yes	158
244-2/8	Montrose Co.	1974	Jim Herndon	Mrs. Jim Herndon	No	No	
244-2/8	Oak Creek	1961	Scott C. Hinkle	Scott C. Hinkle	No	No	
244-1/8	Mesa Co.	1960	Edward B. Walsh	Mrs. Edward B. Walsh	No	No	
244-1/8	Grand Co.	1966	Kenneth H. Newbury	Kenneth H. Newbury	No	No	
243-6/8	San Miguel Co.	1939	Ben Crandell	Ben Crandell	No	Yes	329
243-5/8	Gunnison Co.	PR 1970	Unknown	Dana Hollinger & Bob Howard	No	No	
243-4/8	Clear Creek Co.	1981	Louis I. Kingsley	Louis I. Kingsley	Yes	Yes	159
243-2/8	Colorado	1954	Unknown	Dana Hollinger & Bob Howard	No	No	
243-1/8	Harrison Gulch	1958	George R. Mattern	Aly M. Bruner	No	No	
242-6/8	Middle Park	PR 1961	Picked Up	Karl H. Knorr	No	Yes	329
242-4/8	Hinsdale Co.	PU 1991	Picked Up	Rick House	No	No	
242-3/8	Meeker	1938	John T. Crook	Meeker Hotel and Café +	No	Yes	329
242-2/8	Rabbit Ears Pass	1964	Douglas Valentine	Douglas Valentine	No	No	
242-1/8	Hinsdale Co.	1973	Bill Crose	Bill Crose	No	No	
242	Garfield Co.	1981	Daniel J. Stanek	Daniel J. Stanek	No	No	
241-7/8	Grand Co.	1978	Ricky Dixon	Dana Hollinger & Bob Howard	No	Yes	329
241-7/8	La Plata Co.	1984	Randall N. Bostick	Randall N. Bostick	No	No	
241-4/8	Douglas Co.	1994	Donald E. Ditmars	Donald E. Ditmars	No	No	
241-4/8	Summit Co.	1974	Robert R. Ross	Robert R. Ross	No	No	
241-2/8	Oak Creek	1967	Richard J. Peltier	Richard J. Peltier	No	No	
241	Colorado	PR 1969	Nolan Allen	Aly M. Bruner	No	No	
240-7/8	New Castle	1960	Harold F. Auld	Harold F. Auld	No	No	
240-6/8	Colorado	1935	Eddie Miller	Meeker Hotel and Café +	No	Yes	330
240-6/8	Eagle Co.	1982	Steve B. Humann	Steve B. Humann	Yes	Yes	160
240-6/8	Colorado	PR 1970	Unknown	Darryl Powell	No	Yes	330
240-4/8	Eagle Co.	1979	James P. Hale	James P. Hale	No	No	
240-4/8	Garfield Co.	1983	James E. Powell, Jr.	James E. Powell, Jr.	No	No	
240-4/8	La Plata Co.	1976	Cullen D. Wagoner	Cullen D. Wagoner	Yes	Yes	161
240-2/8	Yuma Co.	1995	Vernon E. Young	Vernon E. Young	Yes	Yes	162
240	Garfield Co.	1962	Ed Peters, Jr.	Ed Peters, Jr.	Yes	Yes	163
240	San Juan Wild.	1967	Tommie Cornelius	Tommie Cornelius	No	No	
240	Garfield Co.	1956	Wayne Anderson	Dana Hollinger & Bob Howard +	No	No	
239-6/8	La Plata Co.	1977	David Blake	David Blake	Yes	Yes	164
239-1/8	Summit Co.	1959	Fred H. Palmer	Fred H. Palmer	Yes	Yes	165
238	Uncompahgre NF	1969	James D. Greer	James D. Greer +	Yes	Yes	166
237-3/8	Douglas Co.	Prior to 1970	Unknown	Dana Hollinger & Bob Howard	No	No	
237-2/8	Colorado	PR 1996	Unknown	Aly M. Bruner	No	No	
235-2/8	Yuma Co.	1998	Dusty T. Walters	Dusty T. Walters	No	No	
237-1/8	Grand Co.	1949	Clayton Hill	Clayton Hill +	No	Yes	330
235-6/8	Montezuma Co.	PU 1992	Pick Up	Tom Broderick	No	Yes	330
235-2/8	Yuma Co.	1998	Dusty T. Walters	Dusty T. Walters	No	No	
235-1/8	Garfield Co.	1997	Mark Martin *	—	No	No	
234-5/8	Colorado	1925	Bill Henry	Bill Henry +	No	Yes	330
234-1/8	Gunnison Co.	1970	Jack E. Moermond	Jack E. Moermond	Yes	Yes	167
233-7/8	Colorado	PR 1992	Unknown	Darryl Powell	No	Yes	330
233-6/8	Rio Blanco Co.	1960	Robert E. Buckles	Robert E. Buckles	Yes	Yes	168
232-5/8	Rio Blanco Co.	1979	Harold Boyack *	—	No	No	
232-3/8	Arapahoe Co.	1974	James R. Verney *	—	No	No	
232-3/8	Colorado	PR 1900	Unknown	Melvin A. Mitchell, Jr.	Yes	Yes	169
232	Grand Co.	1986	William L. Henry	William L. Henry	No	No	
231-1/8	Eagle Co.	1996	Mike Crites	Mike Crites	No	No	
230-3/8	Eagle Co.	1996	Ted R. Ramirez	Ted R. Ramirez	Yes	Yes	170

Score	Location	Year	Hunter	Owner	Story	Photo	Page in Book
230-2/8	Summit Co.	1929	Dave Doig	Howard Doig +	No	Yes	330
228-3/8	Kiowa Co.	1982	Lilia Winkler	Lilia Winkler	No	No	
228-3/8	Archuleta Co.	1958	Harold Zesch	Harold Zesch	No	No	
228-2/8	Mesa Co.	1998	Mathew M. Gilson	Mathew M. Gilson	Yes	Yes	171
228	Greeley	1954	Vern Williams	Dana Hollinger & Bob Howard +	No	No	
228	Garfield Co.	1994	Leo W. Bange *	—	No	No	
228	Southern Ute IR	1977	Cullen D. Wagoner	Cullen D. Wagoner	No	Yes	161
225-2/8	Garfield Co.	1972	Dennis Quinn *	—	No	No	
223-7/8	Uncompahgre Mtns.	1972	Steve Haynes *	—	No	No	
223-5/8	Garfield Co.	PR 1978	Picked Up	Jack Thompson	No	No	
223-2/8	Moffat Co.	1999	Bradley D. Herman	Bradley D. Herman	Yes	Yes	172
222-1/8	Montrose Co.	1975	Lavern Rucker *	—	No	No	
220-6/8	Mesa Co.	1962	John O. Garvin	John O. Garvin	Yes	Yes	173
220-5/8	Rio Blanco Co.	1974	Anthony L. Weiss	Anthony L. Weiss	Yes	Yes	174
220-2/8	Carbondale	1966	Calvin Turner	Calvin Turner	Yes	Yes	175
220-2/8	Uncompahgre Pl.	1971	Michael T. Schwitters *	—	No	No	
220	Delbert Co.	1992	Jim Early *	—	No	No	
219-5/8	Mesa Co.	1980	Roger Lewis *	—	No	No	
219-5/8	Yuma Co.	1993	Garry Neuschwanger *	—	No	No	
218	Garfield Co.	1979	Bob Hill *	—	No	No	
216-6/8	Garfield Co.	1975	Richard Lepak *	—	No	No	
216-2/8	Jefferson Co.	1996	Steve L. Kyle	Steve L. Kyle ***	Yes	Yes	176
215-7/8	Weld Co.	1993	Jon Brodie *	—	No	No	

TYPICAL WHITETAIL DEER

Score	Location	Year	Hunter	Owner	Story	Photo	Page in Book
194	Logan Co.	1981	Stuart Clodfelder *	—	No	No	
186-3/8	Adams Co.	1996	David A. McCracken	David A. McCracken	Yes	Yes	178
182-5/8	Yuma Co.	1978	Ivan W. Rhodes	Ivan W. Rhodes	Yes	Yes	179
180-2/8	Yuma Co.	1989	Jeff L. Mekelburg	Jeff L. Mekelburg	Yes	Yes	180
178-4/8	Yuma Co.	1979	Terry M. Scheidecker	Terry M. Scheidecker	No	No	
176-3/8	Boulder Co.	1989	Picked Up	Michael J. Scrivner	No	No	
175-7/8	Logan Co.	1971	Picked Up	Marvin Gardner	Yes	Yes	181
175-1/8	Otero Co.	1992	Kenny D. Mills	Kenny D. Mills	No	No	
174-5/8	Larimer Co.	1990	George S. Sumter, Jr.	George S. Sumter, Jr.	No	No	
173-3/8	Bent Co.	1994	Rick J. Tokarski	Rick J. Tokarski ****	Yes	Yes	182
173-3/8	Prowers Co.	1997	Les F. Ohlhauser	Les F. Ohlhauser	Yes	Yes	183
171-2/8	Yuma Co.	1985	John O. Cletcher, Jr.	John O. Cletcher, Jr.	Yes	Yes	184
170-5/8	Prowers Co.	1987	Douglas W. Kuhns	Douglas W. Kuhns	No	No	
170-2/8	Lincoln Co.	1992	Joseph C. Fox	Joseph C. Fox	Yes	Yes	185
170-2/8	Crowley Co.	1993	Judy F. Hallman *	—	No	No	
164-5/8	Sedgwick Co.	1973	Brad Ham *	—	No	No	
164-2/8	Lincoln Co.	1995	Richard J. Larson	Richard J. Larson	No	No	
163	Lincoln Co.	1994	Dennis Goody *	—	No	No	
162-7/8	Elbert Co.	1993	Michael A. Franek	Michael A. Franek	Yes	Yes	186
160	Otero Co.	1995	Troy Cunningham *	—	Yes	Yes	187
160	Pueblo Co.	1993	Kenneth H. Karbon *	—	No	No	
160	Weld County	1994	Michael Yearly *	—	No	No	

NON-TYPICAL WHITETAIL DEER

Score	Location	Year	Hunter	Owner	Story	Photo	Page in Book
258-2/8	Cheyenne Co.	1992	Michael J. Okray	Bass Pro Shops	Yes	Yes	188
239-2/8	Prowers Co.	1997	Scott M. Tenold	Scott M. Tenold	Yes	Yes	189
233-3/8	Pueblo Co.	1994	Raymond A. Vertovec	Raymond A. Vertovec	Yes	Yes	190
229-7/8	Yuma Co.	1986	David Jake Powell *	—	No	No	
228	Las Animas Co.	1998	Brad C. Hardin	Brad C. Hardin	No	No	
209-1/8	Prowers Co.	1997	Paul D. Mirley	Paul D. Mirley	Yes	Yes	191
204-2/8	Yuma Co.	1986	Jeff L. Mekelburg	Jeff L. Mekelburg	Yes	Yes	180
201-3/8	Kiowa Co.	1991	Dale A. Dilulo	Dale A. Dilulo	No	No	
200-3/8	Logan Co.	PU 1994	Picked Up	Dennis D. Reid	No	No	
200	Baca Co.	1996	David Sanford	David Sanford	Yes	Yes	192
199-1/8	Morgan Co.	1997	Michael L. Furcolow	Michael L. Furcolow	Yes	Yes	193
197-6/8	Prowers Co.	1988	Samuel S. Pattillo	Samuel S. Pattillo	No	No	
187-6/8	Bent Co.	1991	Chris Malden *	—	No	No	

TYPICAL AMERICAN ELK

Score	Location	Year	Hunter	Owner	Story	Photo	Page in Book
442-3/8	Dark Canyon	1899	John Plute	Ed Rozman	Yes	Yes	204
427-3/8	Colorado	PR 1906	Unknown	Meeker Hotel and Café #	Yes	Yes	205
407	Summit Coo	1967	Robert G. Young	Robert G. Young	No	Yes	331
402-3/8	San Miguel Co.	1954	Lewis Frederickson	Jay Scott	No	No	
400-4/8	Routt Co.	1953	Lewis Frederickson	Lewis Frederickson	No	No	
397-2/8	Gunnison Co.	1970	John R. Burritt	John R. Burritt	Yes	Yes	206
394-2/8	Baca Co.	1994	David B. Martin	David B. Martin	No	No	
393-1/8	Montrose Co.	1986	Wayne Bradley *	—	No	No	
393	Las Animas Co.	1996	Ron D. Velarde	Ron D. Velarde +	No	Yes	331
392-4/8	Buford	PR 1967	Picked Up	Robert T. Fulton	No	No	
392	Jackson Co.	1969	James A. Baller	North Park State Bank	Yes	Yes	207
391-6/8	Slater	1963	W.J. Bracken	W.J. Bracken	No	No	
391-4/8	Mt. Evans	1874	Unknown	Frank Brady	Yes	Yes	209
391-3/8	Grand Lake	1949	John Holzwarth	John Holzwarth Family	Yes	Yes	210
391	Meeker	PR 1906	Unknown	Meeker Hotel and Café +	No	Yes	331
390-2/8	Las Animas Co.	1993	Robert A. Schnee	Robert A. Schnee	No	No	
388-6/8	Larimer Co.	PR 1890	John Zimmerman	Fort Collins Museum	No	No	
387-5/8	Douglas Co.	1999	Hit by Van	Colorado Div. of Wildlife	Yes	Yes	211

Score	Location	Year	Hunter	Owner	Story	Photo	Page in Book
386-4/8	Larimer Co.	1997	David McCormick *	—	No	No	
386-2/8	Delta Co.	1974	Bert Johnson	Bert Johnson	Yes	Yes	212
385-1/8	Trappers Lake	1954	Byron W. Kneff	Byron W. Kneff	No	Yes	331
384-3/8	Clear Creek Coo.	1973	John Wallace	John Wallace	No	Yes	331
384-1/8	Gilpin Co.	1850	William C. Wheeler	James W. Wheeler	No	No	
384	Costilla Co.	1967	William E. Carl	William E. Carl	No	No	
383-6/8	Las Animas Co.	1993	Michael W. Marbach	Michael W. Marbach	No	No	
382-4/8	Summit Co.	1966	Marshall Sherman	Marshall Sherman	Yes	Yes	213
382	Little Cimmaron	1957	Newell Beauchamp	Bud Lovato	No	Yes	331
381-3/8	Larimer Co.	1972	Earl L. Erbes	Earl L. Erbes	Yes	Yes	214
380-5/8	Chaffee Co.	1972	Anton Purkat	Anton Purkat	Yes	Yes	215
380-5/8	Hayden	1966	Mike Holliday	Mike Holliday	No	No	
380-2/8	Las Animas Co.	PU 1987	Pick Up	Crawford Ranch	No	No	
379-7/8	Routt Co.	1961	Walter R. Ducey	Walter R. Ducey	Yes	Yes	216
379	Moffat Co.	1996	Rod B. Morrison	Rod B. Morrison	Yes	Yes	217
378-2/8	White River	1953	Art Wright	Art Wright	No	Yes	331
378	Gunnison	1966	Ed Lattimore, Jr.	Ed Lattimore, Jr.	No	No	
378	Dolores Co.	2000	Andrea Holley	Andrea Holley	No	Yes	332
377-6/8	Routt Co.	1959	Tom Nidey	Tom Nidey	No	Yes	332
377-4/8	Gunnison Co.	1972	Leo Welch	Leo Welch	Yes	Yes	218
376-7/8	Routt Co.	1963	J.L. Bailey	J.L. Bailey	No	No	
376-5/8	Granby	1961	Melvin Van Lewen	Colorado Div. of Wildlife	Yes	Yes	219
376-3/8	Radium	1964	Bill Mercer	Bill Mercer	No	No	
376-3/8	Gunnison Co.	1986	Gerald J. Obertino	Gerald J. Obertino	Yes	Yes	220
376-3/8	White River	1957	Ron Vance	Ronald Crawford	No	No	
376	Almont	1961	John Schwartz	John Schwartz	No	Yes	332
375-6/8	Crow Valley	1961	Dale R. Leonard	Dale R. Leonard	Yes	Yes	221
375-2/8	Craig	1960	Kenneth W. Cramer	Kenneth W. Cramer	No	No	
375-1/8	Jackson Co.	1976	Vincent Kvidera *	—	No	No	
368-4/8	Rio Blanco Co.	1953	P.R. Hays & J. Cook	Perry R. Hays	No	No	
367-3/8	Larimer Co.	1970	H. Troxell & B. Alexander *	—	No	No	
366-6/8	Eagle Co.	1961	Hank Hinton	Hank Hinton +	No	Yes	332
365-5/8	Rio Blanco Co.	1995	Jay Verzuh *	—	No	No	
365-3/8	Dolores Co.	1973	Renay Neely	Renay Neely	No	Yes	332
364-6/8	Las Animas Co.	1991	Ralph T. Geer	Ralph T. Geer	No	No	
364-4/8	Larimer Co.	1993	Darrel D. Lemon	Darrel D. Lemon	No	Yes	332
364-4/8	Fraser	PR 1970	Larry Yager	Larry Yager +	—	No	No
364-3/8	La Plata Co.	1992	Carl L. Absher	Carl L. Absher	No	No	
362-3/8	Grand Co.	1960	J.R. Barnes, Jr.	J.R. Barnes, Jr. +	No	Yes	332
362-2/8	Jackson Co.	1972	Alfred H. O'Brien *	—	No	No	
362	Rio Grande Co.	1998	Joseph D. Medina	Joseph D. Medina	No	No	
362-1/8	Sangre De Cristo Mtns.	1996	Tom C. Smith	Tom C. Smith	Yes	Yes	222
360	Las Animas Co.	1992	Rob Lucero *	—	Yes	Yes	223

NON-TYPICAL AMERICAN ELK

Score	Location	Year	Hunter	Owner	Story	Photo	Page in Book
447-2/8	Meeker	1936	Paul Dunn	Meeker Hotel and Café #	Yes	Yes	224
441-3/8	Meeker	PR 1918	Robert Helvey	Meeker Hotel and Café +	Yes	Yes	225
404-1/8	Jefferson Co.	1993	Chris White	Chris White ***	Yes	Yes	226
400-6/8	Mesa Co.	1994	William C. Parrish	William C. Parrish	Yes	Yes	227
400	Routt Co.	1939	William E. Goosman	Mrs. William E. Goosman	Yes	Yes	228
389-5/8	Douglas Co.	1998	Mark Martin *	—	Yes	Yes	229

SHIRAS MOOSE

Score	Location	Year	Hunter	Owner	Story	Photo	Page in Book
194-4/8	Jackson Co.	1995	Jack A. Anderson	Jack A. Anderson	Yes	Yes	238
189-4/8	Larimer Co.	1997	Brad B. Schwindt	Brad B. Schwindt	No	No	
177-2/8	Jackson Co.	1995	Steven P. Kugler	Steven P. Kugler	Yes	Yes	239
175-2/8	Park Co.	1996	Virgil A. Lair	Virgil A. Lair	No	No	
171-7/8	Jackson Co.	1994	Nancy A. Sommer	Nancy A. Sommer	Yes	Yes	240
163-6/8	Grand Co.	1992	Steve R. Countway	Steve R. Countway	No	No	
162	Jackson Co.	1991	Dennis W. Macy	Dennis W. Macy	Yes	Yes	241
162	Jackson Co.	1998	Michael R. Tucker	Michael R. Tucker	No	Yes	333
161-7/8	Jackson Co.	1992	Kirt Krieger *	—	No	No	
161-2/8	Jackson Co.	1999	Wayne R. Kroft	Wayne R. Kroft	Yes	Yes	242
160-6/8	Jackson Co.	1994	Robert T. Goettl	Robert T. Goettl	Yes	Yes	243
160-4/8	Jackson Co.	1996	Ronald W. Madsen	Ronald W. Madsen ****	Yes	Yes	244
159-4/8	Jackson Co.	1987	Donald I. Poeschl	Donald I. Poeschl	No	No	
159-4/8	Jackson Co.	1998	Steven M. Weinberg	Steven M. Weinberg	No	No	
159-1/8	Grand Co.	1998	Richard F. Karbowski	Richard F. Karbowski	No	Yes	333
158-1/8	Grand Co.	1993	Ronald R. Pomeroy	Ronald R. Pomeroy	No	No	
158-1/8	Jackson Co.	1994	Bill L. Olson	Bill L. Olson	No	No	
155-7/8	Jackson Co.	1992	Thomas A. Yukman	Thomas A. Yukman	No	No	
153-4/8	Jackson Co.	1993	Scott Koester *	—	No	No	
147-4/8	Jackson Co.	1993	Dan Plannenstiel *	—	No	No	
146-5/8	Jackson Co.	1993	Roy L. James	Roy L. James	No	No	
146-3/8	Jackson Co.	1993	Dave Hughes *	—	No	No	
142	Jackson Co.	1994	Glenn M. Smith	Glenn M. Smith	No	No	
140	Jackson Co.	1999	Ronald L. Elkins	Ronald L. Elkins	Yes	Yes	245

BIGHORN SHEEP

Score	Location	Year	Hunter	Owner	Story	Photo	Page in Book
197-7/8	Costilla Co.	1998	West Ward	West Ward	No	No	
195	Cuchara Peaks	2000	Donald W. Snyder	Donald W. Snyder	Yes	Yes	249
193-6/8	Cameron Pass	1954	F. Cotter	Herbert J. Havemann	No	No	

Score	Location	Year	Hunter	Owner	Story	Photo	Page in Book
191-7/8	Lake Co.	1901	Emory Whilton	Kern Co. CA Museum	No	No	
191-3/8	El Paso Co.	1983	Gene Moore *		Yes	Yes	250
191-2/8	Huerfano Co.	1997	Timothy K. Rushing	Timothy K. Rushing	Yes	Yes	251
190	Jackson Co.	1999	Tracy Atkinson	Tracy Atkinson	Yes	Yes	252
187-6/8	El Paso Co.	2000	Steven J. Behunin *		No	Yes	333
187-5/8	El Paso Co.	PU 1988	Picked Up	Michael D. Swanson	Yes	Yes	253
187	Colorado	PR 1964	Picked Up	E.H. Brown	No	No	
185-3/8	Fremont Co.	1955	Leonard L. Kiser	Leonard L. Kiser	No	No	
185-2/8	Fremont Co.	1978	Robert W. Wallace	Robert W. Wallace	No	No	
184-7/8	Glenwood Spgs.	1960	Pick Up	Mark E. Cook	No	No	
184-6/8	Area 57	1991	Todd Clyncke +	Todd Clyncke	No	No	333
184-3/8	Gunnison Co.	1915	Billy Prior	Daniel C. Harrington	No	No	
183-7/8	Huerfano Co.	1997	Mark D. Thomson	Mark D. Thomson	No	No	
183-7/8	Clear Creek Co.	1988	Ray Alt *		No	No	
183-5/8	Pitkin Co.	1998	D.Dean Spatz	D. Dean Spatz	No	No	
183-2/8	El Paso Co.	1979	Bob Renner *		Yes	Yes	254
183-2/8	Larimer Co.	1992	Jim Black *		No	No	
183-1/8	S. Platte Canyon	1957	Harold C. Eastwood	Harold C. Eastwood	No	No	
182-7/8	El Paso Co.	1989	Fred Church *		No	No	
182-4/8	Waterton	1956	William D. Jenkins	William D. Jenkins	No	No	
182	Saguache Co.	1992	Ralph G. Hejny	Ralph G. Hejny	Yes	Yes	255
182	Las Animas Co.	PR 1994	Pick Up	U.S. Army	Yes	Yes	256
181-6/8	Gunnison Co.	1986	Paula D. Darner	Paula D. Darner	No	No	
181-4/8	Saguache Co.	1994	Darrel L. Moberly	Darrel L. Moberly	Yes	Yes	257
181-3/8	Park Co.	1963	Richard L. Rudeen	Richard L. Rudeen	No	No	
181-1/8	Clear Creek Co.	1982	Gary Renfro *		No	No	
180-6/8	Texas Creek	1963	Picked Up	Jack D. Putnam	No	No	
180-1/8	Sugarloaf Mtn.	1947	Picked Up	Henry H. Zietz Family	No	Yes	333
180-1/8	Clear Creek Co.	1990	Charles W. Hanawalt	Charles W. Hanawalt ****	Yes	Yes	258
179-7/8	Huerfano Co.	1996	Dennis Gardner *	—	No	No	
179-5/8	El Paso Co.	1977	Doy K. Curtis *	—	No	No	
179-2/8	El Paso Co.	1982	Thomas H. States *	—	No	No	
177-6/8	El Paso Co.	1990	John Diedrich *	—	No	No	
177-2/8	Larimer Co.	1992	Mark Montgomery *	—	No	No	
177-1/8	Gunnison Co.	1999	P. Craig Pierce	P. Craig Pierce	Yes	Yes	259
176-7/8	El Paso Co.	1996	Brian Nicely *	—	No	No	
176-2/8	Clear Creek Co.	1989	Dominic Florian *	—	No	No	
176-1/8	El Paso Co.	1977	Tony Seahorn *	—	No	No	
176	El Paso Co.	1982	Gary Eastwood *	—	No	No	

DESERT BIGHORN SHEEP

Score	Location	Year	Hunter	Owner	Story	Photo	Page in Book
169-5/8	Mesa Co.	1996	Steven K. Allen	Steven K. Allen	No	Yes	333

ROCKY MOUNTAIN GOAT

Score	Location	Year	Hunter	Owner	Story	Photo	Page in Book
52-6/8	Park Co.	1988	Lyle K. Willmarth	Lyle K. Willmarth ****	No	Yes	334
51	Clear Creek Co.	1988	Janice L. Hemingson	Janice L. Hemingson	Yes	Yes	261
50-6/8	Mt. Antero	1965	Leroy C. Wood	Leroy C. Wood	No	No	
49-2/8	Clear Creek Co.	1994	Gayle Lippold *	—	No	No	
48-4/8	Chaffee Co.	1978	Marvin Clyncke *	—	No	Yes	334
47-2/8	Clear Creek Co.	1984	Don Stiles *	—	No	No	
47-2/8	Clear Creek Co.	1990	Richard A. Devrous, Jr. *	—	No	No	
47	Chaffee Co.	1981	Calvin Farner *	—	No	No	
47	La Plata Co.	1987	Mark Wuerthele *	—	No	No	

PRONGHORN

Score	Location	Year	Hunter	Owner	Story	Photo	Page in Book
91-4/8	Weld Co.	1965	Bob Schneidmiller	Bob Schneidmiller	Yes	Yes	263
89-2/8	Moffat Co.	1982	Gerald Scott	Gerald Scott	No	No	
87-4/8	Moffat Co.	1997	Preston J. Essex	Preston J. Essex	Yes	Yes	264
86-6/8	Jackson Co.	1995	Scott E. Raubach	Scott E. Raubach	Yes	Yes	265
86-6/8	Bent Co.	1992	Rodney D. Glaser	Rodney D. Glaser	Yes	Yes	266
86-4/8	Moffat Co.	1972	Joseph R. Maynard	Joseph R. Maynard	No	No	
86-4/8	Las Animas Co.	1996	Nicholas R. Russo	Nicholas R. Russo	Yes	Yes	267
86-2/8	El Paso Co.	1981	Maurice Cutting	Maurice Cutting	Yes	Yes	268
86	Gunnison Co.	1995	James R. Dawson	James R. Dawson	Yes	Yes	269
85	Moffat County	1983	Judd Cooney *	—	No	No	
84-6/8	Otero Co.	1992	Larry C. Hansen *	—	No	No	
84-6/8	Moffat Co.	1975	James C. MacLachlan	James C. MacLachlan	No	No	
84-4/8	Moffat Co.	1998	Patrick G. Diesing	Patrick G. Diesing	Yes	Yes	270
84-2/8	Weld Co.	1989	M. Wayne Hoeben	M. Wayne Hoeben ***	Yes	Yes	271
84-2/8	Baca Co.	1997	William R. Kincade	William R. Kincade	Yes	Yes	272
84-2/8	Moffat Co.	1999	Doug Palmer	Doug Palmer	No	No	
84-2/8	Jackson Co.	1991	Jerrald L. Copple	Jerrald L. Copple	No	No	
84-2/8	Moffatt Co.	1999	Kenneth M. Appelgren	Kenneth M. Appelgren	No	No	
84	Washington Co.	1967	Christian Heyden	Christian Heyden	No	No	
84	Jackson Co.	1993	Barry A. Weaver	Barry A. Weaver	No	No	
83-6/8	Jackson Co.	1983	Cylestine A. Manguso	Cylestine A. Manguso	No	No	
83-6/8	Jackson Co.	1994	Stephen H. Porter	Stephen H. Porter	Yes	Yes	273
83-4/8	Craig	1969	Albert Johnson	Albert Johnson	No	No	
83-4/8	Jackson Co.	1982	Cynthia L. Welle	Cynthia L. Welle	No	No	
83-4/8	Moffat Co.	1991	Rodney R. Hall, Jr.	Rodney R. Hall, Jr.	No	No	
83-4/8	Moffat Co.	1990	Brad A. Winder	Brad A. Winder	No	No	
83-4/8	Boone	1966	Mahlon T. White	Mahlon T. White	No	No	
83-4/8	Moffat Co.	1992	L. Dale Adkins *	—	No	No	
83-3/8	Weld Co.	1993	Delmar Brewer	Delmar Brewer	Yes	Yes	274

Score	Location	Year	Hunter	Owner	Story	Photo	Page in Book
83-2/8	Baca Co.	1993	Earl Leon Hollenback *	—	No	No	
83-2/8	Jackson Co.	1975	James R. Mosman	James R. Mosman	No	No	
83-2/8	Jackson Co.	1999	Stanley W. Bouse	Stanley W. Bouse	Yes	Yes	275
83	Moffat Co.	1989	Mike Wallers	Mike Wallers ****	No	No	
83	Washington Co.	1979	Gina R. Cass	Gina R. Cass	No	No	
83	Moffat Co.	1971	Michael Coleman	Michael Coleman	No	No	
83	Jackson Co.	1988	Douglas A. Weimer	Douglas A. Weimer	No	No	
83	Boyero	1965	Henry H. Zietz	Henry H. Zietz Family	No	Yes	334
83	Thatcher	1965	M.A. May	M.A. May	No	No	
83	Moffat Co.	1987	Marvin L. Shepard	Marvin L. Shepard	Yes	Yes	276
83	Weld Co.	1993	Gregory A. Peters	Gregory A. Peters	No	No	
83	Las Animas Co.	1993	Mike R. Caldarella	Mike R. Caldarella	No	No	
83	Jackson Co.	1985	Charles J. Cesar	Charles J. Cesar	Yes	Yes	277
83	Moffat Co.	1989	Mike Wallers	Mike Wallers	No	No	
82-6/8	Rocky Ford	1967	Henry A. Helmke	Henry A. Helmke	No	No	
82-6/8	Larimer Co.	1986	James D. Brink	James D. Brink	No	No	
82-6/8	Rio Grande Co.	1995	Hammond R. Collins	Hammond R. Collins	Yes	Yes	278
82-6/8	Weld Co.	1978	Chester N. Erwin	Chester N. Erwin	No	No	
82-4/8	Moffat Co.	1996	Kim Steven Hussong *	—	No	No	
82-4/8	Park Co.	1964	Mrs. Cotton Gordon	Mrs. Cotton Gordon	No	No	
82-4/8	Moffat Co.	1994	Brad A. Winder	Brad A. Winder	No	No	
82-4/8	Jackson Co.	1989	Loren D. Reid	Loren D. Reid	No	No	
82-4/8	Moffat Co.	1992	Brad A. Winder	Brad A. Winder	No	No	
82-4/8	Weld Co.	1999	Bob Chapman	Bob Chapman	No	No	
82-4/8	Saguache Co.	1986	Michael J. Atwood, Sr.	Michael J. Atwood, Sr.	Yes	Yes	279
82-4/8	Moffat Co.	1981	Charles W. Klaassens	Charles W. Klaassens	Yes	Yes	280
82-4/8	Moffat Co.	1991	S. Wayne Olson	S. Wayne Olson	No	No	
82-4/8	Washington Co.	1998	Timothy A. Baker	Timothy A. Baker	No	No	
82-2/8	Weld Co.	1955	James Gertson, Jr.	James Gertson, Jr.	No	No	
82-2/8	Weld Co.	1967	Mrs. Paul Goodwin	Mrs. Paul Goodwin	No	No	
82-2/8	Morgan Co.	1977	Kenneth L. Kelly	Kenneth L. Kelly	No	No	
82	Las Animas Co.	1994	Gary L. Cleaver *	—	No	No	
82	Moffat Co.	1998	Marvin Clyncke *	—	No	Yes	334
82	Moffat Co.	1990	Len H. Guldman	Len H. Guldman	No	No	
82	Limon	1958	Walt Paulk	Walt Paulk	No	No	
82	Logan Co.	1997	Andrew R. Paxton	Andrew R. Paxton	No	No	
81-4/8	Rio Blanco Co.	1998	Rodney S. Cook	Rodney S. Cook ***	No	Yes	334
81-4/8	Jackson Co.	1985	Steve Jackson *	—	No	No	
81-2/8	Baca Co.	1989	Charles A. Grimmett	Charles A. Grimmett	No	No	
81	Larimer Co.	1993	Allen Muirhead *	—	No	No	
81	Saguache Co.	1996	Thomas Torrez *	—	No	No	
81	Moffat Co.	1991	Terry N. Oman	Terry N. Oman	Yes	Yes	281
80-6/8	Rio Grande Co.	1997	John R. Olson	John R. Olson	Yes	Yes	282
80-4/8	Park Co.	1991	Joseph D. Malik	Joseph D. Malik	No	No	
80-4/8	Yuma Co.	1993	Randy Wilkins *	—	No	No	
80-4/8	Jackson Co.	1991	Beryl J. Palmer	Beryl J. Palmer	No	No	
80-4/8	Park Co.	1993	Tracy L. Downare	Tracy L. Downare	No	No	
80-4/8	Moffat Co.	1989	Glen A. Filener	Glen A. Filener +	No	Yes	334
80-4/8	Rio Blanco Co.	1998	George J. Tidona	George J. Tidona	No	No	
80-2/8	Moffat Co.	1993	Pamela S. Coburn	Pamela S. Coburn	Yes	Yes	283
80-2/8	Yuma Co.	1982	Mark Sievers *	—	No	No	
80-2/8	Rio Blanco Co.	1993	Don Collier *	—	No	No	
80-2/8	Rio Blanco Co.	1993	Gary L. Hinaman *	—	No	No	
80	Moffat Co.	1992	Breck Johnson *	—	No	No	
80	Weld Co.	1995	Rick Parish *	—	No	No	

COUGAR

Score	Location	Year	Hunter	Owner	Story	Photo	Page in Book
15-12/16	Meeker	1901	Theodore Roosevelt	Smithsonian Institution	Yes	Yes	285
15/12/16	Mesa Co.	1978	Robert R. Meyer	Robert R. Meyer	No	No	
15-11/16	Eagle Co.	1990	Layne K. Wing	Layne K. Wing	No	No	
15-11/16	Montrose Co.	1992	Randell Thompson *	—	No	No	
15-10/16	San Miguel Co.	1994	Robert D. Parker *	—	No	No	
15-9/16	Mesa Co.	1997	Darryl Powell	Darryl Powell ****	Yes	Yes	286
15-8/16	Huerfano Co.	1971	J.D. Dodge	J.D. Dodge	No	No	
15-8/16	Montrose Co.	1988	Kendall Hamilton	Kendall Hamilton	No	No	
15-8/16	Rio Blanco Co.	1985	Robert L. Raley	Robert L. Raley	No	No	
15-6/16	Garfield Co.	1997	Richard A. Mowles *	—	No	No	
15-7/16	Huerfano Co.	1971	J.D. Dodge *	—	No	No	
15-7/16	Coal Canyon	1967	Larry Bamford	Larry Bamford	No	No	
15-7/16	Rio Blanco Co.	1970	Ronald D. Vincent	Ronald D. Vincent	No	No	
15-6/16	Sedalia	1961	Walt Paulk	Walt Paulk	No	No	
15-6/16	Mesa Co.	1980	Jack Harrison	Jack Harrison	No	No	
15-6/16	West Salt Creek	1964	Hartle V. Morris	Hartle V. Morris	No	No	
15-6/16	Dolores Co.	1998	Thadius Countess *	—	No	No	
15-5/16	Las Animas Co.	PR 1994	Picked Up	Phillip L. Ehrlich	Yes	Yes	287
15-5/16	Delta Co.	1995	William E. Kallister	William E. Kallister ****	Yes	Yes	288
15-5/16	Rio Blanco Co.	1987	Rocky O. Alburtis	Rocky O. Alburtis	No	No	
15-5/16	Mesa Co.	1969	John Lamicq, Jr.	John Lamicq, Jr. ****	No	No	
15-5/16	Larimer Co.	1976	Glenn Schmidt *	—	No	No	
15-5/16	Rio Blanco Co.	1985	Bob Raley *	—	No	No	
15-4/16	Dolores Co.	1984	Bruce Nay	Bruce Nay	No	No	
15-4/16	Rio Blanco Co.	1989	William E. Pipes III	William E. Pipes III	No	No	
15-4/16	San Miguel Co.	1987	G. Merrill Jones *	—	No	No	
15-3/16	Fremont Co.	1976	Art Heinze *	—	No	No	
15-3/16	Douglas Co.	1977	Donald R. Looper *	—	No	No	
15-3/16	Huerfano Co.	1987	Bob Sigman *	—	No	No	
15-3/16	Archuleta Co.	1991	Charles T. Ames	Charles T. Ames ****	No	No	
15-3/16	Clear Creek Co.	1995	Mark Turner *	—	Yes	Yes	289
15-3/16	Eagle Co.	1991	Jeffrey S. Shoaf	Jeffrey S. Shoaf	No	No	
15-3/16	Meeker	1968	Jack Cadario	Jack Cadario	No	No	

Colorado's Biggest Bucks and Bulls

Score	County	Year	Hunter	Owner	BC	P&Y	Pg
15-3/16	Moffat Co.	1991	Robert W. Dager	Robert W. Dager	No	No	
15-3/16	Larimer Co.	1990	Peter A. Larson	Peter A. Larson	No	No	
15-3/16	Rio Blanco Co.	1983	Robert L. Raley	Robert L. Raley	No	No	
15-3/16	Garfield Co.	1996	Daryl G. Speck	Daryl G. Speck	No	No	
15-2/16	Rio Blanco Co.	1963	Leonard Cardinale *	—	No	No	
15-2/16	Conejos Co.	1987	Wayne Miller *	—	No	No	
15-2/16	Mesa Co.	1987	Frank P. Alaneno *	—	No	No	
15-2/16	Larimer Co.	1994	Don Watowa *	—	No	No	
15-2/16	Mesa Co.	1996	M. David Bennett, Jr. *	---	No	No	
15-2/16	Delta Co.	1996	Ray Kennedy *	---	No	No	
15-2/16	Allison	1962	Georgianna Etheridge	Georgianna Etheridge	No	No	
15-2/16	Garfield Co.	1983	Leslie H. Brewster	Leslie H. Brewster	No	No	
15-2/16	Park Co.	1990	Jack P. Van Vianen	Jack P. Van Vianen	No	No	
15-2/16	Archuleta Co.	1982	Judd Cooney	Judd Cooney	No	No	
15-2/16	San Miguel Co.	1991	Charles M. Karp	Charles M. Karp	No	No	
15-2/16	Archuleta Co.	1997	Dolores E. Adams	Dolores E. Adams	No	No	
15-2/16	La Plata Co.	1998	Brad F. Pfeffer	Brad F. Pfeffer	Yes	Yes	290
15-2/16	Montezuma Co.	1999	Terry D. Amrine	Terry D. Amrine	No	Yes	335
15-1/16	Montrose Co.	1993	Kevin W. Smith	Kevin W. Smith	No	No	
15-1/16	Douglas Co.	1969	C.R. Anderson & E.H. Brown	C.R. Anderson & E.H. Brown	No	No	
15-1/16	Dolores Co.	1990	Anthony S. Wagner	Anthony S. Wagner	Yes	Yes	292
15-1/16	Garfield Co.	1987	Joseph S. Arrain	Joseph S. Arrain	No	No	
15-1/16	Las Animas Co.	1996	Norman R. Noe	Norman R. Noe	Yes	Yes	293
15-1/16	Garfield Co.	1985	Jay H. Kneasel	Jay H. Kneasel	No	No	
15-1/16	Grand Co.	1996	Ken A. Krien	Ken A. Krien	No	No	
15-1/16	Grand Co.	1997	Richard F. Karbowski	Richard F. Karbowski ****	No	Yes	
15-1/16	Rio Blanco Co.	1990	Gerald L. Dowling	Gerald L. Dowling	No	No	
15-1/16	Grand Co.	1999	Paul T. Jones	Paul T. Jones	No	No	
15-1/16	Archuleta Co.	1982	Judd Cooney *	—	No	No	
15-1/16	Ouray Co.	1989	Steven A. Rider *	—	No	No	
15-1/16	Rio Blanco Co.	1990	Gerald L. Dowling *	—	No	No	
15-1/16	Eagle Co.	1990	Richard E. Davis *	—	No	No	
15-1/16	Rio Blanco Co.	1994	Bruce R. Schoeneweis *	—	No	No	
15-1/16	Eagle Co.	1997	David TerMaat *	—	No	No	
15	Rio Grande Co.	1986	Richard J. Dugas *	—	No	No	
15	Montezuma Co.	1993	John L. Gardner *	—	No	No	
15	Montrose Co.	1993	Corey W. Murray *	—	No	No	
15	Montezuma Co.	1993	Robert D. Crask *	—	No	No	
15	Las Animas Co.	2000	Barry Gene Hasten	Barry Gene Hasten	Yes	Yes	296
15	Dotsero	1887	J.T. Meirer	Univ. of KS Museum	No	No	
15	Canon City	1970	Glen Rosengarten	Glen Rosengarten	No	No	
15	Eagle Co.	1992	Dwain Spray	Dwain Spray	No	No	
15	Eagle Co.	1991	James R. Johnston	James R. Johnston	No	No	
15	Mesa Co.	1985	Lawrence C. Glass	Lawrence C. Glass	Yes	Yes	295
15	Clear Creek Co.	1989	Garry E. Fry	Garry E. Fry	No	No	
15	Antelope Pass	1971	Phil Nichols	Phil Nichols	No	No	
15	Routt Co.	1997	Tavis D. Rogers	Tavis D. Rogers	No	No	
15	Dolores Co.	1987	Richard S. Inman	Richard S. Inman	No	No	
15	Canon City	1969	Dale R. Leonard	Dale R. Leonard	No	No	
15	Dolores Co.	1986	Ray E. Ables	Ray E. Ables	No	No	
15	San Miguel Co.	1985	Jerry J. Jergins	Jerry J. Jergins	No	No	
15	Las Animas Co.	1974	Marion M. Snyder	Mike Powell	No	No	
15	Las Animas Co.	1992	Rick E. Tenreiro	Rick E. Tenreiro	No	No	
15	San Miguel Co.	1981	James N. McHolme	James N. McHolme	No	No	
15	Routt Co.	1997	Bob Barnes	Bob Barnes	No	No	
15	Rio Grande Co.	1986	Richard J. Dugas	Richard J. Dugas	No	No	
15	Rio Grande Co.	1996	Lyle R. Sigg	Lyle R. Sigg	No	No	
15	Huerfano Co.	1977	Sheila D. Bisgard	Sheila D. Bisgard	No	No	
15	Mesa Co.	1965	John Adams	John Adams	No	No	
15	Archuleta Co.	1999	H. Michael Hocker	H. Michael Hocker	Yes	Yes	294
14-15/16	Rio Blanco Co.	1971	Jack Pawlak *	—	No	No	
14-15/16	Rio Blanco Co.	1971	Stanley R. Winslow *	—	No	No	
14-15/16	Montezuma Co.	1984	Roy Keefer *	—	No	No	
14-15/16	Ouray Co.	1988	Doug McCauley *	—	No	No	
14-15/16	Garfield Co.	1989	Bruce R. Schoeneweis *	—	No	No	
14-15/16	San Miguel Co.	1991	Monroe A. Hare *	—	No	No	
14-15/16	La Plata Co.	1994	Valerie Gardner *	—	No	No	
14-15/16	Moffat Co.	1995	Rob Bathurst *	—	No	No	
14-15/16	Rio Blanco Co.	1998	Clare Streeter *	—	No	No	
14-15/16	Mesa Co.	1993	Laverle Dan Fair **	—	No	No	
14-15/16	Garfield Co.	1987	Oliver G. McCutchan, Jr.	Oliver G. McCutchan, Jr.	No	No	
14-14/16	Montezuma Co.	1983	Ms. Charlie White *	—	No	No	
14-14/16	Moffat Co.	1993	Mike Camilletti, Sr.	—	No	No	
14-14/16	Rio Blanco Co.	1994	Frank L. Fackovec *	—	No	No	
14-14/16	San Miguel Co.	1995	Wyatt C. Watson *	—	No	No	
14-14/16	Montezuma Co.	1998	Ronald R. Grenadier *	—	No	No	
14-14/16	Chaffee Co.	1965	Paul F. Gabel	Paul F. Gabel	Yes	Yes	297
14-14/16	Fremont Co.	1999	Randy L. Pfaff	Randy L. Pfaff	No	No	
14-14/16	Eagle Co.	1992	Swain Sperry **	—	No	No	
14-13/16	Rio Blanco Co.	1994	Frank L. Fackovec *	Frank L. Fackovec	No	No	
14-13/16	San Miguel Co.	1990	Tommy L. Winters	Tommy L. Winters	No	No	
14-13/16	Rio Blanco Co.	1999	Steve W. Chin	Steve W. Chin	Yes	Yes	298
14-13/16	Montezuma Co.	1985	George Wells	George Wells	No	No	
14-13/16	Archuleta Co.	1992	Sam B. Ray	Sam B. Ray ****	Yes	Yes	299
14-13/16	Garfield Co.	1994	James E. Rydell	James E. Rydell	No	No	
14-13/16	Garfield Co.	1971	Albert L. Heise *	—	No	No	
14-13/16	Chaffee Co.	1973	Phillip B. Grable *	—	No	No	
14-13/16	Huerfano Co.	1974	William F. Eikleberry *	—	No	No	
14-13/16	Mesa Co.	1981	Jim R. Lewis *	—	No	No	
14-13/16	Moffat Co.	1982	John A. Lee *	—	No	No	
14-13/16	San Miguel Co.	1985	David E. Smith *	—	No	No	
14-13/16	Montezuma Co.	1987	Richard Kimball *	—	No	No	
14-13/16	Dolores Co.	1990	Robert R. Hoffa, Jr. *	—	No	No	
14-13/16	Fremont Co.	1992	Robert W. Allen *	—	No	No	

Score	County	Year	Hunter	Owner	Pope&Young	B&C	Page
14-13/16	Delta Co.	1993	Dennis Hayden *	—	No	No	
14-13/16	Las Animas Co.	1994	J. Richard Bland III *	—	No	No	
14-13/16	Saguache Co.	1995	Mike Haynes *	—	No	No	
14-13/16	Rio Blanco Co.	1997	Roger C. Trout *	—	No	No	
14-12/16	Rio Blanco Co.	1965	LeRoy Wood *	—	No	No	
14-12/16	Boulder Co.	1984	Doug Beck *	—	No	No	
14-12/16	Larimer Co.	1985	Jim Johnson *	—	No	No	
14-12/16	Moffat Co.	1985	Michael B. Moline *	—	No	No	
14-12/16	Custer Co.	1986	David Waldrop *	—	No	No	
14-12/16	Saguache Co.	1988	Mark Wuerthele *	—	No	No	
14-12/16	Archuleta Co.	1988	Leo F. Neuls *	—	No	No	
14-12/16	Saguache Co.	1989	Roger Maurice Tyler *	—	No	No	
14-12/16	Mesa Co.	1990	Kerry Kammer *	—	No	No	
14-12/16	Rio Blanco Co.	1981	Ross L. Talbott *	—	No	No	
14-12/16	Garfield Co.	1993	Jay R. Rasch*	—	No	No	
14-12/16	La Plata Co.	1993	Michael Falcone *	—	No	No	
14-12/16	Huerfano Co.	1994	David Hinton *	—	No	No	
14-12/16	Rio Blanco Co.	1994	Stephen W. Greer *	—	No	No	
14-12/16	San Miguel Co.	1995	Fritz A. Brennecke *	—	No	No	
14-12/16	Jefferson Co.	1995	Dan Eaton *	—	No	No	
14-12/16	Rio Grande Co.	1997	Tobias Dellamano *	—	No	No	
14-12/16	Montezuma Co.	1997	Tommy L. Tucker	Tommy L. Tucker	Yes	Yes	300
14-12/16	La Plata Co.	1993	Michael Falcone	Michael Falcone	No	No	
14-12/16	Custer Co.	1998	John Pete Pitrowski	John Pete Pitrowski	Yes	Yes	301
14-12/16	Mesa Co.	1987	Joe B. Owen	Joe B. Owen	No	No	
14-11/16	Custer Co.	1979	Philip Stegenga *	—	No	No	
14-11/16	San Miguel Co.	1981	Judd Cooney *	—	No	No	
14-11/16	Chaffee Co.	1983	Reggie Spiegelberg *	—	No	No	
14-11/16	Montezuma Co.	1987	Carla D. Coval *	—	No	No	
14-11/16	Montezuma Co.	1990	Phil M. Elmore *	—	No	No	
14-10/16	Rio Blanco Co.	1976	Paul Janke *	—	No	No	
14-10/16	Fremont Co.	1979	Pete J. Santi *	—	No	No	
14-10/16	Las Animas Co.	1980	Glenn R. Kukick *	—	No	No	
14-10/16	Fremont Co.	1981	Johnny J. Lama *	—	No	No	
14-10/16	Fremont Co.	1981	Carolyn E. Lama *	—	No	No	
14-10/16	San Miguel Co.	1982	James Yuds *	—	No	No	
14-10/16	Montezuma Co.	1983	Mike Morgan *	—	No	No	
14-10/16	Chaffee Co.	1983	Tom Bowman *	—	No	No	
14-10/16	Montrose Co.	1987	David Ernest Nesler *	—	No	No	
14-10/16	Alamosa Co.	1987	Tim Walters *	—	No	No	
14-10/16	Gilpin Co.	1988	Garry V. Woodman *	—	No	No	
14-10/16	Montezuma Co.	1989	Steven J. Vittetow *	—	No	No	
14-10/16	La Plata Co.	1993	Edward A. Petersen *	—	Yes	Yes	302
14-10/16	Clear Creek Co.	1994	Connie Renfro *	—	No	No	
14-10/16	Pueblo Co.	1994	Tommy Chambliss *	—	No	No	
14-10/16	Moffat Co.	1995	Dave Burke *	—	No	No	
14-10/16	Larimer Co.	1995	Thomas H. Harris *	—	No	No	
14-10/16	Montrose Co.	1996	Lisa A. West *	—	No	No	
14-10/16	Clear Creek Co.	1997	David L. Skiff *	—	No	No	
14-10/16	Las Animas Co.	1998	Pat Powell *	—	No	No	
14-10/16	Jefferson Co.	1991	Michael R. Memmer	Michael R. Memmer	No	No	
14/10/16	La Plata Co.	1993	Edward A. Peterson	Edward A. Peterson	Yes	Yes	
14-10/16	Archuleta Co.	1985	M. Howard Payne	M. Howard Payne	No	No	
14-10/16	Rio Blanco Co.	1988	Stephen C. LeBlanc	Stephen C. LeBlanc	No	No	
14-10/16	Montrose Co.	1987	David E. Nesler	David E. Nesler	No	No	
14-9/16	Jefferson Co.	1984	Lee Veldhouse *	—	No	No	
14-9/16	Rio Blanco Co.	1984	Don Waechtler *	—	No	No	
14-9/16	Douglas Co.	1986	Wayne Kraft *	—	No	No	
14-9/16	Fremont Co.	1986	Bill Goodspeed *	—	No	No	
14-9/16	Chaffee Co.	1988	David Douty *	—	No	No	
14-9/16	Grand Co.	1993	Barry J. Smith *	—	No	No	
14-9/16	Larimer Co.	1994	Jay Ervin *	—	No	No	
14-9/16	Montezuma Co.	1995	Robert Hermann *	—	No	No	
14-9/16	Delta Co.	1998	Scott Hargrove *	—	No	No	
14-9/16	Mesa Co.	1989	Clayton C. French	Clayton C. French	No	No	
14-9/16	Rio Blanco Co.	1992	Dennis A. Swanson	Dennis A. Swanson	Yes	Yes	303
14-9/16	Garfield Co.	1984	Douglas E. Starks	Douglas E. Starks	No	No	
14-9/16	Montezuma Co.	1988	Eric M. Stevens	Eric M. Stevens	No	No	
14-9/16	Boulder Co.	1993	Harley L. Johnson	Harley L. Johnson	No	No	
14-9/16	Costilla Co.	1997	Michael R. Treinen	Michael R. Treinen	No	Yes	291
14-8/16	Saguache Co.	1982	J. Keith Chastain *	—	No	No	
14-8/16	Garfield Co.	1984	Douglas Starks *	—	No	No	
14-8/16	Archuleta Co.	1985	Howard Payne *	—	No	No	
14-8/16	Fremont Co.	1985	Oney Cole *	—	No	No	
14-8/16	Larimer Co.	1987	David Skiff *	—	No	No	
14-8/16	Chaffee Co.	1987	Scott Pelino *	—	No	No	
14-8/16	Saguache Co.	1987	William Larry Wray *	—	No	No	
14-8/16	Garfield Co.	1988	Roy M. Goodwin *	—	No	No	
14-8/16	Larimer Co.	1989	John D. Lindell *	—	No	No	
14-8/16	Montrose Co.	1990	Jimmy C. Garner *	—	No	No	
14-8/16	Montezuma Co.	1991	Mark D. Thomson *	—	No	No	
14-8/16	San Miguel Co.	1992	DeWayne Mullins *	—	No	No	
14-8/16	Garfield Co.	1992	Carroll Thomas Roach *	—	No	No	
14-8/16	San Miguel Co.	1993	Steve Mazur *	—	No	No	
14-8/16	Chaffee Co.	1993	Terry J. Krause *	—	No	No	
14-8/16	Mesa Co.	1995	Mark Richards *	—	No	No	
14-8/16	Moffat Co.	1996	Russell S. Overton *	—	No	No	
14-8/16	Rio Blanco Co.	1997	Paul J. Chackan *	—	No	No	
14-8/16	Rio Blanco Co.	1985	Albert A. Meyers	Albert A. Meyers	No	No	
14-8/16	Fremont Co.	1986	Terry L. Ellison	Terry L. Ellison	Yes	Yes	304
14-8/16	Rio Blanco Co.	1998	Robert Dee Owens	Robert Dee Owens	Yes	Yes	305
14-8/16	Rio Blanco Co.	1999	Dennis L. Roehl	Dennis L. Roehl	No	No	
14-8/16	Mesa Co.	1992	Michael Fullmer **	—	No	No	

BLACK BEAR

Score	Location	Year	Hunter	Owner	Story	Photo	Page in Book
22-4/16	Sinbad Ridge	1978	Ray Cox *	—	No	Yes	335
22-2/16	Delta Co.	1998	James B. George	James B. George	No	No	
22	Hahns Peak	1964	W.L. Cave	W.L. Cave	No	No	
22	Garfield Co.	1977	Joseph R. Maynard	Joseph R. Maynard	No	No	
21-12/16	Delta Co.	1967	Quincy M. Hines	Quincy M. Hines	Yes	Yes	308
21-12/16	Huerfano Co.	1988	Harvey R. Newcomb	Harvey R. Newcomb	No	No	
21-9/16	Mesa Co.	1962	Hartle V. Morris	Hartle V. Morris	No	No	
21-9/16	Ouray Co.	1993	Lee Gabardi	Lee Gabardi	No	No	
21-9/16	Ouray Co.	1978	Thomas C. Middleton	Thomas C. Middleton	No	No	
21-9/16	Garfield Co.	1955	Robert C. Maurer	Robert C. Maurer	No	No	
21-9/16	Williams Fork River	1958	C. Stehle & J. Grove	Clyde Stehle	No	No	
21-9/16	Collbran	1957	O.K. Clifton	O.K. Clifton	No	No	
21-8/16	Garfield Co.	1980	Robert W. Jackson	Robert W. Jackson	Yes	Yes	309
21-8/16	Mesa Co.	1986	Rem B. Bennett, Jr.	Rem B. Bennett	No	No	
21-7/16	Garfield Co.	1985	Norman J. O'Bryan *	—	No	No	
21-6/16	Pitken Co.	1980	Chris Green	Chris Green	No	No	
21-5/16	Gunnison Co.	1998	Brian Curtis	Brian Curtis	No	No	
21-5/16	Rio Blanco Co.	1987	Jason Steiner	Jason Steiner	No	No	
21-5/16	Colorado	1897	E.T. Seton	Smithsonian Institution	No	No	
21-5/16	Garfield Co.	1995	Ted R. Bina	Ted R. Bina	No	No	
21-5/16	Buffalo Park	1958	John L. Howard	John L. Howard	No	No	
21-4/16	Snowmass	1974	Ronald D. Vincent	Ronald D. Vincent	No	No	
21-3/16	Eagle Co.	1971	Charles T. Coffman	Charles T. Coffman	No	No	
21-3/16	Routt Co.	PU 1981	Picked Up	Steven R. Beckwith	No	No	
21-3/16	Mesa Co.	1987	Marilyn J. Scott	Marilyn J. Scott	No	No	
21-2/16	Montrose Co.	1970	Earl L. Markley	Earl L. Markley	No	No	
21-2/16	Collbran	1965	R.R. Lyons & H.V. Morris	Raymond R. Lyons	No	No	
21-2/16	Mesa Co.	1966	Waldemar R. Kuenzel, Jr.	Waldemar R. Kuenzel, Jr.	No	No	
21-2/16	Mesa Co.	1996	Stephen J. Gray	Stephen J. Gray	No	No	
21-2/16	Gunnison Co.	1977	Dick Cooper	Dick Cooper	No	No	
21-2/16	Trinidad	1999	Roger L. Bell	Roger L. Bell	Yes	Yes	310
21-1/16	Teller Co.	1982	Samuel T. Harrelson, Jr.	Samuel T. Harrelson, Jr.	No	No	
21-1/16	Steamboat Spgs.	1964	Norman W. Garwood	Norman W. Garwood	No	No	
21-1/16	Paonia	1960	William O. Good	William O. Good	No	No	
21	Uncompahgre NF	1974	James Emerson *	—	No	No	
21	Garfield Co.	1974	J.D. Liles	J.D. Liles	No	No	
21	Routt Co.	1980	Jerome W. Keyes, Jr.	Jerome W. Keyes, Jr.	No	No	
21	Collbran	1967	Cecil E. Alumbaugh, Jr.	Cecil E. Alumbaugh, Jr.	No	No	
21	Montezuma Co.	1998	Joe W. Brunner	Joe W. Brunner	Yes	Yes	311
21	Garfield Co.	1985	Gordon L. Haxton	Gordon L. Haxton	No	No	
20-15/16	Routt Co.	1982	Mark A. Chapman *	—	No	No	
20-14/16	Mesa Co.	1973	Richard A. Schreiber *	—	No	No	
20-14/16	Routt Co.	1984	Lonny Vanatta *	—	No	No	
20-14/16	Eagle Co.	1987	Willis D. Bassett	Willis D. Bassett	No	No	
20-13/16	Eagle Co.	1982	Terry L. Pierce	Terry L. Pierce	Yes	Yes	312
20-12/16	San Miguel Co.	1978	John W. Rowe *	—	No	No	
20-11/16	Pitkin Co.	1975	Dale W. Gray *	—	No	No	
20-11/16	Rio Blanco Co.	1976	Walter Krom *	—	No	No	
20-10/16	Rio Blanco Co.	1969	Frank Rit Heller *	—	No	No	
20-9/16	Grand Co.	1973	Curt Lynn *	—	No	No	
20-9/16	Delta Co.	1982	Steve McCarthy *	—	No	No	
20-8/16	Pitkin Co.	1992	Stanley E. Lauriski *	—	No	No	
20-8/16	Mesa Co.	1995	Michael R. Elliott	Michael R. Elliott	Yes	Yes	313
20-8/16	Dolores Co.	1999	Woody Ott	Woody Ott	Yes	Yes	314
20-7/16	Montezuma Co.	1974	Bryan C. Neeley *	—	No	No	
20-7/16	Garfield Co.	1985	Roger Bolander *	—	No	No	
20-7/16	Routt Co.	1987	Bill Grammer *	—	No	No	
20-6/16	Garfield Co.	1970/	Steve Bergman *	—	No	No	
20-6/16	Saguache Co.	1975	Ed Wiseman *	—	No	No	
20-6/16	La Plata Co.	1991	Paul Nichols *	—	No	No	
20-5/16	Montezuma Co.	1975	Stanley A. Coval *	—	No	No	
20-5/16	Montrose Co.	1976	Jack Cassidy *	—	No	No	
20-5/16	Archuleta Co.	1985	Ronald J. Murphy *	—	No	No	
20-5/16	Mesa Co.	1989	Paul Alan Seidelman *	—	No	No	
20-5/16	Garfield Co.	1988	Paul H. Prather	Paul H. Prather	No	No	
20-4/16	Mesa Co.	1971	M.R. James *	—	No	No	
20-4/16	Mesa Co.	1982	Larry A. McIntosh *	—	No	No	
20-4/16	Garfield Co.	1990	Robert J. Witt	Robert J. Witt	No	No	
20-4/16	Fremont Co.	1985	Carl B. Mockensturm	Carl B. Mockensturm	No	No	
20-4/16	Pueblo Co.	1998	Steve West	Steve West	Yes	Yes	315
20-3/16	Dolores Co.	1979	Randy E. Dossey *	—	No	No	
20-3/16	Dolores Co.	1979	Marvin Reichenau*	—	No	No	
20-3/16	Garfield Co.	1995	William H. McCarty	William H. McCarty	No	No	
20-3/16	Mesa Co.	1984	Rob Keck	Rob Keck	No	No	
20-2/16	Delta Co.	1976	Bill Izon *	—	No	No	
20-2/16	Montrose Co.	1978	John Brandt *	—	No	No	
20-2/16	Del Norte Co.	1978	Fred D. Davis, Jr. *	—	No	No	
20-2/16	Montezuma Co.	1978	Floyd H. Hicks *	—	No	No	
20-2/16	Mesa Co.	1979	Dennis Behn *	—	No	No	
20-2/16	Delta Co.	1981	Scott Dillon *	—	No	No	
20-2/16	El Paso Co.	1988	Russ Nily *	—	No	No	
20-2/16	Garfield Co.	1987	Terry L. Smalec	Terry L. Smalec	Yes	Yes	316
20-2/16	Moffat Co.	1998	Delbert L. Schmidt	Delbert L. Schmidt	No	No	
20-1/16	Montrose Co.	1978	Mike Barber *	—	No	No	
20-1/16	Archuleta Co.	1980	Len Cardinale *	—	No	No	
20-1/16	Archuleta Co.	1980	Judd Cooney *	—	No	No	
20	Grand Co.	1981	Randy O. Vineyard *	—	No	No	
20	Garfield Co.	1990	Gus Sexauer *	—	No	No	
20-1/16	Huerfano Co.	1997	Charles M. Betters	Charles M. Betters	Yes	Yes	317
20	Larimer Co.	1993	Patrick T. Stanosheck	Patrick T. Stanosheck	Yes	Yes	318